Financial Markets and Institutions

Written for undergraduate and graduate students of finance, economics, and business, the fourth edition of *Financial Markets and Institutions* provides a fresh analysis of the European financial system. Combining theory, data, and policy, this successful textbook examines and explains financial markets, financial infrastructures, financial institutions, and the challenges of financial supervision and competition policy. The fourth edition features not only greater discussion of the financial and euro crises and post-crisis reforms, but also new market developments like FinTech, blockchain, cryptocurrencies, and shadow banking. On the policy side, new material covers unconventional monetary policies, the Banking Union, the Capital Markets Union, Brexit, and the Basel III capital adequacy framework for banking supervision and macroprudential policies. The new edition also features wider international coverage, with greater emphasis on comparisons with countries outside the European Union, including the United States, China, and Japan.

Visit the companion website at www.cambridge.org/de_Haan4e for exercises and solutions for each chapter, and copies of the figures and tables used in the book.

Jakob de Haan is Head of Research of De Nederlandsche Bank and Professor of Political Economy at the University of Groningen.

Dirk Schoenmaker is Professor of Banking and Finance at the Rotterdam School of Management, Erasmus University Rotterdam.

Peter Wierts is Senior Economist at the Payments and Market Infrastructures Division of De Nederlandsche Bank and Associate Professor of Finance at VU University Amsterdam.

Financial Markets and Institutions

A European Perspective

Fourth Edition

Jakob de Haan

Dirk Schoenmaker

Peter Wierts

CAMBRIDGE
UNIVERSITY PRESS

CAMBRIDGE
UNIVERSITY PRESS

University Printing House, Cambridge CB2 8BS, United Kingdom

One Liberty Plaza, 20th Floor, New York, NY 10006, USA

477 Williamstown Road, Port Melbourne, VIC 3207, Australia

314–321, 3rd Floor, Plot 3, Splendor Forum, Jasola District Centre,
New Delhi – 110025, India

79 Anson Road, #06–04/06, Singapore 079906

Cambridge University Press is part of the University of Cambridge.

It furthers the University's mission by disseminating knowledge in the pursuit of
education, learning, and research at the highest international levels of excellence.

www.cambridge.org
Information on this title: www.cambridge.org/9781108494113
DOI: 10.1017/9781108643849

First edition © Jakob de Haan, Sander Osterloo and Dirk Schoenmaker 2009
Second edition © Jakob de Haan, Sander Osterloo and Dirk Schoenmaker 2012
Third edition © Jakob de Haan, Sander Osterloo and Dirk Schoenmaker 2015
Fourth edition © Jakob de Haan, Dirk Schoenmaker and Peter Wierts 2020

First published 2009
Second edition 2012
Third edition 2015
Fourth edition 2020

Printed in the United Kingdom by TJ International Ltd, Padstow Cornwall

A catalogue record for this publication is available from the British Library.

Library of Congress Cataloging-in-Publication Data
Names: Haan, Jakob de, author. | Schoenmaker, Dirk, author. | Wierts, Peter J. author.
Title: Financial markets and institutions : a European perspective / Jakob de Haan, Dirk
Schoenmaker, Peter Wierts.
Description: Fourth edition. | Cambridge, UK ; New York, NY : Cambridge University Press, 2020. |
Includes bibliographical references and index.
Identifiers: LCCN 2019042017 (print) | LCCN 2019042018 (ebook) | ISBN 9781108494113
(hardback) | ISBN 9781108643849 (ebook)
Subjects: LCSH: Financial institutions – Europe. | Europe – Economic policy. | Europe – Economic
integration.
Classification: LCC HG186.A2 H33 2020 (print) | LCC HG186.A2 (ebook) |
DDC 332/.0415094–dc23
LC record available at https://lccn.loc.gov/2019042017
LC ebook record available at https://lccn.loc.gov/2019042018

ISBN 978-1-108-49411-3 Hardback
ISBN 978-1-108-71392-4 Paperback

Additional resources for this publication at www.cambridge.org/de_Haan4e

Contents

Part I   Setting the Stage

Part II   Financial Markets

Figures

Tables

Boxes

Preface

As a team of authors we have followed the building of the European financial system from different angles. We have contributed to the academic literature on this topic. Moreover, one of us has been teaching a course on European Financial Integration, from which this book has emerged. On the policy side, the authors have been directly involved in the work of national administrations (i.e. the Ministry of Finance, the Ministry of Economic Affairs in the Netherlands, and the Dutch central bank) as well as the European institutions (i.e. the Council, the European Commission, and the European Central Bank). As part of our job, two of us have participated in many meetings in Brussels discussing the future of European financial markets and institutions, and negotiating new European financial services directives.

The authors would like to thank Wilco Bolt, Patty Duijm, Jean Frijns, Jon Frost, Ronald Heijmans, Nicole Jonker, Thomas Lambert, Iman van Lelyveld, Albert Menkveld, Arco van Oord, Almoro Rubin de Cervin, Martijn Schrijvers, Peter Tjeerdsma, and Casper de Vries for their advice on specific chapters. We thank Martin Admiraal, Rene Bierdrager, and Henk van Kerkhoff for their statistical support and Kelley Friel for copy-editing. The authors are in particular grateful to Sander Oosterloo, as co-author of the first three editions of this book.

What Is New in the Fourth Edition?

Since the first edition of this book, the world's financial system has been through its greatest crisis for a century. What made this crisis unique is that severe financial problems emerged simultaneously in many different countries, and its economic impact was felt throughout the world as a result of the increased interconnectedness of the global economy. Financial innovation also played an important part in the financial crisis. Two chapters deal with (1) financial crises, including an overview of the causes and consequences of the 2007–2009 financial crisis as well as the more recent euro crisis, and (2) financial innovation, including the role of securitisation and the shadow banking system.

In the fourth edition, the chapters on financial markets and institutions have been updated with new data through 2018 whenever possible. These extensive updates illustrate the impact of the financial crisis and the euro crisis on the process of European financial integration: a breakdown of integration, followed by a partial reversal. New market developments of FinTech, blockchain, and cryptocurrencies are covered in the fourth edition. On the policy side, the fourth edition features an extensive analysis of unconventional monetary policies, the Banking Union, the Capital Markets Union, Brexit, the Basel III capital adequacy framework for banking supervision, the Solvency 2 capital adequacy framework for insurance supervision, and macroprudential policies. Compared to the previous editions, more emphasis is put on the comparison with countries outside the European Union. The fourth edition includes coverage of the Chinese financial system. China has become a major player alongside the United States, the European Union, and Japan in the global financial system.

How Does This Textbook Compare with Other Books?

Different from other textbooks, *Financial Markets and Institutions: A European Perspective* has a wide coverage dealing with the various elements of the European financial system supported by recent data and examples. This wide coverage implies that we treat not only the functioning of financial markets where trading takes place but also the working of supporting infrastructures (clearing and settlement) where trades are executed. Turning to financial institutions, we cover the full range of financial intermediaries, from institutional investors to banks and insurance companies. Based on new data, we document the gradual shift of financial intermediation from banks towards institutional investors, such as pension funds, mutual funds, and hedge funds. In this process of re-intermediation, the assets of institutional investors have quadrupled over the last 25 years. As to policy making, we cover the full range of monetary policy, financial regulation and supervision, financial stability, and competition. We deal with the challenges of European financial integration for monetary, financial supervision, and financial stability policies. Competition and state aid is a new topic for a finance textbook.

The existing textbooks in the field of financial markets and institutions generally describe the relevant theories and subsequently relate these theories to the general characteristics of financial markets. An excellent example of a more in-depth textbook is *The Economics of Financial Markets* by Roy E. Bailey. The broad coverage of our book is comparable to the widely used textbook *Financial Markets and Institutions* by Frederic S. Mishkin and Stanley G. Eakins. Whereas our book focuses on the EU (with international comparisons to the United States and China), Mishkin and Eakins analyse the US financial system. The early European textbooks (e.g. *The Economics of Money, Banking and Finance – A European Text*, by Peter Howells and Keith Bain) typically contain chapters on the UK, French, and German banking systems, but do not provide an overview of European banking. More advanced textbooks that do discuss the specifics of the European financial system mostly do this in the context of monetary policy making.

Finally, the excellent *Handbook of European Financial Markets and Institutions*, edited by Xavier Freixas, Philipp Hartmann, and Colin Mayer, has a broad coverage of the European financial system, but deals with topics on a stand-alone basis in separate chapters and is not constructed as an integrated textbook. Nevertheless, this handbook contains very useful material for further study of particular aspects of the European financial system.

How to Use This Book

Financial Markets and Institutions: A European Perspective is an accessible textbook for both undergraduate and graduate students of Finance, Economics, and Business Administration. Each chapter first gives an overview and identifies learning objectives. Throughout the book we use boxes in which certain issues are explained in more detail, by referring to theory or practical examples. Furthermore, we make abundant use of graphs and tables to give students a comprehensive overview of the European financial system. At the end of each chapter we provide suggestions for further reading. Cambridge University Press provides a supporting website for this book. This website contains exercises (and their solutions) for each chapter. The website also provides regular updates of figures and tables used in the book, and identifies new policy issues.

A basic understanding of finance is needed to use this textbook, as we assume that students are familiar with the basic finance models, such as the standard Capital Asset Pricing Model (CAPM). The book can be used for third-year undergraduate courses as well as for graduate courses. More advanced material for graduate students is contained in special boxes marked by a star (*). Undergraduate students can skip these technical boxes.

Countries

Member States of the European Union

1	Austria	AT	1995
2	Belgium	BE	1951
3	Bulgaria	BG	2007
4	Croatia	HR	2013
5	Cyprus	CY	2004
6	Czech Republic	CZ	2004
7	Denmark	DK	1973
8	Estonia	EE	2004
9	Finland	FI	1995
10	France	FR	1951
11	Germany	DE	1951
12	Greece	EL	1981
13	Hungary	HU	2004
14	Ireland	IE	1973
15	Italy	IT	1951
16	Latvia	LV	2004
17	Lithuania	LT	2004
18	Luxembourg	LU	1951
19	Malta	MT	2004
20	Netherlands	NL	1951
21	Poland	PL	2004
22	Portugal	PT	1986
23	Romania	RO	2007
24	Slovakia	SK	2004
25	Slovenia	SI	2004
26	Spain	ES	1986
27	Sweden	SE	1995

The European Union (EU) consists of 27 Member States as of 2020 after Brexit (the new EU-27). Before the accession of the New Member States in 2004, 2007 and 2013, the EU consisted of 15 Member States, which are usually indicated by EU-15. The 10 New Member States in 2004 are indicated by NMS-10, the total of 12 New Member States in 2004 and 2007 are indicated by NMS-12 and the total of 13 New Member States in 2004, 2007, and 2013 are indicated by NMS-13. EU-28 refers to the EU-15 and NMS-13 before Brexit.

There are 19 countries in the euro area.

Countries in the Euro Area

	Country	Year of accession
1	Austria	1999
2	Belgium	1999
3	Cyprus	2008
4	Estonia	2011
5	Finland	1999
6	France	1999
7	Germany	1999
8	Greece	2001
9	Ireland	1999
10	Italy	1999
11	Latvia	2014
12	Lithuania	2015
13	Luxembourg	1999
14	Malta	2008
15	Netherlands	1999
16	Portugal	1999
17	Slovakia	2009
18	Slovenia	2007
19	Spain	1999

Abbreviations

ABP	Algemeen Burgerlijk Pensioenfonds
ABS	Asset-Backed Securities
ACP	Asset-Backed Commercial Paper
ACP	Autorité de Contrôle Prudentiel
AI	Artificial Intelligence
AIFs	Alternative Investment Funds
AIFMD	Alternative Investment Funds Managers Directive
AIG	American International Group
ALM	Asset and Liability Management
AMF	Autorité des Marchés Financiers
API	Application Programming Interface
APP	Asset Purchase Programme
ASC	Advisory Scientific Committee
ATM	Automated Teller Machine
BaFin	Bundesanstalt für Finanzdienstleistungsaufsicht
BCBS	Basel Committee on Banking Supervision
BIS	Bank for International Settlements
BME	Bolsas y Mercados Españoles
BMR	Benchmarks Regulation
BoE	Bank of England
BoJ	Bank of Japan
BOJNET	Bank of Japan Financial Network System
BRRD	Bank Recovery and Resolution Directive
BU	Banking Union
CalPERS	California Public Employees Retirement Scheme
CAPM	Capital Asset Pricing Model
CB	Central Bank
CBPP	Covered Bond Purchase Programme
CCP	Central Counterparty
CD	Certificate of Deposit

CDC	Collective Defined Contribution
CDO	Collateralised Debt Obligation
CDS	Credit Default Swap
CEA	Comité Européen des Assurances
CEO	Chief Executive Officer
CESR	Committee of European Securities Regulators
CET1	Common Equity Tier 1
CFO	Chief Financial Officer
CLS	Continuous Linked Settlement
CMBS	Commercial Mortgage-Backed Securities
CMU	Capital Markets Union
CoCo	Contingent Convertible
CRA	Credit Rating Agency
CRAAC	CRA Assessment Centre
CRD	Capital Requirements Directive
CRO	Chief Risk Officer
CRR	Capital Requirements Regulation
CSD	Central Securities Depository
DB	Defined Benefit
DC	Defined Contribution
DEAB	Debt Euro-Area Bias
DG	Directorate General
DGS	Deposit Guarantee Scheme
DHB	Debt Home Bias
DMO	Debt Management Office
DNB	De Nederlandsche Bank (Dutch central bank)
DTB	Deutsche Terminbörse
EBA	European Banking Authority
EBRD	European Bank for Reconstruction and Development
EC	European Commission
ECB	European Central Bank
ECFI	European Court of First Instance
ECJ	European Court of Justice
ECN	European Competition Network
Ecofin	Council of Economic and Finance Ministers
ECSC	European Coal and Steel Community
ECU	European Currency Unit
EDP	Excessive Deficit Procedure
EEA	European Economic Area

EEAB	Equity Euro-Area Bias
EEC	European Economic Community
EFAMA	European Fund and Asset Management Association
EFSF	European Financial Stability Facility
EFSM	European Financial Stabilisation Mechanism
EHB	Equity Home Bias
EIOPA	European Insurance and Occupational Pensions Authority
ELA	Emergency Liquidity Assistance
ELB	Effective Lower Bound
EMI	European Monetary Institute
EMIR	European Market Infrastructure Regulation
EMMI	European Money Markets Institute
EMS	European Monetary System
EMU	Economic and Monetary Union
EOE	European Options Exchange
EONIA	Euro Overnight Index Average
EP	European Parliament
EPC	European Payments Council
ERM	Exchange Rate Mechanism
ESA	European Supervisory Authority
ESCB	European System of Central Banks
ESFS	European System of Financial Supervisors
ESM	European Stability Mechanism
ESMA	European Securities and Markets Authority
ESRB	European Systemic Risk Board
ESTER	Euro Short-Term Rate
ETF	Exchange Traded Funds
EU	European Union
Euratom	European Atomic Energy Community
EUREPO	Repo Market Reference Rate for the Euro
EURIBOR	Euro Interbank Offered Rate
FCA	Financial Conduct Authority
FDI	Foreign Direct Investment
Fed	Federal Reserve
FESE	Federation of European Securities Exchanges
FOMC	Federal Open Market Committee
FPC	Financial Policy Committee
FRA	Forward Rate Agreement
FSA	Financial Services Authority

FSAP	Financial Services Action Plan
FSB	Financial Stability Board
FSOC	Financial Stability Oversight Council
FSR	Financial Stability Review
FTO	Fine Tune Operation
FX	Foreign Exchange
GDP	Gross Domestic Product
GIIPS	Greece, Ireland, Italy, Portugal, Spain
GLAC	Gone-Concern Loss-Absorbing Capacity
GMI	Governance Metrics International
G-SIB	Globally Systemically Important Bank
G-SII	Globally Systemically Important Insurer
GVA	Gross Value Added
HFT	High Frequency Trading
HI	Herfindahl Index
HQLA	High Quality Liquid Assets
IAIS	International Association of Insurance Supervisors
IAS	International Accounting Standards
IASB	International Accounting Standards Board
ICI	Investment Company Institute
ICMA	International Capital Market Association
ICSD	International Central Securities Depository
IFRS	International Financial Reporting Standards
IMF	International Monetary Fund
IOSCO	International Organisation of Securities Commissions
IPO	Initial Public Offering
IRS	Interest Rate Swap
ISD	Investment Services Directive
ISDA	International Swaps and Derivatives Association
IT	Information Technology
JSTs	Joint Supervisory Teams
LCR	Liquidity Coverage Ratio
LI	Lerner Index
LIBOR	London Interbank Offered Rate
LIFFE	London International Financial Futures and Options Exchange
LoLR	Lender of Last Resort
LR	Leverage Ratio
LSE	London Stock Exchange

LTCM	Long-Term Capital Management
LTI	Loan-to-Income
LTRO	Longer-Term Refinancing Operation
LTV	Loan-to-Value
LVPS	Large-Value Payment System
M&As	Mergers and Acquisitions
MBS	Mortgage-Backed Securities
MC	Marginal Cost
MCR	Minimum Capital Requirement
MFI	Monetary Financial Institution
MIF	Multilateral Interchange Fee
MiFID	Markets in Financial Instruments Directive
MiFIR	Markets in Financial Instruments Regulation
MMF	Money Market Fund
MoU	Memorandum of Understanding
MPC	Monetary Policy Committee
MR	Marginal Revenue
MREL	Minimum requirements for own funds and eligible requirements
MRO	Main Refinancing Operation
MSCI	Morgan Stanley Capital International
MTF	Multilateral Trading Facility
MTO	Medium-Term Objective
NAV	Net Asset Value
NCA	National Competition Authority
NCB	National Central Bank
NFC	Non-Financial Corporations
NMS	New Member States
NSA	National Supervisory Authority
NSFR	Net Stable Funding Ratio
NYSE	New York Stock Exchange
OECD	Organisation for Economic Co-operation and Development
OFT	Office of Fair Trading
OIS	Overnight Interest Rate Swap
OMTs	Outright Monetary Transactions
OMX	Options Maklarna Exchange
O-SIIs	Other Systemically Important Institutions
OTC	Over-the-Counter
P&C	Property and Casualty

PCA	Prompt Corrective Action
PSD	Payment Services Directive
QE	Quantitative Easing
RAROC	Risk Adjusted Return on Capital
RMBS	Residential Mortgage-Backed Securities
ROE	Return on Equity
RQMV	Reverse Qualified Majority Voting
RTGS	Real-Time Gross Settlement
RWAs	Risk-Weighted Assets
RWCRs	Risk-Weighted Capital Ratios
SBA	Stand-by Arrangement
SCP	Structure-Conduct-Performance
SCR	Solvency Capital Requirement
SEA	Single European Act
SEC	Securities and Exchange Commission
SEPA	Single Euro Payments Area
SETS	London Stock Exchange's premier Electronic Trading System
SFTs	Securities Financing Transactions
SGP	Stability and Growth Pact
SIB	Systemically Important Bank
SIFI	Systemically Important Financial Institution
SIV	Structured Investment Vehicle
SMEs	Small and Medium Enterprises
SMP	Securities Markets Programme
SOFFEX	Swiss Options and Financial Futures Exchange
SPO	Secondary Public Offering
SPV	Special Purpose Vehicle
SRB	Single Resolution Board
SRF	Single Resolution Fund
SRI	Socially Responsible Investing
SRM	Single Resolution Mechanism
SSM	Single Supervisory Mechanism
SSNIP	Small, but Significant Non-transitory Increase in Prices
SSP	Single Shared Platform
STP	Straight-Through Processing
TARGET	Trans-European Automated Real-Time Gross Settlement Express Transfer System
TBTF	Too Big To Fail

TEU	Treaty on European Union
TFEU	Treaty on the Functioning of the EU
TIPS	TARGET Instant Payment Settlement
TLAC	Total Loss-Absorbing Capacity
TLTROs	Targeted Longer-Term Refinancing Operations
T2S	TARGET2-Securities
TSCG	Treaty on Stability, Coordination and Governance in the Economic and Monetary Union
UCITS	Undertakings for Collective Investments in Transferable Securities
UK	United Kingdom
US	United States
VaR	Value-at-Risk

Part I

Setting the Stage

1

Functions of the Financial System

OVERVIEW

Having a well-functioning financial system in place that directs funds to their most productive uses is a crucial prerequisite for economic development. The financial system consists of the financial infrastructure and all financial intermediaries and financial markets, and their relationships with respect to the flow of funds to and from households, governments, business firms, and foreigners.

The main task of the financial system is to channel funds from those with a surplus to sectors that have a shortage of funds. In doing so, the financial sector performs two main functions: (1) reducing information and transaction costs and (2) facilitating the trading, diversification, and management of risk. This chapter discusses both of these functions at length.

The importance of financial markets and financial intermediaries differs across Member States of the European Union. An important question is how these differences affect macroeconomic outcomes. Atomistic markets face a free-rider problem: when an investor acquires information about an investment project and behaves accordingly, he reveals this information to all investors, thereby dissuading other investors from devoting resources to acquiring information. Financial intermediaries, particularly banks, may be better able to deal with this problem than financial markets.

This chapter discusses these and other pros and cons of market-based and bank-based systems. A specific element of this debate is the role of corporate governance, i.e. the set of mechanisms that arrange the relationship between stakeholders of a firm, notably equity holders, and the management of the firm. Investors (the outsiders) cannot perfectly monitor managers acting on their behalf, since managers (the insiders) have superior information about the performance of the company. Therefore mechanisms are needed to prevent company insiders from using the firm's profits for their own benefit rather than transferring them to outside investors. This chapter outlines the various mechanisms in place.

While there is considerable evidence that financial development up to some point is good for economic growth, there is no clear evidence that one type of financial system is better for growth than another. However, various recent studies suggest that differences in financial systems may influence the type of activity in which a country specialises, because certain systems may more easily facilitate particular types of economic activity than others. In addition, some evidence suggests that the economies of market-based systems are less affected by financial crises.

Before the financial crisis, the traditional banking model, in which issuing banks hold loans until they are repaid, was increasingly replaced by the 'originate and distribute' model, in which banks pool loans (like mortgages) and then tranch and sell them via securitisation. Therefore this chapter discusses the recent growth of non-bank financial intermediaries.

Finally, the chapter describes the 'law and finance' view, according to which legal system differences are key to explaining international variations in financial structure. According to this approach, distinguishing countries by the efficiency of their national legal systems in supporting financial transactions is more useful than categorising them based on whether they have bank-based or market-based financial systems.

LEARNING OBJECTIVES

After you have studied this chapter, you should be able to:
- explain the main functions of a financial system
- differentiate between the roles of financial markets and financial intermediaries
- explain why financial development may stimulate economic growth, and why this relationship may be non-linear
- explain why government regulation and supervision of the financial system is needed
- describe the advantages and disadvantages of bank-based and market-based financial systems
- explain the various corporate governance mechanisms
- explain the 'law and finance' view.

1.1 Functions of a Financial System

The Financial System

This section explains why financial development affects economic welfare. To understand the importance of financial development, the essentials of a country's *financial system* will first be outlined. The financial system

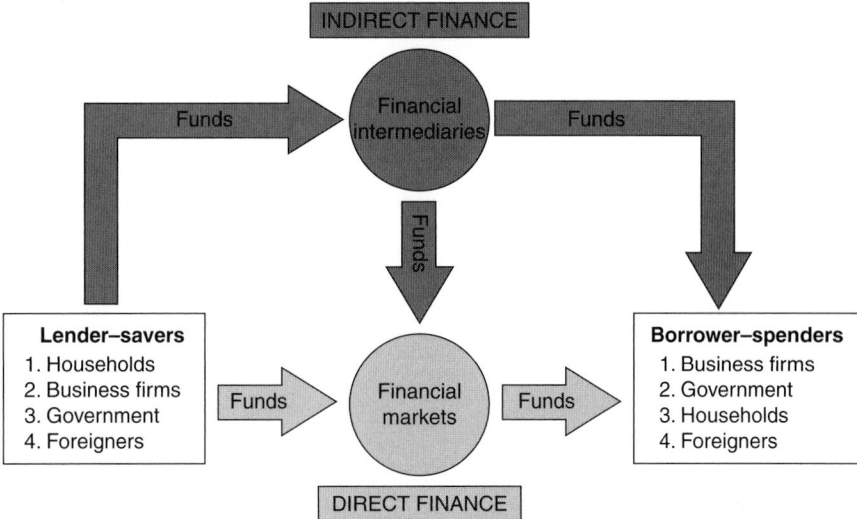

Figure 1.1   Functioning of the financial system
Source: Mishkin (2006)

encompasses the financial infrastructure and all financial intermediaries and financial markets, and their relationships with respect to the flow of funds to and from households, governments, business firms, and foreigners. *Financial infrastructure* is the set of institutions that enables the effective operation of financial intermediaries and financial markets, including payment systems, credit information bureaus, and collateral registries.

The main task of the financial system is to channel funds from sectors that have a surplus to those with a shortage of funds. Figure 1.1 explains the working of the financial system. Sectors that have saved and are lending funds are on the left, and those that must borrow to finance their spending are on the right. The bottom of the figure illustrates the process of *direct finance*, when one sector borrows funds from another sector via a *financial market* – a market in which participants issue and trade securities. The top of the figure depicts an *indirect finance* transaction, in which a financial intermediary obtains funds from savers and uses these savings to issue loans to a sector in need of finance. *Financial intermediaries* are (coalitions of) agents that provide financial services, such as banks, insurance companies, finance companies, mutual funds, and pension funds (Levine, 1997). In most countries, indirect finance is the main route for moving funds from lenders to borrowers. These countries have a *bank-based system*, while those that rely more on financial markets have a *market-based system*.

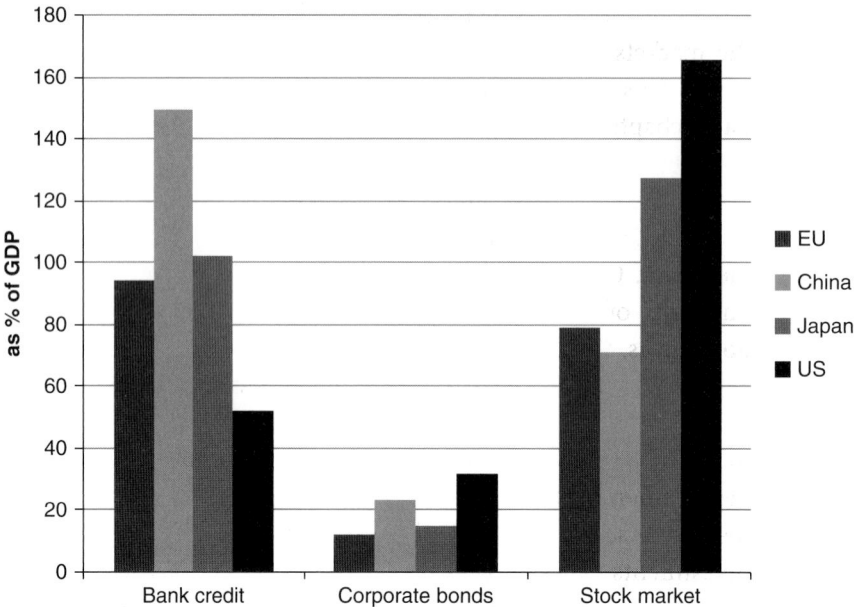

Figure 1.2   Bank credit and corporate bond and stock market capitalisation in the EU, China, Japan, and the US, 2017 (% of GDP)
Source: Authors' calculations based on data from World Bank, BIS, and WFE

Figure 1.2 shows the importance of bank credit, bond, and equity finance in the EU, China, Japan, and the US in 2017 as a percentage of GDP. It shows that banks are a more important source of finance for non-financial corporations in the EU than in the US, but China and Japan have higher levels of bank credit to non-financial firms than the EU. Stock and bond market capitalisation are highest in the US.

The financial system transforms household savings into funds that are available for investment by firms. However, the importance of financial markets and financial intermediaries varies across EU Member States, as will be explained in detail below. The types of assets held by households also differ among European countries. Yet EU countries' financial systems share one common feature – the importance of *internal finance*: most investments by firms in industrial countries are financed through retained earnings, regardless of the relative importance of financial markets and intermediaries (Allen and Gale, 2000).

The structure of the world's financial markets and institutions has experienced revolutionary changes over the last 30 years. Some financial markets have become obsolete, while new ones have emerged. Similarly, some financial institutions have gone bankrupt, while new entrants have emerged.

However, the functions of the financial system have been more stable than the markets and institutions used to accomplish these functions (Merton, 1995). This chapter discusses the functions of the financial system in detail. Later chapters will discuss the changes in Europe's financial markets and financial institutions over the last generation.

Major disruptions sometimes occur in the financial system that are characterised by sharp declines in asset prices and the failure of financial intermediaries. Capitalist economies have experienced such financial crises for hundreds of years. Often, these crises are followed by severe economic downturns. Chapter 2 will discuss financial crises, focusing on the banking and debt crises that have hit the euro area since 2008.

Having a well-functioning financial system in place that directs funds to their most productive uses is a crucial prerequisite for economic development. If sectors with surplus funds cannot channel their money to sectors with good investment opportunities, many productive investments will never take place. Indeed, cross-country, case-study, industry-, and firm-level analyses suggest that the functioning of financial systems is vitally linked to economic growth. Countries with larger banks and more active stock markets have higher growth rates, even after controlling for many other factors underlying economic growth (Levine, 2005; Popov, 2017). However, others have questioned the importance of finance for economic growth. For instance, Lucas (1988: 6) argues: 'I believe that the importance of financial matters is very badly over-stressed.' Furthermore, several recent studies conclude that the relationship between financial and economic development may be non-linear. For instance, Arcand *et al.* (2015) report that at intermediate levels of financial depth, there is a positive relationship between the size of the financial system and economic growth, but at high levels of financial depth, more finance is associated with less growth. In fact, the marginal effect of financial depth on output growth becomes negative when credit to the private sector reaches 80–100 per cent of GDP. This reflects the fact that higher levels of financing increase the likelihood of financial crises (see Chapter 2), which may depress economic growth. In addition, a large financial sector may lead to a misallocation of resources, as the financial sector may attract talent from more productive sectors of the economy, which may be inefficient from society's point of view. Finally, some types of finance, like mortgage credit, are considerably less conducive to sustainable economic development than other types, such as enterprise credit.

Main Functions

The two main *functions of the financial system* are (1) to reduce information and transaction costs, and (2) to facilitate the trading, diversification, and management of risk. This section discusses each of these functions in turn to explain why the financial sector may stimulate capital formation and/or technological innovation, two of the driving forces of economic growth.

Reducing Information Asymmetry and Transaction Costs

The financial system helps overcome the information asymmetry between borrowers and lenders that can occur *ex ante* and *ex post*, i.e. before and after a financial contract has been agreed upon. *Ex ante* information asymmetry arises because borrowers generally know more about their investment projects than lenders. The borrowers that are most eager to engage in a transaction are the most likely ones to produce an undesirable outcome for the lender (*adverse selection*). It is difficult and costly to evaluate potential borrowers. Individual savers may not have the time, capacity, or means to collect and process information on a wide array of potential borrowers. Thus, high information costs may prevent funds from flowing to their highest productive use. Financial intermediaries may reduce the costs of acquiring and processing information and thereby improve resource allocation. Without intermediaries, each investor would face the large fixed costs associated with evaluating investment projects. Financial markets may also reduce information costs. Economising on information acquisition costs facilitates the gathering of information about investment opportunities and thereby improves resource allocation. In addition to identifying the best investments, financial intermediaries may also boost the rate of technological innovation by identifying entrepreneurs with the best chances of successfully initiating new goods and production processes (Levine, 2005).

The information asymmetry problem occurs *ex post* when borrowers, but not investors, can observe actual behaviour. Once a loan has been granted, there is a risk that the borrower will engage in activities that are undesirable from the perspective of the lender (*moral hazard*). Financial markets and intermediaries also mitigate the information acquisition and enforcement costs of monitoring borrowers. For example, equity holders and banks will create financial arrangements that compel managers to manage the firm in their best interest (see Section 1.2 for more details).

Credit rating agencies (CRAs) play an important role in financial markets by producing information about credit risk and its distribution to market participants (see Box 1.1). CRAs assess the credit risk of borrowers (governments, financial, and non-financial firms) by providing credit ratings. A *credit rating* can be defined as an opinion regarding the creditworthiness of a financial instrument, or the issuer of a financial instrument, using an established and defined ranking system of rating categories. A rating only refers to the credit risk; other risks, like market risk (the risk due to unfavourable movements in market prices) and liquidity risk (the risk that a given security or asset cannot be traded quickly enough in the market to prevent a loss), are not taken into account. Ratings play a crucial role in financial markets, as investors use them to evaluate the credit risk of financial instruments. Since assessing these instruments requires specific knowledge and is very time consuming, individual investors often rely on CRA ratings. The ratings thus have an important influence on the interest rate that borrowers have to pay. The downgrading of a rating generally leads quickly to a higher interest rate on loans. Portfolio manager performance is often benchmarked against standard indices that are usually constructed on the basis of credit ratings.

Box 1.1 Credit rating agencies

Since John Moody started in 1909 with a small rating book, the rating business has developed into a multi-billion-dollar industry. CRAs essentially provide two services. First, they offer an independent assessment of the ability of issuers to meet their debt obligations, thereby providing 'information services' that reduce information costs, increase the pool of potential borrowers, and promote liquid markets. Second, they offer 'monitoring services' through which they encourage issuers to take corrective actions to avert downgrades via 'watch' procedures.

There are around 150 CRAs, but the three largest competitors (Standard & Poor's Ratings Services, Moody's Investors Service, and Fitch Ratings) share roughly 95 per cent of the market. While most CRAs are regional or product-type specialists, the three biggest players are truly global and broad in their product coverage. What is more, the sovereign rating coverage of the big three dwarfs that of other CRAs.

Credit ratings are expressed on a scale of letters and figures (see Figure 1.3). Standard & Poor's rating scale is, for example, as follows: AAA (highest rating), AA, A, BBB, BB, B, CCC, CC, C, D (lowest rating). Modifiers are attached to further distinguish ratings within classifications. Whereas Fitch and Standard & Poor's use pluses and minuses, Moody's uses numbers. CRAs typically signal their intention to consider rating changes in advance, using 'outlooks' and rating reviews (so-called watchlists). Whereas outlooks represent agencies' opinions on the development of a credit rating over the medium term, watchlists focus on a much shorter time horizon – three months, on average. The watch and outlook procedures

Box 1.1 (cont.)

Interpretation	Fitch and S&P	Moody's
Highest quality	AAA	Aaa
High quality	AA+	Aa1
	AA	Aa2
	AA−	Aa3
Strong payment capacity	A+	A1
	A	A2
	A−	A3
Adequate payment capacity	BBB+	Baa1
	BBB	Baa2
	BBB−	Baa3
Likely to fulfil obligations ongoing uncertainty	BB+	Ba1
	BB	Ba2
	BB−	Ba3
High-risk obligations	B+	B1
	B	B2
	B−	B3
Vulnerable to default	CCC+	Caa1
	CCC	Caa2
	CCC−	Caa3
Near or in bankruptcy or default	CC	Ca
	C	C
	D	D

Figure 1.3 Credit ratings
          Source: IMF (2010)

are considered to be generally strong predictors of rating changes relative to other publicly available data.

CRAs are mainly paid by the issuers of these instruments to publish a rating. This may give agencies an incentive to overstate the creditworthiness of a particular product in order to build a good relationship with the issuer, thereby creating a conflict of interest. However, CRAs must safeguard their credibility with investors, as otherwise their ratings would be of no value in the market. Yet it is doubtful whether the potential loss of reputation sufficiently restrains CRAs and can indeed function as an effective form of sanction. CRAs may be manipulated by issuers, which shop for a higher rating.

CRAs have come under attack due to their role in the recent financial crisis. It is widely believed that CRAs' poor credit assessments of complex structured credit products con-tributed to both the build-up and the unfolding of the crisis. Many analysts have concluded that CRAs assigned high ratings to complex structured subprime debt based on inadequate historical data and, in some cases, flawed models. The agencies have also come under fire for their sovereign rating activities, which involve assessments of a government's ability and willingness to repay its public debt (both the principal and interest) on time. CRAs were condemned for exacerbating the European debt crisis (see Chapter 2) when they

---

Box 1.1 (cont.)

downgraded the countries in the midst of the financial turmoil, thereby worsening the fiscal problems of countries like Greece, Ireland, Portugal, and Spain.

Before the global financial crisis, CRAs were mainly governed by the Code for Conduct Fundamentals for Credit Rating Agencies of the International Organisation of Securities Commissions (IOSCO), which sets international standards for security markets. The IOSCO code is based on voluntary compliance and lacks enforcement mechanisms (self-regulation). CRAs were supposed to follow the code or explain why they did not do so (i.e. comply or explain). In the wake of the financial crisis, the EU introduced regulation for CRAs, focusing on registration, enhanced oversight, and transparency. While the European Commission considers the revised IOSCO code to be 'the global benchmark', it maintained that its substance had to be made more specific, to make it easier to apply in practice, and more efficient. Therefore, the Regulation on Credit Rating Agencies (1060/2009/EC), which has been changed twice (by Regulation 513/2011 and Regulation 462/2013), determines that CRAs are supervised by ESMA (see de Haan and Amtenbrink (2012) for details). The European Securities and Markets Authority (ESMA) is, among other things, responsible for the registration and ongoing supervision of registered credit rating agencies. ESMA is an independent EU authority that helps safeguard the stability of the EU's financial system by ensuring the integrity, transparency, efficiency, and orderly functioning of securities markets, and enhancing investor protection (see Chapter 12).

In addition to reducing information costs, the financial system reduces the time and money required to carry out financial transactions (*transaction costs*), for example by *pooling* – the process of agglomerating funds from disparate savers for investment. By pooling the funds of various small savers, large investment projects can be financed. Without pooling, savers would have to buy and sell entire firms (Levine, 1997). Mobilising savings involves (1) overcoming the transaction costs of collecting savings from different individuals, and (2) overcoming the informational asymmetries associated with making savers feel comfortable about relinquishing control of their savings (Levine, 2005).

Pooling can take place via either financial markets or financial intermediaries. Firms can raise funds to finance large-scale projects by issuing securities (such as bonds and equities) in small denominations on public markets (stock exchanges) to tap a larger pool of savers. Savers generally prefer to invest in liquid instruments, i.e. instruments that can be converted into purchasing power quickly and inexpensively to ensure easy access to their funds. If claims on the firm can be traded in liquid secondary markets, savers will be more willing to relinquish their funds to finance long-term projects. Financial intermediaries such as banks offer an alternative way of pooling. They transform the funds collected from savers into short-term (liquid) and relatively safe bank deposits and invest these funds in portfolios of more profitable long-term (illiquid) risky projects by granting loans to diverse firms (ECB, 2018).

By reducing information and transaction costs, financial systems lower the cost of channelling funds between borrowers and lenders, which frees up resources for other uses, such as investment and innovation. In addition, financial intermediation affects capital accumulation by allocating funds to their most productive uses.

Facilitating Trading, Diversification, and Management of Risk

The second main service the financial sector provides is facilitating the trading, diversification, and management of risk. Financial systems may mitigate the risks associated with individual investment projects by providing opportunities for trading and diversifying risk, which may affect long-run economic growth. In general, high-return projects tend to be riskier than low-return projects. Thus, financial systems that make it easier for people to diversify risk by offering a broad range of high-risk (like equity) and low-risk (like government bonds) investment opportunities tend to induce a portfolio shift towards projects with higher expected returns. Likewise, the ability to manage a diversified portfolio of innovative projects reduces risk and promotes investment in growth-enhancing innovative activities (Levine, 2005).

Financial intermediaries and markets can reduce risk by providing *liquidity*, which refers to the ease and speed with which agents can convert assets into purchasing power at agreed prices (Levine, 1997). Savers are generally unwilling to delegate control over their savings to investors for long periods, so less investment is likely to occur in high-return projects that require a long-term commitment of capital. However, the financial system makes it possible for savers to hold liquid assets – like equity, bonds, or demand deposits – that they can sell quickly and easily if they need access to their savings. Without a financial system, all investors would be locked into illiquid long-term investments that yield high payoffs only for those who consume at the end of the investment. Liquidity is created by financial intermediaries as well as financial markets. For instance, a bank transforms short-term liquid deposits into long-term illiquid loans, therefore making it possible for households to withdraw deposits without interrupting industrial production. Similarly, stock markets reduce liquidity risks by allowing stockholders to trade their shares, while firms still have access to long-term capital.

Risk measurement and management is a key function of financial intermediaries. The traditional role of banks in monitoring borrowers' credit risk has evolved towards the use of advanced models by all types of financial intermediaries to measure and manage financial risks. Progress in information technology has facilitated the development of advanced risk management models, which rely on statistical methods to process financial data (see Chapters 10 and 11 for more details).

Securitisation is the packaging of particular assets and the redistribution of these packages by selling securities, backed by these assets, to investors (see also Section 1.3). It is an important way for the financial system to perform the function of trading, diversification, and management of risk. For instance, an intermediary may create a pool of mortgage loans (bundling) and then issue bonds backed by those loans (unbundling). Securitisation thereby converts illiquid assets into liquid assets. While residential mortgages were the first financial assets to be securitised, many other types of financial assets have undergone the same process.

While the focus of finance is traditionally on fostering investment, more attention has recently been paid to social and environmental factors. A new subfield of finance and sustainability stresses the role of finance in accelerating the transition towards a sustainable economy (see Box 1.2).

Box 1.2 Finance and sustainability

The allocation role of finance is an important part of the transition towards a sustainable economy. Sustainable development can be defined as development that meets the needs of the present generation without compromising the ability of future generations to meet their own needs. Resource scarcity and climate change are reaching planetary boundaries and may reduce the consumption of future generations. Population growth is speeding up this process. Sustainable finance also takes social and environmental factors into account (see Figure 1.4). Social factors encompass inequality and (child) labour conditions, while environmental factors include the intensity of resource use, pollution, and ecosystem decline. Although the impact of economic activities on the environment is typically felt in the long term, conventional finance is mostly focused on the short term, which is reinforced by quarterly reporting of financial results (an exception is life insurance companies and pension funds, which tend to have a long-term focus; see Chapter 9).

Box 1.2 (cont.)

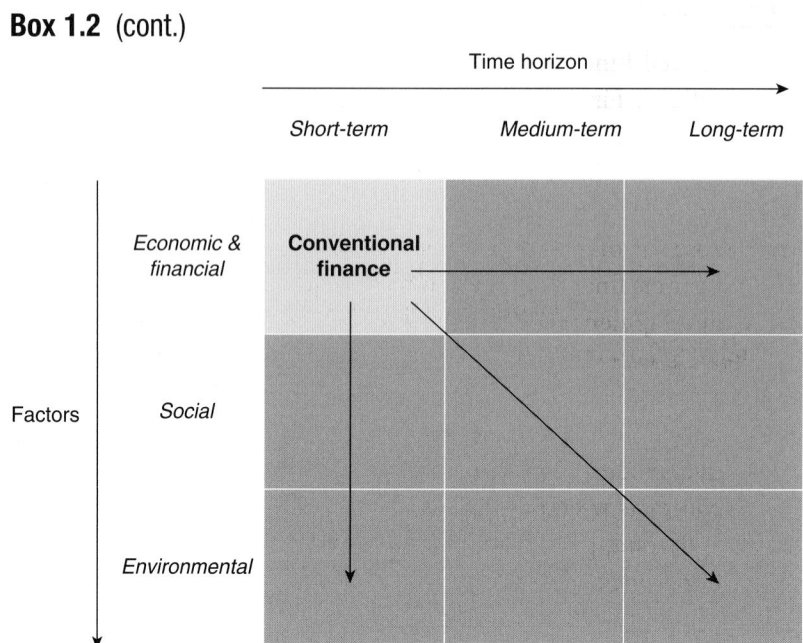

Figure 1.4   Time horizon and factors in sustainable finance
            Source: Sikken (2014)

Companies are increasingly integrating sustainability principles into their business strategies. Some institutional investors have adopted a socially responsible investing (SRI)
approach, which incorporates environmental, social, and governance (ESG) information
into investment decisions. While environmental and social reports used to be stand-alone
reports (and were therefore largely ignored), newly emerging integrated reports show how
a company's strategy, governance, performance, and prospects, in the context of its external
environment, lead to the creation of value in the short, medium, and long term.

The materiality (or lack thereof) of the ESG dimension within and between industries depends
on the nature of the industry, the specific company's business model, and local conditions
(Schoenmaker and Schramade, 2019). New evidence indicates that there may be a business
case to take ESG information into account when making investment decisions. There is also
evidence suggesting that companies that perform well on ESG issues exhibit a superior financial
performance (Khan *et al.*, 2016). But the evidence on the link between ESG and financial
performance is mixed. In a meta-study, Friede *et al.* (2015) conclude that some 90 per cent of
the studies considered find a non-negative relationship between ESG and company financial
performance, while the large majority of studies reports positive findings. However, in another
meta-study, Revelli and Viviani (2015) find that SRI has no real cost or benefit.

Role of Government

A well-functioning financial system requires four types of government actions. First, government regulation is needed to protect *property rights* and to *enforce contracts*. Property rights refer to control over the use of the property, the right to any benefit from the property, the right to transfer or sell the property, and the right to exclude others from the property. The absence of secure property rights and enforcement of contracts severely restricts financial transactions and investment, thereby hampering financial development. If it is not clear who is entitled to perform a transaction, an exchange will be unlikely. As the financial system allocates capital across time and space, contracts are needed to connect the providers and users of funds. If one of the parties does not adhere to the content of a contract, an independent enforcement agency (for instance, a court) is needed; otherwise contracts would be useless.

Second, government regulation is needed to encourage proper information provision (*transparency*) so that providers of funds can take better decisions on how to allocate their money. Government regulation can reduce adverse selection and moral hazard problems in financial systems and enhance their efficiency by increasing the amount of information available to investors, for instance, by setting and enforcing accounting standards. However, borrowers have strong incentives to cheat, so government regulation may not always be sufficient, as various corporate scandals, such as WorldCom, Parmalat, and Ahold, illustrate.

Third, in view of the importance of financial intermediaries, governments should arrange for the regulation and supervision of financial institutions in order to ensure their *soundness*. Savers are often unable to properly evaluate the financial soundness of a financial intermediary, as that requires extensive effort and technical knowledge. Financial intermediaries have an incentive to take too many risks because high-risk investments generally bring in more revenues that accrue to the intermediary, while if the intermediary fails the depositors bear a substantial part of the costs. Government regulation may prevent financial intermediaries from taking too many risks. Depositors may also be protected by a deposit guarantee system, but this may provide the intermediary with an even stronger incentive to engage in risky behaviour. Finally, there is a risk that a sound financial intermediary may fail when another intermediary goes bankrupt due to taking too many risks (*contagion*). Since the public cannot distinguish between sound and unsound financial institutions, they may withdraw their money once one financial intermediary fails, thereby perhaps destroying a sound institution. Chapter 12 discusses *financial supervision* in the EU, while Chapter 13 deals with *financial stability* in the EU. A stable financial system is capable of withstanding shocks and the unravelling of financial imbalances, thereby mitigating the likelihood of disruptions in the financial intermediation process that are severe enough to significantly impair the allocation of savings to profitable investment opportunities (ECB, 2006). An important prerequisite for financial stability is a well-functioning financial infrastructure, which is discussed in Chapter 7.

New regulatory and supervisory policies are increasingly designed at the global level. The Basel Committee on Banking Supervision, the International Association of Insurance Supervisors, and the IOSCO traditionally set the international standards. The Financial Stability Board (FSB), which comprises G20 ministers of finance, central banks, and supervisors, has set the international financial reform agenda since the financial crisis. The FSB has addressed the problem that some financial institutions may be 'too big to fail', i.e. their failure may have such serious consequences that governments will always come to their rescue. The FSB has produced a list of global systemically important financial institutions that have to follow stricter regulations (see Chapters 12 and 13).

Fourth, governments are responsible for *competition policy* to ensure competition. There are many ways that competition may be hampered. For instance, competitors may agree to sell the same product or service at the same price (*price fixing*), leading to profits for all the sellers. Or banks may receive support from the government (*state aid*), leading to an unfair advantage over their competitors. In the EU, competition policy is based on the Treaty on the Functioning of the European Union, particularly Articles 101 (Restrictive practices), 102 (Abuse of dominant market power), and 107 (State aid control). The treaty states: 'The following shall be prohibited . . . : (a) directly or indirectly fix purchase or selling prices . . . (b) limit or control production . . . (c) share markets or sources of supply'. Chapter 14 provides further details on EU competition policy for the financial sector.

Foreign Participants

Figure 1.1 assumes that foreigners also participate in the financial system and that domestic sectors can borrow from or lend to foreigners. What are the benefits of lending or borrowing in foreign financial markets and doing business with foreign financial intermediaries? Following Mishkin (2006), we may differentiate between the direct and indirect effects of (international) *financial liberalisation*, i.e. the opening up of domestic financial markets to foreign capital and foreign financial intermediaries.

Allowing foreign capital to freely enter domestic markets increases the availability of funds, thereby stimulating investment and economic growth. Furthermore, competition in the financial system may be enhanced when foreign financial intermediaries enter a country, stimulating domestic financial intermediaries to become more efficient.[1] Finally, opening up to foreign capital and foreign financial institutions may lead to implementing institutional reforms that stimulate financial development (see Box 1.3). For instance, when domestic financial intermediaries lose customers to foreign intermediaries, they may support institutional reforms, such as improved transparency regulation, helping them to compete better (Mishkin, 2006).

As will be explained in some detail in Chapter 3, the EU has gone beyond financial liberalisation and has taken various steps to promote the creation of a single market for financial services. Chapter 6 will analyse *financial market integration* in the EU. According to Baele *et al.* (2008), a market for a given set of financial instruments or services is fully integrated when all potential market participants in such a market (1) are subject to a single set of rules for dealing with those financial instruments or services, (2) have equal access to this set of financial instruments or services, and (3) are treated equally when they operate in the market.

1.2 Bank-Based versus Market-Based Financial Systems

There are important differences among the financial systems of the EU Member States. For instance, the size of financial markets and the importance of bank and non-bank financial intermediaries (such as mutual funds, private pension funds, and insurance companies) differ substantially across countries (Bijlsma and Zwart, 2013). Based on the ratio of bank credit to market capitalisation, three groups of countries can be distinguished:
1. Belgium, Finland, France, Ireland, Luxembourg, the Netherlands, Sweden, and the United Kingdom (market-based countries);
2. Austria, Bulgaria, Croatia, the Czech Republic, Denmark, Estonia, Germany, Greece, Hungary, Italy, Latvia, Lithuania, Malta, Poland, Portugal, Romania, Slovakia, Slovenia, and Spain (bank-based countries);
3. Cyprus (outlier).

Countries in the first group are closer to the US than other EU Member States. The second group consists of EU countries that resemble China more

Box 1.3 The political economy of financial reform

Reforming the financial system may foster financial development, which in turn may stimulate economic growth. For instance, Bekaert *et al.* (2005) report that countries that liberalised their equity markets experienced an overall increase in annual per capita GDP growth of approximately 1 per cent.

Some countries have reformed earlier and more extensively than others. What explains these policy differences? A small but very relevant line of research has examined the forces driving financial reform. These studies are based on the assumptions that there are winners and losers in financial reform, and that the status quo will persist as long as the benefits of not reforming outweigh the costs of not reforming for those who determine the timing and pace of policies. Fernandez and Rodrik (1991) explain the tendency to retain the status quo if individuals affected by the reform are uncertain of its benefits. If it is not known *ex ante* who will benefit from the reform, a majority may oppose the policy change even if they would benefit *ex post* from it. So, although several financial institutions may prosper after a reform, uncertainty regarding the identities of the winners and losers may cause the sector as a whole to oppose it. Learning, made possible by the accumulation of new information, is particularly relevant in this context (Abiad and Mody, 2005). If the reform takes place in stages, then the early stages of the reform may help agents assess whether they will benefit or lose; therefore they may change their views. Consequently, some agents who initially opposed reforms may become advocates for further reforms.

Abiad and Mody (2005) use a newly constructed financial reform index, covering 35 countries over the period 1973–1996, to examine the driving forces of financial reform. The index captures six dimensions of financial liberalisation, including the degree of controls on international financial transactions. On each dimension, a country is classified as being fully repressed, partially repressed, largely liberalised, or fully liberalised. When they relate their index to various explanatory variables, Abiad and Mody (2005) find that countries with highly repressed financial sectors tend to stay that way, but once reforms are initiated, the likelihood of additional reforms increases. This suggests that learning plays an important role. Various types of crises also influence the process. While balance-of-payments crises tend to increase the likelihood of financial reforms, banking crises tend to increase the likelihood of reversals of reform. According to Abiad and Mody (2005), left-wing and right-wing governments are seen to operate similarly in similar situations, and openness to trade does not, on average, increase the pace of reform.

closely and includes the Eastern European countries that joined the EU more recently. Recent entrants generally have smaller financial systems than those in the old Member States, where firms rely more on financing by banks than on market finance. Finally, Cyprus is classified as an outlier since it has a very

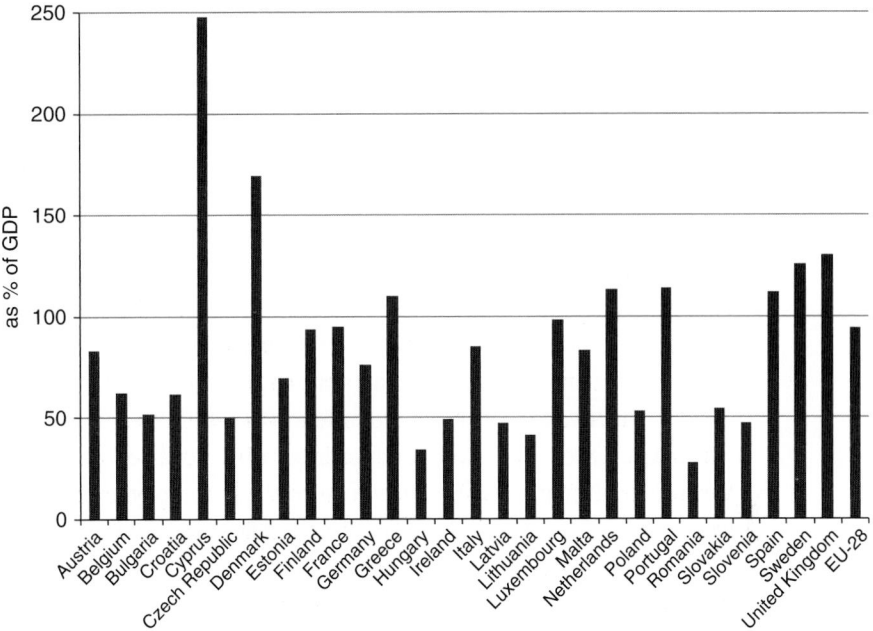

Figure 1.5   Bank credit in EU Member States, 2016 (% GDP)
Source: Authors' calculations based on World Bank data

large banking sector that extends a large amount of credit relative to the size of its economy. Arguably, it could also be classified as bank-based, given the size of its banking sector.

However, there are sometimes important differences even within each group. For instance, among bank-based countries the importance of bank credit for financing non-financial firms differs substantially, as shown by Figure 1.5. For instance, bank credit to non-financial firms was higher in Spain than in Germany or Italy.

A key question is how these differences in financial systems affect macro-economic outcomes. For instance, do bank-based financial systems (like that of Germany) lead to higher rates of economic growth than market-based systems (like that of the UK)?

Providing Financial Functions

What are the theoretical reasons explaining the differences in the growth performance of countries with bank-based vs. market-based systems? As Levine (2005) pointed out, the case for a bank-based system refers to the role of markets in fulfilling financial roles. As discussed above, atomistic markets face a *free-rider problem*: when an investor acquires information about an investment project and behaves accordingly, he reveals this information to all investors, thereby dissuading others from devoting resources to acquiring information. Thus investors lack strong incentives to properly acquire information, as they cannot keep the benefits of this information for themselves. Consequently, innovative projects with the potential to foster growth may not be identified. Banks, however, may exclusively benefit from the information they acquire, often by maintaining long-term relationships with firms, and use it in a profitable way. Since banks can make investments without revealing their decisions immediately in public markets, they have an incentive to research potential investment projects. Furthermore, banks with close ties to firms may be more effective than atomistic markets at exerting pressure on firms to repay their loans. Often, firms obtain a variety of financial services from their bank and also maintain checking accounts with it, thereby increasing the bank's information about the borrower. For example, the bank can learn about the firm's sales by monitoring the cash flowing through its checking account or by keeping track of the firm's accounts receivables. Firms may profit from these long-term relationships in the form of access to credit at lower prices.

However, banks' informational advantage may induce them to appropriate a sizeable share of their borrowers' profits, thus thwarting borrowers' incentives to perform. This *hold-up problem* can be mitigated if a borrower also has access to market-based funding. However, many firms, especially small and medium-sized enterprises, have no access to market-based funding, and therefore remain vulnerable to the hold-up problem (Langfield and Pagano, 2016).

The problem of free riding in financial markets that occurs due to diffuse shareholders may be less severe in the case of large, concentrated ownership. However, concentrated owners may maximise the private benefits of control at the expense of minority shareholders. Furthermore, large equity owners may stimulate the firm to undertake higher-risk activities since shareholders benefit on the upside, while debt holders share the costs of failure. Finally, the concentrated control of corporate assets produces market power that may distort public policies (Levine, 2005). The available empirical evidence does not suggest that international differences in concentrated ownership are associated with disciplining firms' management (Carlin and Mayer, 2000).

Corporate Governance

A second element in the debate about the pros and cons of bank-based vs. market-based systems refers to *corporate governance*, i.e. the set of mechanisms regulating the relationship between a firm's stakeholders (notably equity holders) and its management. Principal–agent theory predicts that the managers (i.e. the agents) may not always act in the best interest of the owners (i.e. the principal) (Jensen and Meckling, 1976). Investors (the outsiders) cannot perfectly monitor the managers acting on their behalf, since managers (the insiders) have superior information about the performance of the company. Thus mechanisms are needed to prevent company insiders from using the firm's profits for their own benefit rather than returning the money to outside investors. Corporate governance systems differ across EU Member States (see Box 1.4).

Investors can use several tools to ensure that firm managers act in their interest. The most important of these are the appointment of the board of directors, executive compensation, the market for corporate control, concentrated holdings, and monitoring by financial intermediaries (Allen and Gale, 2000).

Appointing the board of directors[2] gives shareholders an instrument with which to control managers and to ensure that the firm is run in their interest. The way that boards are chosen differs across countries. In many countries, firm managers effectively determine who is nominated for the board, which may create an incestuous relationship between boards of directors and management (Jensen, 1993). Boards may, for instance, approve various protection mechanisms that reduce the attractiveness of a takeover, one of the mechanisms in the market for corporate control (see below).

Box 1.4 Corporate governance in EU Member States

Governance Metrics International (GMI) publishes ratings of firms' corporate governance on a scale of 1.0 (lowest) to 10.0 (highest). Each GMI rating report includes a summary of the company's overall governance profile and commentary on six research categories: board accountability, financial disclosure and internal controls, shareholder rights, executive compensation, market for control and ownership base, and corporate behaviour and corporate social responsibility. All company ratings are calculated relative to the 3,400+ companies rated by GMI worldwide (global rating). A GMI rating of 9.0 or higher is considered to be well above average. A rating of 7.5–8.5 is above average, 6.0–7.0 is average, 3.5–5.5 is below average, and 3.0 or less is well below average.

The number of firms with a GMI rating differs across countries, ranging from 14 in Spain to 394 in the UK. Figure 1.6 shows the average GMI score for various EU Member States. The figure shows that the corporate governance regimes differ substantially. While the average score for Spain is only 3.97, for the UK it is 7.60.

Box 1.4 (cont.)

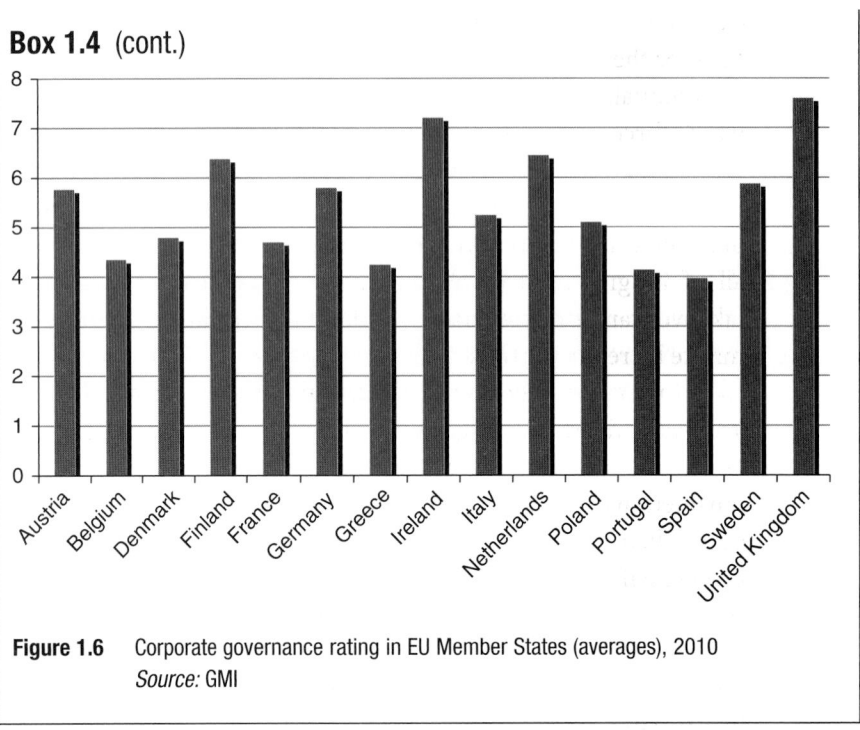

Figure 1.6   Corporate governance rating in EU Member States (averages), 2010
Source: GMI

A second method of ensuring that managers pursue the interests of share-holders is to base managers' compensation on the firm's performance. Examples include direct ownership of shares, stock options, and bonuses dependent on the share price. However, contingent compensation may also incentivise managers to take excessive risks, as they benefit handsomely from good performance but face limited penalties for poor performance (Allen and Gale, 2000).

The most important mechanism with which to control firm management is the market for corporate control, which can operate in three ways: proxy contests, friendly mergers and takeovers, and hostile takeovers. In *proxy contests*, a shareholder tries to persuade other shareholders to act in concert with him to force the management of the firm to change course or even to unseat the board of directors. The success of proxy contests depends, among other things, on the dispersion of shareholding. The more dispersed share-holdings are, the more difficult such contests will be.

Friendly mergers and takeovers occur when the management of both firms agree that combining the firms would create additional value. The transaction can occur in various ways, such as an exchange of stock or a tender offer by one firm for the other firm's stock (Allen and Gale, 2000).

Potentially the most important device in the market for corporate control, which forces managers to behave in accordance with stockholders' interests, is a hostile takeover. A *takeover bid* is an attempt by a potential acquirer to obtain a controlling block of shares in a target firm, and thereby gain control of the board and, through it, the firm's management. If a firm does not exploit all of its growth potential, some outsiders may consider it an attractive takeover target. After a takeover, they will try to improve the firm's performance by replacing the current management. This threat gives managers the right incentives to behave in the interest of current stockholders. However, a takeover threat may not be successful for three reasons. First, there may be an information asymmetry between insiders and outsiders: ill-informed outsiders will outbid relatively well-informed insiders for control of firms only when they pay too much. Second, there may again be a free-rider problem: if an outsider spends resources to obtain information, other market participants will also benefit from the results of this research when the outsider bids for shares of the firm. Third, firms often take actions that deter takeovers, and thereby weaken the market, as a disciplining device. For instance, a firm may issue rights to existing shareholders to acquire a large number of new securities.

Since the market for corporate control may not always ensure that managers behave in accordance with shareholders' interests, proponents of a bank-based system argue that monitoring by financial institutions may be more effective. The agency problem is solved by financial institutions acting as the outside monitor for firms (Allen and Gale, 2000). By investing their funds with a financial intermediary that, in turn, provides funds to firms, individual savers de facto delegate the monitoring function to the financial institution. The intermediary can realise economies of scale in monitoring costs, and may eliminate the free-rider problem for individual savers because it performs a monitoring function for all savers. The main characteristics of this system are a long-term relationship between banks – but potentially other financial intermediaries like institutional investors as well (see Chapter 9) – and firms, financial intermediaries that hold both equity and debt, and active intervention from the financial intermediary should the firm become financially distressed.

However, it is not clear that banks are better at mitigating borrowers' moral hazard than securities markets. Banks can discipline borrowers by punishing defaults with a refusal of further credit. However, even though the threat of such punishment may be optimal *ex ante*, it is not fully credible: once a firm gets into default, the bank's costs are sunk. If the borrower has another profitable project, the bank will want to finance it, and will thus renege on its threat not to extend credit – a practice known as 'ever-greening' or forbearance. Securities markets tend to be more credible: defaulting borrowers typically find it difficult to restructure their bonds and obtain further funding due to the high transaction costs of renegotiating with many bondholders, rather than a single bank. Moreover, each bondholder has the incentive to do nothing and let other bondholders renegotiate. As a consequence, no renegotiation occurs (Dewatripont and Maskin, 1995; Langfield and Pagano, 2016).

Proponents of a market-based system also point to the problems created by powerful banks. While firms with close ties to a 'main bank' have greater access to capital and are less cash constrained than firms without such ties, dependence on an influential bank may have various negative effects. Bankers act in their *own* best interests, not necessarily in the best interests of all stakeholders. For instance, banks with power can extract part of the expected future profits from potentially profitable investments, which may reduce the firm's effort to undertake innovative investments. Influential banks may also prevent outsiders from removing inefficient managers if these managers are particularly generous to the bankers. In addition, bank managers may be more reluctant to bankrupt firms with which they have had long-term ties (Levine, 2005).

Furthermore, it may be difficult to govern the banks themselves. For instance, if large banks are also incorporated as joint stock companies, the same informational frictions (namely asymmetric information and incentive distortions) will impair the effective monitoring of bank managers by the banks' shareholders (ECB, 2018).

Finally, proponents of market-based financial systems claim that markets provide a more effective set of instruments with which to manage risks. While bank-based systems may provide inexpensive, basic risk management services for standardised situations, market-based systems provide greater flexibility to tailor make products.

Types of Activity

While there is considerable evidence that financial development is good for economic growth, early research concluded that there is no clear evidence that a particular kind of financial system is best for growth. For instance,

Levine (2002) finds that the quality of the financial services produced by the entire financial system (intermediaries and markets) affects economic growth. However, some more recent studies suggest that while both bank-based and market-based financial systems support economic growth on average, their contribution varies according to the extent of economic and financial development (Popov, 2017). For instance, Demirgüç-Kunt *et al.* (2013) use a large cross-country sample and show that as countries develop economically, there is a weaker association between an increase in economic output and an increase in bank development, and a stronger link between an increase in economic output and an increase in securities market development. The difference between market-based and bank-based systems may also matter for other reasons, which are discussed further in Box 1.5.

Box 1.5 Does the type of financial system matter after all?

Securities markets have the advantage of aggregating the diverse views of a large number of market participants, and are therefore more likely to support activities in which there is a high degree of uncertainty in production. Banks are more likely to support activities in which uncertainty is low but gestation periods are long (Carlin and Mayer, 2000). Banks may be effective at eliminating the duplication of information gathering and processing, but securities markets may be better able to gather and process information in new, uncertain situations involving innovative products and processes.

Gambacorta *et al.* (2014) show that differences in financial structures are related to the sectoral composition of output. Sectors with tangible and transferable capital (such as agriculture), as well as those in which output is easier to pledge as collateral (such as construction), will rely more on bank loans. By contrast, sectors that rely heavily on human capital, or those in which output is hard to collateralise, will tend to rely more on equity or bonds. Likewise, firm size is related to the funding mix: small firms typically depend on bank finance because of the fixed costs involved in tapping capital markets.

Gambacorta *et al.* (2014) also show that banks and markets behave differently in relation to moderating business cycle fluctuations. Drawing on their long-term relationships with clients, banks are more inclined to offer credit during a downturn, while markets are more inclined to pull back during a recession. However, a financial crisis can impair banks' shock-absorbing capacity. When banks are under strain, they are less able to help their clients through difficult times. In addition, during a financial crisis, banks may put off necessary balance sheet restructuring but instead roll over credit in an effort to postpone loss recognition (so-called zombie lending). Capital market investors cannot afford to do this. In a financial crisis, therefore, systems that are more market oriented may speed up the necessary deleveraging, thereby paving the way for a sustainable recovery.

Box 1.5 (cont.)

The differing responses of banks and markets can also affect the severity of recessions. While the average cost, in terms of forgone output, of normal recessions is lower for countries with a bank-based system than those with a market-based system, the opposite is true when recessions coincide with a financial crisis. If these events coincide, countries with a bank-based system tend to have recessions that are three times as severe as those with a market-based system (Gambacorta *et al.*, 2014). Langfield and Pagano (2016) find that housing market crises may have a particularly large impact in bank-based systems. When the value of assets that banks have as collateral drops, banks may deleverage their balance sheet and implement more conservative lending approaches, which in turn reduces bank financing.

Complements

Some authors argue that financial markets and financial intermediaries may provide complementary growth-enhancing financial services to the economy. On the one hand, financial intermediaries may be necessary for the successful functioning of financial markets. On the other hand, financial intermediaries' business models may depend on the existence of well-functioning financial markets. Mutual funds, for instance, rely on the existence of liquid securities markets.

Financial markets have not developed spontaneously. The earliest financial transactions involving loans were handled by financial intermediaries. The Amsterdam Bourse, founded at the start of the seventeenth century, was the first formal financial market (Allen and Gale, 2000). Stock markets may complement banks by spurring competition for corporate control and by offering alternative means of financing investment, thereby reducing the potentially harmful effects of excessive bank power. Indeed, banks have increasingly moved away from their traditional deposit-taking and lending role towards fee-generating activities, such as the securitisation of loans and the sale of risk management products (see Section 1.3). Financial markets, of course, also compete with banks. Consumers can invest directly in securities (government and private bonds, and stocks) rather than leaving their money in savings accounts, while borrowers can access capital markets rather than banks. Direct customer access to these markets is often called *dis-intermediation*.

Allen and Santomero (1997) forcefully argue that financial intermediaries reduce *participation costs*, i.e. the costs of learning about and effectively using financial markets. As financial markets have become increasingly complex, financial intermediaries offer various services to uninformed investors, such as providing information, investing on their behalf, or offering a fixed income claim against the intermediary's balance sheet. Investors obtain access to financial markets through the intermediary's services, which add value to the transaction by reducing the (perceived) participation costs of uninformed investors. Allen and Santomero (1997) argue that financial intermediaries' and firms' greater use of such services has increased the breadth and depth of financial markets. The increased size of financial markets has coincided with a dramatic shift away from individuals' direct participation in financial markets towards participation through various intermediaries. The importance of different types of intermediaries has also undergone a significant change. While the share of assets held by banks has fallen, institutional investors now hold dramatically more (see Chapter 9 for a further analysis). In countries with a bank-dominated financial system, like France and Italy, the role of institutional investors has increased, which has made these actors more dominant in corporate governance issues.

Legal Systems

Recent research suggests that differences in legal systems are key to explaining international differences in financial structure. Each country's financial system comprises a set of contracts that is defined and made more or less effective by legal rights and contract enforcement mechanisms. A well-functioning legal system facilitates the operation of both financial markets and intermediaries. According to this literature, distinguishing countries according to the efficiency of their national legal systems in supporting financial transactions is more useful than categorising them by whether they have bank-based or market-based financial systems. La Porta et al. (1997) argue that countries' financial systems offer different levels of creditor and shareholder protection. Common law countries of the English tradition protect both shareholders and creditors the most, French civil law countries the least, and German and Scandinavian civil law countries fall somewhere in the middle. However, countries with German or Scandinavian legal origins are said to have the highest level of contract enforcement. La Porta et al. (1997: 1149) find that 'civil law, and particularly French civil law, countries, have both the weakest investor protections and the least developed capital markets, especially as compared to common law countries'.

Table 1.1 summarises some of the measures developed by La Porta et al. (1997) and extended and updated by Djankov et al. (2007, 2008) for the EU Member States. Column (2) shows the legal family to which the country

Table 1.1 Indicators of investor and creditor protection, 2003

(1)	(2)	(3)	(4)	(5)
Country	Law family	Creditor rights	Shareholder rights	Anti-self-dealing index
Austria	German	3	2.5	0.21
Belgium	French	2	3	0.54
Bulgaria	German	n.a.	3	0.65
Czech Republic	German	3	4	0.33
Denmark	Scandinavian	3	4	0.46
Finland	Scandinavian	1	3.5	0.46
France	French	0	3.5	0.38
Germany	German	3	3.5	0.28
Greece	French	1	2	0.22
Hungary	German	1	2	0.18
Ireland	English	1	5	0.79
Italy	French	2	2	0.42
Latvia	German	3	4	0.32
Lithuania	French	2	4	0.36
Luxembourg	French	n.a.	2	0.28
Netherlands	French	3	2.5	0.20
Portugal	French	1	2.5	0.44
Slovakia	German	2	3	0.29
Slovenia	German	3	n.a.	n.a.
Spain	French	2	5	0.37
Sweden	Scandinavian	1	3.5	0.33
United Kingdom	English	4	5	0.95

Note: n.a. = not available
Source: Djankov *et al.* (2007, 2008)

belongs. The rationale for the other measures is as follows. Those who control a firm – managers, controlling shareholders, or both – can use their power to deliver firm wealth to themselves, without sharing it with other investors. The measures quantify the extent to which various investors are protected. Column (3) presents a creditor rights index that measures the powers of secured lenders in bankruptcy (Djankov *et al.*, 2007). The index is scored from 0 (poor creditor rights) to 4 (strong creditor rights). For their full sample, Djankov *et al.* report that the index of creditor rights for 2003 is lowest in French legal-origin countries and highest in German legal-origin ones.

Column (4) shows an index reflecting shareholder rights. A number of scholars have criticised the original index, reported in La Porta *et al.* (1997), for its ad hoc nature, mistakes in its coding, and conceptual ambiguity in the definitions of some components. Therefore, Djankov *et al.* (2008) developed a revised and extended index that is shown in column (4) of Table 1.1. This index is available for 72 countries and is based on laws and regulations applicable to publicly traded firms as of May 2003. The index summarises the protection of minority shareholders in the corporate decision-making process, including the right to vote. It is scored from 0 (poor shareholder rights) to 6 (strong shareholder rights). For their full sample, Djankov *et al.* (2008) report that the index of shareholder rights is lowest in French legal-origin countries and highest in English legal-origin ones.

A more recent alternative measure quantifies the level of shareholder rights' protection from expropriation by corporate insiders through self-dealing (see Djankov *et al.*, 2008). Various forms of such self-dealing include executive perquisites to excessive compensation, transfer pricing, self-serving financial transactions such as directed equity issuance or personal loans to insiders, and outright theft of corporate assets. This index ranges between 0 (poor protection) and 1 (high protection) and is shown in column (5) of Table 1.1. For their full sample, Djankov *et al.* report that the index is lowest in French legal-origin countries and highest in English legal-origin ones.

Various conclusions can be drawn from Table 1.1. First, EU Member States clearly have different legal traditions. So, if the finance and law view is correct (see Box 1.6 for a discussion), financial differences in the EU are likely to be sustained despite attempts to create a single financial market (see Chapter 3 for further details on the various policy initiatives to create a single market). Second, the various indicators vary widely across EU Member States, suggesting that the degree to which investors are protected differs substantially across these countries. For instance, the creditor rights index ranges between 0 (France) and 4 (the UK), while the shareholder index ranges between 1 (Luxembourg) and 5 (Spain and the UK).

Box 1.6 Legal origin, endowments, or political institutions?

According to the law and finance literature, countries' financial development can be traced to their legal origins (La Porta *et al.*, 1997). Beck *et al.* (2003) test the law and finance theory and the *endowments theory* based on Acemoglu *et al.* (2001). The endowments theory focuses on the disease and geography endowments encountered by colonisers, and how these endowments shaped both colonisation strategy and the construction of long-lasting institutions. Acemoglu *et al.* (2001) argue that the mortality rates of European settlers in different parts of the world after 1500 affected the colonisation strategy and their willingness to establish settlements. Places that were relatively healthy for them were more likely to receive better economic and political institutions, while places that European

Box 1.6 (cont.)

settlers were less likely to go were more likely to have 'extractive' institutions imposed, which did not protect private property or prevent expropriation. The main purpose of colonisation was to transfer resources from the colony to the colonising state. This early pattern of institutions has persisted, and influences the extent and nature of modern institutions. Acemoglu *et al.* (2001) propose using estimates of potential European settler mortality as an instrument for institutional variation in former European colonies today.

Although Acemoglu *et al.* (2001) focus on general institutional development, their theory is applicable to the financial sector. As Beck *et al.* (2003) point out, in an extractive environment, colonisers will not construct institutions that favour the development of free, competitive financial markets because these may threaten the position of the extractors. By contrast, in settler colonies, colonisers will be much more likely to construct institutions that foster financial development. Using settler mortality as a proxy for endowments, Beck *et al.* (2003) find supporting evidence for both theories. However, their evidence also suggests that initial endowments explain more of the cross-country variation in financial intermediary and stock market development than legal origin. Furthermore, initial endowments are more robustly associated with financial intermediary development than legal origin.

In a more recent study, Keefer (2007) concludes that political institutions drive financial development, proxied by total credit extended to the private sector by banks and other financial institutions. Keefer reports that various political variables, including his measure of political checks and balances (i.e. how many political actors can block proposed legislation, therefore tracking whether formal institutions can constrain arbitrary executive branch behaviour) and newspaper circulation (a proxy for the extent of voter information), have a significant influence on financial sector development. More importantly, these variables remain significant determinants of financial sector development, even after controlling for legal origin. In fact, the legal-origin variables often become insignificant once political variables are included in the regression model.

1.3 Rise of Alternative Finance

Securitisation

Banks do not follow the standard description of the loanable funds model, in which financial institutions intermediate between savings and investment (Jakab and Kumhof, 2015). Instead, banks provide loans by creating money (see Box 10.1 for a discussion of money creation). When a bank provides a loan, it can simultaneously create a bank deposit that represents purchasing power. This allows banks to adjust their balance sheets rapidly and flexibly to the demand for investment financing (Goodhart, 2017). But this process faces two primary constraints. A first constraint is set by prudential requirements, in particular bank capital requirements (see Chapter 12). Monetary authorities set a second constraint, especially the interest rate that central banks charge to banks on their refinancing operations (see Chapter 4).

Before the financial crisis (which is discussed in Chapter 2), the traditional banking model, in which issuing banks hold loans until they are repaid, was increasingly replaced by the '*originate and distribute*' model, in which banks pool loans (like mortgages) and then tranch and sell them via securitisation. Starting with mortgages, securitisation gradually grew to encompass trade receivables, credit card receivables, lease payments, and even future royalty payments.

To facilitate securitisation, banks often set up off-balance-sheet vehicles, like conduits and *special purpose vehicles* (SPVs), which are shell companies that hold financial assets such as securitised mortgages. They generally have no employees or headquarters. Their management is outsourced to an administrator, typically a commercial bank that set up the conduit in the first place. The administrator manages the asset portfolio according to pre-specified investment guidelines and issues asset-backed commercial paper to finance the conduit's assets. Banks often provide liquidity enhancement and credit enhancement to these off-balance-sheet vehicles. So, if the quality of their assets deteriorates, the investors in these off-balance-sheet vehicles often have recourse to banks. The economic rationale for setting up these vehicles is to reduce the capital requirements imposed by bank regulation. Banks are not required to hold equity capital for these vehicles' assets, but instead need to hold equity only against the liquidity and credit enhancement provided to them (see Box 2.6). And these capital requirements were lower (Acharya and Schnabl, 2009).

Under the 'originate and distribute' model, banks pool and repackage loans and then pass them on to other financial investors (including conduits created for this purpose). Banks create 'structured' products often referred to as *collateralised debt obligations*. They first form diversified portfolios of mortgages and other types of loans. Next they slice these portfolios into different tranches, which are then sold to investors. The safest tranche – known as the 'super senior tranche' – offers investors a (relatively) low interest rate, but it is the first to be paid out of the portfolio's cash flows. By contrast, the most junior tranche – referred to as the 'equity tranche', 'toxic waste', or 'stub' – is paid only after all other tranches have been paid. The mezzanine tranches are between these extremes. The most junior security, or

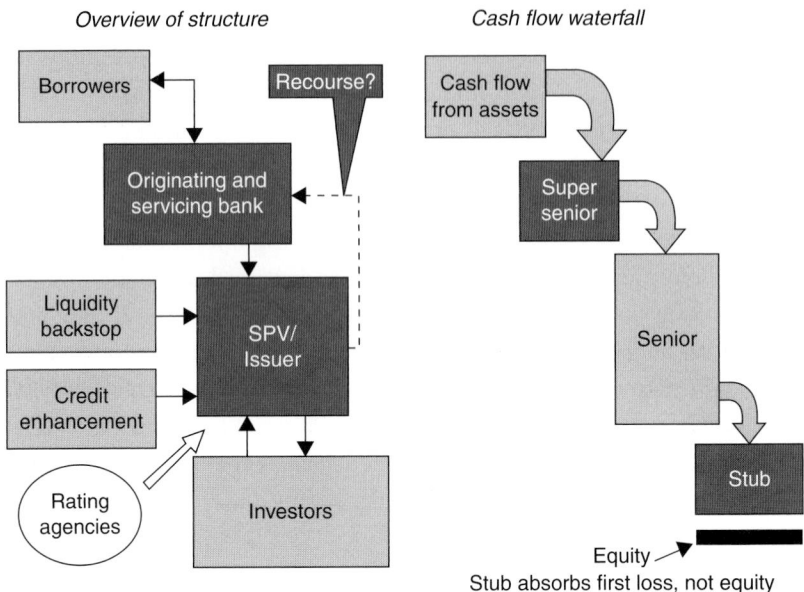

Overview of structure   *Cash flow waterfall*

Figure 1.7   Securitisation
Source: Huertas (2010)

stub, absorbs the first loss; once this class of security is wiped out, the mezzanine securities bear loss; then the senior securities, and then finally the super-senior securities.

The exact cut-offs between the tranches are typically chosen to ensure a specific CRA rating for each tranche (see Box 1.1). The top tranches are constructed to receive the highest rating. The more senior tranches are then sold to various investors, while the issuing bank usually (but not always) holds the toxic waste (see Figure 1.7).

The increasing complexity of securitised credit led to the application of credit rating techniques to new varieties of structured security, where no historic record existed. These ratings proved highly imperfect predictors of risk and were subject to rapid rating downgrades once the financial crisis broke (see Chapter 2).

Buyers of securitised instruments can protect themselves by purchasing *credit default swaps* (CDSs), which are contracts insuring against default. The buyer of these contracts pays a periodic fixed fee in exchange for a contingent payment in the event of a credit default. Those who purchased a tranche of a collateralised debt obligation with the highest rating combined with a CDS had reason to believe it was a low-risk investment because the probability of the CDS counterparty defaulting was considered to be small (Brunnermeier, 2009). However, the financial crisis proved this assumption wrong (see Chapter 2).

A growing proportion of aggregate maturity transformation has occurred outside regulated banks with central bank access via channels other than SPVs and conduits. Investment banks increasingly fund holdings of long-term maturity assets with much shorter-term liabilities. In addition, particularly in the US, mutual funds increasingly perform a bank-like form of maturity transformation. They have held long-term credit assets against liabilities to investors, which promise immediate redemption (Turner, 2009).

Adrian and Shin (2010) assert that such changes in the financial systems of some countries, notably the US, have altered the mode of financial intermediation as well. A characteristic feature of financial intermediation that operates through the capital market is the long chain of financial intermediaries involved in channelling funds from the ultimate creditors to the ultimate borrowers. Figure 1.8, taken from Adrian and Shin (2010), illustrates this feature by showing one possible chain of lending relationships in a market-based financial system.

In this illustration, banks issue mortgages that are then pooled. These pooled mortgages are packaged to form mortgage-backed securities (MBS), which are liabilities issued against the mortgage assets. The MBS might then be owned by an SPV that pools and tranches them into another layer of claims, such as collateralised debt obligations. A securities firm (e.g. an investment bank) might hold collateralised debt obligations on its own books for their yield, but will finance such assets by collateralised

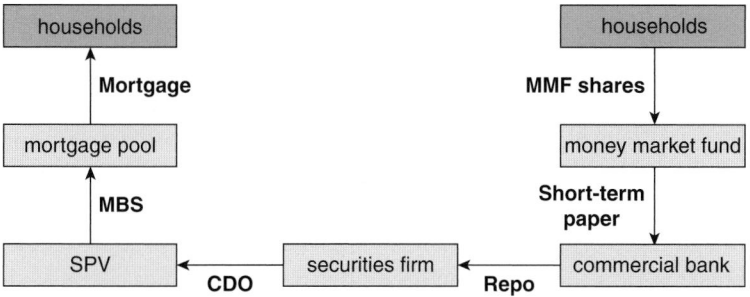

Figure 1.8   Long intermediation chain
Source: Tobias Adrian and Hyun Song Shin, 'The Changing Nature of Financial Intermediation and the Financial Crisis of 2007-09', Staff Reports, no. 439 (April 2010), available at www.newyorkfed.org /research/staff_reports/sr439.html. Reproduced with permission

borrowing through repurchase agreements (i.e. repos) with a larger commercial bank. (In a repo, the borrower sells a security today for below the current market price based on the understanding that it will buy it back in the future at a pre-agreed price. The difference between the current market price of the security and the price at which it is sold is called the haircut in the repo.) In turn, the commercial bank funds its lending to the securities firm by issuing short-term liabilities. Money market mutual funds are natural buyers of such short-term paper, and, ultimately, the money market fund completes the circle, as household savers would own shares of these funds.

Non-Bank Financial Intermediation

Tightening banking regulation spurs the growth of non-bank financial intermediaries, which are less regulated. Non-bank financing provides a valuable alternative to bank financing and helps support real economic activity. For many firms and households, it is also a welcome source of diversification of credit supply, and provides healthy competition for banks. However, if non-bank financing involves bank-like activities, such as transforming maturity/liquidity and creating leverage, it can become a source of systemic risk, both directly and through its interconnectedness with the banking system. Chapters 12 and 13 discuss the need for functional regulation, whereby equivalent activities (regardless of the type of financial intermediary) are regulated similarly to prevent regulatory arbitrage.

Figure 1.9 presents the main components of the global financial system: banks, pension funds and insurers, investment funds and other financial intermediaries, such as money market funds, hedge funds, broker/dealers, and structured finance vehicles. While banks make up slightly more than half of the financial system, annual growth of total banking assets has been relatively low at 4 per cent since the 2007–2009 financial crisis. The detailed breakdown in Table 1.2 indicates that investment funds grew 10 per cent year on year from 2010 to 2016. Pension funds and insurers grew at a more modest rate of 6 per cent. Other financial intermediaries show a mixed picture. While securitisation through structured financial vehicles has declined sharply since the financial crisis (-6 per cent), hedge funds have grown at an annualised rate of 31 per cent. The spectacular rise of hedge funds and private equity has prompted regulation of this sector through the Alternative Investment Fund Managers Directive 2011/61/EU (see Chapter 12).

Table 1.2 Breakdown by financial intermediary of the global financial system, 2016 (in € trillion)

Financial intermediary	Total assets (in € trillion)	Annualised growth rate 2010–2016 (in %)
Banks	139.2	4.3
Pension funds and insurers	59.6	5.7
Investment funds	38.0	10.0
Other financial intermediaries	21.9	6.6
– Money market funds	5.0	2.7
– Hedge funds	3.6	30.8
– Broker-dealers	8.7	3.0
– Structured finance vehicles	4.6	−5.8
Total financial system	258.7	5.7

Source: FSB (2018)

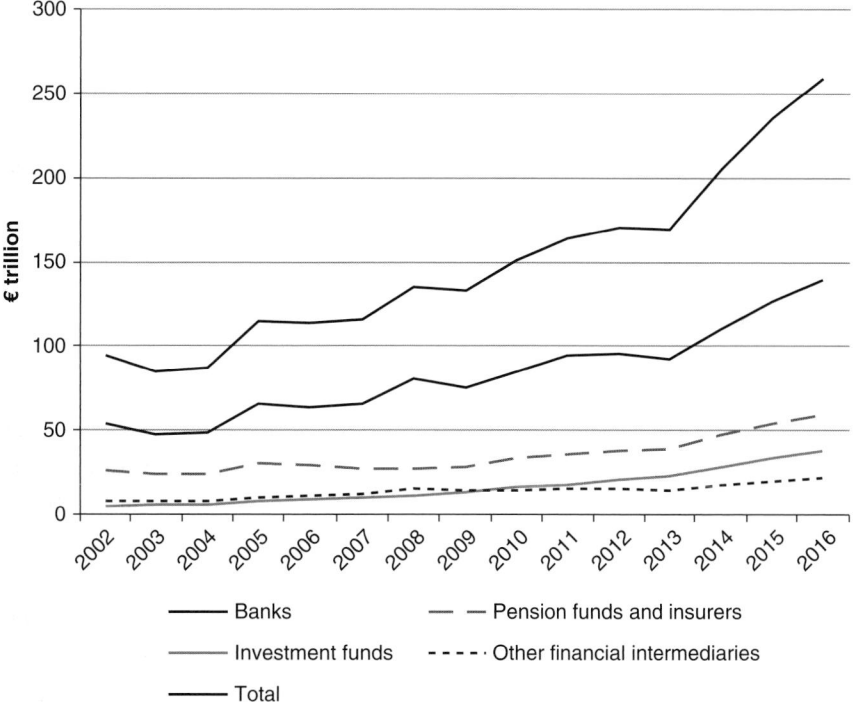

Figure 1.9   Growth of the global financial system, 2002–2016 (in € trillion)
Note: The total assets of the financial system are based on 21 jurisdictions and the euro area: Argentina, Australia, Brazil, Canada, Cayman Islands, Chile, China, Euro Area, Hong Kong, India, Indonesia, Japan, Korea, Mexico, Russia, Saudi Arabia, Singapore, South Africa, Switzerland, Turkey, the UK, and the US. These countries represent slightly more than 80 per cent of global GDP.
Source: FSB (2018)

Chapter 9 will discuss the role and size of various institutional investors, like pension funds, insurers, investment funds, hedge funds, and private equity, in more detail. It also documents the shift from banking to institutional investment.

1.4 Conclusions

The financial system encompasses the financial infrastructure as well as all financial intermediaries and financial markets, and their relationships with respect to the flow of funds to and from households, governments, business firms, and foreigners. Its main task is to channel funds from sectors that have a surplus to those that have a shortage of funds. The importance of financial markets and financial intermediaries differs across EU Member States. However, most investments by EU firms are financed through retained earnings, regardless of the relative importance of financial markets and intermediaries.

The financial system helps overcome the information asymmetry between borrowers and lenders, and reduces the time and money spent carrying out financial transactions. As discussed above, information asymmetry can occur *ex ante* and/or *ex post*: the former because borrowers generally know more about their investment projects than lenders, and the latter because borrowers (but not investors) can observe actual behaviour.

A well-functioning financial system requires particular government actions. First, government regulation is needed to protect property rights and to enforce contracts. Second, government regulation is needed to encourage proper information provision so that providers of funds can take better decisions on how to allocate their money. Third, government should regulate and supervise financial institutions to ensure their soundness. Finally, governments are responsible for implementing policies to ensure competition.

An important question is how differences in financial systems affect macroeconomic outcomes. Atomistic markets face a free-rider problem: when an investor acquires information about an investment project and behaves accordingly, he reveals this information to all investors, thereby dissuading other investors from devoting resources to acquiring information. Financial intermediaries may be better able to deal with this problem than financial markets.

Another element in the debate on the pros and cons of bank-based vs. market-based systems refers to corporate governance, i.e. the set of mechanisms regulating the relationship between a firm's stakeholders (i.e. equity

Table 1.3 Bank-based vs. market-based financial systems

	Bank-based	Market-based
Economic growth	++	++
Resilience	—	+
High-uncertainty investment	—	++
Low-uncertainty investment	++	—

holders) and its management. Investors (the outsiders) cannot perfectly monitor managers acting on their behalf since managers (the insiders) have superior information about the performance of the company. Therefore mechanisms are required to prevent company insiders from using firm profits for their own benefit rather than returning the money to outside investors.

There is considerable evidence that financial development – up to a point – is good for economic growth. Recent research suggests that recessions following a financial crisis in countries with a bank-based system are more severe than those in countries with a market-based financial system. Differences in financial systems may influence the type of activity in which a country specialises, because different forms of economic activity may be more easily provided by one financial system than the other (see Table 1.3).

Some authors argue that financial markets and financial intermediaries provide complementary growth-enhancing financial services to the economy. Intermediaries are necessary for the successful functioning of markets. Due to several recent changes, market-based financial intermediaries have become very important in some countries, notably the US, making the chain of intermediation much longer.

Finally, according to the 'law and finance' view, legal system differences are key to explaining international differences in financial structure. Therefore, distinguishing countries according to the efficiency of their national legal systems in supporting financial transactions is more useful than categorising them by whether they have bank-based or market-based financial systems.

Notes

1. Whether competition increases depends on the entry strategy of foreign intermediaries. For instance, if a foreign intermediary acquires various domestic intermediaries and merges them, competition may decrease.

2. There are two main types of boards of directors. The UK and the US have a so-called one-tier board, which consists of a mix of outside (non-executive) directors and inside (executive) directors, who are the top executives of the firm. The management is responsible for implementing the business policies that the board has determined. Continental European countries apply a two-tier board system, with a supervisory board and a management board. The supervisory board is the controlling body and is elected by the shareholders (and sometimes also by the employees). The management board is appointed by the supervisory board.

Bibliography

Suggested Reading

Allen, F. and D. Gale (2000), *Comparing Financial Systems*, MIT Press, Cambridge (MA).

Levine, R. (1997), Finance and Growth: Theory, Mechanisms and Evidence. In: P. Aghion and S. N. Durlauf (eds.), *Handbook of Economic Growth*, Elsevier, Amsterdam, 865–923.

Schoenmaker, D. and W. Schramade (2019), *Principles of Sustainable Finance*, Oxford University Press.

References

Abiad, A. and A. Mody (2005), Financial Reform: What Shakes It? What Shapes It? *American Economic Review*, 95, 66–88.

Acemoglu, D., S. Johnson, and J. A. Robinson (2001), The Colonial Origins of Comparative Development: An Empirical Investigation. *American Economic Review*, 91, 1369–401.

Acharya, V. V. and P. Schnabl (2009), How Banks Played the Leverage Game. In: V. V. Acharya and M. Richardson (eds.), *Restoring Financial Stability: How to Repair a Failed System*, Wiley, Hoboken (NJ), 83–100.

Adrian, T. and H. S. Shin (2010), The Changing Nature of Financial Intermediation and the Financial Crisis of 2007–09. Federal Reserve Bank of New York Staff Reports 439. www .newyorkfed.org/research/staff_reports/sr439.html.

Allen, F. and D. Gale (2000), *Comparing Financial Systems*, MIT Press, Cambridge (MA).

Allen, F. and A. M. Santomero (1997), The Theory of Financial Intermediation. *Journal of Banking and Finance*, 21, 1461–85.

Arcand, J.-L., E. Berkes, and U. Panizza (2015), Too Much Finance? *Journal of Economic Growth*, 20, 105–48.

Baele, L., A. Ferrando, P. Hordahl, E. Krylova, and C. Monnet (2008), Measuring European Financial Integration. In: X. Freixas, P. Hartmann, and C. Mayer (eds.), *Handbook of European Financial Markets and Institutions*, Oxford University Press, 165–94.

Beck, T., A. Demirgüç-Kunt, and R. Levine (2003), Law, Endowment and Finance. *Journal of Financial Economics*, 70, 137–81.

Bekaert, G., C. R. Harvey, and C. T. Lundblad (2005), Does Financial Liberalization Spur Growth? *Journal of Financial Economics*, 77, 3–55.

Bijlsma, M. J. and T. J. Zwart (2013), The Changing Landscape of Financial Markets in Europe, the United States and Japan. CPB Discussion Paper 238.

Brunnermeier, M. K. (2009), Deciphering the Liquidity and Credit Crunch 2007–2008. *Journal of Economic Perspectives*, 23, 77–100.

Carlin, W. and C. P. Mayer (2000), How Do Financial Systems Affect Economic Performance? In: X. Vives (ed.), *Corporate Governance: Theoretical and Empirical Perspectives*, Cambridge University Press, 137–68.

de Haan, J. and F. Amtenbrink (2012), Taming the Beast? New European Regulation for Credit Rating Agencies. *Zeitschrift für Staats- und Europawissenschaften (ZSE)* [Journal for Comparative Government and European Policy], 4, 433–58.

Demirgüç-Kunt, A., E. Feyen, and R. Levine (2013), The Evolving Importance of Banks and Securities Markets. *World Bank Economic Review*, 27, 476–90.

Dewatripont, M. and E. Maskin (1995), Credit Efficiency in Centralized and Decentralized Economies. *Review of Economic Studies*, 62, 541–55.

Djankov, S., R. La Porta, F. Lopez-de Silanes, and A. Shleifer (2008), The Law and Economics of Self-Dealing. *Journal of Financial Economics*, 88, 430–65.

Djankov, S., C. McLiesh, and A. Shleifer (2007), Private Credit in 129 Countries. *Journal of Financial Economics*, 84, 299–329.

European Central Bank (2006), *Financial Stability Review* (December), ECB, Frankfurt am Main. (2018), *Financial Integration in Europe* (May), ECB, Frankfurt am Main.

Fernandez, R. and D. Rodrik (1991), Resistance to Reform: Status Quo Bias in the Presence of Individual-Specific Uncertainty. *American Economic Review*, 81, 1146–55.

Financial Stability Board (2018), *Global Shadow Banking Monitoring Report 2017*, FSB, Basel.

Friede, G., T. Busch, and A. Bassen (2015), ESG and Financial Performance: Aggregated Evidence from more than 2000 Empirical Studies. *Journal of Sustainable Finance and Investment*, 5, 210–33.

Gambacorta, L., J. Yang, and K. Tsatsaronis (2014), Financial Structure and Growth. *BIS Quarterly Review*, March, 21–35.

Goodhart, C. (2017), The Determination of the Money Supply: Flexibility versus Control. *The Manchester School*, 85, 33–56.

Governance Metrics International (2006), *Ratings on 3800 Global Companies*, GMI, New York.

Huertas, T. F. (2010), *Crisis: Cause, Containment and Cure*, Palgrave Macmillan, Basingstoke.

International Monetary Fund (2010), The Uses and Abuses of Sovereign Credit Ratings. Chapter 3 of *Global Financial Stability Report*, IMF, Washington, DC.

Jakab, Z. and M. Kumhof (2015), Banks Are not Intermediaries of Loanable Funds – and Why this Matters. Bank of England Working Paper 529.

Jensen, M. (1993), The Modern Industrial Revolution, Exit, and the Failure of Internal Control Systems. *Journal of Finance*, 48, 831–80.

Jensen, M. and W. Meckling (1976), Theory of the Firm: Managerial Behavior, Agency Costs, and Capital Structure. *Journal of Financial Economics*, 3, 287–322.

Keefer, P. (2007), Beyond Legal Origin and Checks and Balances: Political Credibility, Citizen Information and Financial Sector Development. World Bank Policy Research Working Paper 4154.

Khan, M., G. Serafeim, and A. Yoon (2016), Corporate Sustainability: First Evidence on Materiality. *Accounting Review*, 91, 1697–724.

La Porta, R., F. Lopez-de-Silanes, A. Shleifer, and R. Vishny (1997), Legal Determinants of External Finance. *Journal of Finance*, 52, 1131–50.

Langfield, S. and M. Pagano (2016), Bank Bias in Europe: Effects on Systemic Risk and Growth. *Economic Policy*, 31, 51–106.

Levine, R. (1997), Financial Development and Economic Growth: Views and Agenda. *Journal of Economic Literature*, 35, 688–726.

(2002), Bank-Based or Market-Based Financial Systems: Which is Better? *Journal of Financial Intermediation*, 11, 398–428.

(2005), Finance and Growth: Theory, Mechanisms and Evidence. In: P. Aghion and S. N. Durlauf (eds.), *Handbook of Economic Growth*, Elsevier, Amsterdam, 865–923.

Lucas, R. (1988), On the Mechanics of Economic Development. *Journal of Monetary Economics*, 22, 3–42.

Merton, R. C. (1995), Financial Innovation and the Management and Regulation of Financial Institutions. *Journal of Banking and Finance*, 19, 461–81.

Mishkin, F. S. (2006), *The Next Great Globalization*, Princeton University Press.

Popov, A. (2017). Evidence on Finance and Economic Growth. ECB Working Paper 2117.

Revelli, C. and J. Viviani (2015), Financial Performance of Socially Responsible Investing (SRI): What Have We Learned? A Meta-Analysis. *Business Ethics: A European Review*, 24, 158–85.

Schoenmaker, D. and W. Schramade (2019), *Principles of Sustainable Finance*, Oxford University Press.

Sikken, B. J. (2014), Lecture Series Finance & Sustainability, Duisenberg School of Finance, Amsterdam.

Turner, A. (2009), *The Turner Review: A Regulatory Response to the Global Banking Crisis*, Financial Services Authority, London.

2

Financial Crises

OVERVIEW

Financial crises have occurred repeatedly throughout history. This chapter starts by exploring the different types of crises: banking crises, sovereign debt crises, and currency crises. A banking crisis indicates that a significant part of a country's banking sector has become insolvent after heavy investment losses, banking panics, or both. A sovereign debt crisis/default occurs when a government fails to meet interest or principal payments on its debt obligations. Finally, a currency crisis causes the value of a country's currency to fall precipitously.

The chapter provides facts and figures about financial crises, and discusses some theoretical models. A first set of models is related to the liability side of banks. Since banks use short-term deposits to finance long-term loans, they are vulnerable to massive withdrawals culminating in a banking run. A second set of models looks at the asset side of banks. Shocks to fundamentals (e.g. a collapse in real estate prices or increased bankruptcies in the non-financial sector) can upset the business cycle, resulting in deteriorating asset quality that can trigger further banking problems.

In 2007–2009, the world's financial system experienced its greatest crisis for at least a century. What made this crisis unique was that severe financial problems emerged simultaneously in many different countries, and its economic impact was felt throughout the world as a result of the increased interconnectedness of the global economy. The second part of this chapter offers an overview of the causes and consequences of this crisis, which triggered the euro crisis (a sovereign and banking crisis in Europe), discussed in the final part of this chapter.

LEARNING OBJECTIVES

After you have studied this chapter, you should be able to:
- explain the characteristics of different types of financial crises
- understand the link between sovereign and banking crises

- explain the main theoretical models of banking crises
- understand the pro-cyclicality of the financial system
- explain the main drivers and contagion mechanisms of the 2007–2009 financial crisis
- explain the euro crisis.

2.1 Introduction

Financial crises have occurred periodically since the development of money and financial markets. They come in three main forms: banking crises, sovereign debt crises, and currency crises.

In a *banking crisis* a significant part of a country's banking sector has become insolvent after heavy investment losses, banking panics, or both. They can be systemic or non-systemic. Laeven and Valencia (2018) define a *systemic banking crisis* as a situation in which a country's corporate and financial sectors experience a large number of defaults, and financial firms face great difficulties repaying contracts on time. As a result, non-performing loans increase sharply and all (or most) of the aggregate banking system capital is exhausted.

A *sovereign debt crisis* involves an outright default on payment of debt obligations, i.e. the repudiation or restructuring of debt into terms less favourable to the lender than in the original agreement. A sovereign default occurs when a government fails to meet interest or principal payments on its debt obligations. A distinction can be made here between external and domestic debt obligations. External debt consists of loans issued under another country's jurisdiction and is often denominated in a foreign currency and held by foreign creditors. Domestic debt is issued under a country's own jurisdiction, typically denominated in the local currency, and held by domestic creditors. In a default, countries may repudiate their debt, but it is more common for a government to restructure its debt on terms less favourable to the lender than those in the original contract (e.g. a longer maturity and a lower interest rate). Although debt crises are often believed to occur mainly in emerging countries, only a few industrial countries (like Denmark and the US) have managed to avoid defaulting on their government debt (Reinhart and Rogoff, 2009).

Finally, a *currency crisis* causes the value of a country's currency to fall precipitously. Countries maintaining an (almost) fixed exchange rate regime are vulnerable to sudden crises of confidence, leading to speculative attacks that can destabilise seemingly stable regimes overnight. Although currency crises are often believed to be a phenomenon of emerging countries, they have also occurred in the European Union (EU). Before the start of the Economic and Monetary Union (EMU) in 1999 (see Chapter 4), several European countries tried to stabilise their exchange rates using the Exchange Rate Mechanism (ERM), which had mixed success. In 1992–1993, the currencies of several participating countries plummeted vis-à-vis the German mark, the anchor of the system (see Box 2.1).

These different types of crises may be related. For example, if a government defaults on its sovereign debt, which is widely held by domestic banks, this can lead to a sudden loss of capital in the banking system, and potentially trigger a banking crisis. Alternatively, a banking crisis can lead to capital flight, which can give rise to an exchange rate crisis. And if a government supports banks considered too big to fail, this may lead to an unsustainable debt position and a sovereign debt crisis (Elson, 2017).

The remainder of this section will focus on debt and banking crises. Figure 2.1 plots the incidence of government external debt defaults and banking crises for a large sample of countries, accounting for about 90 per cent of world income. The graphs show the percentage of all independent countries that experienced a crisis from 1800 through 2008–2009.

The first graph identifies five episodes with many external debt defaults. The first is during the Napoleonic War, while the second runs from the 1820s through the late 1840s, when nearly half the countries in the world were in default. The third episode begins in the early 1870s and lasts for two decades, while the fourth begins in the Great Depression of the 1930s and extends through the 1950s, when almost 50 per cent of all countries stood in default. The most recent default episode encompasses the emerging market countries' debt crises of the 1980s and 1990s. The median duration of default spells after the Second World War is three years (Reinhart and Rogoff, 2010).

The second graph shows that the highest incidence of banking crises occurred during the Great Depression of the 1930s. The share of countries with banking difficulties began to expand in the 1970s, while in the early 1980s there were severe banking crises in emerging economies, notably in Latin America. During the early 1990s, the Nordic countries as well as Japan experienced some of the worst banking crises. In the second half of the 1990s, crises in Mexico and Argentina (in 1994–1995) were followed by the Asian crisis of 1997–1998. A brief tranquil period came to an abrupt halt in the summer of 2007 when the US subprime crisis began (see Section 2.3 for further details). Although the frequency of banking crises in advanced

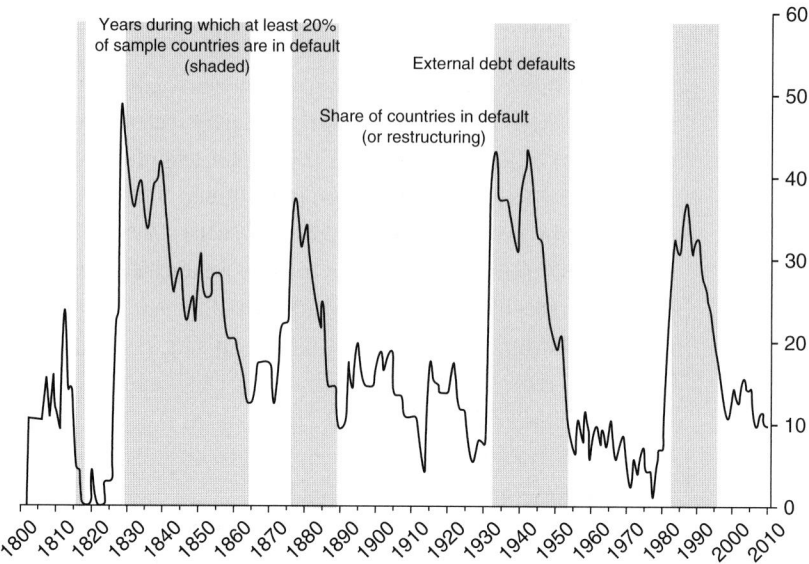

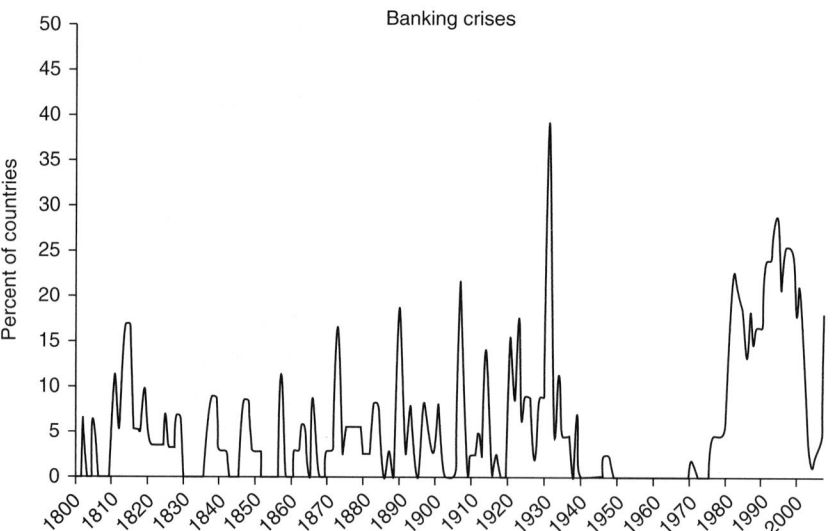

Figure 2.1   Incidence of financial crises, 1800–2009
Source: Reinhart and Rogoff (2010) and Qian *et al.* (2010)

economies drops off markedly, all (except for Portugal) experienced at least one post-war crisis prior to the current episode.

Systemic banking crises, such as the 2007–2008 crisis, are typically preceded by *credit booms* (growth of credit above GDP growth) and *asset price bubbles*

Box 2.1 The EMS crisis

The European Monetary System (EMS) was created in March 1979. Its cornerstone was the *Exchange Rate Mechanism* (ERM), which kept each currency within a band defined by a grid of central rates for the various pairs of currencies. For most countries, this band was defined as plus or minus 2.25 per cent of the central parity; these parities could be changed by mutual consent. If an exchange rate reached the edge of the band, the central banks of both countries were expected to intervene on the foreign exchange market.

The ERM went through a number of phases:
- a turbulent start, 1979–1983
- a calmer intermediate phase, 1983–1987
- no realignments, 1987–1992
- crises, 1992–1993
- tranquillity restored, 1993–1998.

Initially, there were frequent and substantial realignments. For instance, by September 1979 a number of currencies had already been devalued vis-à-vis the German mark. This pattern was repeated many times. Although some devaluations occurred in the second phase, both their frequency and magnitude were substantially lower than in the previous phase. As there were no devaluations during the period 1987–1992, the ERM's parities and bands were considered very credible. There were new entries during this third phase: the Spanish peseta in June 1989, the British pound in October 1990, and the Portuguese escudo in April 1992. Perceptions during this period that exchange rates were almost fixed were destroyed with the onset of the very turbulent fourth phase of the ERM, which was marked by a severe currency crisis. In August 1992 the British pound fell close to the ERM floor and the Italian lira fell below it. Eventually, the two currencies left the system. Except for the Dutch guilder, all remaining currencies in the ERM came under attack between September 1992 and August 1993. It was only after the fluctuation margins were increased to 15 per cent that the foreign exchange markets become more tranquil. During the fifth phase, ERM membership broadened again as participation in the exchange rate system was one of the convergence criteria for participation in the EMU (see Chapter 3).

Source: Eijffinger and de Haan (2000)

(a rise in asset prices above their fundamental economic value) (Reinhart and Rogoff, 2009). Such crises produce, on average, a 35 per cent real drop in housing prices spread over a period of six years, while equity prices decline by 55 per cent over 3.5 years. Box 2.2 describes the high costs of banking crises in terms of output lost and fiscal costs. Many financial crises, especially those in countries with fixed exchange rates, are *twin crises*: large currency depreciations exacerbate banking sector problems through foreign currency exposures

---

Box 2.2 Costs of banking crises

Laeven and Valencia (2018) compiled a database of 151 banking crises from 1970–2017, four of which occurred after 2011: Cyprus (2011), Guinea Bissau (2014), Moldova (2014), and Ukraine (2014). They use their database to estimate the output losses and fiscal costs of a crisis (computed as the direct fiscal outlays due to financial sector rescue packages as a percentage of GDP) and the increase in public debt. Output losses are computed as deviations in actual GDP from their trend. They are reported in cumulative terms; t denotes the starting year of the crisis. Laeven and Valencia (2018) find that output losses in high-income countries (median is 34.95 per cent of trend income) tend to be much larger than those in low- and middle-income countries (median is 13.63 per cent of trend income). The larger output losses in high-income countries could be explained by the presence of larger and deeper financial systems, the disruption of which has stronger effects on the real economy. Laeven and Valencia (2018) find substantial variation in the fiscal costs of systemic banking crisis episodes in both high-income and low- and middle-income economies. Still, the median cost of crises in high-income countries is 6.7 per cent of GDP, and 10 per cent of GDP for low- and middle-income countries. The median increase in public debt, measured over $t-1$, $t+3$, where t is the starting year of the banking crisis, reaches 21.1 per cent of GDP in high-income countries, compared to 16.4 per cent of GDP in low- and middle-income countries. While increases in public debt during banking crises in emerging and developing economies are mostly due to the fiscal outlays associated with financial sector intervention policies, in advanced economies such outlays constitute a relatively small fraction of the overall increase in public debt. In these countries, discretionary fiscal policy and the impact of reduced economic growth on government revenues and outlays play a much more important role.

The financial crisis of 2007–2009 (see Section 2.3) led to the Great Recession – the most severe since the Great Depression. The effects from the financial markets spread to the real economy through at least three channels. The first was the decline in financial wealth, which dampened the confidence of consumers and investors in the future outlook of the economy and their willingness to maintain current spending levels. A second channel has been called the 'financial accelerator'; this refers to the amplifying and dampening effect on spending that occurs when troubled banks reduce the amount of new credit creation. This balance sheet effect was a particularly potent force in the financial crisis given the high degree of leverage of the banking system. The third channel of negative spillover from the financial crisis to the broader economy is known as 'debt deflation', which refers to the negative impact on consumer spending arising from the heavy debt burden assumed by many households. When the housing bubble burst and interest rates started to rise, many households (and businesses) were faced with debts they could not sustain and began to cut back on non-debt-related spending to avoid bankruptcy (Elson, 2017).

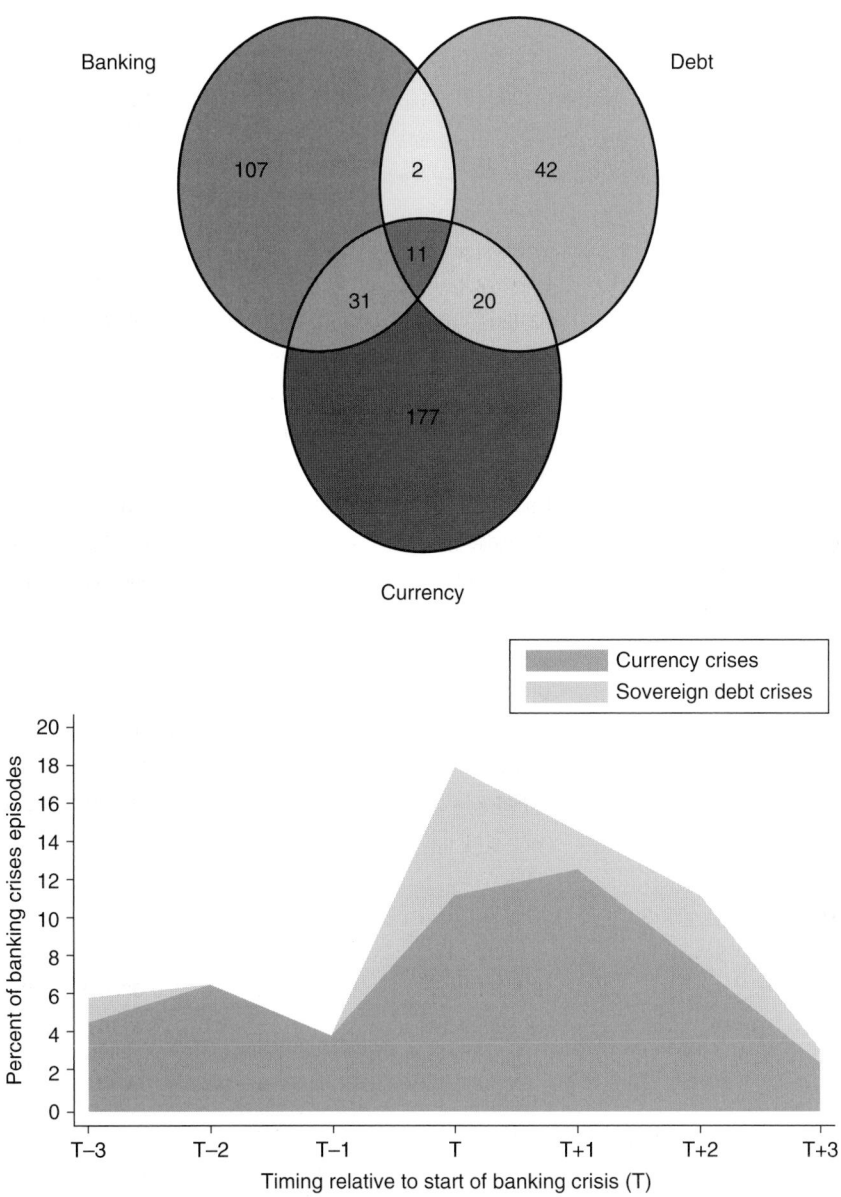

Figure 2.2   Financial crises by type and their sequencing
Source: Laeven and Valencia (2018)

of borrowers or banks. Likewise, banking crises often precede or accompany sovereign debt crises. Sometimes a country may experience *triple crises* (i.e. simultaneous banking, currency, and sovereign debt crises). Laeven and

Valencia (2018) identify 11 such crises from 1970–2017 (upper part of Figure 2.2). Twin crises seem to consist more of currency/banking and currency/debt crises than banking/debt crises. The lower part of Figure 2.2 examines the sequencing of crises. It suggests that currency and sovereign debt crises tend to coincide or follow banking crises, while currency crises generally peak one year after the beginning of the banking crisis.

The aftermath of a systemic banking crisis frequently involves a protracted and pronounced contraction in economic activity and a worsening of the government's financial position. The government often has to bail out financial institutions in a crisis. However, the most important driver of the worsening fiscal position after a systemic banking crisis is the economic downturn that follows. The data provided by Reinhart and Rogoff (2009) suggest that banking crises cause output to fall by 9 per cent over two years, while unemployment rises 7 per cent over the next four years. The indirect fiscal consequences of a banking crisis are thus much larger than the costs of bank bailouts. Government debt, on average, increases by 86 per cent in the three years after a systemic banking crisis. The experiences of Finland and Sweden stand out in this regard. Both countries experienced a systemic banking crisis at the beginning of the 1990s (see Box 2.3). In Sweden the government's budget balance increased from a surplus of 3.8 per cent of GDP before the crisis to a deficit of 11.6 per cent at the peak of the crisis, i.e. a deterioration of 15.4 per cent. Likewise, Finland's fiscal position worsened by almost 12 per cent (Reinhart and Rogoff, 2009).

Box 2.3 The banking crisis in Sweden

Sweden's financial system was liberalised in the 1980s. At the time, its financial system was dominated by a small number of large commercial banks offering wide-ranging financial services, which led to a predominance of debt financing of the non-financial sector. The financial deregulation and liberalisation of capital flows led to a credit-financed surge in investment. The credit surge also contributed to a jump in asset prices, especially real estate prices. Before the liberalisation, banks relied almost exclusively on deposits for funding, but gradually started to shift towards (more expensive) money market and foreign funding. As monetary policy was unable to stem the credit boom due to its focus on maintaining the stability of the exchange rate, losses from defaulted bank loans began to mount rapidly in the early 1990s after asset prices collapsed and a severe recession set in. While losses on real estate loans represented a significant part of the problem, other sectors also experienced financial distress when economic growth slowed down. The major Swedish banks were hit by massive credit losses totalling around 7 per cent of GDP in 1992. These losses threatened to quickly put all but one of the seven major Swedish

Box 2.3 (cont.)

banks, which controlled most of the Swedish market, below the capital requirement of 8 per cent. Consequently, the conservative government had to intervene heavily to preserve financial stability. It initially dealt with the crisis in an ad hoc manner, but in September 1992 it decided to explicitly guarantee banks' debts in a transparent process. The guarantee did not cover equity capital; in case of financial support by the government, owners generally lost their equity stakes. The guarantee received wide parliamentary support, including from the social-democratic opposition. The Bank Support Authority was created within the Finance Ministry in 1993 to implement the programme.

The banking crisis started with the largest savings bank, Forsta Sparbanken. The Swedish government provided a lending guarantee to the bank but this was later converted into a loan. Eventually, the bank was merged into the Savings Bank of Sweden together with several other savings banks. The second problem bank was Nordbanken, the third-largest commercial bank at the time, which was largely owned by the government. The government guaranteed a new share issue and the bank was restructured. An asset management company, Securum, took over the bad assets, while Nordbanken received in return a capital injection of 1 per cent of GDP. Gota Bank, the fourth-largest commercial bank, also got into difficulties. The government decided to meet all of its commitments but not those of the parent company, which was declared bankrupt. Again, the restructuring involved placing non-performing assets, largely in the form of commercial real estate, in a separate asset management company (Retriva, which merged with Securum in December 1995). In 1993, Gota Bank was merged with Nordbanken, which retained the name Nordbanken. Nordbanken became part of the pan-Nordic bank, Nordea.

Source: De Haan *et al.* (2009)

We next examine crises in Europe. Drawing on the seminal work by Reinhart and Rogoff (2009), Table 2.1 presents four crisis indicators for European countries: the share of years a country has been in default since 1800 (or since the year it became independent), the share of years with a banking crisis, and the number of banking crises since 1800 and 1945. Four conclusions can be drawn from this table. First, the share of years in default varies considerably among European countries. Second, whereas several countries have been able to avoid a debt crisis, all have had a banking crisis since 1800. Third, the average length of time a country spends in a state of average default exceeds the average amount of time spent in a banking crisis. Finally, the number of banking crises dropped off markedly after the Second World War. Nevertheless, except for Portugal, all

Table 2.1 Debt and banking crises in European countries

Country	Share of years in default since independence or 1800 (in %)	Share of years in banking crisis since independence or 1800 (in %)	Number of banking crises since independence or 1800	Number of banking crises since independence or 1945
Austria	17.4	1.9	3	1
Belgium	0	7.3	10	1
Denmark	0	7.2	10	1
Finland	0	8.7	5	1
France	0	11.5	15	1
Germany	13.0	6.2	8	2
Greece	50.6	4.4	2	1
Hungary	37.1	6.6	2	2
Italy	3.4	8.7	11	1
Netherlands	6.3	1.9	4	1
Norway	0	15.7	6	1
Poland	32.6	5.6	1	1
Portugal	10.6	2.4	5	0
Romania	23.3	7.8	1	1
Spain	23.7	8.1	8	2
Sweden	0	4.8	5	1
United Kingdom	0	9.2	12	4

Source: Reinhart and Rogoff (2009)

countries included in Table 2.1 have experienced at least one banking crisis since 1945.[1] One such crisis is described in more detail in Box 2.3.

2.2 Theory

Broadly speaking, theoretical models either focus on the asset or liability side of the bank balance sheet to explain banking crises. We first describe how liability problems may cause a banking crisis, and then discuss some theories focusing on the asset side.

As explained in Chapter 1, banks transform short-term deposit funding into long-term loans. They borrow in the form of short-term savings and demand deposits, which can be withdrawn at short notice. At the same time, they lend at longer maturities in the form of loans to firms and households. This makes them vulnerable. In normal times, banks hold more than sufficient reserves to handle withdrawals of deposits. However, during a run, depositors lose confidence in the bank and withdraw their deposits en masse. As withdrawals increase, the bank is forced to liquidate assets, typically at 'fire sale' prices, especially if the assets are illiquid. As banks often hold broadly similar portfolios of assets, the market can dry up completely if all banks try to sell at once. This typically happens during a systemic banking crisis. Assets that are liquid during normal times can suddenly become highly illiquid when banks need them the most. So even a bank that would be solvent in normal times may see its balance sheet destroyed: if everyone expects a problem and acts as if one is about to occur, then the run becomes a self-fulfilling prophecy. Conversely, if no one expects a bank to be in crisis, this expectation is also self-fulfilling and no run occurs (Reinhart and Rogoff, 2009).

As Chapter 1 explained, modern banking systems have become more complex over the last two decades. Despite running off-balance-sheet vehicles and using various financial instruments to transfer credit risk, banks remained sensitive to panics and runs. In the summer of 2007 holders of short-term liabilities refused to fund US banks, expecting losses on subprime and subprime-related securities, which caused runs on banks. The difference is that modern runs are typically caused by the drying up of liquidity in short-term markets (a wholesale run) rather than retail depositor withdrawals (Allen *et al.*, 2009). Yet classical bank runs still occur, as the example of Northern Rock (described in Box 2.4) illustrates.

Box 2.4 The run on the Rock

Northern Rock was formerly a building society in the UK, but it demutualised on 1 October 1997. At the end of 1997, it had £15.8 billion in consolidated assets, but by 2006 its consolidated balance sheet had grown to £101.0 billion – comprised mainly of secured lending on residential properties. Wholesale markets became an important source of funding, making up some 25 per cent of total funding, of which half had a duration of less than one year. The bank had not anticipated that all of its funding markets could close simultaneously, as happened after 9 August 2007. It had insufficient insurance and standby facilities to cover this risk. It soon became evident that Northern Rock would face severe problems if the markets stayed frozen for long. Initially, the Bank of England (BoE) refused to provide support to financial institutions, including Northern Rock. In a letter dated 12 September 2007, the BoE governor pointed to the risk of 'moral hazard': should the central bank provide extra liquidity against weaker collateral, markets would take it as a signal that the central bank would always rescue them, which would lead to ever more risk taking by banks.

On the evening of Thursday, 13 September 2007, the BBC leaked that Northern Rock had asked for and received emergency financial support from the BoE. The next day, long

> **Box 2.4** (cont.)
>
> queues began to form outside some of its branches; later, its website collapsed and its phone lines were reported to be jammed. The first bank run in the UK since Victorian times was underway. The momentum of the run on Northern Rock deposits once it had begun was caused by two factors. First, depositors were becoming aware that, were the run to continue, Northern Rock would eventually cease to be a going concern. Second, public awareness increased that deposits above £2,000 were not guaranteed in full. Only after four days did the BoE announce that it would guarantee all existing deposits in the bank. On 9 October, the BoE confirmed that 'additional facilities' would be available to Northern Rock, and on 18 December the government granted a further extension of the earlier guarantee arrangements. Eventually, on 22 February 2008 Northern Rock was taken into state ownership as a result of two unsuccessful private sector takeover bids.
>
> *Source:* Treasury Committee (2008)

From a theoretical perspective, events such as those described above imply that there are *multiple equilibria*. A confidence shock can cause a jump from a good equilibrium to a bad equilibrium. According to the Diamond and Dybvig (1983) model, bank runs are self-fulfilling prophecies. In this model, agents have uncertain needs for consumption in an environment in which long-term investments are costly to liquidate. If depositors believe that other depositors will withdraw, then it is rational for them to redeem their claims and a panic occurs. In a good equilibrium, no one believes a panic will occur, and depositors withdraw funds according to their consumption needs; their demands can be met without any costly liquidation of assets (Allen *et al.*, 2009).

According to the second line of argument, banking problems do not arise from the liability side, but from a protracted deterioration in asset quality due to poor fundamentals arising from the business cycle, like a collapse in real estate prices or increased bankruptcies in the non-financial sector. Some authors consider crises to be an intrinsic part of the business cycle, resulting from shocks to economic fundamentals. When the economy enters a recession, borrowers will have difficulty repaying their loans. So, an economic downturn will reduce the value of bank assets, raising the possibility that banks will be unable to meet their commitments. If depositors anticipate financial difficulties in the banking sector, they will try to withdraw their bank deposits. The result is the same as in the panic story, but the cause is different. According to this interpretation, crises are not random events but are caused by depositors' response to negative news about economic circumstances (Allen *et al.*, 2009). Allen and Gale (1998) develop a model in which they assume that depositors can observe a leading economic indicator that provides public information about future bank asset returns. If returns are high, depositors will want to keep their funds in the bank; however, if returns are low, they will withdraw their money in anticipation of low returns, thus causing a crisis (see Box 2.5).

Box 2.5 Bank runs and the business cycle*

Allen and Gale (1998) developed a model to show how cyclical fluctuations in asset values can produce bank runs. Time is divided into three periods: $t = 0, 1, 2$. There are early consumers c_1 at date 1 and late consumers c_2 at date 2, each with a probability of 0.5. The consumer's utility function is as follows:

$$U(c_1, c_2) = \begin{cases} u\ (c_1)\ \text{with probability } 1/2 \\ u\ (c_2)\ \text{with probability } 1/2 \end{cases} \tag{2.1}$$

where c_t denotes consumption at date $t=1, 2$. Consumers want to maximise consumption. Their objective function is given by:

$$\max\ E\left[u(c_1(R)) + u(c_2(R))\right] \tag{2.2}$$

where $c_1(R)$ and $c_2(R)$ denote the consumption of the early and late consumers, conditional on the return on the risky asset R (see below). Let E denote the consumer's total endowment of the consumption good at date 0. The role of banks is to make investments on behalf of consumers. Banks have two types of assets: a safe asset L and a risky asset X. The total amount invested must be less than or equal to the amount deposited:

$$L + X \leq E \tag{2.3}$$

The return r on the safe asset is zero, which is why $r = 1$. The return R on the risky asset X is stochastic, where R is a non-negative random variable. The risky asset is more productive than the safe asset L but cannot be liquidated at date 1. The expected return is thus larger than zero: $E[R] > 1$. At date 1, depositors receive a signal about R, which can be thought of as a leading economic indicator representing the state of the business cycle. The signal is realised at date 2. The holding of the safe asset must be sufficient to provide for the consumption of the early consumers:

$$c_1(R) \leq L \tag{2.4}$$

The consumption of the late consumers cannot exceed the total value of the risky asset plus the amount of the safe asset left over after the early consumers are paid off. Together with the previous constraint in equation (2.4), this condition gives:

$$c_1(R) + c_2(R) \leq L + RX \tag{2.5}$$

Box 2.5 (cont.)

The deposit contract needs to be incentive compatible. For each value of R, the late consumers must be at least as well off as the early consumers. Since late consumers are paid off at date 2, an early consumer cannot imitate a late consumer. But a late consumer can imitate an early consumer, obtain $c_1(R)$ at date 1, and consume that at date 2. It will be optimal to do so unless:

$$c_1(R) \leq c_2(R) \tag{2.6}$$

Until now, the deposit contract is assumed to be contingent on the return on the risky asset R. But a standard deposit contract is non-contingent. Allen and Gale (1998) use a standard deposit contract that promises a fixed amount at each date in their model. In the event that the bank does not have enough liquid assets to make the promised payment, it pays out all available liquid assets, divided equally among those withdrawing. Let $\bar{c}$ denote the fixed payment promised to the early consumers. The amount promised to the late consumers can be ignored, since they are always paid what is available at the last date.

Next, the equilibrium conditions of the standard contract and the possibility of bank runs are analysed. Let c_{21} and c_{22} denote the equilibrium consumption of late consumers who withdraw from the bank at dates 1 and 2. Let $a(R)$ denote the fraction of late consumers who decide to withdraw early, conditional on the risky return R. So, a bank run is dependent on the signal about R and is thus related to the business cycle.

If a run does not occur, the feasibility conditions in equations (2.4) and (2.5) still apply as before. If there is a run, then the early consumers and the early-withdrawing late consumers share the liquid assets available at date 1:

$$c_1(R) + a(R)c_2(R) = c_1(R) + c_{21}(R) = L \tag{2.7}$$

And the late-withdrawing late consumers receive the returns to the risky asset at date 2:

$$(1 - a(R))c_2(R) = c_{22}(R) = RX \tag{2.8}$$

Since early consumers and early-withdrawing late consumers are treated the same in a run, and all late consumers must have the same utility in equilibrium:

$$c_1(R) = c_{21}(R) = c_{22}(R) \tag{2.9}$$

The final condition comes from the standard deposit contract, which promises the early consumers $c_1(R) = \bar{c}$ or, if that is infeasible, an equal share of the liquid assets L. Yet some of the late consumers may want to withdraw early as well. In the latter case $c_1(R) < \bar{c}$, the early withdrawers (including the early-withdrawing late consumers) exhaust the liquid assets of the bank:

Box 2.5 (cont.)

$$\begin{cases} c_1(R) = \bar{c} & \text{no bank run} \\ c_1(R) < \bar{c} \rightarrow c_1(R) + c_{21}(R) = L & \text{bank run} \end{cases} \tag{2.10}$$

The optimal deposit contract is solved for $\bar{c} = L$. In that case, the bank holds exactly sufficient liquid assets to pay the early consumers. The remaining assets are invested in risky assets with a positive expected return. Figure 2.3 illustrates the optimal deposit contract. The figure plots consumption $c_1(R)$ and $c_2(R)$ against the return on the risky asset R. Remember that R can be observed at date 1 but not at date 0. When $R = 0$ the only consumption available is from the safe asset. To maximise expected utility at $t = 0$, this safe asset is split equally between the two groups so $c_1(0) = c_2(0) = L/2$. As R increases, both groups can consume more. At $\bar{R} = L/X$, L is consumed by the early consumers and $\bar{R}X$ is consumed by the late consumers. Note that at $\bar{R} = L/X$, the consumption of the early and late consumers is still equal. As R increases above $\bar{R}$, it is not possible for the early consumers to have more than L since this is the only consumption available at date 1. At date 2, the late consumers are able to consume $RX > L$.

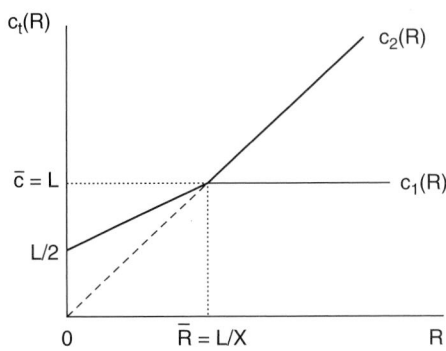

Figure 2.3   The standard deposit contract with bank runs
Source: Allen and Gale (1998)

Minsky's (1986) 'financial instability' hypothesis links the business cycle to financial crises. While his views were initially often regarded as radical, if not crackpot, the credit crisis of 2007–2009 (see Section 2.3) has revived interest in his theory. In his model, the events leading up to a crisis start with a 'displacement' (i.e. an exogenous, outside shock to the macroeconomic system), an invention, or an abrupt change of economic policy that excites investors. He identified five subsequent stages of the boom and eventual bust:
1. credit expansion, characterised by rising asset prices

2. euphoria, characterised by overtrading
3. distress, characterised by unexpected failures
4. discredit, characterised by liquidation
5. panic, characterised by the desire for cash.

The displacement sets in a boom fuelled by credit. As a boom leads to euphoria, banks extend credit to ever more dubious borrowers, often by creating new financial instruments. Then, at the top of the market, some smart traders start to cash in their profits. The onset of panic is usually heralded by a dramatic event, such as a bank not being able to meet its obligations. Losses on loans begin to mount, and the value of the loans falls relative to liabilities, driving down the capital of financial institutions. With less capital, financial institutions cut back on their lending (*deleveraging*).

Minsky's financial instability hypothesis highlights the *pro-cyclicality* of the financial system, which he attributes to four factors. First, the role of risk assessment is important. While risk tends to be underestimated in good times (euphoria with 'low risk'), it is overestimated in bad times (distress with 'high risk'). Moreover, risk can be endogenous. For example, when financial institutions sell a particular asset to reduce their risk, the price of that asset may fall further. Second, the amount of debt (leverage) is a key factor explaining the depth of the financial crisis. The higher the level of debt that is built up in the upswing, the more severe is the deleveraging in the downswing. Third, Gorton and Ordoñez (2014) stress the pro-cyclical role of collateral. Investors are willing to lend in the short term (e.g. via repos) against collateral without collecting costly information about the collateral backing the debt. When the economy relies on such informationally insensitive debt, firms with low-quality collateral can borrow, which generates a credit boom. Financial fragility builds up over time as information about counterparties decays. A crisis occurs when a (possibly small) shock suddenly gives investors an incentive to collect information. Fourth and last, capital requirements play a role. Banks have to maintain minimum capital against new loans (see Chapter 12). In good times, retained earnings boost capital, which enables banks to increase their lending. In bad times, capital shrinks through losses, which may hamper banks' ability to grant new credit.

Figure 2.4 illustrates how the financial cycle (measured by credit and house prices) and the business cycle (measured by GDP) diverge. The amplitude of the financial cycle from 1970 to 2011 is five times that of the business cycle in the US. Moreover, the duration of the financial cycle tends to be longer than that of the US business cycle. While Figure 2.4 represents the US cycle, similar patterns can be found across Europe. Financial cycles may not move

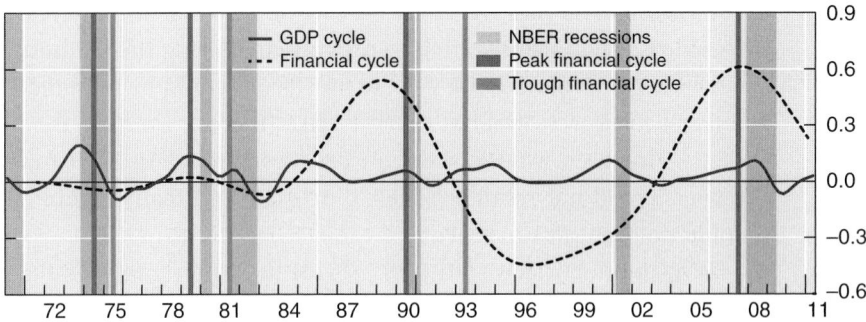

Figure 2.4   Business cycle (GDP) versus financial cycle in the US, 1970–2011
Source: Borio (2014)

synchronously across countries. Section 2.5 explains that one cause of the euro crisis was that the financial cycles in euro-area Member States were not in sync.

Finally, some recent theories on financial instability focus on information problems. For example, Mishkin (1992) argues that a financial crisis is a disruption to financial markets in which adverse selection and moral hazard problems become much worse, such that financial markets are unable to efficiently channel funds to those who have the most productive investment opportunities. Uncertainty about the future (e.g. firms' business prospects) increases during a financial crisis, which exacerbates the information asymmetry between contracting parties (e.g. information on the behaviour or repayment capacity of a counterparty) and worsens parties' incentives. *Adverse selection* occurs when investments that are most likely to produce an undesirable outcome are the most likely to be selected. *Moral hazard* arises when a borrower has an incentive to invest in high-risk projects in which the borrower does well if the project succeeds but the lender bears a substantial loss if the project fails.

2.3 The Financial Crisis of 2007–2009

The crisis of 2007–2009 started after the US housing market bubble burst, which forced banks to write down several hundred billion dollars in bad loans caused by mortgage delinquencies, especially in the subprime part of the market. *Subprime mortgages* are housing loans to high-risk borrowers with a weak or bad credit history who do not qualify for a conventional mortgage. Although these loans are relatively risky, subprime mortgages represented about 20 per cent of all newly issued mortgages in the US in

2005–2006. The mortgages had a low or zero starting interest rate, which would rise significantly after a year or two. During the US housing boom – which began around 2001 – these mortgages could be refinanced before the interest rates were reset at market rates (thereby averting the high interest costs). However, when housing prices started to fall in 2006, many subprime owners could not refinance their mortgage, and many defaulted when they could not continue payments.

Why did financial institutions provide these mortgages? In the years before the crisis, US interest rates were very low due to large capital inflows from abroad, especially from Asia, and the policies of the Federal Reserve, the central bank of the US (known as the Fed). Several Asian countries, including Japan and China, accumulated large current account surpluses prior to the crisis. As China and several other surplus countries were committed to (more or less) fixed exchange rates, the rising claims on other countries due to their current account surpluses took the form of central bank reserves. These are typically invested almost exclusively in risk-free government securities, rather than in a wide array of equity, property, or fixed income assets (Turner, 2009). As inflation was also low, real interest rates in the US were at a historically low level. Low interest rates in turn led to a rapid growth of credit extension, particularly for residential mortgages, which fuelled the property price boom. For banks (and other providers), subprime loans were appealing because a relatively high interest rate could be charged while (at that time) the default rate was very low because of the housing boom.

In 2004, the Fed began to gradually raise interest rates from 1 per cent to 5.25 per cent in order to cool down the economy and keep inflation under control. As a result, it became more expensive to buy a house as mortgage rates increased substantially. This led to a slowdown in the housing market and eventually a housing price crash. As subprime mortgages were sold under the (false) assumption that housing prices would continue to increase, many subprime mortgage holders defaulted when they were unable to refinance their loans. This created a domino effect that spread problems throughout the financial system. The US banking crisis therefore followed Minsky's model, starting with cheap credit ('low risk') and rising house prices, euphoria with overextension, distress with defaults, forced liquidations and fire sales, and finally panic with a freezing of short-term funding markets ('high risk').

But how did problems in the US housing market lead to a global financial crisis? Even though banks initially faced serious losses, they were small compared to the wealth losses of the dotcom bubble, which did not lead to a serious recession. One particular aspect of the subprime crisis made it different from previous financial crises (Brunnermeier, 2009). As discussed in Chapter 1, banks traditionally finance their mortgage loans through the deposits received from depositors and keep the mortgage loans (as well as the associated risks) on their balance sheet. In return, banks receive an upfront fee as well as interest income. However, in this case the providers of subprime loans bundled the mortgage loans and sold them to investors via collateralised debt obligations (CDOs). CDOs were used to package together different tranches or pools of mortgages from different Mortgage-Backed Securities (MBS) that were judged to carry different degrees of risk. As mortgage providers were merely interested in receiving the upfront fee, they tried to sell as many mortgages as possible and there was no incentive to perform a proper credit check as the risks were transferred to third parties. The process of pooling, packaging, and reselling the loans as securities is referred to as *securitisation*.[2] The securitised instruments were in high demand by investors seeking as large a spread as possible above the risk-free rate, to at least partially offset the declining risk-free rate (Turner, 2009).

Before the securitised instruments were sold, they were rated by credit rating agencies (CRAs, discussed in Chapter 1). The agencies reviewed the proposed transactions before they came to market, and placed their seal of approval on the deals by rating the various tranches. The most critical rating was the one for the senior tranche, which was almost invariably AAA, i.e. the highest possible rating. Indeed, deals were constructed to ensure the senior tranches would receive this rating. Although the ratings for securitised instruments were not directly comparable with ratings of sovereign or corporate bonds, the use of the same rating scale suggested that they were. Consequently, AAA-rated securitised instruments were subject to the same investment and regulatory screens as AAA-rated corporate bonds, thereby opening the door to their sale to investors (Huertas, 2010). The crisis was exacerbated by inadequate CRA risk assessments and investor over-reliance on these credit ratings.

Securitisation led to a remarkable growth in the relative size of wholesale financial services within the overall economy; internal banking system activities grew far more rapidly than end services to the real economy (Turner, 2009). This growth in the relative size of the financial sector, particularly securitised credit activities, increased the potential impact of financial system instability on the real economy. This financial sector growth was accompanied by an increase in total system *leverage*, which played an important role in driving the boom and creating vulnerabilities that arguably increased the severity of the crisis (see Figure 2.5). Moreover, there was a maturity transformation, as the Special Purpose Vehicles and conduits through which the securities were distributed

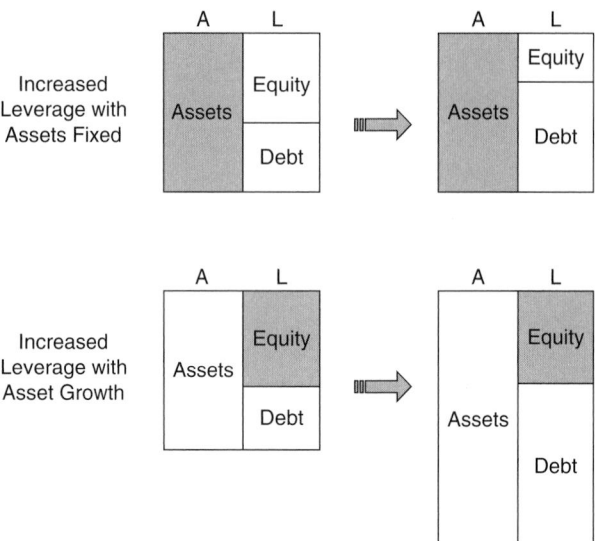

Figure 2.5   Two modes of levering up
Source: Hahm *et al.* (2011)

(see Chapter 1) were often funded with (short-term) asset-backed commercial paper. By contrast, the dotcom bubble was predominantly financed by equity.

The volume of credit derivatives also grew extremely fast – to over $45 trillion in notional value by mid-2007. Credit derivatives (like credit default swaps, CDS, see Chapter 1) allow an investor to take a position with respect to the possibility that the so-called reference entity will default. The investor can either buy protection, in which case he or she will receive a payment if the reference entity defaults, or sell protection, and make a payment if the reference entity defaults. In return for providing this protection, the seller of the protection receives a premium from the buyer (Huertas, 2010). Trading of these derivatives was not subject to any regulation. Nor were issuers of CDS required to hold any reserves to cover the possibility of their redemption in the event of a default in the underlying components of these securities (Elson, 2017).

Financial guarantee insurance performed a similar function to credit derivatives. In exchange for a premium, financial guarantee insurance companies (generally they only sold this type of insurance and were therefore known as monolines) provided protection against the possibility that an issuer would be unable to make timely payments of interest and/or principal on its securities.

When the crisis broke, it became apparent that the diversification of risk holding that securitisation was supposed to deliver had not been achieved.

Many instruments were on the books of banks and bank-like institutions rather than investors who intended to hold the assets to maturity. Instruments were not simply sold through to an end investor, but were bought by the propriety trading desk of another bank, or sold by the first bank but with part of the risk retained via the use of credit derivatives, or 'resecuritised' into increasingly complex and opaque instruments (Turner, 2009). According to Acharya and Schnabl (2009), about 30 per cent of all AAA asset-backed securities in the US remained within the banking system (50 per cent including conduits, see Box 2.6). Consequently, most of the risk was still somewhere on banks' balance sheets (either directly or indirectly via guarantees or insurances) but not always transparently.

Uncertainty regarding who was exposed to these risks disturbed the functioning of many financial markets, including the interbank money market. Problems started to occur in this market due to the damage done to two hedge funds affiliated with the US investment bank Bear Stearns. Banks became increasingly reluctant to lend to each other, which triggered a liquidity crisis. In addition to this so-called *funding*

Box 2.6 Off-balance-sheet vehicles

As explained in Chapter 1, banks used off-balance-sheet vehicles like conduits in the securitisation process. These conduits were funded with some equity and the rest in rollover finance in the form of asset-backed commercial paper. They had recourse to bank balance sheets. *Recourse* is an institutional arrangement through which the risks of the conduit are transferred back to the commercial bank setting up the conduit. This recourse could consist of liquidity enhancement and/or credit enhancement. *Liquidity enhancement* provides a backup credit line or commitment to repurchase non-defaulted assets in case a conduit cannot roll over maturing commercial paper. *Credit enhancement* covers credit losses on a conduit's assets.

Acharya and Schnabl (2009) distinguish between three types of off-balance-sheet vehicles:
1. *Fully supported conduits*, which have liquidity enhancement that covers the entire amount of commercial paper outstanding and credit enhancement that covers all assets in the conduit.
2. *Partially supported conduits*, which have liquidity enhancement and partial credit enhancement.
3. *Structured investment vehicles*, which have only partial liquidity and credit enhancement; their extent varies depending on the underlying assets.

Table 2.2 shows the ten largest conduit administrators in 2007.

Table 2.2 Ten largest conduit administrators by size (January 2007)

	Conduits		Administrator			
	Number	CP (in $ bn)	Assets	Equity	CP/Asset	CP/Equity
Citibank	23	93	1,884	120	4.9%	77.5%
ABN AMRO	9	69	1,300	34	5.3%	202.9%
Bank of America	12	46	1,464	136	3.1%	33.8%
HBOS	2	44	1,160	42	3.8%	104.8%
JPMorgan Chase	9	42	1,352	116	3.1%	36.2%
HSBC	6	39	1,861	123	2.1%	31.7%
Société Générale	7	39	1,260	44	3.1%	88.6%
Deutsche Bank	14	38	1,483	44	2.6%	86.4%
Barclays	3	33	1,957	54	1.7%	61.1%
WestLB	8	30	376	9	8.0%	333.3%

Source: Acharya and Schnabl (2009)

liquidity, market liquidity also became a problem. A wide range of institutions – both banks and near banks – became more reliant on 'liquidity through marketability', believing that it would be safe to hold long-term assets funded by short-term liabilities since these assets could be sold rapidly in liquid markets if needed. This assumption was valid for individual firms in non-crisis conditions, but became rapidly invalid in mid-2007, as many firms simultaneously attempted to liquidate their positions. They often had to sell assets at fire sale prices. In 2007 several hundred non-bank mortgage lenders collapsed, while others were merged into larger banking institutions.

Increased *risk aversion* and *deleveraging* amplified the initial shock. Central banks were forced to inject liquidity into the financial system to ensure that banks were not exposed to long periods of tight liquidity. Banks reported substantial losses as they had invested directly in structured securities or had contracts requiring them to support conduits. Many firms were, however, unable to rapidly assess their exposures as their assets became illiquid when the underlying market imploded. This resulted in a loss spiral for the financial system, as illustrated in Figure 2.6. When banks mark their balance sheet to market, changes in prices lead to losses for all banks holding these assets. Losses worsen funding liquidity for many banks, forcing them to shed even more assets, which further depresses prices and increases losses. A loss spiral can thus lead to sharp asset price movements (Brunnermeier *et al.*, 2009).

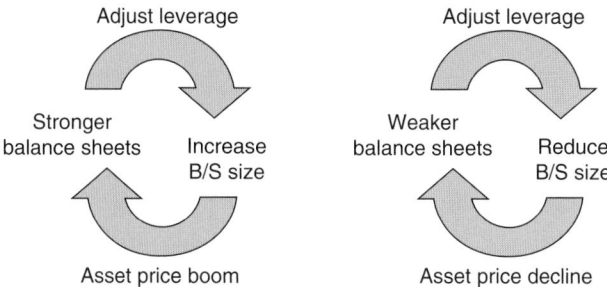

Figure 2.6   Loss spiral through the balance sheet
Source: Brunnermeier *et al.* (2009)

In 2008, problems worsened and the US authorities were forced to bail out Bear Stearns, the country's fifth-largest investment bank. It was highly leveraged and heavily exposed to the subprime mortgage market. The US government helped engineer JPMorgan Chase's purchase of the bank by guaranteeing $29 billion of subprime-backed securities. Later, the mortgage agencies Fannie Mae and Freddie Mac, accounting for nearly half of the outstanding mortgages in the US, were nationalised. When problems occurred at the fourth-largest investment bank, Lehman Brothers, the authorities tried persuading rival institutions to take it over. In the absence of a buyer, the government decided to allow Lehman Brothers to fail in September 2008 to set an example. The subsequent fears over counterparty risk turned to panic, since if Lehman Brothers was not too big to fail, other investment banks might fail as well. In addition, several institutions had an exposure on Lehman that became virtually worthless. For instance, the Reserve Primary Fund, one of the largest money market funds, owned $700 million of Lehman Brothers' short-term paper and came into serious financial difficulties due to its collapse. This, in turn, led to uncertainty about all money market funds. As money market funds are the primary source for funding repos and commercial paper in the US, they came close to a breakdown (Richardson, 2009). Central banks in the US and elsewhere had to step in and eventually became vital suppliers in this market.

EU and US authorities were eventually forced to rescue financial institutions to prevent a systemic meltdown. The world's largest insurance company, American International Group (AIG), received an emergency loan in return for an 80 per cent public stake in the firm. The landscape of American finance radically changed. Bank of America bought investment bank Merrill Lynch. Two investment banks, Goldman Sachs and Morgan Stanley, converted themselves into commercial banks. In a rescue deal backed by US authorities, Washington Mutual and Wachovia were sold to JPMorgan Chase and Citigroup, respectively.

Major banks in Western Europe had taken an active interest in the market for securitised instruments in the US. For example, these banks would commonly borrow on a short-term basis from money market mutual funds through their branches in the US and then purchase MBS/CDOs (Elson, 2017). The crisis in the US therefore quickly spread to Europe, and governments were forced to intervene. For instance, Benelux authorities had to bail out Fortis. The Dutch government eventually nationalised Fortis' Dutch activities, while its other activities were sold to the French banking group BNP Paribas. The French, Belgian, and Luxembourg authorities also had to recapitalise the financial conglomerate Dexia. In the UK, the authorities were forced to take over Bradford & Bingley's mortgages and loans, while its savings operations and branches were sold to the Spanish banking group Santander. The UK authorities also took a major equity stake in two large banks: RBS and Lloyds-HBOS. Germany's Hypo Real Estate, a large commercial property lender, received a €50 billion secured-credit facility from a consortium of German banks and the government. The Icelandic authorities had to nationalise their entire banking system, leading to the country's near bankruptcy.

2.4 The Euro Crisis

The Crisis Unfolded

In 2009 the euro celebrated its tenth anniversary, yet a shock was unfolding in Greece that materialised into a full-blown financial crisis by the end of the year. After several revisions of previously announced deficit figures (even going back to the time of Greece's admission to the euro area) had been published, it became clear that public finances in Greece were unsustainable. The 10-year yield spread between Greek and German government bonds increased strongly, reaching about 1,000 basis points in May 2010. Similar concerns arose in Ireland, Portugal, and, later, Spain and Italy (see Figure 2.7).

On 2 May 2010, the euro countries agreed to provide Greece with €80 billion in bilateral loans to be disbursed from May 2010 to June 2013. The International Monetary Fund (IMF) financed an additional €30 billion under a stand-by arrangement. The European Commission was entrusted with coordinating and administrating the pooled bilateral loans, including

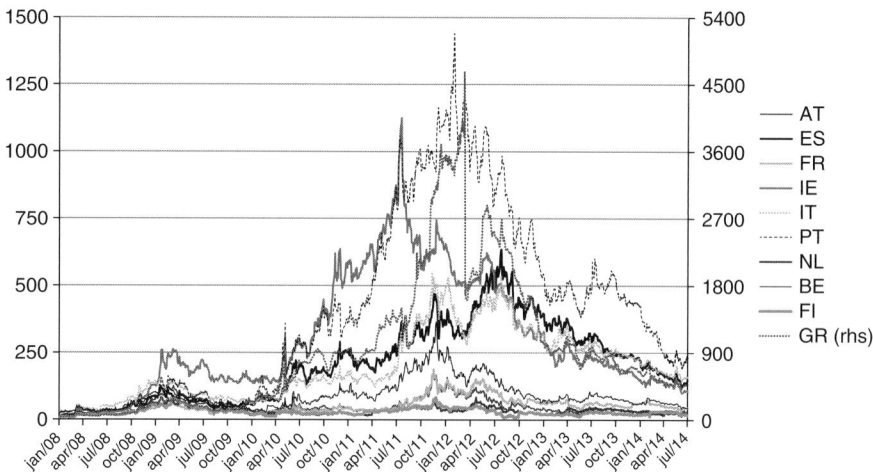

Figure 2.7   Ten-year government bond spreads against German sovereign bonds, 2008–2014
Source: Datastream

their disbursement. The loans were subject to strict conditions aimed at consolidating Greek public finances and restoring competitiveness.

Why was Greece rescued? Several economists argued that it and other countries facing insolvency should default as quickly as possible, to allow for a substantial debt restructuring (haircut) to restore sustainable debt levels and stabilise financial markets. According to this logic, delaying such a decision would worsen the situation. European policy makers did not follow this advice, as they were worried that a Greek default would have two serious consequences in particular. First, a Greek default might spread to other countries (contagion). A worsening of the Greek crisis could further aggravate the situation in Portugal and Ireland – which were also facing severe financial problems at the time – and push them into default. Policy makers were worried that the crisis might even spread to Spain or Italy, pushing them to ask for a rescue. This would overburden the abilities and willingness of the other EU countries to come to the rescue. A major default would also activate CDSs, with unforeseeable consequences for European and global financial markets.

The second potential consequence was that many banks and other financial institutions had a large exposure on Greece. European policy makers feared that a sovereign default would trigger another banking crisis, as many banks were just recovering from the 2007–2009 crisis and would not be able to absorb the substantial losses caused by a Greek default. More generally, financial institutions had extensive exposures to European

Table 2.3 Exposure of euro-area banks on euro-area countries ($ million), March 2011

	Greece	Ireland	Italy	Portugal	Spain
Austria	104	3,193	105,097	187	5,288
Belgium	240	4,689	4,173	465	4,441
Cyprus	11,351	–	1,729	82	92
Estonia	3	–	399	–	12
Finland	2	–	1,271	59	3,014
France	1,675	15,955	41,153	7,411	28,790
Germany	5,246	62,664	266,138	3,910	58,840
Greece	–	773	4,694	10,158	1,265
Ireland	544	–	14,324	22,250	11,052
Italy	537	13,182	–	2,998	35,190
Luxembourg	7,687	3,088	28,598	2,613	8,325
Malta	382	–	890	848	166
Netherlands	4,502	5,986	25,908	13,111	19,892
Portugal	92	2,475	4,331	–	89,932
Slovakia	–	–	19,711	86	167
Slovenia	2	–	8,778	43	110
Spain	361	13,737	31,764	25,616	–

Source: BIS

governments (see Table 2.3) and to each other. In turn, in an effort to contain the banking crisis, governments held considerable participations in banks or stood guarantee for large amounts. This government involvement was essential to preserve market confidence in vulnerable institutions. However, it could also give rise to doubt about the sustainability of fiscal policy, especially if other factors are threatening public finances, like poor economic growth rates. If this happens, risk premiums rise and downgrades occur, jeopardising the (re)financing of debt.

The support provided to Greece was insufficient to stabilise the markets and prevent contagion. Tensions in the financial markets continued to mount, and the euro tumbled to a 14-month low against the US dollar. In May 2011 the euro-area countries thus agreed to establish two facilities to provide financial support to EU countries experiencing severe economic or financial disturbances. First, the European Financial Stabilisation Mechanism (EFSM) was set up, which allowed the European Commission to raise up to €60 billion on behalf of the EU to provide financial assistance to EU Member States experiencing serious financial difficulties. Second, the euro countries established the European Financial Stability Facility (EFSF). The EFSF was set up as a limited liability company authorised to issue debt securities, guaranteed up to a total of €440 billion by euro-area countries on a pro rata basis, for lending to euro-area countries. The IMF committed itself by matching half of the funding provided by Europe. Moreover, the IMF was closely involved in designing adjustment programmes for countries seeking recourse to the safety net (*conditionality*).

The ECB also announced far-reaching measures. On 10 May 2010, it announced the launch of the Securities Markets Programme (SMP), under which it purchased €73.5 billion in secondary public and private bond markets by the end of that year in order to enhance depth and liquidity in dysfunctional markets.

Following the statements by euro-area governments and the ECB, tensions in the financial markets briefly abated. Market sentiment improved in the summer, and new debt issues by European governments were successful. The country risk premiums – most notably in Greece, Ireland, and Portugal – expanded substantially relative to countries with a stronger economic recovery and healthier financial positions, such as Germany and the Netherlands.

Yet on 21 November 2010, Ireland requested EU financial assistance. The problems in Ireland were completely different, although no less serious than those in Greece. For many years, Ireland had experienced high growth rates, and had reached the top 10 richest countries in the world. Until 2007, there were sharp rises in real estate prices, which produced substantial investments in the construction sector. The wide availability of credit created a bubble, which began to deflate when the subprime crisis broke out, causing house prices to fall by close to 40 per cent and commercial real estate prices by more than 50 per cent. This caused an exceptionally deep recession and a doubling of unemployment. The Irish banking sector had to absorb unprecedented losses on mortgage lending, and was confronted with extensive withdrawals from the international liabilities, so state support was unavoidable. Serious concerns arose about the sustainability of Irish public finances when the extent of government support to the banking sector became clear, forcing Ireland to ask for European support. The EU, EFSF, IMF, and some non-euro -area EU countries (UK, Denmark, and Sweden) promised €67.5 billion in financial support in return for Ireland's commitment to an ambitious programme to restructure the financial sector and restore public finances.

In 2011, the problems continued. In April, Portugal had to seek international financial assistance. Its economy had not performed well since its accession to EMU: sluggish growth and pronounced credit expansion had seriously eroded the country's competitiveness, and it was also plagued by excessive government and current account deficits. The EU Council of

Economics and Finance Ministers agreed on a €78 billion financial assistance package on 17 May 2011.

In 2011 it also became obvious that Greece would require a second major rescue package because it would not be able to return to financial markets in 2012 when the first package ran out. At their summit in July 2011, euro-area heads of state or government announced several measures to alleviate the Greek debt crisis and to ensure the financial stability of the euro area as a whole. This support was conditional on the implementation of another austerity package (combined with continued demands for privatisation and structural reforms outlined in the first programme), and demanded that all private creditors holding Greek government bonds should agree to accept lower interest rates and a 53.5 per cent loss in face value. The most contentious part of the deal was the involvement of the private sector. Germany, strongly supported by the Netherlands and Finland, insisted that private investors should be involved in any new package. The new deal was not ratified until February 2012. In mid-May 2012, the crisis and the impossibility of forming a new coalition government after elections led to strong speculation that Greece would leave the eurozone (*Grexit*). A second election in mid-June ended with the formation of a new government that supported continued adherence to the main principles outlined in the signed bailout plan.

Again, the agreement did not have a lasting effect on financial market volatility. This time, interest rates on Italian and Spanish government bonds started to rise, without a clear change in the underlying fundamentals. In response, the ECB Governing Council purchased €22 billion in government bonds under the SMP after the Spanish and Italian governments agreed to additional fiscal consolidation measures.

In July 2012, an 18-month programme was agreed upon to provide external financing to support Spanish banks. The newly established European Stability Mechanism (ESM, see below) disbursed €41.3 billion to the Spanish government to recapitalise the country's banking sector – the ESM's first financial assistance programme. It also was the first time that banks were recapitalised via loans granted to a government. There were no contributions from other lenders.

The Cypriot government requested a bailout on 25 June 2012, citing difficulties in helping its banking sector deal with the exposure to the Greek debt. In May 2013 a €10 billion deal was finally agreed; Cyprus became the fifth country – after Greece, Ireland, Portugal, and Spain – to receive money from the EU–IMF. The deal included measures to prevent the withdrawal or transfer of money. This was necessary, as equity, bond, and deposit holders of the country's two largest banks (the Bank of Cyprus (BoC) and the

Cyprus Popular Bank (Laiki)) also had to contribute to the restructuring of these banks (bail-in). The BoC was capitalised through the full contribution of the bank's shareholders and bondholders and through the conversion of 47.5 per cent of uninsured deposits (over €100,000) into equity. The resolution of Laiki minimised the use of taxpayers' money with a full bail-in of equity shareholders and bondholders, and a partial bail-in of uninsured depositors. Under a *bail-in*, a financial institution is recapitalised by writing down or converting (or both) its unsecured debt, while maintaining the institution's legal entity (Enoch *et al.*, 2014). All deposits under €100,000 were fully protected. Laiki was split into two units: all uninsured deposits were kept in a legacy unit (Legacy Laiki), and the insured deposits were transferred together with certain assets and liabilities to the BoC.

After Dexia's nationalisation in October 2011, Belgian interest rates started to increase. Italian yields also soared, but, at that time, not due to bank problems. Italy had a high debt-to-GDP ratio and relied heavily on foreign investors. Even France was affected: its debt was downgraded and market yields rose substantially above those of other 'core' countries like Germany and the Netherlands. Needless to say, a crisis that threatened Italy and France would jeopardise the common currency.

It was only after ECB President Draghi told an investment conference in London in July 2012: 'Within our mandate, the ECB is ready to do whatever it takes to preserve the euro. And believe me, it will be enough' that bond spreads of *GIIPS countries* (Greece, Ireland, Italy, Portugal, and Spain) started to decline substantially.[3] To fulfil this promise, the ECB introduced the Outright Monetary Transactions programme in September 2012 (see Chapter 4). With this instrument, the ECB guaranteed the survival of the monetary union. After European political leaders finally showed their commitment by agreeing to further support for Greece, the financial markets calmed down. Interest rate spreads between the core countries and the periphery, which had to that point reflected an increased risk of a euro break-up, narrowed sharply in the second half of 2012 (see Figure 2.7).

Causes

Lack of Fiscal Discipline?

Several important fault lines that had existed under the surface since the launch of the euro, notably persistent current account imbalances, unexpectedly became clearly visible during the euro crisis.[4] Especially during its initial

Table 2.4 Pre-crisis imbalances

	Current account and fiscal imbalances		Bank assets	Debt and inflation	
	Cumulative current account balance 1999–2007 (% of own GDP)	Cumulative budget deficit 1999–2007 (% of own GDP)	2000–2008 increase (p.p.)	Bank assets, 2008	Debt–GDP ratio, 2008	Excess inflation (1999–2007)
Portugal	−96	−36	44%	262%	72	7.5
Greece	−84	−47	36%	173%	109	9.9
Spain	−60	2	121%	296%	39	9.2
Ireland	−21	14	464%	783%	43	11.6
Italy	−8	−26	85%	235%	102	1.8
EZ	−2	−17	94%	335%	69	0.0
France	6	−23	180%	395%	68	−2.9
Austria	16	−19	305%	379%	69	−3.2
Germany	27	−19	18%	316%	65	−4.8
Belgium	47	−5	83%	392%	92	−1.1
Netherlands	48	−5	−9%	375%	55	2.8
Finland	61	33	101%	197%	33	−4.9

Source: Baldwin and Giavazzi (2015)

stages, the eurozone crisis was often attributed primarily to a lack of budget-ary discipline. This might be partly due to the fact that the initial phase of the crisis was dominated by Greece, the budgetary troubles of which could indeed be clearly attributed to a lack of discipline (and even deliberate statistical misreporting). Spain and Ireland, however, had relatively low levels of public debt when the crisis erupted before they too ran into budgetary problems (see Table 2.4). So, a lack of budgetary discipline was not the real cause of the crisis. Current account imbalances were the main culprit (Baldwin and Giavazzi, 2015). The euro area's current account as a whole was in balance before the crisis and remained nearly balanced throughout. In other words, there was very little net lending from the rest of the world to euro-area countries. However, there were large current account imbal-ances *within* the euro area. These were reflected in capital flows from core nations like Germany, France, and the Netherlands to periphery nations like Ireland, Portugal, Spain, and Greece. A significant portion of these capital flows was invested in non-traded sectors, like housing (notably in Spain and Ireland). The first column of Table 2.4 shows the cumulated imbalances from the euro's inception until the failure of Lehman Brothers. Except for

Portugal and Greece, these capital flows were not extensively used to finance governments' budget deficits (see column 2).

The remainder of the chapter discusses four aspects of the euro crisis: (1) diverging financial cycles in core vs. periphery countries caused by capital inflows; (2) decreased competitiveness as a result of capital flows to periphery countries, which drove up wages and inflation; (3) the 'doom loop', in which national governments are the ultimate guarantor of their banks, but the banks are key holders of public debt; and (4) policy reactions.

Diverging Financial Cycles

Although the euro crisis was a sovereign debt crisis, it was not primarily caused by unsustainable fiscal policies. In fact, fiscal policies in countries like Ireland and Spain looked relatively healthy when the financial crisis started. Why, then, did the economic downturn following the financial crisis cause such a large swing in the budgetary position of Member States? De Haan *et al.* (2015) argue that this reflects differences in the financial cycle across Member States. As explained in Chapter 2, the three main characteristics of a financial cycle are that (1) it is driven by growth in credit and house prices, (2) it has a much longer duration than business cycles (16–20 years instead of up to 8 years), and (3) it has a wider amplitude than the business cycle, while the correction of a financial cycle is often accompanied by a financial crisis (Drehmann *et al.*, 2012).

In the euro area, the financial cycle was asymmetric (see Figure 2.8). It was strongest in a number of countries in the periphery, notably in Ireland, Spain, and to a lesser extent Greece. In the run-up to the financial crisis, multiple countries had experienced strong credit booms, in part because joining the euro area meant that their banks could raise funds from international sources in their own currency. These countries – at least initially – experienced a process of real convergence, while lower interest rates related to EMU membership fuelled consumption- and property-related borrowing (Obstfeld, 2013). By contrast, the financial cycle was much more contained in Germany and Austria, where interest rates had already been low before EMU membership.

When cross-border financial flows to periphery countries dried up, countries with the greatest reliance on external funding were disproportionately affected. This applies especially to Ireland and Spain, where the resulting decline in construction was a major shock to domestic economic activity, while abandoned projects and falling property prices indicated large

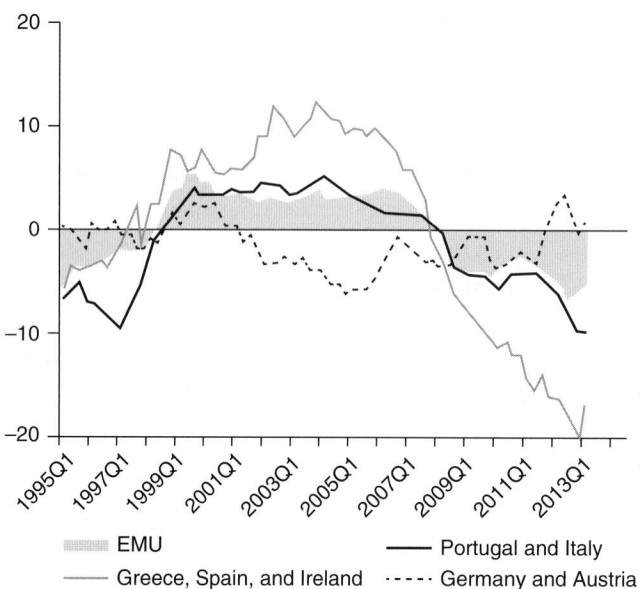

Figure 2.8　Diverging financial cycles in the euro area
Note: A financial cycle is calculated as the first principal component of the output gap, real credit growth, and real house price growth.
Source: De Haan *et al.* (2015)

prospective losses for banks that had made too many property-backed loans (Lane, 2012). Recent research shows that a turn of the financial cycle has a much larger negative impact on public finances than a turn of the normal business cycle (Bénétrix and Lane, 2013). This difference is mostly due to its effect on government revenues. Rising asset prices increase revenues in capital gains and transaction taxes. In addition, high wage growth increases income tax revenue, especially when the system is progressive. Finally, wealth effects stimulate domestic demand and thereby revenues from indirect taxes. All these factors reverse when the financial cycle turns, resulting in a large budgetary deterioration. Even countries that entered the euro crisis with relatively healthy public finances saw their budget deficits rapidly increase. As a consequence, they had to introduce austerity measures, which amplified the recession.

Diverging Competitiveness

The credit boom fuelled by capital inflows in much of Southern Europe and Ireland facilitated another development that would come back to haunt

EMU: diverging competitiveness positions. In the run-up to the crisis, several countries experienced a deterioration in competitiveness. Between 2001 and 2011 per-unit labour costs rose by 33 per cent in Greece, 31 per cent in Italy, 27 per cent in Spain, and 20 per cent in Ireland. By contrast, they grew by only 0.9 per cent in Germany, partly because the country needed to restore its price competitiveness after reunification. Although the large current account deficits of some countries signalled a competitiveness problem, the deficits were relatively easy to finance as financial integration increased the availability of foreign funding (Obstfeld, 2013). In fact, capital inflows continued pushing up money and credit growth, which in turn increased inflation (see Table 2.4) and had further negative effects on competitiveness. Growing current account deficits in the periphery were accompanied by increasing surpluses in core countries like Germany and the Netherlands.

As countries in the euro area can no longer devalue their currency or implement national monetary policy, external imbalances can only be restored by improving competitiveness. However, relative price adjustments without a change in the nominal exchange rate will be difficult when average euro-area inflation is low; it will be a rather slow and painful route to rebalancing (Shambaugh, 2012). The conventional wisdom before the crisis was that individual euro-area countries' balance of payments would become as irrelevant as among regions within a country. Yet the euro crisis eventually challenged this view (Merler and Pisani-Ferry, 2012). The financing of external positions in the monetary union was often interpreted as proof of the successful integration of capital markets and of real convergence. However, if capital inflows fuel investments that have little effect on future productivity growth (such as real estate) and delay adjustment to structural shocks, they pose risks (Giavazzi and Spaventa, 2011).

Doom Loop

Sovereign funding problems were reinforced by a negative feedback loop with the banking sector. The euro area's banking system is large, and grew rapidly in the run-up to the crisis (see Table 4.2). The largest banks in the euro area are large in proportion to their home economies. Furthermore, most banks heavily invested in government bonds, with a home bias that is particularly strong for the banks of troubled sovereigns (Greece, Ireland, Italy, Portugal, and Spain). In Spain, Portugal, and Italy domestic banks owned around 25 per cent of the outstanding stock of government debt – the basis of what came to be known as the 'doom loop' (or 'diabolic loop'). The essence of the problem is that the government may collapse when it is trying to rescue its banks, as happened in Ireland.

During the financial crisis, governments in several euro-area countries engaged in large-scale (and in the case of Ireland, even blanket) financial sector bailouts. Such bailouts involve the immediate issuance of additional debt by the sovereign, causing an increase in the sovereign's credit risk. This has two possible consequences. First, the government runs the risk that this debt overhang will affect the private sector. Households and corporations may anticipate that the high level of government debt will require higher taxes in the future, thereby diluting long-run returns on real sector and human capital investments. The resulting underinvestment in the economy can cause economic growth to slow down, thereby further increasing the sovereign's credit risk. Second, the deterioration in the sovereign's creditworthiness may feed back adversely onto its financial sector through four channels: (1) the market value of the government debt on the balance sheet of the financial institutions reduces, decreasing the financial sector's creditworthiness; (2) higher sovereign risk reduces the value of collateral that financial institutions can use for funding purposes; (3) if CRAs downgrade sovereigns, this normally lowers the ratings of banks located in the downgraded country; (4) as the sovereign's creditworthiness declines, the value of the explicit and implicit government guarantees to the financial sector also declines, which adversely impacts the financial sector's credit quality (Acharya et al., 2012, 2014; Obstfeld, 2013).

During the euro crisis the exposure of foreign banks on sovereign debt of the GIIPS reduced, whereas the exposure of domestic banks increased. For instance, in December 2010, 67 per cent of Greek sovereign debt was held by domestic banks; this rose to 99 per cent by June 2013 (de Haan et al., 2015). This made the problem of the doom loop even more pressing, since funding problems on sovereign bond markets in the periphery were associated with funding problems for banks in these countries. As a result, many countries in the periphery at some point experienced an outflow of capital that constituted a sudden stop in external financing (Merler and Pisani-Ferry, 2012). Most of the capital fled to core countries that were considered safe havens. It made banks in vulnerable countries very dependent on ECB funding, which was reflected in growing imbalances in the Target2 settlement system (see Chapter 7). Target2 liabilities (and assets) reached around €1,000 billion in the summer of 2012.

From 2008 to 2012, EU banks received €413.2 billion in public capital injections (European Commission, 2014). Banks from the UK, Germany, Ireland, and Spain received the largest injections – €60 billion or more each.

In relative terms, total injections represented 3.2 per cent of the EU's GDP in 2012, but they represented more than 10 per cent of the country's GDP in Ireland, Greece, and Cyprus. Problems in the banking systems eroded public finance in those countries, and ultimately led governments to ask for support for their partners. Public capital injections were also significant (over 4 per cent of GDP) in Belgium, Luxembourg, Spain, Denmark, the UK, and Portugal.

Some banks that received support in the early stages of the crisis repaid the capital injected (notably in the Netherlands, Denmark, Germany, and Italy). However, in other Member States (Spain, Greece, Portugal, Belgium, and France, among others), new injections were needed still in 2012 or 2013 (European Commission, 2014).

Policy Reactions

The reaction of European leaders to the crisis was initially to initiate several ad hoc support programmes to support the countries that faced financial difficulties. Later on, more structural measures were taken, including reform of the Stability and Growth Pact, the creation of a permanent fund to support countries facing financial difficulties, and the creation of a Banking Union. Fear that the sovereign debt crisis would spread further, and thereby undermine the stability of the euro area and perhaps even the sustainability of the currency union, created the political willingness to take these steps.

In October 2010 European politicians decided to create a permanent crisis mechanism, the ESM – which replaced the EFSF and EFSM – as of 2013. The ESM is a permanent last-resort rescue mechanism set up among euro-area countries that can issue triple-A bonds to aid euro countries in difficulty on the basis of strict conditionality. ESM assistance will predominantly take the form of loans that will be conditional on agreement to (and compliance with) a strict macroeconomic adjustment programme. The interest rate on the loans will be the sum of the funding cost to the ESM and a charge of 200 basis points. The ESM has an effective lending capacity of €500 billion, which it seeks to supplement with the participation of the IMF and non-euro EU countries. The ESM will only provide financial assistance if this is deemed necessary to safeguard the stability of the euro as a whole. Decisions to activate the ESM, and the terms under which assistance will be made available, will be taken unanimously by its Board of Governors, which is made up of the finance ministers of the euro-area countries. However, abstentions do not prevent decisions from being adopted.

The crisis has made clear that national supervision in a monetary union is not a viable arrangement, notably in an environment with a large banking sector and high interconnectedness among national banking systems as well as between banking systems and sovereigns (Obstfeld, 2013). Furthermore, a banking union with a common safety net can break the doom loop between national governments and banks. Under a common safety net, government support to banks will no longer be provided through national budgets; therefore problems in the banking sector will not immediately affect the governments' fiscal positions. The European Council therefore decided in June 2012 to establish a European Banking Union (see Chapter 12).

2.5 Conclusions

Crises are a permanent feature of the financial system. While a well-functioning financial system can contribute to economic growth as discussed in Chapter 1, crises may temporarily hamper economic growth.

In a systemic banking crisis, a significant part of a country's banking system becomes insolvent after heavy investment losses and/or banking panics. Theory suggests that such banking crises are often rooted in the business cycle. Credit is expanded in an upswing, and reduced in a downswing ('credit crunch'). The financial system can thus amplify the business cycle. Banking crises can have a large impact on the economy. While problem banks may need to be refinanced by the government, the real cost of a banking crisis is the loss of economic growth.

The financial crisis of 2007–2009 was a banking crisis, which started with the bursting of the US housing market bubble. A unique feature of the crisis was the role of securitised credit. In the process of securitisation, subprime mortgages (i.e. housing loans to high-risk borrowers) were repackaged by originating banks and sold to other financial institutions around the world, which caused the crisis to spread very fast and to become very deep.

In a sovereign crisis, governments default on their debt obligations. While countries sometimes repudiate their debt in a default, it is more common for a government to restructure its debt on less favourable terms to the lender. Debt crises are a common feature of emerging countries, but can also happen in industrialised countries. The most important cause of the euro crisis was not a lack of fiscal discipline, but current account imbalances. These were reflected in capital flows from core countries like Germany, France, and the Netherlands to periphery countries like Ireland, Portugal, Spain, and Greece. These capital inflows, in turn, led to diverging financial cycles in core and periphery countries and tended to drive up wages and inflation in periphery countries, thereby making them less competitive. The crisis also featured the doom loop, in which a government may collapse in an attempt to rescue its banks.

Notes

1. Only Austria, Belgium, the Netherlands, and Portugal managed to escape banking crises from 1945 to 2007. Except for Portugal, even these countries had massive bailouts in 2008.
2. While securitised credit has existed for almost as long as modern banking, from the mid-1990s the scale of securitisation increased rapidly. For instance, further adaptations were introduced in the form of 'synthetic' CDOs, which did not contain any mortgage-related assets but were designed to replicate their structure using another form of derivative known as CDS to speculate on the value of the original CDO or MBS. In addition, there was 'an explosion in the complexity of the securities sold, with the growth of the alphabet soup of structured credit products' (Turner, 2009: 14).
3. See www.ecb.europa.eu/press/key/date/2012/html/sp120726.en.html.
4. This and the following sub-sections draw heavily on de Haan *et al.* (2015) and Baldwin and Giavazzi (2015).

Bibliography

Suggested Reading

Allen, F. and D. Gale (1998), Optimal Financial Crises. *Journal of Finance*, 53, 1245–84.

Baldwin, R. and F. Giavazzi (eds.) (2015), *The Eurozone Crisis: A Consensus View of the Causes and a Few Possible Remedies*, Centre for Economic Policy Research, London.

Reinhart, C. M. and K. S. Rogoff (2009), *This Time Is Different: Eight Centuries of Financial Folly*, Princeton University Press.

References

Acharya, V. V., I. Drechsler, and P. Schnabl (2012), A Tale of Two Overhangs: The Nexus of Financial Sector and Sovereign Credit Risks. *Banque de France Financial Stability Review*, 16, April.

Acharya, V. V., I. Drechsler, and P. Schnabl (2014), A Pyrrhic Victory? Bank Bailouts and Sovereign Credit Risk. *Journal of Finance*, 69, 2689–739.

Acharya, V. V. and P. Schnabl (2009), How Banks Played the Leverage Game. In: V. V. Acharya and M. Richardson (eds.), *Restoring Financial Stability: How to Repair a Failed System*, Wiley, Hoboken (NJ), 83–100.

Allen, F., A. Babus, and E. Carletti (2009), Financial Crises: Theory and Evidence. *Annual Review of Financial Economics*, 1, 97–116.

Allen, F. and D. Gale (1998), Optimal Financial Crises. *Journal of Finance*, 53, 1245–84.

Baldwin, R. and F. Giavazzi (2015), Introduction. In: R. Baldwin and F. Giavazzi (eds.), *The Eurozone Crisis: A Consensus View of the Causes and a Few Possible Remedies*, Centre for Economic Policy Research, London, 18–60.

Bénétrix, A. and P. Lane (2013), Financial Cycles and Fiscal Cycles. *Journal of International Money and Finance*, 34, 164–76.

Borio, C. (2014), The Financial Cycle and Macroeconomics: What Have We Learnt? *Journal of Banking and Finance*, 45, 182–98.

Brunnermeier, M. K. (2009), Deciphering the Liquidity and Credit Crunch 2007–2008. *Journal of Economic Perspectives*, 23, 77–100.

Brunnermeier, M., A. Crockett, C. Goodhart, A. Persaud, and H. Shin (2009), *The Fundamental Principles of Financial Regulation*. Geneva Report on the World Economy 11, ICBM, Geneva, and Centre for Economic Policy Research, London.

de Haan, J., J. Hessel, and N. Gilbert (2015), Reforming the Architecture of EMU: Ensuring Stability in Europe. In: H. Badinger and V. Nitsch (eds.), *Routledge Handbook of the Economics of European Integration*, Routledge, New York, 408–32.

de Haan, J., J.-E. Sturm, and E. Zandberg (2009), The Impact of Financial and Economic Crises on Economic Freedom. In: *Economic Freedom of the World Report 2009*, Fraser Institute, Vancouver.

Diamond, D. and P. H. Dybvig (1983), Bank Runs, Deposit Insurance, and Liquidity. *Journal of Political Economy*, 91, 401–19.

Drehmann, M., C. Borio, and K. Tsatsaronis (2012), Characterizing the Financial Cycle: Don't Lose Sight of the Medium Term! BIS Working Paper 380.

Eijffinger, S. C. W. and J. de Haan (2000), *European Monetary and Fiscal Policy*, Oxford University Press.

Elson, A. (2017), *The Global Financial Crisis in Retrospect*, Macmillan, New York.

Enoch, C., L. Everaert, T. Tressel, and J. Zhou (eds.) (2014), *From Fragmentation to Financial Integration in Europe*, IMF, Washington, DC.

European Commission (2014), *European Financial Stability and Integration Report 2013*, EC, Brussels.

Giavazzi, F. and L. Spaventa (2011), Why the Current Account May Matter in a Monetary Union. In: M. Beblavý, D. Cobham, and L. Ódor (eds.), *The Euro Area and the Financial Crisis*, Cambridge University Press, 199–221.

Gorton, G. and G. Ordoñez (2014), Collateral Crises. *American Economic Review*, 104, 343–78.

Hahm, J., H. S. Shin, and K. Shin (2011), Non-Core Bank Liabilities and Financial Vulnerability. Paper presented at Federal Reserve Board conference, Regulation of Systemic Risk, Washington, DC, 15–16 September.

Huertas, T. F. (2010), *Crisis: Cause, Containment and Cure*, Palgrave Macmillan, Basingstoke.

Laeven, L. and F. Valencia (2018), Systemic Banking Crises Revisited. IMF Working Paper 18/206.

Lane, P. R. (2012), The European Sovereign Debt Crisis. *Journal of Economic Perspectives*, 26, 49–68.

Merler, S. and J. Pisani-Ferry (2012), Sudden Stops in the Euro Area. Bruegel Policy Contribution 2012/6, March.

Minsky, H. P. (1986), *Stabilizing an Unstable Economy*, Yale University Press, New Haven (CT).

Mishkin, F. S. (1992), Anatomy of a Financial Crisis. *Journal of Evolutionary Economics*, 2, 115–30.

Obstfeld, M. (2013), Finance at Center Stage: Some Lessons of the Euro Crisis. European Economy – Economic Papers 493.

Qian, R., C. M. Reinhart, and K. S. Rogoff (2010), On Graduation from Default, Inflation and Banking Crisis: Elusive or Illusion? NBER Working Paper 16168.

Reinhart, C. M. and K. S. Rogoff (2009), *This Time Is Different: Eight Centuries of Financial Folly*, Princeton University Press.

(2010), From Financial Crash to Debt Crisis. NBER Working Paper 15795.

Richardson, M. (2009), Causes of the Financial Crisis of 2007–2009. In: V. V. Acharya and M. Richardson (eds.), *Restoring Financial Stability: How to Repair a Failed System*, Wiley, Hoboken (NJ), 57–80.

Shambaugh, J. (2012), The Euro's Three Crises. *Brookings Papers on Economic Activity*, 44, 157–231.

Treasury Committee of the House of Commons (2008), The Run on the Rock. Fifth Report of Session 2007–08, Volume I.

Turner, A. (2009), *The Turner Review: A Regulatory Response to the Global Banking Crisis*, Financial Services Authority, London.

3

European Financial Integration: Origins and History

OVERVIEW

The European Union (EU) has its origins in the European Coal and Steel Community (ECSC), which was formed by six European countries in 1951. Since then, it has grown to 27 members through the accession of new Member States, and has increased its powers by adding new policy areas to its remit. At the time of writing, the EU is negotiating the first exit of a Member State after a majority of the UK electorate voted to leaving the EU on 23 June 2016 in a process that has come to be known as Brexit.

The chapter starts by explaining the functions of the most important EU institutions (European Commission, Council of the EU, European Council, the European Parliament, and the European Court of Justice) and legal instruments (including directives and regulations). It also provides an overview of the EU's supranational and intergovernmental forms of cooperation.

It proceeds by outlining the process of monetary integration, from the agreement in principle in 1969, to the creation of an internal market, and the adoption of the euro in 1999 by 11 Member States. The chapter then discusses the steps taken to coordinate the fiscal and economic policies of EU members, including the Stability and Growth Pact and the Macroeconomic Imbalance Procedure.

The next section addresses the more gradual moves towards financial integration. It describes the harmonisation of banking standards, and the launch of the Financial Services Action Plan (FSAP) in May 1999. The FSAP was created to remove regulatory and market barriers that limit the cross-border provision of financial services and the free flow of capital within the EU, and to create a level playing field among market participants. The section also details the Banking Union (created in 2014) and the emerging Capital Markets Union.

LEARNING OBJECTIVES

After you have studied this chapter, you should be able to:

- outline the various steps in the process of European monetary and financial integration (and disintegration)
- explain the Stability and Growth Pact
- describe the fundamental principles underlying the EU financial integration process
- explain the functioning and responsibilities of the most important EU institutions (European Commission, Council of the EU, European Council, the European Parliament, and the European Court of Justice)
- describe the various EU legal instruments
- explain the main elements of the Banking Union.

3.1 European Integration: Introduction

Although the idea of economic integration of European countries was proposed earlier, it was put into practice only after the Second World War. The major impetus was the Schuman Plan of May 1950 that triggered the establishment of the European Coal and Steel Community (ECSC) the following year as the basis of a permanent Franco-German reconciliation. To ensure that reconstruction in West Germany would not endanger peace, the ECSC sought to integrate the coal and steel sectors, which were considered to be of central importance to the defence industry. The main objective of the ECSC was to eliminate barriers and encourage competition in these sectors.

The ECSC had a limited membership of Belgium, Germany, France, Italy, Luxembourg, and the Netherlands. In 1973 Denmark, Ireland, and the UK joined what was then called the European Community, to be followed by Greece (in 1981), Spain and Portugal (in 1986), and Austria, Finland, and Sweden (in 1995). After the collapse of communism at the end of the 1980s, several Eastern and Central European countries became candidate members of what was by then called the European Union (EU). In 2004, Cyprus, the Czech Republic, Estonia, Hungary, Latvia, Lithuania, Malta, Poland, Slovakia, and Slovenia acceded to the EU, followed in 2007 by Bulgaria and Romania, and in 2013 by Croatia. At the time of writing, the EU is negotiating membership with several other Balkan countries. The UK left the EU on 31 January 2020 (see Box 3.1).

Box 3.1 Brexit

Under pressure from many Eurosceptic Conservative Members of Parliament and the UK Independence Party (UKIP), UK Prime Minister David Cameron announced that his Conservative government would hold a referendum on EU membership before the end of 2017 if it was re-elected in the 2015 election. In the referendum, held on 23 June 2016, a small majority (52 per cent) of those voting supported leaving the EU. As a result, Cameron – who had campaigned for the UK to remain in the EU – resigned and was succeeded by Theresa May. May called for another general election to be held on 8 June 2017. Although the Conservative Party won the election, it did not win a majority, forcing May to broker a deal with the Democratic Unionist Party from Northern Ireland to support a Conservative minority government.

On 29 March 2017, the UK government invoked Article 50 of the Treaty on European Union, which governs withdrawal from the EU. Under Article 50, a Member State notifies the European Council, whereupon the EU is required to negotiate and conclude an agreement with the country leaving, setting out the arrangements for its withdrawal that defines its future relationship with the EU. The negotiation period is limited to two years unless it is agreed upon to extend it. The UK was therefore due to leave the EU on 29 March 2019. The UK government's letter informing the EU of its decision to leave called for a 'deep and special relationship' between the UK and the EU, and stated that the UK would seek a free trade agreement with the EU.

On 29 April 2017, the EU-27 heads of state accepted negotiating guidelines. According to these guidelines, the UK should first agree to a financial commitment and to lifelong benefits for EU citizens living in Britain before negotiations on the future relationship between the EU and the UK can begin. The negotiations were tough, as there were disagreements on many issues, including the border between Northern Ireland and the Irish Republic. In addition, the EU demanded that the European Court of Justice maintains jurisdiction over the rights of EU citizens living in the UK after Brexit. It was also difficult to reach an agreement on the EU-27 demand that the UK should pay a 'divorce bill', in view of the previous agreement on the EU budget for the period 2014–2020. The British parliament rejected on several occasions the withdrawal agreement reached with the EU, after which May resigned and was succeeded by Boris Johnson, who vowed to leave the UK on 31 October 2019, if needed without an agreement with the EU. However, the British parliament accepted a law prohibiting such a 'hard Brexit'. After it had been extended three times, Brexit happened on 31 January 2020.

Most economists agree that leaving the EU will adversely affect the British economy in the medium and long term. For instance, Sampson (2017: 163–4) concludes that 'the research literature displays a broad consensus that in the long run Brexit will make the UK poorer because it will create new barriers to trade, foreign direct investment, and immigration. However, there is substantial uncertainty over how large the effect will be, with plausible estimates of the cost ranging between 1 and 10 per cent of the UK's income per capita.' Using input-output analysis, Chen *et al.* (2018) find that UK regions are exposed to anticipated negative trade-related

> **Box 3.1** (cont.)
>
> consequences in the order of 10–17 per cent of regional GDP. The highest levels of risk are found in the Midlands and the North of England; many of these areas voted for Brexit. For London and Scottish regions, the exposure rates are lower. For Ireland, the exposure risk is approximately 10 per cent of GDP.

Much of the EU's organisational structure is very similar to that of the ECSC (see Section 3.2). For instance, the High Authority, the ECSC's supranational executive organ, was the predecessor of the European Commission. Other ECSC institutions include the Council of Ministers (representing member governments), the Assembly (composed of 68 delegates from the national parliaments, later transformed into the European Parliament, EP), and the European Court of Justice (ECJ).

The 1958 Treaty of Rome (see Box 3.2) created the European Economic Community (EEC) and the European Atomic Energy Community (Euratom). Of the three communities (i.e. the ECSC, the EEC, and Euratom), the EEC was by far the most important in terms of scope and instruments.[1] The treaty paved the way for the creation of a common market in which goods, services, labour, and capital could move freely. It directed Europe towards a single financial market, but major steps were not taken in this direction until the 1980s.

In 1985, the European Commission published a white paper on the Completion of the Internal Market, which called for the free circulation of persons, goods, services, and capital within the EU. The paper predicted that economies of scale and scope would result from decreased border controls, unified technical standards, reduced distribution and marketing costs, and standardised rules and regulations in the manufacturing and services sectors. To provide an economic underpinning of the Internal Market Project, the Cecchini Report (1988) calculated the costs of nationally fragmented markets, i.e. the costs of 'non-Europe', and estimated the benefits of an internal market at approximately 4–7 per cent of GDP. The white paper led to the adoption of the Single European Act (SEA) in 1986 that aimed to create an internal market by 1992.

Another major step in the history of European integration was the publication of the report of the Committee for the Study of Economic and Monetary Union in 1989. The Delors Report – named after the chairman of this committee and then-president of the European Commission, Jacques Delors – proposed a three-phase transition towards monetary unification. Its main conclusions were incorporated into the 1992 Maastricht Treaty. The

---

Box 3.2 The role of treaties

Treaties form the basis of the European integration process. The basic treaty is the Treaty of Rome, which established the European Economic Community. It contains the legal basis for most decisions taken by European Union institutions (see Section 3.2) and is still the main source of communitary legislation. It has been amended by subsequent treaties.

The first major amendment was the Single European Act (1986), which completed the internal market. The act's chief objective was to increase momentum towards the process of European integration. Importantly, it moved away from the principle of unanimity for the harmonisation of legislation. The Maastricht Treaty on European Union (TEU) (1992) created the EU and launched the Economic and Monetary Union.

The Treaty of Amsterdam (1997) placed greater emphasis on security and justice matters, and took steps towards creating a common foreign and security policy. The Treaty of Nice (2001) introduced institutional reforms to allow the EU to continue functioning effectively after its enlargement.

The Treaty of Lisbon (2007), which entered into force on 1 December 2009, further streamlined EU institutions and upgraded the powers of the European Parliament. This treaty amends the EU's two core treaties, i.e. the TEU and the Treaty of Rome. The latter has been renamed as the Treaty on the Functioning of the European Union (TFEU).

Economic and Monetary Union (EMU) was launched on 1 January 1999 with the irrevocable fixing of the exchange rates of the then 11 participating countries and the start of the common monetary policy by the European Central Bank (ECB). Euro notes and coins were introduced in January 2002.

In May 1999, the European Commission launched the Financial Services Action Plan (FSAP), which was designed to remove any regulatory or market barriers that limit the cross-border provision of financial services and the free flow of capital within the EU, and to create a level playing field among market participants. In 2014, a further major step towards financial integration was the start of the Banking Union (see Chapter 12). In September 2015, the European Commission adopted an action plan to establish an integrated capital market in the EU (known as the Capital Markets Union, or CMU).

This chapter outlines the most important steps taken towards European financial integration. The next section explains the most important European institutions and the legal instruments used to shape integration. Section 3.3 describes how monetary integration has evolved. Section 3.4 discusses the coordination of fiscal and economic policies. Section 3.5 sets out the major steps towards financial integration and discusses the Banking Union and the CMU.

3.2 European Institutions and Instruments

There are two basic approaches to integration. In the *supranational approach*, an international institution that is independent from national governments is responsible for policy making, while in the *intergovernmental approach* an international institution basically fulfils a secretariat role for the governments and has no real power. The key difference between the two approaches is the transfer of sovereignty from the Member States to the international institution. Whereas in the intergovernmental approach no sovereignty is transferred, in the supranational approach Member States lose their power to enact legislation. The EU features both types of integration.

Institutions

The *European Commission* is the only EU institution that can submit formal proposals for legislation (the so-called right of initiative). As explained in greater detail below, the Council and Parliament can only request legislation. The European Commission initiates the formal legislative process by presenting a proposal to the EP and the European Council; the EP and Council then begin the process of negotiation.

The Commission consists of 27 commissioners, one from each Member State, who are nominated by the European Council and approved by the EP before being appointed to a five-year term. Commissioners are expected to detach themselves from national interests. In 2014, the president of the European Commission was appointed for the first time under the new provisions established by the Treaty of Lisbon. Jean-Claude Juncker, the lead candidate (or *Spitzenkandidat*) of the European People's Party (EPP), campaigned for this position during the EP elections, in which the EPP won 220 out of 751 seats. The European Council officially nominated Juncker for the position, after which the EP elected him. In 2019, Ursula von der Leyen was appointed as successor of Juncker. In contrast to Juncker, she was not the *Spitzenkandidat* of the Christian Democrats. The European Council selected her and at the same time proposed Christine Lagarde as the new President of the ECB.

The Commission has a relatively small staff of about 32,000 officials, which is sometimes referred to as 'the Brussels bureaucracy'. Each commissioner is responsible for a particular policy area, and politically responsible for a Directorate General (DG).[2] The most important departments for financial services are DG Financial Stability, Financial Services and Capital Markets

Union, DG Internal Market, Industry, Entrepreneurship and SMEs, DG Economic and Financial Affairs, and DG Competition.

The *Council of the European Union* consists of representatives of each Member State at the ministerial level. Council meetings of ministers of economics and finance are known as *Ecofins*. Depending on the issue, council decisions are taken on the basis of unanimity, simple majority, or qualified majority (55 per cent of council members, comprising at least 16 Member States and representing at least 65 per cent of the EU population). Decisions on financial services policy are mainly taken by qualified majority.

The *European Council* has become a very powerful body. Comprised of the heads of state or government and the president of the European Commission, it is tasked with providing 'the Union with the necessary impetus for its development' (Article 15 TEU). Essentially, it defines the EU's policy agenda; it put forward major policy initiatives such as the Internal Market Programme, the Maastricht Treaty, and the Banking Union. It also takes decisions if the ministerial-level Council of the European Union reaches a stalemate on a particular issue.

The role of the EP, which since 1979 has been directly elected by EU citizens every five years (coinciding with the terms of commissioners of the European Commission), is more limited than that of national parliaments. Yet over time, its influence has increased. The EP has veto power over appointments to the Commission and can dismiss the Commission. The EP also has the right to reject the EU budget. It plays an important role in legislation, which may go through four different procedures. Under the *consultation procedure*, the EP only gives its opinion. Under the *cooperation procedure* it has the right to amend or even reject legislation, but the European Council may overrule these decisions. Under the *co-decision procedure*, EP approval is necessary. The Commission presents a proposal to Parliament and the Council, then the EP sends amendments to the Council, which can either adopt the text with those amendments or send back a 'common position'. That proposal may be approved or further amendments may be tabled by the EP. If the Council does not approve the additional amendments, a 'Conciliation Committee' is formed to seek agreement. Finally, under the *assent procedure* the Council is required to obtain the EP's agreement (without amendments) before certain important decisions are taken. The assent principle is based on a single reading: if the EP does not give its approval, the act in question cannot be adopted. The assent procedure applies mainly to the accession of new Member States, association agreements, and other fundamental agreements with third countries. It is also required for specific tasks of the ECB and amendments to the Statutes of the European System of Central Banks and the ECB. Parliament's assent is given by a majority of votes cast, but a majority of Members is also required for decisions on the accession of a new Member State.

The ECJ consists of 27 judges (one judge per Member State) and 9 advocates-general. ECJ judgments on matters relating to the interpretation and application of European law have been very important to the development of the EU. As the supreme court of the EU, the ECJ provides a coherent and uniform interpretation of EU law and ensures Member States' compliance. The ECJ has rejected protectionism in many judgments and has thus contributed significantly to the realisation of the internal market.

Legal Instruments

EU legislative measures are proposed by the European Commission and adopted by co-decision: the Council and EP consider, amend, and agree on the final content. These measures, published in the *Official Journal of the European Union*, can take the form of:

- *Regulations*, which are binding in their entirety and directly applicable in all Member States. They do not require transposition into respective national laws (although changes may be required in Member States' laws to achieve the full effect); or
- *Directives*, which are binding upon each Member State to which they are addressed. National authorities choose the form and methods. Directives must be incorporated into the national law of each Member State, generally by introducing or amending national laws, generally within 18 or 24 months after publication.

The Commission and Council can also take binding *decisions* and *recommendations* or deliver non-binding (but politically important) *opinions*. The Treaty of Lisbon created *delegated acts* under which the legislator delegates the power to the European Commission to adopt acts amending non-essential or technical elements of a legislative act. The treaty also strengthened the Commission's implementing powers by authorising it to adopt *implementing acts*, which are designed to ensure the uniform implementation of specific measures across the EU.

These legal instruments have different impacts on integration (see also Box 3.3). While regulations foster full integration since they supersede national legislation, directives must be implemented by the Member States, which leaves scope for minor or major differences.

The adoption or implementation of legal instruments is only the first element of the legislative framework. The second element is putting in place the necessary administrative arrangements to ensure the new rules are

---

> ## Box 3.3 Dynamics of integration
>
> The combination of the choice of decision-making procedure (supranational or intergo-vernmental) and the choice of legal instrument (regulation or directive) largely determines the degree of integration. In the area of competition policy and monetary policy, the EU uses regulations to ensure uniformity across the EU. For example, the Regulation on the Introduction of the Euro (EC/974/98) stipulates that the national currencies participating in the euro must be converted into the euro in a uniform way. If the euro denomination of the German D-Mark, for example, were calculated differently across countries, there would be scope for arbitrage. A supranational institution (the European Central Bank, ECB) is responsible for policy making in this area (see Chapter 4).
>
> By contrast, the EU has often used directives in the area of financial services policy, which have been implemented in a different way by each Member State. An example is the definition of 'capital' under the Banking Directive (2006/48/EC), which has been replaced by a new legislative package known as CCR/CRD IV, which applies from 1 January 2014 (see Chapter 12). This directive stipulates the amount of capital banks must maintain based on the risks they face, but all Member States use their own definition of capital. Moreover, banking supervision was undertaken by national supervisory authorities. Since the start of the Banking Union in November 2014, the ECB has become responsible for banking supervision, as discussed in more detail in Section 3.5. The EU has also started to use regulations alongside directives for financial services policy to foster uniformity.

observed. The third element, sometimes referred to as enforcement, is ensuring that the new rules work effectively and are complied with across the EU.

3.3 Monetary Integration

During the initial phase of European integration, the emphasis was on the integration of goods markets. The Treaty of Rome only vaguely referenced monetary issues, describing exchange rate policies as a matter of 'common concern'. It was only at the summit in 1969 in The Hague that the European governments agreed on monetary union. Pierre Werner, prime minister of Luxembourg at the time, was appointed to chair a committee to draw up a plan. The Werner Report, completed in 1970, called for the completion of a monetary union by 1980. The Werner Committee proposed a three-stage approach towards monetary union, leading eventually to fixed exchange rates and a common monetary policy.

Although the Council adopted the plan, the turmoil in the currency markets at the time made the mid-1970s a low point in European monetary integration. However, at the end of the 1970s the then French president, Valéry Giscard d'Estaing, and German chancellor, Helmut Schmidt, created the European Monetary System (EMS) with the goal of developing a 'zone of monetary stability' in Europe. The core of this system was the Exchange Rate Mechanism (ERM). Currencies participating in the ERM were supposed to fluctuate vis-à-vis one another within a band of plus or minus 2.25 per cent around agreed-upon central rates that could be adjusted. Although this system brought some stability to the participating currencies, at times there were frequent adjustments of the central rates. Within the system, the German D-Mark functioned as the anchor. Countries that pegged their currency to Germany's had little room for manoeuvre in monetary policy making. If the German monetary authorities decided to change their interest rates in response to the domestic economic situation, the other countries had to follow if they wanted to maintain their peg. Various countries, notably France, felt that the German-dominated ERM did not always serve their interests. A monetary union was often regarded as the solution to this problem.

During the 1980s, the discussion therefore focused again on monetary integration. The signing of the SEA in 1986 and the commitment to establish an internal market by 1992 were important steps towards monetary union and helped create momentum for European integration. The European Commission argued that in order to reap the full gains from the internal market, exchange-rate risks and transaction costs were to be banished by introducing a common currency. For instance, an important European Commission study from that era was called 'One Market, One Money' (Emerson *et al.*, 1992). Although many economists do not subscribe to the view that fixed exchange rates are needed to fully capture the gains from the single market, the argument gained popularity among policy makers.

At the Hanover summit in June 1988, the European Council established a committee to propose the concrete stages leading to EMU, which were put forward in the Delors Report, as discussed above. Although it did not specify a timetable, the committee proposed a gradual process towards EMU, but stressed that the timing of each stage required a political decision. Although not strictly necessary for the creation of monetary union, the Delors Committee advocated a single currency under a new central bank's authority, as this would demonstrate the irreversibility of the union. Since participating countries were expected to coordinate their economic (particularly fiscal) policies as well as their currencies, the system adopted in the 1992 Treaty on

European Union, signed in Maastricht, was called Economic and Monetary Union (EMU) (see Section 3.4).[3]

Many of the Delors Committee's suggestions found their way into the treaty, including a three-stage approach (see Figure 3.1). As suggested in the Delors Report, the first stage of EMU started on 1 July 1990 with the liberalisation of capital controls.

However, ratification of the Maastricht Treaty turned out to be difficult. Denmark's narrow rejection of the treaty in a June 1992 referendum[4] came as a huge shock. France's referendum resulted in a wafer-thin (51 per cent) majority in favour. Ratification was tortuous and contentious in other countries too.

The prospect of EMU dimmed when serious currency crises in 1992–1993 forced governments to broaden the ERM fluctuation band to plus or minus

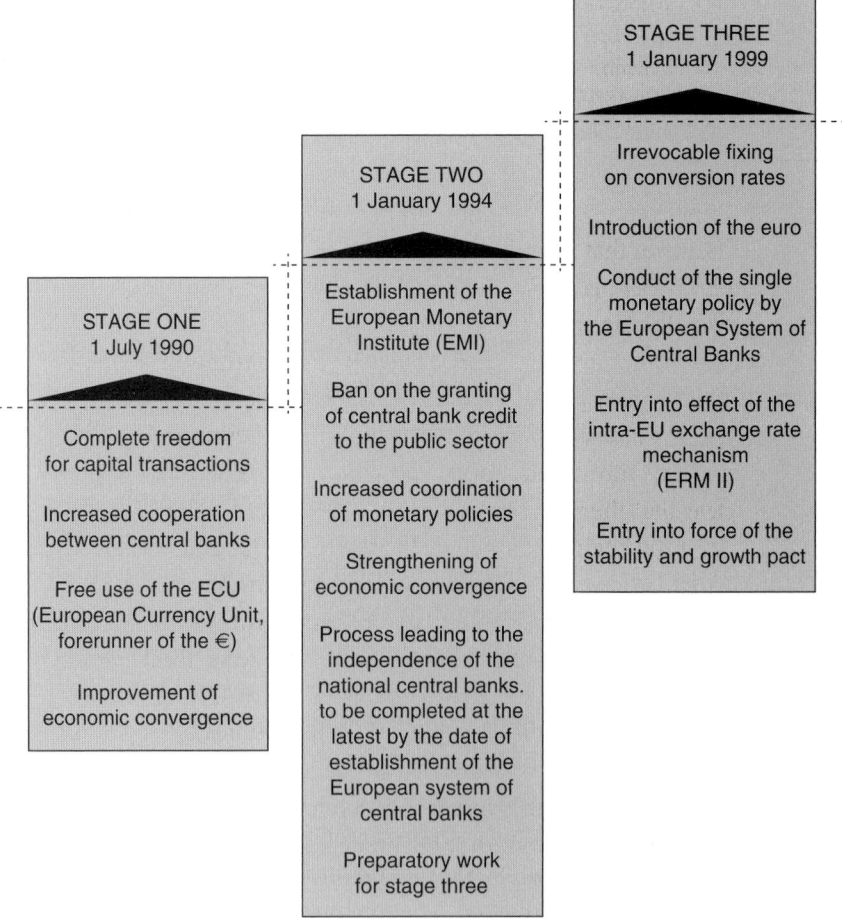

Figure 3.1   The three stages leading to EMU
Source: ECB

Table 3.1 Convergence criteria

Inflation	Member State has a price performance that is sustainable and an average rate of inflation, observed over a period of one year before the examination, that does not exceed by more than 1.5 percentage points that of, at most, the three best-performing Member States in terms of price stability.
Interest rate	Member State has had an average nominal long-term interest rate that does not exceed by more than 2 percentage points that of, at most, the three best-performing Member States in terms of price stability.
Exchange rate	Member State has observed the normal fluctuation margins provided for by the ERM for at least two years, without devaluing against the currency of any other Member State on its own initiative.
Budget deficit	Member State's planned or actual government deficit to GDP ratio must not exceed 3 per cent unless: – either the ratio has declined substantially and continuously and reached a level that comes close to the reference value; or – the excess over the reference value is only exceptional and temporary and the ratio remains close to the reference value.
Debt	Member State's government debt-to-GDP ratio must not exceed 60 per cent, unless the ratio is sufficiently diminishing and approaching the reference value at a satisfactory pace.

15 per cent. Many sceptics questioned the likelihood of monetary union among countries that were unable to keep their national currencies aligned. Sometimes EMU was perceived as an ambitious project that would never fly, just like the emu, the large Australian bird. For instance, the then prime minister of the UK, John Major, wrote in *The Economist* that continuing 'to recite the mantra of full economic and monetary union ... will have all the quaintness of a rain dance and about the same potency'. Although the currency crises produced lingering doubts, with the start of the second stage of EMU on 1 January 1994 it became clear that the project was becoming more and more likely.

At the beginning of 1998, the European Council decided that 11 of the then 15 EU Member States were eligible to join the currency union based on the convergence criteria (i.e. entry requirements) as outlined in the Maastricht Treaty. These criteria related to inflation, long-term interest rates, exchange rate stability, and public deficit and debt-to-GDP ratios (see Table 3.1).

On 1 January 1999, 11 EU Member States adopted a single currency – the euro. This represented an unprecedented example of so many countries voluntarily sharing a currency and pooling their monetary sovereignty. Greece joined the euro area in 2001 and Slovenia in 2007, while Cyprus and Malta introduced the euro in 2008 and Slovakia in 2009. Estonia joined the euro area in 2011, Latvia in 2014, and Lithuania in 2015 (see Box 3.4).

Box 3.4 Lithuania introduces the euro

The European Central Bank and the European Commission published convergence reports on 4 June 2014 that concluded Lithuania met the convergence criteria for entering the currency union (see Table 3.1). Based on these findings, on 23 July 2014 the Council of the European Union took the decision to allow Lithuania to adopt the euro as its currency on 1 January 2015. As explained in more detail in Section 3.5, euro-area countries participate automatically in the Banking Union, and Lithuania therefore also joined the Banking Union on the same date that it adopted the euro. It was the first country to join both the euro area and the Banking Union in this way.

The EU Council also adopted a regulation on Lithuania's irrevocable conversion rate to the euro: 3.45280 Lithuanian litas to one euro, which corresponds to the central rate of the litas in the Exchange Rate Mechanism (ERM) II. (ERM II is the successor of the ERM after the introduction of the euro, which aims to stabilise the exchange rates of participating countries vis-à-vis the euro.) This rate is unchanged from that agreed at the time the litas entered the ERM II in 2004. During the reference period, the litas continued to be stable and did not exhibit any deviation from its central rate within ERM II.

Source: ECB Monthly Bulletin, August 2014

Under the EMU, participating countries relinquished their monetary sovereignty to the ECB. While the ECB is responsible for policy decisions, national central banks play a role in implementing monetary policy (see Chapter 4). The central banks of non-eurozone EU Member States are members of the European System of Central Banks (i.e. the ECB plus the national central banks of all EU Member States), but they do not take part in decisions related to the single monetary policy.

The ECB's primary objective as laid down in the Treaty on the Functioning of the EU is price stability. The ECB defines price stability as maintaining inflation in the euro area below (but close to) 2 per cent in the medium term, and has developed a monetary policy strategy to accomplish this objective (see Chapter 4 for further details).

3.4 Coordination of Fiscal and Economic Policies

Stability and Growth Pact

Whereas monetary policy in EMU is conducted at the supranational level, fiscal policy has remained largely the competence of national governments. According to the ECB (2011), a well-functioning monetary union requires member countries to maintain fiscal discipline. Large deficits can give rise to inflationary pressures that may force the ECB to keep short-term interest rates higher than would otherwise be necessary. Furthermore, fiscal policies may undermine confidence in the ECB's monetary policy if markets come to expect that excessive government borrowing will ultimately be financed through money creation.

Therefore, the Maastricht Treaty contains provisions for monitoring and coordinating EU Member States' fiscal policies, which were further specified in the Stability and Growth Pact (SGP) that was adopted in 1997. The SGP contains a preventive arm that prescribes the path for sound fiscal policies, and a corrective arm intended to prevent 'gross policy errors' by deterring excessive deficits and requiring their prompt correction should they occur.

Under the preventive arm of the SGP, Member States submit stability or convergence programmes in which they detail their medium-term budgetary plans. Under the original SGP, Member States were required to pursue the medium-term objective of budgetary positions that were 'close to balance or in surplus' (this was changed later; see below).

The SGP's corrective arm specifies the Excessive Deficit Procedure (EDP). When the Ecofin decides that a Member State has an excessive deficit, the procedure stipulates a sequence of steps to be taken to intensify pressure on the Member State to take effective action to correct the problem. For each step, the Ecofin has to take decisions on the basis of recommendations from the Commission. If a Member State does not take (sufficient) action to redress its deficit, sanctions may be imposed. Sanctions include requiring the Member State to make a non-interest-bearing deposit that, if non-compliance persists, becomes a fine.

Critics of the SGP pointed to a major weakness of the rules in place: the Ecofin will not automatically impose sanctions, as each step requires a discretionary decision by the Council, thus following an intergovernmental approach. And the same ministers who are responsible for drafting national budgets also have to decide whether one of their colleagues breaches the rules. There are no strong incentives for Member States to prevent other Member States from creating an excessive deficit. Furthermore, Member States have no other means than peer pressure under the preventive arm of the SGP. It is no wonder, therefore, that some Member States did not adhere to their medium-term objectives. At the end of the 1990s, large countries in particular did not sufficiently reduce their deficits. As a consequence, they exceeded the 3 per cent deficit threshold after the economic downturn set in during 2000–2001. It then became clear that the EDP enforcement mechanism is also weak since it depends on the Ecofin, which is not impartial.

In 2005, the SGP was amended to introduce more discretion and flexibility into the surveillance procedures and make the corrective arm slightly more stringent. The amendments included requiring each Member State to present its own country-specific medium-term objective in its stability programme. These country-specific objectives will be differentiated and may diverge from the 'close to balance'/'in surplus' requirement depending on the current debt ratio and potential growth. The adjustment effort should be greater in good times and could be more limited in bad times. As a benchmark, Member States should pursue an annual adjustment in cyclically adjusted terms, net of one-off and temporary measures, of 0.5 per cent of GDP. The amended SGP also places more emphasis on the government debt ratio. This was important, as the Ecofin had previously only focused on the government budget deficit. However, the reform has not introduced any fundamental institutional changes.

The SGP has been reformed several more times since 2005. For instance, since 2011 reverse qualified majority voting (RQMV) has been required for decisions on most sanctions. RQMV implies that a Commission recommendation or proposal is considered adopted by the Council unless a qualified majority of Member States votes against it, which makes the procedure more automatic. Despite these changes, the centrality of the 3 per cent threshold and the importance of the EDP have remained intact.

Macroeconomic Imbalance Procedure

European policy makers have also enhanced the ability to monitor and prevent large macroeconomic and financial imbalances within the euro area, for example by introducing the Macroeconomic Imbalance Procedure (MIP). The MIP is based on a continuous monitoring of a 'scoreboard', consisting of a set of 11 indicators covering the major sources of macroeconomic imbalance. These include the current account balance, price competitiveness as measured by the change in the real effective exchange rate, as well as the growth of credit and house prices. For each indicator, thresholds have been defined to identify potential imbalances. According to the European Commission, the scoreboard and thresholds are not applied mechanically, as the scoreboard is complemented by an economic interpretation. The scoreboard is designed to identify countries that warrant in-depth analysis in order to determine whether the potential imbalances identified in the early warning system are benign or problematic. Like the SGP, the MIP has a preventive arm and a corrective arm. Under the preventive arm the Council can make policy recommendations to tackle imbalances early on. Under the corrective arm an Excessive Imbalance

Procedure may be opened for a Member State if it is deemed to have excessive imbalances. In that case, the Member State will have to submit a corrective action plan with a clear roadmap of concrete policy measures and deadlines for implementing corrective action. Non-compliance with Council recommendations may lead to financial sanctions of up to 0.2 per cent of GDP. All decisions on sanctions are made in the Council via RQMV.

3.5 Financial Integration

The Treaty of Rome of 1957 identified the 'creation of a unified economic area with a common market' as a task of the community. Early policies related to the creation of a single market for financial services focused on the banking system. The first step towards harmonising the prudential standards for the supervision of banks was the First Banking Directive (77/780/EEC). This directive required full harmonisation of relevant banking standards, such as solvency, liquidity, and internal controls. But national approaches to basic prudential standards, including capital requirements, continued to diverge. Major subsequent steps towards financial integration were taken under the Internal Market Programme, FSAP, the Banking Union, and the Capital Markets Union. Each of these steps is discussed in turn below.

The Internal Market Programme

As pointed out in Section 3.1, creating an internal market was high on the agenda of European policy makers in the second half of the 1980s. In the context of banking, the European Commission called for a single banking licence and home-country control. The Second Banking Directive (89/646/EEC) permits a credit institution that is licensed in any EU Member State to establish branches or supply cross-border financial services in other EU Member States. This provision, known as the *single banking licence*, has helped stimulate cross-border banking in Europe. The main limitation of the Second Banking Directive is that the single licence does not extend to subsidiaries in host Member States. This is unfortunate, as cross-border European banking more often takes place via subsidiaries, especially major banking operations (see Chapter 10). After Brexit, UK banks are no longer automatically licensed to operate branches in the EU.

The Second Banking Directive also introduced the principle of *home-country control* of the supervision of branches with some exceptions, notably the supervision of branch liquidity. The authorities in the home country were made responsible for supervision on solvency that extends to the bank itself as well as its foreign and national subsidiaries, which have to be consolidated for supervisory purposes, and its foreign branches. Under this directive, the authorities in the host state have the right to regulate a foreign bank's activities in that state only to the extent that such regulation is necessary for the protection of 'public interest'.

The European legal framework incorporates the international banking standards of the Basel Committee on Banking Supervision (see Box 3.5). An important element of banking supervision is the *capital adequacy requirements*, which stipulate the minimum amount of capital that banks have to maintain. The Solvency and Own Funds Directives (89/647/EEC and 89/299/EEC) that laid down the solvency rules for banks were based on the 1988 Basel Capital Accord. Likewise, Basel III forms the basis of the current EU regulation (see Chapter 12).

An important principle underlying European financial integration is *minimum harmonisation*. Instead of fully harmonising rules, a common minimum is defined that Member States have to implement. However, they are free to move beyond this minimum. For example, the Directive on Deposit Guarantee Schemes (94/19/EEC) that was accepted by the Council in 1994 provides a minimum of €20,000 mandatory coverage per depositor. The directive does not address funding, so the financing must be arranged at the national level (e.g. *ex ante* or *ex post* funding). Branch deposits are covered by the home country's deposit insurance system. All EU countries adopted a compulsory explicit deposit insurance scheme, yet practical arrangements regarding coverage limits, funding, and co-insurance differ substantially across Member States. During the financial crisis, the EU rules were changed. Directive 2009/14/EC of 11 March 2009 requires Member States to increase their level of coverage to €100,000. According to the European Commission, this new level would cover an estimated 90 per cent of deposits.

The fields of insurance and securities have experienced moves towards integration that parallel those discussed in relation to the banking sector. The Third Insurance Directives (92/49/EEC and 92/96/EEC) and the Investment Services Directive (93/22/EEC) also adopted the principles of a single licence, home-country control, and minimum harmonisation of standards.

Another important milestone for European financial integration was the Directive on Liberalisation of Capital Flows (88/361/EEC). Starting from 1 July 1990 – the start of the first phase of EMU – capital controls were only allowed in the case of large, speculative movements.

> ## Box 3.5 Basel Committee on Banking Supervision
>
> The Basel Committee on Banking Supervision provides a forum for regular cooperation on banking supervisory matters. Its objective is to enhance understanding of key supervisory issues and improve the quality of banking supervision worldwide by exchanging information on national supervisory issues, approaches, and techniques. The committee develops guidelines and supervisory standards, such as Standards on Capital Adequacy (Basel I, Basel II, and Basel III), the Core Principles for Effective Banking Supervision, and the Concordat on cross-border banking supervision.
>
> The Basel Committee comprises 45 members from 28 jurisdictions, consisting of central banks and authorities with formal responsibility for the prudential supervision of banking business. It also has nine observers including central banks, supervisory groups, international organisations and other bodies. The committee's secretariat is located at the Bank for International Settlements in Basel, Switzerland.
>
> The committee frequently discusses minimum capital requirements for banks. In 2004 an agreement was reached that is generally referred to as the *Basel II Accord*. It uses a three-pillar concept: (1) minimum capital requirements, (2) supervisory review, and (3) market discipline. Its predecessor, the *Basel I Accord* of 1988, dealt with only parts of each of these pillars. Basel II aimed to improve on the existing rules by aligning regulatory capital requirements more closely with the underlying risks that banks face. In response to the financial crisis, the committee made several changes in 2010, generally referred to as *Basel III* (see Chapter 12 for further details).

The Financial Services Action Plan

In 1998, the European Council of Cardiff underlined the importance of financial market integration as a political priority. In response, the European Commission published a communication entitled 'Financial Services: Building a Framework for Action', which set out a series of measures to strengthen integration. This resulted in the Commission's launch of the FSAP in May 1999. The FSAP, endorsed by the European Council in March 2000, consists of a set of 42 measures to fill gaps and remove remaining barriers to provide a legal and regulatory environment that supports the integration of financial markets across the EU.

The FSAP has four objectives. The first objective is a single EU wholesale market. The Markets in Financial Instruments Directive (MiFID, 2004/39/EC) is, to a large extent, the cornerstone of the FSAP. This directive provides securities firms with an updated EU passport, allowing them to offer a range of financial services across Member States on a 'home-country control' basis. Under the passport principle, a firm licensed to provide financial services in its home country has the right to provide these services throughout the EU, without the need for an additional licence. MiFID applies the passport to a broader range of financial instruments and significantly extends the list of financial services that can be 'passported' across European countries.

The second objective is open and secure retail markets. The Commission acknowledged that certain barriers prevented consumers and suppliers from reaping the single-market benefits of increased choice and competitive terms.

An example of FSAP directives in the domain of retail financial services is the Insurance Mediation Directive (2002/92/EC), which aims to improve choice and reinforce protection for customers while helping insurance inter-mediaries (like insurance brokers and banks) market their services cross-border in the EU. The directive sets common minimum standards across the EU for the regulation of the sale and administration of insurance. It provides rights for an insurance intermediary established in one Member State to operate in another Member State.

The FSAP's third objective is state-of-the-art prudential rules and supervision. The Capital Requirements Directive lays down these new capital adequacy rules for banks and is based on the 2004 Basel II Capital Accord. Similarly, the Solvency II Directive (2009/138/EC) introduces risk-based capital requirements for insurance companies (see Chapter 12). Capital requirement rules stipulate the minimum amount of own financial resources that financial institutions must have in order to cover the risks to which they are exposed. The aim is to ensure the financial soundness of these institutions, thereby protecting depositors and clients, and fostering the stability of the financial system.

The final objective of the FSAP is related to wider conditions for an optimal single financial market, e.g. addressing disparities in tax treatment and creating an efficient and transparent legal system for corporate governance. An example is the Savings Directive (2003/48/EC) that aims to subject interest on savings received in one Member State, by individuals who are resident for tax purposes in another Member State, to effective taxation in accordance with the laws of the latter country. It establishes automatic exchanges of information to combat cross-border tax evasion on savings income.

In 2004, the European Commission concluded that the FSAP was delivered on time, with 40 out of 42 measures adopted before the 2005 deadline.

The Banking Union

Before the global financial crisis (as discussed in section 2.3), national authorities in the Member States were responsible for supervising the banking system and ensuring its stability. The crisis has made clear that this is not a viable arrangement. A decentralised system of bank supervision and resolution is inadequate in an environment with a large banking sector and high interconnectedness among national banking systems as well as between banking systems and sovereigns. Experience of the near failure of cross-border banks in Europe suggests that in times of crisis, national authorities focus on preserving the national elements, while the integrated value of a bank is neglected (Gros and Schoenmaker, 2014).

The European Council therefore decided in June 2012 to create a Banking Union, which involves four elements. First, they created a single rulebook, consisting of a set of harmonised rules that all banks in the EU must comply with. These rules range from capital requirements to rules for the recovery and resolution of banks.

Second, under the *Single Supervisory Mechanism* (SSM), microprudential supervision of banks has moved from national supervisors to the ECB since November 2014. The single supervisor applies a unified approach to supervision by harmonising practices and methodologies, which increases comparability across borders and reduces compliance costs for banks. Under the SSM, every bank is supervised according to a single supervisory model, using the same data-reporting template. This ensures a harmonised and consistent implementation of prudential regulation. Single supervision under the aegis of the ECB also credibly addresses long-standing coordination problems between supervisors in the home and host countries. The supranational structure of decision making aims to diminish the predominance of a 'national bias' (ECB, 2014). Chapter 12 discusses the SSM in more detail.

In the third element of the Banking Union, the council introduced a *Single Resolution Mechanism* (SRM) to deal with bank resolution, i.e. the orderly restructuring and/or liquidation of ailing financial institutions. A situation in which only supervision is delegated to the European level, but in which the resolution mechanism remains national, could give rise to conflicts of interest. For example, a supervisory decision to withdraw a bank's licence would be taken at the central level, whereas the bill of such decisions would be footed at the national level. This would put tremendous pressure on the European supervisor to exercise forbearance. The SRM regulation has been in force since 2016, together with the bail-in provisions under the Bank Recovery and Resolution Directive. Under this mechanism, losses are initially borne by shareholders and creditors. If necessary, a new Single Resolution Board (SRB) can make temporary financing available from the newly established Resolution Fund. Chapter 13 offers a more extensive discussion of the SRM.

Fourth, a European deposit guarantee scheme will be introduced. A first step in this direction was the agreement on the Deposit Guarantee Scheme Directive, which ensures that deposits in all Member States continue to be guaranteed up to €100,000 per depositor and bank. It also aims for faster payouts with specific repayment deadlines, which would gradually be reduced from 20 to 7 working days. The directive also ensures strengthened financing of national deposit guarantee schemes, notably by requiring a significant level of *ex ante* funding (0.8 per cent of covered deposits) to be met in 10 years.

Finally, the European Stability Mechanism (ESM), created as a permanent last-resort rescue mechanism among euro-area countries can, under very strict conditions, recapitalise banks in the Banking Union.

Figure 3.2 illustrates the new governance framework for financial supervision and stability in the Banking Union. The bottom line shows the agency for each function. The first two stages are preventive; the European Commission is responsible for legislation and the ECB for supervision. The latter three stages form the crisis management arrangements. The ECB (in cooperation with the national central banks) is the lender of last resort, just as the national central banks used to be the lenders of last resort under the national regime. This lender of last resort role is typically not written down in legislation to reduce moral hazard. Finally, the SRB is responsible for resolution and the ESM is the fiscal backstop to the banking system in the Banking Union.

The Capital Markets Union

The European Commission (2015) has presented the CMU project to foster the development of capital markets in the EU. The Commission has pointed

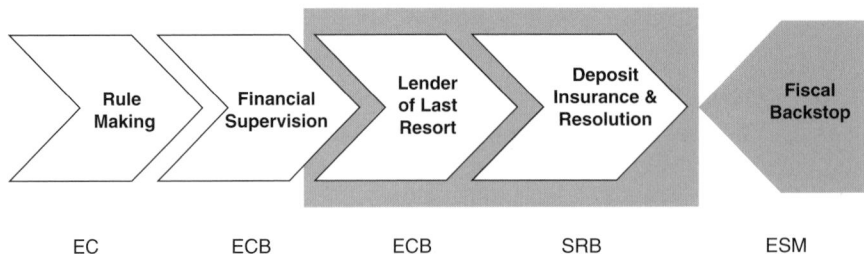

Figure 3.2   European bodies in the Banking Union
Source: Schoenmaker (2013)

out that even though the European economy is as big as the US economy, Europe's equity markets are less than half the size of those in the US, and its debt markets are less than a third of the size of US markets. European small and medium-sized enterprises (SMEs) receive five times less funding from capital markets than those in the US.

The Commission's approach is to remove the barriers to a single capital market, thus 'creating a sense of momentum, and sparking a growing confidence for investing in Europe's future' (European Commission, 2015: 6). Deeper capital markets would help unlock more funding for investment, notably for SMEs. An integrated capital market also offers an important channel for risk sharing. While euro-area Member States no longer have their own currencies, and thus cannot adjust their exchange rates to mitigate the effects of idiosyncratic shocks (i.e. shocks to one or a few states), an integrated capital market can help geographically diversify their income sources. This would allow eurozone countries that are hit by an idiosyncratic shock to smooth their consumption by drawing on income from investments in countries that are not affected by the shock.

The Commission intends to tackle (or has tackled) many diverse issues to stimulate CMU, ranging from increasing the possibilities for crowdfunding, and introducing measures to enhance access to venture capital and remove cross-border tax barriers. For example, the Commission has enacted a regulation that aims to simplify and standardise the prospectuses for the issuing and offering of securities. The new regulation exempts small issuers (below €8 million) from the obligation to publish a prospectus (Xafa, 2017), which streamlines the relevant administrative procedures and makes it cheaper and easier for them to access capital markets.

In 2017, the European Commission published a mid-term review of its progress in implementing its proposals. It stressed the need to ensure consistent supervision across the EU. The objective is to apply the same supervisory standard to financial entities of similar size and with similar risk profiles, regardless of where they are located in the EU, to avoid regulatory arbitrage. The post-Brexit influx of businesses from the City of London to continental Europe gave impetus to this initiative (Xafa, 2017).

While regulatory adjustments as proposed by the European Commission are useful, Darvas and Schoenmaker (2018) suggest taking a more bottom-up approach to creating the CMU by stimulating the demand for and supply of equity and debt securities. For example, employees prepare for old age by setting aside part of their current income as pension savings. They can do this collectively through pension funds (an institutional investor; see Chapter 9) or privately through private pension savings schemes managed by a professional asset manager (another type of institutional investor). Although some EU Member States have very high pension savings, others, like Germany, have almost no pension savings (less than 5 per cent of GDP). Most of the private pension commitments in Germany are still on companies' balance sheets. That is risky for both the (future) pensioners and the companies. If a company fails, pensioners may lose (part of) their pension entitlement. It is thus in the interest of both companies and workers/pensioners to put pension commitments in a separate pension fund vehicle. This would be a boost for capital markets, as it would increase the demand for marketable instruments, such as equity and debt securities. This driver for capital markets development comes from the demand side.

An increasing share of institutional investors increases the demand for marketable securities, such as equities and bonds. Figure 3.3 shows that there is a strong relationship between the amount of assets managed by institutional investors in a country and the size of that country's equity and debt markets.

But there is also a driver from the supply side: firms issuing corporate bonds to replace bank loans. Banks have begun reducing the provision of credit to the private sector, so other channels are needed to finance firms. Moreover, market financing (e.g. corporate bonds) was more stable during the recent financial crisis than bank financing (e.g. bank loans), which reduces firms' reliance on bank financing.

3.6 Conclusions

The EU has its origins in the ECSC, which was formed by six European countries in 1951. Since then, the EU has grown in size through the accession of new Member States, and has increased its powers by adding new policy areas to its remit. Since Brexit, the EU consists of 27 Member States. It has supranational and intergovernmental forms of cooperation.

Legislation – particularly treaties – has been the main mechanism for fostering economic integration. For example, the Maastricht Treaty established the ECB. Within the broader framework of these treaties, legislative measures are proposed by the European Commission and adopted by the Council and the EP. These legislative measures include regulations, which apply directly in each Member State, and directives, which need to be incorporated into the national law of each Member State. While regulations ensure a uniform regulatory framework throughout the EU, the implementation of directives by individual Member States leaves room for differences.

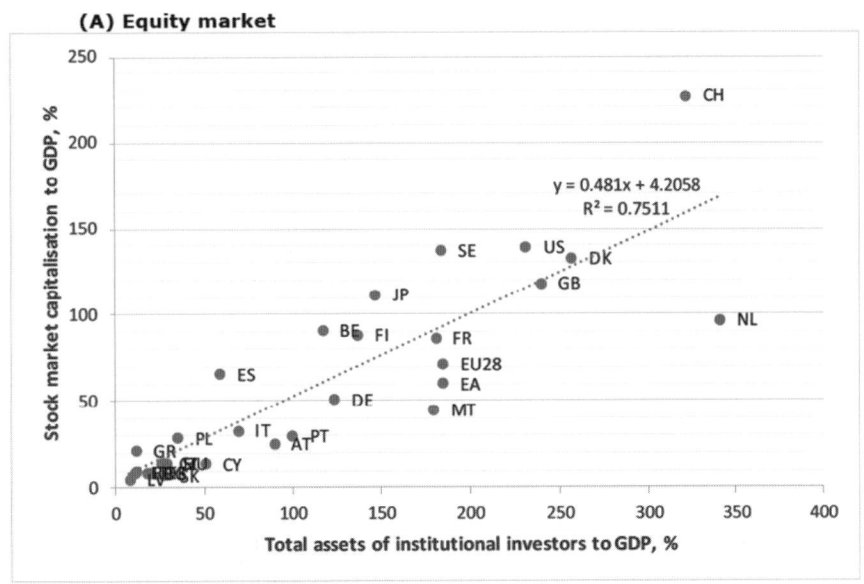

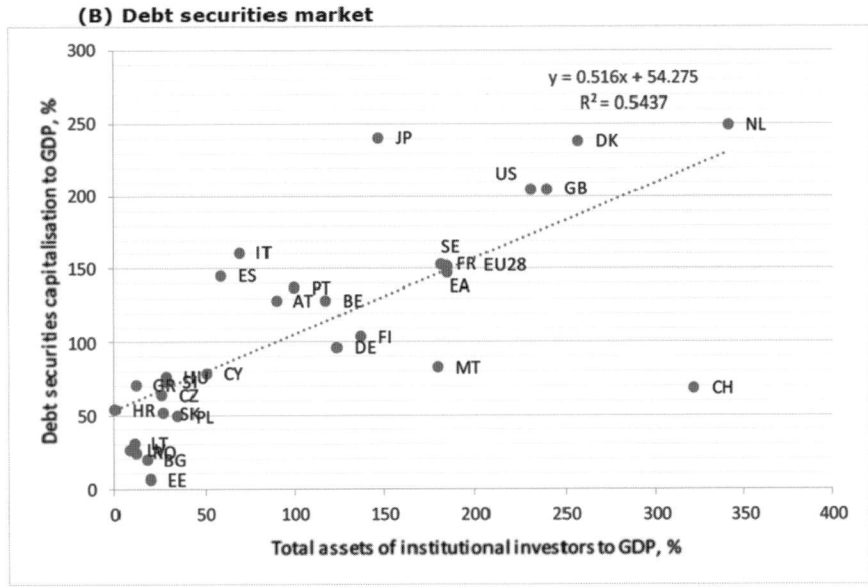

Figure 3.3   Assets managed by institutional investors and market capitalisation (2014 or most recent data; % of GDP)

Source: Darvas and Schoenmaker (2018)

Monetary integration was characterised by two major steps. In 1979, the EMS was introduced. A key element of the EMS was the ERM, within which the currencies of participating countries were supposed to fluctuate within a band of plus or minus 2.25 per cent. As explained in Chapter 2, in the early 1990s, the EMS was strained by the differing economic policies and conditions of its members, and the fluctuation band was subsequently widened to plus or minus 15 per cent. In 1999, the ECB took over responsibility for monetary policy making, and a common currency, the euro, was introduced in 11 EU Member States. Currently, 19 Member States are part of the euro area.

Whereas monetary policy has been delegated to the supranational ECB, fiscal policy has remained largely the competence of national governments. In order to protect monetary policy, the SGP has introduced restrictions on the national fiscal policies of eurozone countries.

While monetary integration in Europe took place with a small number of major steps, financial integration is a more gradual process. In 1992, the EU created an internal market with a system of laws that apply in all Member States, guaranteeing the freedom of movement of people, goods, services, and capital. In the area of financial services, the internal market introduced a single licence and home-country control for financial institutions. With a licence from the home country, financial institutions can expand throughout the EU. To strengthen financial integration, the European Commission launched the FSAP in 1999 to remove any remaining barriers that limit the cross-border provision of financial services. A major step in the financial integration process is the creation of the Banking Union. Under the SSM, the microprudential supervision of banks moved from national supervisors to the ECB in November 2014. The other pillars of the Banking Union are an SRM, a European deposit guarantee scheme, and the ESM. A common deposit guarantee system is considered a low priority, as national schemes were harmonised in the early stages of the financial crisis. A CMU is the next step in the European financial integration process.

Notes

1. The three communities were merged in 1967. After this time, one typically referred to the European Communities, and later to the European Community. Since the Maastricht Treaty one generally refers to the European Union.
2. Sometimes a commissioner is responsible for more than one DG.
3. So EMU does not mean European Monetary Union. Unfortunately, this is how the abbreviation is often explained, sometimes also in academic publications.
4. Denmark attained an 'opt-out clause', which meant that even if it met the convergence criteria for entering the euro area as stipulated in the Maastricht Treaty (see Table 3.1), it

would be up to the Danish government to decide about entry. The Danes voted on the treaty in a second referendum in 1993, in which 57 per cent of the voters favoured ratification.

Bibliography

Suggested Reading

Decressin, J., H. Faruqee, and W. Fonteyne (eds.) (2007), *Integrating Europe's Financial Markets*, IMF, Washington, DC.

Sampson, T. (2017), Brexit: The Economics of International Disintegration. *Journal of Economic Perspectives*, 31, 163–84.

Xafa, M. (2017), European Capital Markets Union Post-Brexit. CIGI Papers 140, Centre for International Governance Innovation, Waterloo (Canada).

References

Cecchini, P. (1988), *The European Challenge, 1992: The Benefits of a Single Market*, Gower, Aldershot.

Chen, W., B. Los, P. McCann, M. Thissen, and F. van Oort (2018), The Continental Divide? Economic Exposure to Brexit in Regions and Countries on Both Sides of the Channel. *Papers in Regional Science*, 97, 25–54.

Darvas, Z. and D. Schoenmaker (2018), Institutional Investors and Development of Europe's Capital Markets. In: D. Busch, E. Avgouleas, and G. Ferrarini (eds.), *Capital Markets Union in Europe*, Oxford University Press, 395–412.

Emerson, M., D. Gros, A. Italianer, J. Pisani-Ferry, and H. Reichenbach (1992), *One Market, One Money: An Evaluation of the Potential Benefits and Costs of Forming an Economic and Monetary Union*, Oxford University Press.

European Central Bank (2011), The Reform of Economic Governance in the Euro Area – Essential Elements, *ECB Monthly Bulletin*, March, 99–119.

European Central Bank (2014), Financial Integration in Europe, ECB, Frankfurt am Main.

European Commission (2011), Regulating Financial Services for Sustainable Growth: A Progress Report, February, EC, Brussels.

European Commission (2015), Action Plan on Building a Capital Markets Union, COM(2015) 468 final, Brussels.

Gros, D. and D. Schoenmaker (2014), European Deposit Insurance and Resolution in the Banking Union, *Journal of Common Market Studies*, 52, 529–46.

Sampson, T. (2017), Brexit: The Economics of International Disintegration. *Journal of Economic Perspectives*, 31, 163–84.

Schoenmaker, D. (2013), *Governance of International Banking: The Financial Trilemma*, Cambridge University Press.

Xafa, M. (2017), European Capital Markets Union Post-Brexit. CIGI Papers 140, Centre for International Governance Innovation, Waterloo (Canada).

4

Monetary Policy of the European Central Bank

OVERVIEW

This chapter describes the monetary policy of the European Central Bank (ECB). Since the start of the monetary union in 1999, the ECB has been responsible for monetary policy making in the euro area. The ECB and the national central banks of eurozone countries make up the Eurosystem. The Maastricht Treaty defines the ECB's primary objective as achieving 'price stability'. The ECB specifies this objective as inflation 'below but close to' 2 per cent in the euro area in the medium term. The ECB has an array of instruments available to realise this objective. Policy decisions are the outcome of the monetary policy strategy. The ECB has a 'two-pillar' strategy that pairs the discussion of a broad-based analysis of the risks to price stability in the short to medium run ('economic analysis') with monetary factors ('monetary analysis').

The ECB adopted several non-standard (or unconventional) policy measures in response to the financial crisis. The primary aim of these measures was to provide liquidity to banks and to keep financial markets functioning. During the euro crisis, the ECB's non-standard measures aimed to address markets' malfunctioning and to reduce differences in financing conditions among euro-area countries. More recently, with short-term interest rates close to zero, the ECB's non-standard measures have aimed to reduce the risk of deflation and to return inflation to a level consistent with the aim of price stability.

Next, the chapter discusses central bank communication, which is widely believed to be integral to the effectiveness of monetary policy. Finally, the ECB's forward guidance (i.e. its communications about its future policies) is discussed.

LEARNING OBJECTIVES

After you have studied this chapter, you should be able to:
- explain the functioning of the ECB
- describe the ECB's monetary policy strategy

- explain the ECB's monetary policy instruments
- describe the ECB's unconventional policy measures and explain why they have been introduced
- describe the ECB's communication policies
- explain the concept of forward guidance and describe the ECB's forward guidance.

4.1 The European Central Bank

After the introduction of the euro on 1 January 1999, the European Central Bank was responsible for monetary policy in the euro area – the second-largest economic area in the world after the US. At the time of writing, the euro is the official currency of 19 EU Member States with around 340 million citizens. Andorra, Monaco, San Marino, and the Vatican City have also adopted the euro as their national currency.

The ECB and the national central banks (NCBs) of eurozone countries comprise the Eurosystem. While the ECB is responsible for monetary policy decisions, these NCBs play a role in implementing monetary policy. In addition to defining and implementing monetary policy in the euro area, the Eurosystem is responsible for:

- conducting foreign exchange operations;
- holding and managing the official foreign reserves of the euro zone countries;
- promoting the smooth operation of payment systems.

Since the creation of the Banking Union in 2014, the ECB has become responsible for supervising banks of Member States in the Banking Union (see Chapter 12). The ECB also plays an important role in the European Systemic Risk Board, an independent EU body responsible for the macro-prudential oversight of the EU financial system. The board's responsibilities are discussed in detail in Chapter 13.

Structure

The three decision-making bodies of the ECB are the Governing Council, the Executive Board, and the General Council (see Figure 4.1).

The *Governing Council* is the European Council's most important decision-making body. It consists of the six members of the Executive Board and the governors of the euro-area NCBs (19 as of 2019), who are appointed by their respective governments. When taking monetary policy decisions, the members

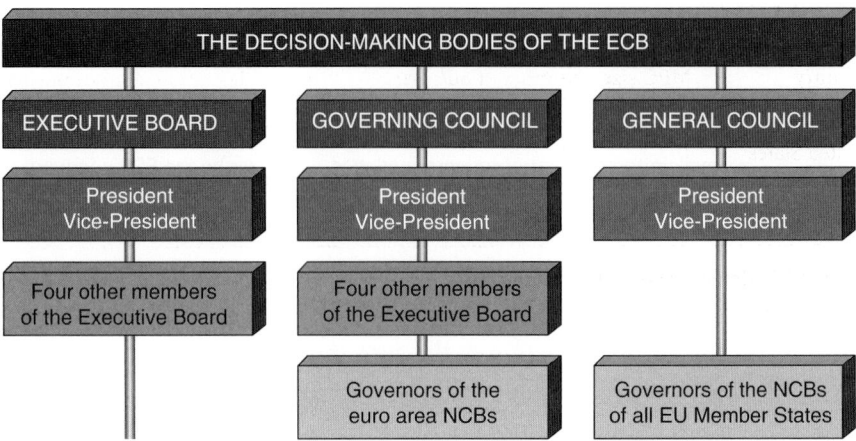

Figure 4.1   Structure of the ECB
Source: ECB (2011)

of the Governing Council are expected to focus on the euro area as a whole and not on their own country. The Governing Council is responsible for formulating monetary policy. After Lithuania's entry in 2015, the council introduced a rotation system for decision making on monetary policy; it now takes such decisions every six weeks rather than every four weeks, as before (see Box 4.1). Compared to other central banks, the ECB's Governing Council is large and contains a higher proportion of outsiders (see Table 4.1). For instance, 7 of the 12 US Federal Reserve Bank presidents do not vote as a result of the rotation system in place at its Federal Open Market Committee (FOMC).

The *Executive Board* of the ECB consists of the president, vice-president, and up to four other members. Its members are appointed by the European Council, voting by qualified majority, on the recommendation of the Council of the European Union. Executive Board members serve a non-renewable, eight-year term in office. The Executive Board prepares the meetings (and implements the monetary policy decisions) of the Governing Council, which may involve issuing instructions to NCBs. Both the Governing Council and the Executive Board are chaired by the president of the ECB or, in his or her absence, by the vice-president (ECB, 2011).

As long as not all EU Member States use the euro as their currency, the *General Council* will also play a role. It consists of the president and vice-president of the ECB and the governors of the NCBs of all EU member countries. The central banks of non-euro-area Member States do not participate in decisions related to the single monetary policy for the euro area. In

Table 4.1 Main characteristics of selected monetary policy committees

Country	MPC size	Number of outsiders	De jure decision rule	Non-voting MPC members
Euro area	25	19	Simple majority	4
United States	19	12	Simple majority	7
Japan	9	6	Simple majority	0
United Kingdom	9	4	Simple majority	0

Note: MPC: Monetary Policy Committee, i.e. the body responsible for monetary policy decisions. Data as of January 2019. 'Outsider' refers to committee members without a full-time managerial position within the central bank.

Box 4.1 Decision making within the ECB Governing Council

According to the Maastricht Treaty, the ECB Governing Council takes monetary policy decisions by a simple majority of the votes cast by the members who are present in person. In practice, most monetary policy decisions reflect a 'consensus' of the members of the Governing Council (ECB, 2011). Each member of the Governing Council has one vote. The principle of 'one member, one vote' reflects the notion that all the members, including the governors of the NCBs, are appointed in their personal capacity and not as representatives of their Member States. At some point in time, most EU Member States will join the euro area.[1] The size of the ECB Governing Council could therefore increase to 33, making it by far the largest monetary policy-making institution among OECD countries. Such an increase in membership would make discussion and voting procedures more time consuming and complicated.

New voting rules were therefore agreed upon in 2002. Since Lithuania's entry as nineteenth member of the euro area in 2015, these new rules are in place. According to the new rules, there are two groups with rotating voting rights. Governors rotate in and out of voting rights every month; the principle of 'one person, one vote' applies for those having voting rights. The first group consists of the five governors of the largest Member States (Germany, France, Italy, Spain, and the Netherlands). They share four voting rights. The second group consists of all other governors, who share 11 voting rights.

When the euro area expands to 22 members, there will be three groups that rotate. The first group, with four votes, will consist of the 'big 5'. The second group, with eight votes, will consist of half of all NCB governors selected from the subsequent positions in a ranking primarily determined by the size of the country's economy. The third group, comprising the remaining governors, will share three votes.

The new decision-making rules have met considerable criticism from academic observers. Gros (2003) argues that the new rules undermine the principle of Member State equality, and make members more likely to act in the interest of their home country.

the General Council, however, they have the opportunity to discuss monetary policy issues and their exchange rate relations with the euro.

It is widely believed that a high level of central bank independence, coupled with an explicit mandate for the bank to restrain inflation, are important institutional devices to assure price stability. According to this logic, an independent central bank can give its full attention to maintaining low levels of inflation. In countries with a more dependent central bank, other considerations (such as politicians' prospects of re-election and ensuring a low unemployment level) may interfere with the objective of price stability. The ECB is one of the most independent central banks in the world. Its independence is based on the Treaty on European Union, which contains several provisions to ensure independence, such as a fixed and non-renewable term of office for Executive Board Members, a separate budget for the ECB, and a prohibition on monetary financing. Furthermore, it prohibits the ECB, NCBs, and any member of their decision-making bodies from seeking or taking instructions from community institutions or bodies, from any government of a Member State, or from any other body. Changing this treaty would require the agreement of every signatory country.

Objectives

The Maastricht Treaty made price stability the ECB's primary objective, but left it to the ECB to define this objective. The treaty stipulates: 'without prejudice to the objective of price stability', the ECB shall 'support the general economic policies in the Community with a view to contributing to the achievement of the objectives of the Community', which include a 'high level of employment', and 'sustainable and non-inflationary growth'. Price stability, first specified by the ECB as inflation less than 2 per cent in the euro area, was made more precise in 2003 following an internal evaluation of the ECB's monetary policy strategy. The ECB has developed a monetary policy strategy to maintain inflation below (but close to) 2 per cent in the euro area over the medium term (see Section 4.2 for further details).

Inflation in the euro area is measured using the Harmonised Index of Consumer Prices (HICP), which is a comprehensive measure of the prices of consumption goods. An inflation rate target of 'below but close to' 2 per cent is considered the maximum rate that is consistent with price stability. Price decreases – deflation – are also not consistent with price stability. Since maintaining price stability is a medium-term goal, price levels may be temporarily distorted by short-term factors. Euro-area-wide developments, rather than specific national or regional factors, are the only determinants of ECB monetary policy decisions. A less than 2 per cent year-on-year increase in the HICP for the euro area as a whole represents price stability, even if annual increases in national price indices are above 2 per cent. Box 4.2 discusses why price stability is considered so important.

Box 4.2 Price stability

Not all central banks have price stability as their primary objective. For instance, the Federal Reserve's mandate is 'to promote effectively the goals of maximum employment, stable prices, and moderate long-term interest rates'. Because long-term interest rates can remain low only in a stable macroeconomic environment, these goals are often referred to as the *dual mandate* – maximum employment and price stability. There are seven reasons why price stability is the ECB's primary objective.

First, price stability makes it easier for people to disentangle changes in relative prices (i.e. movements in prices of any individual good or service) from changes in the general price level. This allows markets to allocate resources efficiently. Second, price stability reassures creditors, and prevents them from demanding an inflation risk premium as compensation for the risks associated with holding nominal assets over the longer term. Third, individuals and firms are less likely to divert resources from productive uses in order to hedge against inflation if prices are stable. For example, high inflation provides an incentive to stockpile real goods since they retain their value better in such circumstances than money or certain financial assets. Fourth, as tax and welfare systems are not fully indexed, inflation (or deflation) exacerbates the perverse incentives of these systems which distort economic behaviour. For instance, an increase in nominal income to compensate for inflation may cause an individual to move to a higher marginal tax rate which, in turn, may affect his or her labour supply. Fifth, inflation acts as a tax on cash holdings, because households have an incentive not to use cash as often in order to reduce transaction costs. These 'shoe-leather' costs arise because individuals have to visit the bank (or cash machine) more frequently to withdraw banknotes. Sixth, unexpected inflation causes a considerable and arbitrary redistribution of wealth and income (e.g. redistribution effects from creditors to debtors). The weakest groups in society often suffer the most from inflation, as they have a limited ability to hedge against it. Finally, inflation leads to sudden revaluations of financial assets, which may undermine the soundness of the banking sector's balance sheets and decrease households' and firms' wealth, leading to financial instability.

Thus maintaining price stability helps achieve broader economic goals, such as high levels of economic activity and better employment prospects (ECB, 2011). Indeed, several empirical studies suggest there is a negative relationship between inflation and economic

Box 4.2 (cont.)

growth. Yet since this relationship is less clear at low rates of inflation, several analysts have argued that the ECB's target of 2 per cent is too low for three reasons (de Haan *et al.*, 2005; Blinder *et al.*, 2017).

First, there may be an upward *measurement bias* in inflation – i.e. the measured inflation may overstate the actual rate. For instance, this may happen because improvements in the quality of goods may cause price changes to be overestimated. Since the quality of goods typically increases over time, goods such as computers bought at two different points in time are not directly comparable. Ignoring this quality change will induce a measurement error in the price index. Likewise, the prices of new goods often fall rapidly in the first years after their introduction. It may be several years before goods are included in the basket of goods used to calculate the price index, and thus the fall in their prices may be missed. According to the Governing Council of the ECB, the quality of the HICP makes it possible to precisely define price stability in the euro area (Issing, 2001).

Second, even if the 2 per cent target seems high enough to prevent deflation in the euro area as a whole, it may occur in an individual country, depending on the variation in inflation rates within the monetary union. Deflation shares many of the costs of inflation. However, Sibert (2003) argues that redistribution due to unexpected deflation may be costlier than if it is due to unanticipated inflation. Defaults may occur if the former happens, and the resulting bankruptcies and restructurings could destroy real wealth. The deterioration in debtors' balance sheets brought about by unexpected deflation may thus lower both consumption and investment demand. Persistent deflation may produce a deflationary spiral of falling prices, output, profits, and employment. Aggregate demand-induced deflation can reduce employment when nominal wages are rigid downwards. With sticky wages, a decline in prices causes real wages to rise, profit margins to fall, and employment levels to decrease. This may set off a deflationary cycle. How large are inflation differentials in the euro area? Before the start of European Economic and Monetary Union (EMU), the inflation dispersion in the founding countries of the EMU decreased over time, especially during the second half of the 1990s. The non-weighted standard deviation declined from around 4 percentage points at the beginning of the 1990s to about 1 percentage point at the start of the union. The standard deviation initially declined afterwards, but inflation dispersion has slightly increased more recently.

Third, some have argued that since nominal interest rates cannot fall (far) below zero, *monetary policy faces a trade-off between a very low level of inflation and stabilising the economy.* If the economy is faced with a recession when inflation is very low, it will be hard for the monetary authority to engineer a negative short-term real interest rate to counter the output loss. This is because the nominal short-term interest rate cannot be lowered (much) below zero, the so-called effective lower bound. This lower bound reflects the fact that people

Box 4.2 (cont.)

will prefer to keep funds in the form of cash rather than deposit them at a bank that charges negative rates on deposits (i.e. customers are charged to deposit their money). Several proponents of raising the inflation objective argue that a higher inflation target makes it less likely to hit the effective lower bound. If inflation is higher, say 4 per cent, it is easier for the central bank to engineer a negative real short-term interest rate. However, opponents of a higher inflation target argue that under the effective lower bound, the central bank may use unconventional monetary policies to influence the real economy (see Blinder *et al.*, 2017 for further discussion of the debate about higher inflation targets).

Finally, Akerlof *et al.* (2000) argue that *a moderate level of inflation provides 'grease' to the price- and wage-setting process*. The economic adjustment of relative prices to shocks can become sluggish in the presence of downward nominal rigidities in wages and prices. For instance, when inflation is zero, individual firms facing an adverse firm-specific shock will not be able to secure real wage reductions in the presence of downward nominal wage rigidity, and will instead lay off workers. Likewise, at low levels of inflation, a significant number of price and wage setters probably ignore or underweight anticipated inflation when setting future prices. A moderate level of inflation provides for some real wage flexibility, which reduces the natural, or long-run, rate of unemployment. According to the ECB (2003), however, the empirical evidence on the importance of downward nominal rigidities for the euro area is not conclusive. Evidence based on the distribution of changes in the euro-area price indices indicates that nominal price cuts are more common than is often assumed. According to micro-based studies, a substantial proportion of wage earners has experienced nominal wage cuts. However, even if downward nominal rigidities were pervasive, one may wonder whether 'accommodating' them with a higher inflation rate further entrenches this undesirable structural feature of some economies (ECB, 2003).

4.2 Monetary Policy Strategy

The ECB's monetary policy is based on a 'two-pillar' strategy that pairs the discussion of monetary factors ('monetary analysis') with a broad-based non-monetary analysis of the risks to price stability in the short to medium run ('economic analysis'). Figure 4.2 provides a schematic overview. According to the ECB (2011: 69), 'the two-pillar approach is designed to ensure that no relevant information is lost in the assessment of the risks to price stability and that appropriate attention is paid to different perspectives and the cross-checking of information in order to reach an overall judgement on the risks to price stability'.

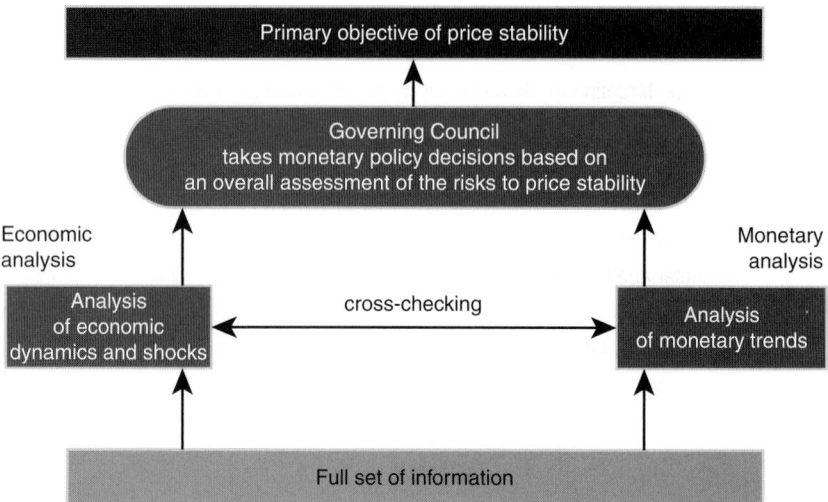

Figure 4.2   The monetary policy strategy of the ECB
Source: ECB (2011)

The two-pillar approach provides a check on the indications that stem from the shorter-term economic analysis using those from the longer-term-oriented monetary analysis, which, according to the ECB, ensures that monetary policy does not overlook important information relevant for assessing future inflation trends. By taking policy decisions and evaluating their consequences not only on the basis of the short-term indications stemming from the analysis of economic and financial conditions but also taking money and liquidity considerations into account, the ECB arguably will not be tempted to take an overly activist role in determining its monetary policy stance (ECB, 2011).

The 'economic analysis' pillar of the ECB's approach to monetary policy focuses on the assessment of current economic and financial developments and the implied short- to medium-term risks to price stability. This analysis is based on economic and financial variables such as developments in overall output; aggregate demand and its components; fiscal policy; capital and labour market conditions; a broad range of price and cost indicators; developments in the exchange rate, the global economy, and the balance of payments; financial markets; and the balance sheet positions of euro-area sectors (ECB, 2011). Macroeconomic staff projections also play an important role (see Box 4.3). The ECB publishes these projections for the euro area four times a year. The Governing Council combines these projections with many other indicators to assess the risks to price stability, but it neither assumes

---

Box 4.3 Inflation targeting

Inflation targeting has become a very popular monetary policy strategy among central banks in Australia, Canada, New Zealand, Norway, Sweden, and the UK, for example, and in several emerging and developing countries (such as Brazil, Indonesia, and South Africa). According to Mishkin and Savastano (2001), *inflation targeting* involves the public announcement of numerical inflation targets, a strong central bank commitment to price stability as the final monetary policy objective, and a high degree of transparency and accountability.

The distinctive feature of this strategy is a forward-looking decision-making process known as 'inflation forecast targeting': the central bank sets its policy instruments in such a way that its inflation forecast eventually equals the inflation target. Although there are different forms of inflation targeting, they all use a published numerical inflation target and a predefined policy horizon. Central banks using this approach communicate monetary policy decisions in terms of a reaction to deviations from a forecast for a particular measure of inflation from the inflation target at a particular horizon. The central bank's inflation forecast is therefore the centrepiece of both its decisions and its public communications.

The ECB (2011) provides several arguments against using this approach. Most importantly, focusing solely on a forecast inflation figure does not provide a comprehensive and reliable framework for identifying the nature of threats to price stability. Given the considerable uncertainty surrounding the structure of the euro-area economy, the ECB therefore uses a diversified approach to the analysis of economic data based on a variety of analytical methodologies.

---

responsibility for the projections nor uses them as its only tool for organising and communicating its assessment, as is done under inflation targeting.

The economic analysis pillar takes into account the need to identify the nature of shocks to the economy, their effects on cost and pricing behaviour, and the short- to medium-term prospects of their propagation in the economy. For example, the appropriate monetary policy response to a temporary rise in the international price of oil might be different from the appropriate response to wage increases that are not in line with productivity growth. The former results in a transient and short-lived increase in inflation which quickly reverses, whereas the latter entails the risk of a self-sustaining spiral of higher costs, higher prices, and higher wage demands. The ECB also carries out several surveys that provide further inputs into its economic analysis. In addition, it analyses asset prices and financial yields to derive information about the expectations of financial markets, including expected future price developments. Likewise, developments related to the exchange rate are closely assessed for their implications for price stability, as exchange rate movements directly affect price developments through their impact on import prices (ECB, 2011).

The monetary analysis pillar of the ECB's approach to monetary policy focuses on a medium- to long-term horizon. When the ECB's monetary policy strategy was introduced in 1998, the ECB Governing Council announced a quantitative 'reference value' for the annual growth rate of a broad monetary aggregate (M3). This focus on money growth was motivated by the view that inflation is considered to be a mostly monetary phenomenon in the long run. The ECB justified its decision to use M3 growth based on its perceived favourable empirical properties, especially its relatively stable relationship with money demand. Furthermore, M3 growth was shown to be a good indicator of future inflation. However, the ECB has always stressed that monetary policy does not react mechanically to deviations of M3 growth from the reference value. Such deviations, however, trigger increased efforts by the ECB to identify and assess the underlying driving forces. Monetary analysis now entails a comprehensive analysis of the liquidity situation, going well beyond M3 growth. For instance, the composition of M3 growth (i.e. the components and sectoral contributions) is extensively analysed.

Although many observers expected the ECB Governing Council to abandon the monetary pillar when it re-evaluated its strategy in early 2003, the council made it clear that the ECB would continue to include monetary analysis in its policy strategy, although it needed some 'clarification'. The council explained that the monetary analysis was designed to serve as a 'cross-check', from a medium- to long-term perspective, on the short- to medium-term indications from the economic analysis. To underscore the longer-term nature of the reference value for monetary growth, the Governing Council discontinued the practice of annually reviewing the reference value for M3 growth.

Since the financial crisis, many central bankers have viewed financial stability as an important objective in its own right because the costs of financial crises are high and their consequences are harmful to both price stability and the monetary transmission mechanism. Some even argue that monetary policy should 'lean against the wind' – i.e. that central banks should be willing to raise interest rates to prevent asset-price bubbles (see Box 4.4).

4.3 Conventional Monetary Policy Instruments

The ECB uses several instruments to affect inflation and output (see Box 4.5 for further discussion of how monetary policy affects the economy). This

---

Box 4.4 Leaning against the wind?

Box 4.4 Leaning against the wind?

Before the financial crisis, many central banks only took financial stability into account if it affected the medium-term outlook for price stability. But several authors argued, even before the crisis, that monetary policy should 'lean against the wind' because it interacts with important drivers of financial imbalances. For example, central banks should be willing to raise interest rates to prevent asset-price bubbles. Borio (2014) argues that policy makers should be able to identify the build-up of financial imbalances in real time if they have a sufficient lead, even out of sample, and raise interest rates if necessary.

Opponents of this pre-emptive approach raise three main objections. First, many doubt that financial imbalances can be identified with reasonable confidence in time to act. Second, they doubt that monetary policy is the most appropriate instrument to address financial imbalances, since the evidence suggests that interest rates would have to be raised substantially to curb risk taking. Finally, Svensson (2016) argues that the full costs of a crisis could be higher under a policy of leaning against wind, because it would weaken the economy before the crisis.

In a speech on asset price bubbles and monetary policy, then ECB President Trichet (2005) argued that 'the circumstances in which a policy-maker will embark with confidence upon an explicit leaning against the wind policy will occur rarely'. But he also argued that monetary analysis helps central banks incorporate emerging financial stability risks that have medium-term implications for price stability: 'The fact that our monetary analysis uses a comprehensive assessment of the liquidity situation that may, under certain circumstances, provide early information on developing financial instability is an important element.' Hartmann and Smets (2018) estimate several reaction functions for the ECB, and find no evidence that it has pursued a leaning-against-the-wind monetary policy approach. However, they also conclude that following the outbreak of the financial crisis, the broadened monetary analysis was increasingly helpful in assessing fragilities in the banking sector and how they influence bank lending.

Source: Blinder *et al.* (2017)

---

section discusses the ECB's most important conventional monetary policy instruments. It starts by describing the ECB policy rates, which signal its monetary policy stance. It then discusses open market operations.

Policy Rates

To understand ECB interest rate decisions, it is first important to define the standing facilities – the deposit facility and the marginal lending facility – that banks use if they need liquidity or if they want to stall liquidity. The

Box 4.5 Monetary policy transmission

Monetary policy decisions affect the real economy and inflation through various channels. Changes in money market rates due to ECB policy measures in turn affect other short-term interest rates (*interest channel*). For example, changes in money market rates have an impact on the interest rates set by banks for short-term loans and deposits.

Furthermore, changes in central bank interest rates may also affect the supply of credit (*credit channel*). The credit channel has three mechanisms: the bank lending channel, the balance sheet channel, and the risk taking channel.

Following an increase in interest rates, the risk that some borrowers cannot safely repay their loans may increase to a level such that the bank will not grant a loan to these borrowers (the *bank lending channel*). Such borrowers are therefore forced to postpone their consumption or investment plans.

Interest rate changes also affect firms' balance sheets. An increase in interest rates lowers the net worth of assets, which means a lower collateral value and thus a reduced ability to borrow (the *balance sheet channel*).

The *risk taking channel* is thought to operate mainly via two mechanisms. First, low interest rates boost asset and collateral values. This, in conjunction with the belief that the increase in asset values is sustainable, leads both borrowers and banks to accept higher risks. Second, low interest rates make riskier assets more attractive, as agents search for higher yields. For banks, these two effects usually translate into a softening of credit standards, which can lead to an excessive increase in loan supply.

Interest rate changes may also affect the exchange rate which, in turn, will normally affect inflation in three ways (*exchange rate channel*). First, exchange rate movements may directly affect the domestic price of imported goods. If the exchange rate appreciates, the price of imported goods tends to fall, thus helping to directly reduce inflation. Second, if these imports are used as inputs into the production process, lower prices for inputs might, over time, lower the prices of final goods. Third, an appreciation in the exchange rate may make domestically produced goods less competitive on world markets, which tends to constrain external demand and thus reduce overall demand pressure in the economy. All else equal, an appreciation of the exchange rate tends to reduce inflationary pressures, and vice versa. The strength of exchange rate effects depends on the economy's openness to international trade, and they are generally less important for large economies than for small open economies. Furthermore, financial asset prices like the exchange rate depend on many other factors in addition to monetary policy.

The *expectations channel* mainly works by influencing the private sector's longer-term expectations. The central bank can, for instance, exert a powerful direct influence on price developments by guiding economic agents' expectations of future inflation and thereby influencing their wage- and price-setting behaviour. If economic agents believe in the central bank's ability and commitment to maintain long-

---

Box 4.5 (cont.)

term price stability, inflation expectations will remain firmly anchored to price stability. This, in turn, will influence wage and price setting, as wage and price setters will not have to adjust their prices upwards due to fears of higher inflation in the future.

  The ECB (2011) notes that monetary policy transmission in the euro area has three main characteristics. First, there are long and uncertain lags in the transmission of monetary impulses to the domestic price level. Second, in normal times, monetary policy works mainly through the interest rate channel: a tightening of monetary policy leads to a transitory decrease in output, which is estimated to reach its maximum one to two years after the interest rate increase. Prices tend to decline more gradually, and respond more sluggishly, than output to the tightening of monetary policy. Third, interest rate changes also affect economic activity via their impact on firms' cash flows and the supply of bank loans, hence confirming the relevance of the credit channel of monetary policy.

Source: ECB (2011)

---

deposit facility is used for mopping up liquidity from banks (usually at substantially below-market rates). The *marginal lending facility* provides liquidity to banks (against collateral) at above-market rates.

  As the interest rates on standing facilities are normally substantially higher (for borrowing) or lower (for depositing) than the corresponding money market rate, banks normally only use standing facilities in the absence of alternatives. As there are no limits on access to these facilities (except for the collateral requirements of the marginal lending facility), the rate on the marginal lending facility and the deposit facility normally provide a ceiling and a floor, respectively, for the overnight rate in the interbank money market. The standing facilities thus constitute a corridor for the interbank money market rate. By setting the rates on the standing facilities, the ECB effectively determines the corridor within which the overnight money market rate can fluctuate.

  Figure 4.3 shows the development of key ECB interest rates since January 1999 and illustrates how the interest rates on the standing facilities have provided a ceiling and floor for the overnight interbank market interest rate, measured by EONIA (euro overnight index average). EONIA represents the average rate on unsecured overnight euro lending transactions in the interbank market. It is the (weighted) average rate on transactions reported to the ECB on a particular day by a representative panel of banks, known as the EONIA Panel.

Key ECB interest rates
Percent

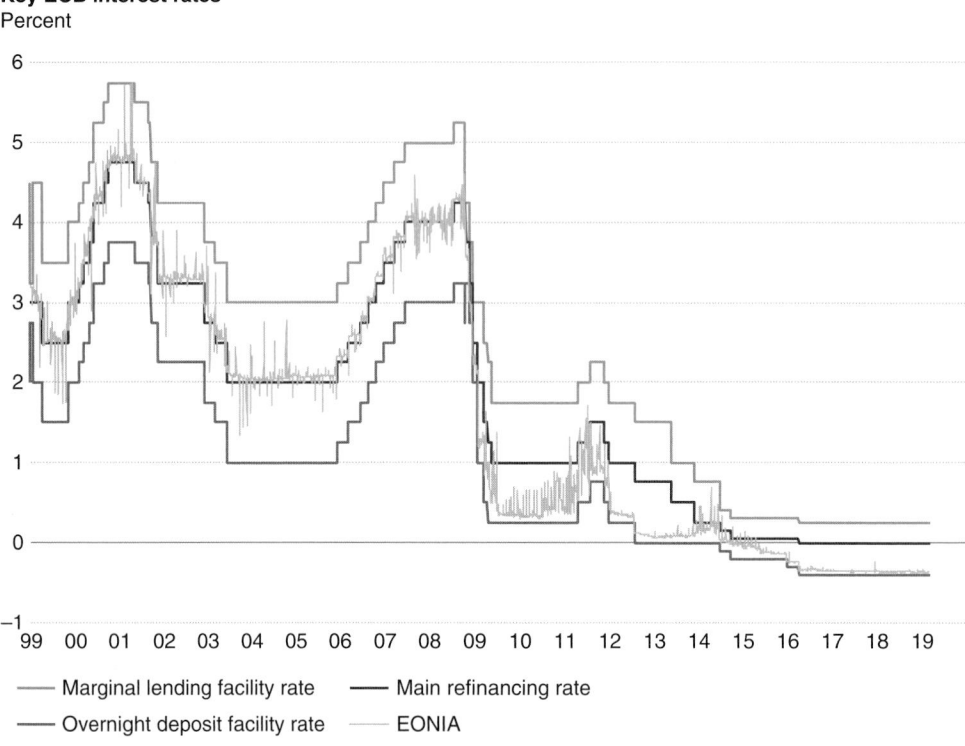

— Marginal lending facility rate   — Main refinancing rate
— Overnight deposit facility rate   ⋯ EONIA

Figure 4.3   ECB policy rates and overnight money market rate
Source: ECB

Figure 4.3 shows that in the past, EONIA generally remained close to the rate on the main refinancing operations (MRO rate), the ECB's most important open market operations, explained in more detail below. This changed in October 2008, when the ECB adopted non-standard (or unconventional) policy measures to counter the negative effects of the financial crisis (see Section 4.4). As shown in Figure 4.3, EONIA dropped below the MRO rate towards the bottom of the corridor given by the deposit facility rate; the latter therefore became the main policy rate (Hartmann and Smets, 2018).

The ECB also changed policy rates when unconventional monetary policies (discussed in Section 4.4) were in place.

Open Market Operations

The Eurosystem affects money market interest rates by providing more (or less) liquidity to banks in order to decrease (increase) interest rates. It allocates an amount of liquidity that allows banks to fulfil their liquidity needs at a price that

Table 4.2 Open market operations

Operations	Liquidity provision	Liquidity absorption	Maturity	Frequency
Main refinancing operations	Reverse transactions	–	One week	Weekly
Longer-term refinancing operations	Reverse transactions	–	Three months	Monthly
Fine tune operations	Reverse transactions	Reverse transactions	Non-standardised	Non-regular

Source: ECB (2011)

is in line with the ECB's policy intentions. To manage liquidity in the money market and steer short-term interest rates, it uses open *market operations*, i.e. it buys (or sells) financial assets. If assets are bought from (sold to) a bank, the reserves of that bank held by the central bank increase (decrease).

Reserve requirements extended the banking sector's liquidity deficit vis-à-vis the central bank. The need for banks to hold reserves with the NCBs increases the demand for central bank liquidity which, in turn, makes it easier for the ECB to steer money market rates through regular liquidity-providing operations. Euro-area banks have to hold a small share of their short-term liabilities (2 per cent until January 2012, 1 per cent thereafter) on their Eurosystem accounts. These required reserves are remunerated at the rate set by the ECB for main refinancing operations (see below). This is only required, on average, over a reserve main-tenance period of a few weeks. Normally the averaging procedure has a stabilising effect, because it encourages liquidity planning and helps mitigate the effects of unexpected short-term liquidity shocks – the main purpose of the reserve requirements (Hartmann and Smets, 2018).

The Eurosystem uses three types of open market operations (ECB, 2011): MROs, longer-term refinancing operations (LTROs), and fine tune operations (FTOs) (see Table 4.2). Lending through open market operations normally takes place in the form of reverse transactions, in which the central bank buys assets from a bank under a repurchase agreement (i.e. the bank buys the asset back) or grants a loan against assets pledged as collateral. Reverse transactions are there-fore temporary open market operations that provide funds for a limited, pre-specified period only. The Eurosystem accepts financial instruments issued by both private and public debtors that meet certain requirements as collateral.

Before the crisis, MROs provided the bulk of liquidity, so the MRO rate constituted the ECB's main policy rate. MROs are liquidity-providing repo operations conducted as variable rate tenders, subject to a minimum bid rate, in which the ECB determines the total amount that is allotted to counterparties, while banks submit bid schedules stating the price they are willing to pay for liquidity in these operations (Hartmann and Smets, 2018).

In addition to the weekly MROs, the Eurosystem also executes monthly LTROs with various maturities (e.g. 6 months or 12 months). These operations are designed to provide longer-term liquidity to the banking system. After October 2008, when the ECB took several measures to combat the financial crisis (see Section 4.4), the weight of the refinancing operations shifted towards LTROs.

The Eurosystem may also carry out open market operations on an ad hoc basis (i.e. FTOs). The frequency and maturity of such operations are not standardised. FTOs aim to manage the liquidity situation in the money market and steer interest rates, particularly in order to smooth the effects of unexpected liquidity fluctuations in the market on interest rates.

4.4 Unconventional Monetary Policy

The ECB's unconventional monetary policies comprise three main phases:
- the global financial crisis, which started in September 2008 (Lehman collapse);
- the euro crisis, which started in May 2010 (Greek crisis);
- declining inflation and sluggish economic recovery after 2013.

At the beginning of the financial crisis, the ECB, like other major central banks, reduced its key interest rates to historically low levels. The main refinancing rate was cut by a total of 325 basis points to 1 per cent between October 2008 and May 2009. In addition, the Governing Council adopted a number of temporary non-standard measures, subsequently referred to as Enhanced Credit Support. These measures focused primarily on banks, reflecting the financial structure of the euro area (see Chapter 1). Later on, the euro crisis forced the ECB to also intervene in sovereign debt markets. In the third phase, worries about deflation became important, at a time when interest rates could not be reduced further. These unconventional policies led to an expansion of the ECB's balance sheet (see Figure 4.4).

Providing Liquidity: Enhanced Credit Support

Before the crisis, the ECB provided a pre-set amount of liquidity to banks through auctions, in which banks put up collateral to guarantee the loans. Banks would also lend to and borrow from each other in the interbank market to fulfil their liquidity needs. This all changed during the financial crisis.

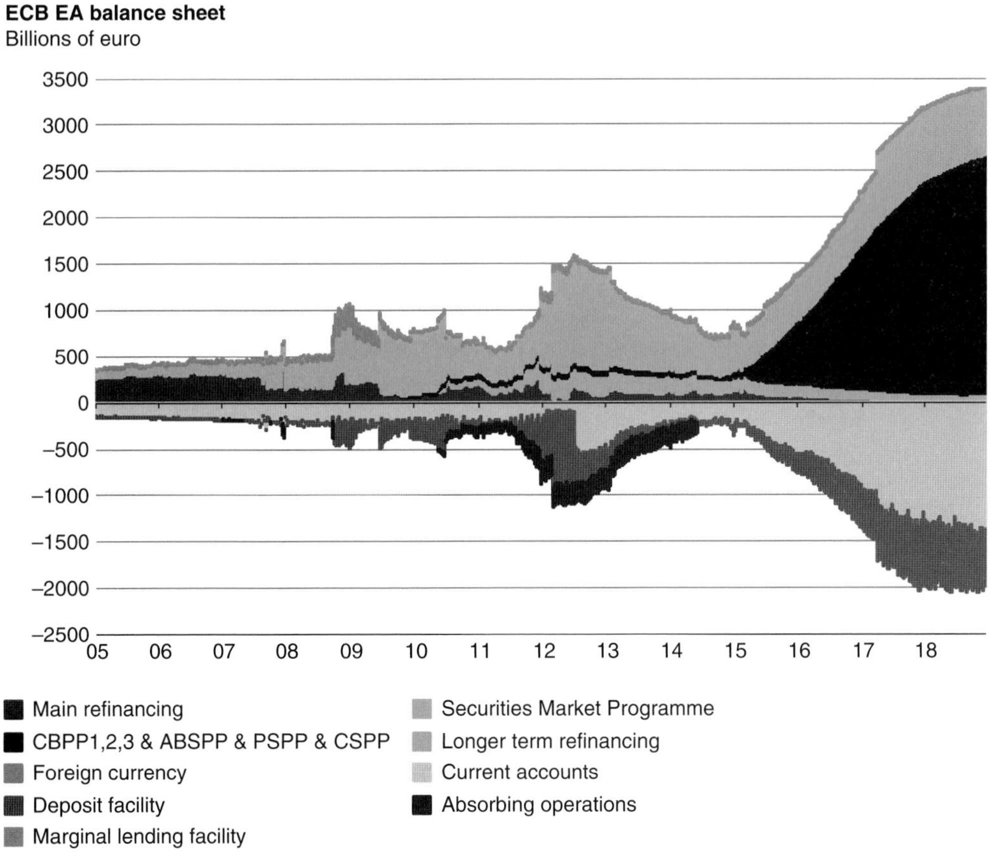
ECB EA balance sheet
Billions of euro
3500
3000
2500
2000
1500
1000
500
0
–500
–1000
–1500
–2000
–2500
05
06
07
08
09
10
11
12
13
14
15
16
17
18
Main refinancing
CBPP1,2,3 & ABSPP & PSPP & CSPP
Foreign currency
Deposit facility
Marginal lending facility
Securities Market Programme
Longer term refinancing
Current accounts
Absorbing operations

Figure 4.4 ECB assets as a percentage of GDP
Source: ECB

The collapse of the US subprime mortgage market led to money market tensions in Europe on 9 August 2007, following the announcement that a number of investment funds had to close. The ECB reacted immediately, providing a fixed-rate overnight FTO the same day. Other measures were then taken to provide liquidity to banks. Despite these difficulties, large bank failures did not occur in the euro area during this period. Only a few mid-sized German banks, which had been particularly engaged in structured credit practices and wholesale funding, received public support.

The financial turmoil escalated in a financial crisis after the collapse of Lehman Brothers on 15 September 2008. This event demonstrated that even prominent and systemically important institutions could fail. As a consequence, financial markets froze. Tensions soon spilled over from

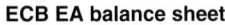

the financial sector into the real economy, leading to the Great Recession, which spread quickly to the euro area as well. The euro area entered a severe recession, which lasted from the second quarter of 2008 until the second quarter of 2009 (Hartmann and Smets, 2018).

In addition to reducing its policy rates, the ECB responded to the crisis with an array of measures to satisfy the high demand for liquidity and help fend off risks of an even more dramatic financial meltdown, which came to be known as Enhanced Credit Support. For instance, from 15 October 2008 onwards MROs and all longer-term refinancing operations were carried out through a fixed-rate tender procedure with full allotment. Thus, the ECB began providing unlimited credit to banks at a fixed interest rate in a practice referred to as *fixed-rate full allotment*. In addition, the (already long) list of collateral assets was extended, allowing banks to use a larger range and proportion of their assets to obtain central bank liquidity. For instance, asset-backed securities, which became illiquid when the market collapsed after the default of Lehman Brothers, were included.

In May 2009, the ECB adopted additional non-standard measures to support the flow of credit to households and corporations. These included announcements of the lengthening of the maximum maturity of refinancing operations (one-year LTROs) and a Covered Bonds Purchase Programme (CBPP) starting in July. The CBPP was the first outright purchase pro-gramme carried out by the ECB (Hartmann and Smets, 2018). The Eurosystem purchased euro-denominated covered bonds issued in the euro area at a value of €60 billion over the period from May 2009 to June 2010. The covered bonds market (see Chapter 5) had virtually dried up in terms of liquidity, issuance, and spreads. The aim of the programme was to revive the covered bond market, which is a very important financial market in Europe and a primary source of financing for banks.

In October 2011, the ECB announced CBPP2. Purchases of about €16 billion were conducted in the primary and secondary markets between November 2011 and October 2012. In September 2014 it announced CBPP3.

Saving the Euro: Securities Markets Programme and Outright Monetary Transactions

The ECB introduced the *Securities Markets Programme* (SMP) in response to tensions that arose in euro-area sovereign bond markets in May 2010 (see Chapter 2). The spreads between the yields on 10-year bonds of some euro-area governments (notably Greece, Ireland, and Portugal) and the German Bund yield increased sharply. Interest rates reached levels that would have quickly become unsustainable for any sovereign. Given the crucial role of government bonds as benchmarks for private sector lending rates and their importance for bank balance sheets and liquidity operations, this development was considered to impair the transmission of policy interest rate decisions to the real economy (Cour-Thiman and Winkler, 2014).

Under the programme, Eurosystem interventions were carried out in the euro-area public and private debt securities markets to ensure depth and liquidity in dysfunctional market segments and to restore the proper functioning of the monetary policy transmission mechanism. Purchases of government bonds were strictly limited to secondary markets. To ensure that liquidity conditions were not affected, all purchases were fully neutralised through liquidity-absorbing operations.

When the sovereign debt crisis struck Italy and Spain in the summer of 2011 and their government bond markets risked becoming dysfunctional, the ECB reactivated its dormant SMP on 7 August 2011. Significant and sustained interventions of varying intensities temporarily eased the situation in government bond markets.

The SMP ran until the end of December 2012 and reached an outstanding nominal amount of around €218 billion (Hartmann and Smets, 2018). Eser and Schwaab (2016) find that the SMP had a significant impact on the yields of the securities purchased. Their baseline model suggests that, on average, a daily SMP intervention of €100 million lowered yields by 0.1 to 2 basis points (bps). Although the SMP was used to enhance monetary policy transmission, it also gave governments time to find a durable solution to the crisis and restore the sustainability of public finances. However, according to Cour-Thiman and Winkler (2014), governments did not use the time effectively. For instance, significant implementation shortfalls emerged in the Greek programme, and the fundamental issues of substantially improving tax collection and strengthening competitiveness were not sufficiently addressed. The SMP was terminated after the introduction of *outright monetary transactions* (OMTs), which are discussed in more detail below.

In 2011 and 2012 the ECB introduced further liquidity-enhancing measures in order to strengthen the liquidity position of European banks, including a further extension of the list of eligible collateral. Moreover, two three-year very long-term refinancing operations, with the option of early repayment after one year, were conducted in December 2011 and February 2012 with a combined gross amount of more than 1 trillion euros (Hartmann and Smets, 2018). Despite these measures, there were signs in the summer of 2012 that banks' ability to provide credit was seriously hampered, with consequences for the real economy. Bank funding costs were pushed up by continued tensions in sovereign debt markets. Some government bond yields started to incorporate the risk that a country might abandon the euro (redenomination risk). In other words, markets had doubts about the sustainability of EMU.

Against this background, on 2 August 2012 the ECB announced its intention to perform OMTs in secondary sovereign bond markets. OMTs represented the implementation of ECB President Draghi's statement on 26 July 2012 that the bank would do 'whatever it takes to preserve the euro'.[2] OMTs require strict and effective conditionality attached to an appropriate European Financial Stability Facility/European Stability Mechanism (EFSF/ESM) programme or a precautionary programme (i.e. Enhanced Conditions Credit Line). Thus, the ECB waited for the euro-area governments to be collectively ready to invest their money first before deciding whether central bank money would be used in the sovereign bond markets, if this was warranted from a monetary policy perspective (Cour-Thiman and Winkler, 2014). Transactions were focused on the shorter end of the yield curve, and in particular on sovereign bonds with a maturity of one to three years. Importantly, no *ex ante* quantitative limits were set on the size of OMTs.

OMTs enabled the ECB to address severe distortions in government bond markets, which originated from unfounded investor fears that the euro would collapse. By signalling its readiness to intervene in government bond markets, the ECB sought to reduce the likelihood of adverse self-fulfilling equilibria.

The ECB has always emphasised that OMTs are designed to ensure the proper transmission of its interest rates to the euro-area economy and the singleness of its monetary policy (Cour-Thiman and Winkler, 2014). The Maastricht Treaty's prohibition of monetary financing prevents the ECB from purchasing government bonds in the primary market. Moreover, it cannot use secondary market intervention to circumvent the prohibition on primary market intervention. According to the ECB, OMTs are consistent with the ECB's mandate as the Governing Council acts independently, which guarantees that OMTs serve a monetary policy purpose. OMTs are limited to transactions in secondary markets for sovereign bonds: the money goes to investors, not to the sovereign issuer. Finally, and most importantly, OMTs require explicit conditionality to ensure that governments make the necessary efforts to restore the sustainability of public finances. The ECB has explicitly committed to suspending OMTs if a government fails to comply with conditionality, or if the OMT objectives are achieved (Cour-Thiman and Winkler, 2014).

In addition to strict conditionality and an explicit reference to an exit, three other modalities distinguish OMTs from the SMP: focus on the short-term maturities in government bond markets, explicit acceptance of *pari passu* status (equal claims on rights), and transparency regarding the disclosure of transactions for the countries concerned. Given these differences, the ECB aimed to address a number of concerns relating to the SMP, which was terminated at the same time that the OMT was announced (Cour-Thiman and Winkler, 2014). So far, OMTs have not been activated.

Persistently Low Inflation: QE

The third phase of unconventional monetary policies was characterised by the ECB's actions to overcome the effective lower bound on interest rates in its attempt to address deflation risks and return inflation to close to but below 2 per cent. It used policies such as quantitative easing (QE), funding for lending as well as explicit forward guidance (discussed in Section 4.6) that had been used before by other central banks such as the Fed and the Bank of England (BoE). The ECB also lowered its policy rates, even into negative territory.

Given the outlook for inflation, in June 2014 and again in September 2014, the ECB lowered the deposit facility rate by 10 bps each time to −0.2 per cent. A negative deposit interest rate means that the ECB will charge banks to park their surplus liquidity with it. The ECB was the first major central bank to introduce negative interest rates; those from smaller countries such as Denmark and Switzerland had taken this step earlier. The ECB also decided to conduct *targeted longer-term refinancing operations* (TLTROs). TLTROs provide financing to credit institutions for periods of up to four years; they are targeted in the sense that the amount banks can borrow is linked to their loans to non-financial corporations and households. These operations offer banks long-term funding at attractive conditions to further ease private sector credit conditions and stimulate bank lending to the real economy. The first series of TLTROs was announced on 5 June 2014 and a second series (TLTRO II) on 10 March 2016. These credit easing measures were complemented by an asset-backed securities purchase programme and CBPP3, discussed above.

In January 2015, the ECB launched an expanded asset purchase programme (APP), encompassing its existing purchase programmes for asset-backed securities and covered bonds.[3] The ECB followed other central banks (such as the Federal Reserve, the BoE, and the Bank of Japan, BoJ), which had used outright purchases as part of their monetary policy for several years by that point. This policy is often referred to as QE. The programme has been expanded several times, as have the amounts of monthly purchases (see Table 4.3).

Table 4.3 Monthly net purchases under the expanded asset purchase programme

From:	Until:	Amount:
March 2015	March 2016	€60 billion
April 2016	March 2017	€80 billion
April 2017	December 2017	€60 billion
January 2018	September 2018	€30 billion
October 2018	December 2018	€15 billion
November 2019		€20 billion

Source: ECB

On 9 December 2015 and 10 March 2016, the ECB further lowered interest rates, bringing the interest rate corridor down to 65 basis points and lowering the deposit facility rate to −0.4 per cent. At the same time, a considerable expansion of the APP was announced; average monthly purchases were increased to €80 billion. The Governing Council extended the net APP several times until the end of 2018, while reducing its monthly pace. It also enhanced its forward guidance on policy rates by stating that it expects these rates to remain at their present levels at least through the summer of 2019 and, in any case, for as long as necessary to ensure the sustained convergence of inflation to levels that are below, but close to 2 per cent (Hartmann and Smets, 2018). The ECB's forward guidance is discussed in Section 4.6, while Box 4.6 summarises research on the effectiveness of the ECB's QE policies.

In September 2019, the ECB Governing Council decided to restart the APP, despite opposition of several council members. From 1 November 2019 onwards monthly purchases amount to €20 billion. It was also decided to further cut the interest rate on the deposit facility to −0.50 per cent. A two-tier system for reserve remuneration was introduced, in which part of banks' holdings of excess liquidity are exempt from the negative deposit facility rate.

4.5 ECB Communication Policies

Theory

Since its inception, the ECB has regarded communication as an integral part of its monetary policy. It has communicated frequently to the public on various issues, such as its objectives, its policy decisions, and the overall economic

Box 4.6 The effectiveness of QE

There is an extensive literature on the impact of asset purchase programmes on financial markets (see Hartmann and Smets, 2018 and de Haan and Sturm, 2019 for reviews). Most such research focuses on two possible channels in which central bank asset purchases can affect financial market prices. The first is the portfolio rebalance channel. If different financial assets are not perfect substitutes in investors' portfolios and changes in the net supply of an asset due to central bank purchases affect its yield, yields on other assets will also be affected as investors have to be persuaded to rebalance their portfolios towards these other assets.[4] Second is the signalling channel: central bank asset purchases may signal to market participants that the central bank has changed either its views on the economic outlook or its policy preference, and investors therefore adjust their expectations of the future path of the policy rate accordingly, thereby lowering long-term bond yields.

Many papers find evidence of declining yields in response to (announcements of) purchase programmes. Altavilla *et al.* (2015) summarise this literature as follows. First, they find that the programmes carried out in the aftermath of Lehman's collapse generally had a stronger impact than subsequent programmes. Second, 'narrow channels' of transmission are generally more important than 'broad channels'. Transmission channels are defined as narrow when the impact is concentrated on the assets directly targeted by the programme, with few spillovers to other market segments. Third, the bulk of the impact of purchase programmes is found to arise at the time of their announcement. The findings of Altavilla *et al.* (2015) suggest that the ECB's QE has significantly lowered yields for a broad set of market segments, with effects that generally increase with maturity and the riskiness of assets. For instance, long-term sovereign bond yields declined by about 30–50 basis points at the 10-year maturity and by roughly twice as much in higher-yield member countries such as Italy and Spain. Because the financial markets expected the January 2015 ECB announcement, the authors consider a broad set of events involving the ECB's official announcements that, starting from September 2014, could have affected market expectations about the programme.

More recently, the debate on the effects of asset purchase programmes has shifted to the transmission of QE from financial markets to the real economy. There is evidence that asset purchase programmes do have non-negligible effects on GDP growth and inflation. For instance, Wieladek and Pascual (2016) assess the macroeconomic impact of the ECB's QE by comparing data outturns to the counterfactual that the policy was not enacted. Using monthly data from June 2012 to April 2016, the authors conclude that without the first round of ECB QE, real GDP and core inflation would have been 1.3 and 0.9 percentage points lower, respectively.

Hartmann and Smets (2018) report that the ECB's estimate of the cumulative effect of its policies on euro-area GDP from 2016 to 2019 is around 1.9 per cent. About one-third of the 5-percentage-point increase in the employment rate (which represents 2–3 million jobs) observed in the euro area as a whole since mid-2014 is estimated to be due to the ECB's

---

Box 4.6 (cont.)

measures. Absent the ECB's policy package, inflation would, on average, have been almost half a percentage point lower each year from 2016 to 2019.

Although most evidence suggests that QE had the desired effect, the ECB's accommodative monetary policy may have three unwanted side effects. First, the prolonged low interest rate may unintentionally reduce governments' incentives to introduce structural adjustments and reforms. Low interest rates dampen the debt burden on the budget, which may trigger governments to postpone measures to restore sound public finances. Likewise, financial institutions, firms, and households may not reduce their indebtedness. Second, accommodative monetary policy could induce investors to take excessive risks in their search for better returns. This may produce an undesirable build-up of bubbles in some market segments. Finally, by prolonging very loose monetary conditions, QE may lead to a misallocation of resources by, for instance, discouraging write-downs of loans that would not be profitable in normal market conditions.

---

outlook. It uses a variety of communication channels. For instance, the ECB extensively uses press conferences to inform the public about its decisions on an almost real-time basis. It also publishes the *Economic Bulletin*, as well as speeches by (and interviews with) ECB policy makers. The ECB has been part of the revolution in central bank openness over the last 20 years.

Central bank communication has two main objectives: first, it enhances the bank's accountability and, second, it helps the bank manage expectations. This section focuses on the second objective (see de Haan *et al.*, 2005 for a discussion of ECB accountability).

Why are expectations relevant? It is now widely accepted that a central bank's ability to affect the economy critically depends on the degree to which it can influence market expectations regarding the *future path* of overnight interest rates. The reason is simple: few, if any, economic decisions hinge on the overnight bank rate, which is the only market interest rate that is effectively controlled by the central bank. Long-term interest rates, which reflect expected future short-term interest rates, affect households' and firms' saving and investment decisions. Therefore, the public's perception of future policy rates is critical for the effectiveness of monetary policy.

Still, from a theoretical point of view, it is not obvious that communication will help the central bank to realise its ultimate objective(s), such as price stability and stable economic growth. For instance, communication has little value added if the central bank credibly commits to a policy rule. Assuming that the public has rational expectations, any systematic pattern in the way that policy is conducted should be correctly inferred from the central bank's observed behaviour (Woodford, 2005). Thus, in order to predict future interest rates, the public merely has to interpret (forecasts of) economic data in view of the central bank's policy rule; there is no role for central bank communication. A central bank can therefore theoretically be fully transparent without any communication.

While this reasoning is highly stylised, it highlights three conditions under which central bank communication may matter: non-rational expectations, absence of commitment to unchanging policy rules, and asymmetric information.

First, the assumption that the public will understand monetary policy perfectly regardless of the efforts made to explain it may be unrealistic. Therefore, it is clearly desirable for the central bank to explain the rule it follows (Woodford, 2005). By communicating to the public, the bank may help anchor inflation expectations.

Second, a central bank is unlikely to stick to an unchanged policy rule for long. Former ECB President Trichet has repeatedly emphasised that the ECB takes its decisions one step at a time, rather than following a rule.

Third, financial market participants generally do not have as much information as monetary policy makers on a number of key inputs to policy making, including the weights policy makers assign to possible objectives, or their assessment of the economic situation. If there is *asymmetric information*, so that the public and the central bank have access to different information, it may be perfectly rational for the public to adjust their expectations if the central bank provides new information. Here it is important to distinguish between the types of information on which asymmetries may exist.

In the first place, the central bank may provide *information about its reaction function*. This should lead, *ceteris paribus*, to an increase in the private sector's ability to forecast the central bank's policy decisions. For example, the central bank may provide information about its long-run inflation target, or on the relative weights it places on its objectives (if it has more than one).

By publicly announcing its monetary policy strategy and communicating its regular assessment of economic developments, a central bank provides guidance to the markets so that expectations can be formed more efficiently and accurately. This helps markets to understand monetary policy's responses to economic developments and shocks, and thus to anticipate the broad direction of monetary policy over the medium term.

Furthermore, the central bank may have better information on the economic outlook. Several studies have found that financial markets react not only to macroeconomic news, but also to *information on the economic outlook* provided by the central bank. Investors tend to update their own views in response to the information conveyed by the central bank. Private agents may lend special credence to the central bank's economic pronouncements, particularly if it has proven to be an effective forecaster of the economy.

Although there are good reasons why communication may be beneficial, it is unclear what constitutes the most effective communication strategy, or the optimal level of transparency. However, the literature on central bank transparency has shown that full disclosure of all available information is often not optimal.

ECB Communications Policy

Most central banks publicly announce their monetary policy decisions on the day they are taken; many release short press statements. The ECB is one of the few to detail the motives behind particular policy decisions at elaborate press conferences after policy meetings. Since 2015 it has also published the minutes (which it calls 'accounts') of its policy meetings four weeks later. Press conferences may provide less detail than minutes, but they are more timely and flexible, and allow the media to ask questions.

The general pattern is as follows. Following a Governing Council meeting, the ECB announces its monetary policy decisions at 13:45 CET. Approximately 45 minutes later, the ECB president and vice-president hold a press conference that comprises a prepared introductory statement on the background considerations for the monetary policy decision and a question and answer (Q&A) session. The introductory statement is understood to reflect the council's joint position, reached by consensus. ECB press conferences are generally less detailed than the minutes of the BoE or the Federal Reserve (Blinder *et al.*, 2008). In particular, the ECB does not provide information on voting.

The ECB also uses other important communication channels including the *Monthly Bulletin* (called the *Economic Bulletin* since January 2015, with a lower frequency than monthly), which provides a detailed and comprehensive analysis of the economic environment and monetary developments, quarterly appearances of the ECB president before the European Parliament's Committee on Economic and Monetary Affairs, and a large number of public speeches and interviews by members of the Executive Board and individual committee members (Blinder *et al.*, 2008; Hartmann and Smets, 2018).

Central bank transparency is thought to help increase the predictability of monetary policy. Such predictability is important for the conduct of monetary policy: while central banks only directly control very short-term interest rates, the expected path of these rates over longer horizons and the premiums for uncertainty are significant for the implementation of monetary policy. If agents can broadly anticipate policy responses, this permits the rapid incorporation of any (expected) changes in monetary policy into financial variables. This, in turn, can shorten the process by which monetary policy is transmitted into investment and consumption decisions, and accelerate any necessary economic adjustments, thus potentially enhancing the policy's effectiveness (ECB, 2011). Indeed, there is empirical evidence that ECB monetary policy has generally been quite predictable. The predictability of ECB policy decisions has also been found to increase over time (see Blattner *et al.* 2008 for an overview).

An important line of research focuses on the impact of central bank communications on financial markets. The underlying notion of this subfield is that if communications steer expectations, asset prices should react. There is a broad consensus that ECB communication affects financial markets. There is substantive evidence that various forms of ECB communication affect volatility, which implies that expectations have changed. This holds true for short-term interest rates, the bond market, the stock market, and the swap markets. The strongest effects are generally found for the president's introductory statements at the ECB press conferences following Governing Council meetings. There is also substantive evidence that financial markets have moved in the intended direction (Blinder *et al.*, 2008).

4.6 Forward Guidance

In recent years central banks have frequently reduced the policy interest rate to the lowest possible level – the *effective lower bound* (ELB). Several economists have argued that if a central bank offers *forward guidance* (i.e. communicates about its future policy rate), monetary policy may be effective even under the ELB. If a central bank can commit to future values of the policy rate, it can work around the ELB constraint by promising monetary accommodation in the future once the ELB ceases to bind (Eggertsson and Woodford, 2003) (see Figure 4.5). The solid line in the figure shows what would happen to the policy rate under the central bank's normal strategy (i.e. without forward guidance). T_0 is the current period. The central bank would prefer a negative policy rate given the economic situation, but cannot reduce its rate further. In period T, the economy has

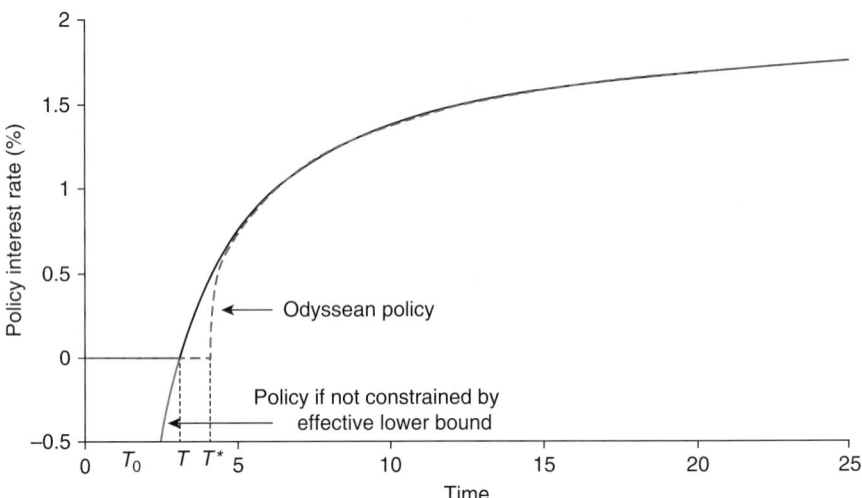

Figure 4.5   Odyssean forward guidance
Source: Den Haan (2013)

recovered to the extent that the bank's reaction function no longer calls for a negative policy interest rate.

Now suppose that the central bank could lower the expected values of future (strictly positive) interest rates. The long-term interest rate reflects expected future short-term rates. So, reducing expected future policy rates would reduce the long-term interest rate in the current period, which would stimulate consumption and investment. The central bank can accomplish lower long-term interest rates by promising to keep the policy interest rate 'lower for longer', i.e. to keep future policy rates below levels consistent with its reaction function. The corresponding time path is the dashed line in Figure 4.5. The policy interest rate remains at zero until T^* and then catches up to the level that is in line with the bank's standard reaction function. However, there is a time-inconsistency problem because between T and T^*, the central bank's normal reaction function calls for a positive interest rate, whereas the bank had promised to keep the interest rate at zero during this period. So, the central bank has an incentive to break its promise. And if markets believe it will do so, they will not adjust their expectations of future policy rates downward so that long-term rates will not come down. In other words, this forward guidance policy can only be effective if the central bank can convince markets that – like Odysseus who tied himself to the mast to withstand the song of the Sirens – it is committed to this policy and will not change course.

Despite its popularity in academic analysis, central banks generally do not engage in the practice of *Odyssean forward guidance*. Instead, central banks use what Campbell *et al.* (2012) call *Delphic forward guidance*.[5] Under this policy, central banks publish their forecasts of macroeconomic developments and their likely monetary policy actions without any commitment. However, this type of forward guidance also may affect private sector expectations. As long-term rates are more relevant for economic decisions than the current level of the overnight rate, any action by the central bank that influences interest rate expectations could be a potential tool of monetary policy, even if current short-term rates cannot be reduced any further (Blinder *et al.*, 2008). As pointed out in Section 4.5, there are several reasons why markets may respond to central bank communication. For instance, the central bank may be perceived to have a superior forecasting ability or better knowledge about its own monetary policy intentions.

In practice, central banks apply three broad forms of Delphic forward guidance (Filardo and Hoffman, 2014): (1) *qualitative* (or open-ended) *forward guidance*, where the central bank does not provide detailed quantitative information about the envisaged time frame for their policy intentions; (2) *calendar-based* (or time-contingent) *forward guidance*, where the central bank refers to a clearly specified time horizon for its policies; and (3) *threshold-based* (state contingent) *forward guidance*, where the central bank links future rates to specific quantitative economic thresholds.

The BoJ was a pioneer in using open-ended forward guidance. In 1999, it announced that interest rates would stay at zero until deflationary concerns were dispelled. When it faced deflationary pressure in 2013, the BoJ again relied on forward guidance, stipulating a two-year time period to achieve the objective of a 2 per cent inflation rate (Den Haan, 2013).

When the BoE's Monetary Policy Committee (MPC) introduced its forward guidance in August 2013 based on a threshold for unemployment, it announced that the guidance would cease to hold if some knockouts were breached. These knockouts were not the issue, however: the unexpectedly strong decline in unemployment to below the threshold forced the BoE to change its forward guidance as early as May 2014. Despite the increased levels of economic activity, the MPC was still worried about the slack in the economy. According to the minutes of the MPC, all members agreed that, 'in the absence of other inflationary pressures, it would be necessary to see more evidence of slack reducing before an increase in Bank Rate would be warranted'.

The Fed has also used different types of forward guidance. For instance, in December 2008, its FOMC announced that '[t]he Committee anticipates that weak economic conditions are likely to warrant exceptionally low levels of the federal funds rate for some time'. In March 2009, 'for some time' was replaced by 'for an extended period'. In August 2011, the Fed switched from open-ended to time-contingent forward guidance, and in December 2012 it shifted to state-contingent forward guidance.

The ECB's forward guidance has mostly been open-ended. While after previous Governing Council meetings it had stated that monetary policy would be accommodative 'for as long as necessary', in July 2013 the ECB announced that interest rates would remain at present or lower levels for 'an extended period of time'. Likewise, in June 2014 the ECB stated that 'key ECB interest rates will remain at present levels for an extended period of time in view of the current outlook for inflation'. More recently, the ECB's forward guidance on interest rates has become state and time dependent. On 14 June 2018, when the Governing Council announced that it would stop QE, it also stated that it expected policy rates to remain at their present levels at least through the summer of 2019 and, in any case, for as long as necessary to ensure the sustained convergence of inflation to levels that are below, but close to, 2 per cent (Hartmann and Smets, 2018).

How did financial markets respond to the ECB's forward guidance? Figure 4.6 displays Bloomberg data on market expectations, which are constructed from forward and interest rate option contracts on Euribor and OIS rates. The figure shows the mean and standard deviation over a 12-month horizon since communication about the APP typically focuses on longer horizons (e.g. the announcement on 14 June 2018 referred to the monetary policy path beyond year-end). The standard deviation can be interpreted as an indicator of market uncertainty. Figure 4.6 suggests that the ECB's forward guidance appears to have successfully reduced uncertainty regarding the policy rate path in the near future, as indicated by the steady decline in the standard deviation of market expectations, even though uncertainty increased at the end of the period.

4.7 Conclusions

Since 1999, the ECB has been responsible for monetary policy making in the euro area. The Governing Council – comprising the ECB's Executive Board and euro-area NCB governors – takes monetary policy decisions. The Maastricht Treaty defines the ECB's primary objective as 'price

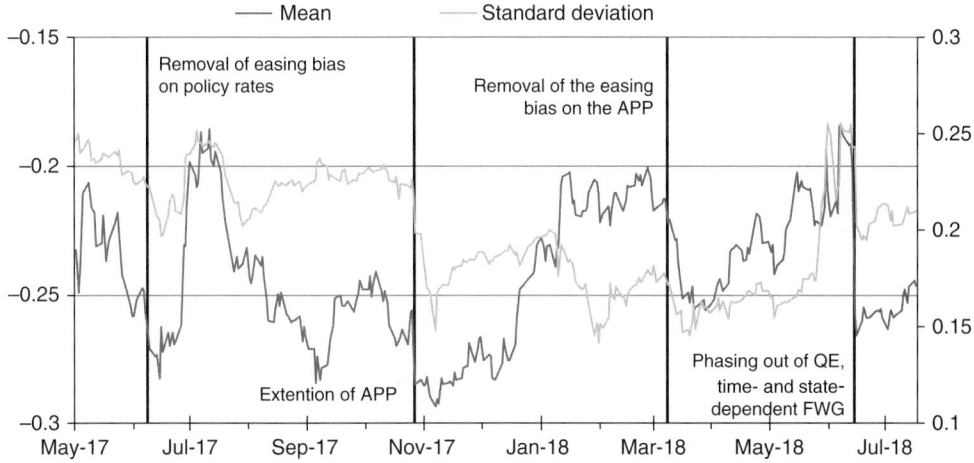

Figure 4.6   Mean and standard deviation of market expectations
Notes: On 8 June 2017, the ECB stopped referring to the possibility of a further easing of its policy rates, while on 8 March 2018 it stopped communicating about a possible extension of the size of monthly net purchases.
Source: De Nederlandsche Bank

stability', which the bank specifies as inflation below (but close to) 2 per cent in the euro area in the medium term. The ECB has been quite successful at keeping inflation (and inflation expectations) in the euro area in line with this target. Its monetary policy is based on a two-pillar strategy that combines the discussion of monetary factors ('monetary analysis') with a broad-based non-monetary analysis of the risks to price stability in the short to medium run ('economic analysis'). The ECB's main policy instruments are (1) policy rates that signal the bank's monetary policy stance; and (2) open-market operations to steer liquidity and thereby money market rates. At the beginning of the financial crisis, the ECB reduced its policy interest rates to historically low levels. It also introduced several temporary non-standard measures, subsequently referred to as Enhanced Credit Support, as the interbank money market does not function properly in times of financial distress. Later it introduced several other non-standard measures, such as OMTs, TLTROs, and QE. Like other modern central banks, the ECB has a very active communication strategy centred on the press conferences following Governing Council policy meetings. In July 2013 the ECB also began providing forward guidance on both the size and duration of QE and future policy rates.

Notes

1. As explained in Chapter 3, Denmark may decide to remain outside the euro area even if it meets the convergence criteria. Initially, also the UK had an 'opt-out' option, but since Brexit (see Chapter 3) this, of course, is no longer relevant.
2. As pointed out by Hartmann and Smets (2018), the ECB could take this step after the institutional reforms that were decided on at the June 2012 European Summit, which aimed to address the EMU's main prudential and fiscal weaknesses.
3. The programme encompassed the asset-backed securities purchase programme and the Covered Bond Purchase Programme (CBPP3), which were both launched in 2014. Under these programmes, assets were bought at a rate of around €10 billion a month. It also included the Corporate Sector Purchase Programme (CSPP) announced on 10 March 2016. In broad terms, the CSPP consisted of purchases by the Eurosystem of investment-grade euro-denominated bonds issued by non-bank corporations established in the euro area. Its most important element was the *Public Sector Purchase Programme.*
4. There are three alternative channels. The first is *capital constraints*: central bank purchases of assets at low prices due to distress in the financial intermediary sector have beneficial effects. The second channel is *scarcity*: central bank purchases of new issuance of, for example, MBS has led to a scarcity premium on the production coupon MBS, driving spreads on MBS down. The scarcity generates incentives for banks to originate more loans. The third is *exchange rate* channels: if markets expect that APPs will drive interest rates low for longer, they will shift their portfolio towards regions with higher yields. This will lead to a depreciation of the currency.
5. Named after Delphi, where, according to ancient Greek mythology, the oracle Pythia predicted the future.

Bibliography

Suggested Reading

Blinder, A., M. Ehrmann, J. de Haan, and D. Jansen (2017), Necessity as the Mother of Invention: Monetary Policy After the Crisis. *Economic Policy*, 32, 707–55.

European Central Bank (2011), *The Monetary Policy of the ECB*, ECB, Frankfurt am Main.

Hartmann, P. and F. Smets (2018), The First Twenty Years of the European Central Bank: Monetary Policy. CEPR Discussion Paper 13411.

References

Akerlof, G. A., W. T. Dickens, and G. L. Perry (2000), *Near-Rational Wage and Price Setting and the Long-Run Phillips Curve*, Brookings Institution, Washington, DC.

Altavilla, C., G. Carboni, and R. Motto (2015), Asset Purchase Programmes and Financial Markets: Lessons from the Euro Area. ECB Working Paper 1864.

Blattner, T., M. Catenaro, M. Ehrmann, R. Strauch, and J. Turunen (2008), The Predictability of Monetary Policy. ECB Occasional Paper 83.

Blinder, A., M. Ehrmann, J. de Haan, and D. Jansen (2017), Necessity as the Mother of Invention: Monetary Policy After the Crisis. *Economic Policy*, 32, 707–55.

Blinder, A. S., M. Ehrmann, M. Fratzscher, J. de Haan, and D. Jansen (2008), Central Bank Communication and Monetary Policy: A Survey of Theory and Evidence. *Journal of Economic Literature*, 46, 910–45.

Borio, C. (2014), Monetary Policy and Financial Stability: What Role in Prevention and Recovery? BIS Working Paper 440.

Campbell, J., C. Evans, J. Fisher, and A. Justiniano (2012), *Macroeconomic Effects of FOMC Forward Guidance*, Brookings Institution, Washington, DC.

Cour-Thiman, P. and B. Winkler (2014), The ECB's Non-Standard Monetary Policy Measures: The Role of Institutional Factors and Financial Structure. ECB Working Paper 1528.

de Haan, J., S. C. W. Eijffinger, and S. Waller (2005), *The European Central Bank: Credibility, Transparency, and Centralization*, MIT Press, Cambridge (MA).

de Haan, J. and J.-E. Sturm (2019), Central Bank Communication: How to Manage Expectations? In: D. Mayes, P. Siklos, and J.-E. Sturm (eds.), *The Oxford Handbook of the Economics of Central Banking*, Oxford University Press, 231–62.

Den Haan, W. (ed.) (2013), *Forward Guidance: Perspectives from Central Bankers, Scholars and Market Participants*, Centre for Economic Policy Research, London.

Eggertsson, G. and M. Woodford (2003), The Zero Bound on Interest Rates and Optimal Monetary Policy. *Brookings Papers on Economic Activity*, 1, 193–233.

Eser, F. and B. Schwaab (2016), Evaluating the Impact of Unconventional Monetary Policy Measures: Empirical Evidence from the ECB's Securities Markets Programme. *Journal of Financial Economics*, 119, 147–67.

European Central Bank (2003), *Background Studies for the ECB's Evaluation of its Monetary Policy Strategy*, ECB, Frankfurt am Main.
    (2011), *The Monetary Policy of the ECB*, ECB, Frankfurt am Main.

Filardo, A. and B. Hoffman (2014), Forward Guidance at the Zero Lower Bound. *BIS Quarterly Review*, March, 37–53.

Gros, D. (2003), Reforming the Composition of the ECB Governing Council in View of Enlargement: How Not to Do It! Briefing paper for the Monetary Committee of the European Parliament, February.

Hartmann, P. and F. Smets (2018), The First Twenty Years of the European Central Bank: Monetary Policy. CEPR Discussion Paper 13411.

Issing, O. (2001), Why Price Stability? In: A. Garcia Herrero, V. Gaspar, L. H. Hoogduin, J. Morgan, and B. Winkler (eds.), *Why Price Stability*? ECB, Frankfurt am Main.

Mishkin, F. S. and M. Savastano (2001), Monetary Policy Strategies for Latin America. *Journal of Development Economics*, 66, 415–44.

Sibert, A. (2003), The New Monetary Policy Strategy of the ECB. Briefing paper for the Committee on Economic and Monetary Affairs of the European Parliament, May.

Svensson, L. E. O. (2016), A Simple Cost-Benefit Analysis of Using Monetary Policy for Financial-Stability Purposes. In: O. J. Blanchard, R. Rajan, K. S. Rogoff, and L. H. Summers (eds.),

Progress and Confusion: The State of Macroeconomic Policy, MIT Press, Cambridge (MA), 107–18.

Trichet, J.-C. (2005), Asset Price Bubbles and Monetary Policy. Speech at Mas lecture in Singapore, 8 June.

Wieladek, T. and A. Garcia Pascual (2016), The European Central Bank's QE: A New Hope. CESifo Working Paper 5946.

Woodford, M. (2005), Central-Bank Communication and Policy Effectiveness. In: *The Greenspan Era: Lessons for the Future*, Federal Reserve Bank of Kansas City, 399–474.

Part II

Financial Markets

European Financial Markets

OVERVIEW

This chapter starts off by reviewing the three primary functions that financial markets perform. First, financial markets release information to aid the price discovery process. Second, markets provide a platform to trade. The main trading mechanisms, quote-driven and order-driven markets, are discussed. Finally, markets provide an infrastructure to settle trades. The remainder of the chapter describes the main financial markets in the EU (the money, bond, equity, derivatives, and foreign exchange markets).

The euro money market trades euro-denominated short-term funds and related derivative instruments. It consists of various segments, including unsecured deposit contracts with various maturities, ranging from overnight to one year, and repurchase agreements (so-called repos, i.e. reverse transactions secured by securities) also ranging from overnight to one year. Banks account for the largest share of the euro money market. The European Central Bank's use of various monetary policy instruments (reserve requirements, standing facilities, and open market operations) has a major influence on the money market. There are three main interest rates for the money market: EONIA (euro overnight index average), EURIBOR (euro interbank offered rate), and EUREPO (the repo market reference rate for the euro).

Euro-area entities issue the bulk of euro-denominated bonds (i.e. debt securities with a maturity of more than one year). Although the share of private sector securities (corporate bonds) in all euro-denominated debt securities outstanding has risen, securities issued by public authorities (government bonds) still form the most important market segment. The introduction of the euro in 1999 created a pan-European capital market in which government debt managers went from being the dominant players in their respective national markets to small to medium-sized players in a larger European market. Before the financial crisis, long-term interest rates were very similar throughout the euro area. After the crisis differentials vis-à-vis the German yield varied considerably across countries, while for each country the yield differential varies considerably over time.

The importance of equity finance in the EU is growing, although there are large differences across exchanges. The market capitalisations of Euronext and the London Stock Exchange are much higher than those of other exchanges in Europe. Despite the increase in equity finance, public equity markets play a limited role as a source of new funds, as firms generally raise external financing via bank loans and, to a lesser extent, debt securities.

Next, the chapter discusses derivatives – financial instruments whose value is derived from the value of the underlying financial instruments. They can be based on different types of assets (such as equities or commodities), prices (such as interest rates or exchange rates), or indexes (such as a stock market index). They are traded either on organised exchanges or over the counter. Derivatives can provide a source of income but are also important risk management tools. The most important derivatives are futures, forwards, options, and swaps.

The final section of the chapter discusses the foreign exchange market.

LEARNING OBJECTIVES

After you have studied this chapter, you should be able to:
- explain the purpose and structure of financial markets
- describe the essentials of the euro money market, including its functions and main interest rates
- explain how the monetary policy of the ECB affects the money market
- discuss the most important developments in the bond markets since the start of the monetary union
- discuss the most important developments in the equity markets since the start of the monetary union
- describe the essentials of the derivatives market
- describe the foreign exchange market.

5.1 Financial Markets: Functions and Structure

Functions

In a *financial market*, individuals issue and trade securities and derivatives. *Securities* are fungible, negotiable instruments representing financial value, and are broadly categorised as either debt securities or equity securities. Financial markets channel funds from those with a surplus, who buy securities, to those with a shortage, who issue new securities or sell existing securities (see Chapter 1). A financial market facilitates trading among its participants by performing the following functions (Bailey, 2005):

- Price discovery: the market facilitates the dissemination of information. Participants who want to buy or sell can find out the prices at which trades can be agreed upon (pre-trading phase).
- Trading mechanism: the market provides a mechanism to facilitate agreements by linking buyers and sellers (trading phase).
- Clearing and settlement arrangements: the agreements are executed. The market must ensure that the terms of each agreement are honoured (post-trading phase).

Price discovery involves the incorporation of new information into asset prices (O'Hara, 2003). Since securities represent a promise of future payments, their value depends on expectations about the size and risk of these future payments. New information can affect these expectations. In an efficient market, prices reflect all (publicly) available information.[1] Although company insiders may have more information than outsiders, regulation typically forbids insider trading (see Chapter 12). Markets also provide liquidity, which refers to the process of matching buyers and sellers (O'Hara, 2003). Liquidity is inter-temporal in nature, as buyers and sellers may enter the market at different times. The trading mechanism is the means of matching buyers to sellers. Below we discuss the primary trading mechanisms in more detail. Finally, clearing and settlement arrangements include: (1) confirmation of the terms of the transactions; (2) clearing of the trades to establish the obligations of buyers and sellers; and (3) settlement of the accounts to finalise the delivery of securities against the payment. These post-trading arrangements are discussed in Chapter 7.

Financial market participants can be classified into three main groups, according to their motive for trading:

1. *Public investors*, who ultimately own the securities and who are motivated by the returns from holding them. Public investors include private individuals and institutional investors, such as pension funds, insurance companies and mutual funds.
2. *Brokers*, who act as agents for public investors and who are motivated by the remuneration they receive (typically in the form of commission fees) for the services they provide. Brokers trade for others, and not on their own account.
3. *Dealers*, who do trade on their own account and whose primary motive is to profit from trading rather than from holding securities. Typically,

dealers obtain their return from the differences between the prices at which they buy and sell the securities over short intervals of time.

In practice, the three groups are not mutually exclusive. Some public investors may occasionally act on behalf of others; brokers may act as dealers and hold securities on their own; and dealers often hold securities in excess of the inventories needed to facilitate their trading activities. The role of these three groups differs according to the trading mechanism used in a particular financial market.

Trading Mechanisms

Financial markets use a trading mechanism to match buyers and sellers. They are often classified according to the type of trading mechanism they use (Harris, 2003). The two main types are quote-driven markets and order-driven markets, while hybrid markets use a combination of the two.

Quote-Driven Markets

In *quote-driven markets* (also known as dealer markets), dealers quote the bid and ask prices at which they are prepared to buy or sell, respectively, specified amounts of the security (Bailey, 2005). Quote-driven markets require little formal organisation, but need mechanisms to publish the dealers' price quotations and regulate dealers' conduct. Stock exchanges normally grant dealers (or market makers) privileged access to certain administrative procedures or market information. In return for these privileges, dealers are obliged to quote 'firm' bid and ask prices at which they guarantee to make trades of up to certain specified volumes. Investors who want to trade in a quote-driven market must trade either directly with a dealer or via a broker.

When a security is traded, the buyer pays the ask price, p_a, and the seller receives the bid price, p_b. The difference is the *bid–ask spread* ($s = p_a - p_b$) received by the dealer. The dealer typically holds an inventory of securities during the day to be able to sell (and buy) immediately. From his return (i.e. the bid–ask spread), the dealer must cover the costs of holding his inventory (e.g. the interest costs of financing the securities inventory) and the risks (e.g. prices may move while the securities are in the inventory). While bid and ask prices are published, dealers may negotiate special prices for large transactions. The spread could be broader for particularly large transactions (i.e. block trades) to cover the price risk of such trades before the dealer can sell on (or buy) the bought (sold) securities to (from) other dealers in the market.

Order-Driven Markets

In *order-driven markets* (also known as auction markets), participants issue orders to buy or sell at stated prices, which can be modelled as 'double auctions'. Participants issue instructions that specific actions should be taken in response to publicly verifiable price observations. An 'auctioneer' then adjusts the price until the total orders to buy equal the total orders to sell (Bailey, 2005). There are different forms of order-driven markets. In call markets, the price is determined at a limited number of specified times: orders can be collected and the auction takes place at the specified time. This type of auction is widely used for new issues of government debt (see Section 5.3) and initial public offerings (IPOs) of equity (see Section 5.4). The call-market mechanism for bonds and equity has been replaced by continuous trading systems in secondary markets.

In *continuous auction markets*, public investors send their instructions (orders) to buy or sell to brokers. The two most common types of orders are the *limit order*, which specifies a purchase or sale at a maximum buying price or minimum selling price, respectively, and the *market order*, which specifies a purchase or sale at the best available price. The outstanding limit orders are generally listed in a limit order book. The existence of a limit order book implies automatic trade matching, though in practice some element of discretion remains (e.g. in setting the priority of orders). Order-driven markets are highly formalised: the auction rules for matching trades are specified in great detail to ensure orderly and fair trading.

Hybrid Markets

Trading mechanisms are often compared with respect to transparency and liquidity (Bailey, 2005). In principle, quote- and order-driven markets should result in the same market prices if all trades are made public. But in practice, quote-driven markets tend to be more fragmented and less transparent. Dealers quote different bid and ask prices, and deals that have been executed are not necessarily made public immediately (to give dealers time to offload large trades in the market).

Liquidity does not depend only on the trading mechanism. In a call market, investors must wait until the next price fixing takes place; they can trade immediately in continuous order-driven markets. The price, however, depends on the availability of sufficient orders on the other side of the market. Investors may therefore sometimes prefer the opportunity to negotiate individual agreements with dealers in quote-driven markets. Quote-driven markets may also permit a delay in the publication of the details of a trade so that deals can be kept secret, if only for a limited time.

Hybrid markets combine characteristics of quote- and order-driven markets. Advances in IT have spurred the development of order-driven markets, particularly for equity trading. The combination of smart trading rules (software) and fast computers (hardware) allows an almost instantaneous matching of orders. Euronext, one of Europe's largest stock exchanges, for example, uses an order-driven trading mechanism with a centralised electronic order book. It also enables small and medium-sized listed companies to hire a designated market maker to act as a 'liquidity provider' in their stock. Similarly, the London Stock Exchange's (LSE's) premier electronic trading system combines electronic order-driven trading with liquidity provision by market makers. While stock exchanges are becoming more order driven, bond markets tend to be more quote driven (i.e. they tend to use dealers). Sections 5.3 and 5.4 discuss the main bond markets and stock exchanges in more detail.

Overview of Financial Markets

A distinction can be made between primary and secondary markets. In a *primary market*, new issues of a security are sold to investors. A *secondary market* trades previously issued securities. Secondary markets can be organised into exchanges, in which buyers and sellers meet in a central location to trade, or *over-the-counter (OTC) markets* in which dealers in different locations stand ready to sell and buy securities.

The remainder of the chapter discusses the five principal financial markets:

- The *money market* trades short-term funds (up to one year). Banks primarily use this market to manage their short-term liquidity positions.
- *Bond markets* trade debt securities with a maturity of more than one year. Governments and firms issue bonds to raise medium- and long-term funds against a fixed or flexible interest rate.
- *Equity markets* trade in equity, which firms issue to raise funds by granting the investor a residual claim on their income.
- The *derivatives market* trades derivatives, which are financial instruments with a value derived from the value of the underlying financial instrument. Derivatives are important risk management tools.
- The *foreign exchange market* determines the relative values of currencies. Figures 5.1 and 5.2 compare the size of the main funding markets – the equity and bond markets – in the EU, China, Japan, and the US. These figures demonstrate the fundamental difference between these financial systems (see also Chapter 1). The US financial system is primarily market based, with a large and growing equity market worth €27 trillion in 2017. The importance

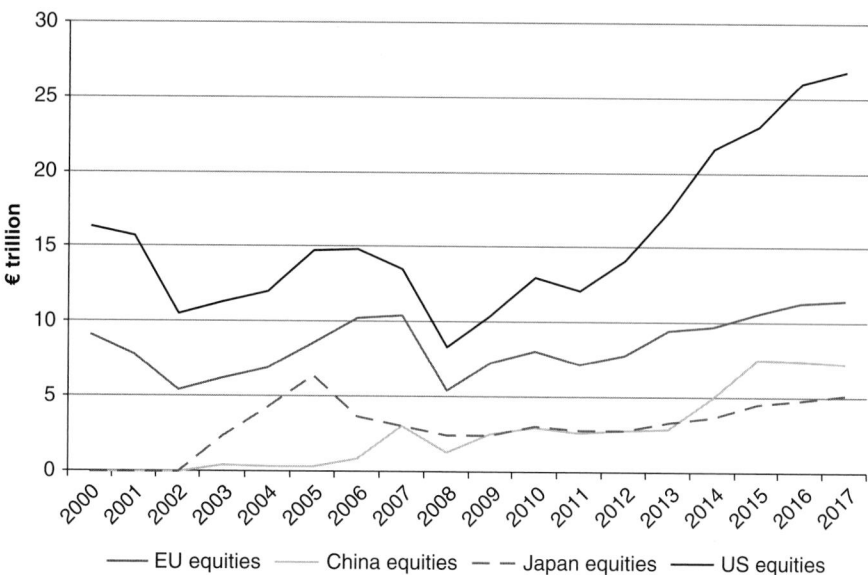

Figure 5.1   Size of equity markets, year-end market value (€ trillion), 2000–2017
Source: World Federation of Exchanges

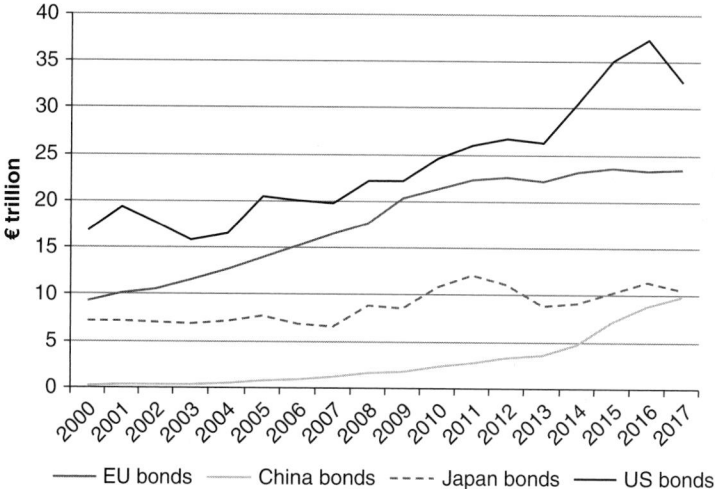

Figure 5.2   Bond markets, amounts outstanding at year-end (€ trillion), 2000–2017
Source: Bank for International Settlements

of equity finance is increasing at a slower rate in the other countries. For instance, the Chinese equity market has been growing since 2013. The large fluctuations in market capitalisation reflect the dotcom bubble in 2000–2001 and the 2007–2009 financial crisis.

Table 5.1 Stock markets vs. (collateralised) debt/money markets

Stock markets	Debt/money markets
Risk sharing	Lending/liquidity provision
Price discovery	Avoiding need for price discovery
Information sensitive	Information insensitive
Transparent	Opaque
Big investments in information	Modest investments in information
Many traders (exchanges)	Few traders (bilateral)
Trading not urgent	Trading urgent
Volatile volume	Stable volume

Source: Holmstrom (2015)

When the euro was introduced, the EU bond market amounted to €9 trillion, compared with €15 trillion in the US (see Figure 5.2). The EU bond market has experienced spectacular growth since then; the EU and US bond markets have become more similar in size: the outstanding value of bonds was €25–30 trillion in 2017. The Chinese bond market is also growing rapidly, reaching €10 trillion in 2017.

Table 5.1 discusses the differences between collateralised debt and equity (Holmstrom, 2015). The key difference between stock markets and collateralised debt/money markets is price discovery. Stock markets are designed to share and allocate aggregate risk, which requires a market that is good at price discovery. Information will quickly be reflected in prices; since prices are common knowledge, additional details are needed in order to generate a profit from trading. The purpose of money markets is to provide liquidity for individuals and firms. The cheapest way to do so is by using enough collateralised debt that the exact price of the collateral does not need to be discovered. When both parties know that there is sufficient collateral, more precise private information about the collateral becomes irrelevant and will not impair liquidity.

5.2 Money Market

In a broad sense, the *money market* trades short-term funds, usually with a maturity of up to one year. The *euro money market* trades euro-denominated short-term funds and related derivative instruments (i.e. contracts, such as options and futures, with a value derived from the value of the underlying instrument). Credit institutions (i.e. banks) account for the largest share of the euro money market. As explained below, these institutions rely on the euro money market to manage their short-term liquidity positions and fulfil their minimum reserve requirements. Other important market participants are money market funds, other financial intermediaries (such as investment funds other than money market funds), insurance companies and pension funds, as well as large non-financial corporations.

This chapter focuses on two money market segments – secured and unsecured.[2] The maturities for both range from overnight to one year. The main difference between these segments is whether the party providing liquidity receives collateral or not (i.e. the amount of risk involved). When providing unsecured interbank deposits, a bank transfers funds to another bank for a specified period of time, during which it assumes full counterparty credit risk.

Transactions are often conducted on a repurchase basis. A *repurchase agreement* (repo) is an arrangement whereby an asset is sold while the seller simultaneously obtains the right and obligation to repurchase it at a specific price on a future date or on demand (ECB, 2008).

In the secured repo market, this counterparty credit risk is mitigated, as the bank that provides liquidity receives collateral (e.g. bonds) in return. In the event of a credit default, the liquidity-providing bank can use this collateral to satisfy its claim against the defaulting bank.

In addition to engaging in transactions with the central bank, money market participants also trade with each other. They take positions in relation to their short-term interest rate expectations, finance their securities trading portfolios (bonds, shares, etc.), hedge their long-term positions using shorter-term contracts, and square individual liquidity imbalances (Hartmann *et al.*, 2001).

As explained in Chapter 4, the euro money market is strongly influenced by the ECB's monetary policy. In addition to taking decisions concerning interest rates, the ECB also influences the euro money market through three monetary policy instruments:

- reserve requirements
- open market operations
- standing facilities.

Euro-area banks must hold *required reserves* of 1 per cent of the total amount of their overnight deposits, other deposits and debt securities with a maturity under two years, and money market paper (excluding interbank liabilities) in reserve accounts with their national central banks. Reserve requirements have to be fulfilled, on average, over a one-month maintenance period.

The minimum reserve system helps to stabilise money market interest rates through the *averaging provision*: a bank's compliance with reserve requirements is judged on the basis of the average of the daily balances on its reserve accounts over a reserve maintenance period. Banks can thus smooth out daily liquidity fluctuations, since transitory reserve imbalances can be offset by opposite reserve imbalances within the same maintenance period. The averaging provision also implies that if institutions believe money market rates will go down later in the maintenance period, they can profit from lending in the market and run a reserve deficit. If they believe money market rates will go up, they can borrow in the market and run a reserve surplus. This mechanism stabilises the overnight interest rate during the maintenance period.

Open market operations are the general instruments used to manage the liquidity situation and to steer interest rates. Under normal circumstances, *main refinancing operations* (MROs) are the most important instrument. During the recent financial crisis, long-term refinancing operations were very important (see Chapter 4 for further details).

Standing facilities provide or absorb liquidity with an overnight maturity when unforeseen liquidity shocks occur. Therefore, they provide a type of insurance mechanism for banks, but at penalty interest rates. The initiative in these transactions is on the side of the credit institution.

In addition to the ECB interest rates on the standing facilities and MROs, there are three main market interest rates for the money market:

- EONIA (euro overnight index average). The *EONIA* is the effective overnight reference rate for the euro. It is computed daily as a volume-weighted average of unsecured overnight euro lending transactions in the interbank market, as reported by a representative panel of large banks.[3] As explained in Box 5.1, EONIA was replaced by the euro short-term rates (ESTER) by January 2020.
- EURIBOR (euro interbank offered rate). The *EURIBOR* is the benchmark rate of the large unsecured euro money market for maturities longer than overnight (one week to one year) that has emerged since 1999. It is based on information provided by a somewhat smaller panel of banks. As explained in Box 5.1, EURIBOR must fulfil the requirements of the EU Benchmarks Regulation (BMR, 2016/1011/ EU). At the time of writing, the European Money Markets Institute (EMMI), which administrates the EURIBOR, is working to bring it into line with the BMR requirements.

Box 5.1 ESTER replaces EONIA

The ECB calculates the daily EONIA (euro overnight index average) based on the weighted average of all overnight unsecured lending interbank transactions of a panel of banks. The number of banks in the panel has fallen sharply in recent years. The European Money Markets Institute (EMMI), a non-profit association based in Brussels, publishes the rate by 19:00 CET each day.

The EMMI has initiated in-depth reforms of the EONIA and EURIBOR (euro interbank offered rate) to bring both into compliance with the new EU Benchmarks Regulation (BMR 2016/11/EU), which was published in 2016 and came into force in January 2018. However, in February 2018 EMMI concluded that 'should market conditions and dynamics remain unchanged, EONIA's compliance with the EU BMR by January 2020 cannot be warranted, as long as its definition and calculation methodology remain in its current format'. EONIA is not expected to meet the BMR criteria, and will therefore see its use restricted as of 1 January 2020.

The ECB Governing Council has developed a euro short-term rate (ESTER) based on overnight unsecured fixed rate deposit transactions over €1 million. ESTER reflects the wholesale euro unsecured overnight borrowing costs of euro-area banks, and serves as a backstop reference rate. ESTER is calculated based on daily confidential statistical information relating to money market transactions that are reported by banks. Unsecured deposits are standardised and are the most frequent means of conducting transactions on the basis of a competitive procedure, which limits the number of idiosyncratic factors that could influence the volatility of the rate. The ECB began publishing ESTER in October 2019.

ESTER is calculated for each TARGET2 day as a volume-weighted trimmed mean rounded to the third decimal, which is calculated by: (1) ordering transactions from the lowest to the highest rate; (2) aggregating the transactions at each rate level; (3) removing the top and bottom 25 per cent in terms of volume; and (4) calculating the mean of the remaining 50 per cent of the volume-weighted distribution of rates.

The transition from EONIA to ESTER, by 1 January 2020 was a complex challenge. Since more than €20 trillion in interest rate derivatives and securities is linked to EONIA, a broad-based coordination across market participants and benchmark users was necessary to prepare the transition to ESTER to guarantee that systems and trading venues can handle the new rate. To support the transition, the ECB published the so-called pre-ESTER, calculated using the new method, once every maintenance period.

Source: ECB

- EUREPO (the repo market reference rate for the euro) is the benchmark rate of the euro repo market and has been released since March 2002. It is the rate at which one prime bank offers funds in euros to another prime bank when the funds are secured by a repo transaction using general collateral.

Developments in Money Market Segments

In January 2019, the ECB started publishing new statistics on the secured euro money market. These statistics complement data on the unsecured money market, which the ECB has published regularly since November 2017. The reported statistics are based on transaction-by-transaction information from the 50 largest euro-area banks (based on the banks' total main balance sheet assets). Unsecured transactions (i.e. those without collateral) include all trades concluded via deposits, call accounts, or short-term securities with financial counterparties including banks, the government sector, and non-financial corporations. Secured transactions cover all fixed-term and open-basis repurchase agreements and transactions entered into under those agreements.

Figure 5.3 shows the turnover data in several segments of the money market, while Figure 5.4 shows the maturity of the transactions. Borrowing (lending) refers to transactions in which the reporting bank receives (provides) euro-denominated funds, irrespective of whether the transaction was initiated by the reporting bank or its counterpart. As the numbers

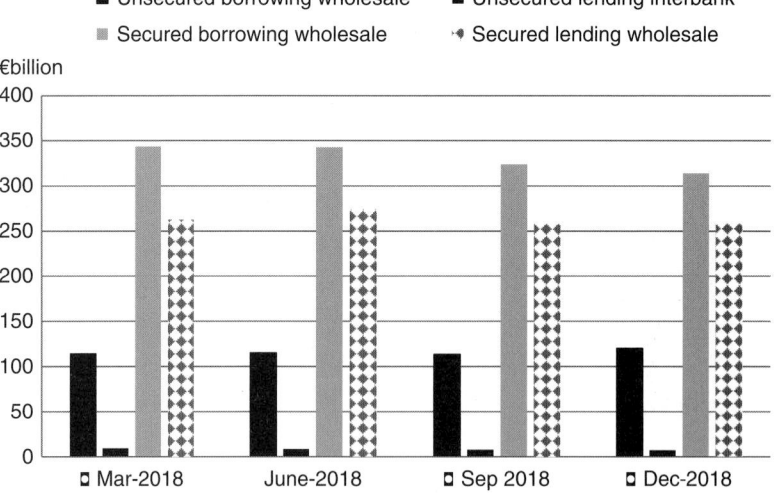

Figure 5.3   Money market: daily turnover, 2018 (in € billion)
Source: ECB

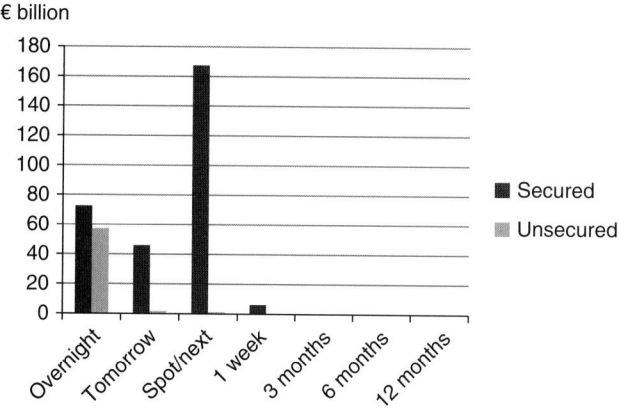

Figure 5.4   Money market: maturity, 2018 (in € billion)
Source: ECB

reported are coming from the 50 largest banks, they do not cover the entire market. This also explains why borrowing and lending differ.

In November/December 2018, the borrowing turnover in the unsecured segment averaged €120 billion per day. Borrowing from credit institutions, i.e. on the interbank market, represented an average turnover of €7 billion per day. This illustrates that the unsecured interbank money market has still not recovered from the financial crisis. In the unsecured market, overnight borrowing transactions represented 51 per cent of the total nominal borrowing amount (see Figure 5.4).

In the same period, the borrowing turnover in the secured segment averaged €314 billion per day. The ECB does not provide figures on the secured interbank market. Most of the turnover in the secured market segment was concentrated in durations ranging from overnight up to one week, with overnight transactions representing around 22 and 26 per cent of the total nominal amount on the borrowing and lending sides, respectively.

5.3 Bond Markets

A *bond* is a debt security that promises that payments will be made periodically for a specified time. The re-denomination of debt from former national currencies into euros at the beginning of the monetary union paved the way for a European debt securities market. The increased role of the euro as an international investment currency has made the market in euro-denominated

Table 5.2 Bonds by issuer, 2017 (€ trillion)

	Government	Financials	Corporates	Total
EU	10.9	10.7	1.8	23.4
of which euro area	*8.0*	*7.3*	*1.3*	*16.5*
China	3.7	3.7	2.4	9.8
Japan	7.9	2.1	0.6	10.6
US	14.6	12.9	5.1	32.6
Total	37.1	29.4	9.9	76.4

Source: Bank for International Settlements

issues attractive to both investors and issuers. The bulk of euro-denominated debt securities is issued by euro-area issuers. However, for issuers outside the euro area it has also become attractive to borrow in euros.

As Table 5.2 shows, debt securities issued by public authorities still form the most important market segment (except for China), closely followed by bank bonds (financials). In Europe, bank bonds are almost as important as government bonds in size. Corporate bonds have become important in the US, but still represent a medium-sized market segment in Europe and China and a small segment in Japan.

Bonds are the main instrument that euro-area governments (mainly central governments, but also regional and local government authorities) use to finance their budget deficits. Government bonds often serve as a benchmark for pricing other assets, and they are frequently used as collateral in various financial transactions.

The non-government bond market in the euro area is dominated by bank debt securities (see Figure 5.5). This segment encompasses numerous different types of bonds, including unsecured bank debt securities and covered bonds. *Covered bonds* are bondholders' claims against the issuing bank that are secured by a pool of cover assets on the bank's balance sheet, such as mortgage loans or loans to the public sector.

Government Bonds

Issuance

The introduction of the euro in 1999 had a major impact on the operations of government debt managers, as the disappearance of exchange rate risks within the euro area created the conditions for a pan-European capital market. As a result, debt managers have become small to medium-sized players in a larger

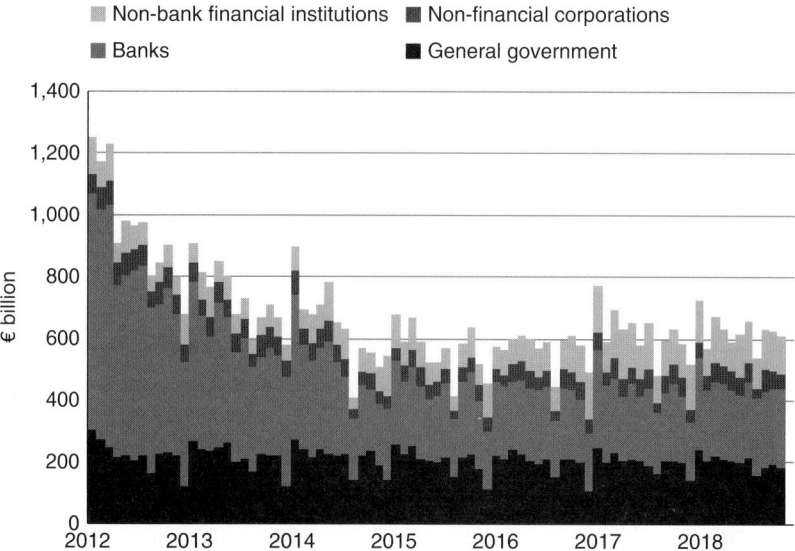

Figure 5.5 Gross issuance of bonds, 2012–2018 (€ billions)
Source: ECB

European market instead of dominant players in individual national markets. Investors now focus more on credit risk and liquidity, while bond portfolios have become increasingly internationally diversified, especially in the smaller euro-area countries. Consequently, competition among debt managers has increased, stimulating a more efficient primary market and a deeper, more liquid secondary market. Governments have put great effort into making their outstanding debt and new issues more attractive to international bond investors. To this end, they have adopted a number of supply-side innovations, which were enabled by the rapid expansion of electronic trading systems (see Box 5.2 for further details). In addition to local systems, the European electronic platform for government securities, EuroMTS, was introduced in 1999, which facilitates the quotation and trading of some European benchmark bonds (see Chapter 7 for further details).

Government Bond Yields

Figure 5.7 shows the euro-area yield curve for AAA-rated government bonds with different remaining maturities at four different dates. Yields of government bonds are influenced by expected short-term interest rates and the term premium. Risk-averse investors demand a risk premium (*term premium*) for investments in long-term bonds to compensate them for the risk of losses due to (unexpected) interest rate hikes; those losses increase with the bond

Box 5.2 Government debt management

The primary objective of debt management agencies in the euro area is to ensure that financing of the government's annual borrowing is at the lowest possible (medium-term) cost with acceptable risks, although precise wordings and emphasis differ by country. The operational targets or guidelines for debt management units differ more substantially. These are often based on asset liability studies or cost-at-risk models, weighing interest costs against budgetary risks. Targets can be based on a range for the average maturity or the (modified) duration,[4] subject to certain restrictions such as quantitative limits on the use of interest rate swaps.

Debt management units were generally given more independence in the 1990s. A stronger focus on 'narrow' debt management goals allowed responsibilities to be delegated to separate units. In addition, greater product complexity and competition among debt managers require a higher degree of operational independence and professionalism, which is easier to accomplish in a non-government unit. Cost considerations also sometimes played a role in decisions to delegate tasks to more independent units (Wolswijk and de Haan, 2005).

The increased competition has led to increasing liquidity of government securities and larger volumes of outstanding issues. While issues of around €2 billion were standard in smaller countries before the start of the Economic and Monetary Union, the minimum is now €5 billion; large euro-area countries have bond issuances of over €20 billion.[5] Governments sometimes focus on 'niches' targeting particular investor needs. For instance, Spain and France have introduced constant-maturity bonds, while France (followed by Greece and Italy) has taken the lead in issuing index-linked bonds (Baele *et al.*, 2004); the returns on these bonds depend on the development of a price index. In 2006, Germany issued an index-linked bond. Outside the euro area, the UK and the USA are major issuers of this type of bond.

Debt managers have also made issuance activity more regular and predictable by introducing pre-announced auction calendars, which has improved market transparency. Increased competition in the primary and secondary government bond markets has also led to changes in distribution channels. Primary dealers and bank syndicates are now popular ways to reach more non-domestic investors. Primary dealers mediate between the debt agency and buyers in both the primary and secondary markets. All euro-area countries (except Germany) now use primary dealers to distribute government bonds. These dealers usually bid at auctions or buy a certain amount of newly issued bonds, promote government debt, and market making. Many foreign financial institutions are considered primary dealers, reflecting the wish to spread ownership of government securities widely. Bank syndicates have also become an increasingly popular way to distribute new government debt, particularly when entering new market segments. Syndicate participants may select investors to whom the government security to be issued may be especially interesting. For smaller countries, a particular advantage is that a significant amount can be placed at once, thus immediately creating liquidity. The financial crisis took a heavy toll on public finances across the euro area, pushing debt-to-GDP ratios from 65 per cent in 2007 to

Box 5.2 (cont.)

78 per cent in 2009. The ensuing euro crisis further deteriorated gross debt-to-GDP ratios to 92 per cent in 2014. Government indebtedness has declined to 86 per cent in 2018, but there are large differences across countries. The highest debt ratios are in Greece (182 per cent), Italy (133 per cent), and Portugal (125 per cent).

Recently, financial markets have provided a favourable funding environment with exceptionally low interest rates and low volatility globally. This has driven sovereign funding costs to very low levels. Some debt management offices (DMOs), including those of France, Germany, and the Netherlands, have even issued negative-yielding debt in recent years. Low interest rates have also enabled debt managers to lengthen the average maturity of issues, which is reflected in the rise in the shares of fixed-rate, long-term issuance in gross marketable borrowing. Looking for ways to mitigate the risks of refinancing, DMOs of several countries, including France, Germany, Italy, and Spain, have been actively issuing securities with maturities of 30 years or more. Furthermore, Austria, Belgium, and Ireland have sold ultra-long bonds with 100-year maturities (OECD, 2018). As a result, the average maturity of government debt has increased slightly (see Figure 5.6). From a risk management perspective, a higher average maturity implies a lower pass-through impact of interest rate changes on government interest. Also, some DMOs have issued alternative instruments, such as green bonds (France and Poland) and *sukuk*, i.e. sharia-compliant bonds (Luxembourg and the UK).

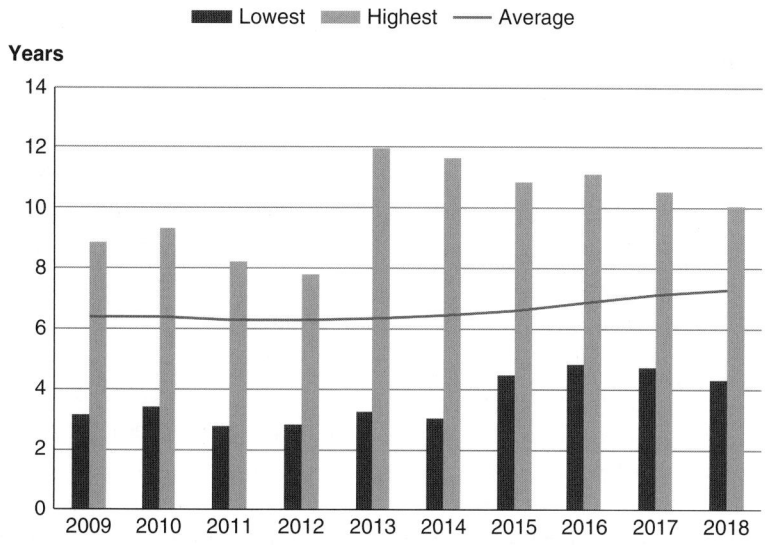

Figure 5.6   Term to maturity of euro-area government debt
Source: ECB

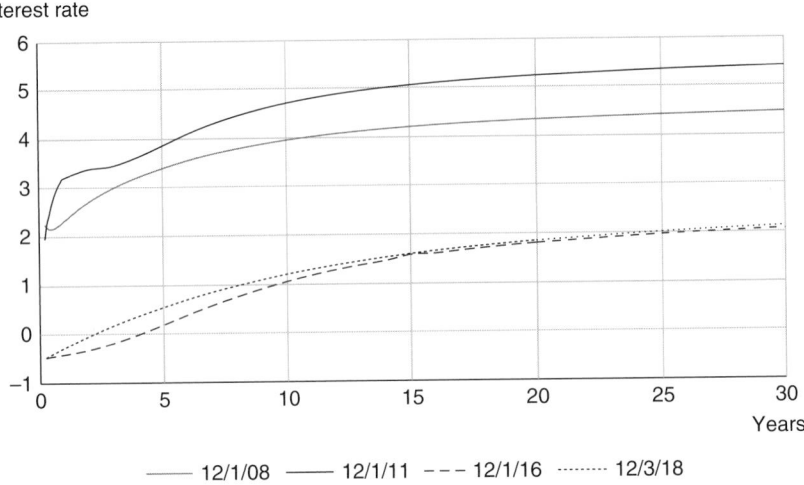

Interest rate

12/1/08 ——— 12/1/11 – – – 12/1/16 ········ 12/3/18

Figure 5.7 Yield curve at 1 December (2008–2018) (%)
Source: ECB

duration. The term premium leads to a positive *term spread*, i.e. the spread of yields for bonds with longer maturity over those with shorter maturity, even when markets expect interest rates to be equally likely to increase or decrease. The term spread in the euro area has been mostly positive since 1999, reflecting what is often called a 'normal' yield curve (ECB, 2007). However, the term spread has changed over time, as shown in Figure 5.7. Due to the unconventional policies of the ECB, the yield curve has shifted down.

In addition to interest rate expectations and the term premium, credit risk and liquidity also influence government bond yields. *Credit risk* is the risk of loss due to the failure of a counterparty to perform according to a contractual arrangement, for instance due to a default by a borrower. The spread between the yield of a particular bond and the yield of a bond with similar characteristics (but without credit risk) is the credit risk premium. Rating agencies – like Moody's, Standard & Poor's, and Fitch – indicate issuers' credit risk by assigning them a rating (see Chapter 1 for further details).

Liquidity is the ease with which an investor can sell or buy a bond immediately at a price close to the mid-quote (i.e. the average of the bid–ask spread, as defined in Section 5.1). The spread between the yield of a bond with liquidity and a similar bond with less liquidity is referred to as the liquidity premium.

Figure 2.7 in Chapter 2 shows that yield differentials vis-à-vis German government bond yields vary considerably across countries, while for each country the yield differential varies considerably over time. Since 2012 the yield spreads of euro-area government bonds vis-à-vis German government bonds have declined. However, spreads have occasionally increased in recent years, often due to political uncertainty in a Member State.

Corporate Bonds

Before 1998, the corporate bond market was dominated by debt issued by highly rated financial corporations; industrial corporations have increasingly found their way to the corporate bond market since then (Baele *et al.*, 2004). Nevertheless, financials are still more important than non-financial firms: they are the second-largest group of issuers of debt securities in the euro-area economy after governments (see Figure 5.5).

The outstanding stock of long-term debt securities of non-financial corporates (NFCs) has increased by around 3.6 times since 2002 (see Figure 5.8). Six countries (France, the UK, the Netherlands, Germany, Italy, and Luxembourg) account for about 80 per cent of all European corporate bonds by value.

During 2009–2016, the European bond market compensated for the decrease in bank loans to euro-area countries. The stock of bank loans extended to corporates decreased by €536 billion, whereas the stock of long-term debt securities increased by €567 billion over this period (European Commission, 2017). Yet NFCs' dependence on debt differs widely among EU Member States. Corporate bonds are the most important source of finance in France (about 11 per cent of NFCs' liabilities), Portugal, and the UK (about 8 per cent each).

Some observers have warned against the increased use of leveraged finance, which comprises leveraged loans and high-yield bonds for non-investment-grade firms that are highly indebted. BIS figures suggest that leveraged finance has doubled in size since the global financial crisis. Debt financing with thin equity stakes is risky: when the economy turns, equity is quickly wiped out, leading to failures.

Although small and medium-sized enterprises (SMEs) can theoretically access the corporate bond market, they are much less frequent issuers given the large size of most transactions in this market. SMEs therefore mostly rely on bank loans for their financing needs, which are normally undertaken by issuers on a syndicated loan basis for larger volumes, or a bilateral basis for smaller and more specific needs. Maturities of bank loans are shorter than maturities in debt capital markets and typically do not extend beyond five

€ billion

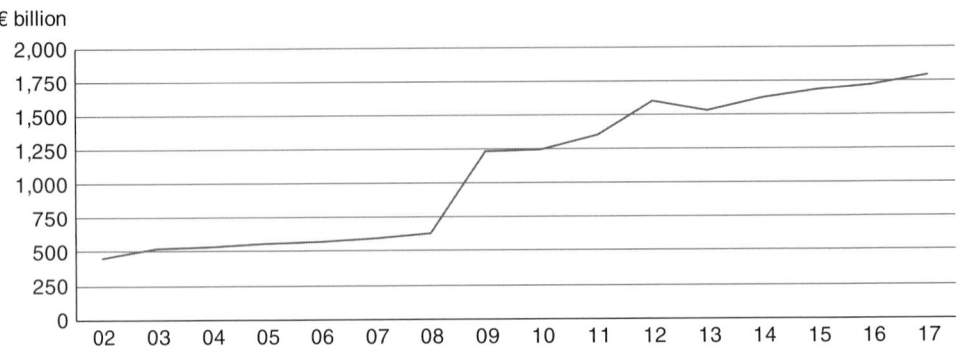

Figure 5.8   Outstanding amounts of long-term debt securities issued by NFCs, EU-28, 2002–2017
Source: ECB

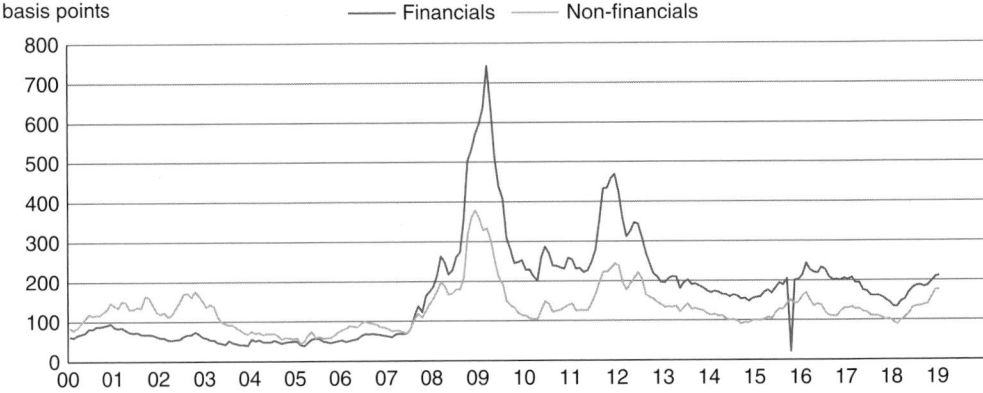

Figure 5.9   Spreads of AAA-rated corporate bonds over German government bonds (percentage points), 1999–2018
Note: 7–10 years' maturity; basis points.
Source: ECB

years and eventually seven years, on an unsecured basis. Furthermore, issuing public securities requires the provision of more financial information. For example, some SMEs may report their financial statements according to local generally accepted accounting principles rather than international standards. There are also requirements associated with corporate bond issuance, which may represent barriers for SMEs, such as the need for a rating or alternative credit assessments (European Commission, 2017).

Yields of AAA-rated corporate bonds are generally higher than AAA-rated government bond yields, mainly due to the perceived credit risk that results from an investment in corporate bonds (see Figure 5.9). When the corporate outlook deteriorates, these spreads increase. For example, spreads were high in 2001 and 2002 when economic growth was low, but decreased significantly in 2003. After the start of the financial crisis, and during the euro crisis, the spreads increased. Corporate bond spreads are higher for bonds of lower-rated issuers than for those of higher-rated issuers. The ECB (2007) identifies two possible explanations for this. First, the default probabilities of lower-rated corporate issuers may be more closely linked to the business cycle than the default probabilities of higher-rated corporations. Second, bond spreads widen when bonds become less liquid. During recessions, lower-rated corporate bonds may suffer and be traded less actively, thus reducing their liquidity and leading to higher liquidity premiums. More generally, there is a trade-off between liquidity and transparency in bond markets, which are quote driven. Dealers quote the prices at which they are prepared to trade bonds. To protect dealers with large positions, deals may be published after a delay. Box 5.3 discusses the optimal level of trade transparency in bond markets.

Covered bonds, i.e. debt securities backed by cash flows from mortgages or public sector loans, are an important type of debt security. The covered bond market has become the most important segment of privately issued bonds on Europe's capital markets: the volume outstanding at the end of 2017 was nearly €2.5 trillion (Grossmann and Stöcker, 2018). Covered bonds provide investors with two layers of protection: recourse to the issuing bank's (1) underlying assets (mainly composed of good-quality instruments) and (2) other unsecured assets. By issuing covered bonds, banks retain the assets on their balance sheet or provide guarantees on dedicated structures to which the assets are transferred (ECB, 2011). Since issuers of covered bonds keep the credit risk of covered bond collateral on their balance sheets (and thus guarantee their stake in the game), they are an efficient and simple alternative to complex originate-to-distribute products. Covered bonds also form an important part of collateral used for Eurosystem operations. In the euro area, German financial institutions are the most important issuers of covered bonds (so-called *Pfandbriefe*), followed by those in Spain and France. However, the outstanding amount of covered bonds in Denmark is the largest in the world.

Another type of bonds that has recently become more popular is *contingent convertible bonds* (CoCos). CoCos are hybrid capital securities that absorb losses or are converted into equity in accordance with their contractual terms when the capital of the issuing bank falls below a certain level. They are attractive for banks due to their potential to satisfy regulatory capital requirements. CoCo issuance activity by banks picked up strongly

Box 5.3 How much transparency is optimal?

Transparency refers to the absence or elimination of information asymmetries. In a fully transparent market, all relevant market information is common knowledge for all participants. According to Dunne *et al.* (2006), the very existence of most financial markets depends on striking a balance between transparency (which is thought to promote competition, fairness, and investor protection) and opacity, in the interest of encouraging the ongoing participation of both end customers and liquidity providers. If market participants do not obtain adequate fairness, protection, and incentives, they will not participate in sufficient numbers and the market will not function properly.

This dilemma can be illustrated by the so-called winner's curse, according to which the highest bidder has probably bid too much. If the highest bidder wants to resell the product immediately after the auction, the best price he will obtain is the underbidder's price. Because of incomplete information or subjective factors, bidders will form a range of estimates of the item's 'intrinsic value'. As a result, the largest overestimation of an item's value ends up winning the auction. With perfect information and fully rational participants skilled in valuation, no overpayments should occur. A number of dealers submit quotes, and the highest-bidding dealer secures the bonds. Typically, the successful dealer enters the inter-dealer market to hedge his risk. The underbidders are aware of this and can benefit by taking up contrarian positions in the market, thereby making it difficult for the successful bidder to square his position. The more transparent the inter-dealer market, the more difficult it is for the successful bidder to hedge his risk. Consequently, an increase in market transparency makes dealers more cautious about participating.

Yet there are powerful arguments in favour of enhancing transparency. For instance, it allows investors to verify whether dealers and others indeed execute orders at the best price available. Goldstein *et al.* (2007) observe a decrease in transaction costs that is consistent with investors' ability to negotiate better terms of trade with dealers once investors have access to broader bond-pricing data. Costs may also be lower for bonds with transparent prices (see Edwards *et al.*, 2007). Greater price transparency can enhance investor protection, as price movements signal default probabilities. Strengthening overall transparency may also create a level playing field between large institutional investors (which may be able to obtain all relevant information) and smaller investors, which are not able to exert the same pressure on dealers.

Finally, transparency may improve liquidity. Harris and Piwowar (2006) argue that ongoing regulatory initiatives to increase transparency in the municipal bond market will lead to liquidity improvements. These improvements should have the greatest impact on retail investors. Goldstein *et al.* (2007) find that enhancing corporate bond markets' transparency has either a neutral or positive effect on liquidity. These findings seem contradictory to what has been argued by Dunne *et al.* (2006). However, Casey (2006) stresses that pre- and post-trade transparency may equally enhance or harm market liquidity and efficiency, depending on how they are applied, by whom, for what instruments, in which markets, and at which latency.

in 2013 and 2014, due to banks' efforts to issue CRR/CRD IV-compliant instruments (see Chapter 12 for further details).

The total outstanding amount of CoCos issued by European banks tripled between 2012 and 2015 to reach a record high of €157 billion. By the end of 2015, 64 European banks (mostly British and Swiss) had raised additional capital by issuing CoCos. Euro-area financial investors in general, including banks, insurers, and pension funds, had very limited direct exposure to CoCos by the end of 2015. Foreign investors outside the euro area, and euro-area investment funds located in Ireland and Luxembourg, hold the large majority of European CoCos (Boermans and van Wijnbergen, 2017).

Securitised Instruments

Despite their similarities, covered bonds are different from securitised products. The key difference is that covered bonds do not involve credit risk transfer. The credit risk stays with the originator, which must hold capital (against the risk of losses) but typically obtains cheaper funding through the covered bond issuance (ECB, 2007).

In the decade prior to the recent financial crisis, there was an unprecedented expansion in the use of *funded securitisation*, a process in which individual bank loans and other financial assets are bundled together into tradable securities, which are then sold on to investors. The most commonly securitised assets were initially mortgage loans, but in the run-up to the global financial crisis, more sophisticated forms of securitisation were developed and/or used more frequently, including synthetic securitisation. *Synthetic securitisation* transfers the risk via a credit protection contract between the originator (the bank) and the investor, leaving the underlying exposures (loans) in the hands of the originator and on its balance sheet. The banks seeking to securitise get the insurance they need but keep the loans they have generated. As a result, banks and other corporations were able to securitise large portions of their credit book (Marques-Ibanez, 2017). Securitisation amounts outstanding peaked at €2 trillion in Europe and US$11 trillion in the US. They have since contracted sharply; in Europe aggregate issuance has been notably lower since the crisis, with only €174 billion issued in 2013 (including retained issuance), equivalent to roughly 40 per cent of the pre-crisis annual rate (BoE and ECB, 2014). As Figure 5.10 shows, also in more recent years securitisation in Europe has not picked up. In particular, new issuance of residential mortgage-backed securities in Europe has fallen markedly. *Mortgage-backed securities* are backed by mortgage loans, both residential and commercial. Figure

€ trillion

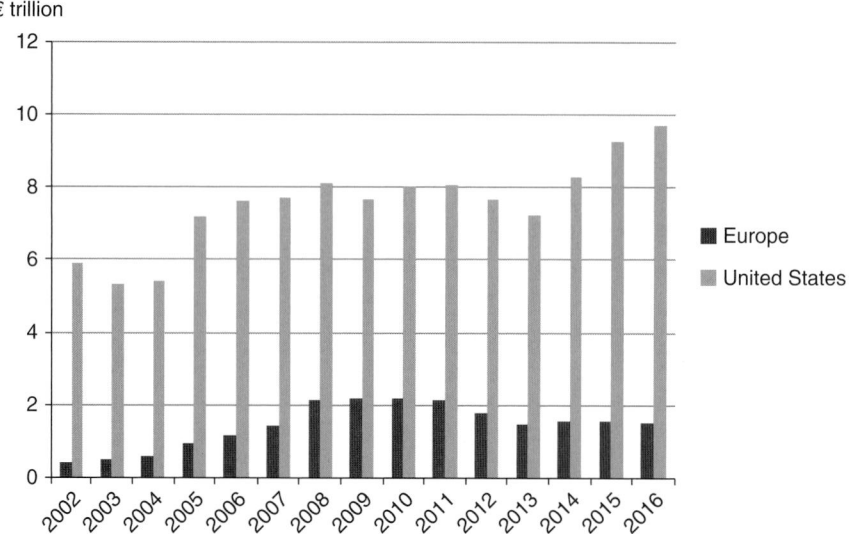

Figure 5.10 Securitisation in Europe and the US, 2002–2016 (outstanding figures, $ billion)
Source: Marques-Ibanez (2017)

5.10 also illustrates that securitisation in the US is at a much higher level and did not drop as much as in Europe after the financial crisis.

5.4 Equity Markets

Equities grant the investor a residual right to receive income from the company's earnings. Equity can be issued either privately (unquoted shares) or publicly via shares that are listed on a stock exchange (quoted shares). Equity finance is less important in the EU than in the US and Asia, as shown in Table 5.3 (see also Figure 5.1). There are also large differences within Europe. As Table 5.3 shows, the market capitalisations of Euronext and the LSE are much higher than those of other exchanges in the EU.

Consolidation

The EU stock market is highly concentrated, perhaps because EU financial exchanges exhibit network externalities, as higher levels of trader participation on both sides of the market positively affect market liquidity and increase traders' utility.

Table 5.3 The world's largest equity exchanges, 2017

	Exchange	Market capitalisation (€ billion)	Traded firms (number)	Turnover (€ billion)
1	NYSE	18,401	2,286	12,113
2	NASDAQ US	8,366	2,949	9,447
3	Japan Exchange Group	5,186	3,604	4,838
4	Shanghai Stock Exchange	4,237	1,396	6,298
5	London SE Group	3,718	2,577	2,241
6	Euronext	3,661	1,255	1,605
7	Hong Kong Exchanges	3,626	2,118	1,633
8	Shenzhen Stock Exchange	3,015	2,089	7,639
9	Toronto Stock Exchange	1,973	3,328	1,037
10	National Stock Exchange of India	1,959	1,897	844
11	Bombay Stock Exchange	1,943	5,616	124
12	Deutsche Börse	1,885	499	1,223
13	Korea Exchange	1,477	2,134	1,584
14	SIX Swiss Exchange	1,405	263	783
15	NASDAQ Nordic	1,278	984	662
16	Australian Stock Exchange	1,257	2,147	689
17	Johannesburg Stock Exchange	1,026	366	318
18	Taiwan Stock Exchange	894	924	644
19	Brasil Exchange	796	343	556
20	BME Spanish Exchanges	741	3,136	582

Source: World Federation of Exchanges

There has been an intensive regional cross-border consolidation of stock exchanges. First, Euronext resulted from a merger of the Paris, Amsterdam, Brussels, and Lisbon stock exchanges during 2000–2002. Next, the stock exchanges of Copenhagen, Stockholm, Helsinki, Tallin, Riga, Vilnius, and Iceland merged between 2004 and 2006, creating the OMX Nordic Exchange. In 2006, the first transatlantic stock exchange merger took place between Euronext and the New York Stock Exchange (NYSE), strengthening its position as the largest securities trading venue in the world. This merger was subsequently unravelled in 2014. Euronext is now the largest stock exchange in the eurozone. In 2008, a merger between Nasdaq and OMX was completed, creating Nasdaq Nordic, while Italy's stock exchange operator Borsa Italiana accepted a takeover from the LSE. In 2011, BATS (Better Alternative Trading System) Global Markets acquired Chi-X Europe, a London-based, order-driven pan-European equity exchange. BATS is the operator of the third-largest stock exchange in the US.

European regulators blocked an attempted merger between the German and British stock exchanges in March 2017 on the grounds that it would generate a monopoly in the processing of bond trades. The European Commission has the duty to assess mergers and acquisitions involving companies with a turnover above certain thresholds and to prevent concentrations that would significantly impede effective competition (see Chapter 14). On 18 June 2019, Euronext acquired Oslo Børs, which became the Group's central exchange in the Nordic region.

Consolidation may have advantages. For example, bigger exchanges enjoy economies of scale that reduce trading costs, which in turn attracts more traders and listed companies (Wharton, 2006). The market capitalisation of Euronext and the LSE has grown faster than that of its smaller competitors (see Figure 5.11). However, consolidation may also reduce competition and thus lower an exchange's incentive for financial innovation (in the form of developing new, cheaper trading mechanisms). While competition may reduce equity trading fees, fragmentation of the order flow between exchanges may reduce the liquidity of equity trading. Examining the competition between Euronext and the LSE in the Dutch equity market, Foucault and Menkveld (2008) find evidence of reduced fees and improved liquidity. Liquidity is improved as some brokers automate the routing decision between the two exchanges to obtain the best execution price, which indirectly combines the order flow at the two exchanges.

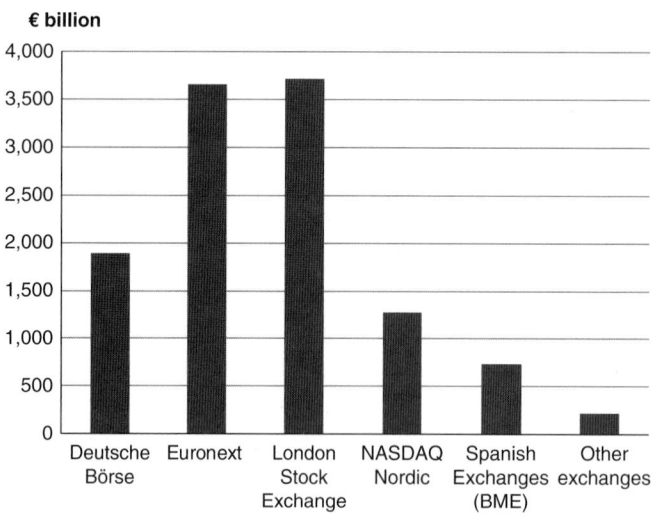

Figure 5.11   Market capitalisation of sample exchanges in the EU, 2017 (€ billion)
Source: World Federation of Exchanges

Yet consolidation produces challenges. First, Europe's clearing and settlement infrastructure remains fragmented. Second, as documented in Chapter 7, post-trading costs per transaction in the EU are substantially higher than in the US. Next, cross-border exchanges like Euronext and OMX force national financial supervisors to cooperate (see Chapter 12).

Initial Public Offerings

In Europe, public equity markets play a limited role as a source of new funds for listed corporations. Debt financing via bank loans or bonds is more important than financing via quoted shares. This pattern is in line with the pecking-order theory (Myers and Majluf, 1984), which suggests that companies adopt a hierarchy of financial preferences. Due to asymmetric information, companies prefer internal financing (i.e. retained earnings) to external financing. If external financing is needed, they first seek debt funding. Equity is issued only as a last resort.

When issuing public equity, a firm may obtain a listing on a stock exchange for the first time, the *initial public offering* (IPO). If a firm is already listed and issues additional shares, this is called a *seasoned equity offering* or *secondary public offering*. A firm issuing equity at a stock exchange may decide to substitute existing unquoted shares for quoted ones (in which case the proceeds go to the initial investors), or to issue newly created shares (the funds raised accrue to the firm).

Firms have a variety of motivations to hold an IPO, the most obvious of which is to obtain funds to finance investment. Listing a firm's shares on a stock exchange also increases its financial autonomy, as it becomes less dependent on a single financial provider (such as a bank). Further, by issuing equity, the firm's owners can diversify their investment risk by selling stakes in the company in a liquid market. Another advantage of public issuance is increased recognition of the company name. In addition, from the time of the IPO, investors receive better information due to improved transparency and the disclosure requirements that are part of the listing conditions. At the same time, the price of a company's stock serves as a measure of its value and as a disciplining mechanism for managers.

However, there are a number of disadvantages for a company inherent in listing its shares on a stock exchange. For instance, equity issuance is expensive, involving costs such as underwriters' commission, legal fees, and other charges resulting primarily from the need to satisfy the additional disclosure requirements. From an investor's perspective, going public implies that the ownership of the company is likely to be shared more widely, resulting in a larger gap between external investors and managers. This separation of ownership and control could cause agency problems, in which company insiders hold more accurate information on the firm's prospects than external equity investors, resulting in a divergence between managers' and outside investors' interests. Lastly, going public exposes a company to scrutiny by shareholders, who may be excessively focused on short-term results.

While it is difficult to disentangle the different factors motivating a company's decision to issue public equity, the economic cycle is likely to play a significant role because equity is often used to finance capital formation, which fluctuates over the business cycle. Furthermore, significant increases in stock market prices generally precede increases in equity issuance. In the literature on behavioural finance (Shiller, 2003), investor sentiment also helps explain the timing of equity issuance. Developments in investor optimism over time may affect the cost of equity, thereby influencing the amount issued. For example, an excessive focus on risk aversion that resulted in falling stock market prices could raise the cost of equity, thereby dissuading companies from issuing it. Although investor sentiment will inevitably change over time, it is difficult to measure risk aversion empirically, and/or investors' willingness to invest in the stock market. Companies also issue equity to finance the acquisition of other companies, either by using the cash proceeds of public offerings or by issuing shares, which are subsequently exchanged for the shares of a target company. Consequently, merger and acquisition cycles can also be expected to correlate with equity issuance activity.

Figure 5.12 shows that the IPO market contracted in 2009 (in line with the economic downturn after the financial crisis) and again in 2012 and 2013 (after the euro crisis). The IPO market only started to recover in 2014. European IPO proceeds reached €36.6 billion in 2018, down from €45.1 billion in 2017. IPO proceeds on the top two exchanges, the LSE and Deutsche Börse, were nearly identical (€10.8 billion and €10.7 billion, respectively), but represented 17 and 82 IPOs, respectively (source: PwC).

5.5 Derivatives

Derivatives are financial instruments with a value derived from the value of the underlying financial instruments. They can be based on different types of assets (such as equities or commodities), prices (such as interest rates or

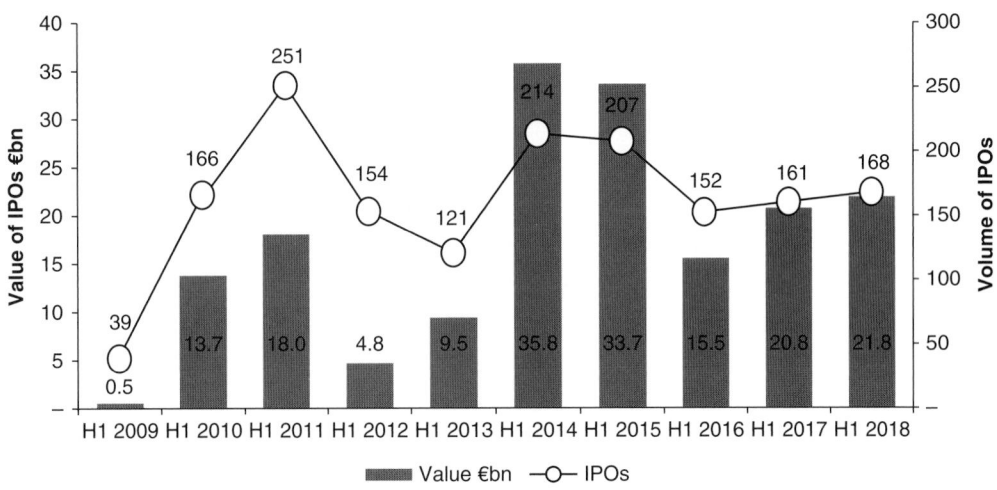

Figure 5.12　IPOs in Europe: value (left) and number (right), 2009–2018 (up to Q2) (€ billion)
Source: PwC

exchange rates), or indexes (such as a stock market index). Derivatives can be used as a source of revenue, but are also important risk management tools (see Batten *et al.*, 2004). The BIS (1994) stresses that derivatives allow parties to identify, isolate, and manage the market risk associated with financial instruments and commodities, i.e. changes in the market prices of financial instruments and shifts in interest and exchange rates. When used properly, derivatives can reduce risks through hedging by transferring the cost of bearing the risk from one party to another; the former wants to reduce its exposure to risk, whereas the latter is willing to assume exposure to risk since it expects to make a profit (Reilly, 2005).

Financial innovation and increased market demand led to a rapid growth in derivatives trading until 2007 (see Figure 5.13). After the onset of the financial crisis, the global derivatives markets stabilised, albeit at a very high level, and decreased after 2013. After the financial crisis, reforms to encourage central clearing of OTC derivatives were introduced to reduce bilateral counterparty risk (which could cause a cascade of failures among major OTC traders). The central counterparty clearing parties provide netting and compression, which reduces the number of outstanding trades. In 2017 the notional amount of outstanding OTC derivatives was around $500 trillion, while exchange traded derivatives totalled $80 trillion.

Trading in derivatives has a major impact on asset management and risk management. Derivatives are a low-cost tool for risk management. A portfolio

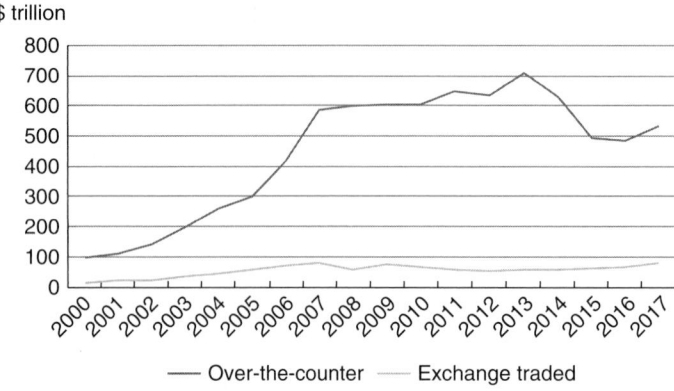

$ trillion

— Over-the-counter — Exchange traded

Figure 5.13 Global derivatives markets ($ trillion), notional amounts, 2000–2017
Source: Bank for International Settlements

manager can change its risk profile through derivative transactions at a very low cost. Transactions in the underlying cash markets (i.e. money, bond, or equity markets), including the transfer of securities, are much more expensive. Moreover, derivatives can be tailor-made in the OTC market (see below). The spectacular growth of hedge funds can also be explained by the rise of low-cost derivatives markets. Hedge funds typically exploit small price differences of similar financial products, as explained in Chapter 9. Only when the transaction cost is smaller than the price differential will they take a position.

There are two broad types of derivatives: forwards and options. A *forward contract* obliges the holder to buy or sell a certain underlying instrument (like a bond) at a certain date in the future (the delivery or final settlement date), at a specified price (the settlement price). Two examples are futures and swaps. *Futures contracts* are forward contracts traded on organised exchanges. *Swaps* are forward contracts in which counterparties agree to exchange streams of cash flows according to predetermined rules. For example, an *interest rate swap* is a derivative in which one party exchanges a stream of interest payments for another party's stream of cash flows. *Options*, by contrast, give the holder the right (but not the obligation) to buy or sell a particular underlying instrument at a certain date in the future at a specified price (Hull, 2018).

Derivatives are traded on *organised exchanges* or *OTC*. The oldest official derivatives market in Europe is the European Options Exchange in Amsterdam, which started to trade stock options in 1978; it later became part of the Amsterdam Exchanges and subsequently Euronext. The London International Financial Futures and Options Exchange (LIFFE) began its operations in 1982 using a system of open-outcry floor trading, but eventually moved to electronic trading. Derivatives exchanges were later opened in continental Europe; some used open-outcry floor trading, and others such as the Deutsche Terminbörse (DTB) introduced electronic trading. DTB, founded in 1991, introduced trading of futures on the Bund, i.e. German government bonds, in direct competition with a contract already trading at LIFFE. By 1998, the DTB had competed the Bund contract away from LIFFE (Anderson and McKay, 2008).

EUREX is a serious competitor to LIFFE in the area of bond and short-term interest rate futures and options trading in Europe. This German–Swiss joint venture was created by the merger of the DTB and the Swiss Options and Financial Futures Exchange (SOFFEX) in 1998. Today, it trades a wide range of bond and money market derivative products. Access to the market is available in a number of major cities, including Chicago, New York, London, and Tokyo (Batten *et al.*, 2004).

OTC contracts are traded (and privately negotiated) directly between two parties. All contract terms, such as delivery quality, quantity, location, date, and price, are negotiable (Anderson and McKay, 2008). As Figure 5.13 shows, the trade in OTC derivatives dwarfs the trade in derivatives via exchanges. The UK is the leading OTC derivative market in the world. Derivatives such as swaps and forward rate agreements are generally traded on OTC markets. Derivative contracts (such as futures contracts and options) that are transacted on an organised futures exchange are standardised. However, Anderson and McKay (2008) point out that the traditional distinction between exchange-based and OTC derivatives has become less clear. For instance, the International Swaps and Derivatives Association has provided a contract with standard pre-conditions, which has made OTC markets more accessible. Furthermore, OTC trades are increasingly being cleared through clearinghouses in much the same way as exchange-based contracts.

Table 5.4 shows the outstanding amounts of the different types of OTC derivatives. Interest rate derivatives dominate the market, followed by foreign exchange (FX) derivatives. Financial institutions, corporations, and government agencies use these derivatives to manage their interest rate and FX risks. Credit derivatives are discussed below. The reduction of outstanding OTC derivatives from 2013 to 2017 reflects the netting and compression of OTC trades at central counterparty clearing parties.

Figure 5.14 shows that the average daily turnover in the various OTC derivatives markets increased rapidly at the beginning of the 2000s. In

Table 5.4 Amounts of outstanding OTC derivatives ($ trillion), 2005–2017

	2005	2009	2013	2017
Interest rate derivatives	229	490	601	427
Foreign exchange derivatives	38	60	79	87
Credit derivatives	20	43	22	10
Equity-linked derivatives	7	7	7	7
Commodity derivatives	6	4	3	2
Total OTC derivatives	300	604	712	533

Source: Bank for International Settlements

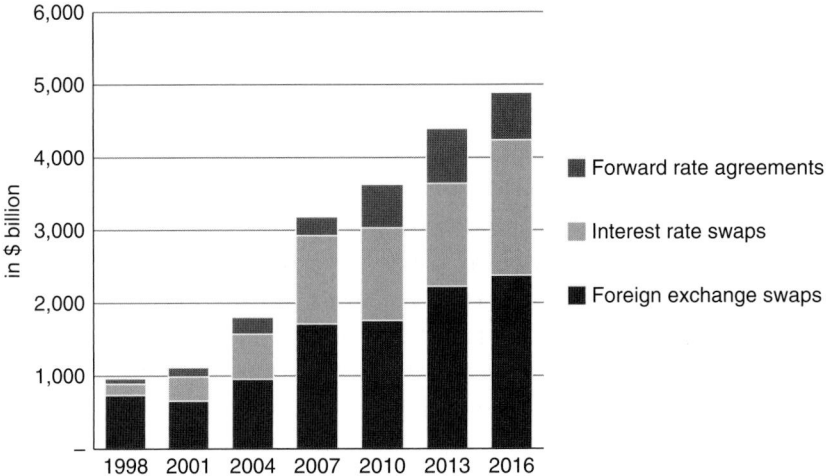

Figure 5.14   Average daily turnover in various OTC derivatives markets ($ billion), 1998–2016
Source: BIS Triennial Central Bank Survey

addition to the forward rate agreement and interest rate swap (IRS) markets – comprising overnight interest rate swaps (OISs, also referred to as EONIA swaps) and other IRSs – the figure shows the share of OTC derivatives linked to the FX market, comprising FX swaps and cross-currency swaps (Xccy swaps). Measured by volume, FX swaps are by far the most important OTC derivatives market segments, followed by other IRSs.

Credit Derivatives

Table 5.4 illustrates that the emergence of credit derivatives has been an important development in the OTC derivatives markets. A *credit derivative* is a contract in which a credit-protection seller promises a payment to a credit-protection buyer contingent upon the occurrence of a credit event (Anderson and McKay, 2008). The types of contracts differ according to the terms and conditions that govern the promised payment, such as the definition of the 'credit event'. Various definitions are used, including formal bankruptcy and default. Increasingly diverse and complex products have appeared, but the most popular type of credit derivative is the single-name *credit default swap* (CDS), in which the protection seller promises to buy a specified bond at par from the protection buyer (Anderson and McKay, 2008). A CDS requires fixed and regular premium payments from the protection buyer to the protection seller until a credit event occurs or the CDS matures. The premium is calculated as a percentage (called *credit spread*) of the nominal value of the reference obligation (the *notional amount*). Multi-name CDSs refer to more reference entities (i.e. the underlying names on which credit risk is exchanged). A CDS resembles an insurance contract, in that it protects the 'protection buyer' against predefined credit events, particularly the risk of default in return for a periodic fee paid to the protection seller. Following a credit event, contracts settle either physically (i.e. through the delivery to the protection buyer of defaulting bonds and/or loans for an amount equivalent to the notional value of the swap) or in cash, with the net amount owed by the protection seller determined after the credit event. CDSs are an attractive instrument for risk management. Protection buyers can transfer credit risks without transferring credit claims or debt securities, while protection sellers can assume credit risks without granting credit or buying debt securities. So, both sides can optimise credit risk portfolios relatively efficiently (ECB, 2007).

Data on notional amounts of CDSs on euro-denominated reference obligations are not available. Table 5.5 describes the development in notional

Table 5.5 Notional amounts of CDSs outstanding ($ trillion), 2005–2017

	2005	2009	2013	2017
Credit default swaps	13.9	35.8	21.1	9.4
– Single-name instruments	10.4	22.9	11.4	4.6
– Multi-name instruments	3.5	12.8	9.7	4.8
– of which index products	–	–	8.7	4.4

Source: Bank for International Settlements

CDS amounts outstanding worldwide. The data indicate initial growth in this market, but after 2009 it shrank very quickly.

The most common maturities of CDSs are 3, 5, 7, and 10 years; 5 years serves as a benchmark. The most active market participants in CDS markets, both as protection buyers and sellers, have been banks, hedge funds, and insurance companies. The majority of reference obligations are bonds or loans rated A or better (ECB, 2007).

5.6 Foreign Exchange Market

Funds transferred from one country to another have to be converted if the countries do not share the same currency. This takes place at the FX market, an OTC market in which banks engage in most of the trading. If countries have a floating exchange rate regime, transactions at the FX market determine the rate at which currencies are exchanged. These transactions consist of buying and selling different currencies. There are two types of transactions: *spot* and *forward transactions*. Spot transactions involve the immediate exchange of currency, while forward transactions involve the exchange of currency at a specified future date.

When a country's currency appreciates, i.e. rises in value vis-à-vis other currencies, its goods become more expensive in other countries, while foreign goods become cheaper. Likewise, a depreciation makes foreign goods more expensive. In other words, the exchange rate affects the rate of inflation. That is why central banks keep a close eye on the exchange rate. Box 5.4 discusses the role of the euro–dollar exchange rate in the ECB's monetary policy.

Figure 5.15 shows the euro exchange rate vis-à-vis the US dollar, the British pound, and the Japanese yen between 1999 and 2018. After 1999 the euro initially depreciated against the dollar, but between 2002 and 2008 it appreciated. During the recent financial crises, the euro strongly fluctuated, reflecting the changing market perceptions of the financial problems in the US and the euro area. In the beginning of 2015, the euro strongly depreciated against the dollar, reflecting the ECB's quantitative easing policies (see Chapter 4).

Not all countries have a floating exchange rate regime. Until 1971 most countries pegged their currency to the dollar. After the demise of the Bretton Woods system, several countries decided to peg their currency to another currency, like the euro. Other countries have a 'floating' or 'crawling' peg, the value of which is adjusted periodically.

Box 5.4 The role of the euro–dollar exchange rate in the ECB's policies

The euro–dollar exchange rate is one indicator of future inflationary developments in the ECB's monetary policy strategy. The ECB has on multiple occasions made it clear that it closely monitors this rate. Several studies have examined the *exchange rate pass-through* (ERPT), i.e. the degree to which exchange rate changes are passed through in (domestic) prices. The ERPT is defined as the percentage change in import prices (in local currency) resulting from a 1 per cent change in the exchange rate between the exporting and importing countries. Firms may choose to pass exchange rate alterations fully into their selling prices (*complete* ERPT) or to absorb the shock by reducing their profit margins, so the selling prices will be unchanged (*no* ERPT). The relationship between exchange rates and prices is given by the following equation:

$$P_t = a + \delta X + \gamma E_t + \psi Z_t + \varepsilon_t \qquad (5.1)$$

where P is the local currency import price and X is a measure of the export costs. Z may include import demand-shifting factors, such as competing prices or income, and E is the exchange rate (importer's currency per unit of exporter's currency). Taking the logarithm of both sides yields the elasticity of ERPT with which γ is referred to as the *pass-through coefficient*. Campa and Goldberg (2005) report that in the long run ERPT is higher than in the short run, but for all European countries in their sample the ERPT is less than 1 in both the short and long run. They also find huge differences in ERPT across euro-area countries.

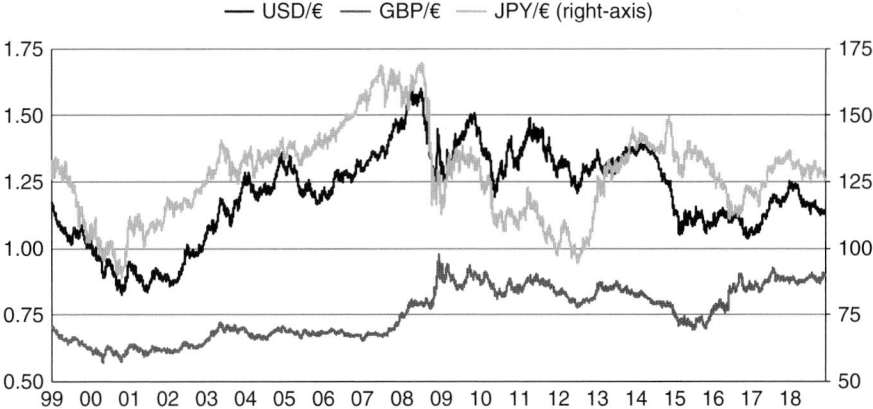

Figure 5.15   The euro exchange rate, 1999–2018
Source: ECB

The *real exchange rate* is the rate at which domestic goods can be exchanged for foreign goods, i.e. the price of domestic goods relative to the price of foreign goods denominated in the domestic currency. So, the real exchange rate (r) can be defined as the nominal exchange rate (e) adjusted by the ratio of the foreign price level (P_f) to the domestic price level (P):

$$r = e * P_f/P \tag{5.2}$$

5.7 Conclusions

Financial markets (1) release information to aid the price discovery process, (2) provide a platform via which to trade, and (3) provide an infrastructure with which to settle trades. The main trading mechanisms are quote- and order-driven markets.

Euro-denominated short-term funds and related derivative instruments are traded on the euro money market. It consists of various segments, including unsecured deposit contracts with various maturities, ranging from overnight to one year, and repurchase agreements (repos, i.e. reverse transactions secured by securities) also ranging from overnight to one year. Credit institutions account for the largest share of the euro money market. The ECB has a major influence on the money market via its use of various monetary policy instruments (reserve requirements, standing facilities, and open market operations). There are three main market interest rates for the money market: EONIA (euro overnight index average), EURIBOR (euro interbank offered rate), and EUREPO (the repo market reference rate for the euro). Recently, EONIA has been replaced by ESTER.

The EU bond market has experienced spectacular growth since the introduction of the euro and is now as large as the US bond market. The bulk of euro-denominated bonds (i.e. debt securities with a maturity of more than one year) is issued by euro-area issuers. Although the share of corporate bonds in all euro-denominated bonds outstanding has risen, government bonds still form the most important market segment. Yield differentials have varied considerably both across and within countries since the introduction of the euro. The issuance of asset-backed securities has increased rapidly over the last decade.

The importance of equity finance in the EU is growing, although there are large differences across exchanges. The market capitalisation of Euronext and the LSE, which are the biggest exchanges in terms of turnover, is much higher than those of other exchanges in the EU. Despite the increase in equity finance, public equity markets play a limited role as a source of new funds for corporations, which generally raise external financing via bank loans or debt securities.

Derivatives are financial instruments with a value derived from the value of underlying financial instruments. They are traded on organised or OTC exchanges. Derivatives can provide a source of income, but are also important risk management tools. The most important derivatives are futures, forwards, options, and swaps. In the run-up to the financial crisis, credit derivatives became important, but declined afterwards. Credit derivatives are contracts in which a credit-protection seller promises a payment to a credit-protection buyer contingent upon the occurrence of a particular credit event.

If countries have a floating exchange rate regime, transactions on the FX market determine the rate at which currencies are exchanged. Central banks closely monitor changes in the exchange rate, since they affect the rate of inflation.

Notes

1. Since company insiders may have more information than outsiders, regulation typically forbids insider trading (see Chapter 12).
2. In addition, the derivatives market has become increasingly important in recent years. The derivative money market segments can be grouped into exchange-traded instruments, such as short-term interest rate futures and options, and instruments that are typically traded OTC. This section will focus on unsecured deposit markets and secured repo markets.
3. See www.emmi-benchmarks.eu/euribor-eonia-org/panel-banks.html for an overview of the banks in the panel.
4. The modified duration measures the change in the current value of the debt portfolio when the yield of the portfolio changes by 1 basis point.
5. The lower limit for government securities to be eligible for trading on EuroMTS is €5 billion.

Bibliography

Suggested Reading

Harris, L. E. (2003), *Trading and Exchanges: Market Microstructure for Practitioners*, Oxford University Press.

Hull, J. C. (2018), *Options, Futures, and Other Derivatives*, 10th edition, Pearson Education, New York.

References

Anderson, R. W. and K. McKay (2008), Derivatives Markets. In: X. Freixas, P. Hartmann, and C. Mayer (eds.), *Handbook of European Financial Markets and Institutions*, Oxford University Press, 568–96.

Baele, L., A. Ferrando, P. Hordahl, E. Krylova, and C. Monnet (2004), Measuring Financial Integration in the Euro Area. ECB Occasional Paper 14.

Bailey, R. E. (2005), *The Economics of Financial Markets*, Cambridge University Press.

Bank of England/European Central Bank (2014), *The Case for a Better Functioning Securitisation Market in the European Union*, BoE/ECB, London/Frankfurt am Main.

Bank for International Settlements (1994), *Risk Management Guidelines for Derivatives*, BIS, Basel.

Batten, J., T. Fetherson, and P. G. Szilagi (eds.) (2004), *European Fixed Income Markets: Money, Bonds, and Interest Rate Derivatives*, John Wiley & Sons, Chichester.

Boermans, M. and S. van Wijnbergen (2017), Contingent Convertible Bonds: Who Invests in European CoCos? DNB Working Paper 543.

Campa, J. M. and L. S. Goldberg (2005), Exchange Rate Pass-Through into Import Prices. *The Review of Economics and Statistics*, 87, 679–90.

Casey, J. P. (2006), Bond Market Transparency: To Regulate or Not To Regulate. Policy Brief, European Capital Markets Institute, Brussels.

Dunne, P., M. Moore, and R. Portes (2006), *European Government Bond Markets: Transparency, Liquidity, Efficiency*, CEPR, London.

Edwards, A. K., L. E. Harris, and M. S. Piwowar (2007), Corporate Bond Market Transaction Costs and Transparency. *Journal of Finance*, 62, 1421–54.

European Central Bank (2007), *The Euro Bonds and Derivatives Markets*, ECB, Frankfurt am Main.

(2008), *Bond Markets and Long-Term Interest Rates in Non-Euro Area Member States of the European Union – Statistical Tables*, ECB, Frankfurt am Main.

(2011), *Recent Developments in Securitisation*, ECB, Frankfurt am Main.

European Commission (2017), *Analysis of European Corporate Bond Markets*, EC, Brussels.

Foucault, T. and A. J. Menkveld (2008), Competition for Order Flow and Smart Order Routing Systems. *Journal of Finance*, 63, 119–58.

Goldstein, M. A., E. Hotchkiss, and E. Sirri (2007), Transparency and Liquidity: A Controlled Experiment on Corporate Bonds. *Review of Financial Studies*, 20, 235–73.

Grossmann, R. and O. Stöcker (2018), Overview of Covered Bonds. In: *ICBC Factbook 2018*, European Covered Bond Council, Brussels.

Harris, L. E. (2003), *Trading and Exchanges: Market Microstructure for Practitioners*, Oxford University Press.

Harris L. E. and M. S. Piwowar (2006), Secondary Trading Costs in the Municipal Bond Market. *Journal of Finance*, 61, 1361–97.

Hartmann, P., M. Manna, and A. Manzanares (2001), The Microstructure of the Euro Money Market. ECB Working Paper 80.

Holmstrom, B. (2015), Understanding the Role of Debt in the Financial System. BIS Working Paper 479.

Hull, J. C. (2018), *Options, Futures, and Other Derivatives*, 10th edition, Pearson Education, New York.

Marques-Ibanez, D. (2017), Securitisation, Credit Risk and Lending Standards Revisited. Research Bulletin 32, European Central Bank, Frankfurt am Main.

Myers, S. and N. Majluf (1984), Corporate Financing and Investment Decisions when Firms Have Information that Investors Do Not Have. *Journal of Financial Economics*, 13, 187–221.

O'Hara, M. (2003), Presidential Address: Liquidity and Price Discovery. *Journal of Finance*, 58, 1335–53.

Organisation for Economic Co-operation and Development (2018), *OECD Sovereign Borrowing Outlook*, OECD, Paris.

Reilly, A. (2005), Over-the-Counter Derivatives Markets in Ireland – An Overview. *CBFSAI Quarterly Bulletin*, Dublin, July.

Shiller, R. J. (2003), From Efficient Markets to Behavioral Finance. *Journal of Economic Perspectives*, 17, 83–104.

Wharton (2006), LSE, NYSE, OMX, Nasdaq, Euronext … Why Stock Exchanges Are Scrambling to Consolidate. Knowledge@Wharton, Wharton School, University of Pennsylvania.

Wolswijk, G. and J. de Haan (2005), Government Debt Management in the Euro Area: Recent Theoretical Developments and Changes in Practices. ECB Occasional Paper 25.

6

The Economics of Financial Integration

OVERVIEW

This chapter begins by defining financial integration and identifying its drivers. Financial integration is a situation without frictions that discriminate between economic agents in their access to – and investment of – capital, particularly on the basis of their location. Market forces as well as collective action and public action drive financial integration.

The second part of the chapter describes different methods of measuring the degree of financial integration, and distinguishes between price-based and quantity-based measures. Price-based indicators measure discrepancies in prices or returns on assets caused by the geographic origin of the assets. Quantity-based indicators measure the effects of frictions on quantities, like cross-border activities or listings, and statistics on investors' cross-border holdings.

The third part of the chapter gives an overview of the extent to which various financial markets in the EU are integrated. The financial crisis and the euro crisis represent serious setbacks for European financial integration. An important reason why the EU placed the creation of a single financial market and the Capital Markets Union high on the policy agenda is that it widely believed that financial integration would stimulate economic growth. The chapter concludes by discussing this growth effect and other consequences of financial integration.

LEARNING OBJECTIVES

After you have studied this chapter, you should be able to:

- define financial integration
- explain what drives financial integration
- describe the various ways to measure financial integration, and discuss their short-comings and underlying reasoning

- assess the extent to which various financial markets in the EU are integrated
- discuss the consequences of financial integration

6.1 Financial Integration: Definition and Drivers

Definition of Financial Integration

While legal restrictions on international capital flows were abolished in the late 1980s (see Chapter 3), financial market segmentation due to exchange rate risk persisted until the start of monetary union in 1999. The introduction of the euro was a powerful catalyst for the creation of integrated financial markets, since it removed one of the most important obstacles to the cross-border provision of financial services. Yet it became clear that there were other impediments to creating truly integrated financial markets, such as different regulations and institutions across EU Member States.

This chapter adopts the definition of an *integrated financial market* from Baele *et al.* (2008). The market for a given set of financial instruments and/or services is fully integrated if all potential market participants with the same relevant characteristics meet three criteria:

- face a single set of rules when deciding whether to use those financial instruments and/or services;
- have equal access to these financial instruments and/or services; and
- are treated equally when they are active in the market.

Full integration requires equal access to banks or trading, clearing, and settlement platforms for both borrowers and lenders, regardless of their country of origin. There can be no discrimination among comparable market participants based solely on their location (Baele *et al.*, 2004).

Drivers of Financial Integration

According to the ECB (2003), there are three primary drivers of financial integration: (1) market forces, (2) collective action, and (3) public action. Each of these is discussed in turn below.

Market Forces

Enhanced competition reduces the cost of capital, which benefits firms by reallocating capital more efficiently to the most productive investment

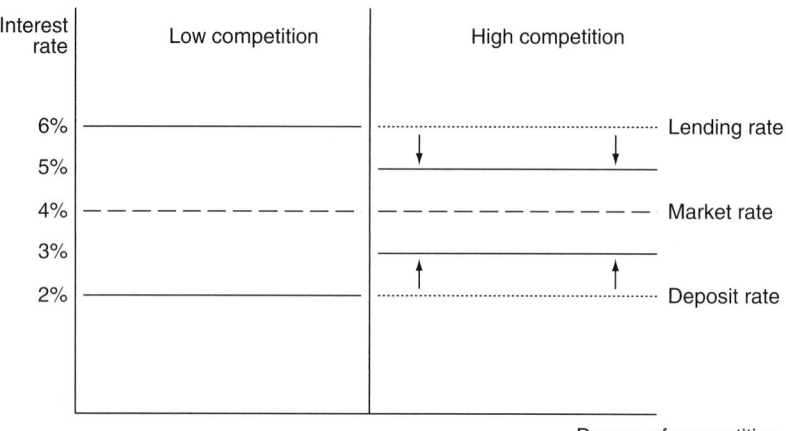

Figure 6.1   Impact of enhanced competition

opportunities. Investors also benefit from access to a broader range of financial instruments and more opportunities to diversify their portfolios. The complete elimination of barriers to trading, clearing, and settlement platforms will allow firms to choose the most efficient platforms. Financial intermediaries may profit by exploiting the potential economies of scale and scope that a larger market offers; yet they may also face pressure on their profit margins.

Figure 6.1 illustrates the impact of enhanced competition. The starting position is a market rate of 4 per cent. In a segmented market with low competition, a bank lends to firms at 6 per cent and offers depositors a return of 2 per cent. The bank earns a margin of 4 per cent. As markets integrate, increased competition forces the bank to reduce its lending rate to 5 per cent and to increase its deposit rate to 3 per cent. The lending firms experience lower capital costs, while depositors receive a higher return. The margin for the bank is reduced to 2 per cent. The bank can (partly) offset the reduction of its profit margin by increasing its business in an integrated market.

Since investors and financial intermediaries may benefit from financial integration, market forces could lead to the elimination of market segmentation. For instance, the issuance practices of government bond issuers converged towards what was perceived to be 'best' practice because they had to compete to attract investors (see Box 5.2). Likewise, mergers of stock exchanges, clearinghouses, and securities settlement systems are often motivated by attempts to exploit the economies of scale and scope potentially available within a broader market. Of course, market forces can foster integration only if there are no legislative or regulatory obstacles standing in the way.

Collective Action

Sometimes market forces alone cannot remove obstacles to integration, particularly those caused by network externalities in the financial system. The greater the number of participants that use a particular market, the more benefits it generally brings to its users. These benefits include greater depth and liquidity, reduced transaction costs, as well as easier and more effective opportunities for risk management (ECB, 2003). Individual market participants will not take these externalities into account. Through collective action, market participants can, for instance, agree on standard technical features of financial instruments, the definition of common practices and conventions, or the establishment of reference indices. However, the existence of powerful network externalities may also hamper integration, as strong network effects are often associated with high switching costs, i.e. the cost of switching from one set of organisation, practices, conventions, rules, and infrastructure to another. A switch to a pan-European market entails costs – at least in the short term – for participants in national markets (ECB, 2003).

In 1998 a series of market conventions sponsored by several market organisations stimulated the process of financial integration. One such convention was the rules applicable to the EURIBOR (the rate at which euro interbank term deposits are offered by one prime bank to another at 11:00 CET), which at the time served as the basic market interest reference rate. A similar initiative permitted the establishment of the other basic interest reference rate for overnight unsecured interbank deposits, the EONIA, which was replaced by ESTER in 2020. In 2002, another market convention added a new reference index, the EUREPO – the rate at which one prime bank offers funds in euros to another prime bank if in the exchange the lender receives eligible assets as collateral from the borrower (see Chapter 5 for further details).

Another good example of collective action is the creation of the Single Euro Payments Area (SEPA) that allows customers to make non-cash euro payments to any beneficiary located anywhere in the euro area using a single bank account and a single set of payment instruments. This is a major step towards integration. Despite the introduction of the euro in 1999 and the development of TARGET (the EU-wide large-value payment system operated by the European System of Central Banks; see Chapter 7), retail payments continued to be processed differently throughout the euro area until 2002, when the banking industry created the European Payments Council, which defined the new rules and procedures for euro payments.

SEPA's goal is to create an integrated, competitive, and innovative retail payments market for all non-cash euro payments.

Public Action

While financial integration first and foremost affects financial markets, it affects the rest of the economy as well, which justifies the involvement of public authorities to support its development towards an optimal outcome. For example, where a public good cannot be supplied privately or where a market or coordination failure occurs (ECB, 2003), neither market forces alone nor collective action within the private sector is sufficient to deliver the desirable level of integration. In such a situation, action by public authorities can serve as a catalyst or facilitator of collective action to help overcome coordination problems. Public action can also extend to direct intervention, as in the case of the development of TARGET. The public authorities' primary responsibility is to establish an appropriate legislative and regulatory framework.

An example of such public intervention is the European Commission's Financial Services Action Plan (FSAP), described in Chapter 3, which aimed to create a single wholesale market and an open and secure retail market. FSAP involved the regulation of cross-border euro payments. Regulation No. 2560/2001, later replaced by Regulation No. 924/2009, guarantees EU consumers that when they make a payment in euros up to €50,000 to an account in another EU Member State, it will cost the same as it would in their own Member State. According to the European Commission (2006), prior to this regulation, charges for cross-border euro payments were often excessive: a €100 transfer cost the consumer an average of €24; the same transfer now costs less than €2.50 on average.

Another recent example of public action is the Capital Markets Union initiative as discussed in Chapter 3. This policy initiative aims to catalyse financial integration and development in the EU. The initiative entails regulatory and non-regulatory measures to ensure the completion of the single market for capital, thereby establishing the conditions for the development and deeper integration of capital markets.

6.2 Measuring Financial Integration

The level of integration of financial markets can be assessed using two categories of measures. The first broad category consists of *price-based indicators*, which measure discrepancies in prices or returns on assets generated by the geographic origin of the assets. Most empirical research on financial market integration in Europe compares the rates of return on assets. For return differentials to be a reliable test of integration, the assets concerned should have identical cash flows and risk characteristics but be traded in different countries. The risk of an asset's return is composed of a systematic part and an idiosyncratic part; the latter can be diversified away, while the former cannot. While this type of risk may be considered negligible in some cases, for example in the money market before the crisis, it is crucial to control for it in the corporate bond and equity markets (Baele *et al.*, 2004). The fact that changes in asset price differentials may reflect divergences in domestic macroeconomic fundamentals or issuer-specific factors should generally caution against interpreting price dispersion measures as direct evidence of the state of financial integration (ECB, 2018).

The second category of measures consists of *quantity-based indicators*, which quantify the effects of frictions faced by the demand for and supply of investment opportunities. Examples include statistics related to the ease of market access, such as cross-border activities or listings, and cross-border holdings of securities. Increased cross-border traffic typically indicates an increase in integration. However, in a fully integrated market, where prices are the same everywhere, there is no need for cross-border activity. The remainder of this section provides further details on particular measures of financial integration.

Price-Based Measures

The construction of price-based integration measures for the money and government bond markets is facilitated by the fact that relatively homogeneous assets are available across countries. A widely used measure in research on the integration of government bond markets is the *difference between local yields and a given benchmark*, which is often the German yield. In the market for 10-year government bonds, for instance, market participants consider German bonds as the reference bond. Consequently, it seems reasonable to measure integration in this segment of the bond market by calculating the spread between the yield on a local asset and the German benchmark asset. In perfectly integrated markets, the spread should be equal to zero. The time variation in the size of the spread is often used as an indicator of how integration is proceeding in a particular country and market. However, price-based measures may be problematic under stressed market conditions, because they may not adequately control for underlying risk characteristics, and therefore do not clearly distinguish effects stemming from changes in issuers' credit standing from the effects of financial integration (ECB, 2011).

A second group of price-based indicators of financial integration refers to the *dispersion of prices*. This can, for instance, be calculated by taking the standard deviation of yields across countries. If the cross-sectional standard deviation $sd(i)_t$ is zero, the law of one price applies fully. The degree of financial integration increases when the cross-sectional standard deviation has a downward trend (moves towards zero).

$$sd(i)_t = \sqrt[2]{\frac{(R_{i,t} - \bar{R}_t)^2}{n}} \tag{6.1}$$

where $R_{i,t}$ is the yield in country i at time t and $\bar{R}_t$ is the average yield across countries at time t.

Another indicator measuring price dispersion is the interquartile range of a particular interest rate. The ECB (2018) employs this proxy to assess the integration of the money markets in the euro area. It is calculated by first putting a country's daily money market rates, like EONIA or EURIBOR, in ascending order. The interquartile range is the difference between the third and first quantiles. A lower (higher) dispersion indicates higher (lower) money market integration.

One of the indicators the ECB (2018) uses to assess the integration of equity markets is based on a segregation (i.e. the opposite of integration) measure proposed by Bekaert *et al.* (2011). The index is constructed as follows. For each calendar month and industry sector, the absolute difference is calculated between the stock market valuation (based on analyst forecasts) of a specific sector for a given country, and the euro area average for that sector. These absolute differences are then aggregated by calculating, for each country, the average of absolute differences, weighted by each industry's share in the country's total stock market capitalisation.

More formally, the segmentation measure for country i is computed as:

$$Seg_i = \sum_{k \in K} \omega_k^i \left| EY_k^i - EY_k^{eur} \right| \tag{6.2}$$

where EY_k^i is the average earnings yield (the inverse of the price/earnings ratio) based on analyst forecasts for industry sector k in country i, K is the total number of sectors, EY_k^{eur} is the respective euro area average, and ω_k^i is the share of sector k in the stock market capitalisation of country i. A higher value indicates a higher level of market segmentation (i.e. a lower level of market integration), because industries in different countries in an integrated market may be expected to have similar business prospects and, therefore, similar valuations. A measure of zero implies perfect integration.

Quantity-Based Measures

Baele *et al.* (2004) classify quantity-based measures into two groups. The first group includes measures dealing with cross-border activities in a specific market, and the second group refers to measures of the home bias.

One way to assess the progress made towards financial integration is to consider whether the barriers to entry for foreign economic agents willing to invest in a specific region have been reduced over time. If so, cross-border ownership of securities should increase over time. Chapters 10 and 11 discuss the cross-border activity of banks and insurers.

As for the second group of measures, Baele *et al.* (2004) regard the extent of the *home bias*, i.e. the degree to which agents invest in domestic assets even though risk is shared more effectively if foreign assets are held, as a sign that financial integration is not complete. Chapter 9 discusses the home bias of institutional investors' portfolios.

6.3 Integration of European Financial Markets

This section summarises the main findings of empirical research on European financial integration. The evidence suggests that the degree of integration varies depending on the market segment. The financial crisis and the euro crisis affected various financial markets to different degrees, resulting in a retrenchment of market activity within domestic borders (ECB, 2011). Despite substantial recent improvements, most market segments remain highly fragmented at the time of writing (ECB, 2018).

Money Markets

To assess the extent to which various segments of the money market rate are integrated, Figure 6.2 shows the interquartile range of a selection of money market interest rates.

(average interquartile range per maintenance period, in basis points, Jan. 2000–Mar. 2018)

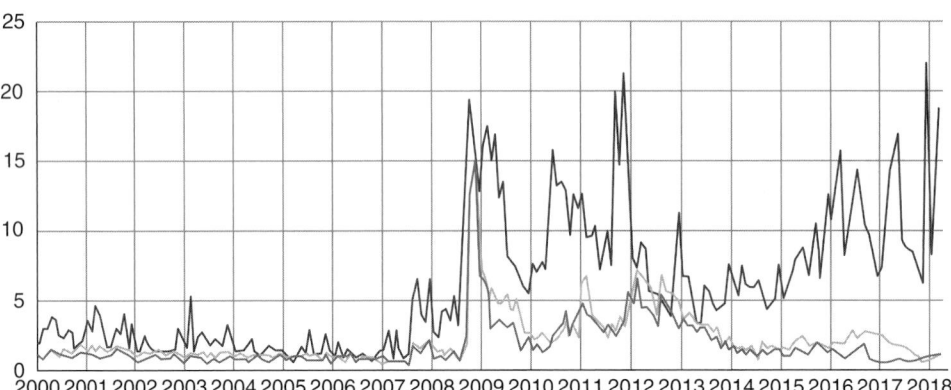

Figure 6.2   Integration of the money market: interquartile range of euro area countries' average unsecured
interbank lending rates (January 2000 – March 2018)
Source: ECB (2018)

As Figure 6.2 shows, the money market reached a stage of 'near-perfect'
integration almost immediately after the introduction of the euro. The
dispersion of the EONIA lending rates and the 1-month and 12-month
EURIBOR rates across euro-area countries remained stable until the financial crisis. After increasing strongly during the crisis, the dispersion of the
EURIBOR rates has declined, but the dispersion of the overnight EONIA rate
is still volatile and high. According to the ECB (2018), the dispersion in repo
market rates reflects a growing demand for high-quality collateral to secure
these transactions.

Figure 6.3 shows a quantity-based measure of integration. This indicator reflects the degree of financial integration in money markets by considering the geographical location of the counterparties (domestic, euro
area, and other). The higher the share of transactions with non-domestic
counterparties, the higher the level of financial integration. In recent
years, the secured segment of the money market showed a broadly stable
share of cross-border activity within the euro area, which remained below
pre-crisis levels. The ECB data for 2017 show that the share of cross-
border trading with counterparties from other euro-area countries was
20 per cent in the unsecured market segment and 25 per cent in the
secured segment.

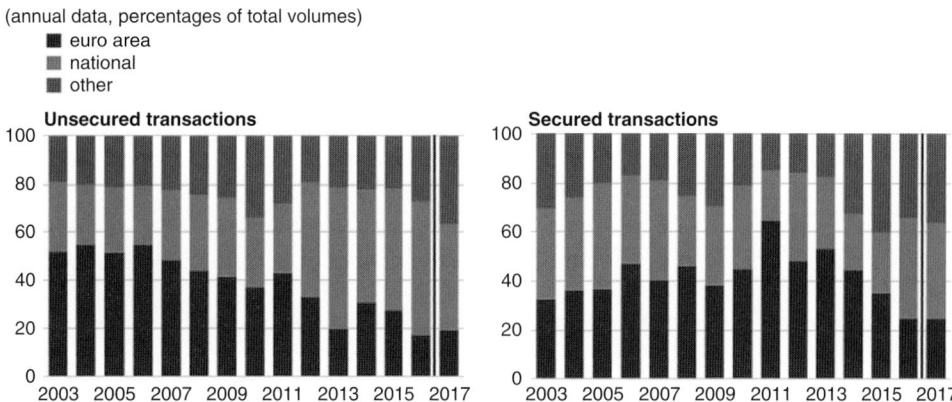

Figure 6.3   Geographical counterparty breakdown of secured and unsecured transactions, 2003–2017
Source: ECB (2018)

Bond Markets

After the introduction of the euro, differences in government bond yields among euro-area countries were never more than 50 basis points until the financial crisis. After August 2007, some sovereign bond markets benefited from a 'flight to safety', while other euro-area sovereign bond spreads rose sharply relative to the German benchmark (see Figure 2.7).

Euro-area government bond market integration, as measured by the dispersion of euro-area sovereign bond yields, dropped in recent years until 2015, and has not returned to pre-financial crisis levels (Figure 6.4). Furthermore, the dispersion of euro-area sovereign bond yields increased from late 2015 until the beginning of 2017. In the remainder of 2017, sovereign bond yields generally converged, reflecting the dissipation of perceived political uncertainty in some euro-area countries and a significant improvement in the macroeconomic outlook for the euro area (ECB, 2018). In particular, Standard & Poor's upgrade of Portugal's rating (to investment grade) produced large reductions in the yield on its government debt. In 2017 and 2018, Italian spreads were impacted by political uncertainty and weaknesses in the Italian banking sector.

According to the ECB (2018), spread convergence in non-financial corporate bonds can largely be explained by issuer-specific factors. The estimated default risk for issuers of corporate bonds (not shown here) has generally tracked changes in the trend for corporate bond spread convergence quite closely in recent years (shown in Figure 6.4).

(monthly data; standard deviation, percentage points)

— non-financial corporate bonds
— sovereign bonds

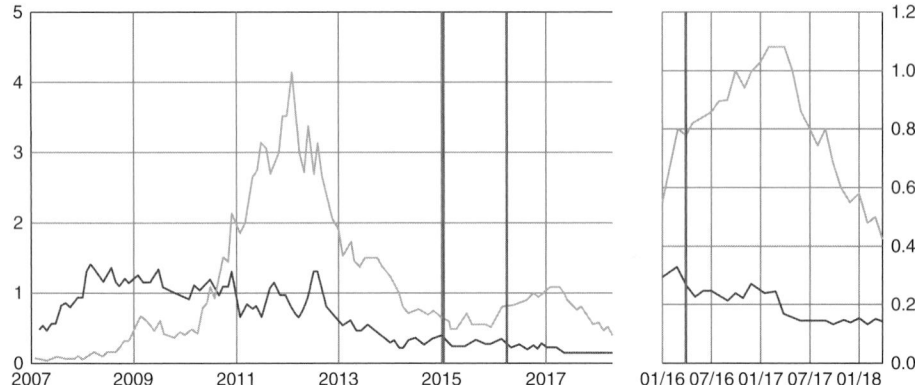

Figure 6.4   Cross-country dispersion of euro-area sovereign and non-financial corporate bond yields
Source: ECB (2018)

Equity Markets

Figure 6.5 shows ECB estimates of the segmentation of equity markets based on equation (6.2). According to this measure, the recent segmentation of euro-area equity markets is comparable to that of the period from 2005 up to the first half of 2007, which is far below the peaks witnessed at the height of the global financial crisis or the euro-area sovereign debt crisis (ECB, 2018).

European financial integration is biased towards debt finance, and especially towards intermediation by banks (ECB, 2018). However, the composition of intra-euro-area asset holdings has shifted in recent years towards a growing foreign share of equity investment and a declining share of foreign debt instruments (Figure 6.6). The top line in Figure 6.6 plots the evolution of holdings by euro-area investors of equity (foreign direct investment and portfolio equity stock liabilities) issued by other euro-area countries as a percentage of the total euro-area holdings of equities. The bottom line plots the evolution of holdings by euro-area investors of debt securities issued by other euro-area countries as a percentage of the total euro-area holdings of debt securities. The middle line plots the ratio of the two shares. The figure shows that this ratio has been increasing since the third quarter of 2014. This rise has been driven by a 5 per cent increase in the numerator and a 9 per cent decrease in the denominator.

(monthly data, Jan. 1995 – Dec. 2017)

— median
▨ interquartile range
■ min-max range

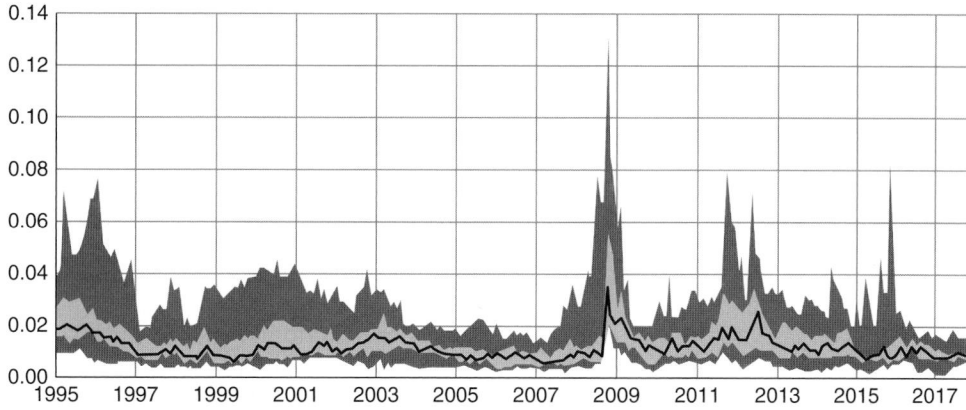

Figure 6.5   Equity market segmentation, January 1995 – December 2017
Source: ECB (2018)

— Intra-euro area debt securities holdings (left axis)
— Intra-euro area equity holdings (left axis)
— Ratio equity to debt intra-euro area asset holding (right axis)

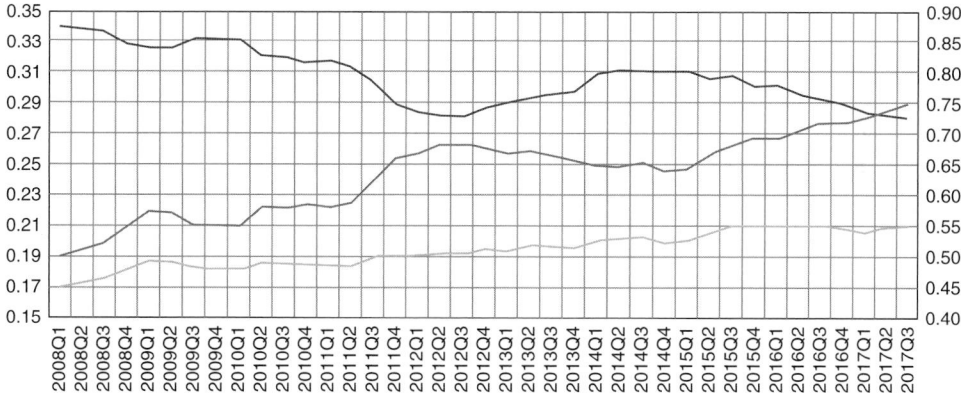

Figure 6.6   Intra-euro-area asset holdings: foreign equity investment versus foreign debt investment
Source: ECB (2018)

This is an important development, given the differences between the risk-sharing properties of these instruments (see Box 6.1 for a discussion of risk sharing). According to the ECB (2016), there is evidence that debt tends to be more prone to runs than equity; liquidity crises have often been triggered by sudden stops in debt investment, rather than equity-like forms of finance.

Furthermore, debt finance tends to be more pro-cyclical than equity finance. Equity payoffs tend to be lower during recessions, whereas debt payoffs are generally independent of economic conditions and hence tend to exacerbate the adverse effects of a recession. Moreover, the main contingency of debt contracts – default risk – makes borrowing more difficult during recessions, which is precisely when countries need insurance the most. The pro-cyclical nature of debt finance can magnify the adverse impact of negative shocks on economic growth.

6.4 The Consequences of Financial Integration

According to Baele *et al.* (2004), financial integration produced three potential benefits: (1) more opportunities for risk sharing and diversification, (2) better allocation of capital, and (3) higher economic growth. It may also have implications for (4) financial stability and (5) the structure of the EU financial system. All five of these consequences will be discussed in turn.

Financial integration enables consumption smoothing, making regions less sensitive to idiosyncratic shocks. This is because financial integration leads to cross-regional asset holdings, the resulting income streams of which can improve the consumption smoothing of economic agents. Regions experiencing an economic downturn would receive income streams from investments from regions enjoying an upturn, thus dampening the impact of idiosyncratic regional shocks. The economic literature on federal states suggests that private financial risk sharing can greatly help smooth consumption (ECB, 2018). As discussed in Box 6.1, recent research by the ECB suggests that risk sharing in the euro area is far from perfect.

Greater financial integration may also facilitate the more efficient allocation of capital. Due to the elimination of barriers to trading, clearing and settlement platforms, firms will be able to choose the most efficient platforms. Investors can also invest their funds wherever they believe they will be allocated most productively (Baele *et al.*, 2004).

Financial integration may also affect economic growth. Integration will stimulate local financial markets and foster internal competition, as well as open these markets to competitive pressure from foreign intermediaries. Guiso *et al.* (2004) argue that financial integration should increase the supply of funds in less financially developed countries of the integrating area. This may occur for two reasons. First, integration facilitates the entry of more

Box 6.1 Risk sharing in the euro area

The ECB (2018) indicator of risk sharing in the euro area measures the extent to which shifts in domestic consumption co-move with changes in domestic GDP, controlling for changes in relative prices. In a situation of perfect risk sharing, domestic consumption would not correlate with domestic output. Figure 6.7 plots point estimates (dots) and confidence intervals (whiskers) from a panel regression of changes in country per capita consumption on changes in country per capita GDP, controlling for changes in relative prices. (Ireland is excluded from the calculation of this indicator due to the unusually large revisions to its GDP growth figure for 2015.) A coefficient for the change in domestic output of zero would indicate perfect risk sharing.

While the indicator clearly shows that euro-area risk sharing is not perfect, the measured reduction of the correlation between domestic consumption growth and domestic GDP growth since 2012 suggests a gradual improvement in risk sharing. Yet, according to ECB (2018) estimates, as of 2017 almost 80 per cent of the idiosyncratic shocks to a country's GDP growth remained unsmoothed.

Financial integration can improve risk sharing via either the capital channel or the credit channel. The first channel runs via cross-border ownership of productive assets, while the second runs via cross-border borrowing and lending by individuals and governments. The ECB (2018) has quantified the importance of both channels, and concludes that in recent years the contribution of capital markets to risk sharing almost halved, and that the contribution of credit markets even turned negative. The contribution of another channel for risk sharing, namely the fiscal channel that runs via cross-border fiscal transfers to both individuals and governments, has always been negligible in the euro area. In the light of these findings, the ECB

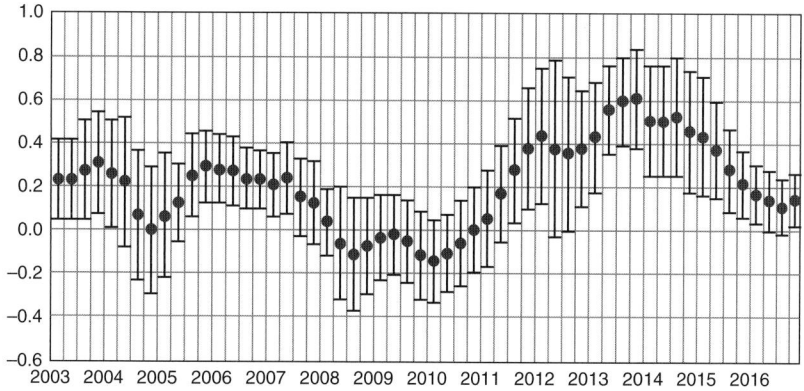

Figure 6.7   Correlation between consumption and output across euro-area countries (quarterly data, 2003.Q4 – 2017.Q3)
Source: ECB (2018)

> **Box 6.1** (cont.)
>
> (2018) maintains that capital and credit markets could make much larger contributions to risk sharing. One way to enhance private risk sharing is by encouraging more widespread investment in private pension and life insurance schemes. As discussed in Chapters 3 and 9, pension systems vary across the euro area. Several countries still rely on substantial intergenerational 'pay as you go' pensions. Furthermore, only a small fraction of pension fund investments is allocated to equity, even though equity has relatively favourable risk-sharing properties.

efficient intermediaries to firms in less developed areas. Second, integration enables these firms to access more distant financial markets. In both cases, firms in less financially developed countries will enjoy easier and cheaper access to external finance (see Figure 6.1), which should spur capital accumulation and economic growth. Financial integration may also affect financial development through improved regulation (Guiso *et al.*, 2004). A level regulatory playing field is an essential prerequisite for an integrated market, and this convergence in regulatory standards is likely to improve the regulatory standards in less developed financial markets. All such developments will contribute to further financial development, which in turn may stimulate economic growth. However, as pointed out in Box 6.2, integration may also hamper growth.

Financial integration may also have an impact on financial stability, although its direction is not clear. On the one hand, a larger and more diversified financial system will be better able to absorb economic shocks than financial systems in individual countries. The process of financial market integration facilitates consumption-smoothing and risk-sharing opportunities. Integration allows households to hold more diversified equity portfolios, and particularly to diversify the portion of risk that arises from country-specific shocks. Furthermore, integration spurs the efficiency of financial intermediaries and markets in countries where the financial system is less developed and more heavily regulated, which fosters the growth of domestic financial markets and the entry of foreign banks, and improves households' access to credit. As a result, country-specific shocks have a smaller effect on consumption when international financial markets are integrated, since they can be diversified away by borrowing abroad or holding foreign assets. At the same time, easier access to credit helps domestic borrowers to buffer specific shocks to their incomes (Jappelli and Pistaferri, 2011).

Box 6.2 Financial integration and economic growth

Theoretically, international financial integration has ambiguous effects on economic growth. On the one hand, integration facilitates risk sharing and thereby enhances production specialisation, capital allocation, and economic growth. It also eases the flow of capital to capital-scarce countries with positive output effects. Finally, financial integration may enhance the functioning of domestic financial systems by intensifying of competition and importing financial services, which is likely to have positive growth effects. On the other hand, if there are pre-existing distortions, integration can slow growth. For instance, in countries with weak institutions – like weak financial and legal systems – integration may induce capital outflows from capital-scarce countries to capital-abundant countries with better institutions. This line of reasoning suggests that financial integration will promote growth only in countries with sound institutions.

Empirical research on the impact of integration on growth is complicated by the difficulty of measuring integration across diverse countries that may impose a complex array of price and quantity controls on a broad assortment of financial transactions. Researchers have used (1) proxies for government restrictions on capital flows, (2) measures of actual international capital flows, and (3) the accumulated stock of foreign assets and/or liabilities.

The most widely used index for measuring capital account restrictions is the Chinn–Ito index. Based on information provided by the IMF on government restrictions on international financial transactions, this index measures the openness of a country's capital account (Chinn and Ito, 2008). This variable proxies directly for government impediments, but the difficulty of accurately gauging the magnitude and effectiveness of government restrictions is a limitation of this approach (Edison *et al.*, 2002).

Measures of actual international capital flows are also employed to proxy for international financial openness. These measures assume that more capital flows indicate more integration. The advantage of these measures is that they are widely available and are not subjective measures of capital restrictions, but a disadvantage is that many factors influence capital flows, including economic growth (Edison *et al.*, 2002).

Lane and Milesi-Ferretti (2007) have computed the accumulated stock of foreign assets and liabilities for an extensive sample of countries. These stock measures are less sensitive to short-run fluctuations in capital flows associated with factors that are unrelated to integration.

The empirical evidence yields conflicting conclusions about the effects of financial integration on economic growth. Quinn (1997) finds that his measure of capital account openness is positively linked with growth. Bekaert *et al.* (2005) report that, on average, equity market liberalisations lead to a 1 per cent increase in economic growth over a five-year period. Other studies report less support for the view that financial integration spurs economic growth. For instance, Edison *et al.* (2002) find that international financial integration does *not* accelerate economic growth, even when controlling for particular economic, financial, institutional, and policy characteristics. Likewise, Bussière and Fratzscher (2008)

Box 6.2 (cont.)

report that capital account opening led, on average, to 1.5 per cent higher growth during the first five years after liberalisation in 45 industrialised and emerging market economies, but that growth subsequently returned to (or fell below) its pre-liberalisation rate. A study by Schularick and Steger (2010) focuses on the period 1880 to 1913, covering 24 countries from all world regions that accounted for more than 80 per cent of world output at the time. The authors conclude that the first era of financial globalisation generated a positive relationship between international financial integration and economic growth. But their study also suggests that a comparable effect cannot be found today. However, Abiad *et al.* (2007) find that financial integration in the new EU Member States raises growth in these countries and thus helps accelerate the convergence process.

Bumann *et al.* (2013) conduct a meta-analysis of the empirical literature on the relationship between financial liberalisation and economic growth, based on 441 *t*-statistics reported in 60 empirical studies. Their findings weakly indicate that, on average, financial liberalisation has a positive effect on growth.

On the other hand, financial integration may also increase the risk of cross-border contagion as the recent crises have shown (ECB, 2011). Economic shocks will spread more easily and rapidly in an integrated financial system. The degree of financial integration can affect how shocks are transmitted, as it enhances the similarity of each country's portfolio. Suppose a shock negatively affects the market value of financial assets on the balance sheets of institutions in several countries with common exposures that, as a consequence, suffer losses. If these institutions are forced (either by regulation or by market pressure) to meet certain constraints on their balance sheets (e.g. leverage ratios, liquidity, etc.), they may be forced to sell assets, which would exert additional downward pressures on prices and may even ignite a fire sale (ECB, 2018). Likewise, financial integration may increase the interconnectedness of financial markets (see Chapter 13 for a discussion).

Financial integration may also affect the structure of the financial system, which in turn may have implications for financial stability. Although financial integration will improve the supply of finance in less financially developed markets and increase the size of local financial markets, it will not necessarily cause the financial structures of the participating countries to converge. Guiso *et al.* (2004) note that the most financially developed countries may share the services provided by their financial system with the other integrating countries. The economies of scale and scope may fuel the expansion of the established intermediaries and markets of the more developed markets. For instance, if banks based in more developed countries provide cross-border loans to firms in less advanced countries, the additional provision of credit will not show up in the private domestic credit of the latter countries. Likewise, firms of less financially developed countries can list their shares on foreign stock exchanges. Pagano *et al.* (2001) identify a variety of reasons for doing so: overcoming equity rationing in the domestic market, reducing their cost of capital by accessing a more liquid market, and signalling their quality by accepting the scrutiny of more informed investors or the rules of a better corporate governance system.

6.5 Conclusions

This chapter defines financial integration as a situation without frictions that discriminate between economic agents in their access to – and their investment of – capital on the basis of their country of origin. Market forces are an important driver of financial integration. Competition can initiate the elimination of segmentation between national markets, resulting in lower prices. Collective action by trade associations is also driving integration. The setting of reference rates, such as the overnight rate (ESTER) and the interbank rate (EURIBOR), is an example of collective action. Finally, public authorities can foster integration. The ECB's establishment of an integrated large-value payment system (TARGET) was, for instance, crucial to creating a single money market. Likewise, the European Commission's FSAP contributed to completing the internal market for financial services.

There are different categories of financial integration measures. Price-based measures are widely used to identify differences in returns due to the geographic origin of the assets. Quantity-based measures examine cross-border activities. More cross-border business is often used to indicate increased integration. However, both ways of measuring financial integration have shortcomings. Asset price differentials may reflect divergences in domestic macroeconomic fundamentals or issuer-specific factors. If asset prices are the same everywhere, there is no need for cross-border activity.

Examining the integration of Europe's financial markets reveals that the money market and the government bond market were fully integrated before the financial crisis. The corporate bond market also appeared to be quite well integrated. The empirical evidence suggests a rising degree of integration of equity markets. Due to the financial crisis and the euro crisis, the integration of financial markets seems to have reached a standstill and has in some cases, such as the money and sovereign bond markets, been reversed. While some indicators suggest a recent improvement, in many market segments financial integration has not returned to pre-crisis levels.

Finally, financial integration enables better risk sharing and the more efficient allocation of capital. The result is a more efficient and competitive financial system that may promote economic growth. Yet there is also a downside to financial integration. While a well-diversified financial system can better absorb economic shocks, these shocks can also spread more easily in an integrated financial system. It is therefore important for financial stability policies to stay in tune with advances in financial integration (see Chapter 13).

Bibliography

Suggested Reading

Baele, L., A. Ferrando, P. Hordahl, E. Krylova, and C. Monnet (2008), Measuring European Financial Integration. In: X. Freixas, P. Hartmann, and C. Mayer (eds.), *Handbook of European Financial Markets and Institutions*, Oxford University Press, 165–94.

Enoch, C., L. Everaert, T. Tressel, and J. Zhou (eds.) (2014), *From Fragmentation to Financial Integration in Europe*, IMF, Washington, DC.

Guiso, L., T. Jappelli, M. Padula, and M. Pagano (2004), Financial Market Integration and Economic Growth in the EU. *Economic Policy*, 19, 524–77.

References

Abiad, A., D. Leigh, and A. Mody (2007), International Finance and Income Convergence: Europe is Different. Working Paper 07/64, IMF, Washington, DC.

Baele, L., A. Ferrando, P. Hördahl, E. Krylova, and C. Monnet (2004), Measuring Financial Integration in the Euro Area. Occasional Paper 14, ECB, Frankfurt am Main.

(2008), Measuring European Financial Integration. In: X. Freixas, P. Hartmann, and C. Mayer (eds.), *Handbook of European Financial Markets and Institutions*, Oxford University Press, 165–94.

Bekaert, G., C. R. Harvey, and C. T. Lundblad (2005), Does Financial Liberalization Spur Growth? *Journal of Financial Economics*, 77, 3–55.

Bekaert, G., C. R. Harvey, C. T. Lundblad, and S. Siegel (2011), What Segments Equity Markets? *Review of Financial Studies*, 24, 3841–90.

Bumann, S., N. Hermes, and R. Lensink (2013), Financial Liberalization and Economic Growth: A Meta-Analysis. *Journal of International Money and Finance*, 33, 255–81.

Bussière, M. and M. Fratzscher (2008), Financial Openness and Growth: Short-Run Gain, Long-Run Pain? *Review of International Economics*, 16, 69–95.

Chinn, M. D. and H. Ito (2008), A New Measure of Financial Openness. *Journal of Comparative Policy Analysis*, 10, 309–22.

Edison, H. J., R. Levine, L. Ricci, and T. Sløk (2002), International Financial Integration and Economic Growth. *Journal of International Money and Finance*, 21, 749–76.

European Central Bank (2003), The Integration of Europe's Financial Markets. *Monthly Bulletin*, October, 53–6.

(2011), *Financial Integration in Europe*, ECB, Frankfurt am Main.

(2016), *Financial Integration in Europe*, ECB, Frankfurt am Main.

(2018), *Financial Integration in Europe*, ECB, Frankfurt am Main.

European Commission (2006), Commission Staff Working Document Addressed to the European Parliament and to the Council on the Impact of Regulation (EC) No. 2560/2001 on Bank Charges for National Payments, EC, Brussels.

Guiso, L., T. Jappelli, M. Padula, and M. Pagano (2004), Financial Market Integration and Economic Growth in the EU. *Economic Policy*, 40, 524–77.

Jappelli, T. and L. Pistaferri (2011), Financial Integration and Consumption Smoothing. *The Economic Journal*, 121, 678–706.

Lane, P. and G. M. Milesi-Ferretti (2007), The External Wealth of Nations Mark II: Revised and Extended Estimates of Foreign Assets and Liabilities, 1970–2004. *Journal of International Economics*, 73, 223–50.

Pagano, M., O. Randl, A. Roëll, and J. Zechner (2001), What Makes Stock Exchanges Succeed? Evidence from Cross-Listing Decisions. *European Economic Review*, 45, 770–82.

Quinn, D. (1997), The Correlates of Change in International Financial Regulation. *American Political Science Review*, 91, 531–51.

Schularick, M. and T. Steger (2010), Financial Integration, Investment and Economic Growth: Evidence from Two Areas of Financial Globalization. *The Review of Economics and Statistics*, 92, 756–68.

7

Financial Infrastructures

OVERVIEW

This chapter discusses the EU's payment and post-trading (i.e. securities clearing and settlement) systems. Over the past decade, the volume and value of transactions that are processed via these systems have grown tremendously. Stable and efficient payment and post-trading systems have become very important for the operation of financial markets and the economy in general. For a long time, these infrastructures were fragmented along national lines and were exposed to limited competition. But integration is continuing in the context of the single currency, the Single Euro Payments Area, and technological innovations.

The chapter starts by examining the different elements of (retail and wholesale) payment and post-trading systems. Given the growing importance of card-based retail payment systems, the main focus will be on the set-up of the existing card schemes. The various steps of the post-trading process, which arranges the transfer of ownership and the payment between buyers and sellers in security markets, will also be discussed. Finally, the role of central banks in the regulation and oversight of payment and settlement systems will be clarified.

The second part of the chapter gives an overview of the economic features of the payment and securities market infrastructures. These infrastructures are characterised by economies of scale and scope, and network externalities. Understanding these characteristics helps to comprehend (future) developments within the EU payment and security market infrastructures.

The third part of the chapter describes the current situation in the payment and post-trading industry and recent initiatives to promote further integration, and addresses weaknesses exposed by the financial crisis.

LEARNING OBJECTIVES

After you have studied this chapter, you should be able to:

- define what a payment system is

- explain the difference between wholesale and retail payment systems
- describe the various steps of the post-trading process
- understand the economic characteristics of the payment and securities market infra-structures, and explain how these characteristics influence the EU market structure
- assess the extent to which the different elements of the EU financial infrastructure are integrated
- understand the growing importance of central counterparties (CCPs) and the related concentration risk.

7.1 Payment Systems and Post-Trading Services

Payment Systems

A *payment* is a transfer of money between economic actors, for example between a consumer and a merchant to pay for delivered goods or services, using cash or non-cash money. Cash payments require no systems for settlement between economic actors. Settlement is immediately final when banknotes or coins are handed over. In order to settle non-cash transactions, such as bank transfers, one bank account has to be debited and another has to be credited. Multiple systems are in place to ensure that this transfer is completed safely and efficiently. If a transaction takes place between accounts held at the same bank, the bank's internal administrative system can settle it. In general, however, economic agents hold accounts at different banks and therefore non-cash payments require cooperation between banks. A *payment system* is a combination of technical, legal, and commercial instruments, rules, and procedures that ensure the transfer of money between banks. A distinction can be made between (1) retail payment systems and (2) wholesale payment systems.

Retail Payment Systems

Retail payment systems are used for the transaction, clearing, and settlement of relatively low-value and non-time-critical payments initiated through payment instruments such as cheques, credit transfers, direct debits, and payment cards (BIS, 2001). Retail payments are generally made in large numbers (mass payments) by many economic actors and typically relate to the purchase of goods and services in the consumer and business sectors (BIS, 2002). Such payments are made using a wide range of instruments and in varied contexts. Generally, private sector systems are used for the transaction process and the clearing of retail payments.

Each retail payment system consists of:

- payment instruments used to initiate and direct the transfer of money between the accounts of the payer and the payee (see Box 7.1 for an overview of the main payment instruments available);
- payment infrastructures for transacting and clearing payment instruments, processing and communicating payment information, and transferring payment information between the paying and receiving institutions;
- financial institutions that provide payment accounts, instruments, and services to consumers, and organisations that operate payment transaction, clearing, and settlement service networks for those institutions;
- market arrangements (or payment schemes) such as conventions, regulations, and contracts for producing, pricing, delivering, and acquiring the various payment instruments and services in order to maintain a minimum level of efficiency and security between all payment service providers in a market. A *payment scheme* is the set of interbank rules, standards, and practices for the provision or operation of specific payment instruments. The scheme defines the characteristics of a payment instrument, such as the authorisation procedures, fee structure, and maximum time frame within which a payment is processed, thereby stipulating the rules with which all participating payment service providers must comply. These rules ensure predictability, security, and efficiency in the provision of the payment instrument;
- laws, standards, rules, and procedures set by legislators, courts, and regulators that define and govern the mechanics of the payment process and the conduct of payment service markets to ensure that payment service providers meet public policy goals (BIS, 2006).

A payment starts with a transaction initiated by either the payer (*push transaction*) or the payee (*pull transaction*) and ends when the payee has received the agreed amount of money in good order. Depending on the payment instrument used and the organisation of the banking sector, the payment instruction travels through one or more of the following: from an entry bank (paying/receiving bank or branch) to a settlement bank (bank head office or correspondent bank) and then to a clearinghouse or processing centre (see Figure 7.1). The latter is a central processing mechanism through which financial institutions agree to exchange payment instructions. Settlement takes place at a designated time based on the rules and procedures of the clearinghouse (explained in the next section on wholesale payment systems). In most cases the actual settlement of the payment takes place at the

---

Box 7.1 Core payment instruments

Credit transfers: a payment initiated by the payer. The payer sends a payment instruction to his or her bank. The bank debits the payer's account and advises the receiver's bank to credit the beneficiary's account. This can happen through different channels and via intermediaries.

Direct debit: a payment initiated by the creditor, who sends the instructions to collect money via his or her bank or via a central processing entity (automated clearinghouse) to the debtor's bank(s). Direct debits are often used for recurring payments, such as for utilities. They require a pre-authorisation ('mandate') from the payer. They are used less often for one-off payments.

Payment card: there are three main types of payment cards: (1) *debit cards*, which allow the cardholder to charge purchases directly to an account as long as sufficient funds are available in the account; (2) *credit cards*, which allow purchases under a certain credit limit. The balance is settled partly or in full by the end of a specified period. Any remaining balance is taken as extended credit on which the cardholder must pay interest; and (3) *stored value (prepaid) cards*, which allow users to pay merchants with funds transferred in advance to a prepaid account.

Cash: in the euro area, only the ECB has the right to authorise the issue of banknotes. The national central banks in the euro area bring banknotes into circulation by providing them to the banking sector. Banknotes are mainly distributed to the public via ATMs (automated teller machines). Euro banknotes come in seven denominations: 5, 10, 20, 50, 100, 200, and 500 euro. The Eurosystem stopped issuing €500 banknotes at the beginning of 2019; these notes will retain their value and can be exchanged at national central banks.

Cheque: a written order from one party (the drawer) to another (the drawee, normally a credit institution) requiring the drawee to pay a specific sum to the party specified by the drawer.

Source: ECB

---

central bank (or in some cases a private entity) where the respective settlement banks have their accounts. The distribution of the payment to the payee completes the payment process. Payment finality, i.e. the guarantee of a payment to the payee, is critical in this respect.

The efficiency of retail payment systems has been enhanced over time by:

- the distribution of cash via ATMs instead of bank branches;
- the use of electronic payment systems instead of paper-based payments;
- automated end-to-end processing (or straight-through processing) instead of manually processed payments.

Strengthening the efficiency of retail payment systems is essential, as such payments entail private and social costs that average nearly 1 per cent of GDP

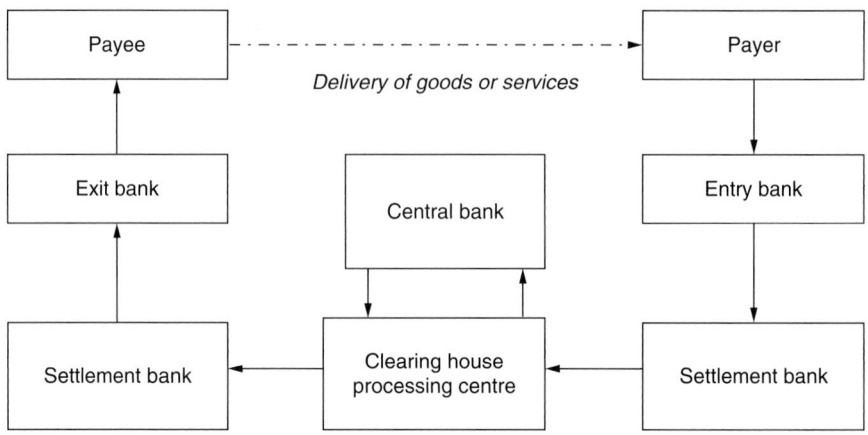

Figure 7.1   The process of initiating and receiving payments (push transaction)
Source: Khiaonarong (2003)

(ECB, 2012).[1] Private costs are those incurred by individual parties in the payment chain, such as banks and retailers. Social costs are the total costs of production, taking into consideration that one party's revenue is another party's costs (see Table 7.1). Cash payments have the lowest social costs of €0.42, followed by debit cards at €0.70 per transaction. This does not necessarily mean that cash is the most cost-effective payment instrument, because the low unit costs may be due to the high volume of cash payments. In the Netherlands, for example, debit card payments have become less costly than cash payments (Jonker, 2013). In 2012 an average cash payment there costs €0.44, compared to €0.30 for the average debit card payment. Between 2002 and 2012, the number of debit card payments more than doubled to 2.5 billion, while cash usage declined to 3.75 billion payments. This changing payment behaviour decreased the total costs of cash and debit card payments to society by 10 per cent from over €2.6 billion in 2002 to less than €2.4 billion in 2012. The social costs dropped from 0.57 per cent to 0.40 per cent of GDP.

The second part of Table 7.1 shows that cheques, credit transfers, and direct debits have the lowest social costs. This is not surprising, as these payment instruments are mostly used for high-value transactions.

Cash is still the preferred means of payment for many people in many countries. It is fast and easy to use, and facilitates the monitoring of expenses. It also preserves privacy and anonymity from both the state and transaction partners (see Beer *et al.*, 2016 for further discussion). It is therefore particularly important for young, old, less-educated, and lower-income groups. Yet

Table 7.1 Unit social costs and social costs per euro of sales for retail payment instruments (in €, 2009 figures)

Measure	Cash	Cheque	Cards	Debit cards	Credit cards	Direct debits	Credit transfers
Unit social costs							
Minimum	0.13	2.39	0.22	0.18	0.48	0.14	0.30
Median	0.39	3.46	0.63	0.45	1.97	1.14	1.01
Maximum	0.78	6.10	8.07	3.40	8.65	2.49	12.07
Average	0.41	3.86	1.34	0.81	2.79	1.07	2.22
Weighted average	0.42	3.55	0.99	0.70	2.39	1.27	1.92
Social costs per €1 of sale							
Minimum	0.013	0.000	0.008	0.008	0.018	0.002	0.000
Median	0.020	0.002	0.016	0.012	0.030	0.004	0.002
Maximum	0.034	0.012	0.081	0.035	0.137	0.011	0.006
Average	0.023	0.004	0.024	0.017	0.052	0.005	0.002
Weighted average	0.023	0.002	0.017	0.014	0.034	0.004	0.002

Source: ECB (2012). The sample includes Denmark, Estonia, Finland, Greece, Hungary, Ireland, Italy, Latvia, Netherlands, Portugal, Romania, Spain, and Sweden.

it is costly and inefficient, and can facilitate criminal activity, money laundering, and tax evasion. It also limits the degree to which monetary policy can drive nominal interest rates deeply into negative territory: individuals may withdraw cash from their bank accounts and hold on to it if banks start paying negative rates on bank accounts.

The number and value of electronic payments is rapidly increasing around the world. This can be illustrated by the increased use of *card payments* – electronic payments by a card at point-of-sale terminals (BIS, 2018). In most countries, the value of card payments more than doubled during 2000–2017, and in China it increased by more than eight times relative to GDP (Table 7.2). Cards are the most widely used cashless payment instrument in the EU. The number of card payments per inhabitant has roughly quadrupled in the EU, from an average of 33 payments per inhabitant in 2000 to 135 in 2017 for a total of nearly 70 billion payments in 2017. But card usage varies significantly across EU Member States (Figure 7.2). In 2017, the average number of payments made per year and per inhabitant ranged from 18 in Bulgaria (up from 2 in 2008) to 366 in Denmark (up from 170 in 2008). There is even a large discrepancy within the euro area; cards are most frequently used in Finland, the Netherlands, Luxembourg, and Estonia and are less popular

Table 7.2 Use of cash and cards in selected countries

	Cards (% of GDP)		Cash (% of GDP)	
	2000	2016	2000	2016
Euro area	7.8	15.6	5.1	10.7
Sweden	9.6	22.8	4.4	1.4
United Kingdom	16.9	45.5	3.2	3.9
China	8.6	75.7	14.6	9.2
Japan	4.4	10.1	13.5	20.0
United States	15.8	31.7	6.0	8.1

Source: BIS (2018)

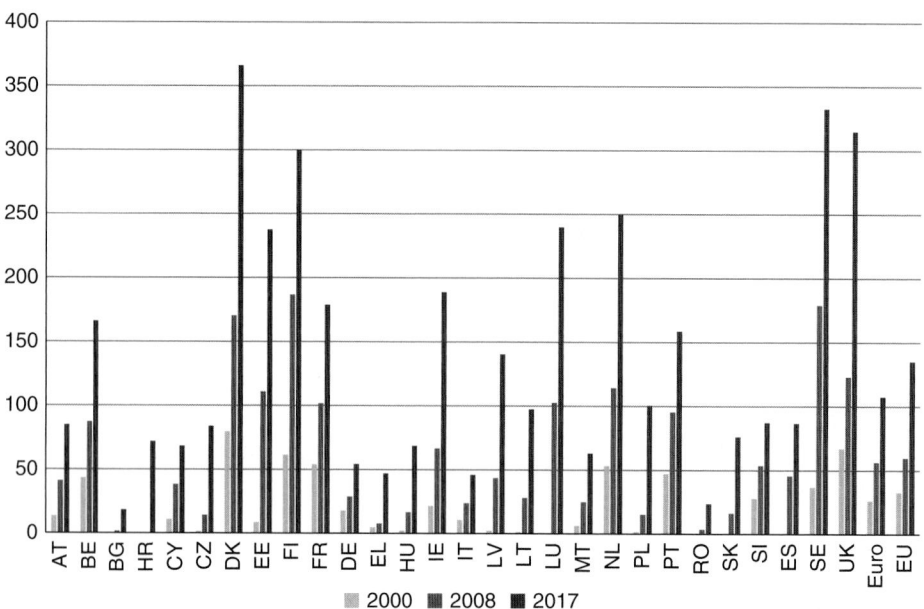

Figure 7.2   Number of card payments per inhabitant and per year, 2000–2017
Source: ECB

in Italy, Greece, and Germany. As illustrated in Figure 7.3, from 2000 to 2017 card payments increased by more than 10 per cent per year, while direct debits and credit transfers grew by approximately 5 per cent.

Cash in circulation is often used as a proxy for cash demand (BIS, 2018). Overall demand for cash has risen in many countries. Since 2000 it has roughly doubled in the euro area, from 5.1 to 10.7 per cent of GDP and has also increased in the UK, Japan, and the US (see Table 7.2). But in China it

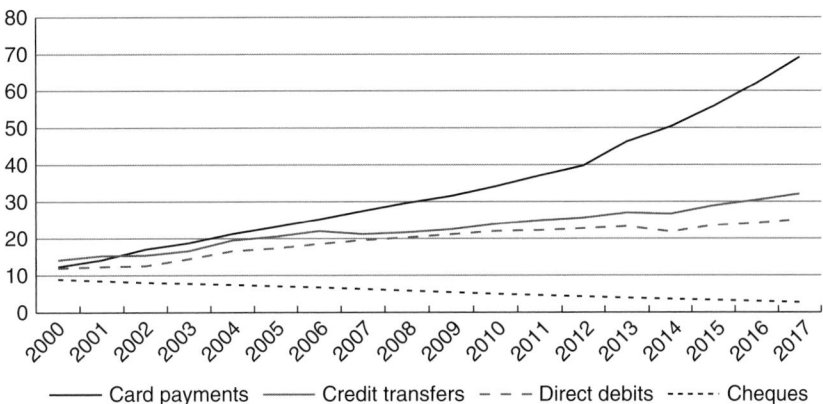

Figure 7.3   Use of payment instruments in the EU, 2000–2017 (billions of transactions per year)
Source: ECB

has decreased substantially, from 14.6 to 9.2 per cent of GDP. Sweden may become a cashless society: cash in circulation has dropped to a meagre 1.4 per cent of GDP. The Riksbank (2018) is therefore considering the introduction of a 'central bank digital currency' as an alternative to cash.

The Bank for International Settlements (2018) has investigated the drivers of this increase in cash demand, and finds a relative increase in the demand for large-denomination banknotes. This suggests that cash is increasingly being used to store value rather than for payments. This is confirmed in the BIS (2018) study by regression results that indicate that the low interest rate environment has been an important driver of the demand for cash, as it produces low opportunity costs of holding cash.

Card-Based Payment Systems

In principle, each debit or credit card payment involves the following four parties:
- the *cardholder*: the person who has received the payment card from the issuer and uses it to pay for goods and services;
- the *issuer*: the payment service provider that issues the payment card to the cardholder;
- the *merchant*: the person accepting the card payment in return for goods or services;
- the *acquirer*: the payment service provider that provides payment services to the merchant.

Interbank payment arrangements are in place to transfer funds between the two intermediaries. Figures 7.4 and 7.5 illustrate the two most common

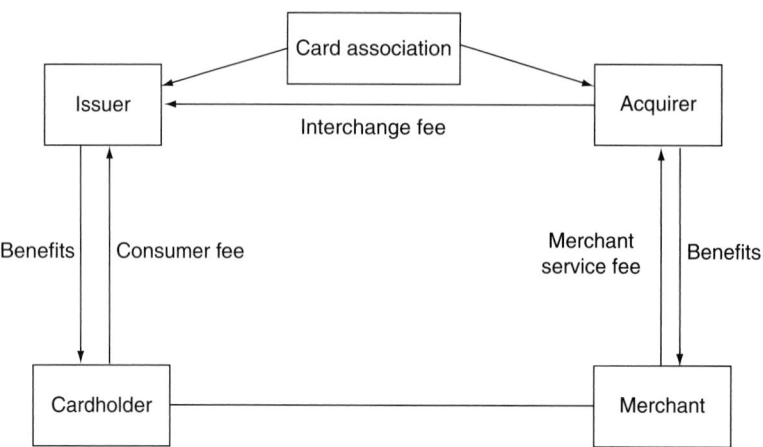

Figure 7.4   Four-party payment scheme
Source: Harper *et al.* (2006)

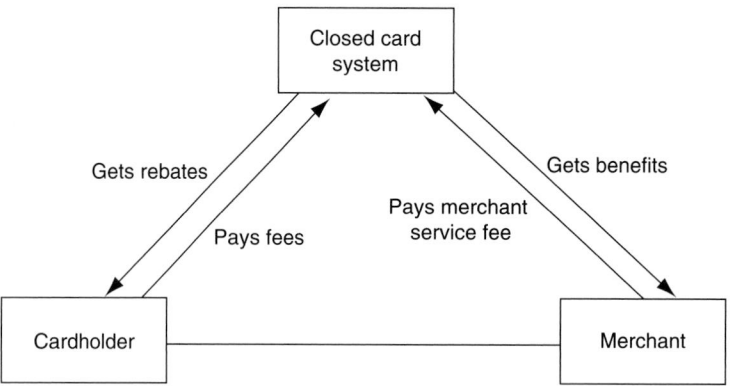

Figure 7.5   Three-party payment scheme
Source: Harper *et al.* (2006)

arrangements for processing a card payment. Figure 7.4 depicts the *four-party payment scheme* (cardholder – issuer – acquirer – merchant). Such a scheme (as used, for instance, by Visa and MasterCard) is often referred to as 'open', as the issuer and acquirer can be any financial institution. Figure 7.5 shows a *three-party ('closed') scheme* (cardholder – payment service provider – merchant), in which the same payment service provider issues *and* acquires (as used, for instance, by Diners Club and American Express).

The interchange and merchant service fees charged by card issuers are the subject of several regulatory and antitrust investigations. The *interchange fee* is paid by an acquiring institution to an issuing institution for each payment card transaction at the point of sale of a merchant. A merchant pays a *merchant service fee* for each transaction to an acquirer, who processes the merchant's transaction through the network and obtains the funds from the cardholder's bank (European Commission, 2007). In a four-party card scheme, the merchant receives the amount of the transaction, minus the merchant fee.

Interchange and merchant service fees are controversial for three reasons. First, they may be seen as a collective agreement between competitors that distorts competition in the market for payment cards. Second, the non-transparent pricing of card payments creates very few incentives to use more efficient payment instruments. Third, as merchants adjust their prices for goods and services to accommodate these fees, cross-subsidisation occurs, i.e. consumers who use other (more efficient) means of payment subsidise the use of expensive (credit) cards.

Wholesale Payment Systems

Wholesale payment systems are used to make large-value and/or time-critical funds transfers between financial institutions within the system (for their own account or for their customers). Although no minimum value is set for these payments, the average value of payments passed through such systems is normally relatively high (BIS, 2001). For a long time, correspondent banking played an important role in processing large-value payments, notably foreign currency payments. A *correspondent banking payment* is a payment between two banks that is made through an intermediary, i.e. the correspondent bank. Since the introduction of the euro, there has been a significant decline in the use of corresponding banking systems within Europe. Central infrastructure payments are, however, becoming more and more important. In *real-time gross settlement (RTGS) systems*, each individual payment is immediately settled on a gross basis when it is received (rather than at a later stage).

TARGET2 (Trans-European Automated Real-Time Gross Settlement Express Transfer System) is the most important central infrastructure payment system for real-time processing of cross-border transfers throughout the EU. It offers a centralised Single Shared Platform to process all payments on behalf of the entire Eurosystem. It settles payments in central bank money related to monetary policy operations, interbank and customer payments, and payments related to the operations of all large-value net settlement systems and other financial market infrastructures handling the euro (such as securities settlement systems or central counterparties). In 2017, TARGET2 processed an average of €2.2 trillion each day. It is the most important RTGS in

€ trillions

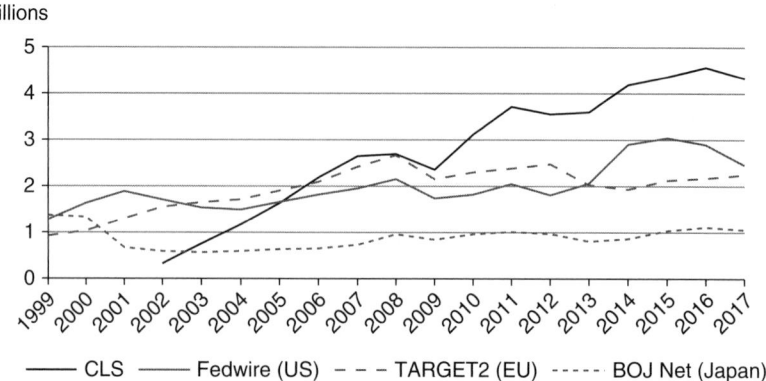

──── CLS   ──── Fedwire (US)   – – – TARGET2 (EU)   ····· BOJ Net (Japan)

Figure 7.6   Major large-value payments systems (average daily turnover in € trillions)
Note: Data in euro are affected by exchange rate fluctuations, since Fedwire Funds and CLS publish their turnover in US dollars and the BoJ NET in Japanese yen.
Source: ECB (2018)

the EU and one of the four largest wholesale payment systems in the world, alongside Fedwire in the US, the Bank of Japan Financial Network System (BoJ NET) in Japan, and Continuous Linked Settlement (CLS), the international system for settling foreign exchange transactions (Figure 7.6). TARGET2 is jointly operated by the Deutsche Bundesbank, the Banque de France, and the Banca d'Italia, on behalf of the Eurosystem.

TARGET2 has been operational since 2008 and is the successor of TARGET, which linked the national-level RTGS structures. TARGET was launched in 1999 to: (1) provide a safe and reliable mechanism for the settlement of euro payments, (2) increase the efficiency of cross-border payments in euros, and (3) serve the needs of the monetary policy of the ECB and to promote the integration of the euro money market. The full integration of the large-value payment systems has been instrumental in achieving this result.

The largest *net settlement system* in Europe is EURO1, a private multilateral, large-value payment system for euro payments established by more than 60 major European banks. This system processes credit transfers and direct debits throughout the day and balances are settled at close of business via a settlement account at the ECB.

Post-Trading Services

The smooth functioning of (and confidence in) securities markets depends in part on the efficiency and reliability of their infrastructure. In particular, the transfer of ownership from the seller to the buyer in exchange for a payment

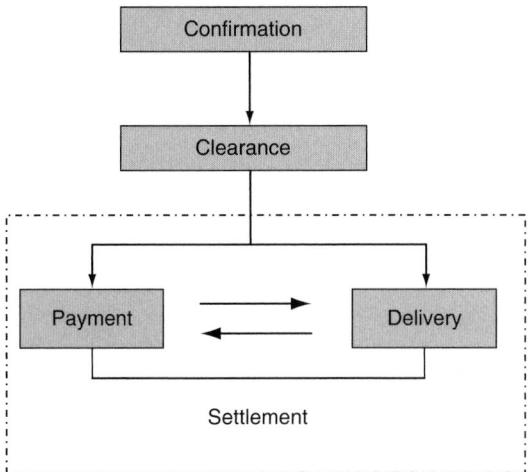

Figure 7.7   Clearing and settlement of a securities trade
Source: Giovannini Group (2001)

must take place in a safe and efficient manner (Kazarian, 2006). The clearing and settlement or *post-trading process* enables the transfer of ownership and payment between buyers and sellers in a security market.

The post-trading process begins when a securities trade has been executed. The subsequent securities settlement process encompasses a number of complementary steps and actions. Figure 7.7 illustrates the four main activities that comprise the post-trading process:

- confirmation of the terms of the trade as agreed upon by the buyer and seller;
- clearance: establish the respective obligations of the buyer and seller;
- delivery: transfer the securities from the seller to the buyer;
- payment: transfer the funds from the buyer to the seller.

Figure 7.7 shows that the post-trading process starts by confirming the terms of the securities transaction. This can be done either directly between the buyer and seller ('over the counter' or OTC) or indirectly through the securities exchange or a clearing agent.

The next step is the clearing of the obligation of the counterparties resulting from the matching process. Clearance of a securities transaction establishes the respective obligations of the buyer and seller, and may be achieved on a gross (trade-for-trade) or net basis (offsetting of mutual obligations). The latter reduces the number of actual transfers. Clearance services can be provided by a clearinghouse, a national central securities depository (CSD), or an international central securities depository (ICSD).[2] The latter two hold securities and allow them to be processed by book entry (rather than by physically moving the securities between buyers and sellers).

Securities markets can also use *central counterparties* (CCPs), which serve as intermediaries between the buyers and sellers of securities. These entities can also offer netting arrangements, which facilitate the management of securities and payment transfers.[3]

The subsequent step is the *settlement* process, which involves delivering the securities and the payment of funds between buyers and sellers. The payment is usually made via a banking or payment system, while the securities are typically delivered via a CSD or ICSD. According to the BIS (1992), the largest financial risks in securities clearance and settlement occur during the settlement process, especially if there is no mechanism to ensure that delivery occurs if – and only if – a payment is received. Without such a mechanism counterparties are exposed to *principal risk*, i.e. the risk that the seller of a security delivers but does not receive payment, or that the buyer makes a payment but does not receive the securities. A securities transaction is settled once the securities are delivered to the buyer and the seller has received the payment. However, formal registration of the transfer of ownership by a CSD is often needed to assure settlement.

Role of the Eurosystem

Stable and efficient payment and security settlement systems are crucial for:

- maintaining trust in a currency's value;
- the conduct of monetary policy operations;
- processing the current volume and value of transactions in financial markets;
- preventing the transmission of problems in payment or security settlement systems to other financial institutions, which could lead to financial instability.

Central banks therefore have an interest in the design and management of payment and security settlement systems. The Eurosystem has the statutory task of promoting the smooth operation of such systems in five ways. (1) *Providing payment and securities settlement facilities:* the Eurosystem runs a settlement system for large-value payments in euros (TARGET2) and thereby functions as a 'banker to the banks'. Banks hold funds on their account at the central bank, and payments between banks are made by debiting and crediting these accounts. In June 2015 the Eurosystem launched Target2-Securities (T2S), which provides a single platform for securities settlement in central bank money in order to deepen financial integration in Europe. Each transaction is settled on a delivery-versus-payment basis, by simultaneously accessing accounts in central bank money and securities accounts at CSDs in 20 European countries. By December 2017, the platform was settling more than 570,000 securities transactions per day on average. (2) *Overseeing the euro payment and settlement systems:* the Eurosystem applies internationally agreed standards to ensure the soundness and efficiency of systems handling euro transactions. It also assesses the continuous compliance of euro payment and settlement systems with these standards.

Additional Eurosystem responsibilities include (3) *overseeing compliance with the standards for securities clearing and settlement systems*; (4) *ensuring an integrated regulatory and oversight framework for securities settlement systems*; and (5) *promoting efficiency in payment systems and securities markets* by encouraging integration through the removal of barriers.

7.2 Economic Features of Payment and Securities Market Infrastructures

Payment and securities market infrastructures benefit from economies of scale and scope and network externalities.

Economies of scale arise when fixed costs are spread over a higher output: the cost per unit falls as output increases. Securities infrastructure providers seek a 'critical mass' of issuers and participants in order to distribute the set-up costs over a larger number of transactions. Similarly, there are strong economies of scale in the production of payment services. In a European cross-country study, Humphrey *et al.* (2003) find that costs increase by only 2 per cent when volumes rise by 10 per cent. Bolt and Humphrey (2007) estimate payment scale economies using a panel of payment and banking data for 11 European countries over 18 years and find that a doubling of payment volume increases total costs by only 27 per cent. Figure 7.8 shows that the unit payment costs decline as the volume of payments processed increases.[4]

Economies of scope refer to the reduction in the per-unit costs resulting from the production of a wider variety of goods and services (i.e. when it is cheaper to produce good A and good B together rather than separately). So,

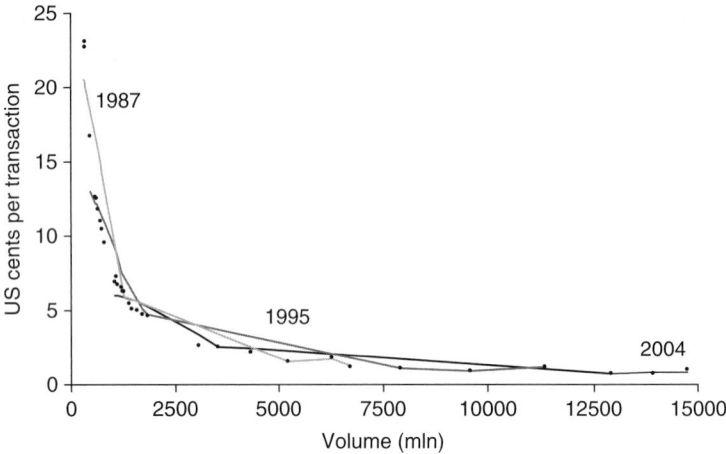

Figure 7.8 Economies of scale in the payment market
Source: Bolt (2007)

integrated financial infrastructures can develop new products and services at a lower unit cost if it is possible to share (certain) input factors for the production of different goods and services.

Economies of scope for CSDs and CCPs can be created by expanding the number of financial instruments or trading platforms for which they provide services. Since there is a strong complementary relationship between the various components of securities settlement (Kazarian, 2006), economies of scope can be achieved by integrating along the value chain of a securities transaction, i.e. by combining trading, clearing, and settlement into one firm. A supplier offering all of these services can do so at a lower cost than different suppliers providing them separately. Deutsche Börse is one such vertically integrated entity (or 'silo'). Serifsoy and Weiß (2007) argue that vertical integration can generate a (natural) monopoly from one stage of the value chain upstream or downstream to other stages. An integrated supplier may cross-subsidise its trading costs – and thereby attract customers from other platforms – through its monopoly profits on the clearing and settlement stage, or vice versa. It may also exclude competitors from the market as users can be forced to 'buy' another service from the same institution.

Payment systems may enjoy economies of scope if they handle more than one type of payment instrument or service. This allows the operator of the system to spread out the fixed costs of the system over a wider range of payment instruments. Generally, the demand for payment services is largely inelastic, as payments in themselves do not generate value. A payment is made to purchase a good or service, or to pay off a debt or financial obligation. Payment services are therefore a convenience good rather than a primary good. However, payment service users may be (very) sensitive to relative payment prices (i.e. price differences between individual payment instruments).

Network externalities are another important economic feature of market infrastructures. A *network* is a large system of many similar (or complementary) parts that are connected to allow movement or communication between the parts or between the parts and a centre. The addition of a new participant to a network can increase the value of the network for all participants. Therefore, the value of the services and products offered to the participants depends on how many other participants are purchasing the same services and products (*network externalities*). For example, consider a simple network consisting of a central junction S and side branches A, B, C, and D, as shown in Figure 7.9 (based on Economides, 1993). The goods in this network are composite goods, each comprising two complementary components – for example, ASB is comprised of the complements AS and SB. If the network consisted of the three side branches A, B, and C, it would create six products (i.e. ASB, ASC, BSA, BSC, CSA, and CSB). Economides (1993) shows that the addition of a new side branch to a network composed of n side branches creates $2n$ new products. Thus, the addition of side branch D would create six new products. This economy of scope in consumption is called a *network externality*. Network externalities can be found in a variety of industries, such as telecommunications, airlines, railroads, etc. (Shy, 2001). The externality directly increases consumer utility through the provision of new goods, and it may also affect consumers indirectly through price decreases.

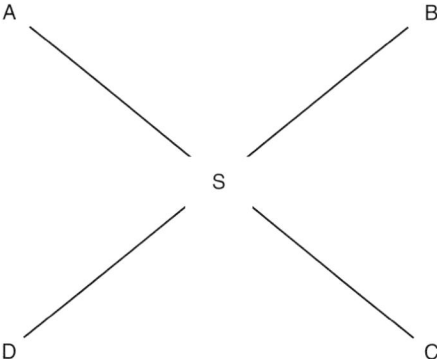

Figure 7.9   Simple network consisting of four side branches

Financial markets exhibit positive size externalities, as increasing the size of an exchange market increases the expected utility of all participants. The higher participation of traders on both sides of the market decreases the variance of the expected market price and increases the expected utility of risk-averse traders. *Ceteris paribus*, higher liquidity increases traders' utility. Thus, financial exchange markets exhibit network externalities (Economides, 1996).

Payment and securities market infrastructures also have characteristics of network industries, as the benefits to one market participant using a specific platform or system increase when another participant also chooses to do business in that network. The nature of these networks creates scope for formal cooperation among market players. The European Commission (2007) argues that certain types of cooperation (e.g. creating and operating common standards and platforms) may be necessary to generate efficiencies. However, cooperation that extends to strategies, pricing, or selling policies could lead to collusion and limit competition and/or exclude third parties.

Markets can be one sided or *two sided*. A market is two sided if the platform or system can affect the volume of transactions by charging one side of the market more and reducing the price paid by the other side by an equal amount. In other words, the price structure matters, and platforms must design it so as to bring both sides on board (see Rochet and Tirole, 2006). For example, consider a platform charging per-transaction charges a^B and a^S to buyers and sellers, respectively. The market for interactions between the two sides is one sided if the volume V of transactions realised on the platform depends only on the aggregate price level $a = a^B + a^S$, i.e. V is insensitive to reallocations of this price between the buyer and seller. However, if V varies with a^B while a is kept constant, the market is said to be two sided (see Figure 7.10). Generally, payment and security settlement

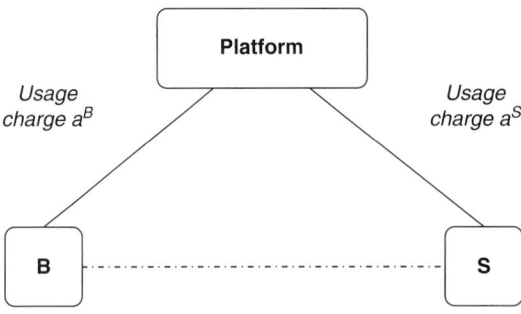

Figure 7.10   Two-sided market
Source: Rochet and Tirole (2006)

systems are two-sided markets. For example, Figures 7.4 and 7.5 show that the market for payment cards is two sided, i.e. one side of the market is subsidising the other. This subsidy is made up of the *interchange* and *merchant fees* that the acquiring bank pays to the issuing bank. Ultimately, these fees raise the price that the merchant pays for a card transaction and reduce the price for the cardholder, thereby increasing the cardholder's willingness to pay by card. As a result, the volume of transactions within the card network is higher than if the cardholder faced higher (visible) costs.

While these platforms were developed to ensure efficient cooperation on standards and practices, and to share costs between suppliers, over time they created an opportunity to exploit the least elastic side of the market (originally the merchants). However, the elasticity in the market may change, and it could become necessary to shift the 'taxation'. This often leads to heavily 'skewed' prices in two-sided markets, where the consumer pays no fee while the merchant pays a high fee (Bolt and Tieman, 2007).

The presence of network externalities often leads to oligopolies or monopolistic markets. This does not necessarily have to be a problem, as the marginal social benefits from network expansion may be larger than the benefits of a perfectly competitive market. Perfect competition will generally lead to a network that is smaller than socially optimal. However, given their dominance in certain markets, network providers may be tempted to abuse their economic position and charge monopoly prices, leading to greater inefficiency than under perfect competition.

Finally, network industries are often characterised by *switching costs*, i.e. customers face substantial costs when they want to switch from one network provider to the other. High switching costs may 'lock in' users and prevent them from switching to another network, thus obstructing innovation as users are prevented from using new and more efficient services.

7.3 Integration of Financial Market Infrastructures

Financial integration has progressed substantially in financial market infrastructures in recent years. In the era of one-click Internet shopping, consumers expect almost instant settlement of payments at any time of day or night, both nationally and across borders. Technological innovation has led to new private payment platforms, such as Adyen, which connect different payment methods around the world on a single platform that supports transaction platforms, such as Booking.com, Netflix, or Uber (see Chapter

8 on innovation in retail payment systems). Yet such 'fitting pipe' solutions between different payment methods across the globe do not necessarily imply full market integration, since the transaction costs are still likely to be (much) higher than for domestic payments.

As discussed in the previous section, financial market infrastructures are characterised by economies of scale and scope, as well as network effects. The consolidation of national systems into single platforms therefore has the potential to lower the cost of post-trading activities and lead to a more efficient allocation of capital, thereby furthering economic growth. But it can also lead to oligopolies and natural monopolies. Markets should therefore remain contestable, which implies an important role for policies that foster competition.

In the context of the single market and common monetary policy, the EU seeks to integrate payments and post-trading clearing and settlement systems. Such systems are intended to be stable (i.e. no materialisation of systemic risk) and efficient (i.e. lowering the transaction costs and bringing benefits to the end user instead of monopoly rents to owners). The following section examines the current state of affairs in the payment and post-trading industry, highlights recent initiatives to promote further integration and competition, and addresses the weaknesses exposed by the financial crisis.

Single Euro Payments Area

Until recently, the EU consisted of 28 heterogeneous payment areas. All national payment systems had their own membership criteria, standards, and practices, which made them more efficient at the national level but cumbersome to integrate, thus preventing the realisation of economies of scale. Replacing the national systems with a single European system not only runs the risk of not being able to satisfy all user requirements; it also requires substantial investments to launch and develop a new Europe-wide network (Salo, 2006).

There is some evidence of convergence for most payment instruments in Europe from 1995 to 2011 (ECB, 2013). This suggests that the cross-country dispersion in the use of payment instruments has declined over time, notably since the introduction of the single currency. But payment behaviours are slow to change, and the differences in payment habits across Europe remain significant, as illustrated in Figure 7.2.

Despite these differences in the use of payment instruments across countries, market fragmentation has been reduced for three payment instruments of the Single Euro Payments Area (SEPA): credit transfers, direct debit, and cards. SEPA has been developed as a result of cooperation between European institutions and the European banking industry. While the EU set out the legal framework, the industry developed common business rules and technical standards. Consequently, all electronic payments are affected and national credit transfers, direct debits, and card payments have migrated to interoperable formats and processes. SEPA enables customers to make electronic payments to any account located in the SEPA area, using a single IBAN account number and the same charges for domestic and cross-border electronic payment transactions in euros (EU Regulation 924/2009/EC). In principle, opening a foreign bank account when studying or working abroad should not be needed. However, in practice national habits often still require a separate bank account.

Since 2008, the new SEPA payment instruments (credit transfers, direct debits, and cards) have operated alongside national processes. In February 2014 credit transfers and direct debits migrated to SEPA in a 'big bang'; compliance with the SEPA format quickly increased to almost 100 per cent. SEPA instant credit transfer was launched in November 2017, which allows payees' accounts to be credited within 10 seconds. But the migration is not yet complete, as market segments such as mobile and online payments require further harmonisation (EPC, 2018).

To facilitate the clearing and settlement of SEPA transfers, the European banking community has defined principles that providers must comply with. The list of compliant clearing and settlement organisations includes national central banks, the ECB and EBA Clearing (a private (bank-owned) pan-European company) (EPC, 2018). EBA Clearing operates EURO1: a private sector large-value payment system for single same-day euro transactions at the pan-European level. It also operates the STEP2 platform, a pan-European automated clearinghouse for mass payments in euros, which has been offering SEPA services since January 2008 (EBA Clearing, 2018). The ECB also supports the move towards instant payments. It launched TIPS (TARGET Instant Payment Settlement) in November 2018 as an extension of TARGET2 and offers final and irrevocable settlement in central bank money in euros in real time and around the clock, every day of the year.

SEPA has been developed within the legal framework of the Payment Services Directive, as revised in 2015 (PSD2, 2015/2366/EU) and has been in use since early 2018. It creates a legal foundation for an EU-wide single market in electronic payments. PSD2 regulates the authorisation of payment institutions and opens up the market to non-bank payment providers, such as FinTech companies. Consumers may decide to give licensed payment institutions access to their bank accounts, including the possibility to transfer money online or at the point of sale. Moreover, PSD2 sets out rules for security requirements for electronic payments and the protection of consumers' financial data, information provision to payers, and the rights and obligations of the users and providers of payment services. In combination with technological innovation, PSD2 is expected to help drive innovation across the entire value chain in retail payment services, as discussed in Chapter 8.

Post-Trading Clearing and Settlement

As with retail payment systems, post-trade services were previously segmented into nationally based systems that tend to be monopolistic, i.e. all trades in a given type of security were cleared and settled by a single national entity. The Giovannini Group (2001) concluded that fragmentation in the EU clearing and settlement infrastructure significantly complicated the post-trade processing of cross-border securities transactions relative to domestic transactions. Complications arose because of the need to access several national systems, whereby differences in technical requirements/market practices, tax regimes, and legal systems act as barriers to the efficient and safe delivery of post-trading services. This led to cross-border prices and costs that are considerably higher than those of domestic transactions (Table 7.3).

But just as in retail payments, post-trade services have rapidly evolved in recent years. While securities trades are usually settled within two days in Europe, derivatives contracts have much longer maturities, of up to several years (for example, an interest rate swap exchanging fixed for floating, or

Table 7.3 Studies examining per-transaction post-trading costs for users

	EU cross-border	US	Ratio	EU domestic	US	Ratio
Lannoo and Levin (2001)	3.10	0.40	7.75	1.74	0.40	4.35
LSE/OXERA (2002)	3.41	0.53	6.43	2.04	0.53	3.85
Giovannini Group (2001)	2.86	0.46	6.22	1.49	0.46	3.24
NERA (2004)	n.a.	n.a.	n.a.	0.10–0.65	0.10	1.00–6.50
DBG (2005)	n.a.	n.a.	n.a.	0.30–0.60	0.10	1.50–3.00

Source: Schulze and Baur (2006)

a credit default swap). Most derivatives were traded on the OTC market, which is subject to bilateral clearing. The market was also strongly interconnected and lacked transparency. No collateral was exchanged in some transactions, leading to a high counterparty risk. Accordingly, when the financial crisis erupted, there was great uncertainty among market participants and policy makers about the risks to which institutions and the financial system as a whole were exposed (DNB, 2018).

Therefore, efforts have been undertaken at the international level (G20/ FSB) to increase the transparency of the derivatives market and reduce counterparty risks. In Europe, these policy initiatives have been incorporated into the European Market Infrastructure Regulation (EMIR, 648/2012/EU), the revised Directive on Markets in Financial Instruments (MiFID II, 2014/ 65/EU), and the Capital Requirements Regulation (CRR, 575/2013/EU). The reforms increase transparency through the central clearing of derivatives and the mandatory registration of transactions in trade repositories; they also promote the mandatory provision of collateral. In order to encourage clearing via CCPs, bilaterally cleared contracts are required to meet higher capital requirements than centrally cleared contracts, and central clearing is mandatory for standardised derivatives.

Access to CCPs is provided to clearing members, which are often banks. Individual clearing members can only settle transactions for their own account, while general clearing members can also offer access to their customers. The CCP then cancels out opposite positions in the same security until a single net position remains (Figure 7.11). In a process known as novation, the original bilateral contract between the buyer and seller is terminated and replaced by separate contracts with the CCP, for both the buyer and seller. As the CCP then becomes the counterparty to every buyer and seller, its positions are exactly offset under normal circumstances. However, if one clearing member can no longer fulfil its obligations, the CCP is exposed to counterparty risk since it guarantees settlement. Hence, CCPs specialise in risk management, especially market risk and default risk. Variation margin, calculated and paid on a daily or intra-day basis, covers changes in the market value of the clearing members' positions under normal market circumstances. To manage default risk, CCPs use several lines of defence, including an initial margin to cover counterparty risk, a default fund to which all clearing members contribute (and replenish if necessary), and requiring the CCP to put up its own capital in order to give it a stake in the outcome ('skin in the game'). Figure 7.12 shows the sequence in which the CCP risk waterfall is activated if a clearing member cannot meet its obligations.

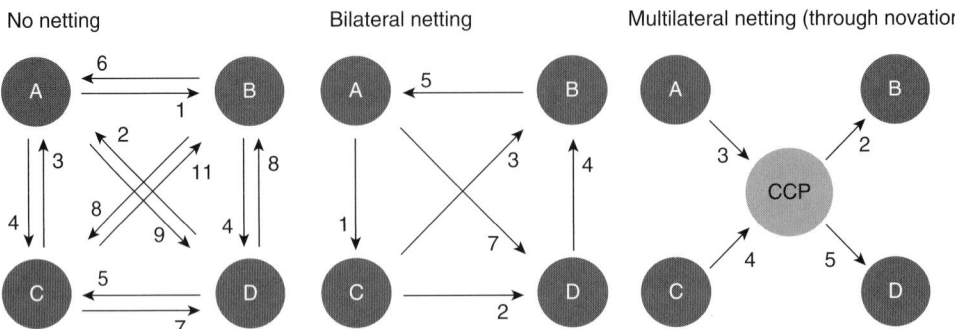

Figure 7.11 Netting and novation in CCPs
Source: DNB (2018)

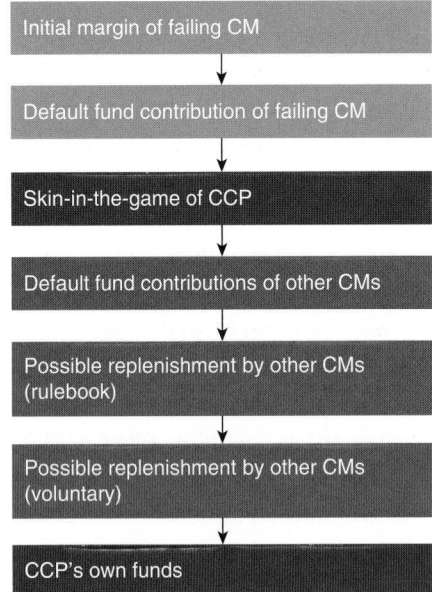

Figure 7.12 CCP risk waterfall
Source: DNB (2018)

While these reforms address some post-trading problems, they also create new risks within the financial system, notably concentration risk. This is related to the central role that CCPs play as intermediaries in transactions between parties (see Figure 7.11) and the fact that mandatory central clearing of standardised contracts increases the risk for financial institutions due to the rising exposures of CCPs and clearing members. These risks were highlighted in September 2018 when a Norwegian individual clearing member defaulted due to strong spread movement in the European power derivatives market (Stafford, 2018). Losses from this event entered deeply into the risk waterfall of its CCP, i.e. all the way through the CCP's skin in the game and the default contributions of other clearing members. This led to a call by its CCP, i.e. EMIR-authorised Nasdaq Clearing, which falls under the supervision of the Swedish Financial Supervisory Authority Finansinspektionen, on all clearing members to replenish the fund with €100 million. Since this was an idiosyncratic case related to a single trader, it seems unlikely that the CCP would have been able to withstand simultaneous defaults from more and larger clearing members at the same time. It will therefore likely trigger a debate on the appropriateness of the default waterfall, including the CCP's own funds. According to EMIR, CCPs should be able to absorb the failure of their two largest clearing members.

The majority of central clearing transactions are likely to be performed by a few large CCPs in the future due to the economies of scale and network effects. As illustrated by this incident, these concentration risks place high demands on CCPs' risk management and resilience. Moreover, as a CCP's bankruptcy can never be entirely ruled out, it is key to reduce the impact of such an event on financial markets. It is therefore important to ensure that a CCP can be resolved in an orderly manner in the event of bankruptcy, and that critical activities can be maintained without threatening financial stability. A European-level regulation for recovery and resolution of CCPs is therefore being developed (DNB, 2018).

The settlement of securities and derivatives contracts is also affected by the harmonisation of CSDs and consolidation in TARGET and T2S. While generally safe and efficient within national borders, settlement across borders presents higher risks and costs for investors than domestic operations (European Commission, 2018). The CSD Regulation (909/2014/EU) therefore aims to increase the safety and efficiency of securities settlement and settlement infrastructures in the EU. It harmonises both the timing and conduct of securities settlement in Europe and the rules governing CSDs, and creates a common EU framework for the regulation, authorisation, and supervision of CSDs.

The launch of T2S provides all CSDs with a single platform for security settlement in Europe, which harmonises all interactions between CSDs. It makes the cost, technical processing, and efficiency of cross-border settlement identical to domestic settlement. A single set of rules, standards, and tariffs apply to all transactions in Europe, thereby reducing complexity and contributing to financial integration. TARGET and T2S are in the process of being consolidated into a single system that allows enhanced functionality and integrated liquidity management across all TARGET services. It is expected to go live in 2021. Moreover, Coeuré (2018) suggests that non-bank payment institutions as regulated under PSD2 could be given access to TARGET as well. This could stimulate innovation and safety by allowing settlement in risk-free central bank money.

7.4 Conclusions

Payment systems are composed of instruments, procedures, and transfer systems that ensure the transfer of money from one economic actor to another. Relatively low-value and non-urgent mass payments are processed through retail payment systems, while wholesale payment systems process large-value and/or high-priority payments between financial institutions.

In securities markets, the clearing and settlement (or post-trading) process provides for the transfer of ownership and payment between buyers and sellers of securities. This process involves four main activities: (1) confirmation of the terms of trade as agreed by the buyer and seller, (2) clearance, by which the respective obligations of the buyer and seller are established, (3) the transfer of securities from the seller to the buyer, and (4) the transfer of funds from the buyer to the seller.

Payment and securities market infrastructures are characterised by economies of scale and scope, and network externalities. The introduction of SEPA should allow providers of payment services to benefit from these economies, thereby increasing overall economic efficiency for citizens as users of these payment services. Moreover, competition is expected to increase in payment services since the market is opening up to non-bank players.

The integration of EU large-value payment systems has been quite remarkable. Various initiatives have been launched to remove existing barriers to integration in these markets and address problems exposed by the financial crisis. However, these reforms also create new risks, notably concentration risk due to the growing importance of CCPs for securities and derivatives transactions.

Notes

1. Denmark, Estonia, Finland, Greece, Hungary, Ireland, Italy, Latvia, Netherlands, Portugal, Romania, Spain, and Sweden. The ECB study provides a snapshot of the social and private cost situation in 2009.

2. Examples of ICSDs are Euroclear and Clearstream International.
3. Netting can be carried out on either a bilateral or multilateral basis. While bilateral netting is an arrangement between only two parties to net their bilateral obligations, multilateral netting is arithmetically achieved by summing each participant's bilateral net positions with those of the other participants to arrive at a multilateral net position vis-à-vis all other participants (Kazarian, 2006).
4. Although the curves in Figure 7.8 are not average cost curves, they reflect how payment unit costs change with payment volume. The curves refer to estimates for three different years.

Bibliography

Suggested Reading

Bank for International Settlements (2018), Payments are a-changin' but cash still rules. *BIS Quarterly Review*, March.

Beer, C., E. Gnan, and U. Birchler (eds.) (2016), *Cash on Trial*, SUERF Conference Proceedings 2016/1.

De Nederlandsche Bank (2018), *The CCP: A Pivotal Player in the Financial System*, DNB, Amsterdam.

References

Bank for International Settlements (1992), *Delivery Versus Payment in Securities Settlement Systems*, BIS, Basel.

   (2001), *Glossary No. 7*, BIS, Basel.

   (2002), *Policy Issues for Central Banks in Retail Payments*, BIS, Basel.

   (2006), *General Guidance for National Payment System Development*, BIS, Basel.

   (2018), Payments are a-changin' but cash still rules. *BIS Quarterly Review*, March.

Beer, C., E. Gnan, and U. Birchler (eds.) (2016), *Cash on Trial*, SUERF Conference Proceedings 2016/1.

Bolt, W. (2007), Retail Payments and Card Use in the Netherlands: Pricing, Scale, and Antitrust. *Competition Policy International*, 3, 257–70.

Bolt, W. and D. Humphrey (2007), Payment Network Scale Economies, SEPA, and Cash Replacement. *Review of Network Economics*, 6, 453–73.

Bolt, W. and A. Tieman (2007), Heavily Skewed Pricing in Two-Sided Market. *International Journal of Industrial Organisation*, 26, 1250–5.

Coeuré, B. (2018), The Future of Financial Market Infrastructures: Spearheading Progress without Renouncing Safety. Speech given on 26 June 2018 at the Central Bank Payments Conference, Singapore. www.ecb.europa.eu/press/key/date/2018/html/ecb.sp180626.en.html (accessed 14 December 2018).

De Nederlandsche Bank (2018), *The CCP: A Pivotal Player in the Financial System*, DNB, Amsterdam.

Deutsche Börse Group (DBG) (2005), *The European Post-Trade Market: An Introduction.* Deutsche Börse Group White Paper.

EBA Clearing (2018), Who We Are. ebaclaring.eu.

Economides, N. (1993), Network Economics with Application to Finance. *Financial Markets, Institutions & Instruments*, 2, 89–97.

(1996), The Economics of Networks. *International Journal of Industrial Organization*, 16, 673–99.

European Central Bank (2012), The Social and Private Costs of Retail Payment Instruments: A European Perspective. ECB Occasional Paper 137.

(2013), Convergence in European Retail Payments. ECB Occasional Paper 147.

(2018), *TARGET Annual Report 2017*, ECB, Frankfurt am Main.

European Commission (2007), *Report on the Retail Sector Inquiry*, EC, Brussels.

(2018), *Central Securities Depositories*, EC, Brussels. https://ec.europa.eu/info/business-economy-euro/banking-and-finance/financial-markets/post-trade-services/central-securities-depositories-csds_en (accessed 13 December 2018).

European Payment Council (2018), *Clearing and Settlement Mechanisms*, EPC, Brussels. www.europeanpaymentscouncil.eu/what-we-do/sepa-payment-scheme-management/clearing-and-settlement-mechanisms (accessed 13 December 2018).

Giovannini Group (2001), *Cross-Border Clearing and Settlement Arrangements in the European Union*, Giovannini Group, Brussels.

Harper, I., S. Rimes, and C. Malam (2006), The Development of Electronic Payment Systems. In: R. Cooper, G. Madden, A. Lloyd, and M. Schipp (eds.), *The Economics of Online Markets and ICT Networks*, Springer, New York, 25–40.

Humphrey, D. B., M. Willesson, T. Lindblom, and G. Bergendahl (2003), What Does It Cost to Make a Payment? *Review of Network Economics*, June, 159–74.

Jonker, N. (2013), Social Costs of POS Payments in the Netherlands 2002–2012: Efficiency Gains from Increased Debit Card Usage. *DNB Occasional Studies*, 1102, Netherlands Central Bank, Research Department.

Kazarian, E. G. (2006), Integration of the Securities Market Infrastructure in the European Union: Policy and Regulatory Issues. IMF Working Paper 06/241.

Khiaonarong, T. (2003), Payment Systems Efficiency, Policy Approaches, and the Role of the Central Bank. Bank of Finland Discussion Paper 1.

Lannoo, K. and M. Levin (2001), The Securities Settlement Industry in the EU: Structure, Costs and the Way Forward. CEPS Research Report.

London Stock Exchange/Oxera (2002), Clearing and Settlement in Europe – Response to the First Report of the Giovannini Group.

NERA Economic Consulting (2004), The Direct Costs of Clearing and Settlement: An EU–US Comparison. City Research Series 1.

Riksbank (2018), Special Issue on the E-Krona, *Sveriges Riksbank Economic Review*.

Rochet, J.-C. and J. Tirole (2006), Two-Sided Markets: A Progress Report. *The RAND Journal of Economics*, 35, 645–67.

Salo, S. (2006), Promoting Integration of European Retail Payment Systems: Role of Competition, Cooperation and Regulation. Paper presented at the SUERF Seminar 'The Adoption of the Euro in New Member States: Challenges and Vulnerabilities on the Last Stretch', Malta, 4 May.

Schulze, N. and D. Baur (2006), Annex II of Economic Impact Study on Clearing and Settlement, EC, Brussels. http://ec.europa.eu/internal_market/financialmarkets/docs/clearing/draft/annex_2_En.pdf (accessed 13 February 2012).

Serifsoy, B. and M. Weiβ (2007), Settling for Efficiency: A Framework for the European Securities Transaction Industry. *Journal of Banking and Finance*, 31, 3034–57.

Shy, O. (2001), *The Economics of Network Industries*, Cambridge University Press.

Stafford, P. (2018), How Clearing Houses Aim to Avert Market Disasters. *Financial Times*, 14 September.

8

Financial Innovation

The financial sector performs two main functions: (1) reducing information and transaction costs, and (2) facilitating the trading, diversification, and management of risk. Financial innovation ensures that the financial system can provide these functions more efficiently if the social benefits outweigh the social costs. Such innovation involves creating and popularising new financial instruments, as well as new financial technologies, institutions, and markets. While it can help foster growth and economic prosperity, some new instruments have been blamed for their role in the global financial crisis. This chapter discusses the causes and consequences of financial innovation.

Competition, regulation and deregulation, and technological advances are important drivers of financial innovation. Competition stimulates financial institutions to develop new products and processes. Since regulation may forbid or otherwise restrain financial innovation, deregulation may spur innovation. Indeed, several innovations have been the result of attempts to circumvent regulation. Finally, technological advances have made new instruments possible.

There has been a recent increase in financial technology (FinTech), which combines changes in customer contact, for instance using mobile apps, with big data and new methodologies for handling the data. Taken together, such innovations may affect the entire value chain in retail payments, credit provision, and other services. A specific class of innovations is related to cryptocurrencies and distributed ledger technologies, which provide an alternative to traditional forms of value transfer through central trusted parties. However, their ultimate impact on the efficiency of financial intermediation is not known.

Financial innovations may improve payments, offer new savings and investment opportunities, and increase risk sharing. The first part of this chapter examines the main drivers of such innovation. The second part analyses some recent innovations such as FinTech, cryptocurrencies, and exchange traded funds. The third part assesses the pros and cons of financial innovation.

LEARNING OBJECTIVES

After you have studied this chapter, you should be able to:
- explain the drivers of financial innovation
- analyse recent financial innovations such as financial technology (FinTech), cryptocurrencies, distributed ledger technology, and exchange traded funds (ETFs)
- understand the advantages and disadvantages of financial innovation
- explain the risks of financial innovation and its impact on financial fragility.

8.1 Financial Innovation: Drivers

Financial innovation involves developing and popularising new financial instruments, as well as new financial technologies, institutions, and markets. They are sometimes categorised as either product or process innovations. Product innovations are exemplified by new cryptocurrencies, derivative contracts, or new corporate securities, while process improvements include new means of online distribution of financial services, processing transactions, or pricing transactions. In practice, however, these innovations are often linked (Lerner and Tufano, 2012).

Financial innovation differs from other types of new product development in three main ways (Lerner and Tufano, 2012). First, since the financial system is highly interconnected, financial innovation is likely to generate a complex web of externalities, both positive and negative. Therefore, assessing the social consequences of financial innovation can be very challenging. Second, financial innovations are very dynamic. As an innovation diffuses from pioneering adopters to more general users, these products frequently change in their underlying structure, the way they are marketed, and how they are used. Thus, the consequences of an innovation may change over time. Finally, the complexity of regulating new financial products and services may lead to a cat-and-mouse game between the regulator and the industry, with several rounds of reregulation.

Financial innovations have the potential to enhance the efficiency of financial services provision. For instance, they provide households with new choices for investment and consumption and reduce the costs of raising and deploying funds. Similarly, financial innovations may enable firms to raise capital in larger amounts and at a lower cost than they could otherwise.

At the same time, financial innovations have been blamed for the global financial crisis (see Chapter 2). Nobel Prize laureate Paul Krugman (2007) explains:

[T]he innovations of recent years – the alphabet soup of C.D.O.s and S.I.V.s, R.M.B. S. and A.B.C.P. – were sold on false pretences. They were promoted as ways to spread risk, making investment safer. What they did instead – aside from making their creators a lot of money, which they didn't have to repay when it all went bust – was to spread confusion, luring investors into taking on more risk than they realised.

Where does financial innovation come from? Generally, it is driven by investor demand for a particular set of cash flows. Intermediaries recognise this demand and engineer securities that have the desired characteristics. By splitting up or combining the cash flows of existing securities, the intermediaries can create profits for themselves. This may increase social welfare if it decreases the costs of financial intermediation and improves resource allocation (Lerner and Tufano, 2012). But if there are impediments to competition, it may also lead to higher private returns for shareholders and employees, with little overall costs savings for the end users of financial services (Philippon, 2016).

According to Gennaioli *et al.*'s model (2012), financial innovations can address client demands for a particular set of cash flows and thus be socially beneficial. But they suggest that investors may systematically underestimate the risks associated with these new products' cash flows, which may trigger an exodus back to traditional, safer products and thus threaten the stability of the overall financial system.

In addition to profit maximisation and competition, financial regulation and technological change are important drivers of innovation. Regulation can drive financial innovation when there are differences across sectors or economies. This can be illustrated by the differences in the development of ETFs between the US and Europe (see Box 8.1). ETFs are investment funds that are traded on an exchange. Whereas in Europe synthetic ETFs have developed very rapidly, in the US physical ETFs are dominant. *Physical ETFs* replicate the index by simply reconstituting the basket of physical securities underlying the index. *Synthetic ETFs* obtain the desired return by executing an asset swap instead of physically replicating the index. One of the main factors explaining this difference between the US and Europe is differences in regulation. European regulators take a more liberal stance on the use of derivatives in investment funds, while the conservative US approach has limited the development of synthetic ETFs (FSB, 2011).

Box 8.1 Exchange traded funds (ETFs): features and risks

ETFs are one of the more successful financial innovations in recent decades. They are investment funds that are traded on an exchange and often track an index (e.g. S&P 500). As such, they offer low-cost diversification, liquidity, and tradability. As there is a direct link between the security and its underlying components, ETFs do not require fund managers to choose securities; thus they tend to have lower fees than other mutual funds.

Although ETFs are generally open-ended, unlike other open-end funds, ETF investors generally do not sell or redeem fund shares directly from the fund. Only 'authorised participants' purchase and redeem ETF shares directly from the fund, but only in large blocks called creation units. In addition, market makers provide liquidity by: (1) investing in ETFs through authorised participants in the primary market and (2) trading with investors in the secondary market. Since arbitrage opportunities can be exploited, the value of ETF shares on the stock exchange does not vary significantly from the NAV of the ETF under normal circumstances.

Unlike traditional open-end funds, redemption from an ETF is typically 'in kind' – i.e. delivering the underlying securities – rather than in cash. Since ETF shares are traded on an exchange, investors can buy them as long as the exchange is open – in contrast to mutual funds, which can only be purchased at the close of the market each day.

The ETF market has grown rapidly over the past decade, expanding globally from $0.7 trillion in 2008 to $4.8 trillion in 2018 (ETFGI, 2018). In the US, ETFs represent 15 per cent of total investment fund assets, compared to about 5 per cent in the euro area. The market is highly concentrated: more than 70 per cent of all euro-area ETFs are managed by just three asset management companies (ECB, 2017). ETF products primarily track the more liquid market segments. Euro-area ETFs most frequently track the S&P500, EURO STOXX, and MSCI World stock market indices.

There are two types of ETFs. *Physical ETFs* replicate the index by simply reconstituting the basket of underlying physical securities (e.g. the basket of S&P 500 stocks) with appropriate weights. They are the dominant form of ETF, especially in the US, and are mainly provided by large independent asset managers. *Synthetic ETFs* enter into an asset swap, i.e. an over-the-counter derivative, rather than replicate the index physically. They are typically provided by banks' asset management arms. According to the FSB (2011), one factor supporting their growth is the synergies created within banking groups if the derivative trading desk acts as swap counterparty to the asset management arm providing the ETF. Another factor is the more liberal stance of European regulation on the use of derivatives in investment funds; the US regulator has adopted a more conservative approach, de facto limiting the development of synthetic ETFs. Synthetic ETFs represent approximately one-fifth of the market in the euro area, but only a negligible proportion in the US. The majority of euro-area ETFs use synthetic replication strategies for the more illiquid markets (ECB, 2017).

Box 8.1 (cont.)

In a synthetic ETF (see Figure 8.1), the provider (typically a bank) sells ETF shares to investors in exchange for cash, which is then invested in a collateral basket, the return of which is swapped by the derivatives desk of the same bank for the return of an index. Since the swap counterparty is typically the bank also acting as the ETF provider, investors may be exposed if the bank defaults. Therefore, problems at banks that are most active in swap-based ETFs may constitute a powerful source of contagion and systemic risk. As there is no requirement to hold collateral to match the assets of the tracked index, the synthetic ETF creation process may be driven by the possibility for the bank to raise funding against an illiquid portfolio that cannot otherwise be financed in the repo market (FSB, 2011).

Finally, the set-up of ETFs implies pros and cons for the liquidity of ETF shares. Intra-day liquidity on the secondary market is an attractive feature of ETFs. Since most authorised participants accept redemption of the underlying securities instead of cash, traditional concerns related to first-mover advantages are mitigated. This occurs when a fund sells assets in response to redemption requests, so that price decreases are amplified and investors have an incentive to exit. But liquidity transformation in ETFs may entail some risk to financial stability (ECB, 2017). Liquidity is determined, on the one hand, by the supply in (and demand for) ETF shares on exchanges (i.e. secondary markets), and on the other hand by the willingness and ability of market makers to provide liquidity by creating or redeeming shares through authorised participants in the primary market. *A priori*, the possibility cannot be ruled out that this function will be impaired when market makers are under stress, and/or the underlying assets become illiquid. Liquidity risks are therefore ultimately borne by the end investors, who may have to accept a widening of the NAV spread if the underlying market becomes illiquid.

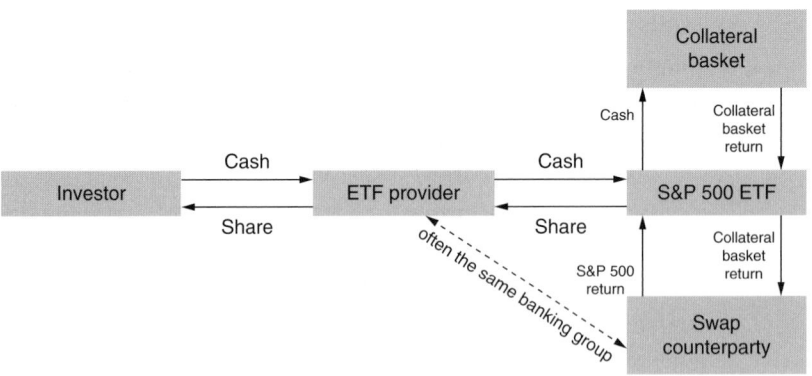

Figure 8.1   Simplified functioning of a synthetic ETF on the S&P 500
Source: FSB (2011)

Yet the relationship between financial innovation and regulation is complex. Innovators look for opportunities to exploit regulatory gaps. For example, bank capital rules have encouraged banks to use off-balance-sheet vehicles (see Chapter 2). Thus, regulation may give rise to certain innovations, but then regulators frequently 'catch up' with the products in a cat-and-mouse process (Dewatripont and Tirole, 1994). The revised bank capital rules give banks few opportunities to use off-balance-sheet vehicles. However, even a well-staffed regulatory agency will struggle to keep up with entrepreneurs and innovators, and will be forced to react to innovations with a lag.

Advances in information technology have made customer contact and payment services possible through mobile apps, as well as the low-cost collection, processing, and dissemination of household and business financial data. This, in turn, allows for the ever-faster evaluation of creditworthiness, identification of prospective borrowers, and management of existing accounts. For example, this may lead to financial innovation through the emergence of online platforms for product comparison (so-called e-aggregators), apps that provide investment advice ('robo-advisers') or a holistic view of personal financial management, and online credit approval. From the consumer's perspective, this provides easier access to (and management of) core personal financial services.

8.2 Recent Financial Innovations

Financial innovation has always been driven by technological change. In 1866 the transatlantic telegraph cable enabled a period of financial globalisation that lasted until 1916 (Arner *et al.*, 2017). There were rapid advances in electronic payments systems in the 1960s and 1970s. For example, the establishment of the Inter-Bank Computer Bureau in 1968 in the UK formed the basis of modern automated clearing services. And the first cash automated teller machine (ATM) was introduced in London in 1967; the advent of the networked ATM proved to be more useful for consumers than the machines themselves. Once ATMs were networked, bank customers no longer had to wait in line at a bank: they could access their money any time across a wide geographical area. Another example is the Internet, which has drastically changed the way consumers and businesses buy and pay for goods and services. Internet banking has enabled consumers to make payments or use other banking services anywhere in the world, at any time. Over time, innovations often become standard financial products as described elsewhere in the book, e.g. derivatives in Chapter 5, or credit card payments in Chapter 7.

As explained in Chapter 1, the financial sector performs two main functions: (1) it reduces information and transaction costs, and (2) it facilitates the trading, diversification, and management of risk. Financial innovations affect both functions. For example, online customer contact, payment services, and credit approval may reduce information and transaction costs. And ETFs or relatively new types of derivatives such as credit default swaps (CDS) affect the trading, diversification, and management of risk. This section analyses more recent innovations from this perspective.

FinTech

In recent years, the scale of investment in technology and the pace of financial innovation have increased considerably. *FinTech* refers to the latest wave of financial innovations (Arner *et al.*, 2017). It has been defined as technologically enabled innovation in financial services that could result in new business models, applications, processes, or products that have an associated material effect on financial markets and institutions and the provision of financial services (FSB, 2017).

At the heart of FinTech are advances in information technology that change the nature of customer contact, particularly mobile apps and online platforms. Moreover, decreases in data handling costs have facilitated the low-cost collection, processing, and dissemination of household and business financial data. As a result, many FinTech innovations target services related to customer contact and operations management, based on these new technologies.

Regulation is an important complementary driver of FinTech. This can be illustrated by the interaction between the EU Second Payment Services Directive (PSD2) and innovation in payment systems. PSD2 allows third-party service providers access to consumer bank account data (see Chapter 7). This gives non-bank FinTech start-ups an opportunity to access this market, thereby increasing competition and improving the efficiency of retail payments for consumers. Another example is the growth of RegTech solutions, which aim to reduce the cost of complying with financial regulations.

FinTech start-ups often operate with relatively small balance sheets and rely heavily on equity (e.g. venture capital) funding due to the uncertainty surrounding future cash flows. Services that rely on large debt-funded balance sheets (i.e. traditional banking, insurance companies, and pension funds) largely remain in the realm of traditional industry for now, for instance due to their large customer bases which take time to build up. In some economies, including China, large technology companies ('BigTech') have become major providers of financial services.

Many FinTech innovations also rely on networks (either in professional networks or through PCs or mobile phones by retail customers), data-handling infrastructures, and the development of methodologies to extract relevant information from the data, especially through open source software. Table 8.1 introduces key terms in the field.

These innovations affect all components of the financial services value chain, i.e. customer acquisition and retention, the production of financial products, and the back office and infrastructure (see Figures 8.2 and 8.3). Such innovations can be developed by existing financial institutions, across

Table 8.1 FinTech terminology

Algorithm	A process or set of rules to be followed in calculations or other problem-solving operations, especially by a computer.
Artificial intelligence	The theory and development of computer systems that can perform tasks normally requiring human intelligence, such as visual perception, speech recognition, decision making, and translation between languages.
Big data	A generic term that refers to the massive volume of data generated by the increasing use of digital tools and information systems.
Blockchain	A system in which a record of transactions made in bitcoin or another cryptocurrency is maintained across several computers that are linked in a peer-to-peer network.
Cryptocurrency	A digital currency in which encryption techniques are used to regulate the generation of units of currency and verify the transfer of funds, independently from a central bank.
Cryptography	The art of writing or solving codes.
Distributed ledger	A digital system in which records of transactions (typically using bitcoin or similar cryptocurrencies) are simultaneously maintained at multiple points throughout a network.
Machine learning	A computer's capacity to learn from experience, i.e. to modify its processing based on newly acquired information.
RegTech	Any range of FinTech applications for regulatory and compliance requirements and reporting by regulated financial institutions.
Robo-advice	Applications that combine digital interfaces and algorithms, and sometimes machine learning, to provide services ranging from automated financial recommendations to contract brokering to portfolio management to clients.

Sources: Oxford Dictionary; Investopedia; FSB (2017)

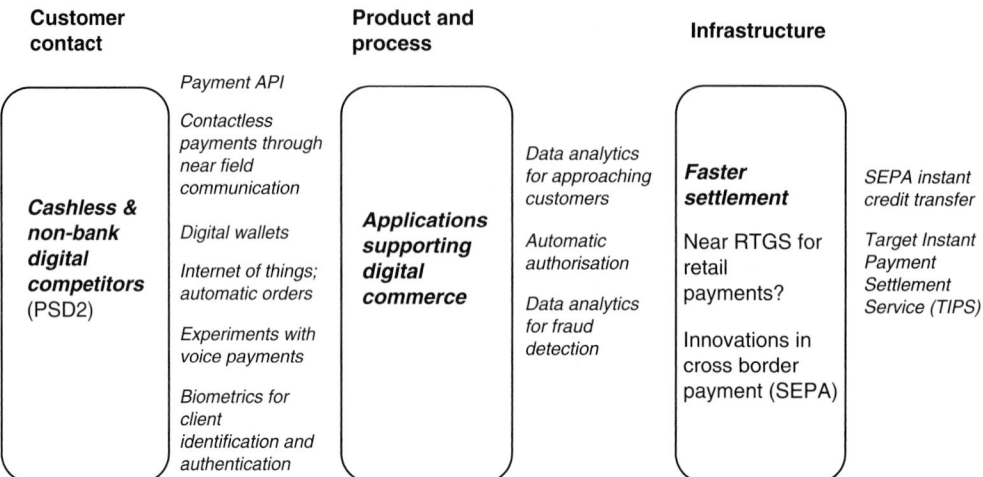

Figure 8.2   Retail payment systems value chain

the value chain, or by new FinTech firms that target a specific niche within the value chain.

Figure 8.2 shows examples of such innovations for retail payment systems, an area that has been disrupted by FinTech. Customer contact is affected by the shift towards digital money; cash is continuing its downward trend in some economies. PSD2's provision to permit the entry of non-bank competitors, including FinTech start-ups and BigTech players, has changed the playing field. The new players have developed products and services to address the inefficiencies associated with Internet shopping, for example by connecting payment methods from different countries. The digitalisation of the payment process provides a wealth of new data, which new algorithms can use to detect fraud. Moreover, innovations in netting, clearing, and settlement allow faster settlement of the resulting payments between financial institutions in the large-value payment infrastructure (Chapter 7).

Figure 8.3 provides a similar perspective on FinTech innovations in credit provisions. The number of bank branches continues to decline, as most customer contacts take place online. This trend is supported by personal financial management apps that give a holistic overview of one's finances, and platforms that compare different products. Big data can also be used to screen customers, inform credit decisions, and monitor compliance, which supports the shift from relationship banking to transaction banking. Internet platforms facilitate the role of non-banks in providing peer-to-peer (P2P) lending. Likewise, back-office functions are potentially aided by new

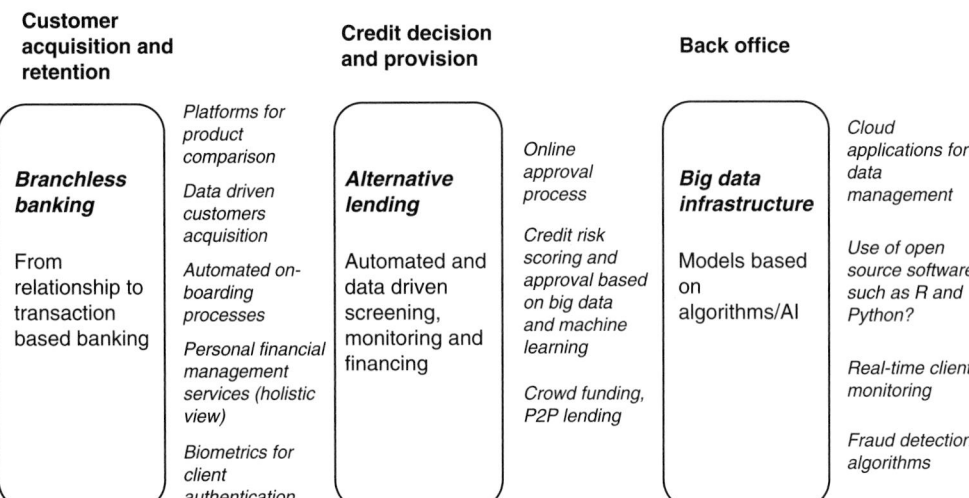

Figure 8.3 Credit provision value chain

applications for data management and new data-handling techniques related to the use of algorithms. P2P lending is growing rapidly, and is already sizeable in some niche markets such as unsecured consumer loans or lending to very small businesses in the UK, but remains relatively small in comparison to the traditional banking sector (Claessens *et al.*, 2018; FSB, 2018).

The impact of regulation on FinTech firms' competitive position is unclear. On the one hand, it could be argued that the current financial regulation is mainly tailored to traditional financial institutions. Hence, FinTech firms may be at a disadvantage and face barriers to entry, unless supervisors manage to lower these barriers, for example by creating special 'regulatory sandboxes' that permit experiments under lighter regimes. On the other hand, tighter regulation after the financial crisis, e.g. for banks, may give FinTech firms that operate just outside the regulatory boundary a competitive advantage in disrupting existing functions, such as credit provision through Internet platforms, aided by new technology related to big data.

Gomber *et al.* (2018) map the financial innovation landscape based on the effect on functions and markets, with competition as a driver (replicated in Table 8.2). The effect on functions is measured as: (i) customer experience with improvements in functionality, and (ii) new functionality (Table 8.2, top rows). The effect on markets is measured as: (i) complementary versus (ii) disruptive effects from innovations (Table 8.2, first columns).

FinTech innovations that complement existing financial products and services are shown in the last row of Table 8.2. These include, for example,

Table 8.2 Classification of FinTech innovation

MARKETS AND COMPETITION	**Contrast between the effects of FinTech innovations**	CUSTOMER EXPERIENCE WITH THE NEW FINANCIAL SERVICES	
		Enhancing experience with new products, new services, and new functionality	Supplementing experience with improvements in existing functionality
	Disruptive effects from		
	• New business models	Block-chain based markets, initial coin offerings, cryptocurrencies, global remittances, FX applications, high-frequency trading, crowdfunding, P2P lending, online brokerage, cross-border payments, open banking	Open banking/APIs, faster payment settlement, increased settlement efficiency with blockchain, smart contracts in trade services and lending, cross-border custody services, e-services piggybacking, higher functionality payment cards
	• New market mechanisms		
	• Shared tech infrastructures		
	• Dis-intermediation of banks		
	• Segment-of-one marketing		
	• Cross-border innovations		
	Complementary effects from		
	• Enhanced business models	Social trading, digital wallets, robo-advisory services, branchless banking services, big data-supported customer intimacy, personal financial management, financial research exchanges	Investment communities, mobile payments, blockchain-based general ledger functionality, risk management technology, RegTech solutions, account deposits without branches, FinTech trade support
	• Extended access by customers		
	• Hybridised services by firms		
	• Shared tech infrastructures		
	• Open APIs		

Source: Gomber *et al.* (2018)

branchless banking and digital wallets, which represent enhancements of business models through improved functionality. The more disruptive types of FinTech are shown in the upper-left corner. These include blockchain technology, high-frequency trading, and crowdfunding, which represent new business models and offer new services and functionality. But in practice the distinction is not always clear-cut, as crowdfunding often complements traditional finance for start-ups.

Can FinTech lead to better value for money for end users, and truly improve the efficiency of resource allocation (as discussed in Chapter 1)? Philippon (2016) analyses the scope for efficiency improvements in the financial sector, measured by the unit costs of financial intermediation. He approximates overall financial services provision using the aggregate size of intermediated financial services based on the balance sheets of the non-financial private sector, i.e. consumer credit, liquidity services, and intermediated corporate assets. By relating this to finance industry income, one can calculate the unit cost of financial intermediation for the end users. The data show that this number has been relatively stable at around 2 per cent. This implies that for intermediated financial services, the spread between the return for savers and borrowers is 2 per cent on average. This has not decreased in recent decades despite large-scale, ongoing financial innovation.

Hence, FinTech has a considerable potential to improve the efficiency of resource allocation in the financial system. But why? Philippon (2016) argues that financial innovations often lead to private returns for employees and shareholders, but less often to improvements in social welfare, as we have seen with innovations before the financial crisis. This could be explained by impediments to entry, which lead to concentration, market power, and a lack of competition (see also Chapter 10 on consolidation in banking). Policy-induced distortions also play a role, such as those related to too-big-to-fail subsidies, the tax deductibility of interest payments (which incentivises risk taking through the use of leverage) and perhaps even financial regulation to the extent that it creates barriers to entry (Chapter 12). As a result, established players in banking, insurance, and pensions retain a competitive advantage in financial intermediation due to their large balance sheets, which take time to build up. FinTech disruptions occur mainly where large debt-funded balance sheets are not needed, for example in improving customer interfaces through Internet platforms or payment systems, or improving the management of large databases.

Ultimately, the extent to which FinTech innovations will benefit end users depends on the social costs of innovations, risks, and regulatory responses. For example, experiences in the securitisation and subprime markets and cryptocurrencies (discussed in the next section) show that price increases that start with financial innovations can become bubbles due to amplification effects. Moreover, automated trading algorithms can improve efficiency costs, but may also amplify market spirals, and facilitate a flash crash. And will P2P lending really hold up in the event of heavy credit losses during a financial crisis? Past experience has shown that innovations have not always lasted, bubbles have burst, flash crashes have occurred, private attempts to create safe collateral (in the form of asset-backed securities) have broken down around the global financial crisis, and governments have already started to put restrictions on cryptocurrencies. In the meantime, both supervisory and competition policies will remain vital for translating the FinTech opportunity into more effective and efficient forms of financial intermediation while addressing the stability risks.

Cryptocurrencies and Distributed Ledger Technologies

Cryptocurrencies were created as a private alternative to money provided by commercial banks and central banks. They are based on a fundamentally different decentralised structure than payment systems: they rely on cryptography rather than a central authority (Nakamoto, 2008). Users can trade cryptocurrencies with each other in exchange for traditional currency or goods and services without the need for a third party (like a bank). Nor is their creation controlled by a central bank. With conventional bank deposits, banks hold the digital record and are entrusted to ensure its validity. Cryptocurrencies, by contrast, have a publicly available ledger that stores all transactions. Rather than requiring users to trust special institutions, reliance is placed on the network and the rules established to reliably verify entries into the ledger.

The adoption of cryptocurrencies like bitcoin appears to be driven by three factors (Ali *et al.*, 2014): (1) ideology, as they are designed to avoid any central control and to minimise the degree of trust that participants need to place in any third party, (2) financial returns, as some view cryptocurrencies as an asset class for financial investment, driven by an interaction between the schemes' planned fixed supplies and their increasing publicity, and (3) the pursuit of lower transaction fees than those of electronic retail payment systems or international transfers.

Cryptocurrencies exist as entries in distributed private ledger systems, outside the regular banking system; they are not backed by any government. There is widespread agreement that their main technological innovation is the decentralised transfer of value between peers in the network, without the need for a trusted third-party intermediary (e.g. Ali *et al.*, 2014; BIS, 2018). Digital entries can be copied, which can lead to fraud, i.e. selling the same currency more than once. Bitcoin's innovative solution has been to incentivise decentral nodes (called miners) to verify transactions, which are then added to the history of the ledger (Figure 8.4). In this example, all

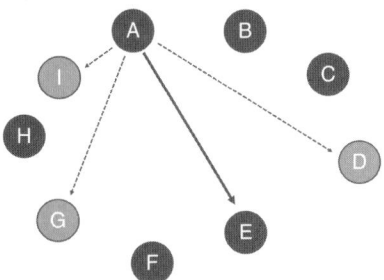

Figure 8.4   Decentral verification of transactions
Source: Ali *et al.* (2014).

participants have access to all accounts (and their entire history). Payments pass directly between users – shown here by the arrow from A to E – but are verified by other users: in particular, new transactions are broadcasted to 'miners' (shown here as participants D, G, and I).

A distributed ledger has three essential characteristics (Benos *et al.*, 2017):

1. Decentralised access to (and control of) the database: each node in the system holds a synchronised copy of the database, and updating is performed by some or all nodes in the system.
2. Reliability in situations without trust: a consensus mechanism ensures the consistency and integrity of the database.
3. The use of cryptography to deliver (1) and (2).

This differs from a distributed database, which is shared across nodes, but a centralised administrator still controls access to the trusted nodes, and updates and synchronises the database.

Blockchain as used by bitcoin is a form of distributed ledger technology. Data are gathered in blocks of transactions, which are linked to each other using cryptographic tools. This dependence of the various blocks of data on the previous blocks makes it very hard to change the data. Thus, the blockchain forms a perpetual chain of immutable records (Benos *et al.*, 2017). The key to building trust in this open system is updating it, i.e. adding blocks to the blockchain. Miners gather blocks of transactions, which are then added to the existing history if they believe they represent the consensus of a majority of miners regarding which transactions are correct. Since miners do not know in advance who will add the next block, they are forward looking: they want their block to be verified by the next group of miners so it will represent the new consensus. If the other miners believe the transaction to be incorrect (i.e. not representing the consensus), they will not add the new block of transactions to it. The underlying mechanism is that miners have to show proof of work to win the competition, which allows them to add the next block of transactions and get the reward, i.e. a transaction fee and/or newly issued currency. The competition involves solving algorithms that require a lot of computing power, but the answers are easy to check. Hence, the expectation is that on average, the miner with the greatest computing power will win the competition and thereby represent the consensus in the network. This is called the 51 per cent rule: on average, attackers need more than half of the mining power to be able to change the consensus.

How have cryptocurrencies affected the functioning of the financial system? How well have they functioned as money? History is full of attempts to create new currencies. Before governments started to regulate the use of fiat money, or where fiat money was not available, different private tokens with intrinsic value have functioned as money, such as salt, shells, glass beads, gold and silver (Ali *et al.*, 2014; BIS, 2018). But base erosion – i.e. over-issuance – has often led to a loss of trust in money. This is why most central banks currently strive to achieve a steady purchasing power of fiat money. Today, most money exists in digital form, as a claim either on commercial banks or the central bank, and the use of coins and banknotes is declining (see Chapter 7). Cryptocurrencies have no underlying physical value (as gold or silver do), and there is no recourse to government or commercial bank assets in case of a default. They are simply a digital entry in an accounting system, or ledger. Base erosion is prevented through fixed supply rules, such as the 21 million maximum supply in bitcoin. Like all money, cryptocurrencies rely on social convention, i.e. the extent to which people trust and use them. They derive value from network externalities. This can lead to a market value that is higher than its intrinsic value, which in principle is zero for a digital account entry.

Economists evaluate the size of these network externalities through the functions of money as (1) a store of value, (2) a medium of exchange, and (3) a unit of account. Using this definition, several authors conclude that cryptocurrencies do not function very well as money (Ali *et al.*, 2014; BIS, 2018). First, their value has been very volatile (Figure 8.5). One reason for this is the absence of a central authority that adjusts the supply to maintain its value: since there is a fixed supply, the level of demand determines the value. Cryptocurrencies have also been vulnerable to theft from their digital storage, which has shaken confidence and added to price volatility. Second, they have been used as a speculative asset, but have not been widely used as a medium of exchange. Moreover, bitcoin has been used as a means of payment in niche markets related to criminal activities, since it operates

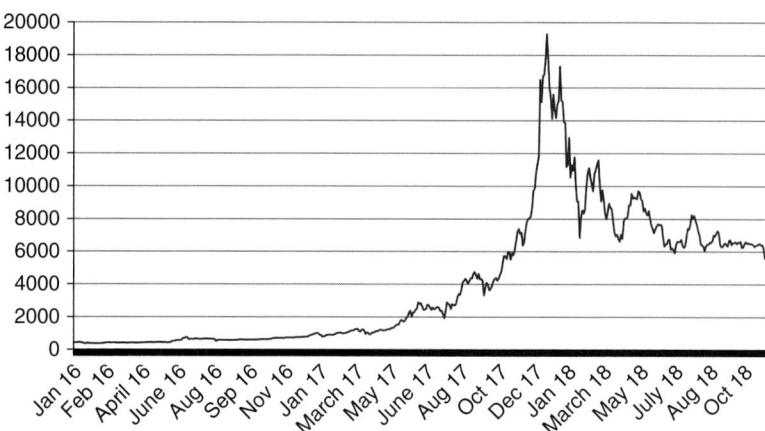

Figure 8.5   Value of bitcoin in US$
Source: Blockchain.com

outside the traditional financial system. Due to their limitations as a stable store of value and widely used medium of exchange, however, cryptocurrencies have not been a generally accepted unit of account.

In addition to being ineffective, cryptocurrencies have also been inefficient at generating trust in a decentralised manner through the use of computer power as a proof of work. The total electricity costs of bitcoin mining equalled that of a mid-sized economy like Switzerland (BIS, 2018). Moreover, when transaction demand is high and the capacity limits of mining are reached, transaction fees spike (to $140 per transaction at their peak). Electricity use, settlement capacity, and decentral storage limits would all prevent bitcoin from handling the transaction volumes required for generally accepted means of payment.

According to Fatás and Weder di Mauro (2018), this analysis of economists overlooks the potential for the underlying technology to serve as a catalyst for innovation in payment systems. For example, it promises the safe and efficient transfer of value within a P2P network. They argue that the role of money as a store of value should be seen separate from its role as a medium of exchange. They also point out that distributed ledger technology, on which cryptocurrencies are based, can be used to store and transfer value in any digitalised asset. It has the potential for much wider applications within the financial system (and beyond, for example, in legal contracts). Rather than serving as an alternative to existing financial intermediation, it can be applied within existing structures. And instead of being a permission-less distributed ledger technology, in which anybody can validate entries, this function can be made private and restricted to specific trusted nodes to give only approved participants access to the data (BIS, 2018). The transaction costs could be much lower in such a system, as trust does not rely on proof of work or other validation methods. Such modifications would allow for more gradual application in specific segments of the financial system, especially those that rely heavily on data storage and transfer of value. In doing so, smart contracts could also help to automatically enforce the terms of financial contracts, e.g. by enforcing the payment legs in a derivatives contract. Potential broader applications of distributed ledger technology include the storage of securities, clearing and settlement of securities, cross-border payments including remittances, trade finance, repo markets, leveraged loan markets, anti-money laundering, and know-your-customer regulations (BIS, 2018).

Special attention has been paid to the potential application of distributed ledger technology in the post-trade clearing and settlement of securities (ESMA, 2016; Benos *et al.*, 2017). In the EU, significant market integration has been achieved through Target2-Securities, where connected central securities depositories (CSDs) can hold their accounts. But there is still significant fragmentation in the way different layers of the market interact with each other (Pinna and Ruttenberg, 2016). The main intermediaries are the trading platforms that confirm the trades; the clearing agents and central clearing parties (CCPs) responsible for matching trades, netting and margin calculations; CSDs responsible for the exchange of payment and securities, collateral management, and reconciliation of positions, and custodians maintaining ownership records and managing changes in positions during the lifecycle of contracts. All these institutions hold their own databases, which prevents straight-through processing. Moreover, the need for reconciliation between different databases leads to risks such as chains of settlement failures, human errors, and less efficient use of collateral. Overall, post-trade processes represent a substantial cost to end users.

In a hypothetical decentralised settlement structure based on distributed ledger technology, securities transactions are cleared and settled bilaterally between buyers and sellers, who are part of the distributed ledger network. Information on ownership and transactions is stored in every node of the network, and trades are validated via a consensus mechanism (Benos *et al.*, 2017). Smart contracts would automatically execute periodic exchanges of value over the lifetime of derivatives contracts. This approach would cut out several intermediaries and therefore lead to lower costs, which could at least be partly passed on to end users.

Yet such a settlement structure would require overcoming several challenges. For instance, since securities transactions are mostly confidential, their validation may still require the restricted involvement of a single trusted node. Continued centralisation also seems likely for other functions: access management, identification of participants, and matching of trades could also be conducted in separate trusted nodes. And CCPs are likely to continue to play a role in transactions with a counterparty credit risk, such as derivatives transactions. Attention has thus shifted to the possible application of private and permissioned ledgers. But beyond these general features, it is unclear how the post-trade landscape would evolve in the future due to the application of distributed ledger technology.

Innovations in Savings and Investments

Over the last four decades there has been a proliferation of new ways to save, such as *mutual funds*. Mutual funds have been one of the most successful financial innovations of the twentieth century, based on their growth rates, adoption rates, fraction of capital intermediated in the economy, or importance to household balance sheets (Lerner and Tufano, 2012). They pool the savings of many small investors by selling them shares in the fund and using the proceeds to buy equity, bonds, money market instruments, or other securities. Mutual funds allow investors to buy or redeem shares on a daily basis at net asset value (NAV) that is calculated by dividing the fund's assets minus liabilities by the number of shares outstanding. This is usually calculated at the end of every trading day. The shares of *closed-end funds* are listed on a stock exchange. Investors cannot sell their shares back to the fund as they can with an *open-end fund*; they must sell their shares in the market. The price they receive may be significantly different from NAV: it may be at a 'premium' (higher) or, more commonly, at a 'discount' (lower). Open-end mutual funds have two advantages that contributed to the growth of mutual funds. First, as the fund agrees to redeem shares at any time, they are very liquid. Second, the open-end character allows the fund to grow as long as investors are willing to put money into it.

A *money market fund* (MMF) is a fixed-income mutual fund that invests in debt securities that are characterised by their short maturities and minimal credit risk. They give ordinary people access to interest-bearing short-term assets that even have transaction-like features (one could write a cheque on them). MMFs were created to circumvent regulatory restrictions in several countries that prohibited banks from paying interest on checking accounts. In addition, money market instruments can generally only be bought in large amounts. MMFs ingeniously avoided these restrictions and limitations by buying large batches of money market instruments and then selling shares to investors who could buy in with a limited amount of money. In Europe, MMFs are an important source of short-term financing for financial institutions, corporations, and governments. Total European money fund assets totalled over $1.2 trillion at the end of 2016 (source: IMMFA).

Innovation also occurred in various kinds of financial limited partnerships: hedge funds, private equity funds, and venture capital funds. *Hedge funds* use investors' money to borrow still more money, and to make various kinds of leveraged investments, all in an effort to achieve a superior return (adjusted for risk) for the investors. The funds they use come from 'sophisticated investors' – wealthy individuals or institutions (pension funds or endowments). Hedge funds are like mutual funds, in that they place investors' money in markets for liquid financial instruments (stocks, bonds, derivatives). The liquid nature of their investments distinguishes hedge funds from *private equity funds*, which tend to buy large or controlling interests in companies, and to hold these positions for sale after several years. Today's typical private equity fund evolved from the leveraged buyout partnerships popular in the 1980s, and is still typically financed heavily with debt. According to Litan (2010), *venture capital funds* have done the most over the last four decades to improve the allocation of savings towards productive investment. These funds make money by investing in young or emerging firms that usually have a novel technology or business model in high-technology industries. As these firms often have a limited operating history, they cannot raise capital in the public markets and are unable to secure a bank loan.

One important financial innovation in the last two decades is the introduction of government bonds with principal amounts indexed to inflation. Such bonds were first sold by the British government in the 1980s; other governments later issued these instruments (see Chapter 5). Until such bonds were offered, investors had no (relatively) safe instrument that offered a hedge against inflation.

Financial Innovations in Risk Sharing

A considerable portion of financial innovation in recent decades has come in the area of derivatives, which are financial contracts with a value derived from some underlying asset (see Figure 5.13). These assets can include equities, bonds, exchange rates, commodities, and residential and commercial mortgages. The more common forms of these contracts include options, forwards/ futures, and swaps. The benefits of derivatives relate to:

- hedging and risk management
- price discovery
- enhancement of liquidity.

'Swap' arrangements are heavily used to reallocate financial risks. A swap is a contract arranging an exchange of cash flows between two parties. An *interest rate swap* involves the exchange of loan payments with a fixed interest rate for another payment stream defined by a floating rate of interest. A *currency swap* involves the exchange of payments in different currencies (where both interest rates could be fixed, both variable, or one fixed and the other variable). Parties enter into such arrangements because they want to reduce or change their risk exposure from the assets on their balance sheets. Swaps enable them to do this without having to sell the underlying assets (Litan, 2010).

A more recent innovation is the CDS. It is an insurance instrument: the purchaser of a CDS receives payment upon some defined event of default on a loan or bond. The CDS market has become dominated by a handful of major banks, which use these instruments to hedge against the default of their borrowers, thereby reducing the amount of capital they are required to hold. Banks also trade these instruments among one another, on their own account or on behalf of customers who want to hedge against the possibility that their supplier or borrower might default, or speculate on this outcome.

A potential future innovation is *home equity insurance.* Shiller and Weiss (1999) have proposed insurance policies to enable individuals to protect themselves against the risk of a decline in the prices of their homes, often people's most important asset. Since this risk is far greater than the risk of fire or other physical disaster, this could be a much larger market than the existing homeowner's property insurance industry. The creation of the Case–Shiller price index for real estate in major metropolitan areas of the US could form the basis of such an industry.

8.3 Pros and Cons of Financial Innovation

In the aftermath of the 2007–2009 financial crisis, financial innovation has become controversial. Litan (2010) argues that on balance there are more good than bad financial innovations. Individually and collectively, these innovations have improved access to credit, made life more convenient, and in some cases probably allowed the economy to grow faster. But some innovations, such as collateralised debt obligations (CDOs) and structured investment vehicles (SIVs), were poorly designed, while others, such as CDSs and adjustable rate mortgages, were misused and contributed to the financial crisis and/or amplified the downturn in the economy when it started.

Litan (2010) analyses the net impact of recent financial innovations using three criteria:

- access to finance
- convenience for users of financial services
- performance of productivity or total output.

This approach allows an impartial assessment of financial innovations. The fact that many were created to circumvent financial regulation does not automatically make them bad. Indeed, the opposite is true if the regulations are impeding productive activity. Some financial innovations have been useful for this purpose (Litan, 2010). Table 8.3 presents the net impact of financial products classified according to the different functions of finance (i.e. payments, saving, investment, risk bearing).

Most financial innovations score positively on the criteria in Table 8.3. On the payments side, they have helped to move away from cash. In the saving category, new products offer more convenient, safer, and potentially more rewarding ways of saving. According to Litan (2010), MMFs have a neutral net impact on GDP, as it is not clear that they benefit the economy. Hedge funds and private equity are organised as financial limited partnerships; their overall impact is therefore difficult to access. Private equity has a positive impact on economic growth. A typical private equity firm holds most of its investments for longer than five years. While on average jobs fall at private equity-controlled firms during the first two years after they are acquired, employment grows afterwards. Moreover, private equity-controlled firms are good at controlling costs. Litan (2010) thus concludes that private equity contributes positively to productivity.

Moving to investment, credit scoring has improved banks' ability to assess credit risk. This has allowed banks to price risk by reflecting it in the risk premium in the interest rate. Credit scoring has facilitated the extension of credit to individuals and small businesses. While adjustable rate mortgages increase access to mortgages, they also contribute to an increase in overall household debt. In addition, underwriting standards on these mortgages lapsed preceding the financial crisis. CDOs and SIVs permitted subprime mortgages to be created and sold to investors, who did not fully appreciate the risks (see Chapter 2). This securitised mortgage credit allowed access and convenience to individuals who previously would not have qualified for a regular mortgage. Cheap mortgage finance helped fuel the housing boom

Table 8.3 Net impact of recent financial innovations

	Access	Convenience	Productivity/GDP
Payments			
ATMs	++	++	+
Credit card expansion	++	++	+
Debit cards	++	++	+
Saving			
Money market funds	++	++	0
Exchange traded funds	+	+	0/+
Hedge funds	0	0	0/+
Private equity	0	0	+
Investment			
Credit scoring	++	++	0
Adjustable rate mortgages	++	+	−/−
Asset-backed securities	++	++	−/+
CDOs*	++	++	−
SIVs*	++	++	−
Rise of venture capital	++	++	++ (but future not clear)
Risk bearing			
Options/futures exchanges	++	+	+/++
Interest/currency swaps	++	++	+/++
default swaps	++	+	+

Note: * These positive scores were temporary.
Source: Litan (2010)

(and eventual bust), which had an overall negative impact on GDP. Venture capital has helped to improve the allocation of savings to productive start-ups, which have no access to bank loans or equity markets. Venture capital has financed the launch of famous companies, such as Google and Amazon, but this type of investment is cyclical. In the aftermath of the financial crisis, its contribution has dropped significantly.

Finally, derivatives help to spread or allocate risk to those most willing and able to bear it. These instruments thus allow market participants and traders to manage their risks and take positions. Putting aside the opportunities for traders and market makers in those instruments, derivatives enable firms producing real products in the economy to hedge risks, for instance to lock in the price of oil, or the price they receive for their products, or to hedge against fluctuations in interest rates or currencies (Litan, 2010). Firms can thus reduce various financial risks to their businesses. This risk reduction may, in turn, lower their cost of capital. But firms must have the financial skills to understand the risk profile of derivatives. Otherwise derivatives may introduce unintended risks to their business.

Financial Innovation and Financial Fragility

Financial innovation can lead to financial fragility. Some recent episodes of financial innovation share a common pattern (Gennaioli *et al.*, 2012). It begins with a strong investor demand for a particular, often safe, stream of cash flows. Some traditional securities in the market offer this pattern, but investors demand more, causing prices to rise. In response to demand, financial intermediaries create new securities offering the sought-after pattern of cash flows, usually by carving out of existing securities that are riskier. By virtue of diversification, tranching, insurance, and other forms of financial engineering, the new securities are believed by the investors (and often by the intermediaries themselves) to be good substitutes for the traditional ones. They are consequently issued and bought in great volumes.

When some risks are neglected, securities are over-issued because neglected risks need not be laid off on intermediaries or other parties when manufacturing new securities. Investors thus end up bearing risk without recognising that they are doing so. Markets in new securities are fragile. At some point, the news reveals that the new securities are vulnerable to some neglected risks, and are not good substitutes for the traditional securities. Both investors and intermediaries are surprised by the news, and investors sell these false substitute securities, moving back to the traditional securities that have the cash flows they seek. As investors fly to safety, financial institutions are stuck holding the supply of the new securities. The prices of traditional securities rise while those of the new ones fall sharply, leading to financial fragility.

One example is the rise of MMFs. The innovation of prime MMFs has arguably created substantial instability by encouraging investors to expect to get their money back on demand at par, even though it is invested in securities that are far from riskless. Gennaioli *et al.* (2012) suggest that it might be better to help investors form more realistic expectations by requiring these funds to be marked to market. With more realistic expectations of net asset value fluctuations, breaking the buck (i.e. suspending or stopping the return of money on demand at par) would no longer be a dramatic event that sparks a run on these funds and creates financial fragility.

A second example is the securitisation of subprime mortgages. Securitisation is the technology that encouraged the unbundling of the production processes for many credit services; separate financial institutions could originate, service, fund, and assume the credit or market risks of a portfolio of loans or other assets (Greenspan, 1997). Until the financial crisis, the benefits of securitisation had been unquestioned. Numerous types of assets were routinely securitised, including residential mortgages, commercial mortgages, auto loans, and credit card loans. By bundling illiquid loans into packages on which securities could be issued, securitisation was thought to considerably expand the supply of funds available for lending and to distribute the risks of lending throughout the financial system.

According to Litan (2010), the main reason that securitisation now has a bad name is because of the financial mutation known as CDOs. CDOs allowed subprime mortgages to be originated and sold to investors because of an innovation in the way investors were paid. The subprime sector lends to individuals with a high level of default risk, because they have a low income or a less-than-perfect credit history relative to the standards of 'prime' borrowers. The share of subprime mortgages agreed rose steadily between 2001 and 2006, from 7.2 to 20.1 per cent. When housing prices started to decline while interest rates increased, losses on these loans rapidly increased, and totalled an estimated $1.4 trillion in 2008. The magnitude of these losses was by no means unprecedented: the losses from the dotcom crash wiped out $5 trillion in the market value of technology companies between March 2000 and October 2002.

What led to the subsequent financial turmoil was the securitisation of these mortgages. Instead of passing the principal and interest payments made on the underlying mortgages directly through to all holders of the securities, as was common for mortgage-backed securities, the CDO divides securities purchasers into groups or 'tranches' with different risks. The CDO structures a 'waterfall' of payments that flows first to the most risk-averse investors, and then in stages to investors with higher risk appetites. To provide additional comfort to investors, especially those in the first tranche, insurance is often arranged via, for instance, CDSs. By structuring the payments in a waterfall-like fashion and layering them with insurance, issuers of CDOs were able to take subprime mortgages that separately would have received low ratings by the ratings agencies, and to repurpose them into higher-rated securities, the first tranche of which even typically received an AAA rating. CDOs were often purchased at market value by off-balance-sheet vehicles.

When the housing price bubble burst, this chain of securities, derivatives, and off-balance-sheet vehicles was so complicated that most investors could not determine the location and size of the risks (Gorton, 2008). For CDO investors and investors in other financial instruments that have CDO tranches in their portfolios, it was impossible to unravel the chain and value the underlying mortgages, i.e. information was lost because of the difficulty of penetrating to the core assets. Similarly, it was impossible for those at the start of the chain to use their information to value the chain 'upwards'. So due to the complexity of the financial instruments that were sold, it was unclear who was actually affected by losses on these instruments and to what extent.

Overall, Gai *et al.* (2008) suggest that financial innovation and greater macroeconomic stability may have made financial crises in developed countries less likely than in the past. But should a crisis occur, its impact could be greater than was previously the case. Macroeconomic volatility is generally higher in developing countries than in advanced economies, but maximum loan-to-value ratios are invariably lower. Crises in emerging market economies should therefore be more frequent, but less severe than in developed countries. Hoggarth *et al.* (2002) find empirical evidence showing that crises in developed countries do indeed tend to be costlier than those in emerging market economies. While recent innovations have caused damage, Box 8.2 suggests that financial innovation is essential for long-term economic growth.

Box 8.2 Financial innovation and long-run economic growth

According to Levine (2011), financial innovation is essential for growth. As firms become more complex, it is more difficult to screen and monitor them. Therefore, without corresponding innovations in finance that match the increases in complexity associated with economic growth, the quality of financial services diminishes, which slows economic growth. Several historical examples illustrate the crucial role of financial innovation in sustaining economic growth. For example, there were financial impediments to US railroad expansion in the nineteenth century. The novelty and complexity of railroads made pre-existing financial systems ineffective at screening and monitoring them. As only local investors with close ties to those operating the railroad provided capital during the early decades of this new technology, limited finance restricted growth. So, financiers innovated. Specialised financiers and investment banks emerged to mobilise capital from individuals, to screen and invest in railroads, and to monitor the use of those investments. Based on their expertise and reputation, these investment banks mobilised funds from wealthy investors, evaluated proposals from railroads, allocated capital, and governed the operations of railroad companies for investors.

Box 8.2 (cont.)

The information technology revolution of the twentieth century provides another example (Levine, 2011). Traditional commercial banks were reluctant to finance nascent high-tech information and communication firms in the 1970s and 1980s because they did not yet generate sufficient cash flows to cover loan payments. Furthermore, these firms were run by scientists with little experience in operating profitable companies. Conventional debt and equity markets were also wary because the technologies were too complex for investors to evaluate. Again, financiers innovated: venture capital firms arose to screen entrepreneurs and provide technical, managerial, and financial advice to new high-technology firms. In many cases, venture capitalists had become wealthy through their own successful high-tech innovations, which helped them evaluate and guide new entrepreneurs. Venture capitalists typically took large, private equity stakes that established a long-term commitment to the enterprise, and became active investors, taking seats on the board of directors and helping to solve managerial and financial problems.

A final example is the biotechnology revolution of the twenty-first century. Screening biotech firms is difficult because of the scientific breadth of the technologies involved, which frequently require inputs from biologists, chemists, geneticists, engineers, bioroboticists, as well as experts on the myriad laws, regulations, and commercial barriers associated with successfully bringing new medical products to market. Since it was unfeasible to house all of this expertise in banks or venture capital firms, financiers formed new financial partnerships with the only kind of organisation with the breadth of skills to screen biotech firms – large pharmaceutical companies. These companies employ, or are in regular contact with, a large assortment of scientists and engineers, have close connections with those delivering medical products to customers, and employ lawyers versed in drug regulations. According to Levine (2011), financial innovation in this case led to far faster improvements in diagnostic and surgical procedures, prosthetic devices, parasite-resistant crops, and other innovations linked to biotechnology.

Source: Levine (2011)

8.4 Conclusions

Financial innovation involves creating and popularising new financial instruments, as well as new financial technologies, institutions, and markets. It is generally driven by investor demand for a particular set of cash flows, financial regulation (e.g. opportunities to exploit regulatory gaps), or technological change. Financial innovations have the potential to improve payments, offer new savings and investment opportunities, and may increase risk sharing. However, they can also add to the fragility of the overall financial system.

In the aftermath of the 2007–2009 financial crisis, financial innovation has become controversial. While most innovations seem to have improved access to credit, made life more convenient, and in some cases even allowed the economy to grow faster, some innovations, such as CDOs and SIVs, were poorly designed. Others, such as CDSs and adjustable rate mortgages, were misused and contributed to the financial crisis and/or amplified the down-turn in the economy when it started. Moreover, although financial innovation and greater macroeconomic stability may have made financial crises in developed countries less likely, they now have a greater impact than was previously the case. The recent wave of financial innovations related to FinTech, cryptocurrencies, and distributed ledger technology may yet have far-reaching implications for the financial system and financial stability.

Bibliography

Suggested Reading

Bank for International Settlements (2018), Cryptocurrencies: Looking Beyond the Hype. *BIS Annual Report 2018*. BIS, Basel.

Gomber, P., R. J. Kauffman, C. Parker, and B. W. Weber (2018), On the FinTech Revolution: Interpreting the Forces of Innovation, Disruption and Transformation in Financial Services. *Journal of Management Information Systems*, 35, 220–65.

Lerner, J. and P. Tufano (2012), The Consequences of Financial Innovation: A Counterfactual Research Agenda. In: J. Lerner and P. Tufano (eds.), *The Rate and Direction of Inventive Activity Revisited*, University of Chicago Press, 523–78.

Litan, R. (2010), In Defense of Much, But Not All, Financial Innovation. Wharton Financial Institutions Center Working Paper 2010-06.

References

Ali, R., J. Barrdear, R. Clews, and J. Southgate (2014), Innovations in Payment Technologies and the Emergence of Digital Currencies. *Quarterly Bulletin 2014 Q3*, BoE, London.

Arner, D. W., J. Barberis, and R. P. Buckley (2017), FinTech and Regtech in a Nutshell, and the Future in a Sandbox. Research Foundation Briefs, CFA Institute Research Foundation.

Bank for International Settlements (2018), Cryptocurrencies: Looking Beyond the Hype. *BIS Annual Report 2018*. BIS, Basel.

Benos, E., R. Garret, and P. Gurrola-Perez (2017), The Economics of Distributed Ledger Technology for Securities Settlement. Bank of England Staff Working Paper 670.

Claessens, S., J. Frost, G. Turner, and F. Zhu (2018), FinTech Credit Markets around the World. *BIS Quarterly Review*, September.

Dewatripont, M. and J. Tirole (1994), *The Prudential Regulation of Banks*, MIT Press, Cambridge (MA).

ETFGI (2018), ETFGI ETF/ETP growth charts, https://etfgi.com. ETFGI, London.

European Central Bank (2017), Box 8 Exchange-*Traded* Funds in the Euro Area. *Financial Stability Review,* May. ECB, Frankfurt am Main.

European Securities and Markets Authority (2016), The Distributed Ledger Technology Applied to Securities Markets. ESMA Discussion Paper 2016/773.

Fatás, A. and B. Weder di Mauro (2018), Making (Some) Sense of Cryptocurrencies: When Payments Systems Redefine Money. *VoxEU*, 7 May.

Financial Stability Board (2011), Potential Financial Stability Issues Arising from Recent Trends in Exchange-Traded Funds (ETFs), 12 April. FSB, Basel.

(2017), Financial Stability Implications from FinTech. FSB, Basel.

(2018), Global Shadow Banking Monitoring Report. FSB, Basel.

Gai, P., S. Kapadia, S. Millard, and A. Perez (2008), Financial Innovation, Macroeconomic Stability and Systemic Crises. *Economic Journal*, 118, 401–26.

Gennaioli, N., A. Shleifer, and R. Vishny (2012), Neglected Risks, Financial Innovation, and Financial Fragility. *Journal of Financial Economics*, 104, 452–68.

Gomber, P., R. J. Kauffman, C. Parker, and B. W. Weber (2018), On the FinTech Revolution: Interpreting the Forces of Innovation, Disruption and Transformation in Financial Services. *Journal of Management Information Systems*, 35, 220–65.

Gorton, G. (2008), The Subprime Panic+. Yale International Center for Finance Working Paper 08-25.

Greenspan, A. (1997), Remarks by the Chairman of the Board of Governors of the US Federal Reserve System, Mr Alan Greenspan, at the Conference on Bank Structure and Competition of the Federal Reserve Bank of Chicago.

Hoggarth, G., R. Reis, and V. Saporta (2002), Costs of Banking System Instability: Some Empirical Evidence. *Journal of Banking and Finance*, 26, 825–55.

Krugman, P. (2007), Innovating Our Way to Financial Crisis. *New York Times*, 3 December.

Lerner, J. and P. Tufano (2012), The Consequences of Financial Innovation: A Counterfactual Research Agenda. In: J. Lerner and P. Tufano (eds.), *The Rate and Direction of Inventive Activity Revisited*. University of Chicago Press, 523–78.

Levine, R. (2011), Finance, Long-Run Growth, and Economic Opportunity. In: T. Beck (ed.), *The Future of Banking*. Centre for Economic Policy Research, London.

Litan, R. (2010), In Defense of Much, But Not All, Financial Innovation. Wharton Financial Institutions Center Working Paper 2010-06.

Nakamoto, S. (2008), Bitcoin: A Peer-to-Peer Electronic Cash System. bitcoin.org, October.

Philippon, T. (2016), The FinTech Opportunity. NBER Working Paper 22476.

Pinna, A. and W. Ruttenberg (2016), Distributed Ledger Technologies in Securities Post-Trading. ECB Occasional Paper 172.

Shiller, R. and A. Weiss (1999), Home Equity Insurance. *Journal of Real Estate Finance and Economics*, 19, 21–47.

Part III

Financial Institutions

9

The Role of Institutional Investors

OVERVIEW

This chapter starts by discussing the impact of institutional investors on the functioning of the financial system. Institutional investors are pooling funds and transferring economic resources to different asset classes and countries. They also transfer resources over time, and contribute to price discovery and thereby increase the efficiency of the financial system.

In recent decades, the intermediation of financial assets has gradually shifted from banks to institutional investors such as pension funds, insurance companies, and mutual funds. During this process of re-intermediation, the assets of institutional investors of the EU15 countries quadrupled from 49 per cent of GDP in 1990 to 223 per cent in 2017.

This chapter provides an overview of the growth of institutional investors over the last three decades and documents the development of the main types of institutional investors. A small group of countries has large-scale funded pensions (Denmark, Ireland, the Netherlands, and the UK), while others rely more on life insurance and mutual funds. New types of institutional investments, such as hedge funds and private equity, are also discussed.

Both the demand side (growing investments by pension funds to cater for ageing, and by mutual funds to accommodate households' wealth accumulation) and the supply side (shift from bank financing to market financing) point to further growth of institutional investment. While there has not yet been substantial institutional investment in the new EU Member States, institutional investors in these countries are expected to grow in line with economic development.

Institutional investors could be expected to invest according to the principles of finance theory, as implied by the international version of the Capital Asset Pricing Model. This theory demonstrates the gains of international diversification. However, there is a home bias in the investments of institutional investors. Still, this bias has declined, especially in euro-area countries, a trend that can be attributed to the introduction of the euro. With the elimination of exchange-rate risk, investors based in the euro area have reallocated part of their portfolio from their home country to the wider euro area.

LEARNING OBJECTIVES

After you have studied this chapter, you should be able to:
- explain the functions of investment management
- describe the different types of institutional investors
- understand the growth of institutional investment and the factors that explain this growth
- explain the theory of international diversification
- assess the home bias of institutional investments and the change in this bias following the introduction of the euro.

9.1 Functions of Investment Management

Institutional investors play an increasing role in the investment management landscape. *Institutional investors* are (large) financial institutions that manage investments (equities, bonds, and alternative assets) for clients and beneficiaries. As professional parties, they are well placed to perform the key functions of the financial system as identified in Chapter 1 (i.e. trade, manage, and diversify risk, and reduce information and trading costs).

Risk, Maturity, and Liquidity Transformation

Institutional investors pool funds from individual households. Economies of scale allow them to invest these funds more efficiently than individuals. Moreover, institutional investors are able to invest in assets that are indivisible and/or long term (such as property) or difficult to obtain (such as foreign investments) and therefore often not available to small investors. Thus institutional investors provide diversified portfolios at low cost to households. For instance, a mutual fund requires a low level of minimum investment and offers households a chance to invest in a diversified way. The costs of asset management are low, as they are shared among many households, so institutional investors offer an attractive risk-return profile.

Given their objective to hedge exposure and diversify their investments, institutional investors are increasingly using derivatives. Many of the new risk management tools have been developed especially for institutional investors, which increases the efficiency of the financial system. Furthermore, when institutional investors adopt more active trading policies, they enhance the liquidity of markets, leading to higher efficiency and lower transaction costs. According to Davis (2003: 21), 'by demanding liquidity, institutional investors help to generate it'. Institutional investors also provide liquidity to households by allowing them to buy and sell their stake in the investment fund at a low cost.

Information Acquisition and Activism

Institutional investors play an important role in the price discovery of investments. While passive investors buy the market portfolio (see Section 9.4 on portfolio theory), active investors gather information and devise investment strategies to maximise their trading gains. But active investing entails an extra cost – fees for investment managers. As active investors earn the market return on average, active investment is a negative-sum game compared to passive investments that do not incur these extra costs (French, 2008). This does not mean that the cost of active investing is a loss to society. In aggregate, active investors improve the accuracy of financial prices, which in turn improves society's allocation of resources. Moreover, active investment strategies allow institutional investors to fit an investment portfolio to their clients' interests and risk profiles.

With respect to corporate governance, institutional investors have more bargaining power than individual investors, as they are often important shareholders in companies. However, the different types of institutional investors are not equally active in corporate governance. For instance, Gillan and Starks (2003) distinguish between pressure-sensitive and insensitive institutional investors. The former include bankers and insurers that care about current or potential business relations with corporations in which they invest. They are more passive institutions. Pension funds and mutual funds are not sensitive to pressure and are therefore more active. Public pension funds are pioneers in active corporate governance. Well-known examples are Hermes (the UK postal pension fund), the California Public Employees' Retirement System (CalPERS), and the Dutch pension fund ABP (see Box 9.1). More recently, hedge funds have become aggressive players in corporate governance.

9.2 Different Types of Institutional Investors

This section describes the three main types of institutional investors in the EU (pension funds, insurance companies, and mutual funds) and their role in the EU financial system (see Table 9.1). The table shows that the size of institutional investors differs across countries. Most countries in southern Europe are characterised by low institutional saving, while institutional investors have a more important role in north-western Europe. While the EU-15 countries, Japan, Switzerland, and the US have well-developed institutional savings exceeding 100 per cent of GDP, the rates for NMS-13 countries and China are 30 and 60 per cent of GDP, respectively. As Chinese equity and bond markets are growing rapidly (see Chapter 5), Chinese institutional savings are expected to catch up with those in the EU-15 and the US.

Pension Funds

Pension funds collect, pool, and invest funds contributed by sponsors (employers) and beneficiaries (employees and their family members) to provide for the future pension entitlements of beneficiaries. In the EU, pay-as-you-go pensions are a common way to provide a basic (first-tier) pension. This system is not funded: the working generation pays for the pensions of the retired generation. Some countries have accumulated major pension assets, which provide beneficiaries with an additional pension (second-tier). These funded pensions can be based on either a defined benefit or defined contribution (Davis and Steil, 2001; Feldstein and Siebert, 2002). *Defined benefit funds* offer employees a guaranteed rate of return (the risk is borne by the employer), while the market determines the returns of *defined contribution (DC) funds* (the risk is borne by the employees). The latter have gained popularity in recent years, as employers have sought to minimise the risk of their obligations, and employees prefer funds that are easily transferable if they switch jobs. *Collective defined contribution* pensions are a hybrid: they do not guarantee a certain return by the company, but employees are able to save collectively for their pension via their employer and to pool risks.

The role of pension funds in the financial system differs across countries. In countries with large pension assets (relative to GDP), such as Denmark, the Netherlands, Switzerland, the UK, and the US, pension funds are an important vehicle for collective saving for retirement (see Table 9.2). Pension funds in these countries are among the largest investors, with billions of euros in assets under management (for

Table 9.1 Assets of different types of institutional investors (% of GDP), 2017

	Pension funds	Life insurance companies	Mutual funds	Total
Austria	6	40	53	99
Belgium	8	78	42	128
Bulgaria	14	8	1	23
Croatia	28	11	6	45
Cyprus	14	20	24	58
Czech Republic	9	10	10	29
Denmark	80	119	109	308
Estonia	18	6	5	29
Finland	4	37	63	104
France	0	128	70	198
Germany	7	52	72	131
Greece	1	10	4	15
Hungary	5	8	17	30
Ireland	48	111	826	985
Italy	5	58	25	88
Latvia	2	2	1	5
Lithuania	8	5	2	15
Luxembourg	4	340	8,307	8,651
Malta	0	36	75	111
Netherlands	211	68	124	403
Poland	10	9	18	37
Portugal	10	33	16	59
Romania	5	3	5	13
Slovakia	12	9	8	29
Slovenia	7	20	6	33
Spain	13	28	28	69
Sweden	9	104	84	197
United Kingdom	110	97	62	269
EU-15	36	76	110	222
NMS-13	9	9	12	30
EU-28	34	71	101	206
China	1	22	37	60
Japan	28	81	38	147
Switzerland	149	77	122	348
United States	84	34	119	237

Note: EU-15, NMS-13, and EU-28 are calculated as a weighted average.
Source: ECB, OECD

example, the Dutch civil servants' pension fund ABP; see Box 9.1).
Historically, some large EU countries (like Germany, France, and Italy)
have relied on other forms of retirement funding. The lack of a funded

Table 9.2 Assets of pension funds (in € billion and % of GDP), 2001–2017

	2001		2007		2012		2017	
	euro	%	euro	%	euro	%	euro	%
Austria	8	4	13	5	16	5	22	6
Belgium	14	6	14	4	18	5	34	8
Bulgaria	n.a.	n.a.	1	4	3	7	7	14
Croatia	n.a.	n.a.	n.a.	n.a.	n.a.	n.a.	13	28
Cyprus	n.a.	n.a.	n.a.	n.a.	4	24	3	14
Czech Republic	2	3	6	5	11	7	17	9
Denmark	42	23	61	27	185	76	217	80
Estonia	0	0	1	5	2	9	4	18
Finland	0	0	0	0	5	2	8	4
France	0	0	0	0	0	0	0	0
Germany	74	4	115	5	168	6	224	7
Greece	0	0	0	0	0	0	1	1
Hungary	3	4	11	11	4	4	6	5
Ireland	51	44	87	46	81	49	134	48
Italy	10	1	26	2	36	2	87	5
Latvia	0	0	0	0	0	1	1	2
Lithuania	0	0	1	2	1	4	3	8
Luxembourg	n.a.	n.a.	0	1	1	3	2	4
Malta	0	0	0	0	0	0	0	0
Netherlands	451	101	763	134	1,006	168	1,453	211
Poland	6	3	39	13	65	17	43	10
Portugal	15	11	22	13	15	9	18	10
Romania	n.a.	n.a.	0	0	2	2	9	5
Slovakia	n.a.	n.a.	2	4	7	10	10	12
Slovenia	0	1	1	3	2	5	3	7
Spain	45	7	88	8	109	11	141	13
Sweden	59	24	29	8	39	9	41	9
United Kingdom	1,180	74	1,488	72	1,966	102	2,411	110
EU-15	1,949	22	2,706	23	3,643	31	4,793	36
NMS-13	10	3	63	7	101	10	116	9
EU-28	1,959	21	2,769	22	3,744	29	4,909	34

Note: EU-15, NMS-13, and EU-28 are calculated as a weighted average; n.a. = not available.
Source: ECB

pension system in these countries has directed households towards life insurance and mutual funds.

Since the early withdrawal of funds is usually restricted or forbidden, pension funds have long-term liabilities resulting in a long-term-oriented investment strategy. This allows them to hold high-risk/return instruments (for example,

Box 9.1 ABP

The ABP (Algemeen Burgerlijk Pensioenfonds) is the Dutch pension fund for employers and employees of the government and the educational sector. It was founded by the government in 1922 and privatised in 1996. ABP provides its 2.9 million customers (employees, former employees, pensioners) with income security against pension, disability, and death.

ABP is the third-largest pension fund in the world, with around €410 billion of assets at the end of 2017. Given its objective to guarantee an adequate pension at all times at the lowest possible premiums, ABP's investment policy is geared towards a long-term risk-return profile. Diversification is a key element of that policy. The investment mix consists of 63 per cent in equities and alternative investments, such as real estate, private equity, hedge funds, and commodities, and 37 per cent in bonds. Over time, the share of equities and alternative investments has increased (see Figure 9.1). The geographical mix consists of 15 per cent of assets in the Netherlands, 34 per cent in the rest of Europe, and 51 per cent in the rest of the world.

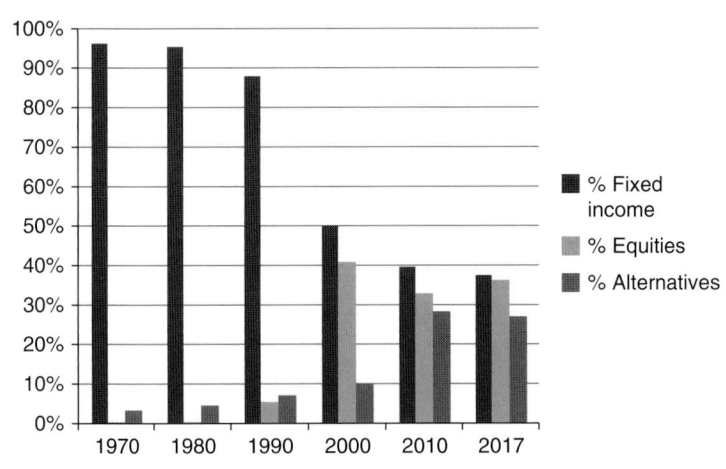

Figure 9.1   Portfolio of ABP (% share), 1970–2017
Source: ABP

investments in commodities, hedge funds, and private equity). Although pension fund clients have no (direct) influence over the fund's investment process, they are protected by regulation, since pension funds have to comply with the 'prudent person' rule (they should, for example, diversify their portfolios). Moreover, pension funds are under the scrutiny of financial supervisors (see Chapter 12). Table 9.2 shows the growth of pension fund assets from 2001 to

2017. Pension fund savings have risen to €4.9 trillion in 2017, which amounts to 34 per cent of EU GDP.

Insurance Companies

Life insurance companies offer a mix of long-term saving and insurance products. These companies have historically provided insurance for dependants against the risk of premature death, but life insurers are increasingly offering long-term saving products as well. Pension funds and life insurance companies therefore often have close ties. Life insurance companies offer annuities for guaranteeing pension benefits, as well as guaranteed investment contracts that may be purchased by pension funds. *Non-life insurance companies* protect against risks such as accidents, illness, theft, and fire. As the asset base of life insurance is far larger than that of non-life insurance, the remainder of this section focuses on life insurance.

All EU-15 countries (except for Greece) have significant life insurance assets relative to GDP. Table 9.3 indicates that life insurance assets are concentrated in the UK, France, and Germany, and to a lesser extent the Netherlands, Italy, and Sweden. Life insurance companies function as retirement saving vehicles in countries with a weak pension sector (such as Belgium, France, Germany, and Italy). They offer a diverse range of products, and therefore have different kinds of liabilities, which allow them a degree of diversification. Life insurance companies sell their products in a competitive market and compete both with each other and with pension funds and mutual funds. This competition may give life insurance companies an incentive to take risks on the asset side.

From a customer point of view, the economic function of life insurance companies is (after offering insurance for dependants) the provision of customised saving schemes. Saving and investing via life insurance is targeted not only at retirement but also at other long-term savings objectives (like dependants' education), which makes them a substitute for *and supplement to* pensions. While pension schemes are more standardised, life insurance products can be tailored towards individual needs. But this advantage comes at a price: the transaction and marketing costs of life insurance policies are far higher than those of pension contracts.

Mutual Funds

The mutual fund industry is among the most successful financial innovations (Khorana *et al.*, 2005). *Mutual funds* are investment vehicles with underlying

Table 9.3 Assets of insurance companies (in € billion and % of GDP), 2001–2017

	2001		2007		2012		2017	
	euro	%	euro	%	euro	%	euro	%
Austria	58	27	88	32	108	35	137	40
Belgium	116	45	217	65	261	69	320	78
Bulgaria	n.a.	n.a.	1	4	3	7	4	8
Croatia	n.a.	n.a.	n.a.	n.a.	n.a.	n.a.	5	11
Cyprus	2	18	n.a.	n.a.	4	23	4	20
Czech Republic	5	8	12	9	17	11	18	10
Denmark	97	54	163	72	246	100	323	119
Estonia	0	3	1	5	1	5	1	6
Finland	32	23	53	30	56	29	78	37
France	837	56	1,374	72	2,077	102	2,760	128
Germany	943	45	1,109	46	1,186	44	1,587	52
Greece	12	9	20	9	16	8	17	10
Hungary	3	6	9	8	8	8	9	8
Ireland	56	48	163	86	231	141	309	111
Italy	307	25	540	35	559	36	931	58
Latvia	0	2	1	2	1	2	1	2
Lithuania	0	1	1	3	1	3	2	5
Luxembourg	29	127	61	161	134	312	177	340
Malta	1	12	1	25	2	29	4	36
Netherlands	297	66	362	64	467	78	468	68
Poland	13	6	33	10	35	9	40	9
Portugal	27	21	53	31	53	32	61	33
Romania	n.a.	n.a.	2	1	4	3	5	3
Slovakia	1	6	5	9	7	10	7	9
Slovenia	1	6	4	12	6	18	8	20
Spain	149	22	243	23	263	26	301	28
Sweden	0	0	276	82	356	87	468	104
United Kingdom	1,740	109	2,098	102	1,927	100	2,114	97
EU-15	4,699	52	6,820	59	7,940	67	10,050	76
NMS-13	27	6	69	8	88	9	107	9
EU-28	4,726	50	6,889	56	8,028	62	10,156	71

Note: EU-15, NMS-13, and EU-28 are calculated as a weighted average; n.a. = not available.
Source: ECB

assets that are identifiable and marked to market on a regular (usually daily) basis. The specific assets of the fund can be created or redeemed upon demand. Mutual funds contractually link investors' claims to the underlying asset. Investors can easily enter and exit the fund and pay or receive current market prices for their investments. Investors in mutual funds are residual claimants and bear all the risk of the fund.

The primary role of mutual funds is to pool funds. In contrast to pension funds, they do not necessarily transfer these funds over time. Many investors in mutual funds have a relatively short investment horizon, i.e. not necessarily intended for retirement saving. The size of mutual funds differs sharply, ranging from small, specialised funds to major players like BlackRock and Vanguard (each had $5–6 trillion in assets under management in 2018). These larger funds also have important stakes in companies, which makes them prominent players in corporate governance.

Investors choose a fund with a specific investment objective (for instance, a bond fund, an equity fund, or an emerging market fund). The fund's asset allocation is generally fixed by the prospectus, while the security selection process is either active or passive. Active asset managers try to 'beat the market' by picking stocks that they consider good investments. Passive funds 'track' the index and do not deviate from the market benchmark. They generally incur lower transaction costs.

Table 9.4 illustrates the growth of mutual funds between 2001 and 2017. Luxembourg and Ireland are outliers due to the favourable tax treatment of these funds. Mutual fund investment in France and Germany is remarkably high. New Member States have the smallest mutual fund market size relative to GDP; the market is also small in Italy and Spain.

Special Types of Institutional Investors

In addition to the three main types of institutional investors described above, two other important institutional asset managers are hedge funds and private equity investors. They have gained popularity over the last two decades since they offer opportunities to diversify risk and increase expected returns.

Originally, *hedge funds* were eclectic investment pools, typically organised as private partnerships and often located offshore for tax and regulatory reasons. Since they operate through private placements and restrict share ownership to wealthy individuals and institutions, most disclosure and regulation requirements that apply to mutual funds and banks do not apply to hedge funds. Hedge funds legally domiciled outside the main financial market countries are generally subject to even fewer regulations. Hedge fund managers, who are paid on a fee-for-performance basis, are free to use a variety of investment techniques, including short positions and leverage, to raise returns and limit the investment risks. In contrast to investment funds, hedge funds concentrate more on absolute than on relative returns. The primary aim of most hedge funds was previously to reduce volatility and risk while attempting to deliver positive returns under all

Table 9.4 Assets of mutual funds (in € billion and % of GDP), 2001–2017

	2001		2007		2012		2017	
	euro	%	euro	%	euro	%	euro	%
Austria	98	45	161	59	150	49	183	53
Belgium	87	34	118	35	87	23	174	42
Bulgaria	n.a.	n.a.	1	2	1	1	1	1
Croatia	n.a.	n.a.	n.a.	n.a.	n.a.	n.a.	3	6
Cyprus	n.a.	n.a.	1	8	2	12	4	24
Czech Republic	3	4	4	3	8	5	19	10
Denmark	38	21	137	60	224	91	294	109
Estonia	0	1	1	8	1	3	1	5
Finland	12	9	49	27	67	35	132	63
France	649	43	1,201	63	1,068	53	1,502	70
Germany	794	38	1,054	43	1,350	51	2,204	72
Greece	17	13	15	6	5	3	6	4
Hungary	3	5	10	9	8	8	20	17
Ireland	182	155	516	272	1,019	622	2,296	826
Italy	395	32	291	19	216	14	402	25
Latvia	0	0	0	1	0	1	0	1
Lithuania	0	0	0	1	0	1	1	2
Luxembourg	854	3,779	1,933	5,156	2,434	5,675	4,320	8,307
Malta	1	12	1	22	15	210	8	75
Netherlands	112	25	100	18	587	98	855	124
Poland	3	2	37	12	38	10	77	18
Portugal	26	20	40	23	28	17	30	16
Romania	n.a.	n.a.	4	3	7	5	10	5
Slovakia	n.a.	n.a.	2	4	4	5	7	8
Slovenia	3	11	4	12	2	5	3	6
Spain	158	23	299	28	148	14	307	28
Sweden	87	35	156	46	200	49	375	84
United Kingdom	362	23	684	33	954	49	1,364	62
EU-15	3,871	43	6,753	59	8,538	72	14,442	110
NMS-13	12	3	66	8	85	8	152	12
EU-28	3,883	41	6,819	55	8,623	67	14,594	101

Notes: Mutual fund data includes both UCITS (equity, bonds, balanced, money market, funds of funds, and other UCITS funds) and non-UCITS (real estate funds, special funds, and other non-UCITS). UCITS are collective investment schemes that can operate freely throughout the EU on the basis of a single authorisation (see Chapter 12). EU-15, NMS-13, and EU-28 are calculated as a weighted average; n.a. = not available.
Source: ECB

market conditions ('hedging'). However, this investment strategy has become riskier over the last decade, including the use of leverage. The aggressive investment style of some hedge funds can land them in financial trouble, as the bailout of the hedge fund LTCM in 1998 illustrates (see Box 9.2).

Box 9.2 The Long-Term Capital Management (LTCM) crisis

LTCM was founded in 1994. Its Board of Directors included Nobel Prize winners Myron Scholes and Robert Merton. The hedge fund's core strategy was convergence trades, which seek to exploit small differences in prices among closely related securities (Jorion, 2000). Compare, for example, a less liquid (called off-the-run) Treasury bond yielding a 6.1 per cent return, versus 6.0 per cent for the more recently issued (on-the-run) Treasury bond. The yield spread represents compensation for the liquidity risk. Over a year, a trade that is long off-the-run and short on-the-run would generate a return of 10 basis points. The key is that the two bonds eventually converge to the same value at maturity. LTCM used this strategy in a variety of markets, such as spreads on different government bonds, mortgage-backed versus government securities, high-yielding versus low-yielding European bonds, and equity pairs (stocks with different share classes). Most of the time, these trades should be profitable except if there is a default or market disruption.

Since such strategies generate tiny profits, leverage must be used to yield attractive returns. At the time of the crisis in 1998, LTCM had borrowed $125 billion but held only $5 billion in equity. This led to a *leverage ratio L*, defined as debt to equity, of 25. The following equation illustrates the impact of leverage: $r_{equity} = r_{assets} + L(r_{assets} - r_{debt})$. When the return on assets (r_{assets}) is higher than the return on debt (r_{debt}), a large leverage would generate a high return on equity r_{equity}. But when the return on assets drops below that on debt, a large leverage would generate sizeable losses.

Initially, this strategy was very productive, with annual profits of almost 40 per cent. But losses occurred due to the Russian financial crisis in August 1998 when the Russian government defaulted on its bonds. Panicking investors sold Japanese and European bonds to buy US Treasury bonds. The profits that were expected to occur as the value of these bonds converged became huge losses as the values diverged. LTCM's equity capital dropped to around $600 million. The Federal Reserve Bank of New York organised a bailout of $3.6 billion by major creditors (14 leading investment banks) to avoid more collapses, without committing its own money. In return, the participating banks received a 90 per cent share in the fund. The fear was that there would be a chain reaction as LTCM liquidated its securities to cover its debt, leading to a drop in prices, which would force other companies to liquidate their own debt. The total losses amounted to $4.6 billion. After the bailout, the panic abated and LTCM former positions were eventually liquidated at a small profit to the bailers (Jorion, 2000). LTCM closed its books in 2000.

Critics have pointed out that this bailout increased moral hazard problems as financial institutions were more able to take risks because there were fewer consequences from a failure (Kho *et al.*, 2000). While central bankers typically argue that a bailout is necessary to prevent contagion and systemic threats, academics stress the moral hazard problem. Furfine (2006) has estimated the potential costs of the central bank's intervention by examining the rates for interbank borrowing between large banks; the spreads on these rates go down if the market believes such banks are 'too big to fail'.

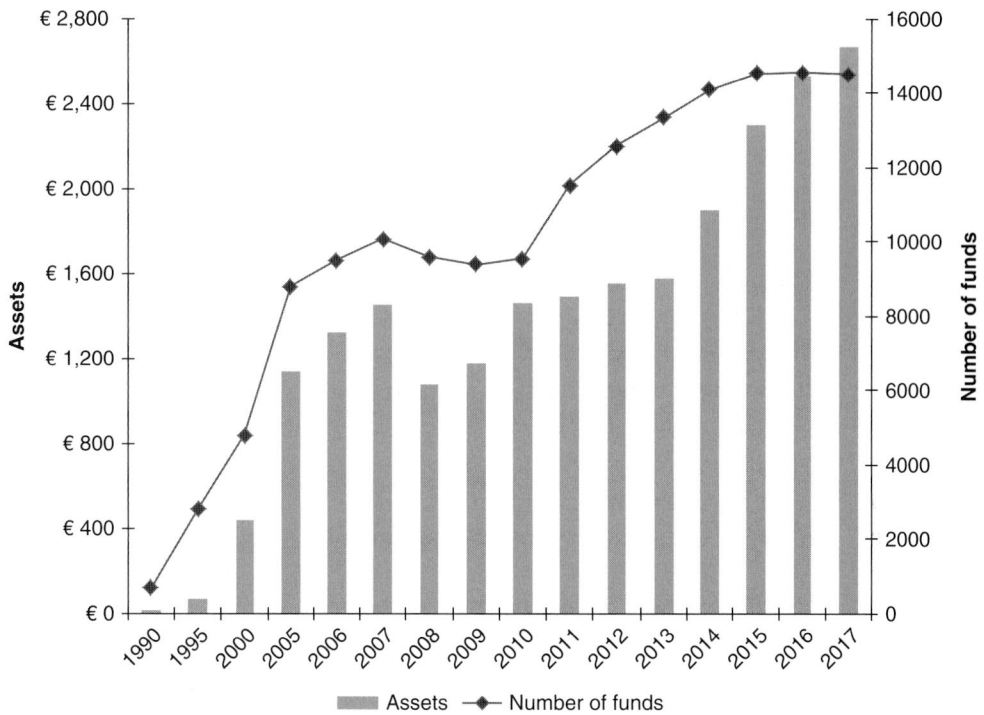

Figure 9.2 Global hedge funds market (number of funds and assets in € billion), 1990–2017
Source: Preqin (2018)

Figure 9.2 illustrates the enormous growth of the hedge fund industry, which was initially driven by investments by wealthy individuals and institutions looking for higher returns. While they experienced a strong decline during the 2008 financial crisis, hedge funds managed an estimated €2.7 trillion in 2017. Their total investment positions are even larger, as they can leverage their assets by borrowing money and through the use of derivatives, short positions, and structured securities. Over the last decade, small investors have been able to invest via *funds of hedge funds*, which are investment funds that invest solely in hedge funds. Pension funds also invest in hedge funds and funds of funds, as illustrated in Figure 9.3.

The distinctions between hedge funds and other types of funds are blurring. Hedge funds are characterised as unregulated private funds that can take on significant leverage and employ complex trading strategies using derivatives or other new financial instruments. Although private equity funds are usually not considered hedge funds, they are also typically unregulated and often use leverage for their investments. However, new regulations for hedge funds and private

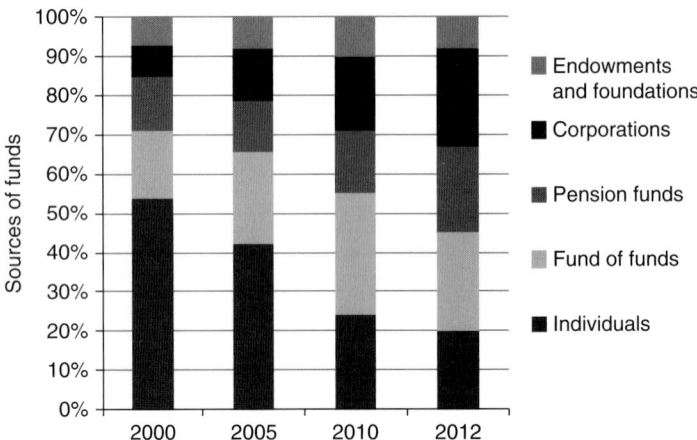

Figure 9.3 Hedge funds' sources of capital (% of total funds), 2000–2012
Source: TheCityUK (2013)

equity were introduced in the aftermath of the financial crisis (see Chapter 12). Traditional asset managers also increasingly use derivatives or invest in structured securities that allow them to take leveraged or short positions.

In general, hedge funds provide liquidity and absorb risk. Moreover, due to their inventive trading strategies, they also play a role in financial innovation (see Chapter 8). Hedge funds thus improve the efficiency of the financial system. At the same time, they have the potential to amplify market price fluctuations if their investment behaviour becomes one-sided or if they concentrate on specific markets, in particular small and low-liquidity markets. Hedge funds fall under the European Alternative Investment Fund (AIF) Managers Directive, which subjects all AIF managers to appropriate authorisation and registration requirements, allows monitoring of macro- and microprudential risks, and introduces several investor protection tools (European Commission, 2014).

Private equity investors invest in non-public companies and often finance these investments with a significant amount of debt, up to 90 per cent in the case of a leveraged buyout. They use investment funds that are open to certain institutions and wealthy individuals to invest in companies and aim at annual returns of 20–25 per cent. This makes them attractive for institutional investors as well, some of which invest in private equity via their own private equity branch. An example is AlpInvest, a private equity company owned originally by two Dutch pension funds (ABP and PGGM, the Dutch pension fund for the healthcare and social work sector). In 2011 AlpInvest was sold to the Carlyle Group.

Table 9.5 Private equity investments by region in 2017

	Total investment value (€ billion)	Market share (%)
North America	194	59
Europe	79	24
Asia	50	15
Rest of world	8	2
Total	331	100

Source: McKinsey (2018)

Table 9.5 illustrates that North America (primarily the US) and Europe (primarily the UK) have the biggest private equity markets, while Asia (primarily China) has rapidly increased towards the third-largest market. Relative to GDP, private equity markets are small (0.5 per cent of world GDP), but growing rapidly, driven by the demand for risky assets and exposure to the non-public market. Private equity funds have become an important source of funds for start-up firms, private middle-market firms, firms in financial distress, and public firms seeking buyout financing (Smit, 2003). As the single shareholder, the private equity holder appoints the management and can intervene directly with the company (Kahle and Stulz, 2017). The private equity model can easily be scaled up, as institutional investors are an important source of capital for private equity. Other sources include family offices and individual investors.

Differences among Institutional Investors

Institutional investors differ along three dimensions. First, the investor's client base can either be captive or determined by the market. In continental Europe, defined benefit pension funds often have a captive client base, as most employers use only one fund. By contrast, mutual funds must compete for clients by offering low fees and/or an excellent track record.

Second, institutional investors' investment horizons differ sharply. While pension funds have a very long horizon, mutual funds can have short-term investment objectives.

Third, the asset allocation process differs across institutional investors. Mutual funds mainly focus on security selection or 'stock picking'; individual investors select the fund that best matches their risk preferences. Pension

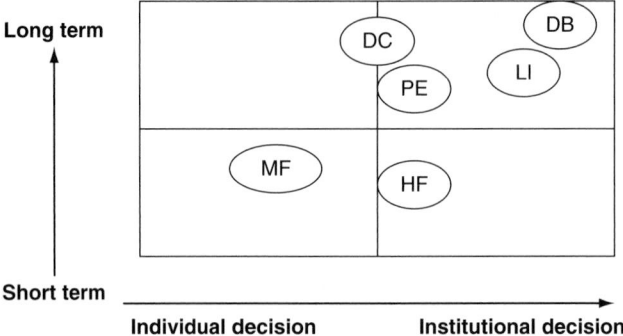

Figure 9.4 Investment horizon and decision power about asset allocation
Note: MF = mutual fund; DC = defined contribution pension scheme; DB = defined benefit pension scheme; LI = life insurance company; PE = private equity; HF = hedge fund.

funds and life insurance companies take investment decisions concerning the percentage of equity and bonds in their portfolios, and diversify the risks within these asset classes. Figure 9.4 illustrates these differences.

9.3 The Growth of Institutional Investors

Re-intermediation

Institutional investors have made banks less important as intermediaries of financial assets, a development that Rajan (2007) calls *re-intermediation* (see Table 9.6). In countries with a bank-dominated financial system, like France, Germany, and Italy, the role of institutional investors has increased, mainly due to the growth of the mutual fund industry. Nevertheless, the largest EU and Asian countries are still mainly bank oriented. In North America, institutional investors are more important financial intermediaries. In the US, institutional claims are almost three times as large as bank claims. Figure 9.5 shows that banking claims (at 58 per cent in 2017) and institutional claims (at 42 per cent in 2017) are converging in the euro area. While banking assets have remained flat since the global financial crisis (see Chapter 10), institutional investors are increasing, as documented in this chapter. As Box 9.3 explains, re-intermediation is less important in the new EU Member States, as institutional investors currently have a limited role in those countries.

Table 9.6 Bank and institutional intermediation ratios (in % of intermediated claims), 1970–2017

		1970	1980	1990	2000	2010	2017	Δ 1970–2017
France	*Bank*	95	94	81	71	71	66	**−29**
	Institutional	5	6	19	29	29	34	**29**
Germany	*Bank*	89	88	83	76	72	66	**−24**
	Institutional	11	12	17	24	28	34	**24**
Italy	*Bank*	94	95	90	67	81	72	**−22**
	Institutional	6	5	10	33	19	28	**22**
United Kingdom	*Bank*	67	71	63	54	73	60	**−7**
	Institutional	33	29	37	46	27	40	**7**
EU4	***Bank***	**86**	**87**	**79**	**67**	**74**	**66**	**−20**
	Institutional	**14**	**13**	**21**	**33**	**26**	**34**	**20**
Canada	*Bank*	66	74	64	52	56	53	**−14**
	Institutional	34	26	36	48	44	47	**14**
Japan	*Bank*	82	78	70	59	51	61	**−21**
	Institutional	18	22	30	41	49	39	**21**
United States	*Bank*	65	65	51	32	33	27	**−39**
	Institutional	35	35	49	68	67	73	**39**
G7	***Bank***	**80**	**81**	**72**	**59**	**62**	**58**	**−22**
	Institutional	**20**	**19**	**28**	**41**	**38**	**42**	**22**
China	*Bank*	n.a.	n.a.	n.a.	n.a.	92	83	n.a.
	Institutional	n.a.	n.a.	n.a.	n.a.	8	17	n.a.

Notes: The intermediation ratio measures the share of financial claims from banks and institutional investors as a percentage of total intermediated claims. The sum of bank and institutional ratios adds up to 100. While data for other EU Member States and time periods are not available, this table illustrates the shift from bank to institutional intermediation. Bolded numbers: EU4 are the largest four European Union countries; G7 are the Group of Seven countries.
Source: Updated from Davis (2003)

Table 9.7 illustrates that the total claims of institutional investors in the EU-15 have increased enormously over the last three decades. The weighted average of assets to GDP rose from 49 per cent in 1990 to 223 per cent in 2017. In the US, institutional investment shows a similar trend, with an increase from 80 per cent of GDP in 1990 to 237 per cent in 2017. China is rapidly catching up, with an increase from 19 per cent of GDP in 2010 to 61 per cent in 2017. When the global stock markets tumbled after the dotcom bust in 2000 and the global financial crisis in 2008–2009, institutional investors' assets declined sharply. The turmoil on the global financial markets reveals the vulnerability of institutional investors (with equity investments of up to 50 per cent of their portfolio) to such downward market

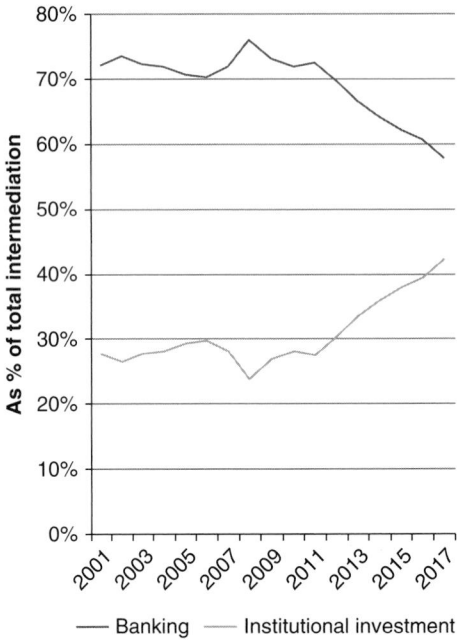

Figure 9.5   Financial intermediation in the euro area, 2001–2017
Note: The graph measures the share of the financial claims of banks and institutional investors as a percentage of total intermediated claims. The sum of bank and institutional ratios adds up to 100.
Source: Authors' calculations based on ECB structural financial indicators

pressures. Nevertheless, institutional investors are long-term investors that tend to keep their equity holdings more or less constant. They recover earlier losses when equity markets bounce back.

Drivers of the Growth in Institutional Investment

The growth in institutional investment can be explained by supply- and demand-side factors. Institutional investors have become more efficient in their function as a financial intermediary, while households have an enhanced need for services provided by institutional investors. As professional parties, institutional investors offer households the advantages of liquidity and diversification, as outlined in Section 9.1.

Supply-Side Factors

Deregulation has spurred the development of institutional investors. For example, fees have been reduced and institutional investors have more freedom to invest internationally and to distribute their products to a wider

Box 9.3 Institutional investment in new EU Member States

Institutional investment can be seen as a luxury good. The most basic household financial needs are the use of currency (coins and banknotes) and bank services (depositing and lending). Only when their income has increased above a critical level do households start to buy insurance and save for retirement. This relationship is presented in Figure 9.6. Institutional investment starts to develop at a GDP per capita of around €15,000 and becomes meaningful beyond levels of €20,000. Currently, the new EU Member States (as well as Greece and Portugal, which entered the EU in the 1980s) have a very small institutional sector, but institutional investment in these countries is expected to grow in line with economic development.

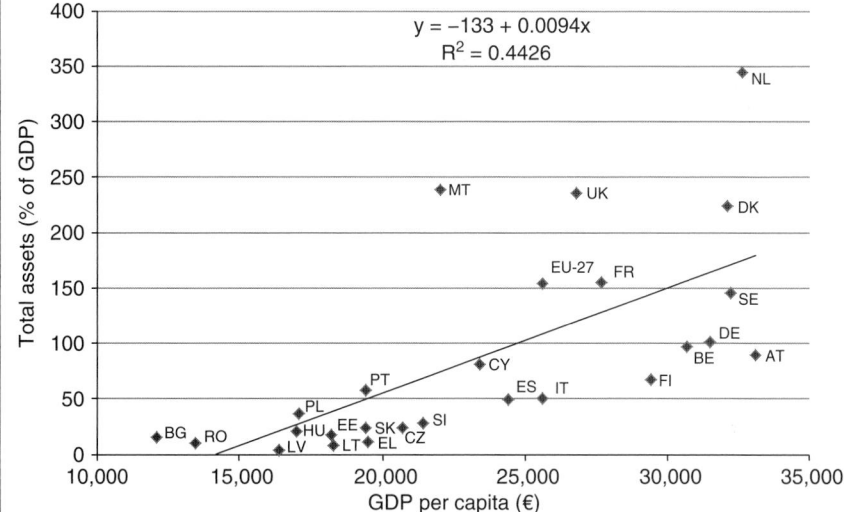

Figure 9.6   Institutional investment and economic development, 2012
Note: Total assets of institutional investment are defined as the assets of pension funds, insurance companies, and mutual funds. Ireland and Luxembourg are excluded, as they attract mutual funds from other countries due to a favourable tax regime.
Source: Own calculations based on ECB and Eurostat data

public. Deregulation has also stimulated competition among asset management institutions, which has lowered the costs for end users, i.e. households. The European Commission plays a crucial role in regulating institutional investors. Because of the ageing problems that EU Member States face (see below), the Commission urged countries to reform their pension schemes. It also proposed a number of directives that would impose severe restrictions

Table 9.7 Assets of institutional investors (% of GDP), 1990–2017

	1990	1995	2000	2005	2010	2017
Austria	22	35	71	99	94	99
Belgium	40	41	83	101	100	59
Denmark	53	69	103	149	189	308
Finland	6	16	43	52	62	104
France	49	76	127	120	154	198
Germany	34	45	81	98	99	131
Greece	1	12	32	20	10	14
Ireland	n.a.	53	199	366	598	985
Italy	12	26	63	61	51	88
Luxembourg	790	2017	4,084	4,853	5,750	8,651
Netherlands	120	151	199	209	293	403
Portugal	8	35	52	65	64	60
Spain	n.a.	43	59	60	50	69
Sweden	47	65	109	157	152	261
United Kingdom	105	167	213	209	234	269
EU-15	49	73	125	137	155	223
China	n.a.	n.a.	n.a.	n.a.	19	61
Japan	n.a.	n.a.	n.a.	n.a.	173	148
Switzerland	107	141	224	248	282	348
United States	80	122	177	185	194	237

Note: EU-15 is calculated as a weighted average; n.a. = not available.
Source: ECB, OECD

on pension funds and life insurance companies. After lengthy negotiations between the Commission, the Member States, and the pension funds, a pension directive was adopted in 2003 to stimulate the single European market for pension funds. This directive promotes the prudential investing of pension funds applied to the portfolio as a whole rather than to individual investments (the 'prudent person' principle). No quantitative restrictions have been imposed on the portfolio composition of EU pension funds, which are thus able to optimise their risk-return profile (see Section 9.4 on portfolio theory and home bias).[1]

In contrast, insurance companies have faced regulatory restrictions on the percentage of equity and the percentage of foreign assets in their portfolio. The new regulatory framework for the insurance industry implemented in January 2016, Solvency II, removes most of these restrictions, which is advantageous for the development of institutional investments in the EU.

Chapter 12 explains the regulatory framework for financial institutions in Europe.

The final supply-side factor furthering the development of institutional investors is related to fiscal advantages. Pension funds benefit from deferred taxation (contributions and investment returns are not taxed, but payouts are). Life insurance contributions also often benefit from deferred taxation, while mutual funds enjoy a favourable tax regime in some EU countries (such as Luxembourg and Ireland).

Demand-Side Factors

Demand-side factors also play an important role in explaining the vast growth of institutional investment. The need to save via institutional investors is linked to the level of social security benefits to which households are entitled. Institutional investment is stimulated when social security provides only a minimum level of income after retirement; the remaining income must be provided via institutional saving.

The demand for institutional savings is mainly fuelled by demographic developments. Figure 9.7 shows that the EU population is ageing, which increases the need to save for retirement; this is done primarily via institutional investors. Which institutions benefit the most from these demographic developments depends on the country. Where pension funds are well

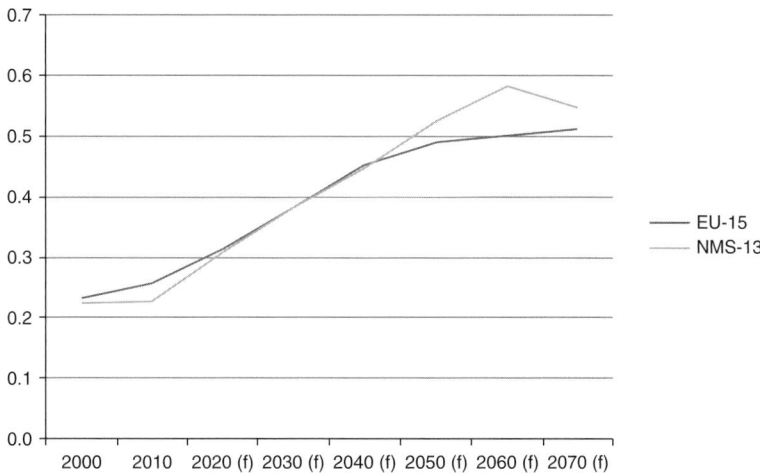

Figure 9.7   Dependency ratio: actual figures and forecasts, 2000–2070
Note: EU-15 and NMS-13 are unweighted averages; (f) = forecast.
Source: Eurostat

established, like the Netherlands and the UK, retirement saving primarily takes place via these funds. Employees in France, where pension funds are practically non-existent, save for their retirement via life insurance companies and mutual funds.

Demographic developments are often captured by the *dependency ratio*, which is calculated as the number of persons of retirement age (65 and over) divided by the number of working-age individuals (15 to 64), expressed as a percentage. Projections for the EU indicate that by 2050 the dependency ratio will be double that in 2010 (when it stood at 25 per cent). Note that the dependency ratios of new and old Member States are converging. The dependency ratio was slightly lower in new Member States at the time of joining, but is forecast to become higher than that of old Member States. The increase in the dependency ratio is due to a decline in fertility rates (from 2.7 children per woman of child-bearing age in 1970 to 1.6 in 2016) and increased life expectancy (from 71.0 years in 1970 to 80.6 years in 2015). It is expected to increase further. To alleviate the impact on the working population and the budget position, Member States have started to increase the retirement age, which is expected to rise in line with life expectancy.

European households have become wealthier over the last two decades, which has increased their investment horizon. Household investors now worry less about the liquidity of their investments, as they are better positioned to absorb liquidity shocks. So, wealthier households will search for the highest risk-return profile in the medium to long run. This means a shift from traditional savings accounts (which can often be withdrawn on demand) to long-term investments that offer a higher return. However, most retail investors are risk averse and are uncomfortable making investment decisions; investing via institutional investors is more convenient for them.

9.4 Portfolio Theory and Home Bias

Portfolio Theory

According to the international version of the Capital Asset Pricing Model (CAPM) derived by Lewis (1999), investors should hold an internationally diversified portfolio, since this will maximise returns given a certain risk profile. Figure 9.8 plots the mean and standard deviation of annualised monthly returns from January 1980 to December 2005 for two different equity portfolios: the MSCI (Morgan Stanley Capital International) USA Index (which proxies for the US stock market) and the MSCI Europe Index (which proxies for the European stock market). Moving along the curve from 100 per cent US stocks to 100 per cent European stocks, the line plots the mean returns and standard deviations. This is a simplified version of the *efficient frontier*, i.e. the portfolio with the minimum standard deviation for a given return.

The mean of the MSCI USA is lower than portfolio C, which has the same standard deviation but includes a fraction of European stocks. In fact, as long as investors prefer higher returns and lower variance, the minimum-variance portfolio at point B (with 40 per cent European equity) is preferable to a portfolio consisting of US shares only. However, as explained below, American investors hold only 7 per cent European stocks in their equity portfolio (point A).

Figure 9.8 illustrates that it is beneficial for investors to diversify geographically. The formal international CAPM can be derived from the standard mean-variance framework modified to include foreign securities (Lewis, 1999). In the mean-variance framework, investors optimise their portfolio by increasing their return (i.e. the mean of their wealth) and decreasing their risk (i.e. the variance of their wealth). When introducing foreign stocks, investors must choose the optimal mix of domestic and foreign stocks in their portfolio. Box 9.4 discusses the international CAPM.

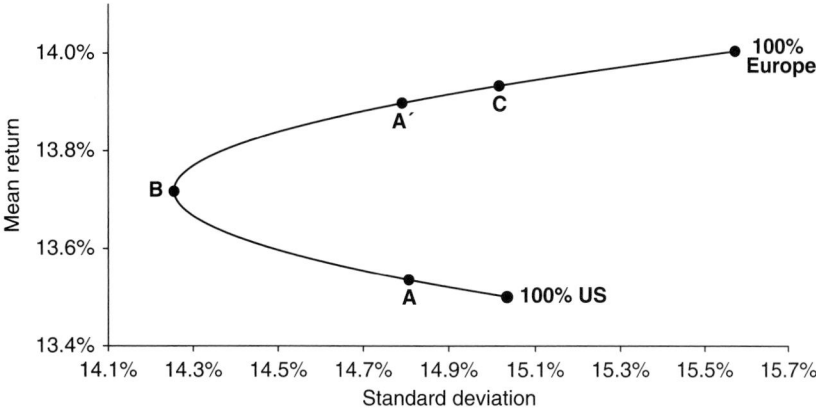

Figure 9.8   The simplified efficient frontier for US and European equities, 1980–2005
Note: This graph is based on returns from the MSCI USA Index and MSCI Europe Index.
Source: Schoenmaker and Bosch (2008)

Box 9.4 The international CAPM

Suppose that domestic investors have access to two risky assets, a domestic and a foreign stock. The domestic investor chooses the proportion of his or her wealth portfolio held in foreign stocks, x (with $0 < x < 1$). The investor's objective is to increase mean wealth, $E(W_1)$, and decrease the variability of wealth, $\text{var}(W_1)$. The investor's objective function is given by:

$$\max \quad V = V(E(W_1), \text{var}(W_1)) \tag{9.1}$$

$$\text{subject to} \quad V_1 > 0, \quad V_2 < 0 \tag{9.2}$$

where W_1 = next-period wealth, and E = the expected value conditional upon information known at time 0. V_1 is the partial derivative of V with respect to the first term, and V_2 with respect to the second term. The one-period return is a combination of the foreign return earned on the fraction of foreign stocks, denoted by x, and the domestic return earned on the fraction of domestic stocks, denoted by $(1 - x)$, and is given by:

$$\begin{aligned} W_1 &= W_0(1 + x \cdot r^f + (1 - x) \ r^h) \\ &= W_0(1 + x \cdot (r^f - r^h) + r^h) \end{aligned} \tag{9.3}$$

where W_0 = current wealth, r^f = foreign return, and r^h = domestic return. The variance of the one-period return is given by:

$$\begin{aligned} \text{var}(W_1) &= \text{var}\left(W_0\left(1 + x \cdot (r^f - r^h) + r^h\right)\right) \\ &= W_0^2 \text{var}\left(1 + x \cdot (r^f - r^h) + r^h\right) \\ &= W_0^2 \left(x^2 \text{var}(r^f - r^h) + 2 \cdot x \cdot (\rho_{fh} \cdot \sigma_f \cdot \sigma_h - \sigma_h^2) + \sigma_h^2\right) \end{aligned} \tag{9.4}$$

where $\sigma_h^2 = \text{var}(r^h) =$ the variance of the domestic stock return, $\sigma_f^2 = \text{var}(r^f) =$ the variance of the foreign stock return to the domestic investor, and $\sigma_{fh} = \rho_{fh} \, \sigma_f \, \sigma_h = \text{cov}(r^f, r^h) =$ the covariance between the domestic and foreign returns. The optimal fraction of foreign stock x^* can be calculated by deriving the first-order condition of the objective function V, given by:

$$\frac{\delta V}{\delta x} = V_1 \cdot W_0 \cdot (r^f - r^h) + V_2 \cdot W_0^2 \cdot (2 \cdot x \cdot \text{var}(r^f - r^h) + 2 \cdot \sigma_{fh} - 2 \cdot \sigma_h^2) = 0 \tag{9.5}$$

Dividing by W_0 and arranging terms leads directly to:

$$\begin{aligned} x^* &= \frac{r^f - r^h}{\text{var}(r^f - r^h)} \cdot \frac{-V_1}{2 \cdot V_2 \cdot W_0} + \frac{\sigma_h^2 - \sigma_{fh}}{\text{var}(r^f - r^h)} \\ &= \frac{(r^f - r^h)/\gamma}{\text{var}(r^f - r^h)} + \frac{\sigma_h^2 - \sigma_{fh}}{\text{var}(r^f - r^h)} \end{aligned} \tag{9.6}$$

where γ is the parameter of risk aversion $\frac{-2 \, V_2 \, W_0}{V_1}$. The interpretation of the demand function for foreign stock is straightforward. The first term on the right-hand side of equation (9.6)

Box 9.4 (cont.)

represents the demand arising from the higher potential returns from the foreign stock. The lower the risk aversion, γ, the greater the response of demand to higher expected returns. However, as γ increases, the importance of relative returns across countries declines. In the limiting case when γ equals infinity, i.e. investors are infinitely risk averse, the first term disappears. The demand for foreign stock then reduces to the second term, i.e. the portfolio share that minimises the variance of the wealth portfolio (point B in Figure 9.8). Thus in general, the demand for foreign stock depends on a combination of the risky portfolio share given by the first term and the minimum-variance portfolio given by the second term.

Source: Lewis (1999)

International Diversification

When investors diversify their portfolio internationally, they can generate extra returns and/or reduce risk. Lewis (1999) calculates that by buying foreign stocks, an American investor can generate an extra return of about 50 basis points per year while also decreasing risk (moving to point B in Figure 9.8), or 80 basis points per year with no change in risk (moving to point A' in Figure 9.8). Empirical evidence for European investors shows an even stronger effect. Schröder (2003) finds that a British investor, holding the optimal portfolio of 80 per cent non-domestic assets rather than 20 per cent non-domestic assets, generates an extra return of 2.2 per cent per year. A German investor, holding the optimal portfolio, generates an extra return of 3 per cent per year. The excess return for European investors is larger than for American investors because the US market is very large so there is less upside potential from investing in foreign markets.

By the same token, international diversification reduces the cost of capital for companies (Stulz, 1999), since investors' required return for investing in equity to compensate them for risk generally falls.

The international CAPM is derived under the assumption that capital markets are perfect – i.e. that there are no barriers. However, several barriers may hamper international capital flows (Karolyi and Stulz, 2003). First, there are traditional barriers including capital controls and trading costs. While capital controls have been abolished in the EU over the past three decades (see Chapter 3), cross-border trading costs are still higher than domestic trading costs (see Chapter 7 on cross-border trading costs in the EU). Second, barriers can be related to different expectations about stock returns, volatilities, and covariances. In particular, investors may be more uncertain about the expected returns on foreign stock. An important risk in the cross-border setting is exchange-rate risk. The degree of risk aversion is captured by γ in equation (9.6). Finally, barriers can emerge from information asymmetry between local and foreign investors. According to the 'corporate insider theory', it is not possible for the home bias to fall sharply if it is optimal for insiders to have large ownership stakes in corporations in a specific country and foreign investors are not corporate insiders (Stulz, 2005). The existence of insider ownership thus limits foreign investors' holdings.

The increasing importance of institutional investors may reduce the home bias. As professional parties, they may have better means of overcoming the barriers to international investment. For example, they employ analysts who can reduce the information asymmetries. Furthermore, due to their size, they can negotiate lower tariffs for large (cross-border) deals.

Measuring the Home Bias

A *home bias* exists when investors underweight foreign assets in their portfolio even though this might not be optimal from a diversification point of view. There is robust evidence across a large range of countries of the existence of such a bias (Chan *et al.*, 2005). This section analyses the extent to which (institutional) investors in Europe diversify their investments geographically. It compares levels of home bias between 1997 and 2014 to determine whether it has declined over time. Two groups of countries are distinguished: euro area countries and non-euro area countries. The home bias may have decreased more in euro area countries after exchange-rate risk was eliminated for these countries.

The international CAPM is used to calculate home bias. The optimal international portfolio with no bias can be calculated under strict assumptions (Elton *et al.*, 2014), including fully integrated capital markets (i.e. investors can buy and sell securities in foreign markets with no restrictions or extra transaction costs) and purchasing-power parity (i.e. currencies' long-run equilibrium exchange rates are equal to their purchasing power). This model is based on the law of one price, which means that identical goods (including securities) in different markets must have the same price. When purchasing-power parity holds, exchange-rate risk is no longer relevant. If there are homogeneous expectations, all investors select the same optimal portfolio. Equilibrium in the international setting is achieved when all investors hold the world market portfolio in which each country portfolio is weighted by its market capitalisation.

The equity home bias, EHB_i, is measured as one minus the *foreign asset acceptance ratio*, which measures the extent to which the share of foreign assets in the portfolio of country i diverges from the relative share of foreign assets in the total world market portfolio (Ahearne *et al.*, 2004). The more the foreign asset acceptance ratio is below unity, the higher the home bias. Equity home bias is given by:

$$EHB_i = 1 - \frac{Share\ foreign\ equity\ in\ country\ i}{Share\ foreign\ equity\ in\ world\ portfolio} \tag{9.7}$$

in which *Share foreign equity in country i* = share of country i's holdings of foreign equity in its total equity portfolio (1 – share of domestic equity); *Share foreign equity in world portfolio* = the share of foreign equity in the world portfolio available to country i (1 – share of country i in the total market capitalisation). The country portfolio is calculated as the domestic market capitalisation plus foreign equity holdings minus foreign owners of domestic equity.

Equation (9.7) measures the extent to which domestic equity is over-weighed compared with foreign equity in the investment portfolio. EHB_i ranges from 0 to 1. Its values can be interpreted as follows:

- $EHB_i = 0$: a neutral portfolio in which there is no home bias. Domestic investors invest in foreign equity securities proportionally to the share of foreign equity in their world portfolio, in line with the international CAPM prediction.
- $0 < EHB_i < 1$: domestic investors have some home bias for domestic equities, but they invest part of their portfolio in foreign equities (the closer to 1, the greater the home bias).
- $EHB_i = 1$: domestic investors invest 100 per cent in domestic equity (complete home bias).

The home bias formula can be illustrated as follows. Country i investors allocate 15 per cent of their portfolio to foreign equity, while the total world market portfolio comprises 75 per cent foreign equity and 25 per cent domestic equity. Country i investors thus exploit international diversification to only one-fifth (15/75) and thus have a home bias of 0.8. Investors' debt home bias (DHB_i) can also be measured.

The *euro-area bias* (Darvas and Schoenmaker, 2018) measures whether the share of investments in the euro area (for non-euro-area countries) or the rest of the euro area (for euro-area countries) in the foreign portfolio is larger than the share of euro-area assets (except home-issued securities in the case of euro countries) in the total foreign equity portfolio available to the country in question (i.e. the sum of equity securities of all countries in the world *except* the country in question). The euro-area bias for equities is given by:

$$EEAB_i = 1 - \frac{Non - Euro\ Area\ equity_i}{Non - Euro\ Area\ Equity\ to\ Foregin\ Market\ Portfolio_i}$$

(9.8)

in which *Non-Euro-Area Equity$_i$* = share of country *i*'s holdings of non-euro-area equity in country *i*'s total foreign equity portfolio; *Non-Euro-Area Equity to Foreign Market Portfolio$_i$* = share of non-euro-area equity in the foreign-equity portfolio which is available for country *i*.

The foreign market portfolio differs per country. For example, as the UK comprises a large part of total EU equity, the foreign equity portfolio for the UK is smaller than that of other countries. While the home bias indicator above considers the total portfolio of the country, the euro-area bias indicator considers only the foreign equity holdings.

$EEAB_i$ can take the following values:

- $EEAB_i$=1 (complete euro-area bias): the country holds no non-euro-area equity in its foreign portfolio.
- $0 < EEAB_i < 1$ (some bias for euro-area equities): euro-area securities are held in a larger proportion than their relative supply.
- $EEAB_i = 0$ (neutral portfolio, with no euro-area bias): the country's holdings of non-euro-area equity are proportional to the supply of non-euro-area equities.
- $EEAB_i < 0$ (non-euro-area bias): the country holds more non-euro area securities than their relative supply.

The same applies to the foreign bond portfolio. It is expected that the debt euro-area bias (DEAB) is higher than the equity euro-area bias (EEAB) for euro-area countries because there is no exchange-rate risk involved, and the international diversification of bonds primarily focuses on credit risk diversification (without incurring major exchange rate risk).

Evidence on the Home Bias

Earlier empirical studies measured the development of the home bias in the EU-15 after the introduction of the euro in 1999 (Schoenmaker and Bosch, 2008; De Santis and Gerard, 2009). These studies show a large decrease in the home bias and an increase in the regional bias for euro-area countries. Updating these earlier studies, Darvas and Schoenmaker (2018) compare the home bias in the EU (for both the euro and non-euro area) and the US.

Table 9.8 gives an overview of the home and euro-area bias in 2014.[2] The equity home bias and debt home bias for the euro-area countries are lower (0.49 and 0.52, respectively) than for non-euro-area countries (0.55 and 0.72, respectively). At the same time, the EEAB and DEAB are higher for euro countries (0.62 and 0.54) than non-euro countries (0.24 and 0.28). Euro-area countries have thus shifted part of their portfolio from domestic securities (reducing their home bias) to securities in other euro-area countries (increasing their euro-area bias). Table 9.9 confirms that the reduction in the home bias is larger for euro-area countries than for non-euro-area countries or the US after the introduction of the euro.

The Netherlands has the lowest equity home bias (0.23 in 2014). This reflects the large proportion of institutional investors in this country, in particular pension funds, that tend to invest in a professional way, applying international diversification. Rubbaniy et al. (2014) find a large decrease in the home bias of pension funds' investments in equities and bonds after the introduction of the euro. The southern European countries, like Spain, Portugal, and Greece, have a bias around 0.80. The equity home and debt home bias in Japan (0.71 and 0.80) and the US (0.60 and 0.85) are still relatively high.

Table 9.9 also illustrates that the debt home bias has declined far more in euro-area countries (−0.35) than in non-euro-area countries (−0.04) or the US (−0.10). The euro-area countries have diversified the credit risk of their bond portfolios to a significant extent, but within the euro area. Based on the exceptionally high US debt home bias (0.85 in 2014), US investors appear to be very domestically focused in their long-term debt portfolios, and allocate only a small percentage of their bond portfolio to foreign bonds. This is partly in line with theory: as the US economy is very large, there is more scope for US investors to diversify credit risk domestically without incurring exchange-rate risk.

The international diversification strategy of institutional investors is illustrated in Figure 9.9 for three regions: the euro area, the non-euro area, and the US. The figure shows that the euro area has the lowest home bias as well as the highest euro-area bias. These results are consistent with the theory of economic integration. Since the introduction of the euro in 1999, investors in euro countries have allocated a larger part of their portfolios to foreign assets than have non-euro countries and the US. At the same time, the

Table 9.8 Home and euro-area bias, 2014

	Equity home bias	Debt home bias	Equity euro-area bias	Debt euro-area bias
Austria	0.35	0.45	0.66	0.51
Belgium	0.43	0.40	0.82	0.70
Cyprus	n.a.	0.51	0.37	0.28
Estonia	0.29	0.15	0.68	0.48
Finland	0.40	0.28	0.37	0.26
France	0.58	0.49	0.55	0.56
Germany	0.46	0.41	0.66	0.52
Greece	0.83	0.48	0.88	0.70
Ireland	n.a.	0.27	0.14	0.17
Italy	0.34	0.80	0.86	0.57
Latvia	0.27	0.30	0.72	0.30
Lithuania	0.64	0.69	0.76	0.17
Luxembourg	n.a.	0.06	0.21	0.27
Malta	n.a.	0.18	n.a.	-0.04
Netherlands	0.23	0.36	0.18	0.58
Portugal	0.51	0.65	0.63	0.79
Slovakia	0.63	0.46	0.52	0.40
Slovenia	0.62	0.54	0.38	0.64
Spain	0.77	0.80	n.a.	n.a.
Euro area	**0.49**	**0.52**	**0.62**	**0.54**
Bulgaria	0.75	0.60	0.62	0.14
Croatia	n.a.	n.a.	n.a.	n.a.
Czech Republic	0.64	0.86	0.70	0.31
Denmark	0.45	0.74	0.19	0.42
Hungary	0.52	0.95	0.71	0.48
Poland	0.91	0.95	n.a.	n.a.
Romania	0.94	0.94	n.a.	0.13
Sweden	0.52	0.73	0.27	0.21
United Kingdom	0.45	0.63	0.18	0.28
Non-euro area	**0.55**	**0.72**	**0.24**	**0.28**
EU-28	**0.50**	**0.58**	**0.52**	**0.47**
Japan	0.71	0.80	0.06	0.00
Switzerland	0.53	0.34	0.45	0.22
United States	0.60	0.85	0.03	-0.32

Note: EU-28, euro area, and non-euro area are calculated as a weighted average; n.a. = not available.
Source: Darvas and Schoenmaker (2018)

regional bias of the euro area has increased, as investors in euro countries have invested their foreign assets mainly in their own region. Investors based in the euro area have thus shifted from a country-based to a sector-based

Table 9.9 Home bias by region, 1997–2014

	Equity home bias			Debt home bias		
	1997	2014	Δ 97–14	1997	2014	Δ 97–14
Euro area	0.86	0.49	−0.37	0.87	0.52	−0.35
Non-euro area	0.84	0.55	−0.29	0.76	0.72	−0.04
EU-28	0.85	0.50	−0.35	0.84	0.58	−0.26
United States	0.84	0.60	−0.24	0.95	0.85	−0.10

Note: EU-28, euro, and non-euro area are calculated as weighted averages.
Source: Schoenmaker and Bosch (2008) and Darvas and Schoenmaker (2018)

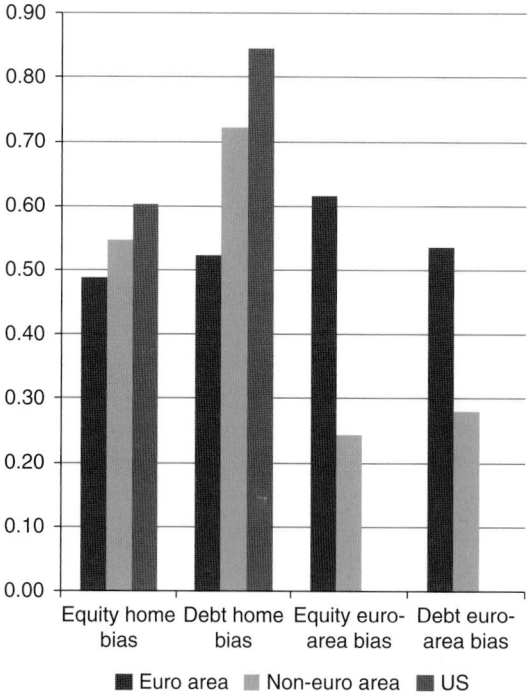

Figure 9.9   Home bias and euro-area bias in the EU and US, 2014

investing strategy. There is a 'euro effect': the euro has caused a decrease in home bias but an increase in euro-area bias.

To compare the risk-sharing capacity of the euro area vs. the US, the home bias of the euro area can be calculated by treating the euro area as a single country (Darvas and Schoenmaker, 2018). As the country composition of the euro area is not constant over our sample period due to new members

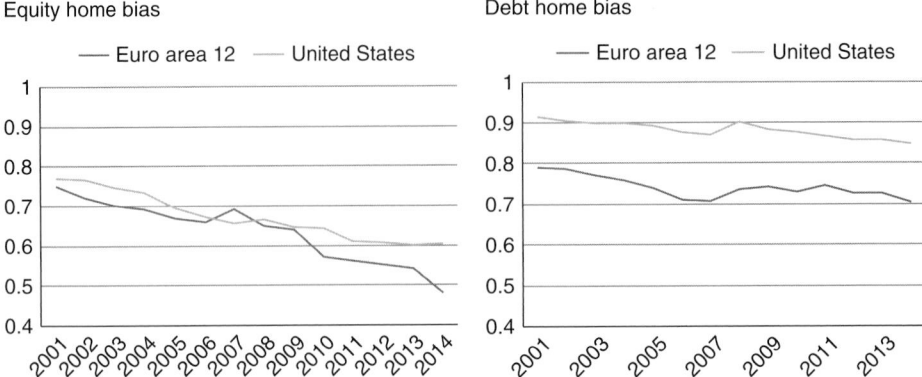

Figure 9.10 Home bias in the euro area vs. the US, 2001–2014
Source: Darvas and Schoenmaker (2018)

joining between 2007 and 2015, only the first 12 members of the euro area (EA-12) are included in this exercise.

Intra-euro-area claims are consolidated as 'domestic claims' from the perspective of the EA-12 aggregate, and only non-euro foreign claims are considered 'foreign' claims. The total market capitalisation of the EA-12 aggregate is simply the sum of the market capitalisations of the 12 countries. By calculating these 'consolidated' EA-12 aggregates, the home bias of the EA-12 group can be calculated using equation (9.7).

Figure 9.10 reports remarkably similar equity home bias in the euro area and the US, and a higher level of debt home bias in the US than in the EA-12 group. As expected, the home bias of the euro area is higher than the (weighted) average of the country-specific home biases of the 12 countries.

Explaining the Home Bias

If the gains of international diversification are positive and significant, why do (institutional) investors not hold the theoretically optimal portfolio? Table 9.10 explains which factors influence the size of the equity home bias.

The first factor is the ratio of total exports to GDP – a proxy for trade. Investors in countries with a large export-to-GDP ratio have less need for international diversification, as the companies in these countries are already diversifying via their international business. However, this ratio could also proxy for the mindset of the country's investors to indicate the openness of the country. If companies tend to do business abroad and diversify their business geographically, investors could act in the same manner.

Table 9.10 Determinants of the equity home bias (OLS regression)

Independent variables	Expected sign	Coefficient	t-value
Constant		0.915***	17.3
Export	+/−	−0.324***	3.9
Institutional	−	−0.146**	2.4
Insider	+	0.127	1.3
Market cap	+	0.159*	2.0
N		42	
Adj. R2		0.69	
F-statistic		16.25	

Notes: Ordinary least squares (OLS) panel regression using EHB_i as the dependent variable. Data for 1997, 2002, and 2004 for the EU-15 and the US are used for this analysis. Period-specific fixed effects are included in the regression. (***), (**), (*) indicate statistical significance at the 1 per cent, 5 per cent, and 10 per cent levels, respectively.
Source: Schoenmaker and Bosch (2008)

First, Table 9.10 reports that export-to-GDP ratios have a significant negative effect on home bias. This supports the theory that countries with relatively large trade volumes can be considered more 'open' and have a lower bias due to the *openness effect*. The domestic companies in these countries have significant exposure to the world market due to their level of international trade. However, investors in these countries are subject to a lower equity home bias, as they also tend to 'trade' (invest) internationally.

The second factor is the size of the institutional sector. Table 9.10 shows that the relative size of the institutional sector has a negative and significant effect on the home bias. Countries in which institutional investors manage a larger percentage of the financial assets exhibit greater international diversification. Indeed, this finding indicates that institutional investors, as professional asset managers, are subject to a lower home bias than non-financial corporations or households. This is the *professionalism effect*.

The third factor is the percentage of shares held by corporate insiders. Insider ownership is expected to increase the home bias in two ways. First, domestic investors hold shares that foreign investors cannot own. Second, domestic investors allocate less to foreign equity, as they have locked up a portion of their portfolio in domestic assets. It should be noted, however, that the theory concerning insider ownership was developed to explain the bias *towards* a country (Stulz, 2005), but not necessarily the home bias *of* a country. The share of corporate insiders is the only variable that is not significant in Table 9.10, although it has the expected positive sign.

Table 9.10 illustrates that the size of the domestic stock market relative to GDP (the fourth factor) has a positive and significant effect on the home bias. Thus, investors are more domestically oriented if their domestic stock market is well developed. This indicates that investors are subject to the *availability effect*, which means they are more eager to invest in domestic assets when these are readily available.

Finally, behavioural approaches may also explain the home bias. Behavioural finance draws upon the psychological effects of individual behaviour. Huberman (2001), for example, argues that familiarity with domestic companies makes it easier for investors to invest in domestic equity. Campbell and Kräussl (2007) find that investors concerned with downside risk tend to hold a larger proportion of their portfolio in domestic equity, due to the greater downside risk of investing abroad.

9.5 Conclusions

Globally, the investment process has become institutionalised: professional market investors are increasingly managing private savings. This chapter examines three main types of institutional investors: pension funds, life insurance companies, and mutual funds. Both the demand side (growing investments by pension funds to cater for ageing and by mutual funds to accommodate households' wealth accumulation) and the supply side (shift from bank-financed to market-financed companies via equity and bonds) point to the future growth of institutional investment.

As in many other financial sectors, the distinctions between the types of institutional investors are blurring. Mutual funds, for instance, are often used as a vehicle for retirement saving and represent a specific asset class for pension funds. Private equity and hedge funds are alternative investments that are increasingly added to pension fund portfolios. Insurance companies launch their own investment funds and are widely involved in pension provision, provision of annuities, and guaranteed investment contracts for pension funds, and also perform asset management services for pension funds.

Institutional investors play an important role in monitoring the companies in which they invest. This promotes good corporate governance, since institutional investors have sufficient clout to influence the management of companies.

Finance theory suggests that investors should aim to diversify their investment portfolio internationally in order to maximise returns given a certain risk profile. Nevertheless, there is a strong home bias in equity and bond portfolios. This chapter shows that the increasing professionalism of institutional investors (compared to individual investors) has led to a decline in the home bias in Europe. The elimination of exchange-rate risk following the introduction of the euro has led to a further decline of the home bias in the euro area.

Notes

1. Davis and Steil (2001) discuss the two main approaches – *prudent person rules*, which enjoin portfolio diversification and broad asset–liability matching, and *quantitative portfolio regulations*, which limit holdings of certain types of asset within the portfolio. Both seek to ensure adequate portfolio diversification and liquidity of the asset portfolio, but in different ways.
2. Data concerning foreign equity and bond holdings are extracted from a country-level dataset of the IMF, the Coordinated Portfolio Investment Survey.

Bibliography

Suggested Reading

Davis, E. P. and B. Steil (2001), *Institutional Investors*, MIT Press, Cambridge (MA).

Elton, E. J., M. J. Gruber, S. J. Brown, and W. M. Goetzmann (2014), *Modern Portfolio Theory and Investment Analysis*, 9th edition, John Wiley & Sons, New York.

Feldstein, M. S. and H. Siebert (eds.) (2002), *Social Security Pension Reform in Europe*, University of Chicago Press.

Gillan, S. L. and L. T. Starks (2003), Corporate Governance, Corporate Ownership, and the Role of Institutional Investors: A Global Perspective. *Journal of Applied Finance*, 13, 4–22.

Kahle, K. and R. Stulz (2017), Is the US Public Corporation in Trouble? *Journal of Economic Perspectives*, 31, 67–88.

Lewis, K. K. (1999), Trying to Explain Home Bias in Equities and Consumption. *Journal of Economic Literature*, 37, 571–608.

References

Ahearne, A. B., W. Griever, and F. Warnock (2004), Information Costs and the Home Bias. *Journal of International Economics*, 62, 313–36.

Campbell, R. A. and R. Kräussl (2007), Revisiting the Home Bias Puzzle: Downside Equity Risk. *Journal of International Money and Finance*, 26, 1239–60.

Chan, K., M. V. Covrig, and L. K. Ng (2005), What Determines the Domestic Bias and Foreign Bias? Evidence from Mutual Fund Equity Allocations Worldwide. *Journal of Finance*, 60, 1495–534.

Darvas, Z. and D. Schoenmaker (2018), Institutional Investors and Development of Europe's Capital Markets. In: D. Busch, E. Avgouleas, and G. Ferrarini (eds.), *Capital Markets Union in Europe*, Oxford University Press, 395–412.

Davis, E. P. (2003), Institutional Investors, Financial Market Efficiency and Stability. The Pensions Institute (London) Working Paper PI-0303.

Davis, E. P. and B. Steil (2001), *Institutional Investors*, MIT Press, Cambridge (MA).

De Santis, R. A. and B. Gerard (2009), International Portfolio Reallocation: Diversification Benefits and European Monetary Union. *European Economic Review*, 53, 1010–27.

Elton, E. J., M. J. Gruber, S. J. Brown, and W. M. Goetzmann (2014), *Modern Portfolio Theory and Investment Analysis*, 9th edition, John Wiley & Sons, New York.

European Commission (2014), *European Financial Stability and Integration*, EC, Brussels.

Feldstein, M. S. and H. Siebert (eds.) (2002), *Social Security Pension Reform in Europe*, University of Chicago Press.

French, K. (2008), Presidential Address: The Cost of Active Investing. *Journal of Finance*, 63, 1537–73.

Furfine, C. (2006), The Costs and Benefits of Moral Suasion: Evidence from the Rescue of Long-Term Capital Management. *Journal of Business*, 79, 593–622.

Gillan, S. L. and L. T. Starks (2003), Corporate Governance, Corporate Ownership, and the Role of Institutional Investors: A Global Perspective. *Journal of Applied Finance*, 13, 4–22.

Huberman, G. (2001), Familiarity Breeds Investment. *Review of Financial Studies*, 14, 659–80.

Jorion, P. (2000), Risk Management Lessons from Long-Term Capital Management. *European Financial Management*, 6, 277–300.

Kahle, K. and R. Stulz (2017), Is the US Public Corporation in Trouble? *Journal of Economic Perspectives*, 31, 67–88.

Karolyi, G. A. and R. M. Stulz (2003), Are Financial Assets Priced Locally or Globally? In: G. M. Constantinides, M. Harris, and R. M. Stulz (eds.), *The Handbook of the Economics of Finance*, Elsevier, Amsterdam, 975–1020.

Kho, B. C., D. Lee, and R. M. Stulz (2000), US Banks, Crises, and Bailouts: From Mexico to LTCM. *American Economic Review*, 90, 28–31.

Khorana, A., H. Servaes, and P. Tufano (2005), Explaining the Size of the Mutual Fund Industry Around the World. *Journal of Financial Economics*, 78, 145–85.

Lewis, K. K. (1999), Trying to Explain Home Bias in Equities and Consumption. *Journal of Economic Literature*, 37, 571–608.

McKinsey (2018), *The Rise and Rise of Private Markets*, McKinsey Global Private Markets Review 2018.

Preqin Global Hedge Fund Report (2018), London.

Rajan, R. G. (2007), Benign Financial Conditions, Asset Management, and Political Risks: Trying to Make Sense of our Times. In: D. D. Evanoff, G. G. Kaufman, and J. R. LaBrosse (eds.), *International Financial Stability: Global Banking and National Regulation*, World Scientific Publishing, Singapore, 19–28.

Rubbaniy, G, I. van Lelyveld, and W. Verschoor (2014), Home Bias and Dutch Pension Funds' Investment Behavior. *European Journal of Finance*, 20, 978–93.

Schoenmaker, D. and T. Bosch (2008), Is the Home Bias in Equities and Bonds Declining in Europe? *Investment Management and Financial Innovations*, 5, 90–102.

Schröder, M. (2003), Benefits of Diversification and Integration for International Equity and Bond Portfolios. In: P. Cecchini, F. Heinemann, and M. Jopp (eds.), *The Incomplete European Market for Financial Services*, ZEW Economic Studies 19, Springer-Verlag, Berlin, 179–86.

Smit, H. T. J. (2003), The Economics of Private Equity. ERIM (Erasmus University, Rotterdam) Report Series EIA-2002-13.

Stulz, R. M. (1999), Globalisation of Equity Markets and the Cost of Capital. NBER Working Paper 7021.

(2005), The Limits of Financial Globalisation. *Journal of Finance*, 60, 1595–638.

TheCityUK (2013), *Hedge Funds*, London.

10

European Banks

OVERVIEW

The traditional business of banking is taking deposits and providing loans. Banks have a comparative advantage over other financial institutions in providing liquidity. They have also developed technologies to screen and monitor borrowers in order to reduce asymmetric information between the lender and the borrower. These liquidity-providing and monitoring functions also give banks a key role in modern capital market transactions, such as underwriting, trading, and derivatives transactions.

Risk is fundamental to the business of banking. Progress in information technology, combined with demands by supervisory authorities, has spurred the development of advanced risk management models. This, in turn, has prompted the centralisation and integration of some management functions such as risk management, treasury operations, compliance, and auditing. This integrated risk management method is designed to ensure a comprehensive and systematic approach to risk-related decisions throughout the banking group. Banks with an integrated risk management unit can exploit diversification opportunities at the group level.

The European banking market is made up of 27 national banking systems. Each national banking system has its own characteristics, such as the number of banks, the level of concentration, and the intensity of competition. Some banking systems are highly concentrated, but this does not necessarily lead to a lack of competition. An important condition for competitive pressure is that the market is open to new entry (contestability). The European Commission therefore promotes the removal of the remaining obstacles to cross-border mergers and acquisitions.

Domestic banking mergers are still very common, while some cross-border mergers have taken place. It is not possible yet to speak of an integrated banking market, as the level of cross-border penetration has returned to the low pre-crisis level. The Banking Union is expected to foster the integration of the 19 national banking systems of the euro-area countries.

LEARNING OBJECTIVES

After you have studied this chapter, you should be able to:
- explain the role of banks as liquidity providers to the economy
- explain the role of banks in screening and monitoring (potential) borrowers
- explain banks' use of risk management models and the trend for banks to centralise the risk management function
- explain the dynamics of domestic and cross-border mergers and acquisitions in banking
- understand the dynamics of the Banking Union.

10.1 Theory of Banking

Drivers of Bank Profitability

Banks perform multiple functions. Their traditional business is lending. Before a bank grants a loan, it screens the creditworthiness of a potential borrower. After the loan is granted, the bank monitors whether the borrower takes excessive risks. The lending business generates income for banks. As loans have to be funded, the difference (or spread) between the lending and borrowing rates determines a bank's profitability. Banks also profit from various fee-earning activities like capital market transactions, such as under-writing and trading, and derivatives transactions. Banks use modern risk management models to measure and control the risks arising from these transactions. These models are built using the monitoring technology that banks use in their lending business.

Lending Business

Banks take deposits from the public and grant loans on their own account. These loans are typically held to maturity (the 'originate and hold' model). Banks thus transform liquid deposits into illiquid loans. Their intermediation function can be illustrated using a simple balance sheet (see Figure 10.1). In this example, banks fund themselves with many small deposits D from the public, shown on the liability side of the balance sheet. The effective deposit rate r_D includes both the explicit interest paid and the cost of free services (for example, free access to ATMs). While deposits are redeemable on demand, depositors usually do not all ask for their money back at the same time. Banks

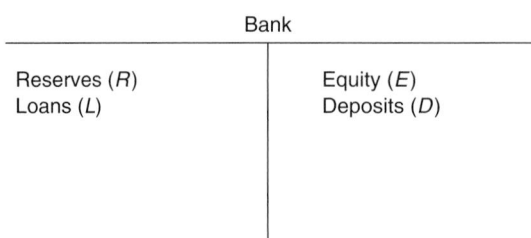

Figure 10.1 Simplified balance sheet of a bank

therefore hold only a fraction of these deposits in the form of liquid reserves R that consist of balances with the central bank or readily tradable assets, such as Treasury securities, that pay the risk-free rate r_F. The remaining funds can be used to provide loans. (As explained in Box 10.1, banks also have other means than the deposits they have received to provide loans.)

Banks provide loans L. The expected loan rate r_L is different from the contracted rate on loans, as some borrowers default on their loans. Assuming a risk-neutral bank, the difference between the contracted loan rate r_C and the expected loan rate r_L is given by:

$$E(1 + r_c) = (1 + r_c)\,(1 - p) + (1 + r_c)\,p \cdot \gamma = 1 + r_L \tag{10.1}$$

where p is the probability of default and γ the recovery rate (the fraction of the principal and interest recovered in case of default). Equation (10.1) can be illustrated with a simple example. Assume a contracted loan rate of 9 per cent, a probability of default of 5 per cent, and a recovery rate of 80 per cent. The expected loan rate is 7.91 per cent, calculated as $(1.09 * 0.95) + (1.09 * .05 * 0.8) = 1.0791$.

The bank's profit π is the interest margin net of cost C and is given by:

$$\pi = L \cdot r_L + R \cdot r_F - D \cdot r_D - C \tag{10.2}$$

An important determinant of bank profitability is the risk premium RP, i.e. the difference between the contracted loan rate and the risk-free rate $(r_C - r_F)$. The risk premium covers the expected loan losses (which are a function of the probability of default p and the recovery rate y), the cost of the loan business, and the reward for risk taking on the loans.

Fee-Based Business

Banks also make profits from fee-earning activities. These off-balance-sheet activities are related to the traditional loan business and include the securitisation of assets (see Chapter 1), credit lines, and guarantees, such as letters of credit. Off-balance-sheet activities also encompass derivative transactions, such as forwards, options, and swaps. Nowadays, large banks are the key players in the derivatives markets.

Asset securitisation involves the sale of income-generating financial assets (such as mortgages, car loans, trade receivables, credit card receivables, and leases) by a bank, the originator of the financial assets, to a *special purpose vehicle* (SPV). The SPV finances the purchase of these financial assets by issuing commercial paper, which is secured by those assets (see Chapter 8). Banks can thus liquefy their illiquid loans. The resulting 'originate and distribute' model separates the functions of granting vs. funding of loans. When the loans on their balance sheet are securitised, banks can provide new loans.

Finally, banks are increasingly involved in fee-earning capital market and asset management activities. European banks deliver services like underwriting securities, advising on mergers and acquisitions (M&As), and managing assets. These activities have helped them recover part of the business lost due to dis-intermediation (see Chapter 9). The non-interest income of banks in the euro area amounts to 38 per cent of total income (ECB, 2017).

Banks as Liquidity Providers

Banks have three advantages over other financial institutions in providing liquidity, which are rooted in the structure of the banking system (Garber and Weisbrod, 1990). First, banks can create money by expanding both sides of the balance sheet simultaneously. When granting a loan to a borrower, the bank increases the deposit balance of that borrower by the same amount, which provides liquid funds to the borrower. Box 10.1 explains the process of money creation by banks. Second, under normal circumstances there is an active and deep interbank market in which banks trade their liquidity surpluses and deficits so that liquidity shocks at individual banks can easily be offset. A bank with a surplus lends to a bank with a deficit, and vice versa. As shown in Chapter 5, the euro interbank market worked smoothly from the first day of the Economic and Monetary Union (EMU) until the crisis. Money market rates quickly converged to a single euro-wide rate. TARGET2 (the wholesale payment system of the national central banks and the European Central Bank) provides the infrastructure for transferring funds in real time (see Chapter 7).

Box 10.1 Money creation

Money is the generally accepted medium of exchange in an economy; it is used as a unit of account and a store of value. A unit of account refers to the thing that goods and services are priced in. Store of value means something that is expected to retain its value in a reasonably predictable way over time. Figure 10.2 shows that coins and banknotes account for only a small portion of the money stock: the vast majority consists of bank balances, mainly current and savings accounts. Money creation is the process by which the money stock increases. Banks play a key role in this process.

Money is brought into existence when banks make loans. For example, when a mortgage agreement is concluded between a bank and customer X, two things happen simultaneously on the bank's balance sheet. On the asset side, the bank enters the amount owed by customer X (the value of the mortgage). On the liability side, the bank records that customer X disposes of a deposit balance equal to the amount of the mortgage loan. As this bank deposit is considered part of the money stock, new money has been created. Thus, banks can create book money simply by making an accounting entry.

Figures 10.3 and 10.4 show simplified bank balance sheets, demonstrating how this process works. Initially, the bank has €450 million in loans outstanding to households and €150 million in liquid reserves, counterbalanced by €580 million in deposits from households and €20 million in equity. Figure 10.4 shows that a mortgage of €10 million induces movements on both the asset and liability sides of the bank's balance sheet. In accounting terms, during the transaction the bank and the customer created reciprocal obligations: the customer has a debt obligation to the bank, and the bank has a debt obligation to the customer in the form of a deposit. The provision of the mortgage leads to an increase in the money stock. This simple example refutes a popular misconception that banks act simply as intermediaries at the time of lending, i.e. that banks can

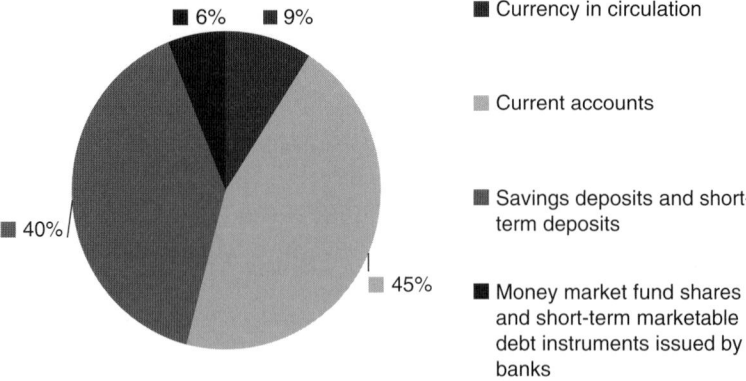

■ 6%   ■ 9%   ■ Currency in circulation

■ Current accounts

■ Savings deposits and short-term deposits

■ 40%

45%   ■ Money market fund shares and short-term marketable debt instruments issued by banks

Figure 10.2 Composition of the money stock in the euro area, 28 February 2017
Note: The figure illustrates the composition of the broadest definition of the money stock generally referred to as M3.
Source: ECB

Box 10.1 (cont.)

only grant credit using funds placed with them previously as deposits by other customers. Repayment of the mortgage reverses the balance sheet movement, which is referred to as money destruction. So, both the creation of money and its destruction are always the outcome of transactions in which domestic banks and non-banks must be involved.

What happens in this simple example if customer X who received the mortgage uses it to purchase a house from customer Y? Customer X transfers the €10 million received as a loan to customer Y. Customer Y exchanges the house for a credit entry on his or her bank account. If X and Y are customers of the same bank, the aggregate balance sheet of the bank does not change. If X and Y are customers of different banks, these banks settle the transaction via their accounts with the central bank. The total amount of deposits in the economy therefore does not change due to the sale of the house.

It is important to point out that banks face limitations in creating money. As unbridled money creation could result in high inflation, central banks aim to ensure price stability by pursuing a monetary policy designed to control commercial banks' money-creating ability. Whenever price stability is at risk, central banks adjust their instruments. They may, for instance, increase key policy interest rates, which in turn dampens demand for credit (see Chapter 4 for details about ECB policies). Money creation is also restricted by supervisory policy measures for safeguarding the stability of the banking sector. When a bank provides new loans, the proportion of the required equity increases, so the bank may run the risk of breaching supervisory capital regulations. Capital regulations force banks to hold a certain amount of capital against their lending, depending on the risks involved. In the case of a leverage ratio of 3 per cent of total assets, the bank can expand its balance sheet to €667 million (see Chapter 12 for details). Finally, banks also have an interest in controlling credit growth, since they are willing to extend loans only to customers whose creditworthiness is sound.

		Bank	
Reserves	150	Equity	20
Loans	450	Deposits	580
Total	600	Total	600

Figure 10.3 Bank balance sheet before the mortgage agreement

		Bank	
Reserves	150	Equity	20
Loans	460 (+10)	Deposits	590 (+10)
Total	610	Total	610

Figure 10.4 Bank balance sheet after the mortgage agreement

The third advantage that banks have over other financial institutions in providing liquidity is that aggregate liquidity shocks are smoothed by the central bank. A central bank conducts open market operations to inject (withdraw) liquidity in the money market if there is an aggregate shortage (surplus). Banks are the usual counterparties of the central bank in these operations. If an individual bank cannot square its position at the end of the day, it can use facilities offered by the central bank. To stimulate banks to do their business as much as possible on the money market, the rates for these standing facilities are slightly off market. At the time of writing in early 2019, the ECB's deposit rate is, for example, 0.40 per cent below the official refinancing rate for open market operations, and the marginal lending rate is 0.25 per cent above the official refinancing rate (see Chapter 4).

These features of the banking system enable banks to provide liquidity to other financial institutions if and when needed. More importantly, banks are also the main provider of liquidity to households and firms. The liquidity pyramid in Figure 10.5 illustrates these relationships. The central bank is at the top of the pyramid, as it can create unlimited liquidity by expanding its balance sheet (granting loans and taking deposits). As explained above, the central bank provides liquidity to banks that in turn provide liquidity to the rest of the financial system and to households and firms. Especially during crises, central banks must act swiftly to provide liquidity. However, banks also play a crucial role under these circumstances, as the examples presented in Box 10.2 illustrate.

During the financial crisis, liquidity became available for banks against collateral. As a consequence, a significant proportion of banks' assets became encumbered. In peripheral euro-area countries, banks increased their asset encumbrance due to central bank lending. However, banks from some core

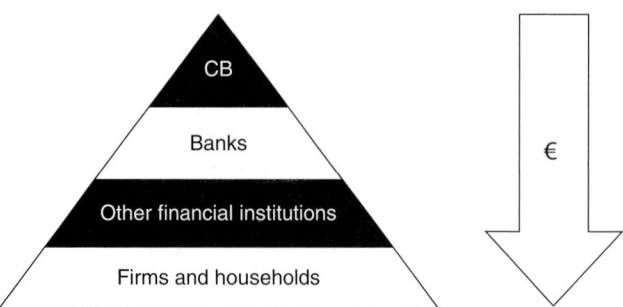

Figure 10.5   Liquidity pyramid of the economy
Note: CB = central bank. In this liquidity pyramid, the central bank provides liquidity to the banking system. Banks, in turn, provide liquidity to other financial institutions and to firms and households.

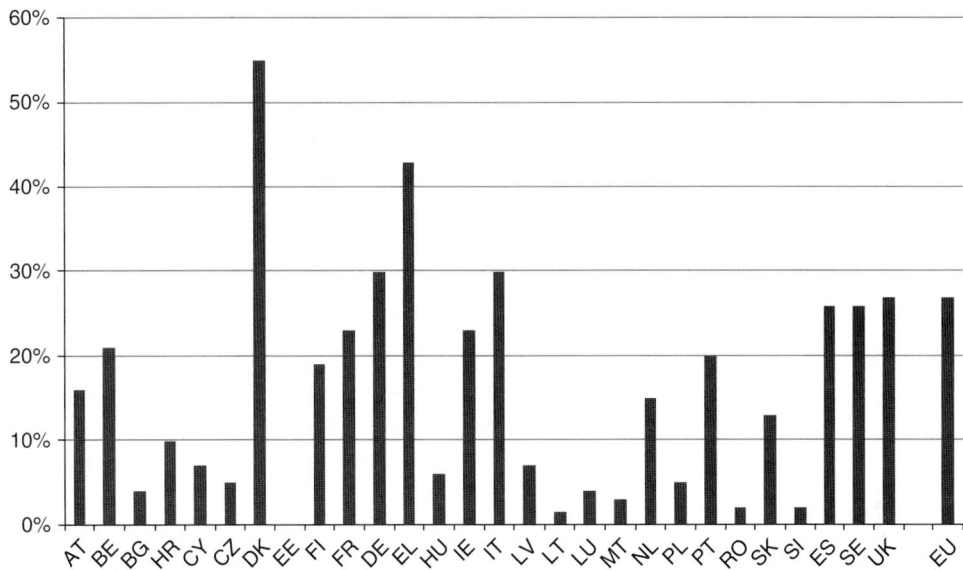

Figure 10.6   Asset encumbrance by country, 2016 (percentage of assets)
Source: European Banking Authority (2017)

Box 10.2 Liquidity management during crises

On 19 October 1987 the US stock market crashed; the S&P 500 stock market index fell by about 20 per cent. The crash exposed the vulnerability of the trading systems, as they were not capable of processing so many transactions at once. Uncertainty about information contributed to a pull-back by investors from the market. *Margin calls* to securities traders that accompanied the large price changes also contributed to the crash. When securities traders buy securities with borrowed money, they have to deposit a margin with the clearinghouse to cover the clearinghouse's credit risk. As the value of securities declined, the clearinghouses called for extra margin. While necessary to protect the solvency of the clearinghouses processing the trades, the size of the margin calls reduced market liquidity as securities traders had drawn on their working capital to meet these margin calls and subsequently had difficulties in continuing trading. The Federal Reserve stepped in by providing highly visible liquidity support through massive open market operations. More importantly, the Federal Reserve also encouraged banks to extend liquidity support to securities traders (brokers and dealers). The extension of credit by banks to securities firms was key to their ability to meet their clearing and settlement obligations and to continue to operate in these markets.

   Another example of liquidity management during a crisis was the subprime mortgage market crisis in the summer of 2007. Many banks, including large banks such as Goldman Sachs, City Group, and Merrill Lynch, announced large losses due to this crisis. As the extent to

---

Box 10.2 (cont.)

which various banks were exposed to these risks was unclear, banks were reluctant to provide short-term loans to each other. The ECB and the Federal Reserve therefore stepped in and provided massive liquidity support. The Bank of England (BoE), however, initially remained on the sidelines. On 12 September 2007 BoE governor Mervyn King said it would be prepared to provide emergency loans to any bank that ran into short-term difficulties as a result of temporary market conditions. But he appeared to rule out following the lead of the ECB and the US Federal Reserve in pumping huge sums into the banking system to ease the liquidity drought. On 13 September, British bank Northern Rock, the country's fifth-largest mortgage lender, applied to the BoE for emergency funds caused by liquidity problems. Concerned customers withdrew an estimated £2 billion in just three days; this was the first run on a British bank in more than a century (see Box 2.4). On 17 September, Chancellor Alistair Darling intervened to try to end the crisis by agreeing to guarantee all deposits held by Northern Rock.

countries and non-euro-area countries also have significant levels of asset encumbrance, although mainly in the form of covered bonds (see Figure 10.6). In particular, Denmark and Germany have a long-standing practice of issuing covered bonds against mortgages.

Banks as Delegated Monitor

Asymmetric information lies at the core of banking. A borrower has private information on the cash flow of an investment project, which is unobservable to outside lenders. Banks therefore monitor (potential) clients. Monitoring is defined here in a broad sense (Freixas and Rochet, 2008) as:

- screening projects *ex ante* (adverse selection);
- preventing opportunistic behaviour of the borrower during the project (moral hazard);
- auditing a borrower who fails to meet its contractual obligation (costly state verification).

Banks have a comparative advantage in monitoring (potential) borrowers if the following three conditions are met (Diamond, 1984). First, a bank can develop economies of scale in monitoring by financing many investment projects. Second, since the capacity of individual lenders is small compared to the size of many investment projects, each project needs several lenders, who would then need to monitor the borrowers. Finally, the costs of delegating this monitoring to a bank are small. Box 10.3 presents the Diamond model of

---

Box 10.3 When is it optimal to delegate monitoring to banks?*

Consider n identical borrowers who need funds for their investment projects. Each invest-ment requires one unit of account, and the returns on the investment are identically independently distributed. The cash flow $\tilde{y}$ that a borrower obtains from his or her investment is unobservable for lenders. The asymmetric information regarding the cash flow gives rise to moral hazard, which can be solved either by monitoring the firm at a cost of K or by signing a debt contract with a cost of C (in case of insufficient cash flow). It is assumed that monitoring is more efficient than using the debt contract: $K < C$. The next assumption is that each lender has only $\frac{1}{m}$ available for investment (i.e. lenders have a small capacity to lend). So, each project needs m lenders. If small lenders provide the funds needed for the investment (direct lending), the total costs of monitoring all projects by all borrowers would amount to $n \cdot m \cdot K$.

Next, a bank is introduced. Facing the same trade-off between monitoring or signing debt contracts, the bank will also choose to monitor borrowers since $K < C$. The bank emerges as a delegated monitor, which monitors the borrowers on behalf of lenders. But who will monitor the bank? It is very costly for all lenders to monitor the bank. The solution is that the bank offers a debt contract (deposit). The lender is promised a nominal amount $\frac{r_D}{m}$ in return for a deposit $\frac{1}{m}$. The bank is liquidated if its announced cash flow $\tilde{z}$ falls below the total sum promised to depositors $n \cdot r_D$. Now, a mechanism is needed to ensure that a bank will truthfully reveal the realised cash flow $\tilde{z} = \sum_{i=1}^{n} \tilde{y}_i - n \cdot K$. The threat of a costly audit in case of failure is used to make the contract incentive compatible.

Suppose that depositors are risk neutral and have access to outside investments with a return of r. The equilibrium repayment on deposits r_D is then determined by:

$$E\left[\min\left(\sum_{i=1}^{n} \tilde{y}_i - n \cdot K, n \cdot r_D\right)\right] = n \cdot r \tag{10.3}$$

Equation (10.3) shows that the return r is equal to the minimum of the expected cash flow of the project minus the monitoring costs and the expected unit return on deposits. In equilibrium, the expected unit return on deposits r_D equals r. Next, the total cost of delegation C_n is equal to the expectation of a costly audit in case of failure:

$$C_n = E\left[\max\left(n \cdot r_D + n \cdot K - \sum_{i=1}^{n} \tilde{y}_i, 0\right)\right] \tag{10.4}$$

Delegated monitoring is more efficient than direct lending if the combined costs of monitoring by the bank and delegation are lower than the cost of monitoring by all lenders:

$$n \cdot K + C_n < n \cdot m \cdot K \tag{10.5}$$

Dividing by n gives:

$$K + \frac{C_n}{n} < m \cdot K \tag{10.6}$$

Box 10.3 (cont.)

Since $m > 1$, monitoring by the bank is less costly than monitoring by all lenders if $\frac{C_n}{n}$ goes to zero when n goes to infinity. Dividing equations (10.3) and (10.4) by n produces:

$$E\left[\min\left(\frac{1}{n}\sum_{i=1}^{n}\tilde{y}_i - K, r_D\right)\right] = r \tag{10.7}$$

and

$$\frac{C_n}{n} = E\left[\max\left(r_D + K - \frac{1}{n}\sum_{i=1}^{n}\tilde{y}_i, 0\right)\right] \tag{10.8}$$

According to the law of large numbers, $\frac{1}{n}\sum_{i=1}^{n}\tilde{y}_i$ converges to $E(\tilde{y})$. Since $E(\tilde{y}) > K + r$,

equation (10.7) shows that $r_D = r$ when n goes to infinity. Substituting these results into equation (10.8) yields:

$$\lim_{n}\frac{C_n}{n} = \max\left(r + K - E(\tilde{y}), 0\right) = 0 \tag{10.9}$$

So, the cost of delegation goes to zero when n goes to infinity.
Source: Freixas and Rochet (2008)

delegated monitoring, which shows that under these conditions it is efficient to delegate monitoring to a bank.

When there are many borrowers, it is efficient to delegate monitoring to one party. In the model shown in Box 10.3, a bank emerges as the delegated monitor for all lenders. Alternatively, lenders may delegate monitoring to a *credit rating agency*, which assigns credit ratings to firms and governments that issue debt obligations, such as bonds (see Box 1.1).[1] A credit rating assesses a firm's creditworthiness based on its ability to repay a loan, which can be derived from observing the firm's cash flows. The resulting credit rating affects the interest rate charged for the bonds.

What determines the choice between direct and intermediated lending? In practice, issuing bonds in the capital market is less expensive than bank lending. So only firms that cannot issue direct debt on financial markets will request bank lending (Freixas and Rochet, 2008). When the uncertainty about the firm's cash flows is relatively low (i.e. the asymmetric information between the firm and the lenders is limited), the firm can borrow on the market. As the uncertainty increases, banks come into play as they are better able than credit rating agencies to ask for information and to intervene when necessary. When the level of uncertainty becomes too high, a firm cannot obtain finance. The resulting equilibrium is that large, well-capitalised firms with a track record of published annual reports finance themselves directly, while smaller and new firms have to turn to banks.

10.2 The Use of Risk Management Models

Risk taking is fundamental to the business of banking. Only by taking calculated financial risks can a bank earn a rate above the risk-free rate of return. Banks unbundle and bundle financial risks. First, risks are decomposed so that they can be managed one by one. For example, the risk on a bank loan with a fixed interest rate can be separated into an interest rate risk (i.e. the risk of loss due to rising interest rates) and a credit risk (i.e. the risk of loss due to a default by a borrower). The bank can separately manage the interest rate risk (e.g. by buying an interest rate derivative with the same maturity as the bank loan) and the credit risk (e.g. by requiring collateral from the borrower). Next, risks are aggregated to reap the benefits of diversification. An example is a diversified portfolio of loans to companies from different sectors and/or geographic regions. The traditional role of banks in monitoring credit risk has evolved towards the use of advanced models to measure and manage risk. Risk management has been broadened from credit risk to market risk (i.e. the risk of loss because of unfavourable movements in market prices) and operational risk (i.e. the risk of loss from inadequate or failed internal processes, people or systems, or from external events). Progress in information technology has facilitated the development of risk management models, which rely on statistical methods to process financial data. The financial services sector is one of the most IT-intensive industries (Berger, 2003).

Modern Risk Management

Economic capital is the amount of capital a bank needs in order to be able to absorb losses over a certain time interval (usually one year) with a certain confidence level. The confidence interval depends on the bank's objectives. The concept of economic capital can be used to compare different types of risks. The main risk types for a bank are credit risk, market risk, and operational risk.

Large international banks usually seek to maintain an AA credit rating (Hull, 2018). Companies rated AA have a one-year probability of default of

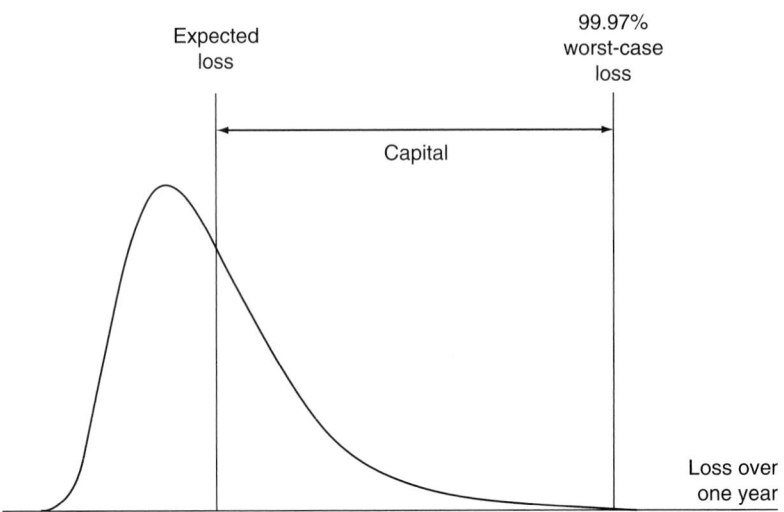

Figure 10.7 Economic capital of an AA-rated bank
Source: Hull (2018)

0.03 per cent, which results in a confidence level of 99.97 per cent. Figure 10.7 illustrates the calculation of economic capital.

Economic capital can be used to calculate the *risk-adjusted return on capital* (RAROC), which is calculated as:

$$\text{RAROC} = \frac{\text{Revenues–Costs–Expected Losses}}{\text{Economic Capital}} = \frac{\pi}{E} \qquad (10.10)$$

Both the numerator and the denominator are adjusted for risk in the RAROC formula. This is an improvement over the widely used standard *return on equity* measure, defined as earned profit divided by available equity. For example, an AA-rated bank estimates its expected losses as 1 per cent of outstanding loans per year on average. The worst-case loss at 99.97 per cent confidence is 4 per cent of outstanding loans. So, the economic capital for €100 of loans is €3 (the difference between worst-case loss and expected loss). The numerator starts with the revenues: the spread between the promised loan rate and the risk-free rate is 2.20 per cent. The costs of the bank amount to 0.75 per cent of the loan. So, the RAROC is $\frac{2.20 - 0.75 - 1.00}{3.00} = 15$ per cent.

RAROC has emerged as the leading methodology for large banks (as well as other financial institutions, such as insurance companies) to measure and manage risk. The use of internal risk models has been stimulated by supervisors allowing banks to use their internal models to calculate capital requirements (see Chapter 12 for the Basel capital adequacy rules). Within the RAROC framework, banks first calculate the risk for credit, market, and operational risk and then aggregate the different risk types for the whole bank. A bank's overall risk profile must account for correlations across risk types (Van Lelyveld, 2006).

Credit risk is the risk of loss because of the failure of a counterparty to adhere to the contractual arrangement, for instance due to a default by a borrower.[2] In a modern bank, counterparties include not only the traditional counterparties on loans (borrowers) but also counterparties in derivatives transactions and in payment and settlement systems. Diversification is an important tool to manage credit risk. By lending to companies in different sectors, banks can reduce the sectoral exposures in their loan portfolio. Similarly, international expansion reduces the business cycle risk. As long as business cycles across euro-area countries are not fully synchronised, there is scope for diversification within Europe. Clearly, geographic (and sectoral) diversification would not protect a bank against a worldwide economic downturn. A second tool to manage credit risk is monitoring counterparties.

The typical time horizon for credit risk is one year. This type of risk thus fits nicely into economic capital models that use a one-year horizon. Figure 10.8 illustrates the loss distribution for credit risk. Its shape is quite skewed, as the vast majority of counterparties will repay (almost) in full; only a minority defaults (partly) on their payment obligation.

Market risk is the risk of loss due to unfavourable movements in market prices like interest rates, foreign exchange rates, equity prices, and commodity prices. This type of risk relates primarily to a bank's trading portfolio and focuses on changes in market value. Losses due to market risk materialise when an adverse price movement causes the market-to-market valuation of a

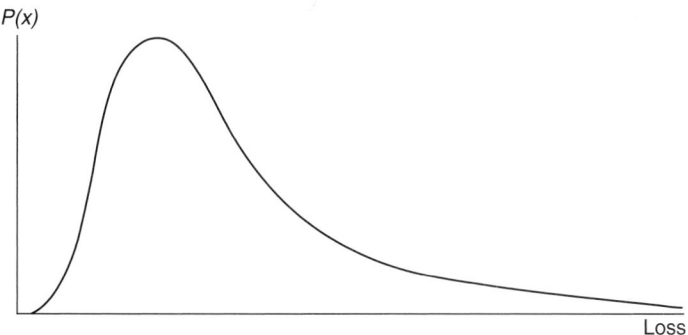

Figure 10.8 Loss distribution for credit risk

trading position to decline. Banks typically manage their trading portfolio within a Value at Risk (VaR) framework with a 10-day time horizon (see Box 10.4). The rationale is that a bank can close its position (e.g. selling a security or taking an opposite position in a new derivative transaction) within 10 business days. Under certain assumptions, the standard deviation of 10-day losses can be translated into the one-year horizon of economic capital models.[3]

Asset and liability management (ALM) risk occurs when assets and liabilities in the balance sheet are not matched. Banks' ALM risk refers to the interest rate risk in the banking book, where long-term assets (loans) are funded by short-term liabilities (deposits). Insurance companies face the opposite problem: their liabilities typically have a longer maturity than assets (see Chapter 11).

The loss distribution for market risk is symmetrical, which is very different from that for credit risk (see Figure 10.9). A good example is the price of equity. According to the efficient market hypothesis, all available information (including information on a company's future prospects) is reflected in the equity price of a company. So, today's stock price is the best predictor of tomorrow's stock price. The stock price will move only with the arrival of new information, which appears randomly. It follows a random walk with an equal likelihood of upward and downward movements.

Operational risk is the risk of loss from inadequate or failed internal processes, people or systems, or from external events. A famous example of operational risk is the failure of Barings Bank in 1995. Nick Leeson, a trader for Barings in Singapore, made money by arbitraging between the Nikkei 225 futures on the Singapore and Osaka exchanges. Barings had no effective risk limits in place, which allowed Leeson to build up large positions. When the

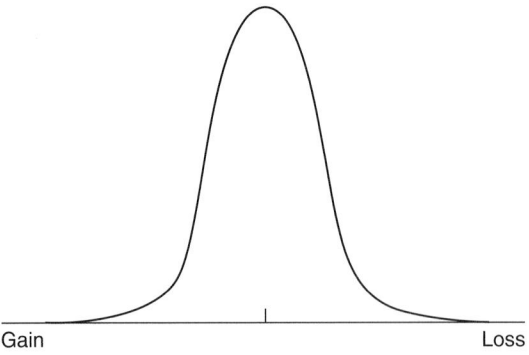

Gain   Loss

Figure 10.9 Loss distribution for market risk

Box 10.4 Value at Risk

A primary tool for measuring market risk is the *VaR methodology*. The VaR measure summarises the expected maximum loss (i.e. Value at Risk) over a target horizon of N days within a given confidence interval of X per cent. As discussed in Chapter 12, the Basel capital framework calculates capital for a bank's trading book using the VaR measure with $N = 10$ and $X = 99$ per cent This means that the bank is 99 per cent certain that the loss level over 10 days will not exceed the VaR measure. So only in 1 out of 100 trading days is the bank's loss expected to exceed the VaR measure.

The main advantage is that the risk of a portfolio comprising various financial assets is contained in a single measure, the VaR. Figure 10.10 illustrates the VaR for a situation in which the change in the value of a portfolio is approximately normally distributed. The basic VaR methodology assumes a normal (bell-shaped) distribution of returns. However, the returns on financial assets are non-normal with heavy tails (Danielsson, 2011). So, VaR underestimates a portfolio's market risk. Extreme value theory, which uses extreme values (e.g. one-day losses of 5 per cent or larger) to measure the tails of a distribution more accurately, is typically applied to more accurately estimate the downside risk of a portfolio of assets. Alternatively, banks can complement the VaR methodology with stress-test scenarios to get a better picture of potential losses.

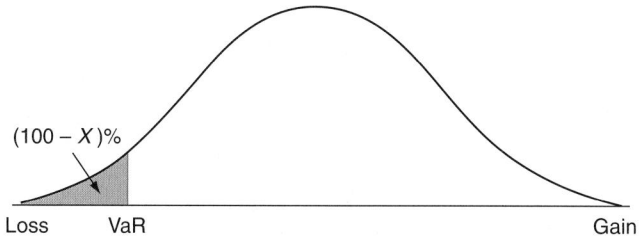

Figure 10.10 Calculation of VaR with a confidence level of X%
Source: Hull (2018)

Source: Hull (2018)

---

market moved against him, Barings' total loss was close to $1 billion. Another example was the rogue trader scandal at Société Générale (SocGen) that cost the bank €4.9 billion. Jerome Kerviel, a junior trader at SocGen, secretly built up huge and risky positions in the derivatives market. He was taking greater and greater risks over a period dating back to March 2007 for large amounts and to 2005 for smaller amounts. SocGen only discovered the fraud between 18 and 20 January 2008. Unwinding the positions over the subsequent three days cost the bank billions. The variety of concealment techniques used, the

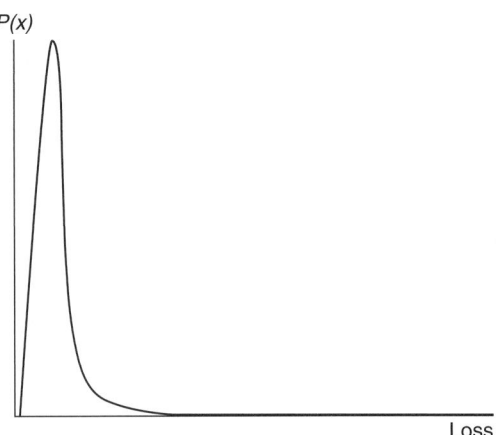

Figure 10.11 Loss distribution for operational risk

lack of systematic checks by staff when warning flags were raised, and short-comings in the control systems all contributed to the late discovery of Kerviel's activities (Hull, 2018).

Other examples of operational risk are IT failures, judicial settlements, and terrorist attacks. The Barings and SocGen examples illustrate that operational risk can interact with credit and market risk. When a trader exceeds limits, losses result only if the market moves against the trader. Figure 10.11 provides the loss distribution for operational risk; it is very skewed, even more than the credit risk loss distribution. Operational losses are usually modest, but occasionally they are very large.

A recent form of operational risk is judicial settlements. Three examples are discussed here. First, French bank BNP Paribas, for example, pleaded guilty to two criminal charges and agreed to pay €6.6 billion in 2015 to resolve accusations that it violated US sanctions against Sudan, Cuba, and Iran. US policy makers used this severe punishment to send a clear message to other financial institutions around the world. Under its new strategy, the US Department of Justice tries to snare more major banks for possible money laundering or sanctions violations. A second example is that several major international banks paid large settlements for their involvement in the Libor fraud. This scandal refers to fraudulent actions connected to the *LIBOR* (London Interbank Offered Rate), an average interest rate calculated based on submissions of interest rates by major banks in London that underpins the lending and derivatives markets. Some banks were found to be falsely inflating or deflating their rates in order to profit from trades or to signal creditworthiness. Third, at several points in time some European and US banks paid large fines for mis-selling packaged mortgage-backed securities that were not as sound as investors were led to believe in the lead-up to the financial crisis: Deutsche Bank paid €6.5 billion, JPMorgan Chase €11.7 billion, and Bank of America €15.0 billion.

While credit, market, and operational risks can each threaten banks' solvency (and are therefore incorporated into the economic capital calculation), banks also incur *liquidity risk* if they have insufficient liquid resources to meet a surge in liquidity demand. (In Chapter 5, market liquidity is defined as the ease with which an investor can sell or buy a security immediately at a price close to the fair price.) The classic case of a surge in liquidity demand for a bank is the sudden withdrawal of deposits. Banks manage their liquid resources in two ways. The first way is to maintain a pool of liquid assets. Central bank reserves are the most liquid assets, but they generate a relatively low return. Other liquid assets are government bonds, which can be easily sold. But a bank typically holds only a fraction of its demand deposits in liquid assets. The remainder is invested in illiquid, but high-return, assets such as loans. These assets can be liquidated immediately only at low prices.

The second way banks can manage liquidity risk is by preserving a diversified funding base (also referred to as *funding liquidity*). As explained in Section 10.1, banks can fund themselves in the interbank market. As long as banks have sufficient confidence in each other, a bank is able to borrow from other banks. Trust is therefore a bank's most important 'asset'. If a bank loses the trust of other banks, it will face liquidity problems and possibly even failure. For example, in May 1984 the Continental Illinois Bank experienced funding difficulties in domestic markets and had to turn to more expensive Eurodollar deposits in London. Rumours that Continental was on the verge of bankruptcy resulted in a run on its wholesale deposits by both domestic and foreign banks.

Criticism of Internal Models

There are severe drawbacks to using internal risk management models, such as RAROC, to calculate regulatory capital. These models focus on day-to-day risk rather than tail risks (Danielsson, 2013). They are typically based on a normal distribution and assume that risks are independent (i.e. no correlation) and exogenous. The financial crisis showed that tail events can – and do – happen. Extreme value theory, which deviates from the normal distribution, can be used to assess tail events. Moreover, most markets went down at the same time, demonstrating the high degree of correlation among risks. The unfolding of the financial crisis also highlighted the endogenous nature of risk – i.e. risk from shocks that are generated and amplified within the system. Exogenous risk refers to shocks from outside the system. While financial markets are subject to both types of risks, endogenous risks incur the greatest damage (Danielsson, 2013).

Another challenge for the use of internal models is model risk – the potential for adverse consequences to decisions based on incorrect or misused model outputs and reports. Regulators require internal model validation procedures to limit model risk. However, model risk can happen with complex financial products if there are no market prices available for model validation and if the calculated value is fully based on the internal model (marked to model instead of marked to market). Moreover, banks have an incentive to reduce risk weights based on internal models, as lower risk weights lead to lower regulatory capital requirements (see Chapter 12).

In response to these shortfalls, regulators are increasingly demanding that banks use stress tests to assess the impact of various severe scenarios on their regulatory capital. The US authorities initiated system-wide stress tests in 2009. Following the US example, the European Banking Authority (EBA) has conducted several stress tests of the European banking system. *Stress tests examine the implications of individual banks' financial positions under several macroeconomic scenarios, taking their exposures and business models into account.* However, these tests have been criticised, as some banks that passed the test got into trouble soon afterwards. With the advance to Banking Union, the EBA and ECB are conducting more demanding stress tests (see Chapter 12).

Centralisation of Risk Management

The organisational structure of international banks is moving from the traditional country model to a business-line model that integrates and centralises key management functions including risk management, internal controls, treasury operations (such as liquidity management and funding), compliance, and auditing (Schoenmaker and Oosterloo, 2008). One of the most notable advances in risk management is the growing emphasis on developing a firm-wide assessment of risk to facilitate a comprehensive and systematic approach to risk-related decisions throughout the financial group. This approach gives senior management a full picture of the group's overall risk profile. RAROC provides the methodology to compare and aggregate different risks.

Although financial groups with a centralised risk management unit could reap economies of scale in risk management, these systems still rely on local branches and subsidiaries for local market data. The potential capital reductions that can be achieved by applying the advanced approaches of the Basel framework (see Chapter 12) encourage banking groups to centralise their risk management activities. A well-constructed risk and capital management framework can deliver significant benefits and substantially strengthen the competitive position of financial groups. The emergence of chief risk officers at the headquarters of large financial groups illustrates this trend towards centralisation.

Most large international financial institutions have adopted a 'hub and spoke' organisational model. The spokes are responsible for risk management within business lines, while the hub provides centralised oversight of risk and capital at the group level. Activities at the spoke level include the credit function within a bank, as local managers are familiar with the local conditions, such as the business cycle relevant to credit risk in a country. Moreover, aggregation across risk factors within a business line also typically takes place in the spokes.

While the hub depends on risk reporting from the spokes, in many cases it is also responsible for overseeing the development of an integrated economic capital framework (such as RAROC) that is then implemented within the spokes. The specific roles of the hub vary, but tend to include assuming responsibility for group-level risk reporting; participating in decisions about group capital structure, funding practices, and target debt rating; acting as liaison with regulators and rating agencies; and advising on major risk transfer transactions, such as collateralised loan obligations and securitisations.

10.3 The European Banking System

Banking Markets across Europe

Domestic banks dominate the banking markets of most EU Member States. The presence of foreign banks can be assessed by the level of *cross-border penetration* – a bank's assets from other EU Member States (or third countries) as a percentage of the country's total banking assets. Average cross-border penetration in the EU gradually increased from 12 per cent in 1997 to 21 per cent in 2007 (Figure 10.12). After the financial crisis, it fell back to 15 per cent in 2017. Cross-border penetration from third countries was 9 per cent in 2017. However, the degree of cross-border penetration is very uneven

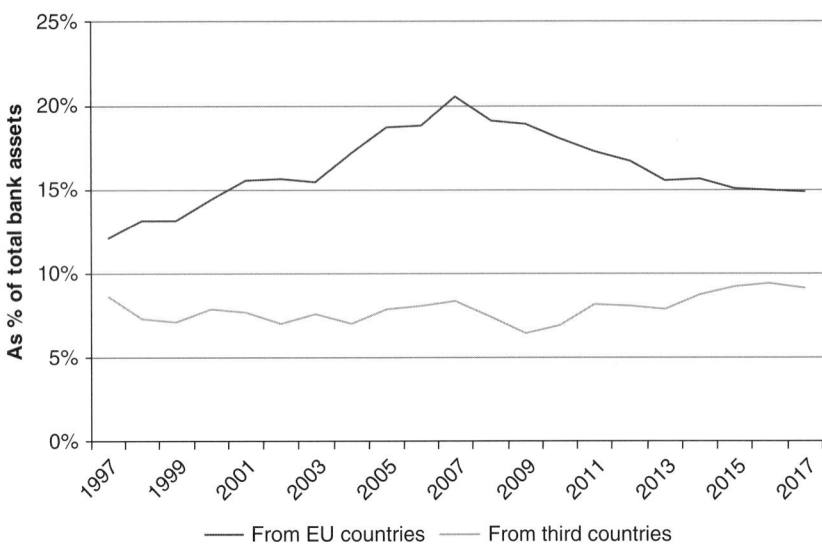

Figure 10.12 Cross-border penetration in European banking (%), 1997–2017
Note: Share of assets from other EU countries and third countries measured as a percentage of total banking assets. The share is calculated for the EU-28.
Source: Authors' calculations based on ECB structural financial indicators

across EU Member States, as Table 10.1 shows. While the banking systems of the new Member States are dominated by banks from other EU countries (which have a penetration rate of 57 per cent), average cross-border penetration in the EU-15 is only 14 per cent. Luxembourg has high cross-border penetration (51 per cent, reflecting the country's favourable tax regime), while the corresponding figures for France, Germany, the Netherlands, Spain, and Sweden are 12 per cent or less.

Table 10.1 also shows that the penetration by banks from third countries is well below 16 per cent for all EU Member States, except for the UK, where it stands at 32 per cent, illustrating London's position as a major international financial centre. Most banking business in London is focused on large firms (i.e. wholesale). There is considerable evidence suggesting that EU wholesale banking markets are highly integrated, in contrast to retail banking, i.e. banking services delivered to consumers and small and medium-sized enterprises (SMEs) (see Box 10.5). Brexit leads to a fragmentation of the wholesale market, as London-based investment banks lose their passport to do business with clients in other EU countries. Some of these investment banks are migrating their EU-related activities to Frankfurt, Paris, Dublin, Luxembourg, and Amsterdam.

Table 10.1 Cross-border penetration in EU Member States, 2017

	(1) Number of banks	(2) Total banking assets (in € billion)	(3) Assets of domestic banks (as % of (2))	(4) Assets of banks from other EU countries (% of (2))	(5) Assets of banks from third countries (as % of (2))
Austria	570	813	72	18	10
Belgium	87	1,017	40	43	16
Bulgaria	26	53	24	75	2
Croatia	28	57	24	75	1
Cyprus	34	80	79	13	8
Czech Republic	56	278	12	88	0
Denmark	99	1,070	85	15	1
Estonia	36	25	6	88	6
Finland	260	449	51	45	4
France	415	8,113	93	6	1
Germany	1,599	7,709	86	12	2
Greece	39	301	98	2	0
Hungary	60	120	53	41	6
Ireland	335	961	72	17	11
Italy	517	3,712	87	12	1
Latvia	52	28	45	54	1
Lithuania	83	29	12	88	0
Luxembourg	138	945	27	51	22
Malta	25	48	75	14	11
Netherlands	91	2,370	92	6	2
Poland	648	445	56	40	4
Portugal	141	393	76	23	1
Romania	37	99	32	68	0
Slovakia	27	78	3	97	0
Slovenia	17	40	65	35	0
Spain	204	2,716	94	6	0
Sweden	155	1,389	90	9	1
United Kingdom	381	8,967	51	16	32
EU-15	5,031	40,925	77	14	9
NMS-13	1,129	1,380	40	57	3
EU-28	6,160	42,305	76	15	9

Notes: Share of business from domestic banks, share of business of banks from other EU countries, and share of business of banks from third countries are measured as a percentage of a country's total banking assets. The shares add up to 100 per cent. Figures are for 2017. EU-15, NMS-13, and EU-28 are calculated as a weighted average (weighted according to assets).
Source: ECB

Box 10.5 Banking market integration

According to Dermine (2006), the 'law of one price' is unlikely to hold in retail banking markets for four main reasons. First, trust and confidence are important in these markets. Customers want to be sure that their money is in safe hands. Knowledge of the bank, the national legal system, language, cultural preferences, and geographic proximity may lead to a preference for a domestic bank. In other words, the services of domestic and foreign banks are differentiated products. Second, retail customers generally buy a package of financial services from the same bank, rather than individual services. Therefore, the 'law of one price' may hold for the bundle of services, but not necessarily for each individual service. Third, asymmetric information in lending is quite important, and local knowledge can help to reduce this information asymmetry. Local banks may therefore be in a better position to lend to SMEs than foreign banks. Fourth, the 'law of one price' assumes the absence of transportation costs and regulatory barriers. But differences in legislation, like tax and consumer-protection rules, may create substantial barriers to foreign bank entry.

Still, there is evidence that EU retail banking markets have also become more integrated until the crisis. However, as Figure 10.13 shows, the standard deviation of bank loans to non-financial corporations increased during the euro-sovereign crisis. Only after the summer of 2012 did the dispersion decline. Figure 10.13 illustrates that the smallest loans have the highest dispersion in interest rates. As these very small loans are typically used by SMEs, the fragmentation appears to affect these companies more than larger companies.

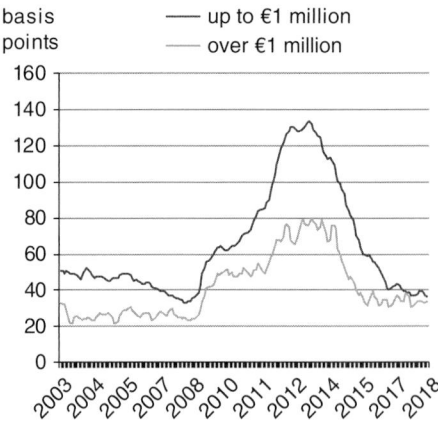

Figure 10.13 Cross-country standard deviation of interest rates on bank loans to non-financial
corporations, 2003–2018
Source: ECB

Table 10.2 Thirty largest banks in Europe, 2017

Banking groups	(1) Total assets (in € billion)	(2) Capital strength[a] (in € billion)	(3) Business in home country (as % of (2))	(4) Business in rest of EU (as % of (2))	(5) Business in rest of world (as % of (2))
Global banks[b]					
1. HSBC (UK)	2,100	126	36	4	60
2. Deutsche Bank (Germany)	1,475	58	35	22	43
3. Barclays (UK)	1,276	61	42	20	38
4. UBS (Switzerland)	782	37	33	24	43
5. BBVA (Spain)	690	47	49	3	48
6. Credit Suisse (Switzerland)	680	44	30	21	49
7. Standard Chartered (UK)	553	37	18	9	73
European banks[c]					
1. BNP Paribas (France)	1,960	84	32	46	22
2. Banco Santander (Spain)	1,444	77	27	43	30
3. ING Bank (Netherlands)	846	45	29	54	17
4. UniCredit (Italy)	837	55	40	57	3
5. Nordea Bank (Finland)	582	28	29	70	1
Semi-international banks[d]					
1. Société Générale (France)	1,275	50	73	17	10
2. Rabobank (Netherlands)	603	37	73	7	20
3. Danske Bank (Denmark)	475	20	54	46	0
4. Commerzbank (Germany)	452	26	53	33	14
5. ABN AMRO (Netherlands)	393	20	73	16	11
6. KBC Bank (Belgium)	292	17	55	40	5
7. Svenska Handelsbanken (Sweden)	282	13	59	38	3
8. DNB Bank (Norway)	275	19	69	22	9
9. SEB Bank (Sweden)	260	13	67	29	4
Domestic banks[e]					
1. Crédit Agricole (France)	1,763	84	81	12	7
2. Groupe BPCE (France)	1,260	59	91	2	7
3. Lloyds Banking Group (UK)	914	41	97	2	1
4. RBS Group (UK)	831	45	91	4	5
5. Intesa Sanpaolo (Italy)	797	43	84	12	4
6. Crédit Mutuel (France)	794	43	89	8	3
7. DZ Bank (Germany)	506	20	83	14	3

Table 10.2 (cont.)

Banking groups	(1) Total assets (in € billion)	(2) Capital strength[a] (in € billion)	(3) Business in home country (as % of (2))	(4) Business in rest of EU (as % of (2))	(5) Business in rest of world (as % of (2))
8. KfW Bankengruppe (Germany)	472	27	81	11	8
9. Caixa (Spain)	383	19	79	17	4
Top 30 European banks	25,253	1,296	56	22	22

Notes:
[a] Top 30 banks are selected on the basis of capital strength (Tier 1 capital (see Chapter 12) as published in *The Banker*).
[b] Global banks: less than 50 per cent of assets in the home country and the majority of their international assets in the rest of the world.
[c] European banks: less than 50 per cent of assets in the home country and the majority of their international assets in the rest of Europe.
[d] Semi-international banks: 50–75 per cent of assets in the home country.
[e] Domestic banks: 75 per cent or more of assets in the home country.
Source: Duijm and Schoenmaker (2017)

Most small customers receive their financial services from domestic suppliers, and the range and terms under which these products are available differ substantially across EU Member States.

In 2017, there were about 6,200 banks in the EU. These banks can be segmented into three groups. The first, very large, group of banks consists of small banks operating in a particular region of a country. For instance, Germany and Austria have many small savings and cooperative banks, most of which have assets of less than €2 billion. The second group consists of medium-sized banks with assets ranging from €2 to €100 billion. These banks often operate on a country-wide scale. The third group comprises large banks with assets up to €2,000 billion; they usually do a significant part of their business abroad.

Table 10.2 ranks the 30 largest banks in Europe, which together represent nearly half of the assets of the European banking system. Schoenmaker (2015) splits large banks into four categories, depending on the composition of their assets. According to this definition, a *global bank* has less than 50 per cent of its assets in the home country and the majority of its international assets in the rest of the world. These banks include HSBC, Barclays, and Standard Chartered from the UK, Deutsche Bank from Germany, BBVA from Spain, and Credit Suisse and UBS from Switzerland.

A *European bank* has less than 50 per cent of its assets in the home country and the majority of its international assets in the rest of Europe. Some European banks focus on a specific region in the EU. The Nordea Group, for example, primarily operates in the Nordic countries. Other European banks, including BNP Paribas, Santander, UniCredit, and ING, operate Europe wide.

A *semi-international bank* has 50–75 per cent of its assets in the home country. Examples are Société Générale from France, Rabobank and ABN AMRO from the Netherlands, Danske Bank from Denmark, Commerzbank from Germany, Svenska Handelsbanken and SEB Bank from Sweden, and KBC from Belgium.

Finally, a *domestic bank* has 75 per cent or more of its assets in the home country. Examples include Crédit Agricole and Groupe BPCE in France, Lloyds Banking Group and RBS in the UK, and Intesa Sanpaolo in Italy.

International Comparison

Table 10.3 compares the geographic segmentation of large banks on other continents with that of the large European banks.

Table 10.3 shows that European banks are the most international; they engage in more than 40 per cent of their business abroad. This may be due to the integrated European banking market. But even when looking at business outside the region, European banks are the most international, with 22 per cent of their business in the rest of the world. American banks are catching up: their business in the rest of the world constituted 14 per cent in 2017.

The picture is very different for Asia-Pacific banks. Their very domestic orientation (Schoenmaker, 2013) has been reinforced in recent years. Business in the rest of the world has declined from 14 per cent in 2000 to 10 per cent in

Table 10.3 Development of international banking by continent, 2000–2017

Continent	2000			2008			2017		
	h	r	w	h	r	w	h	r	w
Europe	55	20	25	51	21	28	56	22	22
Americas	77	8	15	73	9	18	75	11	14
Asia-Pacific	80	6	14	82	7	11	83	7	10

Notes: Share of business in home country (h), rest of the region (r), and rest of the world (w) of the top banks by continent. The top 30 banks for Europe; the top 15 banks for Americas and Asia-Pacific. The shares add up to 100 per cent.
Source: Schoenmaker (2017)

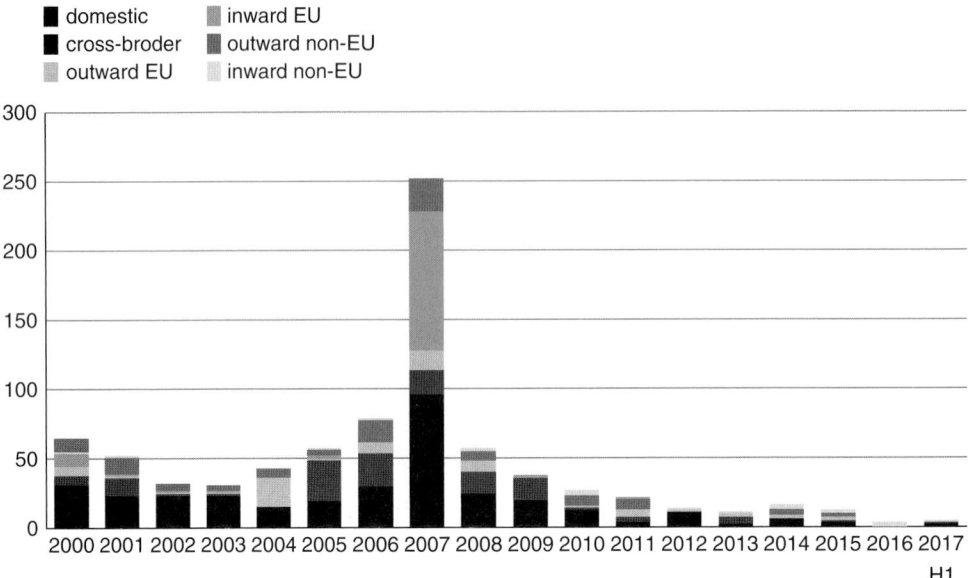

Figure 10.14 Banking M&As in Europe (value of completed deals, € billion), 2000–2017
Source: Dealogic M&A

2017. The composition of the large Asia-Pacific banks is shifting from the major Japanese banks to the major Chinese banks. The Chinese banks have an even stronger domestic orientation than their Japanese counterparts.

Domestic and Cross-Border Mergers and Acquisitions

M&As have changed, and will continue to change, the European banking markets. The Single Market Initiative (see Chapter 3) was widely expected to ease the path for cross-border M&As. Instead, banks prepared themselves by merging with other domestic banks. Cross-border mergers increased only after the start of EMU (see Figure 10.14).

Boot (1999) argues that domestic banks in Europe were often protected as they were regarded as national flagships. A fundamental belief that national financial institutions should not be controlled by foreigners prevented almost any cross-border mergers up to the late 1990s. The shift towards cross-border deals reflected the high concentration in national banking systems; further domestic mergers would be blocked by the competition authorities in some countries. In principle, the European Commission (DG Competition) permits mergers up to the threshold of 2,000 on the Herfindahl Index (see below). Several countries are close to, or even above, this threshold.

Given the shrinking potential for domestic mergers, the number of cross-border bank mergers increased until the financial crisis affected Europe. While early cross-border mergers in the 1990s created regional banks, such as Fortis in the Benelux countries and Nordea in Scandinavia, recent mergers are more widely spread across Europe. Examples are the takeover of Abbey National (UK) by Banco Santander (Spain) in 2004 and the takeover of Bank Austria Credit Anstalt (Austria) and HypoVereinsbank (Germany) by UniCredit (Italy) in 2005. However, as Figure 10.14 illustrates, the transaction value of M&A activity has decreased sharply since 2007. The peak in transaction values in 2007 reflected the merger of the Italian banks Sanpaolo IMI and Banca Intesa and the acquisition of ABN Amro by the consortium of Royal Bank of Scotland (UK), Fortis (Belgium), and Banco Santander (Spain), which resulted in splitting ABN AMRO into three parts. Already seen as having paid too high a price, both Fortis and RBS were among the first large European banks to be affected by the crisis in 2008. After the demise of Fortis, Fortis Netherlands and the Dutch part of ABN AMRO were nationalised and merged into a new bank named again ABN AMRO. BNP Paribas took over the remainder of Fortis (mainly the Belgian and Luxembourg parts). Important domestic deals include the acquisition of Dresdner Bank by Commerzbank and HBOS by Lloyds TSB in 2008 and Banco Popular by Banco Santander in 2017.

Geographic diversification and a potential efficiency improvement are important drivers of cross-border mergers (see Box 10.6 for further details). A good example is Banco Santander's takeover of Abbey National in November 2004, which had strategic problems: it was venturing into corporate banking without success and used outdated IT systems. Abbey National's inefficiency was illustrated by a high cost-to-income ratio of 83 per cent and a negative return on equity of 10 per cent. By contrast, Santander had developed a new payment technology and had a cost-to-income ratio of 63 per cent. After the takeover, Santander successfully introduced this technology with new management at Abbey National, which improved Abbey's cost-to-income ratio to 56 per cent by 2006.

From 2008 to 2017, the overall value of M&A deals decreased to below €10 billion. Significantly, no large cross-border (intra-euro-area) transactions or transactions with a buyer from another EU country (inward EU) have taken place since 2009. M&A activity involving non-EU acquirers has also remained subdued. Likewise, the value of outward transactions of euro-area banks (with these banks as acquirers) in Eastern Europe decreased considerably from the levels observed in 2008–2011 (ECB, 2017).

Box 10.6 The economics and performance of M&As

The classic motive for M&As in financial services is market extension (Walter, 2004). By merging with or acquiring another bank, it becomes possible to expand geographically into markets in which the acquiring bank has been absent or weak. The risk profile of the acquiring bank may be improved to the extent that business is spread across different macroeconomic environments. Or the bank may want to broaden its product range or client coverage because it sees profit opportunities that may complement its current activities (see Chapter 11 for the expansion of banks into insurance activities). In addition, the acquiring bank may seek to increase its market power, thereby imposing better pricing conditions on customers, or may aim to achieve a too-big-to-fail status as that may offer (implicit) government protection.

A key issue is whether it is possible to achieve economies of scale in banking. In an information- and distribution-intensive industry with high fixed costs such as financial services, there may be potential for scale economies. In particular, domestic mergers offer scope for cost synergies, as overlapping branch networks can be rationalised. But there is also potential for diseconomies of scale attributable to disproportionate increases in administrative overheads or management of complexity. Older research did not yield strong support for economies of scale in banking. However, more recent studies report strong evidence of scale economies. For instance, Hughes and Mester (2013) find positive scale economies for even the largest institutions.

Campa and Hernando (2006) examine the performance record of M&As in the European financial industry. Merger announcements imply positive excess returns to shareholders of the target company (the takeover premium), while the returns to shareholders of the acquiring firms are essentially zero around an announcement. They find that one year after the announcement, excess returns are not significantly different from zero for targets or acquirers. Campa and Hernando (2006) also provide evidence on operating performance. Since acquirers usually target banks with lower-than-average operating performance, M&As produce significant improvements in the target bank's performance, beginning on average two years after the transaction.

Beltratti and Paladino (2013) focus on acquisitions in the EU banking sector that were completed or terminated over the period 2007–2010. They report that abnormal returns for bank acquirers were zero, on average, at the announcement but positive after the completion. Abnormal returns are generally larger for more efficient banks and for those with higher profitability and less leverage.

Market Structure and Competition

Table 10.4 shows some indicators of the structure of the EU banking sector. Between 1997 and 2017 the total number of banks in the EU almost halved

Table 10.4 Market structure indicators, 1997 and 2017

	Size		Concentration			
	Number of banks		CR5 (in %)[a]		Herfindahl Index[b]	
	1997	2017	1997	2017	1997	2017
Austria	928	570	44	36	515	375
Belgium	131	87	54	69	699	1,102
Bulgaria	35[c]	26	52[c]	57	721[c]	906
Croatia	n.a.	28	n.a.	73	n.a.	1,387
Cyprus	623	34	92	84	2,747	1,964
Czech Republic	50	56	67	64	2,533	1,028
Denmark	213	99	70	66	1,431	1,123
Estonia	12	36	83	90	4,312	2,419
Finland	348	260	88	74	2,150	1,700
France	1,258	415	40	45	449	574
Germany	3,420	1,599	17	30	114	250
Greece	55	39	56	97	885	2,307
Hungary	286	60	53	50	2,101	802
Ireland	71	335	41	46	500	658
Italy	909	517	25	43	201	519
Latvia	37	52	51	74	1,450	1,235
Lithuania	37	83	84	90	2,972	2,189
Luxembourg	215	138	23	26	210	256
Malta	29	25	98	81	4,411	1,599
Netherlands	648	91	79	84	1,654	2,087
Poland	1,378	648	46	48	859	645
Portugal	238	141	46	73	577	1,220
Romania	39[c]	37	55[c]	59	1,251[c]	909
Slovakia	29	27	63	75	2,643	1,332
Slovenia	34	17	62	62	2,314	1,133
Spain	416	204	32	64	285	965
Sweden	237	155	58	58	830	914
United Kingdom	537	381	24	37	208	453
EU-15[d]	9,624	5,031	34	46	406	656
NMS-13[d]	2,589	1,129	63	61	1,985	1,035
EU-28[d]	12,213	6,160	35	46	445	668

Notes:

[a] CR5 is the share of the five largest banks, measured as a percentage of total assets.

[b] The Herfindahl Index is calculated as the sum of the squares of all the banks' market shares according to total assets, and rescaled from 0 to 10,000.

[c] The figure is for 2003.

[d] EU-15, NMS-13, and EU-28 are calculated as a weighted average (weighted according to assets). n.a. means not available.

Source: Number of banks and concentration from ECB and Allen *et al.* (2006)

from 12,213 to 6,160. The trend in the US is similar, where the number of banks dropped from 9,144 in 1997 to 4,918 in 2017. Due to the decline in the number of credit institutions, the concentration of the national banking markets has increased. Table 10.4 presents two concentration measures: the market share of the five largest banks (CR5) and the Herfindahl Index, defined as the sum of the squares of the market shares of all banks in the sector ($HI = \sum_{i=1}^{n} s_i^2$, where s_i is the market share of bank i). While the CR5 ratio is easily measurable, it does not take into account the remaining banks in the industry, while the Herfindahl Index does. The latter ranges between $1/n$ and 1, reaching its lowest value, the reciprocal of the number of banks (n), when all banks in a market are of equal size, and reaching unity in the case of monopoly. The index as published by the ECB has been rescaled and ranges between 0 and 10,000.

Table 10.4 shows that there are substantial concentration differences across the EU. In Austria, France, Germany, Ireland, Italy, Luxembourg, Poland, and the UK the concentration ratios in the banking markets are relatively low. The highest concentration ratios can be found in Cyprus, Estonia, Greece, Lithuania, Malta, and the Netherlands.[4] From 1997 to 2017, the concentration ratios in the NMS-13 and the EU-15 have converged: the former has gradually declined, while the latter has increased. The convergence is even stronger using the more refined concentration measure of the Herfindahl Index.

Another important feature of markets is the degree of competition. A well-known indicator of competition is the *Lerner Index* (LI), which measures the degree to which a firm is able to price its products above marginal costs using the following formula:

$$LI = (Price - Marginal\ Cost)/Price = 1/\varepsilon \tag{10.11}$$

where ε is the price elasticity of demand [$\varepsilon = -(\Delta Q/\Delta P)(P/Q)$]. The key determinant of market power is the elasticity of demand. The greater ε is, the greater the reduction in the quantity demanded will be when the price rises. Thus, the higher the elasticity of demand, the lower the market power of the respective firm. Under perfect competition, P = MC and LI = 0. Higher values of LI indicate greater firm market power.

As shown in Figure 10.15, since the financial crisis the LI has increased in the three groups of countries considered, suggesting that competition in the European banking sector has decreased.

The *structure-conduct-performance (SCP) paradigm* postulates a connection between market structure, banking behaviour, and profitability based on

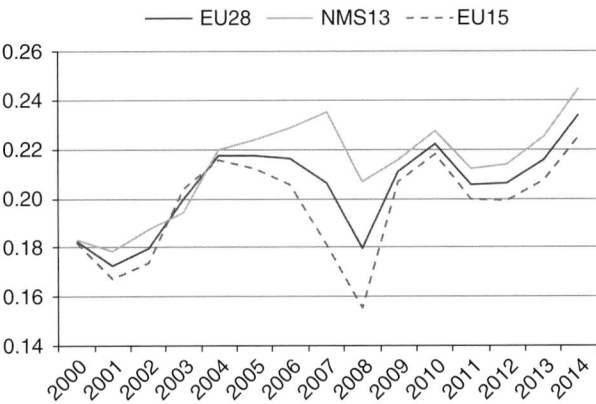

Figure 10.15 The Lerner Index, 2000–2015
Source: De Jonghe *et al.* (2017)

the assumption that in markets with a high degree of concentration, firms have more market power, which allows them to set prices above marginal costs and achieve higher profits. While older studies find a relationship between concentration and profitability, more recent studies suggest that there is no connection between the two (Claessens and Laeven, 2004; Jansen and De Haan, 2006).

Two alternative theories suggest that concentration does not necessarily reduce market competition. According to the *contestability theory*, a concentrated banking market can still be competitive as long as the entry barriers for potential newcomers are low. According to the *efficiency hypothesis*, the most efficient banks increase their market share at the cost of less efficient banks. In other words, high concentration can be a result of fierce competition in a market (Bikker *et al.*, 2006).

Claessens and Laeven (2004) examine the competitiveness of a banking market in a large cross-section of countries and find no evidence that banking system concentration is negatively associated with competitiveness. In fact, they sometimes find evidence that more concentrated banking systems are more competitive.

Concentration is loosely related to bank size. Markets become more concentrated when the number of banks decreases or when the skewness of the size distribution of banks increases (i.e. when the number of large banks increases). But the markets in some countries (e.g. Germany and France) have low levels of concentration and large banks. As Bikker *et al.* (2006) point out, large banks may have market power, as they are probably in a better position to collude with other banks and may benefit from a more established reputation. Furthermore, they are in a better position than small banks to create new banking products due to economies of scale. Indeed, Bikker *et al.* (2006) report that market power increases with bank size. Their research covers 18,467 banks in 101 countries over a period of 16 years.

10.4 The New Banking Union Landscape

The *establishment* of the Banking Union (BU) creates a sub-market within the EU. The BU is expected to ultimately become an integrated market, in which banks can manage their balance sheet at the aggregate BU level and the ECB conducts supervision with a European perspective. However, national supervisors still prevent European banks from operating on a European scale, as they informally request that banks lend or invest in the same country as the deposits are collected. Moving to the demand side, it may take some time before consumers regard a bank from elsewhere in the BU as a domestic bank with which they can entrust their money. When that happens, a truly integrated retail banking market will emerge. Corporations, especially the larger ones, are adapting faster and select their main banks from across the BU.

Table 10.5 compares the major banking systems. China and the euro area (with its BU) have the largest banking systems, with about €28 trillion in total banking assets. The US banking system has fewer assets (€14 trillion), as the US depends less on bank intermediation and more on capital markets (see Chapter 1). China and the US are relatively domestic, with less than 10 per cent of total banking assets abroad. Looking at the largest three banking systems, China and the US are modestly concentrated with a CR5 ratio of around 50 per cent. The BU, which is built from member countries' banking systems, is far less concentrated at 29 per cent. Even in a large country with a dispersed banking system like Germany, the CR5 is 30 per cent (Table 10.4).

As China, the euro area, and the US represent very large economies, the assets of the top three banks are well below 100 per cent of GDP in each. These numbers are far higher for medium-sized countries like the UK, Japan, and Switzerland. It is thus more difficult for these countries to provide a credible fiscal backstop to their banking system. The potential fiscal costs of a banking crisis can be calculated based on a worst-case scenario in which the three largest banks experience severe problems and the cost of replacing equity is standardised at 4.5 per cent of total bank assets (Schoenmaker, 2018). Based on the recent crisis, Schoenmaker (2018) estimates that the hurdle rate for the credibility of the fiscal backstop is around 8 per cent of

Table 10.5 Comparing the major banking systems, end-2015

	Total assets in € billion	Domestic assets in € billion	Activity abroad as % of total assets	CR5 ratio as % of total assets	Assets top 3 banks as % of GDP	Fiscal costs as % of GDP
China	28,226	26,999	4.3	54.5	82.2	3.7
Euro area	27,747	22,757	18.0	28.8	51.1	2.3
United States	14,296	13,044	8.8	46.4	35.6	1.6
United Kingdom	9,349	6,029	35.5	71.0	186.7	8.4
Japan	8,648	6,860	20.7	60.8	146.7	6.6
Switzerland	2,792	1,601	42.7	88.1	300.0	13.5

Note: The total assets comprise the consolidated assets of domestic banking groups and the domestic assets of subsidiaries and branches of foreign banks. To calculate the size of the respective banking systems (labelled as domestic assets), the foreign assets of the domestic banks are deducted. The concentration ratio of the largest five banks (CR5) is their assets as a share of total assets. The assets of the top three banks are taken as a percentage of GDP. The fiscal costs represent the potential fiscal costs of bailing out the three largest banks. *Sources:* Schoenmaker and Véron (2016) and Schoenmaker (2018)

GDP. Above that level, a country's budgetary and political capacity to execute a bailout becomes questionable. Table 10.5 shows that China, the euro area, the US, and Japan face potential fiscal costs below this hurdle rate. The UK and Switzerland are above the hurdle rate and have implemented structural banking reforms to downsize their banking system.

The BU banking system is comparable to that of the US in several ways. Both systems are relatively closed, and have limited inward or outward expansion. The number of banks is about 5,000 to 6,000 in both (see Table 10.5). The major banks are also comparable. Figure 10.16 shows the geographic segmentation of the top 20 banks in the three regions (EU, BU, and US). The large BU and US banks have just over 70 per cent of their assets at home. The rest of the region (i.e. the rest of Europe and the rest of North and South America) accounts for 12 and 3 per cent, respectively. The rest of the world amounts to 16–18 per cent. The large EU banks are more international. They have not only a smaller home base (one country), but also more business in the rest of the world. Examples of major global banks outside the BU are HSBC, Barclays, and Standard Chartered from the UK.

The BU represents a paradigm shift for banks and policy makers. The home market expands for banks from their country to the wider BU. Table 10.6 illustrates the geographic segmentation, categorising Europe's 20 largest banks in terms of business in the BU, the rest of Europe (i.e. the non-BU member

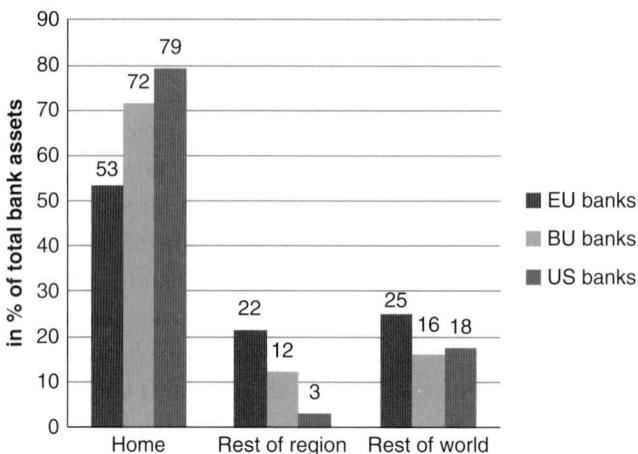

Figure 10.16 Geographic segmentation of top 20 banks in the EU, BU, and US (in %), 2017
Note: The total assets of the top 20 banks are segmented into domestic, rest of the region, and rest of the world.

states), and the rest of the world. Some of the European banks operating on a regional basis (the second group in Table 10.2) have now become pan-Banking Union banks. BNP Paribas, ING Bank, and UniCredit operate throughout the BU, with 65–80 per cent of their assets held within the union. These banks are comparable with the super-regional banks in the US, such as Bank of America, which has a large presence across the whole region. The semi-international and domestic banks (the third and fourth groups in Table 10.2) have also become large players in the BU. The market share of the biggest banks in the BU lingers around 1–5 per cent, which is very low. The top five banks by market share are all French (i.e. Crédit Agricole, BNP, BPCE, Société Générale, and Crédit Mutuel). The market share of the 20 biggest banks amounts to 41 per cent.

Further consolidation within the BU can be expected. The concentration ratio of the five largest banks (CR5) in the BU is 29 per cent. To compare, the CR5 is 46 per cent for the EU-15 countries and 47 per cent for the US. The major US banks were formed after the lifting of restrictions on interstate banking by the Riegle-Neal Interstate Banking and Branching Efficiency Act of 1994. Through several mergers and acquisitions, super-regional banks, such as JPMorgan Chase and Bank of America, emerged with a market share of 13 and 11 per cent, respectively.

Finally, an international perspective can be sketched. The Financial Stability Board has produced a list of *global systemically important banks* (G-SIBs, see Chapter 12 for further details). These banks are the large financial players that can pose a systemic threat to the global financial system (Bertay *et al.*, 2013).

Table 10.6 Twenty largest banks in BU in 2017

Banking Group	Total assets in € bn	Banking Union in %	Rest of Europe in %	Rest of world in %	Market share in %
1. Crédit Agricole	1,763	90	2	8	5.3
2. BNP Paribas	1,960	71	7	22	4.7
3. Groupe BPCE	1,260	92	1	7	3.9
4. Société Générale	1,275	79	11	10	3.4
5. Crédit Mutuel	794	95	3	3	2.5
6. Deutsche Bank	1,475	49	8	43	2.4
7. Intesa Sanpaolo	797	89	7	4	2.4
8. UniCredit	837	80	17	3	2.2
9. ING Bank	846	67	16	17	1.9
10. DZ Bank	506	94	3	3	1.6
11. Rabobank	603	77	2	21	1.6
12. Banco Santander	1,444	32	38	30	1.5
13. KfW Bankengruppe	472	89	3	8	1.4
14. BBVA	690	51	1	48	1.2
15. Caixa	383	91	5	5	1.2
16. ABN AMRO	393	87	3	11	1.1
17. Commerzbank	452	56	30	14	0.8
18. KBC Bank	292	73	23	4	0.7
19. Landesbank Baden-Würt.	238	83	8	9	0.7
20. Nordea	582	21	78	1	0.4
Top 20 banks	14,718	72	12	16	41.0

Note: Total assets are divided by assets in the BU, in the rest of Europe, and the rest of the world. A bank's market share is calculated as its assets in the BU divided by total assets in the BU. The top 20 are ranked by market share.
Source: Updated from Duijm and Schoenmaker (2017)

Table 10.7 provides an overview of the G-SIBs, which have assets up to €3.3 trillion. Remarkably, the BU and the US are home to most of the G-SIBs; each have 8 out of 29, followed by China with 4. The ECB, as supervisor of the G-SIBs from the BU, is thus a major player together with the Federal Reserve in international policy making and supervision.

10.5 Conclusions

Banks are key players in the financial system, providing liquidity to other financial institutions and to firms and households. They have also developed technologies with which to monitor borrowers. Banks have expanded their

Table 10.7 Global systemically important banks (G-SIBs), 2018

Banking groups	Total assets	World assets rank	Capital sur- charge	Home country	Rest of region	Rest of world
	in € bn		in %	% of total assets	% of total assets	% of total assets
Global banks						
1. HSBC (UK)	2,100	7	2.0	36	4	60
2. Deutsche Bank (BU)	1,475	17	2.0	49	8	43
3. Barclays (UK)	1,276	19	1.5	42	20	38
4. UBS (Switzerland)	782	35	1.0	33	24	43
5. Credit Suisse (Switzerland)	680	43	1.0	30	21	49
6. Standard Chartered (UK)	553	51	1.0	18	9	73
Regional banks						
1. Banco Santander (BU)	1,444	18	1.0	32	38	30
Semi-international banks						
1. Bank of China (China)	2,492	4	1.5	74	20	5
2. Mitsubishi UFJ Financial Group (Japan)	2,313	5	1.5	64	9	27
3. BNP Paribas (BU)	1,960	8	1.5	71	7	22
4. Mizuho Financial Group (Japan)	1,543	14	1.0	69	8	23
5. Sumitomo Mitsui Financial Group (Japan)	1,540	15	1.0	67	10	23
6. Citigroup (US)	1,537	16	2.0	64	7	29
7. Royal Bank of Canada (Canada)	858	25	1.0	68	22	10
8. ING Bank (BU)	846	26	1.0	67	16	17
9. Goldman Sachs (US)	764	37	1.5	75	7	18
10. Morgan Stanley (US)	710	40	1.0	62	5	33
11. Bank of New York Mellon (US)	310	79	1.0	70	1	29
12. State Street (US)	199	109	1.0	66	2	32
Domestic banks						
1. ICBC (China)	3,340	1	1.5	89	7	4
2. China Construction Bank (China)	2,833	2	1.0	95	3	2
3. Agricultural Bank of China (China)	2,695	3	1.0	96	1	2
4. JPMorgan Chase & Co (US)	2,113	6	2.5	76	2	23
5. Bank of America (US)	1,902	9	1.5	86	1	13
6. Crédit Agricole (BU)	1,763	11	1.0	90	2	8
7. Wells Fargo & Co (US)	1,627	12	1.5	95	2	3
8. Société Générale (BU)	1,275	20	1.0	79	11	10
9. Groupe BPCE (BU)	1,260	21	1.0	92	1	7

Table 10.7 (cont.)

Banking groups	Total assets	World assets rank	Capital sur-charge	Home country	Rest of region	Rest of world
	in € bn		in %	% of total assets	% of total assets	% of total assets
10. UniCredit (BU)	837	29	1.0	80	17	3
Total G-SIBs	1,484			72	9	19

Notes: The second column presents the assets ranked on the basis of the Top 1,000 World Banks, as published in *The Banker*. Total assets are segmented between the home country, the rest of the region, and the rest of the world. Total G-SIBs is calculated as an average (weighted by assets).
Source: The list of G-SIBs is from the FSB (2018). Assets are taken from *The Banker* (July 2018). Segmentation of assets is calculated by the authors based on annual reports.

business from traditional lending to modern capital market transactions, thereby preserving their role in the financial system.

Banks' use of advanced models to measure, manage, and price market risk has spurred the centralisation of risk management. While the loan business is done by the local bank managers who are familiar with the economic environment in which the local business units have to operate, the influence of the head office on the pricing of bank products is increasing. As the financial crisis illustrated shortcomings in risk management models, banks are complementing them with stress tests.

Cross-border banking had gradually increased to 21 per cent in 2007 and subsequently fell to 15 per cent in 2017. This chapter has documented the emergence of banks that operate Europe-wide. Nevertheless, retail banking markets are still segmented. Customers prefer to do business with banks they 'know', and thus are biased towards domestic banks. Cultural differences appear to be more important than regulatory differences. The policy of the European Commission is shifting from harmonising rules (Chapter 12) to ensuring effective competition (Chapter 14) in turn. The BU has changed the European banking landscape and may spur retail integration within the union.

New evidence suggests that concentration does not necessarily reduce market competition. The contestability theory indicates that a banking market is competitive as long as the barriers for potential newcomers are low. Competition policy is important to open national markets – both to encourage new entrants within a country and to promote foreign entry through cross-border mergers.

Notes

1. There is, however, an important conflict of interest. Credit rating agencies are paid by the firms and governments whose securities they rate. This conflict is unavoidable due to the free-riding problem, i.e. ratings are valuable only if everybody knows them, but lenders (investors) have no reason to pay for information that is available to everyone else too.
2. A *counterparty* is a legal and financial term. It means a party to a contract.
3. Assuming a normal distribution, the time horizon of the standard deviation can be expanded by multiplying by $\sqrt{t}$. Given that there are 252 business days in a year, the standard deviation of the one-year loss distribution equals the standard deviation of the 10-day loss distribution multiplied by $\sqrt{25.2}$ (Hull, 2018).
4. The European Commission investigates a proposed merger when the (rescaled) Herfindahl Index would exceed the threshold of 2,000 after the merger (see Chapter 14).

Bibliography

Suggested Reading

Freixas, X. and J. C. Rochet (2008), *Microeconomics of Banking*, 2nd edition, MIT Press, Cambridge (MA).

Hull, J. C. (2018), *Options, Futures, and Other Derivatives*, 10th edition, Pearson Education, New York.

Schoenmaker, D. (2013), *Governance of International Banking: The Financial Trilemma*, Oxford University Press.

References

Allen, F., L. Bartiloro, and O. Kowalewski (2006), The Financial System of EU 25. In: K. Liebscher, J. Christl, P. Mooslechner, and D. Ritzberger-Griinwald (eds.), *Financial Development, Integration and Stability in Central Eastern and South-Eastern Europe*, Edward Elgar, Cheltenham, 80–104.

Beltratti, A. and G. Paladino (2013), Is M&A Different during a Crisis? Evidence from the European Banking Sector. *Journal of Banking and Finance*, 37, 5394–405.

Berger, A. N. (2003), The Economic Effects of Technological Progress: Evidence from the Banking Industry. *Journal of Money, Credit and Banking*, 35, 141–76.

Bertay, A. C., A. Demirguç-Kunt, and H. Huizinga (2013), Do We Need Big Banks? Evidence on Performance, Strategy and Market Discipline. *Journal of Financial Intermediation*, 22, 532–58.

Bikker, J. A., L. Spierdijk, and P. Finnie (2006), The Impact of Bank Size on Market Power. De Nederlandsche Bank Working Paper 120.

Boot, A. W. A. (1999), European Lessons on Consolidation in Banking. *Journal of Banking and Finance*, 23, 609–13.

Campa, J. M. and I. Hernando (2006), M&As Performance in the European Financial Industry. *Journal of Banking and Finance*, 30, 3367–92.

Claessens, S. and L. Laeven (2004), What Drives Bank Competition? Some International Evidence. *Journal of Money, Credit and Banking*, 36, 563–83.

Danielsson, J. (2011), *Financial Risk Forecasting*, John Wiley & Sons, New York.

(2013), *Global Financial Systems: Stability and Risk*, Pearson, London.

De Jonghe, O., M. Diepstraten, and G. Schepens (2017), Competition in EU Banking. In: T. Beck and B. Casu (eds.), *The Palgrave Handbook of European Banking*, Palgrave Macmillan, London, 187–211.

Dermine, J. (2006), European Banking Integration: Don't Put the Cart before the Horse. *Financial Markets, Institutions & Instruments*, 15, 57–106.

Diamond, D. W. (1984), Financial Intermediation and Delegated Monitoring,. *Review of Economic Studies*, 51, 393–414.

Duijm, P. and D. Schoenmaker (2017), European Banks Straddling Borders: Risky or Rewarding? CEPR Discussion Paper 12159.

European Banking Authority (2017), *Report on Asset Encumbrance*, EBA, London.

European Central Bank (2017), *Report on Financial Structures*, ECB, Frankfurt am Main.

Financial Stability Board (2018), *2018 List of Global Systemically Important Banks (G-SIBs)*, FSB, Basel.

Freixas, X. and J. C. Rochet (2008), *Microeconomics of Banking*, 2nd edition, MIT Press, Cambridge (MA).

Garber, P. M. and S. R. Weisbrod (1990), Banks in the Market for Liquidity. NBER Working Paper 3381.

Hughes, J. P. and L. Mester (2013), Who Said Large Banks Don't Experience Scale Economies: Evidence from a Risk-Return Cost Function. *Journal of Financial Intermediation*, 22, 559–85.

Hull, J. C. (2018), *Options, Futures, and Other Derivatives*, 10th edition, Pearson Education, New York.

Jansen, D. J. and J. de Haan (2006), European Banking Consolidation: Effects on Competition, Profitability, and Efficiency. *Journal of Financial Transformation*, 17, 61–72.

Schoenmaker, D. (2013), *Governance of International Banking: The Financial Trilemma*, Oxford University Press.

(2015), The New Banking Union Landscape in Europe: Consolidation Ahead? *Journal of Financial Perspectives*, 3, 189–201.

(2017), What Happened to Global Banking after the Crisis? *Journal of Financial Regulation and Compliance*, 25, 241–52.

(2018), Resolution of International Banks: Can Smaller Countries Cope? *International Finance*, 21, 39–54.

Schoenmaker, D. and S. Oosterloo (2008), Financial Supervision in Europe: A Proposal for a New Architecture. In: L. Jonung, C. Walkner, and M. Watson (eds.), *Building the Financial Foundations of the Euro: Experiences and Challenges*, Routledge, London, 329–46.

Schoenmaker, D. and N. Véron (2016), *European Banking Supervision: The First Eighteen Months*, Blueprint 25, Bruegel, Brussels.

Van Lelyveld, I. (ed.) (2006), *Economic Capital Modelling: Concepts, Measurement and Implementation*, Risk Books, London.

Walter, I. (2004), *Mergers and Acquisitions in Banking and Finance: What Works, What Fails, and Why*, Oxford University Press.

11

European Insurers and Financial Conglomerates

OVERVIEW

The function of insurance is to protect individuals and firms from adverse events by pooling risks. Life insurance protects against the financial consequences of premature death, disability, and retirement. Non-life insurance protects against risks such as accidents, illness, theft, and fire. Insurance is a risky business, as insurance companies collect premiums and provide cover for adverse events that may or may not arise. The pattern of small claims, such as fire or car accidents, is fairly predictable. However, larger accidents or natural disasters (like hurricanes) involve high-value claims with low probability.

The insurance business is plagued by asymmetric information problems. There is a moral hazard problem when the behaviour of the insured, which can be only partly observed by the insurer, may increase the likelihood that the insurer has to pay. After signing the contract, the insured may behave less cautiously because of the insurance. Another problem is adverse selection: high-risk individuals (for instance, ill people) may seek out more (health) insurance than low-risk persons. The insurer may therefore end up with a pool of relatively high risks. This chapter explains mechanisms used to separate high from low risks.

Insurance companies tend to centralise risk management at their headquarters. Yet local branches can help capture location-specific factors. The same is true for asset management: as insurance companies are large asset managers, they can profit from economies of scale by pooling their assets.

Insurance systems vary considerably across Europe. Life insurance is quite prominent in the EU-15, but far less so in the new EU Member States. Non-life insurance is more evenly spread across the EU. With the creation of the European single insurance market, insurers used mergers and acquisitions – at both the national and European levels – to become large enough to act at the European level. The level of cross-border insurance has gradually increased, but the insurance sector is not yet integrated.

Finally, the chapter analyses financial conglomerates that combine banking and insurance. These conglomerates can cross-sell insurance products through the bank, and may benefit from increased diversification opportunities. Yet it is difficult to manage a complex financial group that runs fairly different lines of business.

LEARNING OBJECTIVES

After you have studied this chapter, you should be able to:
- explain the nature of the insurance business
- explain the economics of insurance risk
- explain insurers' use of risk management models and the centralisation of the risk management function
- describe the structure of the European insurance market
- identify the characteristics of financial conglomerates and the role they play in the financial system.

11.1 Theory of Insurance

Small vs. Large Claims Insurance

Insurance is designed to protect individuals and firms against the financial consequences of adverse events. Insurance companies provide this protection by pooling individual risks to spread them over a large group of clients. There are different types of insurance. *Life insurance* protects against premature death, disability, and retirement. While it is difficult to predict an individual's death, death rates for large populations are fairly stable and therefore easier to predict. *Non-life insurance* protects against risks such as accidents, theft, and fire; it is sometimes called property and casualty (P&C) or property and liability insurance.

The risk dynamics of non-life insurance are more diverse than those of life insurance. Relatively small accidents (like car accidents) are fairly predictable and can easily be pooled. But larger accidents or natural disasters follow a different pattern: they are low-probability but high-impact events. For example, the risk of a catastrophe such as Hurricane Katrina in New Orleans in 2005 is too big for a single insurance company, and is therefore divided among different insurance and re-insurance companies.

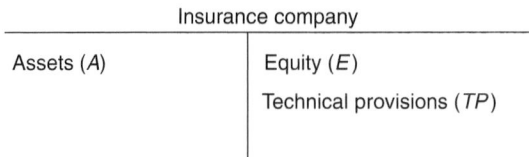

Insurance company	
Assets (*A*)	Equity (*E*)
	Technical provisions (*TP*)

Figure 11.1 Simplified balance sheet of an insurance company

Insurers' intermediation function can be illustrated with a simple balance sheet (see Figure 11.1). Insurers collect premiums *P* from clients and make payouts on claims *C* by these clients when the risk materialises. On the asset side, insurers invest the collected premiums in assets *A*, which earn a return R_A. On the liability side, insurers make technical provisions *TP* to cover expected future claims. In addition, insurers maintain a capital buffer *E* to cover unexpected claims.

Insurers evaluate the risk of prospective clients, which they use to decide how much coverage a client should receive and how much the client should pay for it. The insurance business is viable only when the collected premiums exceed the payout on claims. When a claim is made, the insurer must determine the extent of the loss. Many insurers employ 'adjusters' who determine the insurer's liability and the settlement to be made. The *claim ratio* measures the adjusted claims as a ratio to premiums earned, i.e. *C/P*. A claim ratio of less than 100 per cent means that the premiums earned are sufficient to cover claims.

The insurance company also has to cover its expenses *Exp*. The biggest expenses are commissions paid to insurance agents to acquire business. To avoid having to pay these very high acquisition costs, insurers are increasingly selling insurance to the public directly (*direct writing*). The insurer must also gather information about potential clients to assess the underwriting risk and avoid adverse selection (see below). Finally, insurers incur administrative expenses. The *expense ratio* expresses total expenses relative to premiums earned, i.e. *Exp/P*.

A common economic measure to assess the profitability of non-life insurers is the combined ratio *CR*, which expresses claims and expenses relative to premiums earned:

$$CR = C/P + Exp/P = \frac{C + Exp}{P} \tag{11.1}$$

As the non-life insurance business is inherently risky with fluctuating payouts, the CRs vary across countries and over time (see Figure 11.2). Those for Cyprus and Romania are well above 100 per cent, indicating that the non-life

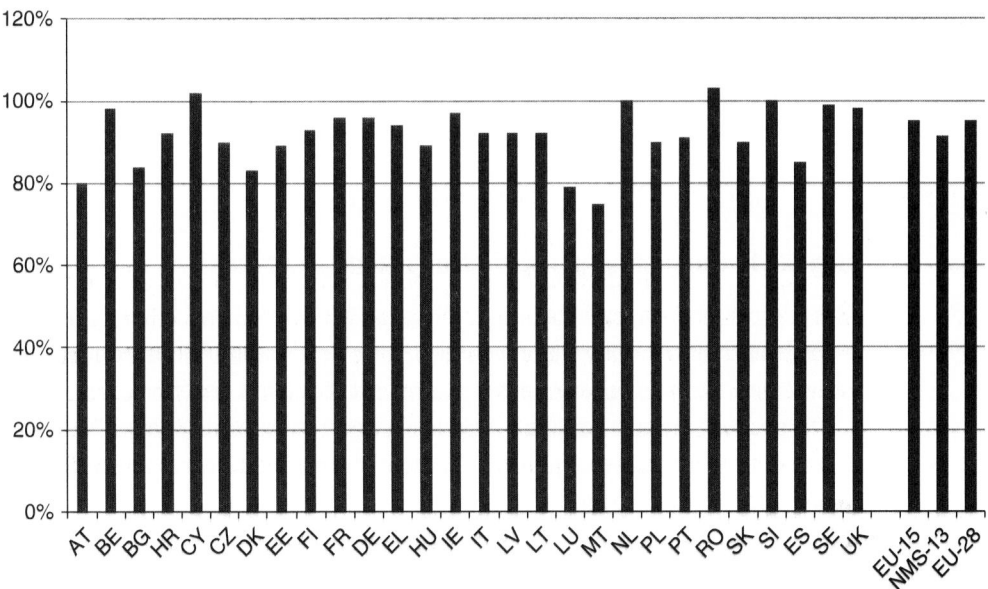

Figure 11.2   Combined ratios across Europe (in %), 2017
Source: EIOPA
Note: Claims and expenses in percentage of premiums.

insurance sector in these countries made a loss in 2017. However, investment returns are not included (see below). In Austria, Luxembourg, and Malta the CR was 75–80 per cent in 2017, indicating a healthy profit. The EU-28 average was 95 per cent in 2017, resulting in a margin of 5 per cent.

Yet the CR provides an incomplete view of a non-life insurer's profitability. Premiums are invested before payouts are made. Investment returns R_A are therefore an important source of income for insurers. The *profitability* π, as a percentage of premium earned, is equal to the results on claims and expenses $(100 - CR)$ and the investment returns:

$$\pi = 100 - CR + R_A/P = 100 + \frac{R_A - C - Exp}{P} \tag{11.2}$$

Equation (11.2) illustrates that the successful management of an insurance company requires making adequate investment returns and properly calculating underwriting risks while keeping acquisition and administrative expenses low. This equation can be illustrated with a simple example. Assume a claim ratio of 65 per cent of earned premiums, an expense ratio of 32 per cent, and allocated investment income of 9 per cent. The profit is 12 per cent of earned premiums $(100 + 9 - 65 - 32 = 12)$.

The stochastic properties of large claims are very different from those of small claims. Small claims have a distribution with light tails (e.g. the normal distribution). In a large portfolio, the expected claim size approaches the average claim size according to the law of large numbers. Box 11.1 describes how small claims risks are calculated.

Box 11.1 The mathematics of small claims insurance*

This box abstracts from expenses, investment returns, and dividend payouts and focuses on the premium setting P and the claims process C. The premium setting follows the dynamics of the claims process. The pattern of small claims is different from that of large claims.

The stochastic properties of the small claim-size model can be formally derived following Mikosch (2004). The total size of the claims $C(t)$ is the product of the number of claims $N(t)$ over period t and the size of the claims X_i:

$$C(t) = \sum_{i=1}^{N(t)} X_i, \quad t \geq 0 \tag{11.3}$$

where N is independent of the claim size. Both the number of claims and their size are random variables. The claim numbers are often described as a *Poisson process* – a stochastic process used to model random events that occur independently of one another. In a homogeneous *Poisson process*, the mean and variance of the distribution are the same. So, for N it is possible to write: $\lambda = E(N) = var(N)$, where λ is the frequency of claims.

Equation (11.3) specifies the realised claims at time t. But an insurer must estimate the expected claims at the time of selling the insurance, i.e. $T = 0$. Exploiting the independence of the claim size sequence X_i and the claim number process $N(t)$, the expected total claim amount is given by:

$$E[C(t)] = E\left[E\left(\sum_{i=1}^{N(t)} X_i | N(t)\right)\right] = E[N(t) \cdot E(X_1)] = \lambda \cdot t \cdot E(X_1) \tag{11.4}$$

Equation (11.4) shows that the expected total claim amount grows linearly with t. Using the properties of the Poisson distribution, i.e. $\lambda \cdot t = E[N(t)] = var(N(t))$, the variance is denoted by:

$$var(C(t)) = \lambda \cdot t \left[var(X_1) + \left(E(X_1)\right)^2\right] = \lambda \cdot t \cdot E(X_1^2) \tag{11.5}$$

An insurer with a large portfolio is interested in the asymptotic behaviour of the total claim amount. Applying the law of large numbers, the mathematical foundation of insurance, the total claim amount is given by:

$$\lim_t \frac{C(t)}{t} = \lambda \cdot E(X_1) \tag{11.6}$$

Box 11.1 (cont.)

Thus, according to the law of large numbers, the total claim amount is the expected claim amount. Put differently, the number of claims is the average number of claims λ and the claim size is the average claim size $E(X_i)$. But the total claim amount may vary in practice. The risk of insurance is determined by the variance of the claims. The claim amount for a large population follows a normal distribution (i.e. a symmetric, bell-shaped curve).

Figure 11.3 visualises the law of large numbers for a portfolio of Danish fire insurance claims (Mikosch, 2004). The data cover the period 1980–1992 and include about 2,500 observations. Because the sample of fire insurance claims contains very large values, the ratio Cn/n converges to $E(X_i)$ very slowly in the figure.

Next, an insurer needs to set a premium $P(t)$ to cover the claims. As the total claim amount varies, it is necessary to choose a premium by loading the expected claim amount by some positive number ρ (called the safety loading). The premium is given by:

$$P(t) = (1 + \rho) \cdot E[C(t)] \tag{11.7}$$

Equation (11.7) shows that the larger the ρ, the safer the insurance business. The safety loading can thus absorb fluctuations in the claim amount. But an overly large safety loading would make the business less competitive.

The final step is to define the portfolio's surplus or risk process. Following Mikosch (2004), $E(t)$ is the insurer's capital or equity balance at time t (see also Figure 11.1) and is given by:

$$E(t) = E(0) + P(t) - C(t), t \geq 0 \tag{11.8}$$

where $E(0)$ is initial capital. A large initial capital is needed and reinforced by supervisors (see Chapter 12). When starting an insurance company, the supervisor requires a large enough initial capital buffer to prevent the business from bankruptcy due to many small (or a few large) claims in the first period, before the premium income can balance the losses and gains.

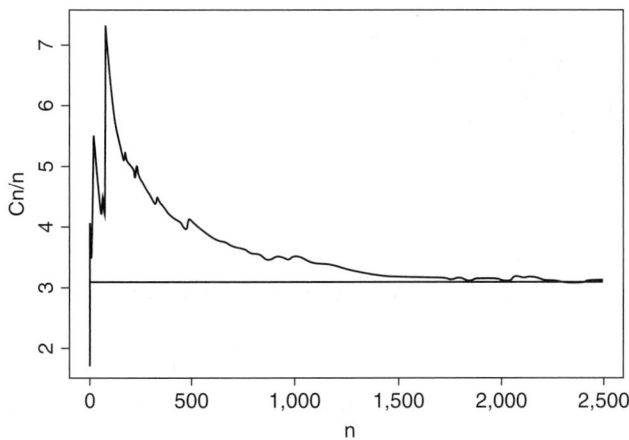

Figure 11.3   The law of large numbers and fire insurance claims
Source: Mikosch (2004)

Box 11.1 (cont.)

What is the risk for an insurer with a sufficient capital balance $E(0)$ and a sufficiently prudent premium rate $(\rho > 0)$? First, there may be an upward drift $\delta > 0$ in the claim amount that the insurer did not expect when it set the premium. The realised claim amount is thus larger than expected: $C(t) = (1 + \delta) \cdot E[C(t)]$. Examples of such a drift are shorter life expectancies due to a new disease or more car accidents due to an unexpected shift in weather conditions (e.g. strong winters with frozen roads). The insurer will incur losses when $\delta > \rho$ and may go bankrupt when cumulative losses wipe out the capital balance $(\delta - \rho) \cdot E[C(t)] > E(0)$.

Second, the principle of independence may be violated. For example, the insurer ING had sold a high proportion of its life policies to people working in the Twin Towers, and experienced an accumulation of payouts after the 2001 terrorist attack.

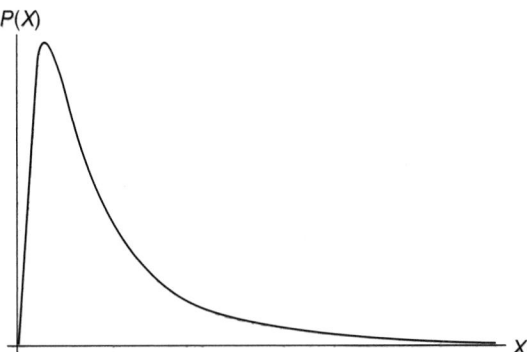

P(X)

X

Figure 11.4 Heavy-tailed distribution

By contrast, large claims are characterised by distributions with heavy tails. Insurance portfolios with heavy-tailed claim sizes are dangerous. Figure 11.4 shows the log-normal distribution, an example of a heavy-tailed distribution. The tail on the right indicates events with a low probability but a large impact on total claims. Extreme value statistics are required to model these large claims. The distribution needs to be fitted from a relatively small number of observations (the excesses over high thresholds). Embrechts *et al.* (1997) provide an overview of modelling extreme events.

Large losses are caused not only by nature (natural catastrophes) but also by man (man-made disasters). Table 11.1 provides an overview of the largest insurance payouts after natural disasters in the last 50 years. Hurricane Katrina in New Orleans caused an insured loss of €69 billion, while the

Table 11.1 Catastrophes: the 25 most costly insurance losses, 1970–2017

Insured loss (in € billion, 2017 figures)	Victims (dead and missing)	Date	Event	Location
68.7	1,836	2005	Hurricane Katrina: storm surge, floods	US, Mexico
31.8	18,451	2011	Earthquake (Mw 9.0) triggers tsunami	Japan
26.7	136	2017	Hurricane Maria	US, Puerto Rico, Caribbean
25.7	237	2012	Hurricane Sandy: storm surge	US
25.0	126	2017	Hurricane Irma	US, Puerto Rico, Caribbean
25.0	89	2017	Hurricane Harvey	US
23.3	65	1992	Hurricane Andrew: floods	US, Bahamas
21.7	2,982	2001	Terror attack on World Trade Center, Pentagon	US
21.1	61	1994	Northridge earthquake (Mw 6.7)	US
19.3	193	2008	Hurricane Ike: floods, damage to oil rigs	US, Caribbean
15.9	185	2011	Earthquake (Mw 6.1), aftershocks	New Zealand
14.0	119	2004	Hurricane Ivan: damage to oil rigs	US, Caribbean
13.6	815	2011	Heavy monsoon rains: extreme flooding	Thailand
13.2	53	2005	Hurricane Wilma: torrential rains, floods	US, Mexico
11.3	34	2005	Hurricane Rita: floods, damage to oil rigs	US, Mexico
9.8	123	2012	Drought in the Corn Belt	US
8.5	36	2004	Hurricane Charley	US, Caribbean
8.5	51	1991	Typhoon Mireille	Japan
7.5	78	1989	Hurricane Hugo	US, Caribbean
7.5	562	2010	Earthquake (Mw 8.8) triggers tsunami	Chile
7.3	95	1990	Winter storm Daria	France, UK, Benelux
7.3	–	2010	Earthquake (Mw 7.0) over 300 aftershocks	New Zealand
7.1	110	1999	Winter storm Lothar	Switzerland, UK, France
6.7	321	2011	Major tornado outbreak: 349 tornadoes	US
6.4	22	2017	Wildland fire 'Tubbs Fires'	US

Note: The losses include property and business interruption, but exclude liability and life insurance losses. The losses are indexed to 2017.
Source: Swiss Re (2018)

total loss (insured and uninsured) amounted to €118 billion. A tsunami, triggered by an earthquake, damaged the nuclear plant at Fukushima (Japan) and caused an insured loss of €32 billion. In 2017, three hurricanes, Maria, Irma, and Harvey, caused devastating combined insured losses (including destroyed homes) of €77 billion in the Caribbean and the US. Hurricane Sandy flooded the southern part of New York in 2012, causing €26 billion of insured losses. The terrorist attack on the Twin Towers and the Pentagon in 2001 led to an insured loss of €22 billion. Winter storms in Europe, such as Daria in 1990 and Lothar in 1999, caused insured losses of close to €7 billion each. The highest insured losses have been in the US, Europe, and Japan due to their higher insurance density. Emerging markets generally have a lower insurance density, so only a small proportion of victims benefit from insurance cover. For example the 2004 Boxing Day tsunami in the Indian Ocean caused the deaths of 220,000 people, but had low levels of insured losses and is thus not reported in Table 11.1.

Re-insurance

Individual insurers cannot bear these large losses on their own: their equity would be wiped out when an extreme event occurs. Insurers therefore share the risks (and premiums) of catastrophe insurance (Rejda, 2005). A common risk-sharing mechanism is *re-insurance*, which shifts part or all of the insurance originally written by one insurer (the ceding company) to another insurer (the re-insurer).[1] The re-insurer may in turn re-insure part or all of the risk with another insurer.

The insurance risk of extreme events is thus sliced into different layers and divided between several insurers. Re-insurance can be designed in different ways. One format is *proportional re-insurance*, in which the insurer cedes a proportion of the premiums and risks to a re-insurer. The ceding insurer retains the remainder of the premiums and risks (the retention amount). Another approach, which is often used for catastrophe insurance, is *excess-of-loss re-insurance*. Losses in excess of a certain limit (i.e. the retention limit) are paid by the re-insurer up to a maximum limit (expressed as an amount of money). Excess-of-loss contracts permit tailor-made slicing of the insurance risk. The terrorist attacks on 11 September 2001 show the importance of re-insurance, since re-insurers paid out at least half of the insured losses (Rejda, 2005).

Traditional insurance and re-insurance may not suffice for large catastrophes. For instance, the financial losses from a large flood can supersede the absorption capacity of individual insurers and re-insurers.

Therefore, many countries have a government programme that covers part of the risk (see Box 11.2). However, government involvement gives rise to moral hazard, as private parties may seek to shift their risk to the government (Loubergé, 2000; Kessler, 2008). There are several ways to mitigate this undesired effect. First, governments could provide cover for only the top layer of risk. Private (re-)insurers then take the first layers of risk of the catastrophe and have an incentive to take appropriate precautionary measures, thereby reducing moral hazard. Second, governments should charge sufficiently high premiums to push the insurance coverage back to the market as much as possible. Private (re-)insurers have a competitive motive to underbid the premium charged by the government. Yet if the risk is too high in relation to the premium, private (re-)insurers will drop out. In that case, the government ends up providing residual coverage for catastrophes.

Box 11.2 Flood insurance

While flooding affects many people worldwide and often causes serious damage (see Table 11.1), insurance cover for the risk of flooding is not widespread. This box reviews the (lack of) flood insurance solutions in selected countries.

The oldest insurance scheme is found in the US. The National Flood Insurance Program (NFIP), set up in 1968, covers losses caused by river flooding. The maximum cover for residential buildings/contents is $250,000/100,000. Premiums are high, and vary based on the flood hazard. Prior to the Mississippi floods of 1993, 15–20 per cent of property in exposed areas was insured under the NFIP. After these floods, these figures went up markedly. There is no cap on insured losses, as the NFIP is government funded.

In France, the flood insurance market is based on private insurers, but is statutorily regulated. The Caisse Centrale de Réassurance is the main re-insurer and is guaranteed by the state; insurance penetration is practically 100 per cent.

The UK has only private insurers and no state insurance. Insurance cover is generally included in homeowners' and household contents policies in conjunction with storm cover. Premium rates are often high for storm/flood and are broken down by individual postcodes. Flood insurance penetration is 95 per cent.

The Netherlands has an enormous loss potential. Some 70 per cent of property is at risk of storm surge as vast areas lie below sea level and/or can be flooded by the Rhine or Maas rivers. Dutch insurers concluded a market agreement in 1965 to exclude flood cover. The result is that the state is expected to pay (partial) compensation in the event of a disaster. When the Rhine and Maas flooded in 1995, causing an economic loss of €900 million, the government paid €180 million.

Source: Swiss Re (1998)

An alternative to traditional re-insurance and government insurance is securitisation of the risk. An example is the catastrophe (cat) bond. *Cat bonds* are corporate bonds that permit the issuer to skip or defer scheduled payments if a catastrophic loss over a certain threshold occurs. If insurers have built up a portfolio of risks by insuring properties in a region that may be hit by a catastrophe, they could create a special-purpose entity to issue the cat bond. Investors who buy the bond make a healthy return on their investment unless a catastrophe (like a hurricane or an earthquake) hits the region; in that case, the principal initially paid by the investors is forgiven and is used by the sponsor to pay the claims of policyholders. The bonds pay relatively high interest rates and help institutional investors to diversify their portfolio, because natural disasters occur randomly and are not correlated with the stock market or other common factors (Rejda, 2005).

Asymmetric Information

Under the assumption of full information, complete insurance is possible at actuarially fair premium rates. But complete coverage is not always available in insurance markets due to asymmetric information (Loubergé, 2000). Insurance is subject to moral hazard when the contract outcome is influenced by the behaviour of the insured and the insurer cannot observe, without costs, the extent to which the reported losses can be attributed to the behaviour of the insured. Complete coverage may not be attainable under moral hazard due to the trade-off between the goals of efficient risk sharing (by allocating the risk to the insurer) and efficient incentives (by leaving the consequences of decisions about care with the decision maker, i.e. the insured).

Insurance is also subject to adverse selection. Information asymmetry arises because the insured generally knows more about his or her risk profile than the insurer. The insured's risk type cannot be determined *ex ante* by the insurer; the insurer can only charge the same premium rate based on aggregate risk. The high-risk types are most eager to buy insurance, producing an undesirable outcome for the insurer.

While both types of asymmetric information (i.e. moral hazard and adverse selection) may lead to sub-optimal insurance outcomes, this section focuses on adverse selection, which is potentially a serious problem in any type of insurance market. Chapter 10 explains moral hazard in more detail. In a seminal paper, Rothschild and Stiglitz (1976) analyse adverse selection in the insurance market. They model the effect of two types of individuals under asymmetric information (i.e. the insurer does not know which type): the high-risk type H with accident probability p^h and the low-risk type L with accident probability p^l. We assume competitive insurance markets so that insurance is offered at actuarially fair premiums, as premiums are competed down to cost price. High-risk types prefer full insurance, as they are keen to get full coverage knowing their risk profile. This insurance contract is too expensive for low-risk types, who are prepared to take partial insurance at a lower premium given their low risk profile.

In equilibrium, the insurance market offers both contracts simultaneously and clients self-select. This two-tier contract structure forces low-risk types to distinguish themselves from high-risk types in order to obtain full insurance at an actuarially fair premium. The low-risk types get partial insurance at a fair premium. In practice, this partial insurance usually takes the form of a 'deductible' (i.e. own risk for the client), which reduces the scale of the compensation by a fixed amount. Alternatively, when losses are variable (rather than the fixed amount assumed here), co-insurance (fractional compensation) can be used. This two-tier market solution with self-selection is known as a *separating equilibrium*.

Box 11.3 illustrates the working of the Rothschild–Stiglitz model. The application of a deductible or co-insurance is one way to separate high- and low-risk individuals. Another mechanism is screening. For example, before issuing health insurance, the insurer can require the potential client to undergo a medical test. The insurer can offer two contracts: one at a low premium for people who pass the medical test and one at a high premium for people who are not willing to do the test or fail the test.

Box 11.3 Rothschild–Stiglitz model

The working of the Rothschild–Stiglitz model can be illustrated with some numerical examples. The first example is with a relatively small proportion of high-risk individuals, so the insurer is still able to offer a single contract to all (both high and low risk). The case in which everybody is charged the same premium is called a *pooling equilibrium*. Table 11.2 describes two types of people: 90 per cent are healthy people with a low risk of illness of 1/1000 ($p^l = 0.001$) and 10 per cent are unhealthy people with a high risk of illness of 1/100 ($p^h = 0.01$). The cost of illness is €100,000 per episode. The cost of insuring the healthy is €100 (= 100,000 * 1/1000) and €1,000 (= 100,000 * 1/100) for the unhealthy. The average cost is €190 (= 0.90 * 100 + 0.10 * 1,000). If insurance is offered at an actuarially fair premium of €190 for the whole population, both types will buy full insurance as the premium is below their assumed reservation prices of €200 and €1,500, respectively.

Box 11.3 (cont.)

In the second example, the proportion of healthy people is 80 per cent (see Table 11.3), which increases the average cost to €280 (= 0.80 * 100 + 0.20 * 1,000). Healthy people are unwilling to buy insurance at this premium as it is above their reservation price of €200. There is *no equilibrium*: only unhealthy people will buy insurance. Since the insurer knows that, it will charge a premium of €1,000. The result is that the healthy population are not insured.

In the third example, we assume that the population is evenly split between healthy and unhealthy people, and the insurer has enough market power to charge premiums above the actuarially fair amount (Table 11.4). The average premium is €150 (= 0.50 * 100 + 0.50 * 200). Since healthy people are not willing to pay this amount (their willingness to pay is assumed to be €140), there is again no pooling equilibrium. We now try to set up a *separating equilibrium* with two different contracts and premiums. The general policy is available for €240. The insurer also offers an insurance policy for €100 to anyone who can pass its medical test, which costs €40. Healthy people will choose the second contract: they pay €100 for the insurance and €40 for the medical test. Unhealthy people can pass the test only if they bribe the doctor, which is costly (€110). So unhealthy people will take the general policy at a premium of €240 rather than the second policy at a cost of €250 (€100 for the insurance and €150 for the test and bribe).

Table 11.2 Pooling equilibrium

Type	% of population	Risk of illness	Cost to insure	Willingness to pay
Healthy people	90	1/1000	€100	€200
Unhealthy people	10	1/100	€1,000	€1,500

Table 11.3 No equilibrium

Type	% of population	Risk of illness	Cost to insure	Willingness to pay
Healthy people	80	1/1000	€100	€200
Unhealthy people	20	1/100	€1,000	€1,500

Table 11.4 Separating equilibrium

Type	% of population	Risk of illness	Cost to insure	Willingness to pay	Cost of medical test
Healthy people	50	1/1000	€100	€140	€40
Unhealthy people	50	1/500	€200	€250	€150

Finally, the government can impose compulsory insurance to enforce a *pooling equilibrium* (Spencer, 2000). It can require all individuals to take out full insurance. The compulsion prevents low-risk individuals from breaking ranks and taking up a partial insurance offer from a rival insurer. A typical example of such compulsory insurance is health insurance. As part of its social policy, a government may find it desirable for all citizens to be fully insured at an affordable premium in case of illness. Without compulsion, low-risk individuals would have partial insurance and high-risk individuals would pay a high premium (the separating equilibrium).

11.2 The Use of Risk Management Models

While underwriting risk is one of their core competencies, insurers use risk management systems and practices in a similar way as banks (Von Bomhard, 2005). In fact, the banking industry imported risk management skills from the insurance sector and developed them further. Several banking crises, like the financial crisis of 2007–2009 and the Scandinavian banking crisis in the 1990s (see Chapter 2), have highlighted the importance of good risk and capital management for banks. There are also similarities between the traditional actuarial thinking that prevails in insurance companies and the financial economic thinking that prevails in banks. Insurers' modern risk management approaches integrate actuarial techniques and total balance sheet management (see below).

Modern Risk Management

The main risks for an insurer are underwriting risk, market risk, credit risk, and operational risk. As explained in Chapter 10, economic capital has emerged as a 'common currency' for risk taking within financial institutions. *Economic capital* is the amount of capital a financial institution needs to absorb losses over a certain time interval with a certain level of confidence. Financial institutions usually choose a time horizon of one year.

The risk-adjusted return on capital (RAROC) for an insurer is given by:

$$\text{RAROC} = \frac{\text{Revenues} - \text{Costs} - \text{Expected Claims}}{\text{Economic Capital}} = \frac{\pi}{E} \qquad (11.9)$$

The revenues consist of premiums P and investment returns R_A (see equation (11.2)). Both the numerator and the denominator are adjusted for risk in the RAROC formula, which divides profit by economic capital.

RAROC can be used to assess past performance as well as forecast future performance. It can thus be applied to determine whether activities should be discontinued or expanded.

RAROC is emerging as the leading methodology for large financial institutions to measure and manage risk. The use of internal risk models has been stimulated by supervisory authorities, who allow insurers to use their internal models to calculate capital requirements (see Chapter 12 on the new Solvency II capital adequacy rules). Within the RAROC framework, insurers first calculate the risk for each risk type (underwriting, market, credit, and operational risk) and then aggregate them.[2]

The first type of risk is *underwriting risk.* Insurers make provisions for future claims, and an unforeseen increase in the size or frequency of claims is a key risk factor. In life insurance, *longevity risk* is the risk that future trends in survival rates prove to be higher than projected. The payout period on annuities or pension contracts may thus be longer than expected. Insurance premiums to cover underwriting risk tend to follow a cyclical pattern. Several studies (e.g. Niehaus and Terry, 1993) identify the existence of an underwriting cycle in insurance markets. Box 11.4 explores different theories explaining the underwriting cycle.

The second type of risk is *market* risk. *Asset and liability management (ALM) risk* is one type of market risk; it occurs when assets and liabilities in the balance sheet are not matched. This type of risk is very important for insurance companies (Van Lelyveld, 2006). ALM risk increases when there is a significant mismatch between assets and liabilities. *Duration* is the effective maturity of an asset or liability; in the life insurance business, asset durations are generally shorter than liability durations. This duration mismatch will cause an interest rate risk, as most assets consist of bonds.[3] Insurers also invest in equities and other investments to increase returns. While equities tend to generate a higher return than bonds in the long run (Dimson *et al.,* 2002), they also generate a considerably higher ALM risk. Insurers use advanced models to optimise their risk-return profile. The ability to invest in equities rather than bonds depends on the size of an insurer's capital buffer. The larger the capital buffer, the more risk (and thus equity investments) the insurer is allowed to take (see Chapter 12 for further details).

The third type of risk is *credit risk.* While banks grant loans, insurers typically invest in traded assets such as bonds. They are exposed to credit risk because the value of bonds may decline as a result of an increase in the perceived likelihood that the issuer will not be able to meet scheduled payments in the future. For most banks, lending activities are typically the

---

Box 11.4 The underwriting cycle

The *underwriting or insurance cycle* is a distinct pattern of upward and downward movements in insurance premiums and their subsequent impact on underwriting profitability. Cyclical patterns, typically running over a period of six to nine years, tend to be particularly pronounced in insurance markets. While the demand for and supply of insurance both vary over time, variations in supply are more important. New financial capital can enter a market quickly to increase the supply when premiums are high, or be withdrawn quickly when returns on insurance are low.

There are three main theories to explain the underwriting cycle (see Niehaus and Terry, 1993). The first is based on fluctuations in profits and assumes a competitive market. If profits are high, some insurers may reduce premiums to attract more clients in expectation of these higher profits. Other insurers, not wishing to lose their market share, may then also reduce premiums.

The second theory is founded on the availability and cost of equity capital. There are two main effects when stock markets rise considerably. First, the cost of capital decreases for existing and new insurers. Second, rising share prices increase the value of an insurer's asset holdings and thereby the value of equity. The increased availability and reduced cost of capital increases the supply and hence exerts a downward pressure on premiums.

The third theory holds that claims, rather than capital market effects, are the key cause of underwriting cycles. It supposes that insurers tend to underestimate the potential for large claims when there are no large individual losses or accumulation of losses. However, when a very large loss occurs, premiums rise sharply. A case in point is car insurance. After a few mild winters without frozen roads, the frequency of car accidents seems to be relatively low and premiums may decrease. But after a cold winter with multiple car accidents, premiums tend to rise again. This theory assumes that insurers have a short memory. It also supposes that following a major loss, insurers will try to recover some of their losses. Of course, exceptionally large losses or accumulations of loss are likely to be more or less random in their timing, but their effects may appear to be cyclical.

---

main source of credit risk. But a typical insurer attributes only 5–10 per cent of total risk capital to credit risk (Van Lelyveld, 2006).

The fourth type of risk is *operational risk* – the risk of loss from inadequate internal processes, people or systems, or from external events. While developments in the insurance industry generally follow those in banking, most insurers model external event risk separately as an underwriting risk. The insurance industry has its own operational risks. Recently, the mis-selling of investment-linked insurance policies has led to large settlements to policyholders in several countries (e.g. the UK and the Netherlands). In the past, insurers have not always been transparent about the investment costs associated with particular policies. Moreover, insurers have not always adequately explained the risks of an investment-linked policy (i.e. that investments may have a negative return), which violates duty-of-care rules (see Chapter 12).

The impacts of the various types of risks differ across the banking and insurance industries. Since the main business of banks is granting loans, credit risk is the most important risk driver in banking, followed by market and ALM risk. ALM risk results from funding long-term assets using short-term deposits. The main risk in life insurance is market risk related to the large asset portfolios. Life insurers collect premiums on life policies, which are invested over a long period. The next most important type of risk for the insurance industry is ALM risk, which is opposite to the banking ALM risk. Life insurers typically invest the premiums on their long-term policies in shorter-lived assets. Insurance or underwriting risk is the main risk driver for P&C insurers. Figure 11.5 illustrates the relative importance of the different types of risk.

As explained in Chapter 10, risk management models have several shortcomings. Given the possibility of large losses due to natural or man-made disasters, it is difficult for P&C insurers to accurately model tail risk. Another risk that is difficult to model is longevity. Unanticipated increases in life expectancy have recently resulted in losses for life insurers as well as pension funds.

Centralisation of Risk Management

The organisational structure of international financial firms is moving from the traditional country model to a business-line model with the integration of key

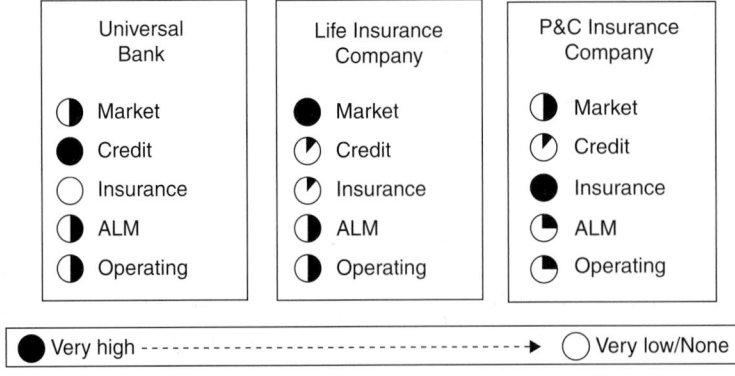

Figure 11.5   The relative role of risk types in banking and insurance
Source: Oliver, Wyman and Company (2001)

management functions. The potential capital reductions that can be achieved by applying the advanced approaches of the Basel II framework encourage banking groups to organise their risk management more centrally (see Chapter 10). The same is true for the Solvency II framework for the European insurance industry (Drzik, 2005). Firms that implement a well-constructed risk and capital management framework can derive significant benefits, and substantially strengthen their medium-term competitive position.

One of the most notable advances in risk management is the growing emphasis on developing a firm-wide assessment of risk. These integrated approaches to risk management aim to ensure a comprehensive and systematic approach to risk-related decisions throughout the financial firm; a centralised risk management approach can also generate economies of scale. Nevertheless, these centralised systems still rely on local branches and subsidiaries for local market data.

Kuritzkes *et al.* (2003) provide evidence that internationally active financial conglomerates are centralising their risk and capital management units. The dominant approach is to adopt a 'hub and spoke' organisational model in which the spokes are responsible for risk management within business lines, while the hub provides centralised oversight of risk and capital at the group level. Activities at the spoke include the credit function within a bank, or the actuarial function within an insurance subsidiary or group, both of which serve the front-line managers for most trading decision making. Both types of activities are described in more detail in the following sections.

Schoenmaker *et al.* (2008) confirm that the European insurance industry has shifted to a more holistic approach. Developments in the field of accounting (for instance, the introduction of International Financial Reporting Standards) and in supervision (Solvency II; see Chapter 12) contribute to the centralisation of risk and capital management processes. Insurance groups that operate in multiple countries are increasingly developing coherent policies regarding risk and capital management; several are hiring chief risk officers (CROs).

Hub Functions

Applying the hub-and-spoke model to a sample of large European insurance companies, Schoenmaker *et al.* (2008) identify which functions are executed at the centre (hub) and which are performed by local branches (spokes). The hub accommodates decisions and responsibilities for the group as a whole at a central level in the organisation. Although all large insurance groups have a distinct central risk management framework in place, their responsibilities and implementation vary widely. In some groups, central risk and capital management processes are in their infancy, while in other groups they are much more advanced and commonly accepted within the organisation.

All groups use their risk management framework to get an overview and to monitor the group-wide risk exposure. Most groups also use their risk framework to specify their risk profile and set risk management, control, and business conduct standards for their worldwide operations (i.e. 'the rules of the game'). Group-wide risk profiles specify risk tolerance levels. Within these boundaries, local units can act more or less independently. Such group-wide policies enable a broadly consistent approach to managing risks at the branch level.

The risk management framework encompasses several bodies tasked with specific responsibilities. At the top is the executive-level group risk committee, headed by the chief executive officer (CEO) or chief financial officer (CFO). This committee is often responsible for setting the strategic guidelines and policies for risk management, for monitoring consolidated risk reports at the group level, and for allocating economic capital to various entities within the group. Some financial groups also have risk committees below this level, such as separate committees for firms that engage in both banking and insurance activities.

Many groups also have central or group risk management teams responsible for developing and implementing the risk management framework, supporting the work of the risk committees, reporting and reviewing risks, and making recommendations concerning risk methodologies. These central/group risk management teams are often headed by a CRO who oversees all aspects of the group's risk management, reports to the CEO or CFO of the group, and attends executive board meetings.

Spoke Functions

In the spokes, decisions are taken at the business/country unit level. Insurance is very much a local business, since there are significant differences between the operational environments of the host countries in which the insurance group is active. Since national conditions and regulations differ (such as fiscal legislation, contracts, social security, consumer protection, and local risks), many decisions must be made at the local level. In general, the actuary determines the specific risk at the local level. These local models are subsequently monitored and assessed at the group level. Although the general conditions for determining local risk models are set at the central level, the local units carry the ultimate responsibility for their risk management.

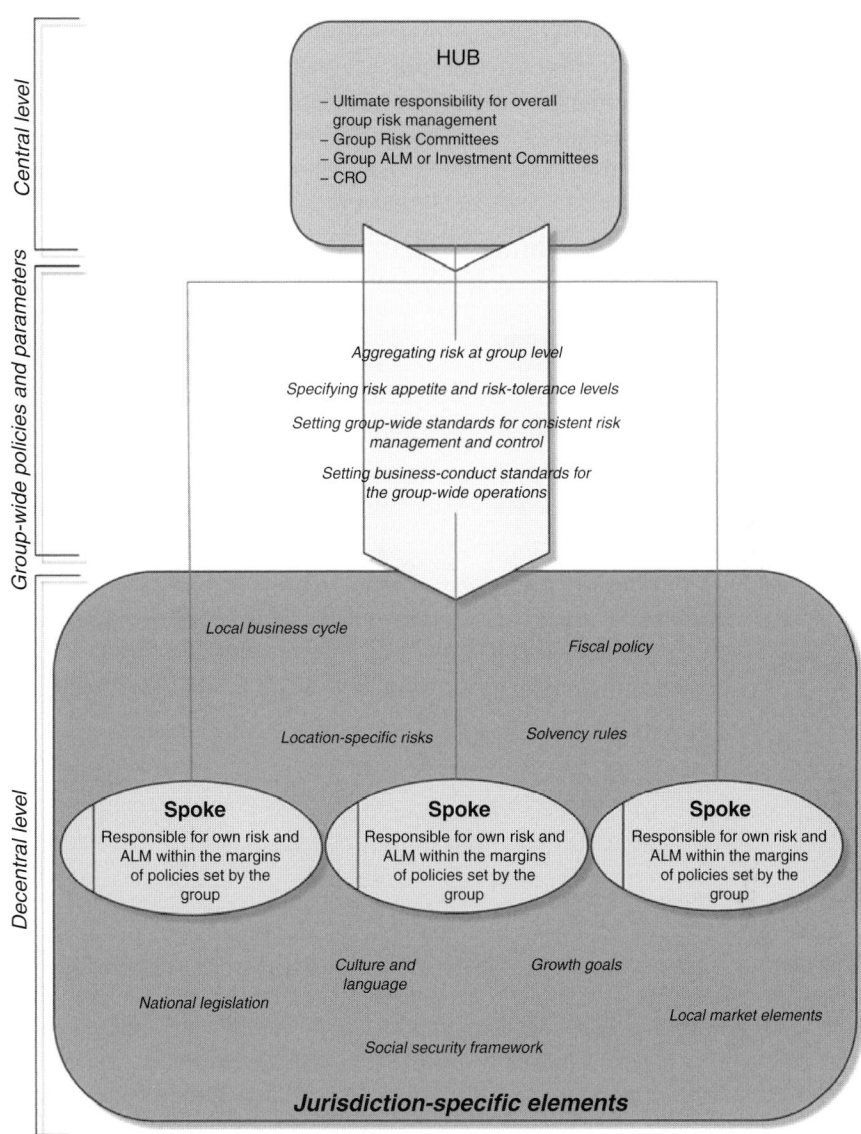

Figure 11.6   Organisation of risk and capital management in insurance groups
Source: Schoenmaker *et al.* (2008)

So, despite the emergence of centralised risk management, the risk management practices of the largest insurance groups are still largely influenced by local policies. Thus, the hub defines the 'rules of the game', and the local managers in the spokes determine 'how the game is played' within the margins of these rules. This general principle is summarised in Figure 11.6, which gives an overview of the roles and responsibilities for each level of the organisation, whereby the spokes are placed within a field of jurisdiction-specific parameters to capture the location-specific factors that influence business decisions.

11.3 The European Insurance System

Insurance Markets across Europe

Insurance markets vary significantly across Europe: *insurance penetration* (i.e. insurance premiums as a percentage of GDP) ranges from 1.1 per cent in Romania to 13.8 per cent in the UK (see Table 11.5). Whereas the penetration rate of life insurance is 5.6 per cent in the EU-15, it is only 1.0 per cent in the new Member States (NMS)-13. Life insurance is basically a savings product for the future, which pays out upon the insured's death. It may therefore be considered a 'luxury' good: only at high income levels do households start to save for retirement (Focarelli and Pozzolo, 2008).

Non-life insurance is less diverse across Europe, since it as seen as a more 'necessary' good offering basic protection against accidents, such as car accidents, fire, or illness. Non-life penetration is 3.1 per cent in the EU-15 and 1.6 per cent in the NMS-13. The differences are also less pronounced than for life insurance at the country level, ranging from 0.9 per cent in Romania to 4.2 per cent in France. The Netherlands, with a non-life penetration ratio of 7.4 per cent, is an outlier as health insurance there has been privatised.

The US also has a high non-life penetration ratio of 7.4 per cent due to high healthcare insurance premiums. Life insurance penetration in Japan is slightly higher than that in the EU-15. China has surpassed the NMS-13 with a total insurance penetration of 3.1 per cent.

Table 11.6 illustrates the major business lines of non-life insurers in the EU. Motor insurance is the largest class of non-life business, but health insurance is catching up. The strong increase in health insurance within the EU reflects the privatisation of the healthcare sector in the Netherlands in 2006. Property insurance is increasing as well, in line with rising property values. Other non-life insurance includes marine, aviation, and transport insurance.

In 2017, some 3,500 insurance companies operated in the EU. Their number has declined since the creation of the European single market, due to mergers and acquisitions at the national and European levels. Insurance companies aim for sufficient critical mass to be competitive at the European level.

Table 11.5 Insurance penetration in the EU, 2017

	Number of insurers	Total premium income (in € billion)	Insurance penetration (in % of GDP)		
			Total	Life	Non-life
Austria	73	17.0	4.6	2.1	2.5
Belgium	123	29.2	6.7	3.4	3.2
Bulgaria	58	1.1	2.2	0.4	1.8
Croatia	24	1.2	2.4	0.8	1.6
Cyprus	35	0.9	4.4	1.8	2.6
Czech Republic	55	5.3	2.8	1.0	1.7
Denmark	106	32.9	11.4	8.2	3.2
Estonia	16	0.7	3.0	0.9	2.2
Finland	62	8.6	3.8	2.0	1.8
France	301	265.3	11.6	7.4	4.2
Germany	463	218.9	6.7	4.4	2.3
Greece	66	3.7	2.1	1.0	1.0
Hungary	46	3.1	2.5	1.2	1.3
Ireland	258	17.7	6.0	3.8	2.2
Italy	220	132.2	7.7	5.8	1.9
Latvia	22	0.4	1.5	0.1	1.4
Lithuania	23	0.6	1.4	0.4	1.0
Luxembourg	91	2.9	5.2	3.2	2.0
Malta	58	0.6	5.6	3.8	1.8
Netherlands	176	70.7	9.6	2.2	7.4
Poland	82	14.5	3.1	1.2	1.9
Portugal	79	10.8	5.6	3.5	2.1
Romania	44	2.1	1.1	0.2	0.9
Slovakia	38	2.2	2.6	1.3	1.3
Slovenia	23	2.0	4.6	1.2	3.5
Spain	315	61.8	5.3	2.7	2.6
Sweden	201	24.6	5.2	3.3	1.9
United Kingdom	402	320.5	13.8	10.2	3.5
EU-15	2,936	1,216.8	8.7	5.6	3.1
NMS-13	524	34.7	2.6	1.0	1.6
EU-28	3,460	1,251.5	8.2	5.2	2.9
United States	4,185	1,994.5	12.2	4.9	7.4
Japan	92	376.4	9.2	6.9	2.3
China	203	313.7	3.1	1.9	1.2

Notes: Insurance penetration is measured as premium income as a percentage of GDP. EU-15, NMS-13, and EU-28 are calculated as a weighted average (weighted according to total premium income).

Source: EIOPA for EU (2017 figures), OECD Insurance Statistics for US and Japan (2016 figures), and World Bank for China (2015 figures)

Table 11.6 Non-life premium income in the EU (in € billion), 1995–2017

	1995	2000	2005	2010	2017
Motor insurance	78	98	119	124	138
Health insurance	51	66	88	108	132
Property insurance	47	54	74	84	101
General liability	17	20	31	32	40
Other non-life	31	31	41	79	92
Total non-life	224	269	353	427	503

Source: Insurance Europe (2018a)

The insurance market has a large number of small and medium-sized insurers with a very small market share, as well as a small number of insurance groups with a large market share. Small insurers, with premium income below €10 million, are more common in the non-life insurance sector. Large insurance groups have premium income ranging from around €5 billion up to €100 billion. Table 11.7 shows the 25 largest insurers in Europe, which account for 60 per cent of the premium income of the European insurance market.

The largest insurers, Allianz, AXA, and Generali, have a premium income of €70–90 billion and operate throughout Europe. They are truly European insurers, with a substantial share of their premium earned in other European countries. There are also global insurers operating on a worldwide scale – Zurich and Chubb from Switzerland, Aegon from the Netherlands, and Prudential and Lloyds from the UK. Schoenmaker *et al.* (2008) define insurers as 'domestic' if they receive 75 per cent or more of their premiums in the home country. Examples are CNP and Crédit Agricole in France and Achmea in the Netherlands.

To operate successfully in a foreign market, an insurer must understand the country's legislation (e.g. on liability), fiscal treatment, and accident statistics (e.g. the number of car accidents). Given the amount of research involved, cross-border insurance is typically issued only by large insurance groups. The preferred method of entering a foreign market is through a subsidiary, usually by acquiring a local insurer. Figure 11.7 illustrates the cross-border penetration of the top 25 insurers in Europe. The cross-border penetration in the EU rose from 30 per cent to 36 per cent between 2000 and 2009 and declined to 31 per cent in 2015. The corresponding figure for the 30 largest banks in Europe was 22 per cent in 2017 (see Chapter 10). Large insurance groups are thus more internationally oriented than their counterparts in banking.

Table 11.7 Twenty-five largest insurance groups in Europe, 2015

Insurance groups	(1) Premium income (in € billion)	(2) Total assets (in € billion)	(3) Premium income in home country (as % of (1))	(4) Premium income in rest of Europe (as % of (1))	(5) Premium income rest of world (as % of (1))
1. AXA (France)	91.9	887	26	40	34
2. Allianz (Germany)	76.7	849	25	52	23
3. Generali (Italy)	70.3	501	34	60	6
4. Prudential (UK)	49.7	525	24	0	76
5. Zurich Insurance Group (Switzerland)	43.7	352	9	33	58
6. Lloyds (UK)	36.2	113	18	14	68
7. Talanx-HDI (Germany)	31.8	153	29	31	40
8. CNP Assurances (France)	31.8	394	78	12	10
9. Crédit Agricole Assurances (France)	31.2	342	81	16	3
10. Aviva (UK)	30.2	526	45	37	18
11. BNP Paribas Cardif (France)	28.0	167	41	36	23
12. MAPFRE (Spain)	22.3	63	34	61	5
13. Chubb (Switzerland)	21.5	94	3	11	86
14. AEGON (Netherlands)	20.3	416	17	30	53
15. Achmea (Netherlands)	19.9	93	94	6	0
16. Poste Vita (Italy)	18.2	106	100	0	0
17. ERGO (Germany)	16.5	129	73	27	0
18. Unipol Gruppo Finanziario (Italy)	15.6	90	100	0	0
19. R+V Versicherung (Germany)	14.5	91	30	50	20
20. Groupama (France)	13.5	107	73	27	0
21. SCOR (France)	13.4	42	15	26	59
22. Swiss Life (Switzerland)	13.0	174	56	38	6
23. Société Générale Insurance (France)	11.9	111	82	18	0
24. Cooperatie VGZ (Netherlands)	10.8	8	100	0	0
25. XL Group (UK)	9.9	54	20	26	54
Top 25 Insurance Groups	742.9	6,387	41	31	28

Notes: The groups are selected based on gross written premium in 2015. Premium in the home country, rest of region, and rest of the world add up to 100 per cent. The geographic segmentation of the top 25 insurance groups is a weighted average, weighted by premium income.

Source: Schoenmaker and Sass (2016)

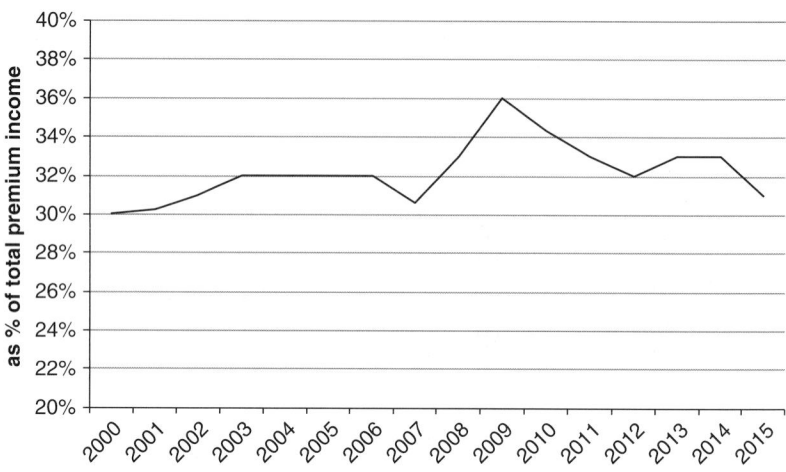

Figure 11.7   Cross-border penetration of top 25 EU insurers (%), 2000–2015
Note: Share of premium income from other EU countries is measured as a percentage of total premium income.
Source: Schoenmaker and Sass (2016)

Portfolios

The investment activities of large European insurers are concentrated in the government bond, bank bond, and corporate bond markets at 84 per cent in 2016. Investments in equity (9 per cent) and alternative investments (7 per cent) are far lower (EIOPA, 2017). Fixed-income portfolios are dominated by highly rated bonds (see Figure 11.8), which allow insurers to limit their credit risk. Nevertheless, the overall amount of AAA bond investments has significantly decreased in favour of lower-quality categories, particularly BBB bonds. This is due to the 'search for yield' in the low interest rate environment, as well as the fact that during this period a large number of countries and corporations in the euro area lost their AAA rating due to downgrades related to the European debt crisis.

Institutional investors, such as insurers and pension funds, are important long-term investors for the real economy. Examples of long-term assets for insurers are (EIOPA, 2013):

- infrastructure financing and other long-term financing through project bonds, other types of debt, and equity;
- financing for small and medium-sized enterprises through debt and equity;
- socially responsible investments and social business financing through debt and equity;

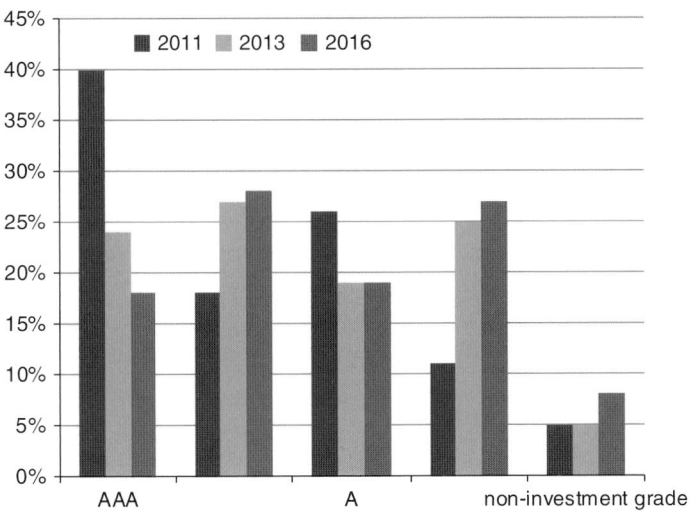

Figure 11.8   Bond investments of European insurers by rating (percentage of total bond investments), 2011–2016
Source: EIOPA (2017)

- long-term financing of the real economy through securitisation of debt serving the above-mentioned purposes.

The demand for high-quality long-term bonds could strengthen as insurance companies economise on capital charges under the new Solvency II regime (see Chapter 12). Liability-driven investment strategies thus tend to raise the demand for risk-free long-term assets, which are used to limit duration gaps without attracting higher risk charges. As such strategies favour government bonds, there is concern about the prospects for corporations, and bank funding in particular, over the medium term. Insurance companies (and pension funds) have continued to reduce their exposure to financial institutions since the crisis.

Market Structure

Between 1994 and 2017 the total number of insurers in the EU decreased from 5,201 to 3,460 (see Table 11.8). This consolidation mainly reflects mergers or acquisitions of small and medium-sized domestic insurers. At the same time, some of the large insurers expanded domestically and elsewhere within Europe.

There are different types of insurance companies. The main model is the *limited-liability* (or joint stock) insurance company owned by shareholders, whose liability for losses is restricted to the share capital. The alternative

Table 11.8 Market structure indicators, 1994/95 and 2017

	Size		CR5[a] (in %)				Competition
	Number of insurers		Life		Non-life		Combined ratio[b]
	1994	2017	1995	2017	1995	2017	2017
Austria	74	73	46	64	54	61	80
Belgium	252	123	64	57	52	54	98
Bulgaria	30	58	n.a.	83	n.a.	69	84
Croatia	n.a.	24	n.a.	64	n.a.	74	92
Cyprus	46	35	89	84	36	39	102
Czech Republic	27	55	97	70	93	73	90
Denmark	250	106	57	56	63	73	83
Estonia	15	16	100	100	65	95	89
Finland	57	62	99	88	88	71	93
France	577	301	50	47	41	21	96
Germany	742	463	31	32	23	35	96
Greece	149	66	68	83	39	43	94
Hungary	13	46	93	63	96	71	89
Ireland	122	258	61	53	50	56	97
Italy	265	220	45	48	34	56	92
Latvia	42	22	n.a.	100	n.a.	100	92
Lithuania	35	23	n.a.	100	n.a.	100	92
Luxembourg	76	91	67	50	82	57	79
Malta	24	58	n.a.	93	n.a.	48	75
Netherlands	492	176	68	59	35	55	100
Poland	34	82	100	64	90	70	90
Portugal	87	79	59	83	53	62	91
Romania	39	44	n.a.	78	n.a.	69	103
Slovakia	11	38	98	75	98	87	90
Slovenia	10	23	90	78	95	79	100
Spain	417	315	29	53	20	42	85
Sweden	494	201	74	60	77	60	99
United Kingdom	821	402	29	50	27	55	98
EU-15[c]	4,875	2,936	44	47	33	44	95
NMS-13[c]	326	524	96	70	91	73	91
EU-28[c]	5,201	3,460	44	48	34	45	95

Notes:

a   CR5 is the share of the five largest life (non-life) insurers, measured as a percentage of total life (non-life) premiums.

b   Combined ratio is measured as claims and expenses as a % of premiums for non-life insurers.

c   EU-15, NMS-13, and EU-28 are calculated as a weighted average (weighted according to premium) for CR5 and the combined ratio.

   n.a. = not available.

Source: EIOPA

mutual insurer model, in which the policyholders own the company, accounts for about 20 per cent of the European market (ACME, 2003); mutuals are more common in some markets, such as France and Germany (about 30 per cent), and less common in others, like the UK (about 10 per cent). There is a current trend towards 'demutualisation' – converting mutuals into limited-liability insurance companies.

Again, there are substantial differences in types of insurance companies between the EU-15 and the NMS-13. First, there are substantially more insurers in the EU-15 than in the NMS-13, largely due to the significant number of small insurers in countries such as France, Germany, Spain, and the UK.

Second, the trend in the number of insurers is different. On average, the number of insurers in the EU-15 declined by about 40 per cent from 1994 to 2017, and increased by 60 per cent in the NMS-13. The change in the number of insurers influences the degree of concentration within national insurance markets. Table 11.8 presents the CR5 ratio, which measures the market share of the top five insurers in the industry. It illustrates that the insurance markets in the NMS-13 are generally more concentrated than those in the EU-15. However, there is convergence: the concentration ratios in the EU-15 are increasing towards 40 to 50 per cent, and decreasing towards 70 per cent in the NMS-13.

Overall, life insurance markets are more concentrated than non-life markets, due to the nature of the product. Life insurance companies carry closely related (savings) products dependent on life expectancy. By contrast, the non-life insurance industry has very different business lines (see Table 11.6); many small companies underwrite only one type of insurance.

There are no direct measures of competition in the insurance industry, partly due to the lack of adequate indices of insurance prices that would allow comparisons. An alternative approach is to rely on indirect measures, such as profitability (European Commission, 2007). A common economic measure to assess the profitability of non-life insurers is the combined ratio (CR; see Section 11.1). However, this method has three major drawbacks. First, when claims are more likely to arise in the future, the matching principle of accounting is not satisfied. For example, clients pay their insurance premium starting in year 1, but may not make a claim until year 2 or 3 (or later). Second, the CR varies over time as payouts fluctuate. Third, the CR does not include investment returns, which are an important source of income, as premiums are invested in financial assets that are held until claims are paid.

The last column of Table 11.8 reports the CRs. The figures indicate that the non-life insurance industry is competitive in Europe, with a CR of 95 per cent (EU-28) yielding a margin of 5 per cent. The margin is higher in the NMS

(9 per cent). At the country level, the picture is more diverse. The majority of EU Member States have a CR of 90–100 per cent. Cyprus and Romania have CRs over 100 per cent and make a loss, while Austria, Luxembourg, and Malta have CRs of 70–80 per cent. These ratios suggest a lack of competition, but the results provide only an indication of the lack of competition and should be interpreted with care.

Insurance is sold through a variety of distribution channels. A growing share of insurance products is sold directly by employees of an insurance company or directly via the Internet (*direct writing*). Internet sales are growing fast, particularly for simple non-life insurance products. Historically, insurance intermediaries (brokers and agents) have played a dominant role. Brokers are fully independent, specialist insurance intermediaries who are not tied to a specific insurance company. Insurance agents are typically less independent than insurance brokers. Agents can work exclusively for one insurance company, but may also offer competing products from a wide range of insurers. A final distribution channel is *bancassurance* (the combination of a bank and an insurance company within a financial institution), where insurance products are sold through the bank.

Distribution channels vary significantly across Europe. The distribution of life insurance is mainly driven by bancassurance networks in Spain, France, Italy, Malta, and Portugal. In Bulgaria, Germany, the Netherlands, Slovenia, and the UK, agents and brokers dominate the distribution of life products (see Figure 11.9). Non-life insurance products are principally distributed via agents in a large number of countries (Germany, Spain, Italy, Poland, Portugal, Slovakia, and Slovenia). The broker channel dominates in Belgium, Bulgaria, the Netherlands, and the UK. The predominance of agents and brokers in almost every market is due to the preference of the insured to use an intermediary during the contract stage and, above all, in the case of a claim. Direct writing is used more for non-life than for life products.

International Outlook

The geographic segmentation of large insurers in the Americas and Asia-Pacific can be compared to the spread of the large European insurers. Table 11.9 shows that European insurers are the most international, with 60 per cent of gross written premium abroad. While this may be largely due to the integrated European insurance market, European insurers are the most international outside the region as well, with 27 per cent of gross written premiums in the rest of the world. American insurers are catching

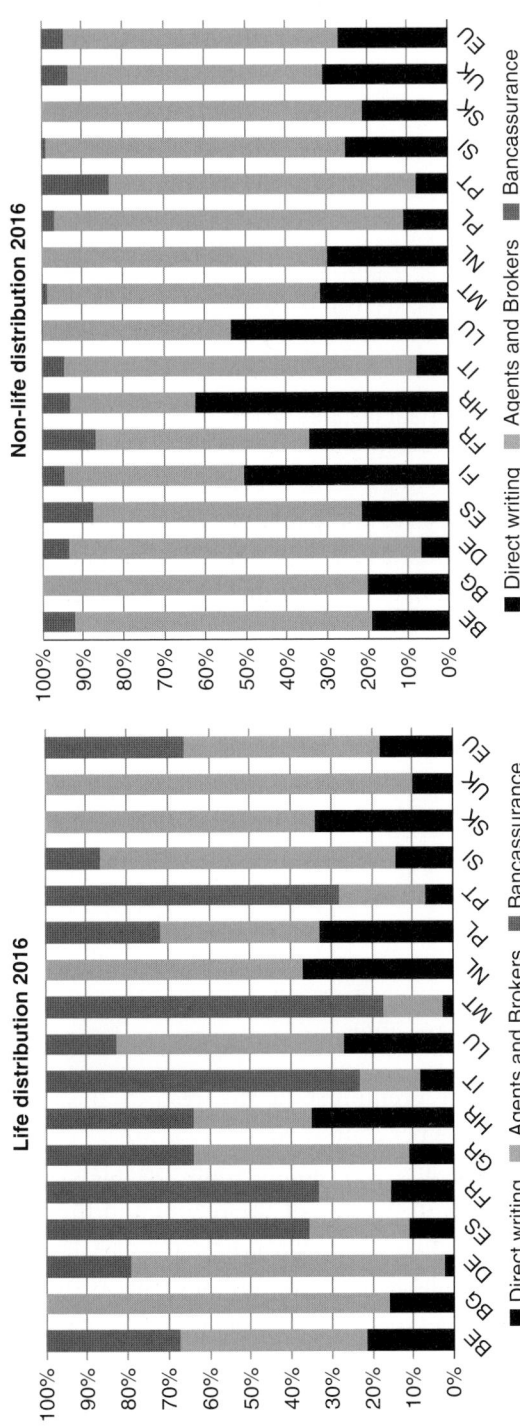

Figure 11.9 Distribution channels in Europe
Source: Insurance Europe (2018b)

Table 11.9 Development of international insurance by continent, 2000–2012

Continent	2000			2004			2008			2012		
	h	r	w	h	r	w	h	r	w	h	r	w
Europe	48	30	22	45	34	21	40	34	26	40	33	27
Americas	80	5	15	76	13	11	74	11	15	78	3	19
Asia-Pacific	–	–	–	97	1	2	95	2	3	96	2	2

Note: Share of gross written premium in home country (h), rest of the region (r), and rest of the world (w) of the top 20 insurers by continent. The shares add up to 100 per cent.
Source: Schoenmaker and Sass (2016)

Table 11.10 Global systemically important insurers, 2017

Insurance companies	Total assets in € bn	Gross written premium in € bn	Of which:		
			Domestic (%)	Region (%)	World (%)
AEGON (Netherlands)	396	23	9	46	45
Allianz (Germany)	901	77	29	47	24
AIG (US)	415	26	70	21	9
Aviva (UK)	499	31	41	44	15
AXA (France)	870	92	28	40	32
MetLife (US)	600	33	67	8	25
Ping An Insurance (China)	832	78	99	1	0
Prudential Financial (US)	693	27	60	8	32
Prudential (UK)	557	50	30	0	70
Total G-SIIs	640	48	48	25	27

Notes: Gross written premium is segmented over the home country, rest of the region, and rest of the world. Total G-SIIs (global systemically important insurers) is calculated as a weighted average (weighted according to gross written premium).
Source: Updated from Schoenmaker and Sass (2016)

up: their gross written premiums in the rest of the world rose from 15 per cent in 2000 to 19 per cent in 2012.

Asia-Pacific insurers are very domestically orientated, with combined gross written premiums in the rest of the region and the rest of the world of only 4 per cent. Similar to banking, the major Chinese insurers are beginning to dominate those from Japan within the region (see also Table 11.10). This shift reflects recent developments in the two countries' GDPs, which illustrates the link between a country's financial institutions and its overall economic performance.

Regional integration became very strong in Europe after the introduction of the single market for both banking (22 per cent in Table 10.3) and insurance (33 per cent in Table 11.9). By contrast, regional integration is very weak in the Americas and Asia-Pacific compared to business in the rest of the world.

The Financial Stability Board (2016) has produced a list of *global systemically important insurers* (G-SIIs). These insurers are the large financial players that can pose a systemic threat to the global financial system. Weiß and Mühlnickel (2014) find that insurers that were most exposed to systemic risk were on average larger, relied more heavily on non-policyholder liabilities, and had higher ratios of investment income to net revenues. Firm size appears to be the most important factor. Table 11.10 provides an overview of these G-SIIs, which have assets up to €900 billion; it includes five insurers from Europe, three from the US, and one from China. Comparing the G-SIBs in Chapter 10 and G-SIIs in this chapter, it is clear that the large systemic insurers are smaller in size and in number than the large systemic banks.

11.4 Financial Conglomerates

Financial conglomerates combine different activities, like banking and insurance. They are argued to provide three main advantages: commercial integration, financial integration, and operational integration. First, *commercial integration* relates to the cross-selling of multiple financial services to clients. The most important form of cross-selling is the provision of insurance services to a bank's customer base (called *bancassurance*). An insurer may also provide banking services to its clients (known as *assurfinance*). Sharing customer databases facilitates cross-selling, which generates economies of scope through reduced client information and transaction costs and consequently higher prices and/or transaction volumes for the financial group (Schmid and Walter, 2009).

Second, *financial integration* is an important motivation for companies to combine banking and insurance activities. There is scope for financial diversification, as the risk profile of insurance activities is different from that of banking activities (see Sections 10.2 and 11.2). The question is how stable these diversification benefits are. Diversification is particularly useful during economic downturns. The normal distribution underestimates the downside risk, since the return series of financial assets has a fat-tailed distribution. Slijkerman *et al.* (2013) apply extreme value theory, which gives a much better description of the downside risk than the normal approximation. For a sample of European financial conglomerates, they find evidence of diversification benefits (see Box 11.5).

Third, *operational integration* can produce efficiencies in the back office to generate economies of scope, for example by sharing costs, such as IT platforms and joint asset management (Schmid and Walter, 2009).

Financial conglomerates also have two primary drawbacks related to managerial complexity (Plantin and Rochet, 2007). Financial conglomerates have a diverse portfolio of business lines that require different expertise and give rise to a variety of risks. It is very demanding to manage such a diversified firm in a coherent way. The first drawback is that cross-subsidisation across business lines may lead to an inefficient allocation of capital and reduced performance. The profits from banking can be used to support underperforming insurance activities, and vice versa. Second, opaque accounts may make it difficult to determine a financial conglomerate's true risk profile. As financial institutions report on a consolidated basis, it is difficult to detangle balance-sheet items as well as profit-and-loss items between the banking and insurance businesses. This may also permit the transfer of (risky) assets within a conglomerate (Schmid and Walter, 2009).

Box 11.5 Functional or geographical diversification?

Financial firms can diversify either functionally (by combining different activities, such as banking and insurance) or geographically. Swiss Re (2007) indicates that Europe has the highest share of financial conglomerates in the world. The combination of banking and life insurance services into such conglomerates accounts for more than half of Europe's life insurance market. In North America and Asia, the penetration of financial conglomerates is much lower, partly due to the previously restrictive regulations on combining banking and insurance. In the US, the Gramm-Leach-Bliley Act of 1999 removed barriers between banks and insurance companies. The Japanese bancassurance market was fully liberalised only in 2007.

Geographic diversification aims to spread a firm's financial activities over different regions. Schoenmaker and Van Laecke (2006) show that the geographical diversification of European banks exceeds that of American and Asian banks.

Van Lelyveld and Knot (2009) find no structural discount for functional diversification, but report that large financial conglomerates appear to trade at a discount. Functional diversification is thus predominantly value destroying for larger conglomerates. Schmid and Walter (2009) report that geographically diversified financial firms trade at a small premium, indicating that this type of diversification is value enhancing.

The empirical literature finds a significant (in both statistical and economic terms) discount for non-financial conglomerates, i.e. the shares of conglomerates seem to be structurally undervalued. Although one would expect financial conglomerates to be formed mainly to create added value generated by the combination of banking and insurance, this value has thus far not been transferred to shareholders. The main arguments for this conglomerate discount are managerial complexity and the lack of focus.

Most studies of financial conglomerates focus on the US. The US definition of a financial conglomerate is a financial institution that is active in at least two of the following areas: commercial banking (lending), investment banking (capital market transactions), insurance, and asset management. In practice, most financial conglomerates combine commercial and investment banking. Schmid and Walter (2009) and Laeven and Levine (2007) report a substantial and persistent discount for US conglomerates. The market values of financial conglomerates that engage in multiple financial activities is about 10 per cent lower than those of comparable financial institutions that specialise in one of these activities.

Van Lelyveld and Knot (2009) focus on the valuation of bank–insurance conglomerates. They compare the valuation of three groups – 45 financial conglomerates, 45 banks, and 45 insurers – and find no structural diversification discount, but they observe considerable variability in the valuation. Large financial conglomerates face a larger discount, which is consistent with the hypothesis that they have more opportunities for inefficient cross-subsidisation.

On balance, financial conglomerates do not appear to represent an advantage over single-market institutions. This is in line with recent market developments of large financial conglomerates. For example, Citigroup (US) grew out of a merger between Citicorp (banking) and Travelers (insurance) in 1998. It has, however, divested most of its insurance underwriting business over the last few years. Likewise, the Swiss bank Credit Suisse formed a financial conglomerate in 1997 with its acquisition of the insurer Winterthur. However, in 2006, Credit Suisse sold Winterthur to the French insurer AXA.

The financial crisis sped up the process of divestment. The European Commission demanded that in order to be eligible for state aid, large financial groups should be downsized and split up (see Chapter 14). The leading Belgian financial conglomerate Fortis was split on product and geographic lines in 2008. The Dutch banking and insurance businesses were separately nationalised by the Dutch government, while the Belgian–Luxembourg banking business was sold to BNP Paribas and the insurance part continued under the name Ageas. In 2013 and 2014, ING sold off its insurance business. Finally, the smallish Dutch conglomerate SNS Reaal was also forced to separate its bank

Table 11.11 Share of financial conglomerates in banking and insurance (%), 2015

Countries	Banking	Insurance
Austria	24	37
Belgium	40	22
Denmark	43	17
Finland	19	82
France	88	22
Germany	27	28
Italy	19	47
Malta	15	0
Netherlands	17	59
Spain	14	3
Sweden	45	27
United Kingdom	10	17
EU-28	31	36

Notes: The table indicates the percentage of banks and insurers in various EU countries that belong to a financial conglomerate. The percentage for the EU is calculated as a weighted average for all 28 EU countries (weighted by banking and insurance assets).
Source: Schoenmaker and Véron (2020)

(SNS) and insurer (Reaal) after it was nationalised in 2013. Reaal, renamed Vivat, was sold in 2015 to the Chinese Anbang Insurance Group.

Financial conglomeration is facilitated by the strong demand for long-term savings products. Growth opportunities in life insurance and pension products have encouraged banks towards these areas, while insurers have established banking subsidiaries to offer bank-type savings products to their clients. Figure 11.9 indicates that the market share of financial conglomerates in distributing life insurance is 34 per cent in selected countries, where bank distribution channels are effective. Spain, France, Italy, and Portugal, in particular, have large financial conglomerates combining banking and life insurance. Examples include BNP Paribas with BNP Paribas Cardif for insurance, and Crédit Agricole with Crédit Agricole Assurances (see Tables 10.2 and 11.7). Penetration in non-life insurance is less pronounced: the market share of financial conglomerates in the distribution of non-life insurance is only 5 per cent.

Table 11.11 shows that financial conglomerates have a substantial presence in the largest EU countries. In Germany, France, and Italy, they comprise

20–90 per cent of the banking and insurance sectors. At the EU level, 31 per cent of banks and 36 per cent of insurers belong to a financial conglomerate.

11.5 Conclusions

Insurance seeks to protect individuals and firms from the financial consequences of adverse events by pooling risks. The business lines are very diverse. Non-life insurance includes car, health, property, and liability insurance, while life insurance provides financial cover for premature death or retirement. Insurance companies collect premiums today and make payments if adverse events happen in the future. Insurance is thus a risky business. This chapter has shown that the pattern of small claims, such as fire or car accidents, is fairly predictable. But larger accidents or catastrophes (like hurricanes) involve high-value claims with a low probability. Since the risk of catastrophes is too large for a single insurance company, it is divided among different insurance and re-insurance companies. Insurance companies tend to centralise risk management using internal risk management models. Insurers and banks are converging with regard to risk management systems and practices.

The insurance markets vary considerably across Europe. Life insurance is prominent in the EU-15 and can be considered a luxury good, while non-life insurance is more evenly spread across the EU and is regarded as a necessary good. The figures indicate that the level of cross-border insurance remains high in the EU, notwithstanding a small decrease after the financial crisis.

Insurance is sold through a variety of distribution channels. A growing share of insurance products is sold directly through the Internet or by employees of an insurance company. Insurance intermediaries such as brokers and agents play a dominant role, which is expected to decrease for simple non-life insurances. A final distribution channel for insurance products is bancassurance.

Financial conglomerates combining banking and insurance cover 31 per cent of the banking and 36 per cent of the insurance markets in Europe. An important driver of financial conglomerates is the cross-selling of insurance products to banking customers. Another driver is the benefits of financial diversification, as the risk profiles are quite different for banking and insurance activities. However, this chapter also indicates that it may be difficult for managers to run a diversified firm with different business lines.

Notes

1. Re-insurance is also used for two other purposes. First, it can be used to increase an insurer's underwriting capacity by allowing the insurer to pass on part of the risk. Second, it can be used to stabilise profits, by helping the insurer to level out the effects of poor loss performance.
2. To assess the overall risk profile of an insurance company, correlations across risk types should be taken into account, but incorporating diversification effects between risk types is still in the early stages (Van Lelyveld, 2006).
3. Bonds are also subject to credit risk. The credit risk of government bonds issued by developed countries is typically very low, while that of corporate bonds is usually higher.

Bibliography

Suggested Reading

Dionne, G. (ed.) (2000), *Handbook of Insurance*, Kluwer, Dordrecht.

Drzik, J. (2005), At the Crossroads of Change: Risk and Capital Management in the Insurance Industry. *The Geneva Papers on Risk and Insurance – Issues and Practice*, 30, 72–87.

Mikosch, T. (2004), *Non-Life Insurance Mathematics: An Introduction with Stochastic Processes*, Springer-Verlag, Berlin.

Rees, R. (2008), Insurance and Re-insurance Companies. In: X. Freixas, P. Hartmann, and C. Mayer (eds.), *Handbook of European Financial Markets and Institutions*, Oxford University Press, 414–35.

References

Association des Assureurs Coopératifs et Mutualistes Européens (2003), *Valuing Mutuality II*, ACME, Brussels.

Dimson, E., P. Marsh, and M. Staunton (2002), *Triumph of the Optimists: 101 Years of Global Investment Returns*, Princeton University Press.

Drzik, J. (2005), At the Crossroads of Change: Risk and Capital Management in the Insurance Industry. *The Geneva Papers on Risk and Insurance – Issues and Practice*, 30, 72–87.

Embrechts, P., C. Klüppelberg, and T. Mikosch (1997), *Modelling Extremal Events for Insurance and Finance*, Springer, Heidelberg.

European Commission (2007), *Business Insurance Sector Inquiry: Interim Report*, EC, Brussels.

European Insurance and Occupational Pensions Supervisors Authority (2013), *Discussion Paper on Standard Formula Design and Calibration for Certain Long-Term Investments*, EIOPA, Frankfurt am Main.

(2017), *Investment Behaviour Report*, EIOPA, Frankfurt am Main.

Financial Stability Board (2016), *2016 List of Global Systemically Important Insurers (G-SIIs)*, FSB, Basel.

Focarelli, D. and A. F. Pozzolo (2008), Cross-Border M&As in the Financial Sector: Is Banking Different from Insurance? *Journal of Banking and Finance*, 32, 15–29.

Insurance Europe (2018a), *European Insurance – Key Facts*, Insurance Europe, Brussels. (2018b), *European Insurance in Figures*, Insurance Europe, Brussels.

Kessler, D. (2008), Insurance Market Mechanisms and Government Interventions. *Journal of Banking and Finance*, 32, 4–14.

Kuritzkes, A., T. Schuermann, and S. Weiner (2003), Risk Measurement, Risk Management, and Capital Adequacy in Financial Conglomerates. In: R. Herring and R. Litan (eds.), *Brookings-Wharton Papers on Financial Services: 2003*, Brookings Institution, Washington, DC, 141–93.

Laeven, L. and R. Levine (2007), Is There a Diversification Discount in Financial Conglomerates? *Journal of Financial Economics*, 85, 331–67.

Loubergé, H. (2000), Developments in Risk and Insurance Economics: The Past 25 Years. In: G. Dionne (ed.), *Handbook of Insurance*, Kluwer, Dordrecht, 3–33.

Mikosch, T. (2004), *Non-Life Insurance Mathematics: An Introduction with Stochastic Processes*, Springer-Verlag, Berlin.

Niehaus, G. and A. Terry (1993), Evidence on the Time Series Properties of Insurance Premiums and Causes of the Underwriting Cycle, *Journal of Risk and Insurance*, 60, 466–79.

Oliver, Wyman and Company (2001), *Study on the Risk Profile and Capital Adequacy of Financial Conglomerates*, Oliver, Wyman and Company, London.

Plantin, G. and J.-C. Rochet (2007), *When Insurers Go Bust: An Economic Analysis of the Role and Design of Prudential Regulation*, Princeton University Press.

Rejda, G. E. (2005), *Principles of Risk Management and Insurance*, 9th edition, Addison-Wesley, Boston (MA).

Rothschild, M. and J. Stiglitz (1976), Equilibrium in Competitive Insurance Markets: An Essay on the Economics of Imperfect Information. *Quarterly Journal of Economics*, 90, 629–49.

Schmid, M. M. and I. Walter (2009), Do Financial Conglomerates Create or Destroy Economic Value? *Journal of Financial Intermediation*, 18, 193–216.

Schoenmaker, D., S. Oosterloo, and O. Winkels (2008), The Emergence of Cross-Border Insurance Groups within Europe with Centralised Risk Management. *Geneva Papers on Risk and Insurance – Issues and Practice*, 33, 530–46.

Schoenmaker, D. and J. Sass (2016), Cross-Border Insurance in Europe: Challenges for Supervision, *Geneva Papers on Risk and Insurance – Issues and Practice*, 41, 351–77.

Schoenmaker, D. and C. van Laecke (2006), Current State of Cross-Border Banking. FMG Special Papers 168, London School of Economics, London.

Schoenmaker, D. and N. Véron (2020), A Twin Peaks Vision for Europe. In: A. Godwin and A. Schmulow (eds), *The Cambridge Handbook of Twin Peaks Financial Regulation*, Cambridge University Press, forthcoming.

Slijkerman, J. F., D. Schoenmaker, and C. G. de Vries (2013), Systemic Risk and Diversification across Banks and Insurers. *Journal of Banking and Finance*, 37, 773–85.

Spencer, P. D. (2000), *The Structure and Regulation of Financial Markets*, Oxford University Press.

Swiss Re (1998), *Floods – An Insurable Risk? A Market Survey*, Swiss Re, Zurich.

(2007), Bancassurance: Emerging Trends, Opportunities and Challenges. *Sigma*, 5.

(2018), Natural Catastrophes and Man-Made Disasters in 2017. *Sigma*, 1.

Van Lelyveld, I. (ed.) (2006), *Economic Capital Modelling: Concepts, Measurement and Implementation*, Risk Books, London.

Van Lelyveld, I. and K. Knot (2009), Do Financial Conglomerates Create or Destroy Value? Evidence for the EU. *Journal of Banking and Finance*, 33, 2312–21.

Von Bomhard, N. (2005), Risk and Capital Management in Insurance Companies. *The Geneva Papers on Risk and Insurance – Issues and Practice*, 30, 52–9.

Weiβ, G. and J. Mühlnickel (2014), Why Do Some Insurers Become Systemically Relevant? *Journal of Financial Stability*, 13, 95–117.

Part IV

Policies for the Financial Sector

12

Financial Regulation and Supervision

OVERVIEW

This chapter reviews the reasons for regulating and supervising the financial services industry. Regulation refers to the process of rule making and the legislation underlying the supervisory framework, while supervision involves monitoring the behaviour of individual firms and enforcing legislation. The case for government intervention is based on market failures. A first market failure is rooted in asymmetric information: financial institutions are generally better informed than their customers. A second market failure involves externalities: the failure of a financial institution may affect the stability of the entire financial system. A third market failure occurs when certain players in the market exert undue market power.

The chapter distinguishes between prudential supervision and conduct-of-business supervision. Prudential supervision aims to protect consumers by ensuring the safety and soundness of financial institutions. For instance, information provisions are designed to ensure that consumers get the right information about financial products. In addition, there are guidelines for objective and high-quality advice to protect customers' interests. Conduct-of-business supervision focuses on how financial institutions deal with their customers and how financial institutions behave in markets. Conduct-of-business rules also promote fair and orderly markets.

Finally, the chapter discusses financial supervision in the EU, including whether national-based supervision is appropriate in an integrating market. The European supervisory structure and the Banking Union are explained, followed by a discussion of several challenges that supervisors face.

LEARNING OBJECTIVES

After you have studied this chapter, you should be able to:

* explain the main market failures in the financial system and the role of government intervention in remedying these failures

- understand the aims and instruments of prudential supervision
- analyse the European microprudential requirements for banks and insurers
- understand the aims and instruments of conduct-of-business supervision
- understand the Banking Union and the need for European financial supervision in an integrated financial market.

12.1 Rationale for Government Intervention

Market Failure

This section reviews the reasons for regulating and supervising the financial services industry. Regulation refers to the process of rule making and the legislation underlying the supervisory framework, while supervision involves monitoring the behaviour of individual firms and enforcing legislation. The case for government intervention is based on *market failures*, which occur when the private sector, if left to itself (i.e. without government intervention) would produce a sub-optimal outcome. Goodhart *et al.* (1998) identify three main reasons for government intervention in the financial sector:

1. *Asymmetric information.* Financial supervision aims to protect customers from being less informed than financial institutions. This chapter analyses how this can be done.
2. *Externalities.* The failure of a financial institution may affect the stability of the entire financial system. Macroprudential policy aims to foster financial stability and to contain the effects of systemic failure. Chapter 13 discusses policies designed to maintain financial stability.
3. *Market power.* Financial institutions or financial infrastructures, such as payment systems, may exert undue market power. Competition policy aims to protect consumers against monopolistic exploitation. Chapter 14 examines this topic.

Why is asymmetric information a rationale for government intervention? Asymmetric information arises in two cases. First, customers generally lack the technical knowledge and time required to properly assess the safety and soundness of a financial institution. Yet given the temptation financial institutions face to make high-risk investments in an attempt to achieve higher returns, some sort of oversight may be needed. Indeed, if a bank fails, a substantial part of the losses will be borne by others (i.e. depositors). Information asymmetry creates problems of adverse selection (a riskier financial institution may make a more attractive offer to potential customers) as well as moral hazard (a financial institution may increase its risk after it has collected funds from customers). The state is the agent that represents the interests of depositors and policyholders who lack the expertise, information, and incentives to monitor financial institutions' balance-sheet and off-balance-sheet activities (Dewatripont and Tirole, 1994). Therefore banks, insurance companies, and pension funds are all subject to prudential requirements, while financial institutions without retail investors are not. Prudential supervision aims to protect customers by ensuring the soundness of financial institutions. Moreover, governments provide direct protection to bank depositors through deposit guarantee schemes with a cover of €100,000 in the EU (see Chapter 3). However, a government safety net may provide banks with an even stronger incentive for risky behaviour. Prudential supervision is thus also needed to counter this incentive by ensuring the banks' soundness (Mishkin, 2000). Sections 12.2 and 12.3 discuss prudential supervision for banks and insurance companies in more detail.

The second case in which asymmetric information arises is that customers may not be able to properly assess the behaviour of a financial institution. This problem is common in professional services (Goodhart *et al.*, 1998). In most cases, private sector mechanisms are used to mitigate this principal–agent problem. The disciplinary body of a privately run medical association can, for example, expel a member who (repeatedly) fails to meet the minimum standards of the medical profession. Why, then, is government supervision of financial services needed? An important explanation draws on the fiduciary nature of financial services. A customer hands over his or her money today, while the service is rendered in the (sometimes distant) future. For example, only after retirement does it become clear whether the recommended pension savings scheme is appropriate to meet the financial needs of the retirees. Moreover, the amount of money at risk is typically larger in financial services than in other professional services. Conduct-of-business supervision focuses on how financial institutions conduct business with their customers and how they behave in markets. Section 12.4 discusses conduct-of-business rules.

In addition to asymmetric information, a second market failure may give rise to government regulation – externalities. There is a risk that a sound financial institution may fail when another financial institution goes bankrupt (spillover effects). This externality is not incorporated into the decision making of the (failing) financial institution. The social costs of a financial institution's failure thus exceed the private costs. Banks are particularly vulnerable to spillover effects, as their balance sheets contain illiquid assets financed by redeemable deposits. When rumours about the quality of banks' assets spread due to the failure of another bank, depositors may withdraw their money. The liquidity, and subsequently the solvency, of these banks will be threatened when they have to liquidate their assets at fire sale prices (i.e. prices well below prices under normal market conditions). The failure of multiple banks may lead to a banking crisis. Macroprudential supervision thus aims to foster financial stability and to contain the effects of systemic failure. The task of maintaining financial stability is usually assigned to a country's central bank. Chapter 13 explains in more detail why the financial system (and especially the banking sector) is more susceptible to systemic risk than other economic sectors and discusses policies used to contain systemic risk.

A third market failure is related to market power. In economic sectors with a monopoly (only one firm) or oligopoly (a few firms that may collude), firms can raise and maintain prices above the level that would prevail under (perfect) competition. Firms' exercise of market power harms consumers, who face higher prices and less choice of products or services. Many economic sectors lack competition. In the financial sector, economies of scale (incentive for mergers) and network economies (e.g. in payment systems (see Chapter 7) or stock exchanges (see Chapter 5)) may reduce competition. Competition policy therefore aims to ensure effective competition by taking a strong line against price fixing, market-sharing cartels, abuse of dominant market positions, and anti-competitive mergers. Chapter 14 explains the EU competition policy for the financial sector.

Government Failure

The presence of market failures does not imply that government intervention is warranted, as the government may fail as well. *Government failure* occurs when government intervention causes a less efficient allocation of goods and resources than would occur without that intervention. Thus the problems of government failure must be weighed against those caused by market failure (Besley, 2007). Government intervention has three main consequences. First, government-induced protection may have a detrimental impact on incentives for consumers. Why should consumers be careful if they are protected against the possible negative outcomes of their actions? Second, government regulation may lead to bureaucracy ('red tape') that restricts the activities of financial institutions. Third, supervisory agencies need information in order to monitor the financial system; the elaborate system of supervisory reporting places a heavy administrative burden on the sector.

Some academics believe government failure is a bigger problem than market failure. For instance, adherents of free banking challenge the justification for any form of government regulation of the financial system. They argue that the financial services industry does not merit an exception to the general rule of free trade (see, for instance, Dowd, 1996). In their view, a *laissez-faire* policy for the financial sector is optimal, as government intervention undermines the market forces that make the financial system safe. Other academics favour limited government intervention. For instance, Benston and Kaufman (1996) advocate minimum prudential standards (particularly capital requirements) to counter externalities, but argue that beyond these standards there is no special need to protect customers. However, most academics and policy makers believe independent financial supervisors are a better way to minimise distortive political interventions (see Box 12.1).

Box 12.1 Supervisory independence

According to Quintyn and Taylor (2003), political interference in the supervisory process was a major factor contributing to the weakening of banks in the run-up to almost all systemic financial sector crises of the 1990s. There are several reasons why the independence of supervisors from political interference may be beneficial for maintaining financial stability. First, independence may help to overcome an *inaction bias*: the incentives for politicians to rescue failing banks are similar to those for inaction in the face of inflation (Quintyn and Taylor, 2003). The decision to close a failing bank is usually unpopular, as costs must be incurred in the short term in order to make long-term gains, which makes forbearance an attractive option (see Box 12.2). Inaction bias may also be caused by uncertainty, which encourages policy makers to prefer to make a type-1 mistake (incorrectly assuming that things will work out well) than a type-2 mistake (incorrectly assuming that things will go wrong). Furthermore, politicians who are eager to avoid a necessary closure may be tempted to pressure supervisors to organise a bailout or to excuse the failing bank from regulatory requirements, even at the risk of worsening the problem and increasing the long-term costs of resolving it.

A second reason why an independent financial supervisor may be beneficial is that there are multiple values and interests at stake in financial market regulation. Politicians may, for instance, want to boost the position of the national financial industry, and pressure the supervisor to take a lenient approach towards national financial firms (Pagliari, 2012). This argument in favour of supervisory independence is comparable to that relating to monetary decisions (see Chapter 4). The regulating authority's independent status is an important means of ensuring that it is at all times able to take the required action. However, there is also the risk that an independent agency might pursue its own agenda, going against the wishes of the political majority, which highlights the need for proper forms of transparency and accountability (see Section 12.5).

12.2 Microprudential Supervision: Banks

Within the EU, a financial institution is authorised and supervised in its home country and can expand throughout the EU by offering cross-border services in other Member States or establishing branches in these countries without additional supervision by host-country authorities (*home-country control*). The host country has to recognise supervision from the home-country authorities (*mutual recognition*), as EU directives have established minimum requirements for prudential supervision (*minimum standards*). However, financial institutions also operate through subsidiaries (separate legal entities) in other countries for reasons of taxation and limited liability (Dermine, 2006). These subsidiaries are separately licensed and supervised by the host-country authorities. Within the Banking Union, the European Central Bank (ECB) is responsible for granting and, where necessary, withdrawing the authorisation of credit institutions.

According to Lastra (2006), *microprudential supervision* is a process with four stages:

1. Licensing, authorisation, or chartering of financial institutions (i.e. entry into the business). Before a person can obtain a licence, supervisors assess their integrity, honesty, reputation, and ability to manage a financial services provider. The Basel core principles for effective banking supervision state that 'the licensing process at a minimum should consist of an assessment of the ownership structure and governance of the bank and its wider group, including the fitness and propriety of Board Members and senior management, its strategic and operating plan, internal controls and risk management, and its projected financial condition, including its capital base' (BIS, 2006).

2. Ongoing monitoring of the health of financial institutions and the financial system, in particular the asset quality, capital adequacy, liquidity, large exposures, management, internal controls, and earnings. Supervision is exercised through a broad range of instruments, including off-site and on-site examinations (or inspections), auditing (internal unpublished audits and external published audits), analysis of statistical requirements, and internal controls. In case of distress in financial institutions, the supervisory authorities have to act. Box 12.2 discusses two different reactions to distress.

3. Sanctioning or imposition of penalties in case of non-compliance with the law, fraud, bad management, or other types of wrongdoing.

4. Crisis management, which comprises the lender of last resort, deposit insurance, and insolvency proceedings (see Chapter 13).

Box 12.2 Forbearance versus prompt corrective action

Once a supervisory authority finds out that a financial institution is in distress, there are two possible ways it can react. First, it can take *prompt corrective action* (PCA) to resolve the distressed institution by requiring capital injections, the sale of assets, a merger with a sound institution, or liquidation once the regulatory capital ratio falls below a predetermined threshold. Alternatively, the supervisor can choose *forbearance* – i.e. allow the distressed financial institution to continue operation even though it is unable to meet the minimum regulatory requirements. Forbearance may dilute banks' incentives to behave prudently and induce undue liquidity support.

Given the emergence of large cross-border banking groups, the European Shadow Financial Regulatory Committee (2005) advocates implementing a PCA system in Europe similar to that in the US. These procedures would reduce the likelihood of a sudden banking crisis and increase host-country supervisors' trust in home-country supervisors.

Nieto and Wall (2007) identify three important aspects of the philosophy underlying PCA: (1) the primary focus of banking supervisory authorities should be on protecting the deposit insurance fund and minimising government losses; (2) banking supervisors should have a clear set of required actions to take as a bank becomes progressively more undercapitalised; and (3) any undercapitalised bank should be closed before the economic value of its capital becomes negative. Moreover, the authors identify several institutional prerequisites for PCA: supervisory independence and accountability, adequate authority, accurate and timely information, and adequate resolution procedures.

According to the BIS (1997), banks face the following key risks (see Chapter 10 for an in-depth discussion):

- *credit risk:* the risk of a loss due to the failure of a counterparty to perform according to a contractual arrangement, for instance due to a default by a borrower;
- *country risk:* the risks associated with the economic, social, and political environment of the borrower's home country;
- *market risk:* the risk due to unfavourable movements in market prices;
- *interest rate risk:* the risk related to unfavourable movements in interest rates. This risk impacts both a bank's earnings and the economic value of its assets, liabilities, and off-balance-sheet instruments;
- *liquidity risk:* this risk arises when a bank has insufficient liquid resources to meet a surge in liquidity demand. In extreme cases, insufficient liquidity can lead to the insolvency of a bank;

- *operational risk:* the risk of loss from inadequate or failed internal processes, people or systems, or from external events;[1]
- *legal risk:* risks stemming from inadequate or incorrect legal advice, changes in laws affecting the bank, new types of transactions, etc.;
- *reputational risk:* this may arise from operational failures, a failure to comply with relevant laws and regulations, or other sources. Reputational risk is particularly damaging in banking, as customer trust is crucial.

Basel III

To cover the risks mentioned above, banks are required to comply with several regulatory ratios. These ratios aim to ensure that banks hold a minimum level of their own financial resources (i.e. *capital*) and a minimum level of liquid assets and stable funding (i.e. *liquidity*). The most important element of the regulatory framework consists of the minimum capital requirements for credit risk, as this is the main risk in banking (Chapter 10). The Basel Committee on Banking Supervision (BCBS) negotiated these rules. It is the primary global standard setter for the prudential regulation of banks, and provides an international forum for cooperation on banking supervisory matters (see Box 3.5).

The Basel III reforms were completed in two phases. The first phase was initiated after the global financial crises; an agreement was reached in 2011 that increased the level of capital, improved the quality of capital, and introduced additional regulatory capital and liquidity requirements, which are discussed below. Within the EU, these rules have been implemented through the Capital Requirements Regulation (CRR; 575/2013/EU) and the Capital Requirements Directive IV (CRD IV; 2013/36/EU), which went into effect on 1 January 2014. The final phase of Basel III was completed in December 2017. It sought to restore the credibility of risk-weighted capital requirements by limiting the extent to which banks can rely on internal models. Overall, the Basel III compromise leads to a mix of relatively complex risk-weighted regulatory ratios complemented by simple non-risk-weighted backstops.

The current set-up results from the evolution of the different capital accords. The Basel I accord, concluded in 1988, introduced a minimum regulatory capital constraint of 8 per cent, subject to a simple risk-weighting structure. Basel II responded to industry demands for a more refined approach, based on internal models, so it could partly determine its own regulatory capital requirements. The mixed approach of Basel III builds on the lessons learned from the financial crisis, in which these more complex risk-weighted measures performed poorly in response to large and unexpected tail risks. Overall, risk-sensitive and insensitive measures have their pros and cons. The former can provide a granular calculation of capital for risks that can be measured, while the latter address model risk and risks that are difficult to quantify.

The current Basel III accord follows the three-pillar structure of the Basel II accord:

- The first pillar covers the minimum capital requirements for credit risk, operational risk, and market risk. This pillar contains the risk-weighted capital ratio, leverage ratio, liquidity coverage ratio and net stable funding ratio (see below).
- The second pillar (supervisory review) requires supervisory authorities to examine the bank's activities and risk profile to assess their need to hold additional capital (in addition to the level of capital calculated under Pillar 1).
- The third pillar aims to enhance market discipline by increasing the transparency of the amount and composition of a bank's capital relative to its risk profile, thereby introducing incentives for banks to conduct their business in a safe, sound, and efficient manner.

The minimum capital requirements in the first pillar serve as a buffer against unexpected losses, thereby protecting depositors and the overall stability of the financial system. The challenge is to determine how much capital banks need to hold in order to ensure that they are sufficiently capitalised.[2] If capital levels are too low, banks may be unable to absorb potential losses. The risk-weighted capital requirement (RWCR) specifies how much capital banks need to hold against risk-weighted assets. Using *risk-weighted assets* (RWAs) in this calculation represents a move from a static capital requirement to a requirement based on the riskiness of a bank's asset classes i. The minimum RWCR is:

$$RWCR = \frac{Capital}{Risk\ Weighted\ Assets} = \frac{Capital}{\sum_{i=1}^{n} Risk\ Weight_i * Assets\ Class_i} \geq 8\%$$

$$(12.1)$$

The first element is the numerator, i.e. the required level of regulatory capital to cover unexpected losses. There are two types of capital:

- *Going concern capital*: this allows an institution to continue its activities and helps to prevent insolvency. It consists of Common Equity Tier 1 (CET1) capital and Additional Tier 1 capital. CET1 is the most loss-absorbing form of capital. It consists of common shares, retained earnings, and other reserves (BCBS, 2017a). Additional Tier 1 capital comprises continuous capital instruments, i.e. they have no fixed maturity. This type of capital includes preferred shares and contingent convertible securities (CoCos). CoCos are meant to be a relatively cheap form of capital, as they only function as capital when it is needed the most, i.e. when there are severe losses. CoCos can be converted into common equity, or suffer from a write-down, but only after a trigger has been pulled. According to CRD IV, the conversion trigger must at least be 5.125 per cent of CET1. This implies that the trigger is rather low, given that such an event is extremely rare.

- *Gone concern capital:* this helps to ensure that depositors and senior creditors can be repaid if the institution fails. This category of capital consists of undisclosed reserves, revaluation reserves, general loan-loss provisions, hybrid instruments, and subordinated debt.

The second element is the denominator – RWAs – which serve as a proxy for the potential to generate unexpected losses. To calculate risk weights for each asset class i, a standardised approach or internal models can be used subject to supervisory approval. A key part of the Basel III reforms is to limit the use of internal models. RWAs calculated using internal models should not be lower than 72.5 per cent of the RWAs as calculated using the standardised approach.

This so-called output floor was introduced for two reasons due to the poor performance of risk weights as *ex ante* indicators of risk during the financial crisis. First, a range of studies shows that simple non-risk leverage ratios (LRs) more accurately predicted bank failure than RWCRs during the global financial crisis (see ESRB, 2015: 13). Second, several studies find a wide variation in RWAs across banks that cannot be explained by differences in the riskiness of their portfolios (BCBS, 2017a). Reforms were therefore needed to restore the credibility of the risk-based capital framework. The new output floor will be phased in very gradually, with half of it to be implemented by 2022 and full implementation by 1 January 2027.

The standardised approach sets risk weights by exposure class. For example, for an exposure of €100, a risk weight of 50 per cent implies that the RWAs are €50. For a minimal capital ratio of 8 per cent, the minimum required regulatory capital would be €4. Basel III sets risk weights for all exposure classes i, which include banks, covered bonds, corporates, project finance, retail exposures, residential real estate exposures, commercial real estate exposures, subordinated debt, and equity (BCBS, 2017b).

Table 12.1 Standardised approach: corporate credit and residential real estate

External rating of counterparty	AAA to AA−	A+ to A−	BBB+ to BBB−	BB+ to BB−	Below BB−	Unrated
Risk weight	20%	50%	75%	100%	150%	100% (85% if corporate SME)
LTV bands	Below 50%	50% to 60%	60% to 80%	80% to 90%	90% to 100%	Above 100%
Risk weight	20%	25%	30%	40%	50%	70%

Notes: The top rows indicate the risk weights for corporate credit and the bottom rows for residential real estate. LTV = loan to value; SME = small or medium-sized enterprise.
Source: adapted from BCBS (2017b)

Table 12.1 provides an example of the risk weights for credit exposures to corporates and residential real estate. The risk weight for corporates depends on their external rating: the lower the rating, the higher the risk weight. Basel III is designed to reduce reliance on external ratings, as it requires banks to conduct sufficient due diligence when using them. Moreover, it facilitates a more detailed risk weighting for commercial and residential real estate (BCBS, 2017a). Table 12.1 shows how risk weights for residential real estate now vary with the loan-to-value ratio of the mortgage.

To estimate their required amount of economic capital, banks may use their own internal models, as discussed in Chapter 10. Basel II allowed the use of such models to calculate regulatory capital requirements, subject to quality requirements, to align the regulatory framework with advances in industry practices. Banks were rewarded for using internal models, as it would lead to a lower capital requirement. This was supposed to incentivise banks to improve their risk management practices. However, it also implied that banks could, to some extent, set their own capital requirements. Some analysts believed that banks that try to maximise their return on equity would be incentivised to manage their RWAs down, for example by concentrating on investments that are treated as safe, such as sovereign exposures (which have a zero-risk weight), or by using derivatives to shift risks off their balance sheet.

For major global banks, the risk weights fell almost continuously from 70 per cent in 1993 to below 40 per cent at the start of the financial crisis in 2008 (BoE, 2014). This decrease in risk weights and capital requirements before the crisis has partly been attributed to the pro-cyclical nature of credit risk models based on limited sample periods. In good times, losses are low, so measured risk is low. In response, the Basel III reforms aim to restore the credibility of the risk-weighted framework. In addition to the output floor, it

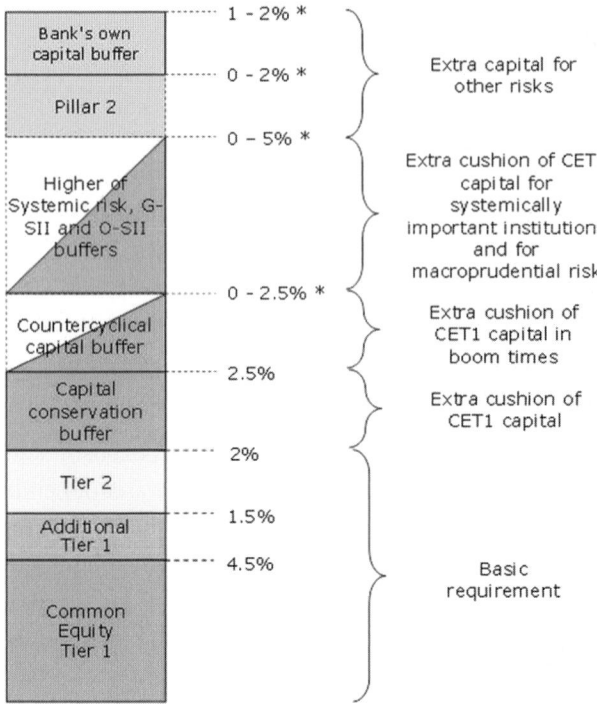

* Assumed upper bounds (values can be higher)

Figure 12.1   CCR/CRD IV capital framework
Source: European Commission (2013)

also places limits on inputs to the models and prohibits using internal models to assess risk that is hard to measure, such as operational risk (BCBS, 2017b).

The 1988 Basel I Accord required banks to ensure that 8 per cent of the RWAs on their balance sheet are backed by own funds. This percentage has not been changed under Basel II and III or CRR/CRD IV. However, Basel III changes the *composition* of the minimum regulatory capital requirement. The minimum requirement for CET1 capital has been increased from 2 per cent to 4.5 per cent, while total Tier 1 capital should be 6 per cent. Tier 2 capital should be at least 2 per cent. Furthermore, several new buffers have been introduced (see Box 12.3). Figure 12.1 presents an overview of the new capital framework, including the new capital buffers.

Figure 12.2 presents an overview of the RWCRs in EU countries, which include the new capital buffers. The average for the EU as a whole as of June 2018 was 16.0 per cent. The figure illustrates the wide differences across countries. Relatively low risk-weighted buffers exist in Spain (13.0 per cent),

Box 12.3 Capital buffers in CRR/CRD IV

Capital Conservation Buffer

The capital conservation buffer is a capital buffer of 2.5 per cent of a bank's total exposures that must be met with an additional amount of the highest-quality capital (i.e. CET1 capital). The capital conservation buffer is in addition to the 4.5 per cent CET1 capital requirement. As its name indicates, the buffer's objective is to conserve a bank's capital. When a bank breaches the buffer, i.e. when its CET1 capital ratio falls below 7 per cent, automatic safeguards kick in and limit the amount of dividend and bonus payments a bank can make. The further the bank 'eats' into the buffer, the stricter the limits become. This prevents the bank's capital from being further eroded by such payments.

Countercyclical Buffer

The countercyclical buffer is designed to counteract the effects of the economic cycle on banks' lending activity, thus making the supply of credit less volatile and possibly even reducing the probability of credit bubbles or crunches. In good times, i.e. when an economy is booming and credit growth is strong, the buffer requires a bank to maintain an additional 0–2.5 per cent of CET1 capital to prevent credit from becoming so cheap that banks lend too much. If a bank lacks sufficient capital to fill this buffer, the same restrictions as for the capital conservation buffer kick in. When the economic cycle turns, and economic activity slows down or even contracts, this buffer can be 'released' (i.e. the bank is no longer required to have the additional capital). This allows the bank to keep lending to the real economy or at least reduce its lending by less than would otherwise be the case.

Global Systemic Institution Buffer

CRD IV includes a mandatory systemic risk buffer of 1–3.5 per cent CET1 capital for globally systemically important banks, which are identified based on G20 criteria that include a financial institution's size, cross-border activities, and interconnectedness (see Chapters 10 and 13). This buffer was implemented on 1 January 2016.

Other Systemically Important Institutions Buffer

CRD IV provides a supervisory option for a buffer on 'other' systemically important institutions. This includes domestically important institutions as well as EU-important institutions. In order to prevent adverse impacts on the internal market, there is framing

> **Box 12.3** (cont.)
>
> in the form of the criteria used to identify these institutions, a notification/justification procedure, and an upper limit on the size of the buffer (2 per cent of RWAs).
>
> ## Systemic Risk Buffer
>
> Each Member State may introduce a systemic risk buffer of CET1 for the financial sector, or one or more subsets of the sector, in order to prevent and mitigate long-term non-cyclical systemic or macroprudential risks that may have serious negative consequences for its financial system and real economy. Since 2015, Member States setting a buffer of 3–5 per cent are required to notify the European Commission, the European Banking Authority (EBA) (see below), and the European Systemic Risk Board (ESRB) (see Chapter 13). The Commission provides an opinion on the measure decided, and if this opinion is negative, the Member States will have to 'comply or explain'. Buffer rates above 5 per cent must be authorised by the Commission through an implementing act, taking into account the opinions provided by the ESRB and EBA.
>
> *Source:* European Commission (2013)

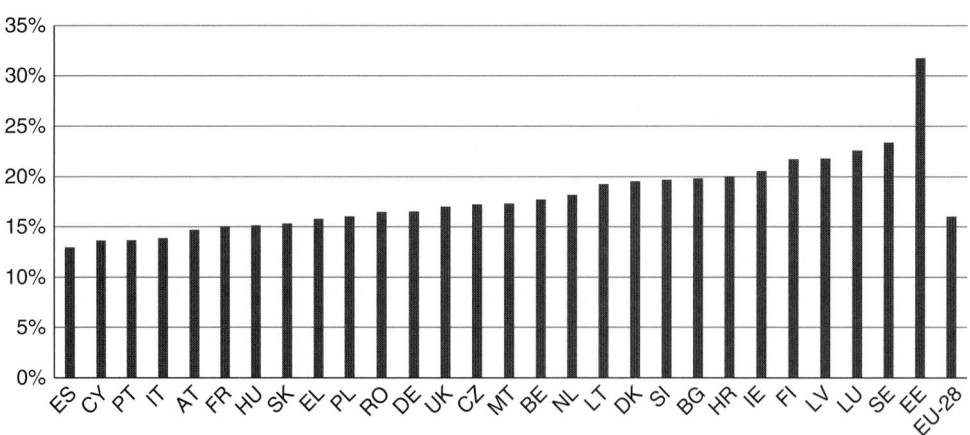

Figure 12.2   Actual risk-weighted capital ratios, 2018
Note: EU-28 is a weighted average.
Source: European Banking Authority (2018), data as of June 2018

Cyprus (13.6 per cent), Portugal (13.7 per cent), and Italy (13.9 per cent). The highest buffers are in Sweden (23.4 per cent) and Estonia (31.8 per cent, which is due to tax reasons).

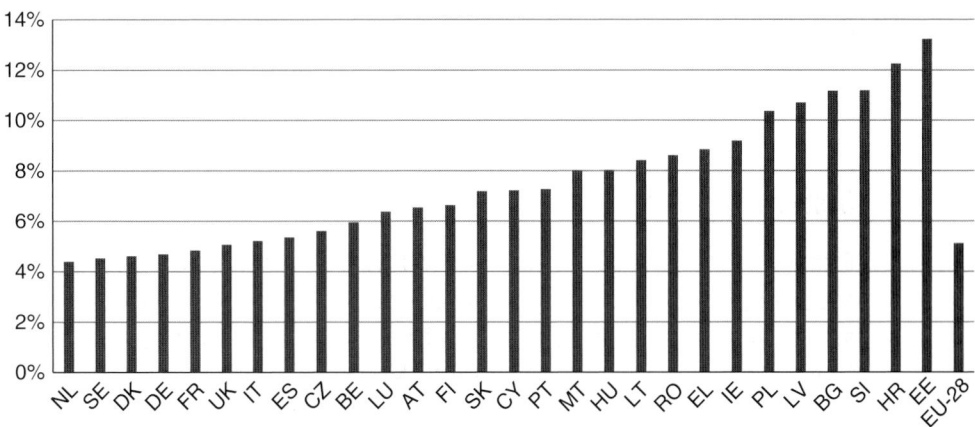

Figure 12.3   Leverage ratios, June 2018
Note: EU-28 is a weighted average.
Source: European Banking Authority (2018)

A minimum *leverage ratio* (LR), i.e. the ratio between a bank's non-risk-weighted total exposures and its Tier 1 capital, has been introduced as a supplementary measure to the risk-based framework. These exposures include total assets (on the bank's balance sheet), derivative exposures, and securities financing transactions (both off balance sheet). The LR is defined as:

$$LR = \frac{Tier\ 1\ capital}{On - and\ off - balance\ sheet\ exposures} \geq 3\%. \tag{12.2}$$

The LR is intended to be a backstop against the risk-based capital requirements (equation (12.1)) and is designed to constrain excess leverage, which was common among many banks before the crisis. The capital measure comprises Tier 1 capital and is set at a minimum of 3 per cent. Figure 12.3 shows the average LR by country in 2018. The average for the EU as a whole is 5.1 per cent. LRs differ widely across countries, and show little correlation with the RWCRs of Figure 12.2, due to differences in risk weights across countries. The Netherlands (4.4 per cent), Sweden (4.5 per cent), Denmark (4.6 per cent), and Germany (4.7 per cent) have the lowest LRs, while Hungary (12.3 per cent), Estonia (13.2 per cent), and Iceland (15.1 per cent) have the highest.

Basel III also introduces two liquidity measures:

- The *liquidity coverage ratio* (LCR), which requires banks to have enough cash (or cash-equivalent securities) to meet net cash outflows over a short (30-day) period of acute stress. The LCR is defined as:

$$LCR = \frac{High\ quality\ liquid\ assets}{Total\ net\ cash\ outflows\ over\ 30\text{-}day\ period} \geq 100\% \qquad (12.3)$$

The LCR aims to ensure that sufficient high-quality liquid assets (HQLA) are available for a bank to survive for one month in case of a stress scenario. Assets are considered to be HQLA if they can be easily and immediately converted into cash with little or no loss of value. This requires assets to be considered relatively safe and have a low correlation with risky assets. Moreover, the market for these assets should be well developed and sizeable, and prices should be relatively stable. Level 1 HQLA assets can be included without limit, while Level 2 assets can only comprise 40 per cent of the stock. In order to account for possible liquidity impediments, Level 2 assets are subject to haircuts.

- The *net stable funding ratio* (NSFR) requires banks to have sufficient available stable funding to support operations over a period of at least one year of less severe stress. The NSFR is defined as:

$$NSFR = \frac{Available\ stable\ funding\ over\ 1\ year\ period}{Required\ stable\ funding\ over\ 1\ year\ period} \geq 100\% \qquad (12.4)$$

Banks can rely on available stable funding for a period of one year or longer. An example is Tier 1 and Tier 2 capital. The funding requirement of a specific asset is determined by its marketability, maturity, and duration of encumbrance. The NSFR aims to limit over-reliance on short-term wholesale funding during times of buoyant market liquidity and encourage better assessment of liquidity risk across all on- and off-balance-sheet items.

Critique on Basel III

The main critique of Basel III is that regulatory capital requirements are still too low given the high social costs of a banking crisis (Admati and Hellwig, 2013). An average LR of 5 per cent in the EU as a whole implies that 95 per cent of banking assets are still funded by debt, and that relatively small shocks can trigger a crisis. As discussed in Chapter 2, bank runs are often related to negative aggregate shocks to the business cycle.

Furthermore, several financial intermediaries are not regulated. As illustrated in Chapter 1, non-bank intermediation has grown rapidly since the financial crisis, and empirical estimations indicate that tighter requirements for banks lead to an increase in non-bank credit (Cizel *et al.*, 2019). For now, such a development supports the evolution towards a capital markets union (Chapter 3). But ideally, such shifts in the regulatory boundary should be based on deliberate policy decisions rather than being an unintended consequence of tighter regulation for banks. Some observers have therefore advocated extending minimum LR requirements to the non-bank financial sector as well (Schoenmaker and Wierts, 2015).

A final issue is the regulatory treatment of sovereign exposures. Within the Basel III framework, sovereign debt kept its status as a lowest-risk asset, and the EU legislative framework provides for zero risk weights for EU sovereign exposures. However, the euro crisis has shown that sovereign exposures can carry significant risk (see Chapter 2), which could lead to a more critical stance with respect to the adequacy of the regulatory framework on sovereign risks. In addition to risk weights, limits on large exposures to sovereigns could be useful to contain the risk of sovereign debt for banks, as some banks tend to invest heavily in sovereign bonds in their home country.

12.3 Microprudential Supervision: Insurers

The EU has also introduced a system for regulatory capital for insurance companies. The Solvency II Directive (2009/138/EC) introduces a risk-based approach to insurance supervision, drawing on the experiences from banking supervision. Its main objective is to enhance policyholder protection across the EU. The directive establishes solvency requirements for insurers in order to guarantee that they have sufficient capital to withstand adverse events such as floods, storms, major catastrophes, or declining values of their assets. This helps increase their financial soundness, and guarantees that insurers can meet their obligations to policyholders.

Solvency II entered into force in the EU on 1 January 2016. It entails a programme of regulatory requirements for insurers, covering authorisation, corporate governance, supervisory reporting, public disclosure, and risk assessment and management, as well as solvency and reserving.

Solvency II follows the three-pillar approach of Basel III. Pillar 1 is designed to ensure that an insurance firm is adequately capitalised. It provides rules for how insurers should value their liabilities (including the money paid to policyholders in the event of a claim) and assets (such as bonds, shares, and property). The rules also cover the amount of own funds insurers need to hold in reserve to make sure they can pay policyholders' claims (see below). Pillar 2 imposes standards of risk management and governance on firms. Each firm is required to undertake its own forward-looking assessment of its risks, solvency needs, and adequacy of capital resources. Pillar 3 details insurers' reporting requirements. Some reports are public, such as annual reports, while others are privately reported to the financial supervisor.

Solvency II introduces a risk-based approach to insurance supervision. It follows a total balance sheet approach that captures both the asset and liability sides, subject to stressed valuations. The solvency requirements are based on a market-consistent valuation. The value of the technical provisions is equal to the sum of a *best estimate* and a *risk margin*. The best estimate is the present value of expected future cash flows to (and from) policyholders. The risk-free interest rate term structure is used to discount future cash flows. For obligations to policyholders, an ultimate forward rate (UFR) extrapolation is used to discount liabilities with maturities of over 20 years. This is because there are relatively few products with such maturities available in the financial markets from which to derive rates, and since it contributes to a more stable solvency ratio. In the current low interest rate environment, the UFR has been consistently well above the market rates (Figure 12.4). This has led to a lower valuation (compared to market rates), and created overly optimistic official solvency capital ratios for insurers with longer-term liabilities.

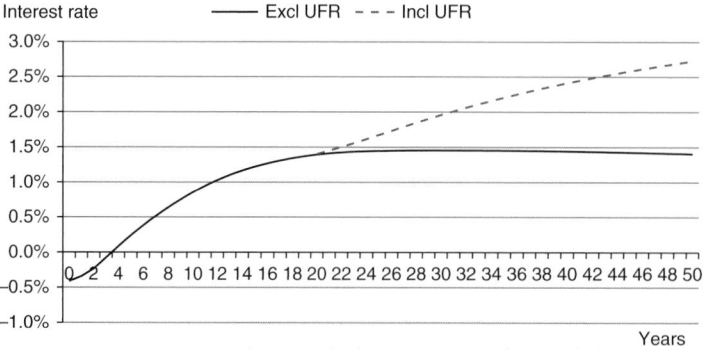

Figure 12.4 Term structure with UFR and market interest rates
Source: EIOPA and market data risk-free interest rate term structure, 31 July 2018

The *risk margin* ensures that the value of technical provisions is equivalent to the amount that insurance and reinsurance undertakings would be expected to require in order to take over and meet the insurance and reinsurance obligations. It reflects the amount of own funds necessary to meet the insurance and reinsurance obligations over their lifetime.

The solvency capital requirement (SCR) is the capital required to ensure that the insurance company will be able to meet its obligations. It is the value at risk (VaR) of the basic own funds of a (re)insurance company subject to a confidence level of 99.5 per cent over a one-year period (see Box 10.3). As in banking, the SCR is calculated using either a standard formula or internal models subject to supervisory approval. A large majority of insurance companies use the standard formula, while the large ones tend to use an internal model (Tucker and Phelan, 2017). The standard formula is a risk-sensitive framework designed to capture the quantifiable risks a firm may face and calculate the capital requirements from these risks. This formula categorises risks into modules for capital purposes: market risk, credit risk, underwriting risk (life, non-life, and health) and operational risk. The overall SCR is calculated as the sum of risks, taking correlations between risk categories into account. With a high correlation, there is little scope for diversification gains or capital savings. By contrast, lower correlations indicate diversification benefits and lead to lower amounts of regulatory capital. The SCR calculation for an insurance company follows a two-step approach:

1. Calculate the individual SCR components based on losses due to pre-specified shocks, using VaR.
2. Sum the individual SCR components, using correlations.

The detailed risk modules are specified in the delegated regulation on Solvency II (Regulation 2015/35/EU) that supplements the Solvency II directive. In the overall SCR, market risk is by far the largest component for insurance companies in the EU (Tucker and Phelan, 2017). The calculation of the individual risk modules is therefore illustrated for this category.

Table 12.2 summarises the different base shocks used to calculate the SCR for all subcomponents of market risk. Market risk is calculated as the sum of all individual subcomponents, i.e. interest rate risk, equity risk, property risk, spread risk, market risk concentrations, and currency risk, taking into account the correlations provided in Table 12.3. The prescribed correlation coefficient of 0.75 between equity and property, for example, indicates that only a limited diversification gain between these two asset classes is allowed. For subcategories i and j, the SCR for market risk is calculated as:

Table 12.2 Market risks

Subcomponent	Value changes due to	Base shock
Interest rate	Changes in the term structure of interest rates or interest rate volatility	Instantaneous increase/decrease in basic risk-free term structure of interest rates (this affects assets as well as liabilities since it changes the discount rate).
Equity	Fluctuations in the level or volatility of equities' market prices	Decrease of 39.0% in the value of type 1 equities (i.e. listed in regulated markets of EEA or OECD countries) and 49.0% for type 2 equities (i.e. listed in other countries or not listed).
Property	Fluctuation in the level or volatility of market prices of property	An instantaneous decrease of 25% in the value of immovable property.
Spread	Changes in the level or volatility of credit spreads over the risk-free interest rate term structure	Differing adjustments for (i) bonds and loans, (ii) securitisation positions, and (iii) credit derivatives. Risk adjustments are based on duration and credit quality.
Concentration	Losses on large investments in individual counterparties and single-name exposures	Applies to single-name exposures above 1.5–3% of assets, depending on credit quality. The SCR is the loss in basic own funds caused by a decrease in value, which depends on a risk factor related to credit quality.
Currency	Changes in exchange rates	An instantaneous increase or decrease of 25% in exchange rates of foreign currency positions.

Source: Adapted from Delegated Regulation under Solvency II (35/2015/EU)

$$SCR_{market} = \sqrt{\sum_{i,j} Corr_{i,j} * SCR_i * SCR_j} \qquad (12.5)$$

The same is done for credit risk, underwriting risk (life, non-life, and health) and operational risk. The final SCR is the sum of these components, again taking correlations into account, but now between the main components.

In addition to the SCR, a minimum capital requirement (MCR) must also be calculated. The MCR follows the same VaR approach, but subject to a confidence level of 85 per cent. For supervisory purposes, the SCR and MCR can be regarded as 'soft' and 'hard' floors, respectively. If an insurer's available resources fall below the SCR, supervisors are required to intervene so that the insurer restores its amount of own funds to the SCR level as soon as possible. For example, one option is to require the insurance company to submit a recovery plan in which the insurer agrees to meet the SCR within six

Table 12.3 Correlation coefficients for the market risk submodule

i \ j	Interest rate	Equity	Property	Spread	Concentration	Currency
Interest rate	1	0 or 0.5*	0 or 0.5*	0 or 0.5*	0	0.25
Equity	0 or 0.5*	1	0.75	0.75	0	0.25
Property	0 or 0.5*	0.75	1	0.5	0	0.25
Spread	0 or 0.5*	0.75	0.5	1	0	0.25
Concentration	0	0	0	0	1	0
Currency	0.25	0.25	0.25	0.25	0	1

Note: * 0 where the capital requirement for interest rate risk is given by an upward shock in the interest rate term structure and 0.5 for a downward shock.

Source: Delegated Regulation under Solvency II (35/2015/EU), article 164

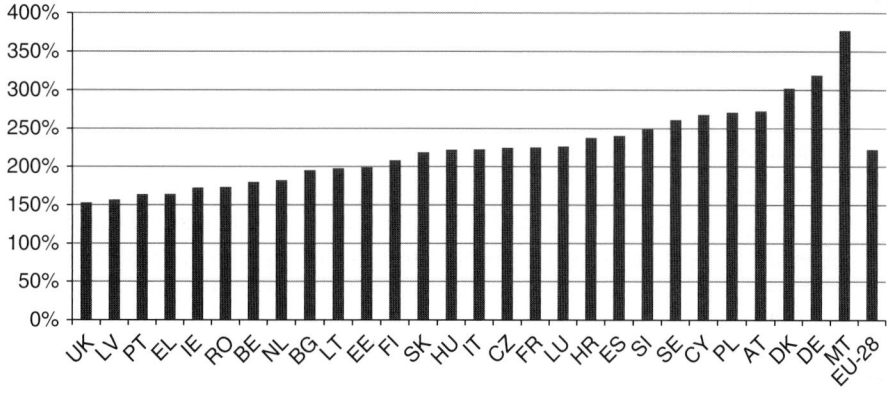

Figure 12.5 Solvency capital ratios

Note: Averages over 2016Q3–2017Q3. Own funds as percentage of required own funds. EU-28 is a weighted average.

Source: EIOPA

months. If, despite supervisory intervention, the available resources of the insurance company fall below the MCR, the supervisory authority may impose a production stop, transfer the portfolio to another insurer, and/or revoke the insurer's authorisation.

Figure 12.5 shows solvency capital ratios for EU countries over 2016Q3–2017Q3. The figure shows that own funds are generally 1.5 to 4 times larger than the required own funds. There are substantial differences between countries, but data cannot be compared directly since countries use different valuation standards. In some countries, insurance companies are allowed to

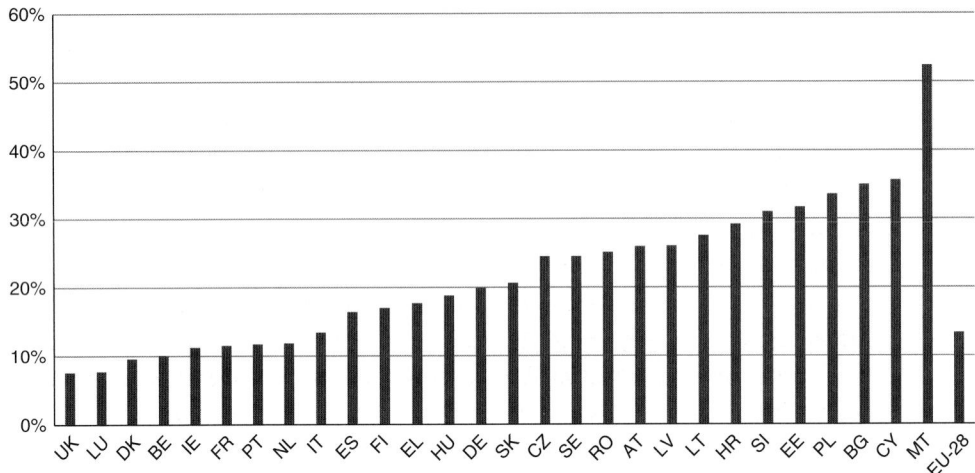

Figure 12.6   Eligible own funds to meet the SCR, as a percentage of total assets
Note: Averages over 2016Q3–2017Q3. EU-28 is a weighted average.
Source: EIOPA

use transitional measures to ensure a smooth transition towards Solvency II. The transition period can take up to 16 years. Figure 12.6 shows eligible own funds as a percentage of total assets. In this case, the values range from 8 per cent in the UK, to around 12–13 per cent in France, the Netherlands, and Italy, 20 per cent in Germany and much higher numbers in a range of smaller countries.

Critique of Solvency II

While Solvency II introduces a much-needed risk-based approach to regulatory capital, there are some challenges associated with the new capital framework for insurance companies. A market-consistent balance sheet directly shows whether or not sufficient assets are available to meet a firm's obligations to its policyholders; a book value balance sheet does not indicate whether sufficient assets are available to meet the liabilities. However, market valuations can lead to large swings in the valuation of an insurer's assets and liabilities that can in turn generate large changes in an insurer's equity, which is the basis for its solvency requirement. In this respect, the volatility of own funds reflects the (market) risk an insurer is exposed to. The Solvency II volatility adjustment is in place to dampen the impact of market value changes due to 'artificial' changes in credit spreads. It is an upward adjustment of the risk-free rate term structure; it is used to counteract short-term volatility due to spreads between the risk-free interest rate term structure and a reference portfolio of bonds, loans, and securitisations. The basic mechanism is as follows. When the spreads go up, the valuation of bonds on the asset side of the balance sheet of the insurance company goes down, which decreases the company's own funds. To dampen this effect, the volatility adjustment allows for a simultaneous upward adjustment to the term structure, so that technical provisions go down as well. An initial assessment of the impact showed that this improved the SCR by 24 basis points on average for insurance companies included in the survey (EIOPA, 2018: 17–18). In some countries the impact was much more substantial. The highest impact on the SCR was found in the Netherlands (29 per cent), Denmark (27 per cent), and Germany (17 per cent).[3]

Another challenge is that the Solvency II capital framework follows the banking approach by applying a one-year holding period. While this holding period may be suitable for banking business that is more short to medium term, it is not suitable for insurance business that is long-term oriented. More broadly, the risk indicators for long-term insurance business should be based on changes in long-term trends affecting the viability of insurers instead of short-term market movements. Yet a short-term period for the capital requirements is typically used, given the difficulties of deriving long-term risk indicators. It is even more important that as long as sufficient capital is available to withstand the risks over a one-year horizon, supervisors have this one year to transfer the liabilities of an insurer to another sufficiently capitalised insurer without having to cut the rights of the policyholder, the main objective of Solvency II.

12.4 Conduct-of-Business Supervision

Conduct-of-business supervision focuses on how financial institutions conduct business with their customers and how they behave in markets, by prescribing rules about appropriate behaviour and monitoring behaviour that can be harmful to customers or the functioning of markets. It is a relatively new activity, which became prominent after the liberalisation of financial markets. In the Big Bang in 1986, fixed commissions for trading on the London Stock Exchange were abolished. The Big Bang was the start of a process of liberalising financial markets across Europe. Liberalisation promotes the entry of new players and may thereby lead to a wider choice of products and services (at lower prices). Conduct-of-business rules are designed to ensure the fair treatment of retail customers in particular in these liberalised markets.

Investor protection approaches have traditionally assumed that actors in the market behave rationally, and thus that market failures related to information asymmetries can be overcome by enhancing the provision of information to investors. But despite the existence of conduct-of-business rules, massive mis-selling occurred in many EU Member States during and after the financial crisis (Alexander, 2018; see also Table 12.4). This led to discussion of an alternative behavioural assumption of bounded rationality. Behavioural finance explains, for example, excessive reliance on investing based on rules of thumb, including short-term performance (Spindler, 2011). Moreover, information provision does not address conflicts of interest such as those related to commission-based adviser business. As in other fields, post-crisis reforms have therefore shifted the balance towards a more interventionist approach.

Conduct-of-business regulation focuses on the activities of financial institutions. The dividing lines between the sub-sectors of banking, insurance, and securities are blurring; the same type of product is increasingly offered by different financial institutions. Alexander (2018) concludes that the sectoral approach to the marketing, sale, and distribution of financial products results in arbitrage risks. He advises harmonising standards across sectors. This recommendation is in line with Merton (1995), who proposes a functional approach towards regulation to prevent regulatory arbitrage between different types of financial institutions. In his view, the same conduct-of-business rules should apply to any institution (i.e. bank, insurer, or investment firm) offering, for example, long-term savings products to retail customers.

Protecting Retail Customers

Conduct-of-business rules protecting retail customers comprise the following elements (Llewellyn, 1999):[4]
- mandatory information provisions
- objective, high-quality advice
- duty of care.

Mandatory information provisions ensure that customers receive the right information at the right time. Proper disclosure and sufficient information (*transparency*) helps retail customers select the appropriate products. Good information helps customers understand the key features of a financial product, including the risks, potential returns, and costs. Mandatory information provisions specify the (minimum) information needed to understand products. These provisions also require financial institutions to present this information in a consistent format to enable comparisons between products.

Developing customers' literacy in financial matters is becoming increasingly important, as individuals take many decisions affecting their financial security and capital markets have become more accessible to consumers. The European Commission (2007) reports that international surveys reveal that customers have a low level of understanding of financial matters. There is a strong correlation between low levels of financial literacy and the ability to make appropriate financial decisions. Customers with poor financial literacy find it hard to understand and use the information they receive when purchasing financial services.

Conduct-of-business rules can also provide guidelines regarding the quality and objectivity of *advice*, which implies a recommendation to a customer to choose a specific product. A financial institution must take steps to ensure that a recommendation is suitable for its customer. This can, for example, be done by creating a customer profile containing information about his or her knowledge and experience relevant to the type of financial product, financial situation, and investment objectives. Advice should be objective, based on the customer's profile, and commensurate with the complexity of the products and risks involved. The requirement of objectivity aims to minimise potential conflicts of interest when financial institutions are better informed than customers.

More generally, financial institutions have a *duty of care* to behave responsibly towards their customers. A financial institution breaches its duty of care when it sells, for example, a high-risk investment product to a customer who cannot afford to bear the financial risk (e.g. a low-income household with limited savings). Table 12.4 provides an overview of actual or suspected mis-selling to retail customers provided by the European Commission (2014).

In summary, on the one hand conduct-of-business rules require proper information provision (transparency) to (potential) customers. This should enable customers to make better decisions. On the other hand, these rules set minimum standards for advice and introduce a duty of care for financial institutions. The challenge for policy makers is to find the right balance between empowering customers by providing information and education (fostering financial literacy) and protecting them by setting minimum standards for financial institutions' behaviour.

Table 12.4 Retail mis-selling of financial products across the EU

TYPE OF PRODUCT	COUNTRY
Highly (and increasingly) complex products, such as structured products	Belgium, Denmark, Estonia, Germany, Italy, Latvia, Spain
Complex hedging products designed to protect borrowers on flexible rate mortagages	Latvia, Spain
Self-certified and interest-only mortgages	UK
Mortgage insurance products	Poland
Loans to individuals that are exposed to exchange rate risks, the extent of which is often unknown to the consumer	France, Hungary
Unregulated collective investment schemes, which invest in assets that are not always traded in established markets and are therefore difficult to value. They may be highly illiquid, and have risks to capital that are generally opaque	UK, Germany
Units in funds based on hedging strategies	Belgium
Product wrapping which prevents consumers from comparing features, prices and charges and thus from making well-informed investment decisions	Finland
Banks placing financial instruments such as hybrid products with their own retail clients, where the risks were in some cases not disclosed or sufficiently explained and some consumers claim that they were given the impression that the investment was a protected deposit	Spain, UK
Insurance products linked to complex underlying structures	France
Expensive and opaque unit-linked insurance and pension products	Netherlands

Source: European Commission (2014)

EU conduct-of-business rules are most advanced in the field of securities. The Markets in Financial Instruments Directive (MiFID; 2004/39/EC), which replaced the Investment Services Directive (93/22/EEC), consists of a set of conduct-of-business, best-execution, and client-order-handling rules, as well as inducements and conflict-of-interest provisions. Specific attention is paid to retail clients, for whom a specific regime has been established, which entails reinforced fiduciary duties upon the firm.

As of January 2018, the Directive on Markets in Financial Instruments, repealing Directive 2004/39/EC (MiFID II; 2014/65/EU) and the Regulation on Markets in Financial Instruments (MiFIR; 600/2014/EU) apply. MiFID II applies to all financial institutions and infrastructure including banks, investment firms, fund managers, exchanges, and other trading avenues. It takes a behavioural finance paradigm approach to investor protection, as bank clients and investors may not be able to process all relevant information and properly assess the risks (Alexander, 2018). This extends to organisational requirements regarding how institutions develop and sell products, to ensure they are suitable to the clients. MiFID II also contains a stronger principle of fair treatment. Investment firms have duty to act honestly, fairly, and professionally in accordance with their clients' best interests. And financial advisers should be able to demonstrate that the products they sell are suitable to their clients, based on a 'know-your-customer' assessment. Moreover, investors should be able to rely on independent and neutral advice; fee and remuneration structures must not conflict with this requirement.

Separate rules apply to consumer credit. The Directive on Consumer Credit (2008/48/ EC) focuses on transparency and consumer rights. It provides for a comprehensible set of information to be given to consumers before a contract is concluded and also as part of the credit agreement. In order to enhance the comparability of different offers and to make the information more understandable, the pre-contractual information must be supplied in a standardised form, e.g. using the annual percentage rate of charge, which is a single figure, harmonised at the EU level, representing the cost of the credit.

The Insurance Distribution Directive (2016/97/EU) regulates how insurance products are sold. It applies to all companies that sell insurance, including insurance intermediaries, and determines the information that should be given to consumers before they sign an insurance contract. It includes a standardised insurance product information document for non-life insurance products. It also contains rules on transparency and business conduct to help consumers avoid buying products that do not meet their needs.

EU directives related to the investment fund sector distinguish between Undertakings for Collective Investments in Transferable Securities (UCITS) and Alternative Investment Funds (AIFs). UCITS are required to be open-ended, liquid, well diversified, only invest in liquid assets and use little leverage (Wegman, 2016). AIFs are all other investment funds, including hedge funds, private equity funds, and other closed-end investment funds. Figure 12.7 illustrates the strong growth in the overall size of the investment fund sector from 2000 to 2018, and particularly in the size of AIFs (see also Chapter 1). While UCITS still represent the largest component, their share in the total investment fund sector has declined from 73 per cent in 2008 to 62 per cent in 2018.

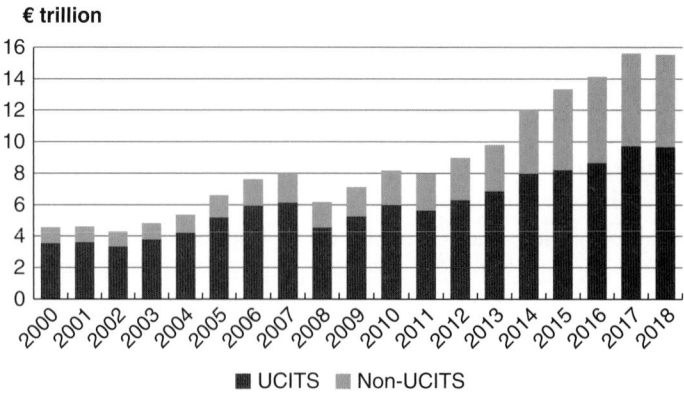

€ trillion

Figure 12.7   Assets of European investment funds (€ trillion), 2000–2018
Source: European Fund and Asset Management Association

The UCITS directive (2009/65/EC) allows such funds to operate freely throughout the EU on the basis of a single authorisation. A collective investment fund may apply for UCITS status in order to allow EU-wide marketing. In 2009 the European Commission completed a programme of improvements to the 2001 UCITS directive, which aimed to establish a new standardised and harmonised disclosure document designed to empower investors to take more effective investment decisions and strengthen the rules of conduct for UCITS management companies, including the prevention, management, and disclosure of conflicts of interest. In 2014 Directive 2014/91/EU was adopted, which amended Directive 2009/65/EC. The 2014 directive introduces rules on UCITS depositaries, such as the entities eligible to assume this role, their tasks, delegation arrangements, and the depositaries' liability as well as general remuneration principles that apply to fund managers.

The Alternative Investment Fund Managers Directive (AIFMD, 2011/61/EU) is part of the regulatory response to the financial crisis. The immediate trigger was the unwinding of leverage in the hedge fund sector, but the scope of the directive extends to all types of non-UCITS. The AIFMD includes transparency requirements, rules for managing potential conflicts of interest, rules on risk management practices, valuation policies, remuneration policies, and leverage restrictions. Managers of AIFs have to set leverage limits for each fund they manage, and demonstrate that they comply with those limits. Moreover, the competent authorities have been given a mandate to impose leverage restrictions to ensure the stability and integrity of the financial system.

Market Functioning

Conduct-of-business regulation promoting fair and orderly markets contains the following elements:

- transparency of trading;
- prohibition of insider trading and market manipulation;
- information requirements for issuers and shareholders, including prospectus and financial reporting.

Rules on the *transparency of trading* require the disclosure of quotes, i.e. the prices at which traders are prepared to sell or buy securities, and the prices at which trades have taken place. Potential investors can only analyse and compare the trading conditions for securities when quotes (pre-trade transparency) are published. Post-trade transparency is also important to provide timely insight into the movement of prices. The transparency requirements seek to achieve an adequate price formation process, to ensure best-practice execution and to provide a level playing field between the different types of trade venues (see Box 5.3).

Insider trading and market manipulation undermine the proper functioning and integrity of markets. *Insider trading rules* ban trading based on material information on the firm that has not been made public. The use of this information by insiders, such as management or employees, may influence the price of the firm's securities. To speed up the release of new information (and thus reduce the potential for insider trading), insider trading rules require listed firms to disclose inside information as soon as possible. It thus promotes transparency and the equal treatment of investors. *Market manipulation rules* prohibit the spread of rumours that may manipulate the price of a security.

Firms that issue securities are required to publish three types of information on a regular basis. First, firms have to publish a prospectus when they are issuing securities. A *prospectus* provides investors with material information about the firm's business, financial statements, biographies of officers and directors, detailed information about their compensation, any litigation that is taking place, a list of material properties, and any other material information. Second, listed firms have to provide annual financial reports; half-yearly or quarterly financial reports may also be required. The purpose of financial reporting is to ensure comparable, transparent, and reliable information about firms. Third, shareholders must disclose acquisitions (and disposals) of shareholdings beyond the 5 per cent threshold to allow firms to identify their major shareholders.

The conduct-of-business rules for markets are laid down in a raft of EU directives. MiFID contains *inter alia* rules on the transparency of trading. It covers trading from regulated markets (i.e. stock exchanges) to multilateral trading facilities (MTFs), i.e. systems that bring together multiple parties (e.g. retail investors or other investment firms) that are interested in buying and selling financial instruments and enable them to do so. MiFID has given MTFs a single passport to operate throughout the EU on the basis of authorisation in their home Member State. MiFID also facilitates in-house matching. Under certain conditions related to pre-trade transparency and best execution, banks and investment firms are allowed to 'match' trades of customers internally. These measures have increased competition among exchanges, MTFs, and investment firms. As already indicated, MiFID II and MiFIR apply from January 2018. The new framework introduces a market structure that closes loopholes and ensures that trading, wherever appropriate, takes place on regulated platforms. It introduces rules on high-frequency trading, improves the transparency and oversight of financial markets – including derivatives markets – and addresses the issue of excessive price volatility in commodity derivatives markets. It also improves the conditions for competition in the trading and clearing of financial instruments.

The Market Abuse Regulation (2014/596/EU), which went into effect in July 2016, replaces the Market Abuse Directive (2003/6/EC). It aims to increase market integrity and investor protection, and enhance the attractiveness of securities markets for capital raising. The regulation is designed to ensure that the EU regulatory framework keeps pace with market developments, such as the growth of new trading platforms, over-the-counter trading, and new technology such as high-frequency trading. The regulation also strengthens the fight against market abuse across commodity and related derivative markets, explicitly bans the manipulation of benchmarks (such as LIBOR), and reinforces regulators' investigative and administrative sanctioning powers. The regulation covers financial instruments traded on EU-regulated markets as well as those traded on a multilateral trading facility. This encompasses broker-operated trading venues and listing venues that are not regulated markets. Moreover, it covers organised trading venues, which were created by MiFID II to trade non-equity instruments such as bonds and derivatives. In this way, the Market Abuse Regulation follows a functional approach.

The Prospectus Regulation (2017/1129/EU) requires that prospectuses provide investors with clear and comprehensive information. It also introduces a single passport for the issuers: once a prospectus has been approved in one EU country, it is valid throughout the EU. As part of the Capital Markets Union Action Plan, the regulation intends to make it easier and cheaper for smaller companies to access capital markets. It also introduces a summary of key information tailored to investors' information and protection needs.

Finally, the Transparency Directive (2004/109/EC), as amended in 2013 (2013/50/EU), requires all securities issuers to publish information including yearly and half-yearly financial reports. The amendment reduces the administrative burden on smaller issuers, particularly by abolishing the requirement to publish quarterly accounts. As for the contents of the financial reports, the EU has adopted the International Accounting Standards (IAS) – now referred to as International Financial Reporting Standards – through IAS Regulation (1606/2002/EC). The IAS provides a single set of comparable global accounting standards issued by the International Accounting Standards Board.

12.5 Financial Supervision in Europe

A key element of the design of the institutional framework for financial supervision is the appropriate level of (de)centralisation. Until the financial crisis of 2007–2009, national supervisory agencies in EU Member States were in charge of supervising all financial institutions. With the start of the Banking Union this has changed for banks in the euro area. Oversight of other financial institutions (insurance companies, pension funds, and banks in non-euro-area countries) is still primarily the responsibility of national supervisors. However, several EU-level supervisory authorities have been created.

Drawbacks of National Supervision

National supervision, within an integrated financial system, has two primary drawbacks. First, even though regulation concerning financial supervision has increasingly become European, various technical rules are still determined at the Member State level, and there are considerable variations between Member States. Even where rules are harmonised, their application can be inconsistent. This fragmented supervision undermines the single market, imposes extra costs on financial institutions, and increases the likelihood of failure for financial institutions, with potential additional costs for taxpayers. Schüler and Heinemann (2005) estimate that a cost-efficient European supervisory framework entails cost savings of 15 per cent over 15 separate national supervisors.

Second, there may be conflicts of interest among national supervisors. While large cross-border financial institutions increasingly operate on an integrated basis, with key decisions taken at the headquarters level, supervisors are examining the national parts of these institutions. The home supervisor, as the consolidated supervisor, is coordinating national supervisory efforts to minimise the potential for regulatory and supervisory arbitrage. The national supervisors also perform joint risk assessments of the large cross-border financial institutions, resulting in a joint supervision plan. But there are no legally binding mechanisms to deal with potential conflicts of national interest.

An example of a potential conflict is the distribution of capital (or liquidity) within a financial services group. The host supervisor may request full capitalisation of the host subsidiary, while the home supervisor may request to maintain capital at the group level and to keep the capitalisation of subsidiaries at the minimum level. Supervisors may also have diverging views on how to remedy a financial institution's shortcomings. Supervisors can easily settle on a joint action when they agree. But when there are (lasting) differences, the various supervisors all have the legal power to take enforcement action under their national mandate, which may result in suboptimal outcomes.

These coordination problems pose the question of whether supervision should take place at the national or European level. The basic argument in favour of moving to a European structure is that it might be difficult to simultaneously achieve an integrated and stable financial system, while preserving national supervision and crisis management with only decentralised efforts at harmonisation (Thygesen, 2003). There is a 'trilemma' in financial supervision (Schoenmaker, 2013); out of three incompatible objectives, one has to be given up: (1) a stable financial system, (2) an integrated financial system, or (3) independent national financial policies (see Figure 12.8 and Box 13.1).

An argument against moving to a European solution for financial supervision and resolution could be that the degree of financial integration does not yet justify such a move. However, as shown in previous chapters, up until the financial crisis, the integration of many financial markets (particularly wholesale markets) was very high. The infrastructures to support financial markets are also integrating, albeit at a slower pace. In addition, there is

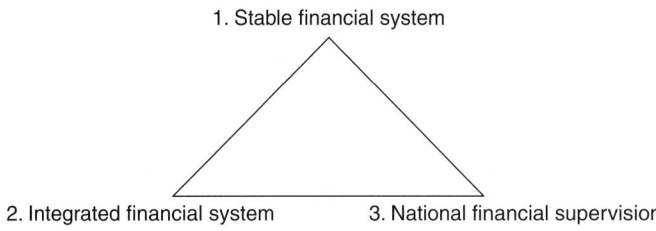

Figure 12.8   The financial trilemma
Source: Schoenmaker (2013)

evidence of increasing cross-border penetration of banks and insurers. Emerging pan-European financial institutions give rise to cross-border externalities arising from the (potential) failure of these institutions. The increasing presence of financial institutions from other EU countries undermines the capacity of host authorities to effectively manage the stability of their financial system.

European Supervisory Authorities

In October 2008 the European Commission mandated a high-level group chaired by the former managing director of the International Monetary Fund, Jacques de Larosière, to give advice on the future of European financial regulation and supervision. The group presented its final report on 25 February 2009, and these recommendations provided the basis for the new European financial supervisory framework.

The de Larosière Report (2009) concluded that the supervisory framework needed to be strengthened to reduce the risk and severity of future financial crises. It recommends creating a European System of Financial Supervisors, comprising three European Supervisory Authorities (ESAs): one for the banking sector (European Banking Authority, EBA), one for the securities sector (European Securities and Markets Authority, ESMA), and one for the insurance and occupational pensions sector (European Insurance and Occupational Pensions Authority, EIOPA). The report also recommended establishing a European Systemic Risk Board (see Chapter 13) to monitor and assess potential threats to financial stability that arise from macroeconomic developments and developments within the financial system as a whole.

The underlying rationale for setting up the ESAs was to ensure closer cooperation and exchange of information among national supervisors, facilitate the adoption of EU resolutions to cross-border problems, and advance the coherent interpretation and application of rules. By preparing uniform standards and ensuring supervisory convergence and coordination, the ESAs should shape the further development of a single rule book applicable to all 28 EU Member States and thus contribute to the single market. The ESAs started their operations in January 2011. Their powers include:

- developing draft technical standards as well as guidance and recommendations;
- resolving disagreements between national supervisors, where legislation requires them to cooperate or agree;
- helping to ensure the consistent application of technical rules of EU law, including through peer reviews;
- a coordination and enforcement role in emergency situations.

In addition to indirect supervisory powers, ESMA also exercises direct supervisory control over financial players with a pan-European profile, currently credit rating agencies (see Chapter 1) and trade repositories. This direct supervisory role may be expanded to other pan-European players, such as central counterparties and cross-border stock markets (e.g. Euronext and OMX, see Chapter 5).

Banking Union: Single Supervisory Mechanism (SSM)

As described in Chapter 3, euro-area leaders decided in June 2012 to establish a Banking Union, which is generally understood to consist of the following four interrelated building blocks:

- A single rulebook, consisting of a set of harmonised legislative texts that all financial institutions in the EU must comply with. These texts range from capital requirements to rules for the recovery and resolution of banks.
- A Single Supervisory Mechanism (SSM), which makes the ECB the central microprudential supervisor of banks in the euro area and in non-euro Member States that choose to join the Banking Union.
- A Single Resolution Mechanism, which applies to all banks covered by the SSM. Its purpose is to ensure the orderly resolution of failing banks with minimal or no costs for the taxpayer (see Chapter 13).
- A financing regime for exceptional situations, including a Single Resolution Fund, European Stability Mechanism (ESM), direct recapitalisation, and, at least, an alignment of deposit guarantee schemes.

Since November 2014, the ECB has directly supervised so-called significant banking groups, while in principle national supervisors will continue to monitor the remaining banks (see Figure 12.9). The main task of the ECB

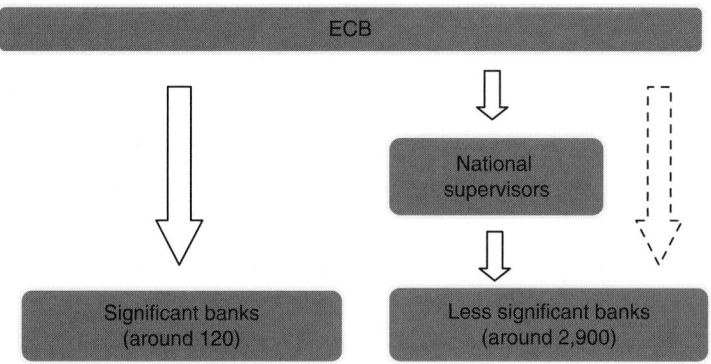

Figure 12.9   The Single Supervisory Mechanism (SSM)

and the national supervisors, working closely together within an integrated system, is to ensure that the single rulebook is applied consistently and coherently and, where necessary, to ensure timely corrective action when a bank is in breach of, or about to breach, regulatory requirements. As such, the ECB is responsible for ensuring the safety and soundness of the European banking system, thereby contributing to financial integration and stability in Europe.

Under the new system, the ECB directly supervises around 120 significant banking groups, representing about 80 per cent of total banking assets in the euro area. The significance of these banking groups is based on: (i) the total value of their assets (€30 billion or more), (ii) their importance in the economy of their home country or the EU as a whole, (iii) the scale of their cross-border activities, and (iv) whether they have requested or received public financial assistance from the ESM. Moreover, in each participating country, at least the three most significant banks are subject to direct supervision by the ECB, irrespective of their absolute size. The ECB indirectly supervises less significant banks in the participating countries, which number approximately 2,900 in the euro area. These banks continue to be directly supervised by the national supervisory authorities, but the ECB can decide at any time to take over the direct supervision of any of these banks.

The ECB has the power, among other things, to grant or withdraw the authorisation of all banks under the SSM, assess acquisition and disposal of holdings in banks, and ensure compliance with all prudential requirements laid down in EU banking rules. While the ECB directly supervises significant banks, national supervisory authorities are still involved in their day-to-day supervision. *Joint Supervisory Teams* (JSTs) represent one of the main forms of cooperation between the ECB and national supervisory authorities. For each significant bank, a team is formed of staff members of the national supervisory authorities involved in supervising that bank and staff members of the ECB. The team is coordinated by the ECB. These teams are responsible for the day-to-day supervision of significant banks and carry out on-site inspections. The main tasks of the JSTs are to perform the risk analysis of the supervised entity or group and to propose a supervisory programme and the appropriate supervisory actions.

Setting up the SSM required changes to the ECB's organisational structure to ensure a separation between monetary policy and supervisory tasks. The SSM is governed by a *Supervisory Board*, acting under the overall responsibility of the ECB's Governing Council. This Supervisory Board consists of: (i) a chair, appointed for a non-renewable term of five years; (ii) a vice-chair, chosen from among the members of the ECB's Executive Board, (iii) three ECB representatives, and (iv) one representative of each participating Member State. The main responsibilities of the Supervisory Board are to plan and execute the ECB's supervisory tasks and propose draft supervisory decisions for adoption by the Governing Council. Decision making within the SSM is based on a procedure known as 'non-objection': if the ECB Governing Council does not object to a draft decision prepared by the Supervisory Board within a defined period of time, the decision is deemed adopted.

Challenges for Financial Supervision

The Banking Union has changed financial supervision in the euro area very rapidly. This section discusses several challenges that financial supervisors face.[5]

Data-Driven Supervision

The Banking Union cuts the ties between national supervisors and the financial institutions under their supervision. The union relies on a more distant data-driven approach, based on a broadened set of regulatory ratios under CRR/CRD IV and a single rulebook. The evolution towards data-driven supervision is also stimulated by the increased data availability that has followed from the regulatory response to the global financial crisis. This includes micro data on derivatives transactions based on the European Market Infrastructure Regulation, securities financing transactions based on the Securities Financing Transactions Regulation (EU/2015/2365), and new data on securities holdings based on the European System of Central Banks' Securities Holdings Statistics dataset.

For supervisors, this poses the challenge to distil the relevant data from the huge amount of potentially available data. Arner *et al.* (2017) argue that new regulatory requirements, together with the decreasing costs of data management, are one of the driving forces behind RegTech. This term refers to technological solutions that streamline and improve regulatory processes. According to these authors, the increasingly data-centric nature of supervision has the potential to prompt a shift from the 'know your customer' paradigm to a 'know your dataset' mindset. Such a development would run parallel with the increasing digitalisation of customer contact in financial services as described in Chapter 8 on the role of FinTech. Moreover, it would affect both microprudential and conduct-of-business supervision.

EU versus Euro Area

Non-euro-area Member States were given the option to participate in the SSM with full membership and voting rights in the Supervisory Board, which places them on an equal footing with euro-area Member States. The role of the ECB Governing Council in the SSM is reduced to the ability to accept or reject the Supervisory Board's decisions. Still, non-euro-area Member States are not involved in ECB Governing Council decisions.

There is a similar tension in the distribution of responsibilities between the ECB and EU-27 institutions, such as the EBA and the European Systemic Risk Board. For instance, as both the EBA and ECB are developing supervisory manuals, overlaps and/or conflicts between the two sets of supervisory rules may occur. The resolution of such tensions is of crucial importance for the future of financial supervision.

Transparency and Accountability

The global financial crisis has raised questions concerning the accountability of financial supervisors. The crisis revealed that information on the supervisory activities and the impact of these activities was inadequate to assess the degree to which supervisors were fulfilling their mandate. Calls were made to give the public and the legislative and executive branches of government more insight as to whether supervisors were performing the right tasks, and whether they were performing them well.

Transparency refers to an environment in which the objectives of policy; its legal, institutional, and economic framework; policy decisions and their rationale; data and information related to policies; and the terms of agencies' accountability are provided to the public in a comprehensible, accessible, and timely manner (IMF, 2000). Transparency is thus a crucial component of ensuring accountability. Although there are other arrangements concerning accountability, information on the conduct of supervisors is essential for an assessment of their performance. As for the SSM, the channels for accountability include: (i) hearings and exchanges of views with the chair of the Supervisory Board in the European Parliament and in the Eurogroup, in the presence of representatives of participating non-euro Member States, (ii) answers to (written) questions from Members of the European Parliament and EU Council members addressed to the Supervisory Board chair, and (iii) the submission of an annual report on its work to the European Parliament, the EU Council, and the Eurogroup.

Transparency of banking supervisors may be beneficial for two reasons (Liedorp *et al.*, 2013). First, transparency may enhance the legitimacy of the supervisor. As a supervisory authority is an independent organisation in which unelected officials take important decisions, ensuring its legitimacy is vital, especially in times of financial turmoil. Transparency may thus also safeguard an adequate degree of independence for the supervisor. Making actions and decisions transparent reduces the chances of undue interference based on an inaccurate perception of the supervisor's conduct. Second, transparency may increase the predictability of the supervisor, which, in turn, may stimulate financial institutions to adhere to existing regulation.

However, there are also two important arguments in favour of secrecy about supervision. First, revealing information about a financial institution does not objectively report its financial position, but may instead trigger events that influence that position. This is the 'reflexive nature' of financial markets: market participants' perspectives on financial markets may in fact drive financial market activity. For instance, exposing liquidity problems at particular firms may freeze the interbank market or trigger bank runs, in effect worsening these firms' liquidity problems, as happened with the money market turmoil that started in the summer of 2007. Second, financial supervisors face more restrictions on being transparent than monetary policy makers. For instance, due to legal restrictions, many supervisors cannot reveal much information on individual financial institutions. However, there seems to be room for improvement, as supervisory transparency in the US is greater than in the EU (Gandrud and Hallerberg, 2014).

Expectations and Demands of Supervision

Supervisors must balance the demands of multiple actors. In fulfilling their mandate, they have to pay attention to the expectations of the legislative and executive branches, the supervised institutions, depositors, and the general public. These demands may conflict and shift over time. The legislative branch may, for example, expect the supervisor to guarantee firms' compliance with existing policy in order to prevent incidents from happening, but may also expect the supervisor not to place an onerous administrative burden on financial firms. The executive branch may focus on achieving maximum results at a minimum cost. The supervised firms expect the supervisor to trust their compliance with rules and norms and therefore not to be too intrusive, but expect the supervisor to guarantee other financial firms' compliance with rules and norms. Depositors expect the supervisor to guarantee that their money is safe – in effect assuming the supervisor will prevent bankruptcies at all times. Finally, the general public presumes the supervisor can guarantee financial stability and prevent financial turmoil.

Based on a survey in the Netherlands, Van der Cruijsen *et al.* (2013) show that 63 per cent of the respondents (totally) agreed with the view that supervisors have to ensure that banks never go bankrupt. Yet given the dynamic nature of financial markets, preventing financial failure at all times is impossible. In fact, it could be highly counterproductive if the supervisor made 'preventing defaults at all times' a core part of its supervisory strategy, as it would introduce moral hazard problems, both at the level of firms and financial services customers.

Van der Cruijsen *et al.* (2013) also report that a majority of their respondents think supervisors should inform the public when a bank has problems. However, such a message could undermine confidence in the financial institution or even the entire financial system. The supervisor will therefore be cautious about communicating problems at financial firms – again failing to fully live up to public expectations.

These findings suggest that supervisory authorities should more actively communicate the limits of their supervision to the public. The timing of this is always difficult. Risks may build up in the financial sector when the economy is on the rise, (over)confidence is gaining the upper hand, and attention to risk mitigation is subdued in favour of potential lucrative opportunities. In such circumstances, the public is less receptive to supervisory warnings, especially when these come with new restrictive powers for the supervisor.

Regulatory Capture

The financial crisis of 2008–2009 demonstrated several shortcomings in existing financial sector regulation and supervision. However, some observers blame financial regulators and supervisors for the crisis. For instance, Barth *et al.* (2012: 5) argue that 'the Guardians of Finance adopted policies that induced financiers to take excessive risk … and the Guardians too often chose not to reform their destabilizing policies, even though they had the power and time to do so'.

One reason for this alleged failure is *regulatory capture*. Nobel laureate Stigler (1971) argued in a seminal article that all regulatory and supervisory agencies tend to respond to the wishes of the best-organised interest groups, in particular the industry they regulate and supervise. When public officials favour the regulated industry's interest over the public interest, these officials are 'captured' by the industry; this is referred to as regulatory capture. Captured regulators and supervisors will thus be lenient towards the sector they are supposed to independently regulate and monitor. Regulators may, for instance, pursue strategies to minimise industry costs rather than strike an appropriate balance between those costs and overall public benefits, while supervisors may apply rules inconsistently and exempt individual firms from regulatory requirements. Indeed, there is evidence that in the run-up to the financial crisis, lobbying by the financial sector affected its level of regulation. For instance, Basel II was influenced by this lobby and thus became much weaker than its predecessor (Claessens *et al.*, 2008).

Capture may not only occur through special interests directly influencing officials, but also through a subtler internalisation of the objectives, interests, and values of the financial sector. Indeed, Barth *et al.* (2012: 38) point out that 'even well-intentioned, incorruptible officials might be subject to the same human psychological factors that induce referees and umpires in sport to conform to the interests of the home crowd'.

12.6 Conclusions

This chapter has identified three market failures in financial services that justify government intervention. First, consumers may be less informed than financial institutions. Financial supervision (both microprudential and conduct-of-business supervision) addresses this problem of asymmetric information. Second, the malfunctioning of one part of the financial system may have an adverse impact on the financial system as a whole. Macroprudential supervision aims to foster financial stability and to contain the effects of systemic failure. Third, certain players in the market may exert undue market power. Competition policy seeks to protect consumers against the exploitation of market power.

Microprudential supervision aims to protect consumers by ensuring the safety and soundness of financial institutions. As financial institutions are becoming more complex, supervisors are moving away from direct control to methods that incentivise financial institutions to behave prudently. The Basel capital adequacy framework allows banks to use their internal models to manage the risks and to assess the minimum capital required to provide a buffer against these risks, as long as risk-weighted assets are at least 72.5 per cent of what they would be under the standardised approach. Solvency II for insurance firms follows the same three-pillar structure of the Basel Capital Accord. It includes rules to ensure that insurance firms are adequately capitalised to pay policyholder claims and introduces full market valuation of insurance firms' assets and liabilities. Conduct-of-business supervision focuses on how financial institutions deal with their customers. Information provisions ensure that consumers get the right information about financial products. In addition, there are guidelines to provide objective and high-quality advice to protect customers' interests. Conduct-of-business rules also promote fair and orderly markets.

The European financial landscape is integrating. In response, financial supervision in the EU has undergone a major reform. The establishment of the ESAs was merely a stepping stone to truly EU-based supervision. With the Banking Union in place since 2014, the ECB is responsible for the day-to-day supervision of around 120 significant banks, representing 80 per cent of total banking assets in the euro area. The ECB will indirectly supervise less significant banks in the participating countries, which numbered approximately 2,900 at the end of 2017. However, the ECB can decide at any time to take over the direct supervision of any of these banks. Finally, supervision has become more data driven; this trend is expected to continue in the future, in line with the digitalisation of financial services more generally.

Notes

1. The €5 billion loss at Société Générale in 2007 due to the alleged fraud of a rogue trader is an exceptional example of the failure of internal bank controls.

2. While prudential supervision aims to minimise the risk of failure, it cannot eliminate the risk of a failing bank in a market economy.

3. Next to the volatility adjustment, other Solvency II instruments with macroprudential impact are the symmetric adjustment in the equity risk module, the matching adjustment, the extension of the recovery period, the transitional measure on technical provisions, and prohibitions or restrictions on certain types of financial activities. See EIOPA (2018) for a full description.

4. The integrity and competence of financial institutions is not listed here as a specific conduct-of-business element. Fit and proper rules are general requirements that are applied in both prudential and conduct-of-business regulation. Section 12.2 explains these rules.

5. This section draws heavily on Cavelaars *et al.* (2013).

Bibliography

Suggested Reading

Admati, A. and M. Hellwig (2013), *The Bankers' New Clothes: What's Wrong with Banking and What to Do about It*, Princeton University Press.

Goodhart, C. A. E., P. Hartmann, D. T. Llewellyn, L. Rojas-Suarez, and S. Weisbrod (1998), *Financial Regulation: Why, How and Where Now?* Routledge, London.

Haldane, A. and V. Madouros (2012), The Dog and the Frisbee. Paper presented at the Federal Reserve Bank of Kansas City's 36th economic policy symposium 'The Changing Policy Landscape', Jackson Hole (WY).

References

Admati, A. and M. Hellwig (2013), *The Bankers' New Clothes: What's Wrong with Banking and What to Do about It*, Princeton University Press.

Alexander, K. (2018), Marketing, Sale and Distribution: Mis-selling of Financial Products. Study requested by the ECON Committee, Directorate-General for Internal Policies, Brussels.

Arner, D. W., J. Barberis, and R. P. Buckley (2017), FinTech and RegTech in a Nutshell, and the Future in a Sandbox. CFA Institute Research Foundation, Research Foundation Briefs.

Bank of England (2014), *The Financial Policy Committee's Review of the Leverage Ratio*, BoE, London.

Bank for International Settlements (1997), *Core Principles for Effective Banking Supervision*, BIS, Basel.

(2006), *Core Principles for Effective Banking Supervision*, BIS, Basel.

Barth, J. R., G. Caprio, and R. Levine (2012), *Guardians of Finance: Making Regulators Work for Us*, MIT Press, Cambridge (MA).

Basel Committee on Banking Supervision (2017a), Finalising Basel III In Brief. BIS, Basel. (2017b), High-Level Summary of Basel III Reforms. BIS, Basel.

Benston, G. J. and G. G. Kaufman (1996), The Appropriate Role of Bank Regulation. *The Economic Journal*, 106, 688–97.

Besley, T. (2007), The New Political Economy. *The Economic Journal*, 117, 570–87.

Cavelaars, P., J. de Haan, P. Hilbers, and B. Stellinga (2013), Challenges for Financial Sector Supervision. *DNB Occasional Studies* 6, De Nederlandsche Bank, Amsterdam.

Cizel, J., J. Frost, A. Houben, and P. Wierts (2019), Effective Macroprudential Policy: Cross-Sector Substitution from Price and Quantity Measures. *Journal of Money, Credit and Banking*, forthcoming.

Claessens, S., G. Underhill, and X. Zhang (2008), The Political Economy of Global Financial Governance: The Cost of Basel II for Poor Countries. *The World Economy*, 31, 313–44.

de Larosière, J. (2009), *Report of the High-Level Group on Financial Supervision in the EU*, European Commission, Brussels. http://ec.europa.eu/internal_market/finances/docs/de_larosiere_report_En.pdf (accessed 13 February 2012).

Dermine, J. (2006), European Banking Integration: Don't Put the Cart before the Horse. *Financial Markets, Institutions & Instruments*, 15, 57–106.

Dewatripont, M. and J. Tirole (1994), *The Prudential Regulation of Banks*, MIT Press, Cambridge (MA).

Dowd, K. (1996), The Case for Financial Laissez-Faire. *The Economic Journal*, 106, 679–87.

European Banking Authority (2018), Risk Dashboard Data as of Q2 2018. EBA, London.

European Commission (2007), *Green Paper on Retail Financial Services in the Single Market*, EC, Brussels.
(2013), *Capital Requirements – CRD IV/CRR – Frequently Asked Questions*, EC, Brussels.
(2014), *Economic Review of the Financial Regulation Agenda*, EC, Brussels.

European Insurance and Occupational Pensions Authority (2018), Solvency II Tools with Macroprudential Impact. EIOPA, Frankfurt am Main.

European Shadow Financial Regulatory Committee (2005), *Reforming Banking Supervision in Europe*, Statement No. 23, ESFRC, Frankfurt am Main.

European Systemic Risk Board (ESRB) (2015), *The ESRB Handbook on Operationalising Macroprudential Policy in the Banking Sector. Addendum: Macroprudential Leverage Ratios*, ESRB, Frankfurt am Main.

Gandrud, C. and M. Hallerberg (2014), Supervisory Transparency in the European Banking Union. Bruegel Policy Contribution 2014/1, Bruegel, Brussels.

Goodhart, C. A. E., P. Hartmann, D. T. Llewellyn, L. Rojas-Suarez, and S. Weisbrod (1998), *Financial Regulation: Why, How and Where Now?* Routledge, London.

International Monetary Fund (2000), *Supporting Document to the Code of Good Practices on Transparency in Monetary and Financial Policies*, Washington, DC, IMF.

Lastra, R. M. (2006), *Legal Foundations of International Monetary Stability*, Oxford University Press.

Liedorp, F., R. H. Mosch, C. A. B. van der Cruijsen, and J. de Haan (2013), Transparency of Banking Supervisors. *IMF Economic Review*, 61, 310–35.

Llewellyn, D. (1999), The Economic Rationale for Financial Regulation. FSA Occasional Paper 1, Financial Services Authority, London.

Merton, R. C. (1995), Financial Innovation and the Management and Regulation of Financial Institutions. *Journal of Banking and Finance*, 19, 461–81.

Mishkin, F. S. (2000), Prudential Supervision: Why Is It Important and What Are the Issues? NBER Working Paper 7926.

Nieto, M. J. and L. D. Wall (2007), Preconditions for a Successful Implementation of Supervisors' Prompt Corrective Action: Is There a Case for a Banking Standard in the EU? Banco de España Working Paper 0702.

Pagliari, S. (ed.) (2012), *Making Good Financial Regulation: Towards a Policy Response to Regulatory Capture*, Grosvenor House Publishing, London.

Quintyn, M. and M. W. Taylor (2003), Regulatory and Supervisory Independence and Financial Stability. *CESifo Economics Studies*, 49, 259–94.

Schoenmaker, D. (2013), *Governance of International Banking: The Financial Trilemma*, Oxford University Press.

Schoenmaker, D. and P. Wierts (2015), Regulating the Financial Cycle: An Integrated Approach with a Leverage Ratio. *Economics Letters*, 136, 70–2.

Schüler, M. and F. Heinemann (2005), The Costs of Supervisory Fragmentation in Europe. ZEW Discussion Paper 05-01.

Spindler, G (2011), Behavioural Finance and Investor Protection. *Journal of Consumer Policy*, 34, 315–36.

Stigler, G. (1971), The Theory of Economic Regulation. *Bell Journal of Economics*, 2, 3–21.

Thygesen, N. (2003), Comments on the Political Economy of Financial Harmonisation in Europe. In: J. J. M. Kremers, D. Schoenmaker, and P. J. Wierts (eds.), *Financial Supervision in Europe*, Edward Elgar, Cheltenham, 142–50.

Tucker, G. and E. Phelan (2017), Solvency Capital Requirement Coverage Ratios. Briefing note, Milliman Insight.

Van der Cruijsen, C. A. B., D. Jansen, J. de Haan, and R. H. J. Mosch (2013), Knowledge and Opinions about Banking Supervision: Evidence from a Survey of Dutch Households. *Journal of Financial Stability*, 9, 219–29.

Wegman, H. (2016), Investor Protection: Towards Additional EU Regulation of Investment Funds? Dissertation, Leiden University.

13

Financial Stability

OVERVIEW

Against the backdrop of the 2007–2009 financial crisis, this chapter discusses the growing importance of macroprudential supervision. In contrast to microprudential supervision, which focuses on the soundness of individual institutions, macroprudential supervision focuses on the stability of the financial system as a whole and on monitoring and assessing so-called systemic risk. This is the risk of a breakdown of an entire financial system rather than the failure of individual parts.

The chapter sets out the key features of the conceptual framework for macroprudential supervision. The framework starts with identifying the two dimensions of systemic risk. The time-series dimension examines financial imbalances, for which a cyclical approach is appropriate. The cross-sectional dimension looks at the distribution of risk within the financial system, for which a structural approach is most useful. The failure of a large financial institution, for example, poses an externality to the financial system. Another externality is the interconnectedness of financial intermediaries.

Next, macroprudential instruments are discussed. On the cyclical side, countercyclical capital buffers and real estate related instruments are applied to contain credit growth and house price rises. On the structural side, capital surcharges and resolution plans are applied to achieve stable, global systemically important financial institutions. Research on the effectiveness of macroprudential instruments is reviewed. The chapter also discusses the emerging institutional architecture for macroprudential supervision in the EU and the US.

Finally, the chapter touches on the issue of crisis management and resolution, discussing the main instruments that can be considered in crisis situations. The new Banking Union crisis management framework is analysed in detail. An important element is transferring responsibility for resolution from the national level to the Single Resolution Board at the European level, mirroring the Supervisory Board of the ECB as discussed in Chapter 12.

LEARNING OBJECTIVES

After you have studied this chapter, you should be able to:

- explain the concept of macroprudential supervision and differentiate it from microprudential supervision
- explain the concept of systemic risk and describe what makes financial systems prone to this risk
- understand the cyclical and structural pillars of macroprudential supervision
- describe the key instruments used by macroprudential authorities to prevent the build-up of systemic risk
- describe the principal features of the crisis management and resolution tools, including bail-in
- explain why improvised cooperation leads to an insufficient level of recapitalisation in the case of a cross-border failure, and why this calls for a Banking Union (BU) approach.

13.1 Financial Stability and Macroprudential Supervision

Macroprudential vs. Microprudential Supervision

Although both types of supervision are closely related, the financial crisis of 2007–2009 highlighted the important distinction between the two (see Hanson *et al.*, 2011).

Microprudential supervision has traditionally been the key focus of supervisory authorities. The intermediate objective of this type of oversight is to limit the distress of individual financial institutions, with the ultimate objective of protecting their customers. It does not focus on the financial system as a whole. However, by preventing the failure of individual financial institutions, microprudential supervision helps maintain confidence in the stability of the financial system as a whole.

Table 13.1 shows the key differences between macroprudential and microprudential supervision. The intermediate objective of macroprudential supervision is to limit financial system-wide distress, with the ultimate objective of protecting the overall economy from significant losses in real output. While risks to the financial system can in theory arise from the failure of one financial institution, common exposure of many financial institutions to the same risk factors is more important.

Table 13.1 Macroprudential versus microprudential supervision

	Macroprudential	Microprudential
Intermediate objective	Limit financial system-wide distress	Limit distress of individual institutions
Ultimate objective	Avoid output (GDP) costs	Consumer (investor/depositor) protection
Correlations and common exposures across institutions	Important	Irrelevant
Characterisation of risk	Seen as dependent on collective behaviour ('endogenous')	Seen as independent of individual agents' behaviour ('exogenous')
Calibration of prudential controls	In terms of system-wide risks; top-down	In terms of risks of individual institutions; bottom-up

Source: Borio (2003)

Macroprudential analysis must therefore pay particular attention to common or correlated shocks as well as to shocks that may trigger *contagion*, i.e. spread the adverse consequences of a financial institution's problems to the rest of the sector. Moreover, macroprudential supervision should take account of the interactions between financial institutions and their environment (i.e. other institutions, financial markets, infrastructure, and the real economy) as well as the dynamics with which imbalances may build up over time.

As such, the macroprudential perspective assumes that the risk of a shock is (partly) generated and amplified within the system (i.e. the risk is *endogenous*), while the microprudential approach focuses on institutions' vulnerability to threats emanating from their environment (i.e. the risk is *exogenous*).

Moreover, in order to avoid financial system-wide distress, the macro-level perspective takes a top-down approach to calibrating prudential controls by identifying risks in the system as a whole and then applying the relevant macroprudential tools. By contrast, the microprudential approach is bottom-up, setting the prudential controls in relation to the risk of each individual financial entity.

Indicators

Central banks regularly develop risk assessments, which are generally reported in their financial stability reports, to identify the sources of systemic risks and their transmission channels. These assessments are typically based on a broad range of information and analytical methods, including macroprudential stress tests. Selecting some key indicators that capture the identified sources of systemic risks helps monitor and assess the build-up of these risks (ESRB, 2014).

An assessment of risks often starts by analysing the financial cycle. Borio (2014) shows that the financial cycle is best described in terms of credit and house prices; it tends to have a lower frequency than the traditional business cycle, and its peaks are closely associated with financial crises (see Chapter 2). Information on the stage and direction of the financial cycle is crucial for assessing vulnerabilities in real time. Mian and Sufi (2014) advise paying extra attention to household credit within the broader category of private credit. Household credit is mainly used for mortgages. In times of rising house prices – often fuelled by the availability of cheap credit – consumers may spend the over-value of their house. In times of declining house prices, consumers restrain spending, in particular when the value of their house falls lower than the mortgage (known as a situation of negative equity). If many homeowners have negative equity, mortgage providers can be faced with an increasing number of non-performing loans. Notably, if homeowners have to sell their property if they lose their job or due to changes in their private life (a divorce, for instance), they may not be able to pay back their loan.

Macroprudential policy has two pillars, depending on the risk dimension focused upon (Schoenmaker and Wierts, 2011; Galati and Moessner, 2018). The first pillar (the time-series dimension) aims to contain financial imbalances, for which a cyclical approach is appropriate. The second pillar (the cross-sectional dimension) focuses on externalities, and thus a structural approach is most effective.

Table 13.2 summarises the objectives and indicators for each pillar. Panel A shows the indicators under the cyclical pillar. The credit-to-GDP gap, housing credit, and housing prices are key indicators of excessive credit growth and leverage. In an empirical test using 38 indicators, Alessi and Detken (2014) find that bank credit to GDP, household credit to GDP, and house price growth rank high in identifying excess credit growth. The structural funding ratio (see Chapter 12) and short-term liquidity indicators are important for detecting maturity mismatches and illiquidity.

Panel B shows indicators under the structural pillar. The indicators of exposure concentration are only indicative; more testing needs to be done to find the appropriate indicators for large exposures, interconnectedness, and price contagion (ESRB, 2014). By contrast, much work has been done on *systemically important financial institutions* (SIFIs) (see below).

Table 13.2 Objectives and indicators: cyclical and structural pillar

A. Cyclical pillar	Excessive credit growth and leverage	Excessive maturity mismatch and market illiquidity
Indicators	Credit-to-GDP gap, housing credit, housing prices	Structural funding ratio, short-term liquidity stress indicators
B. Structural pillar	Exposure concentration	Misaligned incentives (TBTF)
Indicators	Indicators for large exposures, interconnectedness, price contagion	Size, complexity, substitutability, and interconnectedness of SIFIs

Source: Adapted from ESRB (2014)

Systemically Important Financial Institutions

To compute the effect of potential threats to the system as a whole, macro-prudential authorities also need to have a good understanding of the position of SIFIs. These are large, complex, interconnected financial institutions that may cause significant disruption to the wider financial system and economic activity if they fail.

Therefore, these institutions are often considered *too big to fail* (TBTF). Oversight agencies theoretically fear the failure of a large bank more than the failure of a small bank, since the former is more likely to result in macro-economic externalities. TBTF banks receive a de facto government guarantee, which leads to a moral hazard problem. As banks know they will be rescued, they have an incentive to take more risks. Government guarantees also reduce market discipline by decreasing investors' incentives to monitor and price the risk taking behaviour of TBTF banks. As a result, TBTF banks have been able to borrow at costs that do not adequately reflect the risks inherent to their operations (see Strahan, 2013 for a review of the TBTF literature).

SIFIs vary in their structures and activities, and hence in the nature and degree of the risks they pose to the financial system. For example, the collapse of Lehman Brothers, which at the time was not considered to be TBTF by US policy makers, demonstrated that the disorderly failure of a global financial firm may have strong spillovers across markets, affecting financial stability and national economies around the world.

The assessment methodology for identifying SIFIs comprises five broad categories:

1. *Cross-border activity* captures a financial institution's global footprint by measuring its importance outside its home jurisdiction; this dimension captures the international impact of the institution's distress or failure.

2. *Size* can be measured as an institution's assets or equity, either in absolute terms or as a proportion of GDP. Size may serve as an initial indicator of systemic relevance, although it is not sufficient to determine whether an institution is systemically relevant. For example, a large firm may not pose a systemic problem if it is not interconnected or if substitutes are available for its products. Therefore, interactions among the factors also are important in identifying systemically relevant institutions.
3. *Interconnectedness* examines the likelihood that financial distress in one institution or market will spread to others through the provision of funds and services, funding, confidence factors, or exposures through common risk factors.
4. *Substitutability* assesses the extent to which other institutions or parts of the financial system can provide the same services if one or more institutions were to fail. A lack of substitutability could pose a systemic threat if the services provided by the failed institution(s) are critically important to the functioning of other institutions or the financial system (e.g. payment and settlement systems).
5. *Complexity* looks at the group structures and business models of financial institutions, as the complexity and integrated nature of many institutions makes it very difficult not only to manage and supervise SIFIs but also for orderly resolution in the event of their failure.

Stress Testing

Stress tests are an important tool that enhances the authorities' understanding of possible vulnerabilities within individual institutions as well as the overall system. They examine the implications of individual banks' financial positions under several macroeconomic scenarios, taking the banks' exposures and business models into account. The results of such a test reveal a portfolio's sensitivity to one or more shocks. They help fill in the gaps in the historical data, which often do not provide sufficient information about the behaviour of markets during extreme events (Hilbers and Jones, 2004).

System-wide stress tests measure the sensitivity of a group of institutions, or even an entire financial system, to common shocks. They seek to identify common vulnerabilities across institutions that could undermine the system's overall stability. These tests focus on the macroeconomic level, to determine how major changes in the economic environment may affect the financial system as a whole.

System-wide tests can complement individual institutions' stress tests, and act as a cross-check for other types of analysis. Stress tests can also be preceded by an asset quality review, including the adequacy of asset and collateral valuation and related provisions, to enhance the transparency of bank exposures.

13.2 Macroprudential Instruments

The financial crisis of 2007–2009 revealed the need for macroprudential instruments or tools to mitigate the build-up of systemic risk in the financial system. The entry into force of the EU prudential rules (the Capital Requirements Regulation/Capital Requirements Directive (CCR/CRD IV) package, see Chapter 12) on 1 January 2014 gave the EU's macroprudential authorities a set of instruments with which to address systemic risk in the banking sector. Within the BU, macroprudential policy remains the responsibility of the national designated authority; the ECB can impose higher (i.e. more restrictive) requirements if deemed necessary.

Cyclical Pillar

Since the macroprudential instruments under the cyclical pillar can dampen both the upswing and the downswing of the financial cycle (see Figure 13.1), the countercyclical buffers must be increased in order to slow credit growth in the upswing phase. But it is equally important to release buffers in the downswing. This requires a macro approach, as more micro-focused supervisors tend to tighten capital requirements during downturns.

The CCR/CRD IV package offers several instruments:

- the *countercyclical capital buffer*, to counteract the effects of the economic cycle on banks' lending activity (see Chapter 12);
- the *Basel Pillar II* (see Chapter 12) gives authorities the ability to impose additional requirements on a specific bank or group of banks for macroprudential reasons;
- *national flexibility measures* that allow national authorities to impose stricter prudential requirements in order to address systemic risk. If they choose to do so, Member States must notify and justify a more stringent measure to the Commission, European Banking Authority (EBA), and European Systemic Risk Board (ESRB);

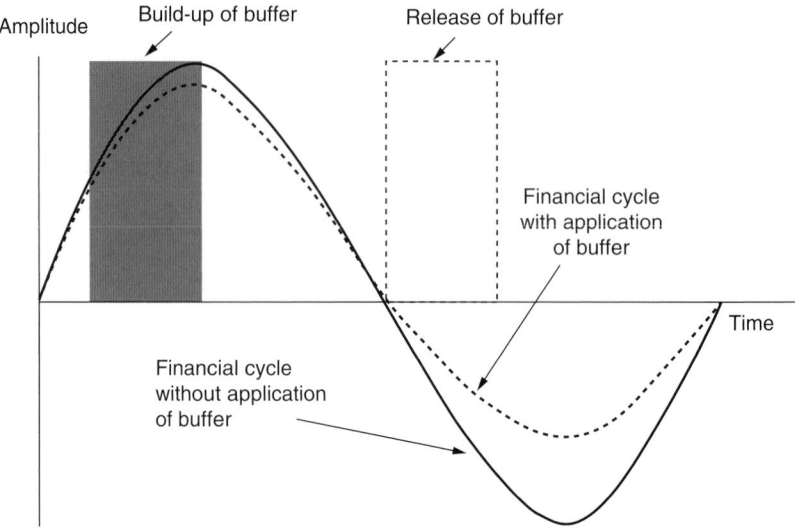

Figure 13.1   Stylised transmission of buffers during the financial cycle
Source: ESRB (2014)

- *real estate-related instruments,* e.g. Member States can set higher risk weights for real estate lending, which allows them to address real estate bubbles;
- two new *liquidity buffers,* i.e. a liquidity coverage ratio and a net stable funding ratio (see Chapter 12);
- a *leverage ratio,* as a backstop mechanism to limit the growth of the total balance sheet compared to available own funds.

Borrower-based instruments that are under national legislation include:

- the *loan-to-value (LTV) ratio,* which limits the extension of mortgage credit beyond a particular fraction of the value of housing collateral, and so restricts losses in the event of a default;
- the *loan-to-income (LTI) ratio,* which limits the extension of mortgage credit beyond a multiple of borrowers' annual income, thereby lowering the probability of default.

A common approach to implementing LTV and LTI restrictions is by prohibiting financial institutions from extending mortgage credit beyond a certain amount. An LTV cap increases the borrower's equity stake in the property, which creates incentives to service the loan and lowers the bank's losses in the event of borrower default ('loss given default'). Both of these effects improve the resilience of the financial system and can also potentially lower mortgage credit growth. A related, but less frequently used, measure is a cap on the LTI ratio, which limits the size of the debt (or the cost of servicing the debt) relative to the borrower's income. These restrictions can thus help mitigate the risk that credit-fuelled bubbles in the housing market will arise. Calibrating and adjusting LTV or LTI restrictions requires national authorities to ensure an appropriate trade-off between financial stability benefits, economic activity, and societal preferences for home ownership (BoE, 2011). An alternative approach would be to require banks to fund high-LTV or high-LTI mortgages through higher amounts of capital, i.e. via higher-risk weights.

Structural Pillar

The structural pillar contains instruments for effectively addressing risks to financial stability due to externalities within the financial system, i.e. financial institutions, financial markets, and financial infrastructures. *Stricter large exposure requirements* (as well as sectoral capital requirements for intra-financial exposures) can be used to address interconnectedness and contagion (ESRB, 2014). These restrictions are microprudential measures that can be further tightened to achieve macroprudential objectives. They can be applied via Pillar II to reduce banks' exposure to a particular sector or asset class. They may target both direct exposures and excessive (indirect) interconnectedness among financial institutions, thereby reducing the risk of contagion.

The second instrument is a *capital surcharge for SIFIs*. Because of their size, complexity, and systemic interconnectedness, the failure of such institutions would jeopardise financial stability. The Financial Stability Board (FSB, 2010) recommends that SIFIs should have higher loss-absorbing capacity than the minimum Basel III levels. The FSB has the authority to designate a financial institution as a SIFI. Chapters 10 and 11 report the list of *global systemically important banks* (G-SIBs) and *global systemically important insurers* (G-SIIs) in 2017. These lists are updated annually. So far, only capital surcharges for G-SIBs have been determined, which range from 1 to 2.5 per cent (see Table 10.7). These surcharges are formulated in risk-weighted terms. The final Basel III reforms as agreed upon in December 2017 also contain a leverage ratio surcharge for G-SIBs that consists of half of the surcharge in risk-weighted terms, e.g. 0.5 per cent for a risk-weighted surcharge of 1 per cent of risk-weighted assets.

Another structural instrument for SIFIs to reduce the moral hazard of TBTF institutions are their resolution plans (Avgouleas *et al.*, 2013). These plans seek to provide authorities with a strategy for resolving a failing bank, with the aim of: (i) ensuring the continuation or orderly wind-down of a bank's critical economic activities, (ii) minimising the disruption of financial stability, (iii) containing moral hazard, and (iv) limiting the risk of exposing taxpayers to losses. It must be possible for a bank to be resolved in a way that ensures that shareholders and unsecured creditors bear losses comparable to those they would suffer in the event of a normal insolvency, rather than benefiting from a public bailout as a consequence of the immediate need to preserve financial stability or the continuation of essential services (see also Section 13.4).

Capital surcharges for SIFIs should reflect the potential losses to society of systemic risk from large and interconnected institutions (ESRB, 2014). The FSB's SIFI framework only applies to global financial institutions; national authorities can designate domestic financial institutions as domestic SIFIs. If needed, national authorities may use the *systemic risk buffer* in response to structural vulnerabilities, including the level of private debt or the size of the banking sector.

Use and Effectiveness of Macroprudential Measures

While the CCR/CRD IV package introduced EU-wide macroprudential measures for banks in 2014, the use of macroprudential instruments is not new. In the period from the Second World War until the financial deregulation of the 1980s, many countries closely regulated credit markets using instruments that resemble current macroprudential policy tools. From the 1990s onwards, macroprudential policy measures have been most actively used in emerging markets, particularly in Asia in the aftermath of the Asian financial crisis. After the global financial crisis, the active use of such instruments also became widespread in Western economies.

The IMF has created a global database on the use of macroprudential policy instruments since the year 2000 (IMF, 2018). The overview in Cerutti *et al.* (2017) shows the rising use of both lender- and borrower-based measures. By 2017, almost all EU Member States had identified systemically important banks, and 17 had imposed capital surcharges on them (ESRB, 2018). Moreover, five EU Member States had activated the countercyclical capital buffer, eight had activated higher risk weights for either residential or commercial real estate, and five had activated some form of liquidity ratio. Concerning borrower-based measures, 19 EU Member States had activated LTV caps, eight used a debt-service-to-income ratio, and three had introduced an LTI cap (ESRB, 2018).

Within the EU, primary responsibility for implementing macroprudential measures is left to the national level, and is subject to guidance on instrument usage and information sharing at the EU level (see Section 13.3). This has led to a lack of consistency in policy implementation across Member States, which have responded very differently to developments in the credit-to-GDP gap for instance (ESRB, 2018). Some countries point to the inadequacy of the credit gap as a risk indicator for the specific post-crisis domestic circumstances, but differences in discretionary decision making also play an important role. Likewise, there are large differences in national approaches to the application of capital surcharges for systemic risk. While the ECB has the power to impose more restrictive requirements, it has not done so as of early 2019.

Galati and Moessner (2018) review the growing literature on the effect of macroprudential policy measures on intermediate financial cycle indicators, such as credit growth and house prices. They conclude that the empirical evidence is clearest on the effects of borrower-based measures, such as LTV caps. Many studies find that these measures reduce credit growth and/or house prices (e.g. Hong Kong Monetary Authority, 2011; Lim *et al.*, 2014). In addition, Cerutti *et al.* (2017) conclude that the use of macroprudential instruments is generally associated with lower growth in credit. But they also find indications of leakages, since the effects are less pronounced in financially more developed and open economies, as well as an increase in cross-border borrowing after the implementation of macroprudential measures. Specific studies indeed suggest that macroprudential policies lead to increased lending by foreign banks (Aiyar *et al.*, 2014) and non-banks (Cizel *et al.*, 2019).

13.3 Macroprudential Architecture

One of the key lessons from the 2007–2009 financial crisis was that the oversight arrangements had placed too much emphasis on the supervision of individual firms, and too little on the stability of the financial system as a whole. The EU and US authorities therefore established new bodies responsible for macroprudential supervision. National macroprudential authorities were created in the EU, the Single Supervisory Mechanism (SSM) was given macroprudential powers, and the ESRB started functioning in 2011. In the US, the Financial Stability Oversight Council (FSOC) was formed, and at the global level G20 leaders established the FSB.

Developments in EU Member States and the SSM

Almost all Member States have a macroprudential authority in place, but the institutional set-up differs across countries (ESRB, 2018). In most cases, it is either the central bank or a committee, with a leading role for the central bank. Committees often have a coordinating role and lack the power to implement instruments; they typically include the central bank, the financial supervisor, and the government. In some Member States such as Sweden and Finland, the supervisory authority has been appointed as the macroprudential authority.

The CRR/CRD IV require Member States to set up a 'designated authority' in charge of macroprudential oversight. In more than half of the Member States, the macroprudential authority is also the designated authority. But for countries with a macroprudential committee that only has a coordinating role, the designated authority is the central bank or the financial supervisory authority. Exceptions include Poland, where the designated authority is the Ministry of Finance, and Denmark, where it is the Ministry of Industry, Business and Financial Affairs. Assigning macroprudential policy to governments may give rise to inaction, as politicians may delay tightening macroprudential policy in the run-up to elections.

The SSM makes the ECB an additional player for members of the BU. While the designated national authorities have the power to apply macroprudential tools, the ECB can set tighter requirements than national authorities. The ECB has established a Financial Stability Committee to advise the SSM Supervisory Board and the ECB Governing Council on macroprudential policy.

European Systemic Risk Board

The ESRB is responsible for macroprudential oversight of the EU's financial system, and is thus responsible for the prevention or mitigation of any systemic risks that arise from macroeconomic developments within the system, in order to prevent widespread financial distress. ESRB recommendations are not binding, but the parties addressed are obliged to either 'comply or explain'.

The ESRB comprises a General Board as its decision-making body, a Steering Committee that sets the agenda and prepares the decisions, a Secretariat, as well as an Advisory Technical Committee and an Advisory Scientific Committee. While all relevant stakeholders are represented within the ESRB, central banks have a prominent role: the majority of the voting members of the General Board are central bankers, and the ECB president chairs meetings of the General Board. The ECB also provides staff for the Secretariat as well as analytical, statistical, administrative, and logistical support to the ESRB.

The tasks of the ESRB include: (1) the collection and analysis of all information relevant to macroprudential oversight; (2) the identification and prioritisation of systemic risks; (3) the issuance of warnings where such risks are deemed to be significant; (4) the issuance of recommendations for remedial action; (5) the monitoring of the follow-up to warnings and recommendations; (6) cooperation with the European Supervisory Authorities, including the development of systemic risk indicators and the conduct of stress-testing exercises; (7) the issuance of confidential warnings on emergency situations addressed to the European Council; and (8) coordination with the IMF and the FSB, as well as other macroprudential bodies.

Financial Stability Oversight Council

The FSOC was established under the Dodd-Frank Act in the US to provide comprehensive monitoring to ensure the stability of the nation's financial system. The Council is charged with promoting market discipline, identifying threats to US financial stability, and responding to emerging threats to this stability. It is chaired by the Secretary of the Treasury and its members comprise representatives from the Federal Reserve, the federal financial regulators, as well as state regulators (the latter are non-voting members).

The FSOC has three sets of powers (Enria and Teixeira, 2011):

1. *Coordination powers:* it has the duty to support coordination and information sharing among its members.
2. *Advisory powers:* it may issue recommendations for regulatory policy. In particular, it may recommend new or stricter standards for interconnected institutions (including non-banks), as well as financial products and markets that pose a threat to financial stability. The FSOC may also recommend that the US Congress close regulatory gaps.
3. *Systemic powers:* it has the authority to require the consolidated supervision of non-bank financial institutions and to designate specific financial market infrastructures (e.g. payment, clearing, and settlement) as systemic in order to subject them to regulatory oversight. The FSOC also plays a role in the possible breaking up of institutions that pose a 'grave threat' to financial stability.

The ESRB and FSOC are broadly similar: they both monitor the emergence of systemic risks, which involves collecting and sharing information on the financial system. The main difference is that the ESRB lacks the authority to intervene directly in the financial system, while the FSOC can bring institutions and market infrastructures within the scope of regulatory oversight and determine whether the Federal Reserve can act in the context of its important new power to break up financial institutions.

Financial Stability Board

G20 leaders established the FSB at their April 2009 summit to coordinate the work of national financial authorities and international standard-setting bodies and to develop and promote the implementation of effective regulatory, supervisory, and other financial sector policies. The FSB gathers national authorities responsible for financial stability in significant international financial centres, international financial institutions, sector-specific international groupings of regulators and supervisors, and committees of central bank experts.

The FSB is the successor to the Financial Stability Forum, with a broadened mandate to promote financial stability. The FSB is working to strengthen the oversight and regulation of non-bank financial intermediaries and to ensure that global systemically important institutions have sufficient loss-absorbing capacity when they fail.

13.4 Crisis Management and Resolution

Bank Recovery and Resolution

The financial crisis of 2007–2009 forced EU Member States to grant public support to banks on an unprecedented scale. According to IMF estimates, crisis-related losses incurred by European banks between 2007 and 2010 are close to €1 trillion or 8 per cent of EU GDP. Between October 2008 and December 2012, the European Commission approved close to €600 billion (4.6 per cent of EU 2012 GDP) in state aid measures in the form of recapitalisation and asset relief measures (EC, 2014).

While clearly necessary at that time to prevent widespread disruption, the financial crisis highlighted the fact that public authorities lacked effective instruments to intervene at an early stage. Moreover, where a bank failed, new instruments were needed to rescue its critical functions, with minimum or no recourse to taxpayer money.

The Bank Recovery and Resolution Directive (BRRD; 2014/59/EU) contains the new crisis management framework for banks in Europe. It provides authorities with more comprehensive and effective arrangements to deal with failing banks at the national level, as well as cooperation arrangements to tackle cross-border banking failures. Key elements of the BRRD are (EC, 2014):

- *Preparation and prevention.* Banks and resolution authorities are required to draw up recovery and resolution plans on how to deal with situations that may lead to financial stress or the failure of a bank. If the authorities identify obstacles to resolvability during the course of this planning process, they can require a bank to take appropriate measures, including changes to corporate and legal structures, to ensure that it can be resolved with the available tools in a way that does not threaten financial stability or involve costs to taxpayers.

- *Early intervention.* Supervisory authorities are granted new powers to intervene if a bank faces financial distress (e.g. when it is in breach of, or is about to breach, regulatory capital requirements), but before the problems become critical and its financial situation deteriorates beyond repair. These powers include the ability to dismiss the management and appoint a temporary administrator, to convene a shareholder meeting to adopt urgent reforms, and to require the bank to draw up a plan to restructure its debt with its creditors.

- *Resolution.* Resolution involves the restructuring of a bank by a resolution authority to ensure the continuity of its critical functions to restore the viability of all or part of that institution, while the remaining parts are put into normal insolvency proceedings. The objective of resolution is to minimise the extent to which taxpayers bear the cost of a bank failure. The resolution authority has the power to sell or merge the business with another bank, to set up a temporary bridge bank to operate critical functions, to separate good assets from bad ones, and to convert to shares or write down the debt of failing banks (*bail-in*). This process occurs at the point when the relevant authorities determine that a bank is failing or likely to fail, that no other private sector intervention can restore the institution to viability within a short time frame, and that normal insolvency proceedings would lead to financial instability.

- *Resolution fund.* Member States are required to establish an *ex ante* funded resolution fund. Contributions are raised from banks in proportion to their liabilities and risk profiles, to reach a target funding level of at least 1 per cent of covered deposits. The fund should primarily be used for resolution costs that cannot be funded via bail-in, e.g. the financing of a bridge bank. However, the BRRD provides that after these stakeholders have borne sufficient losses (i.e. 8 per cent of the liabilities of the bank under resolution) through write-down or conversion, in exceptional circumstances the resolution financing arrangement may bear the remaining losses, but only up to 5 per cent of the bank's liabilities.

- *Cooperation and coordination.* The BRRD provides a framework to improve cooperation between national authorities. If a cross-border banking group fails, this framework should enable national authorities to coordinate their resolution measures and achieve the most effective outcome for the group as a whole. Cross-border resolution may indeed give rise to coordination failures, as countries focus only on their own situations. Box 13.1 explains the financial trilemma model, which facilitates comparisons of the efficiency of the different resolution mechanisms.

Single Resolution Mechanism

The Single Resolution Mechanism (SRM) is the second pillar of the European BU. It introduces centralised decision making and a centralised resolution fund, rather than the decentralised approach based on the BRRD. The SRM Regulation (EU/806/2014) applies to all banks established in the EU Member States participating in the BU.

The main institutional components of the SRM are the Single Resolution Board (SRB) and a Single Resolution Fund (SRF), to which all banks in the BU contribute. The SRB has the status of an EU agency and is based in Brussels. Figure 13.2 provides an overview of the overall structure of the SRM.

The SRB is responsible for the resolution planning and resolution of banks directly supervised by the ECB, as well as cross-border groups. The national resolution authorities remain responsible for all other banks, except where a resolution scheme foresees the use of the SRF. In such a case, the SRB becomes the relevant resolution authority, regardless of the size of the institution.

The SRB operates in two sessions:

- In its *executive session*, the SRB takes the key preparatory and operational decisions for resolving individual banks, including use of the SRF, and the decisions addressed to national authorities, as they are responsible for

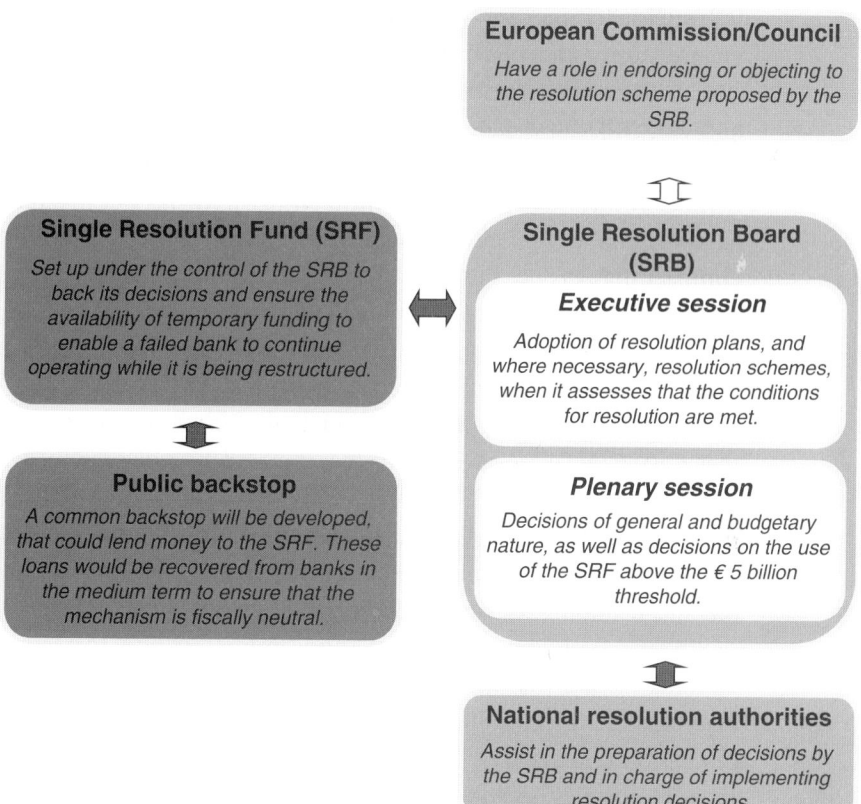

European Commission/Council

Have a role in endorsing or objecting to the resolution scheme proposed by the SRB.

Single Resolution Fund (SRF)

Set up under the control of the SRB to back its decisions and ensure the availability of temporary funding to enable a failed bank to continue operating while it is being restructured.

Single Resolution Board (SRB)

Executive session

Adoption of resolution plans, and where necessary, resolution schemes, when it assesses that the conditions for resolution are met.

Public backstop

A common backstop will be developed, that could lend money to the SRF. These loans would be recovered from banks in the medium term to ensure that the mechanism is fiscally neutral.

Plenary session

Decisions of general and budgetary nature, as well as decisions on the use of the SRF above the € 5 billion threshold.

National resolution authorities

Assist in the preparation of decisions by the SRB and in charge of implementing resolution decisions

Figure 13.2   Structure of the Single Resolution Mechanism

implementing the SRB's decisions. Executive sessions involve the SRB chairman, vice chair, four permanent members, and the relevant national authorities in the countries where the troubled bank is established. Representatives from the ECB and the European Commission participate in the process as permanent observers.

- In its *plenary session*, the SRB takes all general and budgetary decisions. Individual resolution cases are also heard in plenary session if an SRF contribution of more than €5 billion is required. These sessions involve all of the above representatives, in addition to all national resolution authorities participating in the BU.

The SRF is financed by contributions from all banks established in the Member States participating in the BU. The SRF is not designed to replace private investors in absorbing losses and providing new capital to a bank, but to provide temporary financial support through guarantees or loans to ensure the viability of a bank's critical functions while it is being restructured.

The SRF has a target level of €55 billion, to be reached by the end of 2023, and the SRB can decide to borrow from the market or from third parties. During the transitional phase, the SRF is composed of national compartments, which are gradually mutualised. During this period individual Member States can offer bridge financing, and lending between national compartments is possible. The European Stability Mechanism is planned to become available as a common backstop, which would facilitate borrowing by the SRF. These loans are to be recovered from banks in the medium term so that taxpayers' money is not involved.

How does this structure operate in practice? Upon notification from the ECB that a bank is failing or likely to fail, the SRB first determines whether three conditions for resolution are met: (i) a bank is failing or likely to fail, (ii) there are no alternative private solutions, and (iii) a resolution action is necessary in the public interest. Once these have been confirmed, the SRB will adopt a resolution scheme, including relevant resolution tools and the possible use of the SRF.

Since the SRB is an EU agency, the Commission and, to a lesser extent, the Council have a role in endorsing or objecting to any resolution scheme it proposes. If one of them objects, the Board would have to amend the resolution scheme. The overall decision-making process may not last longer than 32 hours, to ensure that a bank can be resolved over the weekend.

National resolution authorities help the SRB prepare its actions, and are tasked with implementing the resolution decisions in line with national company and insolvency law. Member States are thus integrated into the overall structure with respect to the preparatory and implementation stages related to banks in their jurisdiction. The SRB closely monitors the implementation of resolution decisions, and can directly address executive orders to troubled banks if national authorities do not comply with one or more aspects of the resolution decision.

Resolution Tools

The first tool that can be used in the case of a bank failure is private sector acquisition, whereby parts of the bank are sold to one or more purchasers without the consent of the shareholders. In this scenario, the resolution authority can act as an honest broker. This role is important, especially given the time constraints under which most problems have to be solved and the information asymmetries involved.

Box 13.1 The financial trilemma*

Schoenmaker (2013) developed the financial trilemma, which states that (1) a stable financial system, (2) international banking, and (3) national financial policies for supervision and resolution are incompatible. Any two of the three objectives can be combined, but not all three. The financial stability implication of international banking is that national financial policies are no longer adequate. Effective international cooperation for banking supervision and resolution is needed. In Europe, the BU provides the necessary cooperation for banking policies.

The financial trilemma model formalises the systemic effects of bank failure. The policy instrument in this model is a contribution of funds t by the authorities (the Ministry of Finance and/or the central bank) to recapitalise a failing bank. The model considers the *ex post* decision of whether to recapitalise or liquidate a bank in financial distress. This choice is represented by the variable x with values in the space {0,1}, whereby $x^* = 1$ indicates recapitalisation and $x^* = 0$ closure.

Next, B denotes the social benefits of recapitalisation (which include maintaining financial stability and avoiding contagion) and C the costs of continuing the bank's activities. A minor, idiosyncratic bank failure would not pose a systemic problem.

Single-country setting

A social planner recapitalises a failing bank only when the total social benefits of an intervention are larger than the net costs: i.e. when $B > C$. This is the efficient resolution line in Figure 13.3. Private sector solutions are preferable for addressing banking problems to reduce moral hazard. Only when the private sector cannot deal effectively with an emerging banking crisis do the authorities need to get involved.

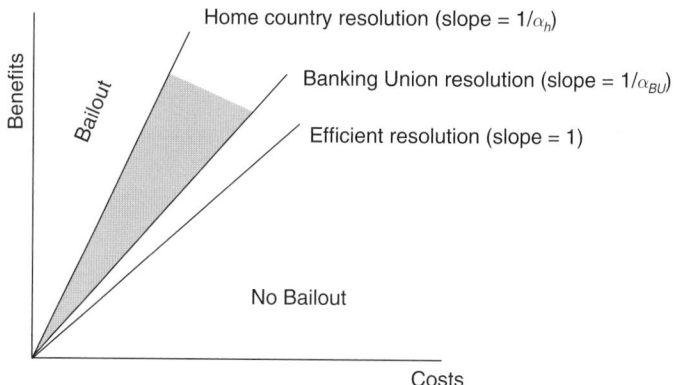

Figure 13.3   Equilibrium outcomes of different resolution mechanisms
Source: Schoenmaker (2013)

Box 13.1 (cont.)

Multi-country setting

In a multi-country setting, the social benefits can be decomposed into the benefits in the home country (α_h), in other European countries (α_e), and in the rest of the world (α_w). These benefits sum up to 1. A cross-border bank is only recapitalised if a sufficient contribution from the different countries can be collected on a voluntary basis. The countries meet to find out how much they are ready to contribute to the recapitalisation, denoted by t. If the total amount they are willing to contribute is larger than the costs, the bank is recapitalised.

The optimal decision for each independent country j is to maximise:

$$x^* \cdot (a_j \cdot B - t_j) \tag{13.1}$$

so that

$$x^* = \begin{cases} 1 & \text{if } \sum_j t_j - C \geq 0 \\ 0 & \text{if } \sum_j t_j - C < 0 \end{cases} \tag{13.2}$$

The only choice variable for country j in this game is the size of its contribution t_j. Equation (13.1) shows that country j can maximise its benefits minus its contribution, by minimising its contribution. If every country only makes a minimal contribution to the recapitalisation, it is difficult to raise sufficient funds to meet the costs (equation (13.2)). This game, in which every country announces its contribution, has a multiplicity of equilibria. In particular, the closure $t_j = 0$, $x^* = 0$ is an equilibrium provided that for no country j,

$$a_j \cdot B - C > 0 \tag{13.3}$$

Equation (13.3) indicates that no individual country is ready to finance the recapitalisation by itself, as the benefits for each country are smaller than the overall costs. In that case, every country reduces its contribution basically to zero. The closure equilibrium can occur (even if recapitalisation is efficient, $B > C$) because some of the externalities fall outside the home country. This is shown in Figure 13.3 as the home country resolution line.

Solutions

Schoenmaker (2013) models two solutions to this coordination problem. The first is a supranational mandate for financial stability. The decision is taken by a supranational body, which can charge the participating countries by applying general criteria to share the burden. The optimal decision for the European supranational body is to maximise:

$$x^* \cdot \left((a_h + a_e) \cdot B - C \right) \tag{13.4}$$

so that

Box 13.1 (cont.)

$$x^* = \begin{cases} 1 \text{ if } (a_h + a_e) \cdot B - C \geq 0 \\ 0 \text{ if } (a_h + a_e) \cdot B - C < 0 \end{cases} \qquad (13.5)$$

The European body improves on the coordination outcome, as all European externalities $(a_h + a_e)$ are taken into account in the recapitalisation decision (see the BU resolution line in Figure 13.3). Chapter 10 quantifies these externalities for the biggest European banks: $a_h = 0.56$ in Table 10.2 and $a_{BU} = 0.72$ in Table 10.6 (note that BU refers to the home country and the other countries in the BU). The BU leads to an efficiency improvement of 51 per cent compared to national decision making, as the latter is at a distance of 0.79 (=1/0.56–1) from the efficient benchmark of 1 and the supranational setting is 0.39 (=1/0.72–1) from 1. Note that 51 per cent = (0.79 – 0.39)/0.79.

A second solution to the coordination failure is to create binding rules among European countries (Goodhart and Schoenmaker, 2009).

If a private sector solution is not immediately at hand, the resolution authority can transfer parts of the bank to a temporary structure (such as a bridge bank) to preserve essential banking functions or facilitate continuous access to deposits.

Another option is a bail-in, which separates assets between a 'good' and 'bad' bank through a partial transfer of assets and liabilities. As a result, the bank in distress is split into a 'good' bank that retains the performing assets, and a 'bad' bank that receives the remaining (toxic) assets that are subsequently restructured or liquidated. Bank creditors can either be left with the 'bad' bank and undergo losses as part of the liquidation or be transferred to the 'good' bank, which may involve their claims being reduced or converted into equity.

The main aim of a bail-in is to stabilise a failing bank so it can continue its critical functions, with minimal or no use of public funds. Bail-in enables authorities to recapitalise a failing bank through the write-down of liabilities and/or their conversion to equity, so that it can continue as a going concern.

To ensure that institutions always have sufficient loss-absorbing and recapitalisation capacity, the BRRD requires resolution authorities to set *minimum requirement for own funds and eligible liabilities* (MREL) targets for each institution, based on its size, risk, and business model. Since 2017, the SRB has set binding bank-specific MREL targets for the banks within its remit, i.e. those under direct ECB supervision and other cross-border groups (SRB, 2017). The basic idea is that it should still be possible to recapitalise a bank in resolution after all going-concern buffers have been written down by bailing in liabilities. Generally, MREL should therefore be at least twice the size of the capital requirements, i.e. twice the size of Pillar 1, Pillar 2, and the combined buffer requirement (see Chapter 12).

In case of resolution, the resolution authority will first write down all share-holders and then follow a predetermined order when bailing in other liabilities. It potentially applies to all liabilities, even beyond MREL, which are not backed by assets or collateral. However, bail-in will not apply to deposits protected by a deposit guarantee scheme, short-term interbank lending, claims of clearing-houses or payment and settlement systems (that have a remaining maturity of seven days), client assets, or liabilities such as salaries, pensions, or taxes. In exceptional circumstances, authorities can choose to exclude other liabilities on a case-by-case basis, if strictly necessary to ensure the continuity of critical services or to prevent widespread and disruptive contagion to other parts of the financial system, or if they cannot be bailed in within a reasonable time.

The write-down will follow the ordinary allocation of losses and ranking in insolvency (see Figure 13.4). Within each class in the hierarchy, all instruments must be treated equally, i.e. *pari passu*. Equity holdings must absorb losses in full before any debt claim is subject to write-down. After shares and other similar instruments, if necessary, losses will be imposed evenly among all holders of subordinated debt. Next in line is senior unsecured debt. This new class was introduced in 2017 through an amend-ment of the BRRD, as regards the Ranking of Unsecured Debt Instruments in Insolvency Hierarchy (2017/2399/EU). It consists of unsecured debt instruments with an initial contractual maturity of at least one year, and excludes derivatives. The addition of senior unsecured debt was intended to improve resolvability by avoiding *pari passu* with all other senior debt instruments. Since the creditor hierarchy for this latter class is not harmo-nised under EU law, the hierarchy of claims in national solvency law applies to these instruments.

Deposits from SMEs and natural persons in excess of €100,000 will be preferred over other senior debt. The Deposit Guarantee Scheme (DGS, see below) will in turn rank above these. In extreme situations, the DGS may have to make a cash contribution equal to the amount of the covered deposits that are exempt from the bail-in tool.

It should be noted that, in order to protect creditors' interests, the BRRD includes the principle that no creditor should be worse off under resolution than it would have been had the bank been wound up under normal insolvency

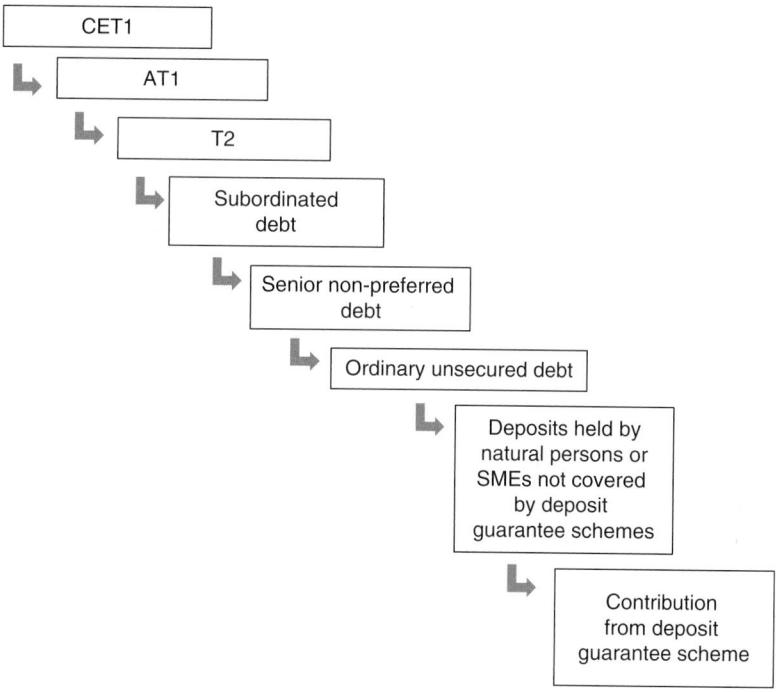

Figure 13.4 Hierarchy of claims in the bail-in procedure
Source: Ranking of Unsecured Debt Instruments in Insolvency Hierarchy (2017/2399/EU) and Bundesbank (2014)

proceedings. This principle entitles creditors to compensation if it is determined that the amount they end up recovering is less than they would have received if the bank had simply been placed into insolvency (for example, because the resolution authority decides to exclude certain liabilities from bail-in).

Goodhart and Avgouleas (2014) provide a critical evaluation of the bail-in process. They argue that despite the bail-in regime, an injection of public funds may still be needed if a number of banks simultaneously enter into difficulties, or if a large complex cross-border bank fails. This view was confirmed by recent experiences in Italy. In July 2017, the Italian government undertook a 'precautionary recapitalisation' of Banca Monte dei Paschi di Siena to remedy a serious economic disturbance and to preserve financial stability. In the previous month, the Italian banks Veneto Banca and Banca Popolare di Vicenza were liquidated under national insolvency rules rather than under the BRRD regime. However, based on the overall evidence, Philippon and Salord (2017) are cautiously optimistic about the future of bail-in in Europe. In their view, the main issue is the transition from the old to the new regime, as the resolution tools will have to be applied before sufficient loss-absorbing and recapitalisation capacity has been created.

Other Relevant Instruments

Emergency Liquidity Assistance

Banks can receive central bank credit not only through monetary policy operations, but also through Emergency Liquidity Assistance (ELA) provided by a central bank. Within the euro area, ELA involves a national central bank providing assistance to a solvent bank or banking group that is facing temporary liquidity problems, without the operation being part of the single monetary policy. While responsibility for the provision of ELA still lies with the national central bank(s) concerned, the Governing Council of the ECB may restrict ELA operations if it concludes that they interfere with the objectives and tasks of the Eurosystem.

Deposit Guarantee Schemes

DGS reimburse depositors whose bank has failed up to a limit. The DGS Directive (2014/49/EU) ensures that deposits are covered up to €100,000. It stipulates that banks must pay in to the schemes on a regular basis (*ex ante*), and not only after a bank failure (*ex post*). The target level of each DGS is a minimum of 0.8 per cent of the covered deposits in a Member State, to be reached within 10 years. The directive also aims to gradually reduce repayment deadlines from 20 to 7 working days. In 2015, the European Commission proposed to introduce a European DGS (COM/2015/0586), but there has not yet been political agreement on this proposal.

13.5 Conclusions

The 2007–2009 financial crisis highlighted the importance of effective crisis management tools as well as macroprudential supervision, focusing on the soundness of the financial system as a whole. Macroprudential supervision focuses on risks that may trigger a loss of economic value or confidence in a substantial part of the financial system that is serious enough to have significant adverse effects on the real economy. This requires the monitoring and analysis of: (1) the distribution of risk in the financial system at a given point in time, i.e. the cross-sectional dimension, and (2) the evolution of aggregate risk, i.e. the time dimension.

Several indicators are used to analyse financial stability. Key variables include credit growth or the credit-to-GDP ratio, the ratio of banks' non-performing loans to total loans, and changes in property or asset prices. Stress tests can be an important tool in this process, measuring the sensitivity of a group of institutions (or even an entire financial system) to common shocks.

Particular attention is being paid to monitoring the possible risks within systemically important financial institutions, the disorderly failure of which may cause significant disruption to the wider financial system and economic activity because of their size, complexity, and systemic interconnectedness.

Various efforts have been launched at the national and regional levels to strengthen macroprudential arrangements, often by establishing new bodies responsible for macroprudential supervision, e.g. the European Systemic Risk Board (ESRB) in the EU, and the Financial Stability Oversight Council (FSOC) in the US.

In Europe, the Bank Recovery and Resolution Directive (BRRD) gives resolution authorities common powers and instruments to resolve a failing bank in an orderly manner, while preserving critical bank operations with minimal or no use of taxpayers' money. In this respect, the bail-in tool enables resolution authorities to write down or convert into equity the claims of shareholders and creditors of banks that are failing or likely to fail. The BRRD also provides resolution authorities with preventive as well as early intervention instruments.

The Single Resolution Mechanism (SRM) is the second pillar of the Banking Union, alongside the Single Supervisory Mechanism (SSM). This ensures that both supervision and resolution are exercised at the same level within the Banking Union. The SRM consists of a Single Resolution Board (SRB), with broad powers in case of bank resolution, and a Single Resolution Fund (SRF), which ensures the availability of temporary funding to support the restructuring of a failing bank.

Bibliography

Suggested Reading

Borio, C. (2010), *Implementing a Macroprudential Framework: Blending Boldness and Realism*, Bank for International Settlements, Basel.

Cerutti, E., S. Claessens, and L. Laeven (2017), The Use and Effectiveness of Macroprudential Policies: New Evidence. *Journal of Financial Stability*, 28, 203–24.

Cizel, J., J. Frost, A. Houben, and P. Wierts (2019), Effective Macroprudential Policy: Cross-Sector Substitution from Price and Quantity Measures. *Journal of Money, Credit and Banking*, 51, 1209–35.

Hanson, S. G., A. K. Kashyap, and J. C. Stein (2011), A Macroprudential Approach to Financial Regulation. *Journal of Economic Perspectives*, 25, 3–28.

Philippon, T. and A. Salord (2017), *Bail-ins and Bank Resolution in Europe: A Progress Report*, Geneva Reports on the World Economy Special Report 4, Geneva.

References

Alessi, L. and C. Detken (2014), Identifying Excessive Credit Growth and Leverage. ECB Working Paper 1723.

Avgouleas, E., C. Goodhart, and D. Schoenmaker (2013), Bank Resolution Plans as a Catalyst for Global Financial Reform. *Journal of Financial Stability*, 9, 210–18.

Aiyar, S., C. W. Calomiris, and T. Wieladek (2014), Does Macro-Prudential Regulation Leak? Evidence from a UK Policy Experiment. *Journal of Money, Credit and Banking*, 46, 181–214.

Bank of England (2011), Instruments of Macroprudential Policy: A Discussion Paper. BoE, London.

Borio, C. (2003), Towards a Macroprudential Framework for Financial Supervision and Regulation? *CESifo Economic Studies*, 49, 181–216.

   (2014), The Financial Cycle and Macroeconomics: What Have We Learnt? *Journal of Banking and Finance*, 45, 182–98.

Bundesbank (2014), Europe's New Recovery and Resolution Regime for Credit Institutions. Monthly Report, June.

Cerutti, E., S. Claessens, and L. Laeven (2017), The Use and Effectiveness of Macroprudential Policies: New Evidence. *Journal of Financial Stability*, 28, 203–24.

Cizel, J., J. Frost, A. Houben, and P. Wierts (2019), Effective Macroprudential Policy: Cross-Sector Substitution from Price and Quantity Measures. *Journal of Money, Credit and Banking*, 51, 1209–35.

Enria, E. and P. G. Teixeira (2011), *A New Institutional Framework for Financial Regulation and Supervision*, University of Milan.

European Commission (2014), *EU Bank Recovery and Resolution Directive (BRRD): Frequently Asked Questions, MEMO/14/297*, EC, Brussels.

European Systemic Risk Board (2014), *Flagship Report on Macro-Prudential Policy in the Banking Sector*, ESRB, Frankfurt am Main.

   (2018), Overview of National Macroprudential Measures. www.esrb.europa.eu/national_policy/html/index.en.html.

Financial Stability Board (2010), *Reducing the Moral Hazard Posed by Systemically Important Financial Institutions*, FSB, Basel.

Galati, G. and R. Moessner (2018), What Do We Know About the Effects of Macroprudential Policy? *Economica*, 85, 735–70.

Goodhart, C. A. E. and E. Avgouleas (2014), A Critical Evaluation of Bail-Ins as Bank Recapitalisation Mechanisms. CEPR Discussion Paper 10065.

Goodhart, C. A. E. and D. Schoenmaker (2009), Fiscal Burden Sharing in Cross-Border Banking Crises. *International Journal of Central Banking*, 5, 141–65.

Hanson, S., A. Kashyap, and J. Stein (2011), A Macroprudential Approach to Financial Regulation. *Journal of Economic Perspectives*, 25, 3–28.

Hilbers, P. and M. Jones (2004), *Stress Testing Financial Systems*, IMF, Washington, DC.

Hong Kong Monetary Authority (2011), Loan-to-Value Ratio as a Macroprudential Tool – Hong Kong SAR's Experience and Cross-Country Evidence. BIS Research Paper 57.

International Monetary Fund (2018), Macroprudential Policy Survey. www.elibrary-areaer.imf.org/Macroprudential/Pages/Home.aspx.

Lim, C., F. Columba, A. Costa, P. Kongsamut, A. Otani, M. Saiyid, T. Wezel, and X. Wu (2014), Macroprudential Policy: What Instruments and How to Use Them? Lessons from Country Experiences. Working Paper 11/238, IMF, Washington, DC.

Mian, A. and A. Sufi (2014), *House of Debt: How They (and You) Caused the Great Recession, and How We Can Prevent It From Happening Again*, University of Chicago Press.

Philippon, T. and A. Salord (2017), *Bail-ins and Bank Resolution in Europe: A Progress Report*, Geneva Reports on the World Economy Special Report 4, Geneva.

Schoenmaker, D. (2013), *Governance of International Banking: The Financial Trilemma*, Oxford University Press.

Schoenmaker, D. and P. Wierts (2011), Macroprudential Policy: The Need for a Coherent Policy Framework. Duisenberg School of Finance Policy Paper 13.

Single Resolution Board (2017), Minimum Requirements for Own Funds and Eligible Liabilities (MREL) – SRB Policy for 2017 and Next Steps. Single Resolution Board, Brussels.

Strahan, P. (2013), Too Big To Fail: Causes, Consequences, and Policy Responses. *Annual Review of Financial Economics*, 5, 43–61.

14

European Competition Policy

OVERVIEW

This chapter provides a concise overview of European competition policy, with a focus on financial services. The chapter first defines competition and describes the objectives of EU competition policy, i.e. maintaining competitive markets and a single market in the EU. The ultimate goal of competition is to offer consumers a greater choice of products and services at lower prices (i.e. to enhance consumer welfare).

The second part of the chapter analyses the economic rationale for competition policy by examining the difference between a perfectly competitive market and a monopoly. In a competitive market, prices are 'competed' down and goods or services are produced in the least costly way. Firms are price *takers*. In a monopoly, there is a single seller in the market who can exert undue market power. The monopolist thus has significant power over the price and is a price *setter*.

The third part of the chapter elaborates on the four tools of EU competition policy: the elimination of agreements that restrict competition and the ability to abuse a dominant position, the control of mergers and acquisitions, the liberalisation of monopolistic sectors, and control of state aid. It also reviews the application of the state aid rules in the 2007–2009 financial crisis.

The fourth part of the chapter discusses a framework for investigating the abuse of dominance. One element of this framework is the Small, but Significant Non-transitory Increase in Prices (SSNIP) methodology, which is used to define the smallest market in which a hypothetical monopolist would be able to impose a small but significant non-transitory price increase (the relevant market). The relevant market for various financial services is discussed.

The final section briefly describes the dual legislative and enforcement system for competition policy in the EU.

LEARNING OBJECTIVES

After you have studied this chapter, you should be able to:
- describe competition and competition policy
- explain the economic arguments for having competition policy
- reproduce the different tools of EU competition policy and explain how these relate to financial markets
- describe the process of assessing a dominant position
- understand the institutional structure of competition policy in the EU.

14.1 What is Competition Policy?

Competition is a market situation in which firms or sellers independently strive for buyers' patronage in order to achieve a particular business objective, e.g. profits, sales, and/or market share (OECD, 1993). Competition forces firms:
- to become (more) efficient
- to offer a greater choice of products and services
- to offer these products and services at lower prices.

Ultimately, competition gives rise to increased consumer welfare and allocative efficiency (the latter is discussed in more detail in Section 14.2). The level of competition is an important aspect of financial sector development and, in turn, economic growth (Claessens and Laeven, 2005).

Generally, *competition policy* aims to ensure that competition in the marketplace is not restricted in a way that is detrimental to society (Motta, 2004). The authorities establish a set of rules and policies aimed at safeguarding competition to enhance economic welfare and ensure the efficient allocation of resources. However, the aim of competition policy should not be to *eliminate* market power, as the prospect of enjoying market power is an important driver of innovation and efficiency. Still, as discussed in Section 14.4, firms are prohibited from *abusing* market power.

Competition policy is a pillar of the EU's internal market policy. By combating distortions of competition between firms, competition policy creates the preconditions for proper market functioning in an attempt to enhance overall consumer welfare. Moreover, safeguarding competition in the EU is an important instrument to promote further market integration, e.g. by removing barriers to entry or exit, and the application of non-discrimination principles for new entrants. The objective of EU competition policy is therefore twofold (EC, 2000). The first objective is to maintain competitive markets. Competition policy is designed to encourage industrial efficiency, the optimal allocation of resources, technical progress, and the flexibility to adjust to a changing environment. In order for the union to be competitive on worldwide markets, it needs a competitive home market. Thus, its competition policy has always taken a very strong line against price fixing, market-sharing cartels, the abuse of dominant positions, and anti-competitive mergers. It has also prohibited unjustified state-granted mono-poly rights and state aid measures that do not ensure firms' long-term viability, but distort competition by artificially keeping them in business.

The second objective is to create a single market. An internal market is essential for the development of an efficient and competitive industry. The European Commission has used its competition policy to prevent the erec-tion of barriers to trade by prohibiting and heavily fining parties to distribu-tion and licensing agreements that prevent parallel trade between Member States, and agreements between competitors to keep out of one another's territories. The provisions of the Treaty on the Functioning of the European Union (TFEU) specifically require EU policy makers to 'act in accordance with the principle of an open market economy with free competition, favouring an efficient allocation of resources'. Roeller and Stehmann (2006) argue that with the progress made towards creating an internal market, the relative importance of the market integration goal has declined. As a result, policy statements increasingly focus on efficiency, consumer welfare, and competitiveness. Nevertheless, competition policy may be an effective instru-ment to strengthen integration in certain financial market segments.

The European Commission's Directorate General for Competition enforces competition law at the EU level, while at the national level the national competition authorities are responsible. Section 14.5 discusses the organisation of EU competition policy in more detail.

14.2 The Economic Rationale for Competition Policy

The two extremes in a marketplace are monopoly and perfect competition.

A *monopoly* is a situation in which: (1) there is a single seller in the market, (2) there are no (close) substitute products or services, and (3) there are barriers to entry for potential sellers. A monopolist is thus a *price setter* rather than a *price taker*; its ability to raise and maintain a price above the level that would prevail under (perfect) competition is referred to as *market* or *monopoly power*. Generally, the exercise of market power leads to reduced output and loss of economic welfare. However, monopolies are not always bad. A good example is a *natural monopoly* in which a single firm can produce at lower costs than if there were two or more firms. According to the Organisation for Economic Co-operation and Development (OECD, 1993), natural monopolies are characterised by steeply declining long-run average and marginal cost curves such that there is room for only one firm to fully exploit available economies of scale and supply the market.

Figure 14.1 shows the welfare effects of market power by comparing the total surplus at the monopoly price with that at the perfect competitive (marginal cost) price.[1] Under perfect competition, the price of the goods or services produced equals marginal cost ($P_c = MC$), and the goods or services will be produced in the least costly way. The monopolist, by contrast, sets output at the level where marginal cost equals marginal revenue ($MC = MR$) in order to maximise its profits. Tirole (1988) shows that the total surplus is equal to the sum of the consumer surplus and the producer surplus (or profit), or the difference between total consumer utility and production costs. In Figure 14.1 this surplus is represented by the area DGAD under marginal cost pricing and by the area DEFAD under monopoly pricing. The

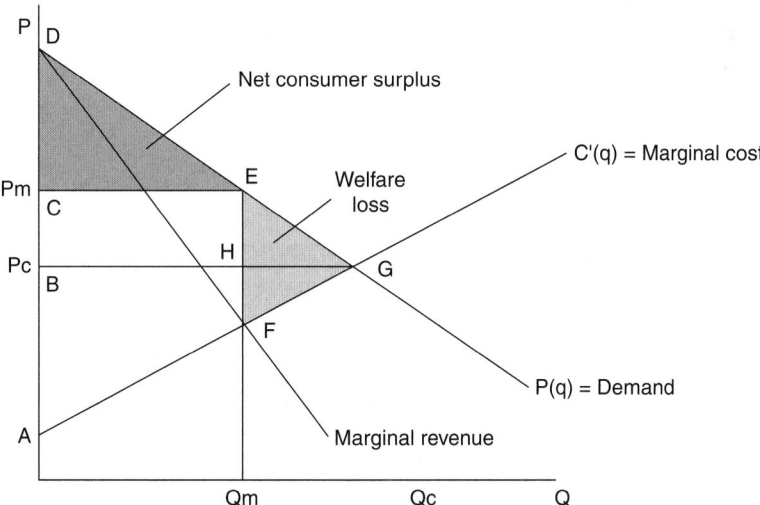

Figure 14.1   Welfare loss from monopoly
Source: Tirole (1988)

difference between the total surplus under monopoly and the surplus under marginal cost pricing is the *welfare* or *deadweight loss* (shown by triangle EFG in Figure 14.1). This welfare loss represents the overall opportunity costs to society arising from monopoly pricing. In addition, part of the consumer surplus under perfect competition, BCEH, is transferred to the monopolist in the form of excess profits.

What are the implications for competition policy? Figure 14.1 shows that having one firm (or very few firms) serving the market generally leads to a welfare loss for society. Competition policy should, however, not try to maximise the number of firms that operate in a market, because firms will then not be able to optimise the scale or magnitude of their output, which results in a higher average cost per unit of output than would be the case in a more concentrated market. Motta (2004) stresses that:

1. competition policy is not concerned with maximising the number of firms; and
2. competition policy is concerned with *defending market competition* in order to increase welfare, not *defending competitors*.

Should competition authorities then strive for perfect competition? Since the notion of perfect competition can in practice be highly restrictive in terms of policy making (OECD, 1993), the goal of competition policy should be a more realistic target such as *workable competition*, i.e. trying to create the preconditions for the proper operation of markets and ensuring that firms do not abuse a dominant position. Although there is no generally accepted definition of workable competition, all authorities involved in competition policy seem to operate using some version of this concept. According to the OECD (1993), the concept of workable competition arises from the observation that since perfect competition does not exist, theories based on it do not provide reliable guides for competition policy. The criteria for judging whether competition is workable are wide ranging, e.g. the number of firms should be at least as large as economies of scale permit, promotional expenses should not be excessive, and advertising should be informative.

Competition authorities should have insight into individual firms' market power and the level of competition in a specific market. There are various ways to quantify the level of market power. A well-known indicator is the *Lerner Index* (LI), which measures the degree to which a firm is able to price its products above marginal costs. The LI is a more accurate measure of market power than concentration measures (such as the Herfindahl Index and the CR5 ratio). Nevertheless, it poses some challenges. For instance, if the LI is relatively high it may still be hard to assesses whether this indicates market power or superior efficiency. Moreover, in practice the LI is hard to determine, as information on marginal costs is often not readily available. The LI is calculated using the following formula:

$$LI = (Price - Marginal\ Cost)/Price = 1/\varepsilon \qquad (14.1)$$

where ε is the price elasticity of demand [$\varepsilon = -(\Delta Q/\Delta P)(P/Q)$]. The key determinant of market power is the elasticity of demand. The greater ε is, the greater the reduction in the quantity demanded will be when the price rises. Thus, the higher the elasticity of demand, the lower the market power of the respective firm. Under perfect competition, P = MC and LI = 0. The higher the value of the LI, the greater the firm's market power.

Another method of assessing competition in a market is the H-statistic of Panzar and Rosse (1987). This test statistic examines the relationship between a change in a firm's input prices and the revenues earned. It is based on the idea that firms employ different pricing strategies in response to changes in input costs depending on the market structure in which they operate.

Even in the absence of a monopoly, dominant positions might arise (Motta, 2004), for example due to *sunk costs*, i.e. costs that, once incurred, cannot be (easily) recovered. Sunk costs lead to barriers to entry as well as to exit, as they increase an incumbent's commitment to the market and may signal a willingness to respond aggressively to other firms' entry (OECD, 1993). In this respect, offering financial services via the Internet or via intermediaries has the potential to improve the contestability of markets by lowering sunk costs and barriers.

In other cases, a dominant position may arise as a result of *lock-in effects* or *switching costs* – i.e. the costs to customers of changing suppliers. The higher these costs, the more difficult it becomes to switch. Thus, switching costs can give substantial market power to existing suppliers. For example, the switching costs in retail banking are relatively high since bank account numbers are not portable (see Box 14.1 for more information on competition in banking).

Finally, dominant positions can be a result of *network* effects. As shown in Chapter 7, the addition of a new participant to a network increases its value for all participants. This means that the value of the services and products offered to the participants depends on the number of other participants purchasing the same services and products. The existence of network externalities can lead to lock-in effects and make it hard for potential competitors to successfully enter the market.

According to Motta (2004), competition policy is also needed because firms may take actions that increase their profits but harm society. For example, *collusion* refers to any formal or informal agreements to raise or fix prices or to

Box 14.1 Competition in banking

Analysing competition in the banking sector is quite complex (OECD, 2009). On the one hand, the general argument in favour of competition in terms of cost minimisation and allocative efficiency applies to the banking industry. On the other hand, as in numerous other markets, the standard competitive paradigm may not fully apply because of features like asymmetric information in corporate relationships, switching costs, and networks in retail banking. In retail banking, switching costs for customers are very important, and reputation and branch networks may act as barriers to entry. In corporate banking, established lending relationships and asymmetric information give financial institutions a degree of market power vis-à-vis both firms and investors.

Thus for a long time, competition policy was applied very cautiously in the EU banking sector. It was treated as a special sector that is heavily influenced by Member States' monetary and regulatory policies rather than by market forces.

An important, and partly unresolved, question concerns the link between competition and stability. Until the 1980s, the prevailing view was that competition worsens stability. Intense competition was perceived to favour excessive risk taking, thus increasing the risk of individual bank failure; regulation was believed to help mitigate this perverse link. Although the view on the potential trade-off between competition and stability has recently become more balanced, the results of empirical studies linking competition and stability remain ambiguous. Structural and non-structural measures of competition are found to be both positively and negatively associated with financial stability, depending on the country and sample analysed and the measure of financial stability used (OECD, 2011). So, while competition may not be *responsible* for fragility, it should take account of the specifics of banking, and not only in crises.

The next section discusses the role of competition policy in crisis situations, which is to keep the markets open, check the distortions introduced by possible rescue packages, weed out inefficient institutions, and remove artificial barriers to entry. In the banking sector particular attention should be devoted to fostering entry during a recovery from a crisis. Vives (2011) argues that all of this calls for close cooperation between supervisory and competition authorities.

Okolelova and Bikker (2018) investigate the effect of the Banking Union on competition in banking. An increase in competition could be expected due to more consistent regulation and supervision in the union. Their results indicate that competition indeed increased during 2015–2016 for the banks under direct ECB supervision, which are large and engage in a significant amount of cross-border activity, but not for banks that fall under national supervision on behalf of the ECB.

reduce output in order to increase profits. When formalised, these agreements are referred to as *cartels*. A firm may also engage in *predatory behaviour* by setting very low prices (sometimes even below costs) to drive out competitors; it can then raise prices and earn higher profits. Other types of *exclusionary behaviour* include investing in extra capacity, obstructing rivals' access to crucial inputs, tying and bundling, and price discrimination. *Tying* refers to the practice of making the purchase of product A conditional on the purchase of product B. *Bundling* refers to the practice of selling two or more products or services in a package. *Price discrimination* occurs when customers in different segments are charged different prices for the same good or service, for reasons unrelated to costs (OECD, 1993). However, this type of exclusionary behaviour is effective only if customers cannot profitably resell the goods or services to other customers. Finally, as discussed in the next section, mergers and acquisitions may also reduce competition.

14.3 Pillars of EU Competition Policy

The objective of EU competition policy was first set out in the Treaty of Rome (1957), which indicated that one of the activities of the community includes establishing 'a system ensuring that competition in the internal market is not distorted'. In general, EU competition policy has the following objectives:
- eliminate (1) agreements that restrict competition and (2) abuses of a dominant position (*antitrust*);
- control mergers and acquisitions between firms;
- liberalise monopolistic economic sectors;
- regulate state aid.

Antitrust

The two main pillars of EU competition law are Articles 101 and 102 of the TFEU. The former prohibits agreements and concerted practices with an anti-competitive objective or effect on the market, while the latter prohibits abuses of a dominant position.

The TFEU prohibits 'all agreements between undertakings, decisions by associations of undertakings and concerted practices which may affect trade between Member States and which have as their object or effect the prevention, restriction or distortion of competition within the common market'. Actions prohibited under Article 101 can take the form of:

- direct or indirect fixing of purchase or selling prices or any other trading conditions;
- limiting or controlling production, markets, technical development, or investment;
- sharing markets or sources of supply;
- applying dissimilar conditions to equivalent transactions with other trading parties, thereby placing them at a competitive disadvantage;
- subjecting the conclusion to acceptance by the other parties of supplementary obligations that, by their nature or according to commercial usage, have no connection with the subject of the contract.

Box 14.2 discusses two decisions related to Article 101 on the use of multilateral interchange fees by MasterCard and Visa[2] (see Chapter 7 for

---

Box 14.2 Article 101 cases: MasterCard and Visa

Chapter 7 indicated that the use of interchange fees is the subject of several regulatory and antitrust investigations. In December 2007, the European Commission published its findings on multilateral interchange fees (MIFs) for cross-border payment card transactions with MasterCard and Maestro branded debit and consumer credit cards in the European Economic Area (EEA). The Commission concluded that MasterCard violated EC treaty rules on restrictive business practices, as its MIF inflated the cost of card acceptance for retailers and did not produce proven efficiencies. Yet the Commission stressed that MIFs are not illegal; a MIF in an open-payment card scheme such as MasterCard's is compatible with EU competition rules only if it contributes to technical and economic progress and benefits consumers. To comply with the Commission's decision, MasterCard reduced its intra-EU cross-border interchange fees to 0.2 per cent for debit cards and 0.3 per cent for credit cards.

The Commission published decisions on interchanges fees for Visa in December 2010 and February 2014. Visa had committed to using the same caps; these Commission decisions made the caps legally binding. Subsequently, in September 2014, the EU Court of Justice confirmed the Commission's analysis in the MasterCard case. The court's interpretation of Article 101 was that interchange fees applied by European banks to cross-border transactions with MasterCard cards indeed limit competition between acquiring banks.

The June 2015 Interchange Fee Regulation (751/2015/EU) gave the 0.2 per cent and 0.3 per cent caps a general legal basis. The regulation aims to ensure that retailers' average costs of card payments are not higher than those of receiving payments in cash (EC, 2015).

In December 2018, the Commission asked for feedback on offers made by MasterCard and Visa to use the same caps for transactions in the EEA using cards issued outside the EEA. Such interregional MIFs fall outside the scope of the Interchange Fee Regulation.

Source: European Commission (2015, 2018)

a discussion of interchange fees). Article 101 applies to horizontal as well as vertical agreements. *Horizontal agreements* are made between competitors in the same product market, while *vertical agreements* are made between firms operating at different stages of a production or distribution chain. However, exceptions can be made for agreements that improve the production or distribution of goods or that promote technical or economic progress. Moreover, such agreements should benefit consumers and should not unnecessarily eliminate competition.

It is not illegal under EU competition law to *hold* a dominant position, since this can be obtained via legitimate means of competition. Article 102 prohibits firms from *abusing* a dominant position: '[A]ny abuse by one or more undertakings of a dominant position within the common market or in a substantial part of it shall be prohibited as incompatible with the common market in so far as it may affect trade between Member States.' A firm is in a dominant position if it has the ability to:

- set prices above the competitive level;
- sell products of an inferior quality;
- reduce its rate of innovation below the level that would exist in a competitive market (European Communities, 2003).

The next section discusses a framework for investigating the abuse of dominance. A well-known recent example of an Article 102 case was the European Commission's decision that Google had abused the dominant market position of its search engine by promoting its own shopping service in search results (EC, 2018). Google was fined €2.4 billion for breaching EU antitrust rules.

Examining Mergers

The second element of the EU's competition policy is the examination of mergers, in order to assess whether they may decrease competition. Merger control regulation has existed since 1989. The EC Merger Regulation[3] adopted in 2004 sets out rules for mergers and acquisitions of companies that could restrict competition. Article 2(3) of the regulation states that: '[A] concentration which would significantly impede effective competition, in the common market or in a substantial part of it, in particular as a result of the creation or strengthening of a dominant position, shall be declared incompatible with the common market.' The European Court of Justice (ECJ) defines *dominance* as 'a position of economic strength enjoyed by an undertaking which enables it to prevent effective competition being maintained on the relevant market by affording it the power to behave to an appreciable extent independently of its competitors, customers and ultimately of its consumers'.[4] However, the new EC Merger Regulation prohibits any merger that significantly impedes effective competition, i.e. the ban is not confined to 'dominant firms'. It therefore takes into account the argument that even in the absence of a dominant position a merger may also have serious anti-competitive effects.

The European Commission investigates mergers with a union dimension – i.e. those for which the combined aggregate worldwide turnover of the merging companies is over €5 billion and the aggregate union-wide turnover of each of at least two of the undertakings concerned is more than €250 million. It conducts in-depth investigations of less than 5 per cent of mergers. During 1990–2014, approximately 0.5 per cent of mergers were prohibited, i.e. 24 of more than 5,000 mergers, six of which were prohibited after 2004 (EC, 2014a). In March 2017 it prohibited the proposed merger between Deutsche Börse and the London Stock Exchange Group, which would have combined the activities of the two largest European stock exchange operators. According to the Commission, this merger would have created a de facto monopoly in the clearing of fixed income instruments in Europe; since sufficient remedies were not offered, it would have significantly impeded competition (EC, 2018). The case is also relevant from the perspective of Chapter 7, which predicts concentration or natural monopolies in clearing based on network effects.

In addition to competitive reasons, potential mergers and acquisitions between financial institutions may also be blocked for prudential reasons. A *prudential carve-out* allows supervisory authorities to block proposed mergers and acquisitions if the 'sound and prudent management' of the targeted firm(s) could be put at risk. Initially, this requirement was defined rather broadly and on several occasions the carve-out was used in a protectionist manner. After the takeover battle for the Italian bank Antonveneta in 2005, in which then-governor of the Italian Central Bank Antonio Fazio tried to block the purchase of Antonveneta by ABN AMRO, the European Council and the European Parliament endorsed a proposal in 2007 to tighten the procedures that supervisory authorities have to follow when assessing proposed mergers and acquisitions. Directive 2007/44/EC, sometimes referred to as the Qualifying Holdings Directive, contains a list of criteria that prudential supervisory authorities should use to assess the acquiring company, e.g. reputation of the proposed acquirer, reputation and experience of the management, financial soundness, compliance with EU directives, and risks related to money laundering and terrorism financing. The directive also reduces the assessment period from three months to 30 days.

Liberalisation of Monopolistic Economic Sectors and State Aid

Governments can also introduce restrictions on competition by granting national businesses exclusive rights to provide certain goods or services, or by providing public aid to businesses.

Article 106 of the TFEU tasks the European Commission with monitoring public undertakings and undertakings to which Member States grant special or exclusive rights (thereby establishing monopolistic sectors). The Commission also has the power to address government actions that may distort competition in the internal market. For instance, the Commission plays a pivotal role in opening up markets such as transport, energy, postal services, and telecommunications to competition.

Firms receiving support from their government are likely to obtain an unfair advantage over their competitors. TFEU Articles 107, 108, 109 therefore forbid state aid unless it is justified by reasons of general economic development. The European Commission is responsible for monitoring state aid. The objective of state aid control is to ensure that government interventions do not distort competition or trade within the EU. The treaty strives to find the right balance between (1) the advantage for the aid recipient and the achievement of a policy objective (e.g. economic development, job creation, financial stability) and (2) the competitive distortion created in the market (i.e. the disadvantage for the competitors). In this respect, state aid is defined as any advantage conferred on a selective basis to undertakings by national public authorities. This does not include subsidies granted to individuals or general measures open to all enterprises.

During the financial crisis and the euro crisis, Member States took several measures to support the European financial sector. Some of these measures were directed towards individual institutions (capital injections, asset solutions; see Figure 14.2), while others were general (guarantee schemes, liquidity operations; see Figure 14.3). They reduced the default risks among financial institutions and thus helped to safeguard financial stability. However, the interventions had distortionary effects, because the rapid unfolding of the crisis and market failures complicated the proper design of support policies.

Since the beginning of the 2007–2009 financial crisis, the European Commission has provided detailed guidance on the criteria for the compatibility of temporary crisis-related support measures with TFEU Article 107. Through the application of state aid rules, the Commission tried to ensure that distortions of competition within the internal market were kept to a minimum despite the significant amounts of state aid being distributed, and that beneficiary banks were restructured when necessary.

Aid instrument	Used	
	In € billion	As a % of 2012 GDP
Recapitalisation measures	413.2	3.20%
Asset relief measures	178.7	1.39%
Total	591.9	4.6%

Figure 14.2 Total recapitalisation and asset relief measures, 2008–2012
Source: European Commission

Aid instrument	Peak outstanding amount (2009)		2012 outstanding amount	
	In € billion	As a % of 2012 GDP	In € billion	As a % of 2012 GDP
Guarantees	835.8	7.10%	492.3	3.82%
Other liquidity measures	70.1	0.59%	42.2	0.33%
Total	906.0	7.7%	534.5	4.1%

Figure 14.3 Total outstanding guarantees and other liquidity measures, 2008–2012
Source: European Commission

Between 1 October 2008 and 1 October 2013, the Commission took more than 400 decisions authorising state aid measures to the financial sector. In the period 2008–2012, overall capital support amounted to €591.9 billion or 4.6 per cent of EU 2012 GDP (see Figure 14.2).

The guarantees and other forms of liquidity support reached their peak in 2009 with an outstanding amount of €906 billion (7.7 per cent of EU 2012 GDP). As shown in Figure 14.3, the outstanding amount dropped to €534.5 billion in 2012 (4.1 per cent of EU 2012 GDP).

Prominent state aid decisions include the Commission's approval of the plan submitted by the Irish authorities to jointly wind down Anglo Irish Bank and the Irish Nationwide Building Society over a period of 10 years. Another example is the German Landesbank WestLB, where it was decided that the bank should be split up, and the remaining assets and liabilities transferred to a bad bank in order to be wound down. WestLB would no longer perform banking activities and only continue to provide asset management services. A small part of its activities was taken over by Landesbank Hessen-Thuringen.

Banks that relied heavily on state aid can be allowed to stay on the market, if parts of their activities have a realistic prospect of returning to viability, provided that they considerably reduce their size and substantially change their business model to focus only on the viable activities (EC, 2012). This approach is illustrated by the approval of the restructuring of the German Bank Hypo Real Estate, which by 2011 had to shrink to 15 per cent of its pre-crisis balance sheet and phase out a number of business activities (EC, 2011).

Table 14.1 lists large banks (assets of more than €250 million in 2007) that received state aid between 2007 and 2011. During the crisis, 14 large banks received state aid. In three cases, two ailing banks were merged as part of the restructuring deal: Lloyds Bank (taking over HBOS), Commerzbank (taking over Dresdner), and Banque Populaire Caisse d'Epargne (renamed Groupe BPCE). The European Commission forced banks to downsize in order to receive state aid. With the exception of Groupe BPCE, recipients of state aid have downsized significantly – overall by 18 per cent from 2007 to 2011. The EU banking system grew over this period by 9 per cent, so the growth difference between the sector as a whole and the banks listed in Table 14.1 is a staggering 27 per cent.

Restructuring during the financial crisis followed three main principles: (1) a return to long-term viability without state aid, based on a sound restructuring plan; (2) burden sharing between the bank/its stakeholders and the state; and (3) limitation of competition distortions, usually through structural (divestitures) and behavioural measures (acquisition bans or limitations on aggressive commercial behaviour). The European Commission adapted its state aid rules for banks in anticipation of the implementation of the Bank Recovery and Resolution Directive and the start of the Single Resolution Mechanism (EC, 2013). The main changes were designed to improve the restructuring process and level the playing field between banks. These changes required banks to devise a sound plan for their restructuring or orderly winding down before they could receive any recapitalisations or asset protection measures. Moreover, in the case of capital shortfalls, bank owners and junior creditors will be required to contribute as a first resort, before banks can ask for public support.

Table 14.1 Large banks receiving state aid, 2007–2011

Banking groups	Assets of separate banks in 2007 in € billion	Total assets in 2007 in € billion	Total assets in 2011 in € billion	Difference 2007–2011 in per cent
1. Royal Bank of Scotland (UK)		2,587	1,801	−30%
2. Lloyds Banking Group (UK)		1,389	1,160	−16%
2a. Lloyds Group (UK)	481			
2b. HBOS (UK)	908			
3. Commerzbank (Germany)		1,116	662	−41%
3a. Commerzbank (Germany)	616			
3b. Dresdner Bank (Germany)	500			
4. ING Bank (Netherlands)		994	961	−3%
5. Fortis (Belgium)		767	Split up	
6. Groupe BPCE (France)		707	1,138	+61%
6a. Caisse d'Epargne (France)	434			
6b. Banques Populaires (France)	273			
7. Dexia Bank (Belgium)		605	413	−32%
8. Landesbank Baden-Wurt (Germany)		443	373	−16%
9. Bayerische Landesbank (Germany)		416	319	−23%
10. KBC Group (Belgium)		356	285	−20%
11. WestDeutsche Landesbank (Germany)		287	168	−41%
Aggregate difference state aid banks		8,900	7,280	−18%
Aggregate difference EU		41,062	44,818	+9%

Note: Banks were selected to receive state aid on the basis of size: assets over €250 million in 2007. In some cases, two banks were merged as part of the restructuring. Assets of the separate banks are reported in the first column. One bank (Fortis) was split up and ceased to exist. Another bank (WestDeutsche Landesbank) was dissolved in summer 2012.

Source: Schoenmaker (2013).

14.4 Assessment of Dominant Positions

TFEU Article 102 and the EC Merger Regulation require competition authorities to examine abuses of dominance. This section discusses how they may do so, using a three-step framework suggested by the UK Office of Fair Trading (OFT, 2001):

1. Assess whether there is a plausible market definition under which the firm under investigation has a high market share.
2. If there is a plausible market in which the firm might be dominant, conduct a full analysis of the economic effects of the practice under investigation.

3. If competition is likely to have been significantly damaged, or if there is a prospect of such damage, issue a decision that describes and demonstrates the adverse economic effects of the business practice. If the conduct is not harmful, issue a decision giving the reasons why the business practice under investigation does not constitute an abuse of a dominant position.

Figure 14.4 depicts an *ex post* investigation of possible abuse of dominance; similar investigations can be conducted *ex ante*, for instance before a proposed merger or acquisition.

Step 1: Identify the Relevant Market

The main purpose of defining the market is to systematically identify the competitive constraints faced by the firms involved. A market is defined in

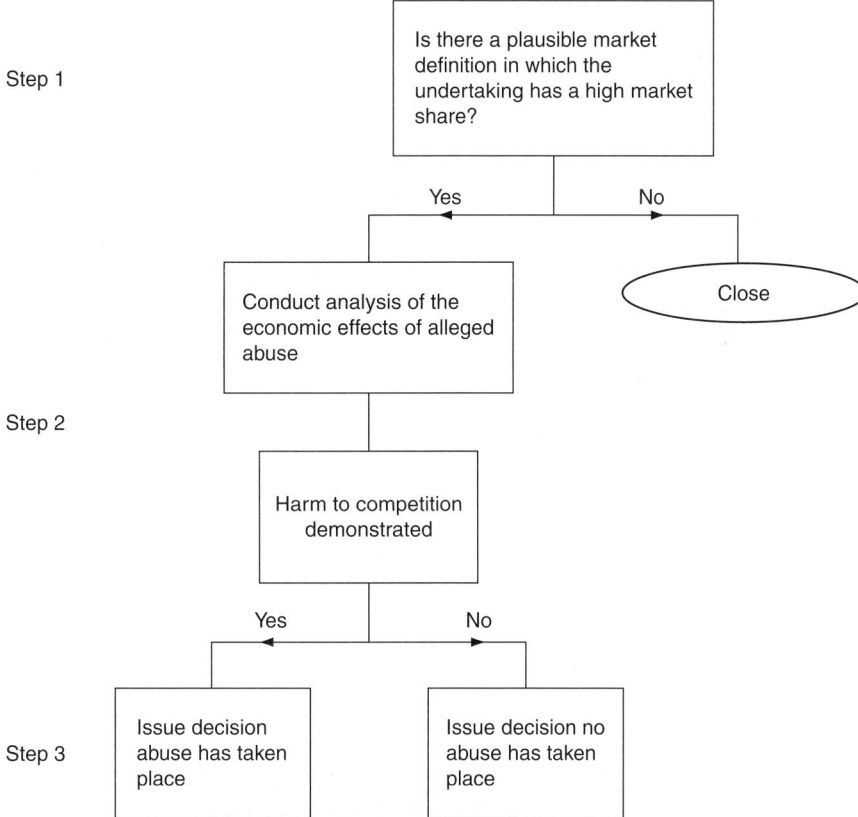

Figure 14.4   Flowchart for undertaking abuse-of-dominance investigations
Source: Office of Fair Trading (2001)

both its product and geographic dimensions (EC, 1997). The relevant *product market* is said to 'comprise all those products and/or services which are regarded as interchangeable or substitutable by the consumer, by reason of the products' characteristics, their prices and their intended use'. The *geographic market* 'comprises the area in which the undertakings concerned are involved in the supply and demand of products or services, in which the conditions of competition are sufficiently homogeneous and which can be distinguished from neighbouring areas because the conditions of competition are appreciably different in those areas'.

A very common methodology to define the relevant geographic market is the *Small, but Significant Non-transitory Increase in Prices* (SSNIP) methodology (EC, 2004). This methodology is used to examine whether some goods produced in a specific area constitute their own relevant geographical market. Assuming that the goods or services in question are produced by a hypothetical monopolist, this approach involves asking whether it is likely that this monopolist can earn a profit by increasing prices by 5–10 per cent (i.e. small but significant) for a period of at least 12 months (i.e. non-transitory).

If the answer is yes, then the candidate goods form their own relevant geographic market. If the answer is no, because consumers substitute away from the candidate markets as they are able to purchase the same good in neighbouring regions or because producers from other regions enter the market, then the relevant geographic market is larger than the goods for the candidate market. The thought experiment is subsequently repeated with a larger geographic area and continued until the answer to the question is affirmative; this area defines the relevant geographic market. When it is difficult to assess whether goods that meet the same needs of the consumer belong to the same market or not, price tests (looking at price co-movements) can be used to evaluate the extent of the relevant candidate market.

Whether or not a price increase is profitable depends on the sales volume that is lost following the price increase, i.e. the extent to which a consumer can substitute away from the candidate market (Box 14.3 explains the algebra of the SSNIP methodology). The quantity of lost sales depends on the following two aspects:

- the availability of substitute products (i.e. *demand-side substitutes*);
- the ability of other firms to supply these products (i.e. *supply-side substitutes*).

After the relevant market is defined, market shares and concentration indices are calculated. There are no thresholds for defining dominance set by law, but the ECJ has argued that dominance can be presumed in the absence of

Box 14.3 Algebra of the SSNIP methodology*

Profits (π) beforehand (denoted with subscript 0) are equal to revenue (price (P) times quantity (Q)) minus total costs (average costs (C) times Q):

$$\pi_0 = (P_0 - C_0)Q_0 \tag{14.2}$$

A change in the price ($\Delta P = P_1 - P_0$) leads to a change in the quantity demanded ($\Delta Q = Q_1 - Q_0$) and may also lead to a change in the average costs of production ($\Delta C = C_1 - C_0$).

This gives a new level of profits:

$$\pi_1 = (P_1 - C_1)Q_1 \tag{14.3}$$

The change in profit is given by:

$$\begin{aligned} \Delta\pi = \pi_1 - \pi_0 &= (P_1 - C_1)Q_1 - (P_0 - C_0)Q_0 \\ &= \Delta P Q_1 + (P_0 - C_0)\Delta Q - Q_1 \Delta C \end{aligned} \tag{14.4}$$

Note that when $\Delta P > 0$, it is expected that $\Delta Q < 0$. The issue is when $\Delta\pi$ will be less than zero. It is convenient to rewrite (14.4) by dividing through P_0 (note that this does not matter as $\Delta\pi < 0$ if $\Delta\pi/P_0 < 0$), yielding:

$$\frac{\Delta\pi}{P_0} = \frac{\Delta P}{P_0}Q_1 + \frac{P_0 - C_0}{P_0}\Delta Q - \frac{Q_1}{P_0}\Delta C. \tag{14.5}$$

Suppose average costs are constant (i.e. they do not depend on the amount produced) so that $\Delta C = 0$. Then,

$$\frac{\Delta\pi}{P_0} = \frac{\Delta P}{P_0}Q_1 + \frac{P_0 - C_0}{P_0}\Delta Q \tag{14.6}$$

Thus, a price rise will be profitable if:

$$\frac{\Delta P}{P_0}Q_1 > \frac{P_0 - C_0}{P_0} - \Delta Q \tag{14.7}$$

that is, if the increased price charged on the new (lower) quantity is greater than the lost margin on the decrease in quantity. If there are economies of scale, it is also necessary to work out:

$$\frac{Q_1}{P_0}\Delta C. \tag{14.8}$$

If, for example, $\Delta C > 0$ when $\Delta Q < 0$, the increase in price on the new quantity needs to be greater than the lost margin on the decreased quantity plus the higher costs of the new quantity.

Source: Geroski and Griffith (2004)

evidence to the contrary if a firm's market share is consistently above 50 per cent. However, a firm with a lower market share may also be dominant, particularly if its competitors are much smaller. The OFT (2001) stresses that despite having a high market share, a firm may not be dominant if one or more of the following conditions hold:

- there are very low barriers to entry into the relevant market, and the threat of potential entry is sufficient to discipline firms with high market shares;
- the nature of competition within the market is such that very intense competition exists even if there are very few players;
- the nature of the buyers in a market, and the volumes they purchase, are such that they can exert significant countervailing pressure against a firm with a high market share.

A high concentration ratio does not necessarily indicate a lack of competition. Claessens and Laeven (2004) estimate competitiveness indicators for banks in a large cross-section of countries and find no evidence that banking system concentration is negatively associated with competitiveness. In fact, they find some evidence that more concentrated banking systems are more competitive. The latter may be the result of fierce competition in the preceding period, as a result of which the overall banking system has become relatively efficient. Claessens and Laeven (2004) conclude that a contestable system may be more important to assure competitiveness than a system with low concentration (see Chapter 10).

Step 2: Abuse of Dominance?

If a market can be defined in which the respective firm has a dominant position, the economic effects of (possible) abuse should be examined. Abusive conduct generally falls into one of two categories (OFT, 2004):

- conduct that exploits customers or suppliers (e.g. through excessively high prices);
- conduct that amounts to exclusionary behaviour, because it removes or weakens competition from existing competitors, or establishes or strengthens entry barriers, thereby removing or weakening potential competition.

In the first case, it may be possible to identify abuse by analysing a firm's profitability. For example, when are profits too high or too low, and what is the relevant time period to consider? And if high profits are found, are they due to market power or to superior efficiency? Profitability figures should therefore be cautiously interpreted, and other economic indicators – such as productivity, the advertise-to-sale ratio, prices, and the level of innovation – should also be analysed.

The economic impact of exclusionary behaviour on the market requires a detailed analysis of, among other things, barriers to entry and switching costs. The challenge is to distinguish between lawful competitive behaviour and abusive practices. In this respect, the OFT (2001) distinguishes between conduct that inflicts harm on *competition* and conduct that inflicts harm on *competitors*. Demonstrating harm to competitors is important only when it leads to adverse impacts on consumers. Harm to competitors does not necessarily have an adverse impact on competition.

Step 3: Issue Decision

If (possible) harm to competition can be proven, competition authorities may impose administrative sanctions, like a fine, prohibiting a proposed merger or acquisition, or requiring additional concessions for a proposed merger or acquisition.

An example of additional concessions is the proposed merger between the two Swedish banking groups Forenings Sparbanken and SEB in February 2001, which would have created Sweden's leading financial group with market shares in a number of markets in the range of 40–60 per cent. According to the European Commission (2001), the merged entity's large customer base and extensive branch network would have placed it well ahead of its closest competitors in Sweden. In reaction to the preliminary views of the European Commission set out in its Statement of Objections, Forenings Sparbanken and SEB announced in September 2001 that they would withdraw their merger application, claiming that the concessions (e.g. forcing the banks to significantly reduce their market shares) would jeopardise the value of the proposed merger.

Defining the market for banking services to households and small and medium-sized enterprises as national is standard practice for antitrust regulators worldwide. In previous cases involving banking mergers, the European Commission has raised concerns where market shares were considerably lower (30–35 per cent). Moreover, in 2001 the UK authorities blocked a merger between Lloyds and Abbey National that presented significantly lower combined market shares (27 per cent for household accounts). The subsequent takeover of Abbey National by the Spanish banking group Banco Santander in 2004 did not raise any competition concerns as these banks were (mostly) active in different countries.

Table 14.2 provides examples of the relevant geographic market for various financial services. The relevant market for retail banking and insurance is national. Retail banking consists of banking services for consumers

Table 14.2 Relevant geographical market for financial services

National	European	Global
Retail banking & insurance		
	Wholesale banking & insurance	Re-insurance
	Stock exchanges	Investment banking

(e.g. payment services, consumer credit, and mortgages) and SMEs (e.g. payment services and loans). Notwithstanding the advance to Banking Union and the Single Euro Payments Area, retail banking is still national, including national deposit insurance schemes. Retail insurance for consumers and SMEs is also very much a local business, with significant differences between countries. The relevant rules for retail insurance products, such as their fiscal treatment, the social security framework, and liability legislation, are national. The relevant market for motor and health insurance is thus clearly national.

Markets for wholesale banking and insurance for large firms are European or even global. Corporate customers are looking for tailor-made solutions for their business and are approached by banks and insurers across Europe. There is a shift to global solutions for more specialised services for large firms. Re-insurance, for example, is a global business. A small group of large re-insurance companies from Europe (in particular Germany and Switzerland) and the US dominates the global market. Investment banking is also a global business. Leading investment banks – located primarily in New York and London – offer underwriting services and advice for mergers and acquisitions. Finally, the relevant geographic market for stock exchanges is shifting. Up until recently, each country had its own stock exchange, on which nearly all domestic companies were listed. The market is now consolidating at the European level (Euronext, NASDAQ Nordic; see Chapter 5).

The border between geographic markets may in practice be less distinct than is suggested by Table 14.2. For instance, the relevant geographic market for large firms can also be defined at the national rather than the European level.

14.5 Institutional Structure

The enforcement of EU competition policy remained largely unchanged from 1962, when a highly centralised authorisation system for all restrictive agreements was established (Monti, 2003a). However, since May 2004 the

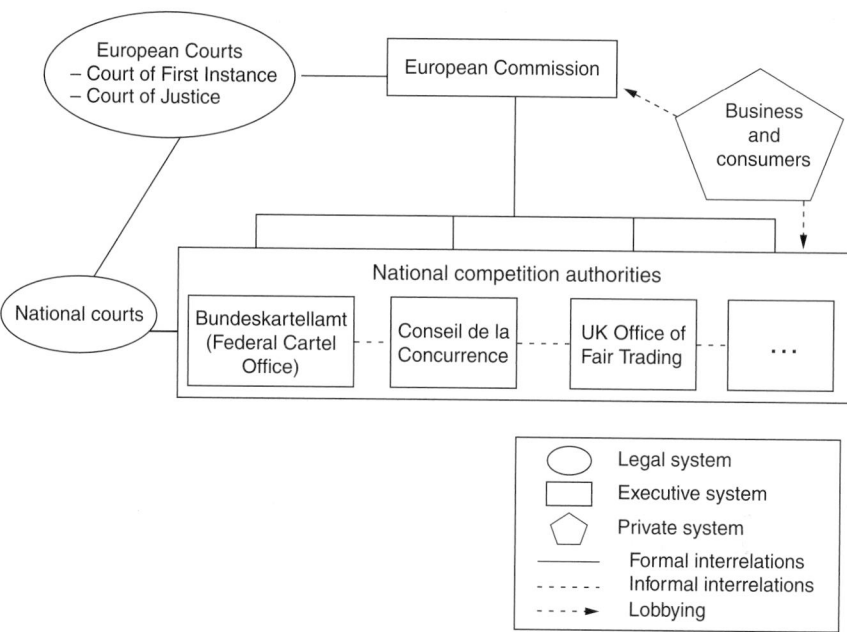

Figure 14.5 Enforcement of EU competition policy
Source: Based on Budzinski and Christiansen (2005)

enforcement system has become more decentralised as the national competition authorities and national courts have become (increasingly) involved in the enforcement of the Community Competition Law. Figure 14.5 gives an overview of the dual legislative and enforcement system in the EU.

Before the introduction of the Community Competition Law in 1958, most Member States did not have a competition policy regime in place. Competition policy has been established at the community level, and many Member States created their own legislation and enforcement agencies, while gradually obtaining more enforcement powers originating from EU legislation. The development of competition policy differs from that of financial supervision. The latter was traditionally organised at the national level and has only recently been centralised with the introduction of the Banking Union. Within the current EU competition policy system, EU institutions occupy a central position. The European Commission enjoys the right of initiative in the legislative process, which includes agenda-setting power (Schmidt, 2000). Moreover, as shown in Section 14.3, the Commission has specific powers in enforcing the Community Competition Law. The application of the law is supervised by the European Court of

First Instance (ECFI) and the ECJ. The ECFI is an independent court attached to the ECJ which rules on competition cases; ECFI decisions can be appealed to the ECJ.

The effective enforcement of EU antitrust rules requires close cooperation between the EU and national institutions. According to Smits (2005), they have to cooperate on finding evidence of infringements and inform each other about investigations, so as to ensure an efficient division of labour and an effective and consistent application of EU competition rules. For this reason, the European Competition Network (ECN) was established in 2004. Within this network, EU competition authorities work together, exchange information, and allocate cases. Monti (2004) argues that the ECN is needed because in an integrated economy, collaborative competition enforcement is more effective than isolated efforts. Given the dual structure of EU enforcement, general principles have been established to ensure an efficient division of work (Monti, 2003b):

- as a rule, competition authorities of the Member States will be well placed to deal with cases that have a major effect on the territory of their Member State;
- where a suspected infringement has its main effects in the territory of two or three Member States, these authorities should consider working together on a case;
- where a suspected infringement has a larger geographic scope, the Commission is likely to be best placed to deal with a case.

In 2014, the European Commission reviewed the experience of 10 years of cooperation within the ECN (EC, 2014b). It concluded that while a substantial degree of convergence had been achieved, progress was needed on the institutional position of national competent authorities and convergence in the application of EU competition rules. The Commission therefore proposed a directive on a minimum toolkit and effective enforcement powers for national competition authorities (2017/142/EC). This includes rules to ensure that national competition authorities can act independently, and have the necessary financial and human resources to do their work, the necessary powers to gather evidence, adequate tools to implement proportionate and deterrent sanctions, and coordinated leniency programmes that encourage companies to come forward with evidence of illegal cartels. In May 2018, the European Parliament and the Council reached a political agreement on this Commission proposal.

The EU's competition policy is different from that in other countries. Box 14.4 compares competition policies in the US and the EU.

Box 14.4 Antitrust policy in the EU and the US

Ginsburg (2005) argues that Sections 1 and 2 of the US Sherman Act cover largely the same ground as Articles 81 and 82 of the Treaty of Rome (now Articles 101 and 102 of the TFEU). Moreover, the US Clayton Act is roughly comparable to the EC Merger Regulation. In practice, EU and US competition policy are exhibiting more and more similarities. In this respect, Martin (2005) poses that the EU is moving along the same path trod by US antitrust 25 years ago: from a reliance on maintaining the ability of equally efficient competitors to compete as a way of ensuring good market performance towards an explicit, case-by-case assessment of the impact of a business practice on market performance, or of a proposed merger/structural change on expected market performance.

However, there are important differences between antitrust policies in the US and the EU. According to Rosch (2007), the policies are based on different schools of thought. While US antitrust policies are based on 'Chicago School economics', EU policies are built on 'post-Chicago School economics'. The basic assumption of the Chicago School is that markets are by nature efficient, and that a monopolist will never be able to keep out competitors. Proponents therefore argue that: (1) firms alleged to be engaged in predatory pricing are more likely to be engaged in profit-maximising conduct that is efficiency *enhancing* rather efficiency *impairing*, and (2) even if a firm is trying to engage in predatory conduct, the market is likely to adjust. However, post-Chicago School scholars assert that firms *do* engage in strategic behaviour to undermine (potential) rivals, which creates the need for active antitrust policies. Rosch (2007) argues that while the Chicago School tends to advocate a hands-off approach, post-Chicago scholars favour a 'light-touch' regulatory approach. Thus, EU enforcement agencies challenge certain actions of monopolists, while US agencies and courts rarely (successfully) challenge certain exclusionary practices, such as vertical restraints and predatory pricing.

14.6 Conclusions

Competition policy is one of the pillars of the EU's internal market policy. It played an important role during the financial crisis of 2007–2009. By combating distortions of competition between firms, competition policy aims to create the preconditions for the proper functioning of markets. Moreover, safeguarding competition is an important instrument to promote further market integration, also within the financial system.

Competition forces firms to become (more) efficient, offer a greater choice of products and services, and offer these products and services at lower prices. Ultimately, competition increases consumer welfare and allocative efficiency.

The level of competition is also an important aspect of financial sector development and, in turn, economic growth. However, firms can benefit from anti-competitive behaviour and may try to scale down competition. The European Commission and the national competition authorities therefore aim to:

- eliminate agreements that restrict competition;
- prevent firms from abusing a dominant position;
- make sure that mergers and acquisitions do not harm competition;
- liberalise monopolistic economic sectors;
- prevent illegitimate state aid, as witnessed during the 2007–2009 financial crisis.

This chapter discusses a framework to detect firms that abuse a dominant position. One element of this framework is the SSNIP methodology, which is used to define the smallest market in which a hypothetical monopolist would be able to impose a small but significant non-transitory price increase (the so-called relevant market). The chapter also explains the institutional structure of EU competition policy. It describes how the enforcement of EU competition policy has become more decentralised, and how the dual enforcement system requires close cooperation between the European Commission and the national competition authorities.

Notes

1. The OECD (1993) defines four conditions of perfect competition: (1) there is such a large number of sellers and buyers that none can individually affect the market price, (2) there are no barriers to entry or exit, (3) buyers and sellers are perfectly informed about production and consumption decisions, and (4) products are homogeneous.
2. The multilateral interchange fee is a fall-back option that can be used when the issuing and acquiring banks are not able to bilaterally agree on an interchange fee.
3. Council Regulation (EC) No. 139/2004 of 20 January 2004 on the control of concentrations between undertakings.
4. Case 27/76 *United Brands Co and United Brands Continental BV v. Commission* [1978] 1 CMLR 429.

Bibliography

Suggested Reading

Bikker, J. A. and L. Spierdijk (eds.) (2017), *Handbook of Competition in Banking and Finance*, Edward Elgar, Cheltenham.

Motta, M. (2004), *Competition Policy: Theory and Practice*, Cambridge University Press.

Vives, X. (2011), Competition and Stability in Banking. *Oxford Review of Economic Policy*, 27, 479–97.

References

Budzinski, O. and A. Christiansen (2005), Competence Allocation in EU Competition Policy as an Interest-Driven Process. *Journal of Public Policy*, 25, 313–37.

Claessens, S. and L. Laeven (2004), What Drives Bank Competition? Some International Evidence. *Journal of Money, Credit and Banking*, 36, 563–83.

(2005), Financial Dependence, Banking Sector Competition, and Economic Growth. *Journal of the European Economic Association*, 3, 179–207.

European Commission (1997), *Commission Notice on the Definition of the Relevant Market for the Purposes of Community Competition Law*, EC, Brussels.

(2000), *Report on Competition Policy 1999*, EC, Brussels.

(2001), Commission Takes Note of Merger Withdrawal by Swedish Banks (SEB/FSB) (press release), EC, Brussels.

(2004), The Internal Market and the Relevant Geographical Market: The Impact of the Completion of the Single Market Programme on the Definition of the Relevant Geographical Market. Enterprise Papers 15, EC, Brussels.

(2011), The Rescue and Restructuring of Hypo Real Estate. Competition Policy Newsletter 3, EC, Brussels.

(2012), *Report on Competition Policy 2011*, EC, Brussels.

(2013), Communication of State Aid Rules to Support Measures in Favour of Banks in the Context of the Financial Crisis ('Banking Communication'), EC, Brussels

(2014a), Towards More Effective EU Merger Control. White Paper, EC, Brussels.

(2014b), Ten Years of Antitrust Enforcement under Regulation 1/2003: Achievements and Future Perspectives. Communication from the Commission to the European Parliament and the Council, EC, Brussels.

(2015), The Interchange Fees Regulation. Competition Policy Brief, EC, Brussels

(2018), *Report on Competition Policy 2017*, EC, Brussels.

European Communities (2003), *Glossary of Terms Used in Competition Related Matters*, EC, Brussels.

Geroski, P. and R. Griffith (2004), Identifying Antitrust Markets. In: M. Neumann and J. Weinand (eds.), *International Handbook of Competition*, Edward Elgar, Cheltenham, 290–305.

Ginsburg, D. H. (2005), Comparing Antitrust Enforcement in the United States and Europe. *Journal of Competition Law and Economics*, 1, 427–39.

Martin, S. (2005), US Antitrust and EU Competition Policy: Where Has the Former Been, Where is the Latter Going? University of Aveiro Working Paper in Economics 27.

Monti, M. (2003a), The New Shape of European Competition Policy. Speech given at the Inaugural Symposium of the Competition Policy Research Center, How Should Competition Policy Transform Itself? 20 November 2003, Tokyo.

(2003b), EU Competition Policy after May 2004. *Presentation to the* Fordham Annual Conference on International Antitrust Law and Policy, New York.

(2004), Competition Policy in a Global Economy. *International Finance*, 7, 495–504.

Motta, M. (2004), *Competition Policy: Theory and Practice*, Cambridge University Press.

Office of Fair Trading (2001), *The Role of Market Definition in Monopoly and Dominance Inquiries*, OFT, London.

(2004), *Abuse of a Dominant Position: Understanding Competition Law*, OFT, London.

Okolelova, I. and J. Bikker (2018), The Single Supervisory Mechanism: Competitive Implications for the Banking Sectors in the Euro Area. DNB Working Paper 621.

Organisation for Economic Co-operation and Development (1993), *Glossary of Industrial Organisation Economics and Competition Law*, OECD, Paris.

(2009), Competition and the Financial Crisis. Paper prepared for the OECD Competition Committee, OECD, Paris.

(2011), Bank Competition and Financial Stability. Report prepared for the G20 workshop 'The New Financial Landscape', OECD, Paris.

Panzar, J. and J. Rosse (1987), Testing for 'Monopoly' Equilibrium. *Journal of Industrial Economics*, 35, 443–56.

Roeller, L.-H. and O. Stehmann (2006), The Year 2005 at DG Competition: The Trend Towards a More Effects-Based Approach. *Review of Industrial Organization*, 29, 281–304.

Rosch, J. T. (2007), I Say Monopoly, You say Dominance: The Continuing Divide on the Treatment of Dominant Firms, Is It the Economics? Paper presented at the International Bar Association Antitrust Section Conference in Florence. www.ftc.gov/speeches/rosch/070908isaymonopolyiba.pdf (accessed 13 February 2012).

Schmidt, S. K. (2000), Only an Agenda Setter? The European Commission's Power over the Council of Ministers. *European Union Politics*, 1, 37–61.

Schoenmaker, D. (2013), Post-Crisis Reversal in Banking and Insurance Integration: An Empirical Survey. *European Economy – Economic Papers* 496, DG ECFIN, Brussels.

Smits, R. (2005), The European Competition Network: Selected Aspects. *Legal Issues of Economic Integration*, 32, 175–92.

Tirole, J. (1988), *The Theory of Industrial Organization*, MIT Press, Cambridge (MA).

Vives, X. (2011), Competition and Stability in Banking. *Oxford Review of Economic Policy*, 27, 479–97.

Index